Collected Works of Northrop Frye

VOLUME 3

Northrop Frye's Student Essays, 1932–1938

The Collected Edition of the Works of Northrop Frye has been planned and is being directed by an editorial committee under the aegis of Victoria University, through its Northrop Frye Centre. The purpose of the edition is to make available authoritative texts of both published and unpublished works, based on analysis and comparison of all available materials, and supported by scholarly apparatus, including annotation and introductions. The Northrop Frye Centre gratefully acknowledges financial support, through McMaster University, from the Michael G. DeGroote family.

Northrop Frye's
Student Essays
1932–1938

VOLUME 3

Edited by Robert D. Denham

UNIVERSITY OF TORONTO PRESS
Toronto Buffalo London

Toronto Buffalo London

Printed in Canada

ISBN 0-8020-4235-X

Printed on acid-free paper

Canadian Cataloguing in Publication Data

Frye, Northrop, 1912–1991
Northrop Frye's student essays, 1932–1938

(Collected works of Northrop Frye ; v. 3)
Includes bibliographical references and index.
ISBN 0-8020-4235-X

1. Literature – History and criticism.   2. Religion.
I. Denham, Robert D.   II. Title.   III. Series.

PN37.F79 1997   C814'.54   C97-931089-X

University of Toronto Press acknowledges the financial assistance to its publishing program of the Canada Council for the Arts and the Ontario Arts Council.

For John P. Fishwick

Contents

Contents

Preface

The student essays of Northrop Frye were among the large body of manuscripts deposited in the Victoria University Library at the University of Toronto following Frye's death in 1991. The essays collected here include all of the extant papers Frye wrote for courses during his final two years at Victoria College (1931–33) and his three years at Emmanuel College (1933–36). Two papers—one on prose fiction and the other on Calvin—are of uncertain date and provenance, but they seem to come from his Toronto student days or shortly thereafter. Two additional essays can be traced to Frye's time at Oxford. I have not included "The Social Significance of Music," a 1935 talk Frye presented to a group in Toronto called the Society of Incompatibles, because practically all of that paper repeats material from part 3 of Frye's essay on Romanticism, written two years earlier. I have also excluded an untitled holograph manuscript on Chaucer which Frye wrote when he was at Merton College: most of that paper was incorporated into the essay on Chaucer that is included here. The headnote for each paper records the course or other occasion for which the paper was written, as best I can determine that information, and gives the location of the paper in the Northrop Frye Papers at the Victoria University Library.

Frye's published works were seldom annotated, and when he did provide notes they were often sketchy at best. This is a practice that began with his student essays. The notes in the present volume focus on Frye's sources—the passages he quotes or paraphrases and the works which he refers to or relies on. The annotations for prose works are ordinarily to editions that are readily accessible, not necessarily the ones Frye himself consulted, although these are sometimes noted; for poetry, I have generally provided only titles, dates, and line numbers. This procedure should enable readers who want to consult Frye's sources to do so fairly easily. In a few cases editing conventions have been adopted for particular essays; these are recorded in the headnotes. The annotations provided by Frye himself are identified with "[NF]" following the note. For seven of the essays Frye provided bibliographies. As these exist in various degrees of completeness, I have supplemented the information he gives, either within square brackets in the bibliography itself or in a separate note. All other material in square brackets is an editorial addition. Information for three of the notes was provided by Jean O'Grady and for two by Marc Plamondon: my debts to them are recorded following the notes for which they were responsible.

I have regularized Frye's spelling, capitalization, and punctuation to conform to current conventions. The titles of works, which Frye sometimes underlined, have been italicized throughout. Frye wrote swiftly, and it is likely that for some of the essays the first draft was the final draft. Five of his Emmanuel College essays, for example, were written during a four-day period. These essays, then, though obviously the fruit of considerable thought, are not the product of careful revision, which was to be Frye's later practice; consequently, the syntax occasionally goes awry. But on the principle that it is better to retain a sense of the original dispatch, I have resisted the temptation to rewrite Frye's prose, except in a few cases where problems of agreement, parallel structure, and the like seemed to call for correction. All such substantive changes, including the occasional addition of an omitted word, are noted in the list of emendations. Some of the essays do contain Frye's holograph corrections and additions. I have retained the changes that he himself made to the typescripts, though I have not noted these changes unless there was some reason for doing so. Marginal comments and other markings made by Frye's instructors have been recorded in the notes.

All of Frye's sources that I could locate have been identified. It should perhaps be noted that, as a student, Frye was often rather careless in following the conventions of scholarly practice. In these essays he frequently misquotes his sources and occasionally gives an incorrect citation, refers to book titles that do not exist, puts paraphrases within quotation marks, and cites sources that argue the opposite of what he claims; and he sometimes gives the impression of having consulted primary texts when in fact he is drawing upon secondary sources. The misquotations have been silently corrected, and the other problems in his handling of his sources are recorded in the notes.

Abbreviations

The abbreviations used in the notes and headnotes are standard. "NF" in the notes signifies Northrop Frye, and "NFF" in the notes and in the headnotes stands for the Northrop Frye Fonds in the Victoria University Library. Four works are represented in the notes with the following abbreviations or shortened forms:

DW = Oswald Spengler, *The Decline of the West*, trans. Charles Francis Atkinson, rev. ed., 2 vols. New York: Knopf, 1928.

GB = Sir James Frazer, *The Golden Bough*, 12 vols. London: Macmillan, 1911–14. References are to the 3rd ed., except for vol. 4, *The Dying God*, which is the 1st ed.

Corrrespondence = *The Correspondence of Northrop Frye and Helen Kemp, 1932–1939*, ed. Robert D. Denham. 2 vols. Toronto: University of Toronto Press, 1996.

Ayre = John Ayre, *Northrop Frye: A Biography*. Toronto: Random House, 1989.

Acknowledgments

These essays are published with the kind permission of the executors of the Northrop Frye estate, Jane Widdicombe and Roger Ball, and the Victoria University Library. I owe debts of gratitude also to the Northrop Frye Centre at Victoria University, which, at the initiative of Dr. Eva Kushner, conceived the idea of publishing Frye's works in a collected edition; to John M. Robson, who served as the first general editor, and to his successor, Alvin Lee; to Roseann Runte, president of Victoria University, for her support of the project; and to Robert Brandeis, librarian at Victoria University, for the assistance he and his staff have continued to provide me. I am also indebted to Christine Cable, who put the texts of Frye's typescripts onto computer disks, to Patricia W. Scott, for tracking down for me scores of books through interlibrary loan, to Margaret Burgess, for her expert copy-editing, and to the following people who have responded to my queries or provided other kinds of assistance: Julia Annas, John Ayre, A.S. Bendall, Daniel Breazeale, Janie Cottis, James Carscallen, Edwin M. Curley, Peter Dale, Scott D. Denham, Douglas John Den Uyl, Bernard F. Dukore, Ian Duncan, Gail Gibson, Bruce Golden, Burkhard Henke, Robin Jackson, Karen James, Douglas Jay,

Kingsley Joblin, Hugh Kenner, Gwin Kolb, James Lawler, William A. Little, Frank Lucash, Maurice Luker, Linda Miller, Hugh Moorhouse, Pierre-François Moreau, Barbara J. Patterson, Linda Peterson, Claude Pichois, Barry Qualls, C.D.C. Reeve, T.G. Rosenmeyer, Florinda Ruiz, Julian Rushton, Tilman Seebass, R. Larry Todd, Stanley Weintraub, Garron Wells, and Thomas Willard. I express my gratitude to the National Endowment for the Humanities for a fellowship that provided a year of uninterrupted time to edit the unpublished Frye papers and to Roanoke College for its support, financial and otherwise, of the project. Finally, the dedication is an imperfect effort to express my thanks to a person whose generous support of his alma mater has played an indirect though substantial role in the publication of this volume, as well as the Frye–Kemp correspondence.

Introduction

I

The twenty-two essays collected here, which come from Northrop Frye's student days, were written over the course of seven years, from 1932 to 1938. Three of the papers are from his last year at Victoria College; fifteen were written for his courses at Emmanuel College, the theology school of Victoria University. Another paper, a talk on Calvin, was written while Frye was at Emmanuel College, though not for an Emmanuel course. Still another, on the forms of prose fiction, cannot be dated with certainty, but it appears to come from the late 1930s. The final two essays are from Frye's years at Merton College: the first is a paper on Eliot that Frye read at the Bodley Club in 1937, and the second, a talk on Chaucer he presented at the Graduate English Club in Toronto in 1938, is an expanded version of an essay he had written for his Merton tutor, Edmund Blunden, two years earlier.

The Emmanuel papers represent a large percentage of the writing Frye did (while a student) in theology, but what has survived from his time at Victoria College and from his Oxford years is only a fraction of what he wrote. The record of his Merton College essays is incomplete, but we do know that during his first year there he wrote two additional papers on Chaucer, one on Wyatt, and one on Fulke Greville. He may have written on Sidney and on Lyly as well.[1] During the tutorials of his second year he read papers on Crashaw and Herbert, on Vaughan, Traherne, Herrick, Marvell, and Cowley, on the Dark Ages, on the character book, on *King Lear*, and on the history of the language; and he also presented a paper to the Bodley Club entitled "A Short History of the Devil."[2] Why these papers were not preserved is somewhat puzzling, especially since Frye had written to Helen Kemp that his Oxford essays were "mostly publishable," adding that he had "collected a lot of material for future books."[3] Yet Frye never seemed particularly interested in keeping any versions of his writing except the published form: the different drafts of the Blake manuscript that he circulated for almost a decade have, except for three chapters of one version, disappeared, and the drafts of essays and books that are found in his notebooks represent only a very small portion of his published work. But the regret we feel over the disappearance of much of his early writing is mitigated by our having those papers that did escape the dustbin.

Frye was a person of uncommon gifts, and very little that came from his pen, even his juvenilia, is without interest. These early essays reveal the growth of a young writer who often has perceptive things to say about the topics he addresses. They also provide a much more complete picture than we have had about the roots of his later work. Frye often remarked that his writing kept circling back to the same issues, and these essays illustrate that his insights into a number of the questions that were to preoccupy him for more than sixty years came to him quite early. They illustrate as well the degree to which he matured as a writer over the course of seven years. "Writing," Frye remarked in a 1934 letter to Helen Kemp, the classmate whom he married three years later, "is an exciting, precise, subtle, difficult business, like a piano recital, but more spontaneous and creative."[4] In a letter written the following year he wished he and Kemp, who was studying art in London, could be together so he could lead her "gently away from the abstract colorless words that crackle to the concrete ones that resound."[5] There are many paragraphs in the present essays, especially the early ones, that make us wish Frye had been more attentive to his own advice about precise and concrete diction. For all of Frye's skill in constructing the periodic sentence and his obvious attention to the rhythm of his prose, his writing is often overly dense and, as one of his professors remarked in a note, "suffers from the half-truth of generalization." Still, whatever the faults of the Victoria College essays, it is worth reminding ourselves that they were written by one who had not yet reached his majority. And seven years later it is clear that Frye has begun to discover the style he perfected in his mature work.

II

As a second-year student at Victoria College Frye was already deeply immersed in Blake, and not long after that his knowledge of the Bible was becoming, as he wrote to Helen Kemp in May 1934, "sound and accurate."[6] Blake and the Bible, when not at the foreground of Frye's later writing, were always hovering in the margins. But the most important influence during these early years was Spengler. In 1930 Frye had happened upon *The Decline of the West* in the library at Hart House, the students' recreational and cultural centre at the University of Toronto, and he had reread it during the summer of 1931 while staying at the YMCA in Edmonton. In an interview Frye remarked that after reading *The Decline of the West* he

> was absolutely enraptured with it, and ever since I've been wondering why, because Spengler had one of those muzzy, right-wing, Teutonic, folk-ish minds. He was the most stupid bastard I ever picked up. But neverthe-less, I found his book an inspired book, and finally I've more or less figured out, I think, what I got from Spengler. There's a remark in Malraux's *Voices of Silence* to the effect that he thought that Spengler's book started out as a meditation on the destiny of art forms and then expanded from there. And what it expanded into is the key idea that has always been on my mind, the idea of interpenetration, which I later found in Whitehead's *Science and the Modern World*, the notion that things don't get reconciled, but everything is everywhere at once. Wherever you are is the center of everything. And Spengler showed how that operated in history, so I threw out the muzzy Teuton and kept those two intuitions, which I felt were going to be very central.[7]

One of Frye's first critical essays was a defence of Spengler against the attacks of Wyndham Lewis, and over the years he kept returning to Spengler.[8] Spengler makes his way explicitly into eight of the papers in this volume, and his influence is present in at least four more. In his paper on Augustine (no. 10), Frye refers to Spengler's *Decline* as "perhaps the most important book yet produced by the twentieth century." What attracted Frye to Spengler was not simply the meditation in the *Decline* on the destiny of art forms and the idea of interpenetration. It was also Spengler's view of the organic growth of cultures and his ability to assimilate a large body of material, to design a mythical structure from it, and to represent his vision of history schematically or creatively. As Frye was to say forty years later, "If *The Decline of the West* were nothing else, it would still be one of the world's great Romantic poems."[9]

Spengler, then, as Frye reported in a notebook from the late 1940s, was one of two thinkers who "focused the subject matter of practically all my theology essays."[10] The other was Sir James Frazer. While other students at Emmanuel College were reading the German theologians, Frye immersed himself in *The Golden Bough*, especially volume 4, *The Dying God*, volumes 5 and 6, *Adonis, Attis, Osiris*, and volume 9, *The Scapegoat*. In his paper on "The Jewish Background of the New Testament" (no. 6), Frye calls *The Golden Bough* "perhaps the most important and influential book written by an Englishman since *The Origin of Species*." What attracted Frye to Frazer, whose imprint can be found in seven of the essays collected here, was the positive value the latter attached to myth and the implications of *The Golden Bough* for the study of symbolism: Frye came to see that the framework for religious studies need not be restricted simply to theology and history. In his essay on prose fiction (no. 19), Frye refers to *The Golden Bough* as "one of the greatest anatomies in the English language," meaning that Frazer had a literary significance for Frye as well. Later he would call Frazer's massive anatomy "a kind of grammar of the human imagination,"[11] the syntax of which Frye spent his entire career diagramming.

The month before he was to return to Toronto from his home in Moncton, New Brunswick, to begin his fourth year at Victoria College, Frye revealed at least part of his objective for the year to Helen Kemp: "I want Romanticism for my topic for Philosophy thesis and Browning for [Pelham] Edgar, and I want to get to headquarters and make sure of getting them. I have already done quite a bit of work on Browning—I suppose, take him all in all, he's my favorite poet. I have very definite heroisms in literature—Donne, Milton, Bunyan, Swift, Blake, Dickens, Browning, and Shaw—and I like writing about them."[12] The "work on Browning" Frye refers to, an essay written during the fall term of his third year for Pelham Edgar's course on "English Poetry of the Nineteenth Century," is one of the three papers that have survived from his Victoria College years. The other two, both written during his final year, are his romanticism thesis, written for George Brett's course in "Modern Philosophy," and the essay on primitivism, written for Edgar's course on "Restoration and Eighteenth-Century Literature." These are the first three papers in the present collection.

Frye's interest in primitivism, that cluster of ideas that gained significance in the eighteenth century as a precursor to romanticism, developed into a long-standing attachment. Primitivism was the set of attitudes neither Augustan nor romantic that prevailed during the age of Blake, and Frye was already deeply engaged with Blake's songs and prophecies.[13] Some of the ideas presented in this early paper (no. 1) were developed in *Fearful Symmetry*,[14] and the paper foreshadows a number of themes that were to preoccupy Frye throughout his career: his defence of primitive and popular literary conventions (in *Anatomy of Criticism*, following Schiller, he calls these "naive"); his conviction that the originality of the great poets was a function of their consciousness of origins; and his interest in the relation between the creative and the critical. *The Decline of the West* is written all over the third paragraph of the essay on "Primitivism," where Frye speaks of the new soul in the metropolis pulling up its roots and experiencing a sense of freedom. Here we can detect perhaps an autobiographical note, as the exhilaration of leaving the "small culture-town" of Moncton for the independence afforded by Toronto was something Frye himself felt as a young man. He often returned to the themes of "The Basis of Primitivism," later writing two essays on the age of sensibility, one in the mid-1950s and the other toward the end of his career.[15]

The long paper on "Romanticism" (no. 2) is the first sustained instance we have of what were to become several of Frye's trademarks: his conceptual expansiveness, his ability to organize a large body of ideas, and his schematic way of thinking. Here Frye tackles practically the entire range of romanticism as a cultural force, not a fashionable topic in the 1930s when Eliot's classicism and the new humanism's anti-romantic doctrines were still a powerful presence in criticism. After an introduction that draws on Spengler's notion of organic cultural growth and decline, Frye examines romantic philosophy from Rousseau to Bergson and Spengler himself, romantic music, and romantic literature, concluding with a glance at the political contexts of romanticism. In a note scribbled on the title-page Frye apologizes to Professor George Brett for the necessary but unmitigated evil of the length of his essay, this remark having been preceded by the wry confession that he has "not had time to deal with the painting or with Continental literature." The omission no doubt pleased Brett, who was faced with a ninety-four-page, marginless typescript.

The essay is an audacious undertaking, especially for a twenty-year-old, and Frye's reach often exceeds his grasp. He begins to discover his voice in his discussion of music and literature in the third and fourth parts of the essay, where the prose is clearer and somewhat more concrete. But in the first two parts, except for the section on Nietzsche, the prose is overly dense, galloping along at a breathless pace; the abstractions are seldom illustrated and never documented; and the voice of authority Frye projects is often unconvincing. In his account of music one feels that Frye is on more familiar territory,[16] but in most of his account of romantic philosophy one is less sure, perhaps because most of the philosophic discussion comes from secondary sources. Still, the paper is a remarkable tour de force, and it contains the seeds of what were to become a number of Frye's basic principles.

The fundamental dialectic of the essay is the space-time opposition. "Obviously all cultural activity," Frye announces, "is comprehended through the two ultimate data of time and space." They are the "ultimate forms of perception." Frye associates time and space with an extensive series of dialectical pairs: the blood and the reproductive faculty versus the sense and reasoning, being versus thought, feeling and intuition versus abstract systems, romanticism versus empiricism and positivism, history versus philosophy, dynamism versus stasis, narrative art versus pictorial art, the compulsion to action (morals) versus the compulsion to thought (logic), the religious period of culture versus the sceptical period, the creative versus the critical, architecture and music versus sculpture and drama, the lyric-essay versus fiction, philosophy of history versus scientific experiment, the world-as-will versus the world-as-idea, and so on. A number of the oppositions appear on the vertical and horizontal axes of the diagram in part 1, section III of the essay. There are various permutations of the dialectic, and the categories here, like the categories that developed in Frye's later work, are fluid, even slippery. But they served Frye well over the years: time and space, the basic categories in the diagram just mentioned, are the principles that lie behind the separation of myth and metaphor, fictional and thematic, and a whole series of other bipolar divisions in *Anatomy of Criticism* and elsewhere. The space-time dialectic is everywhere in both Blake and Spengler, the latter of whom speaks of time as "a counterconception (*Gegenbegriff*) to space,"[17] but Frye was doubtless influenced as well by his readings in the history of philosophy, where time and space had been commonplace categories in philosophical discussion from the Greeks on.

III

Frye had entered Victoria College as a probationary student in the pass course, a nonspecialized program leading to the B.A. degree. But because of his high marks during his first year, he transferred to the more prestigious honour course his second year, choosing what was called "philosophy (English or history option)." Frye took only three honour courses in English, all from Pelham Edgar: Shakespeare his second year, English Poetry of the Nineteenth Century his third, and Restoration and Eighteenth-Century Literature his fourth. He had a heavy concentration in honour philosophy—seven of his eleven honour courses were in philosophy. But somewhat ironically, while we have two of the three papers he wrote for his English honour courses, only his romanticism paper has survived from his philosophy courses. Even if Frye read all or even most of the texts assigned for his philosophy courses, he would have had a substantial undergraduate background in philosophy.[18]

The paper on Browning (no. 3), written for Edgar's nineteenth-century course, ranges far and wide, Frye finding that he cannot consider Browning's poetry until he has located the poet in the cultural upheaval of the times and made an effort to show that Browning was a poet of Victorianism. The argument here meanders and the paragraphs are without much shape, but Frye eventually gets around to what he is mainly interested in: the music of Browning's poetry. In the last half of the essay, as well as in part 3 of the paper on romanticism, Frye hammers out an early form of his ideas on the melody and harmony of poetry—ideas later elaborated, first in an early essay on "Music in Poetry,"[19] and later in an account of the generic rhythm of *epos* in the fourth essay of *Anatomy of Criticism*.

When Frye entered Emmanuel College in the fall of 1933, he was ambivalent about a career in the ministry. In a letter to Helen Kemp the previous summer he had said,

> No, I don't want to be a professor. Theoretically. In practice I should like it well enough. But there is something about such an eminently cultured occupation that would make me feel as though I were shirking something. A professor is, as I think I have said before, an orchid,—highly cultivated, but no roots in the ground. He deals with a crowd of half-tamed little savages who get no good out of him except intellectual training and, in some cases, the radiation of his personality. He is not a vital and essential force in a community of live people. He is not a worker in the elemental sense of that word. Most professors, to gain a reputation, specialize so intensely in their work that they are cut off even from the undergraduate. These are the

pedants. The rest are not so cut off from reality, but they are cut off from life. Oh, well, you get the idea. The ministry is my "vocation," etymologically. I have been "called" to it just as much as any blaspheming fool of an evangelist that ever bragged about what a sinner he was before he was converted. But that doesn't mean that I am fitted for it, necessarily. It doesn't mean that I am not deadly afraid of it and would rather do a hundred other things. . . . I wonder what those writers who talk about relentless and inexorable Fate would say to a man who had two Fates, pulling in opposite directions. The trouble is that I can't quite figure out which one is God.[20]

By the time he was halfway through his theological studies Frye *had* figured it out. In January 1935 he wrote to Kemp, "The ministry, with its requirement of almost absolute versatility at an indefinitely high pitch, compelled me and yet finally frightened me away."[21] But the decision not to become a United Church minister had little effect on Frye's program of study. As John Ayre says, "Comparative theology and Bible studies all belonged to the same mythological universe as the literature of Blake."[22] But the Emmanuel papers illustrate that the circumference of Frye's vision continued to expand, encompassing by the end of his three years a large portion of what Vico called the *verum factum*, the world made by human beings—its literature, philosophy, theology, art, music, religious and political institutions. Still, the centre of this circumference was ultimately religious. Ample support for this view lies in Frye's published works; the unpublished notebooks reveal even more clearly the religious base of Frye's vision. While we await their publication, we now have his Emmanuel College essays, which served as a workshop for Frye to begin formulating his ideas about Christian symbolism, the katabatic and anabatic movements in the religious journey, the Incarnation (which would become for Frye the ultimate metaphor), and a philosophy of history, which, Frye assumes, must by definition have a religious base if it is to be universally applicable. The philosophy of history, he says in his essay on Augustine (no. 10), "is the ultimate theoretical activity of the human race, and can only be worked out by thinkers in the tradition of a true religion"; and in his essay on Calvin (no. 20), he remarks that "the most fundamental intellectual activity of the human race is a philosophy of history, an attempt to find a pattern in existence."

One sees in these essays as well the development of what was to become Frye's characteristic rhetorical mode, an approach he later described as similar to the act of standing back from the brush-strokes of a painting in order to see the large patterns. The only papers in this collection that amount to close readings of texts are Frye's essays on Augustine's *City of God* (no. 10) and Chaucer (no. 22). Typically, Frye is synthetic rather than analytic. He is more interested in the formal and final causes than in the material and efficient ones, more concerned to discover a philosophical generalization than a particular fact, more attracted to the central concept than the casually interesting observation (the word "centre" occurs twenty-seven times in his paper on romanticism). Even in these student papers Frye has an uncanny knack for getting to the kernel of whatever his subject happens to be, and the paper on Chaucer contains, in Frye's reading of *Troilus and Criseyde*, his earliest extended archetypal analysis of a literary work

Readers familiar with Frye will also recognize in these student papers a number of expressions that echo throughout his later work: "Other great poets refused to be bound by conventions, but in being original they were quite conscious of origins" (no. 1). "We are dragged backward into the future" (no. 20). "Art, systematic philosophy, and ethical ideals cannot advance or improve, but history and science do" (no. 13). "What the man is, *per se*, is of no importance; why that type of man should have become prominent in that age is another matter" (no. 2).

Frye's embracing of the *verum factum* was always inclusive, and that attitude is apparent in these early papers. One might not have expected, for example, a student whose roots were in the tradition of Low Church, dissenting Protestantism to engage in such a spirited defense of Calvin (no. 20); or a student whose primary sympathies were already romantic and revolutionary to give considered attention to reactionaries such as Wyndham Lewis and T.S. Eliot. On the other hand, with the hindsight of Frye's sixty-year writing career, we can understand his early attraction to Frazer, to other members of the so-called Cambridge group, to Gilbert Murray (nos. 4, 5, 6 and 9); to a mystery religion such as Orphism (no. 9); and even to Ramon Lull (no. 11). Lull appealed to Frye not only as a visionary but also as a schematic thinker. Certainly this last was part of the attraction of Spengler's *Decline of the West*, the first volume of which had three fold-out tabular diagrams, each more than a foot long. Frye calls Lull's inveterate categorizing a "genuine dialectic," and he was drawn to Lull's numerological schemes as well. With his penchant for systems, taxonomies, and various diagrammatic frameworks, Frye himself, as it turned out, could hardly organize his thoughts

without some underlying schematic structure. This is, of course, obvious in his published work. It is even more obvious in his notebooks,
where he is forever toying with paradigms—colours, mythological characters, musical keys, the zodiac, various ogdoadic formulae—as a way
to give shape to his ideas. Frye's student essays reveal that what became
a typical way of thinking began quite early.

So far as I can determine, Frye never refers to Schleiermacher in his
published work, which, with the expansive range of his interests, is
unusual. Frye's religiously based poetics is not unlike Schleiermacher's,
and their views on the imagination are quite similar.[23] The depth of
Frye's knowledge of Schleiermacher, if it ever was deep, is not apparent
in these essays, but Schleiermacher does make an appearance in four of
them (nos. 2, 15, 17, and 20), and in "The Relation of Religion to the Art
Forms of Music and Drama" Frye identifies his own approach to the
dialogue between religion and art as "Arminian, *via* Schleiermacher."
Less prominent in the papers than Spengler and Frazer are other thinkers who would figure importantly in the development of Frye's thought.
Vico, for example, makes two cameo appearances in the essay on
Augustine (no. 10), and Hegel, whom Frye calls in the same essay "one
of the great seminal minds of the past century," claims an entire section
in the romanticism paper (no. 2). Both turned out to be seminal figures
for Frye, their influence being especially apparent in his two books on
the Bible, *The Great Code* and *Words with Power*.

The Emmanuel College essays naturally focus on topics in church history, theology, and the Bible. One of the cleverest is the fictional narrative, presented in epistolary form and based firmly on the historical
record, about the Franciscan scholar Robert Cowton (no. 12). Frye's
intent is to recreate the sense of medieval life—its history, philosophy,
theology, art, and social conditions—through a letter by Cowton to his
Oxford tutor, which recounts a six-month journey from England to
Rome. Because of references to certain contemporary events and the
jubilee year, as well as to such facts as Cimabue's age and the presence
of Dante in Florence, we can infer that Cowton's trip was made in 1300.
Although the journey Frye recounts is fictional, the character of Robert
Cowton is not. He was a Franciscan who was educated at Oxford in the
late thirteenth century and who wrote a series of *Quaestiones*, much in
demand in the fourteenth and fifteenth centuries, on the four books of
Sentences of Peter Lombard; according to Wycliffe, Cowton authored an
abridgement of Duns Scotus's theological works. Thomas Rondel was

also a Franciscan friar and, like Cowton, had an interest in Peter Lombard, on whose *Sentences* he lectured in Paris. In the closing years of the thirteenth century he lectured at Oxford. As the annotations to this paper indicate, Frye, in recreating a journey Cowton could have taken, fills his Franciscan's letter with a sizeable amount of historical and cultural detail.

Frye's New Testament essays (on the Epistle of James and on the doctrine of salvation: nos. 7 and 8) and his papers on the reformation (nos. 13 and 14) are sketchy and less compelling, perhaps because they were written under the white heat of a deadline.[24] In many of his more substantial Emmanuel essays Frye's focus is dual—both religious and aesthetic. He was to write later, "The religious perspective is essential to the study of literature."[25] In these papers the terms seem to be reversed: the aesthetic perspective is essential to the study of religion. In any case, he frequently manages to bring literature and the other arts into his discussion. He concludes his paper on sacrifice (no. 4) by examining the artistic aspects of the topic. In his paper on the fertility cults (no. 5), he illustrates how the symbol mediates between the religious rite, on the one hand, and music, drama, and the plastic arts, on the other. He says in "An Augustinian Interpretation of History" (no. 10) that Augustine's conception of history was "a fundamentally aesthetic product." He makes clear in "St. Paul and Orphism" (no. 9) that what primarily interests him about the Orphic mysteries is their symbolism. In the essay on "Romanticism" (no. 2) he says that "religious philosophy is an artistic product." In other words, for Frye religion and art interpenetrate, to use one of his own favourite words.

The paper that addresses this interpenetration directly is "The Relation of Religion to the Art Forms of Music and Drama" (no. 17). Here Frye looks back to Frazer and Jung and to the essays he wrote on the Old Testament when he was a twenty-one-year-old, and, though he was, of course, unaware of it at the time, he looks forward to *Anatomy of Criticism*. The relation of art to dream and ritual, the principles of space and time as organizing structures for criticism, the archetypal patterns of art as deriving from "a universal subconscious language of symbolism," the recurrence of the seasons as an analogy for narrative structure—these are all ideas that we associate with Frye's mature critical vision. "The Relation of Religion to the Art Forms of Music and Drama" is, in fact, an embryonic form of the last three essays of the *Anatomy*. The good–beautiful–true triad at the beginning of the paper—it appears in other papers as well—made its way twenty years later into the opening pages of the theory of genres in the *Anatomy*. The structure of the *Anatomy* is, of course, considerably more expansive and complex than what we have here, but the early papers have clearly begun to lay the foundation for the later taxonomies. Frye's comments on Shakespearean comedy and romance seem in retrospect a kind of blueprint for *A Natural Perspective*. Similar examples abound. In the essay on Orphism (no. 9), there is even an early version of Frye's reading of the two creation stories in Genesis that he amplified more than forty years later in *The Great Code*.

One of the most original of Frye's early published works was his 1942 essay, "The Anatomy in Prose Fiction."[26] It was expanded into "The Four Forms of Prose Fiction,"[27] and, with still further revisions, incorporated into the fourth essay of *Anatomy of Criticism*. Frye was almost single-handedly responsible for bringing the anatomy into the discussion of prose fiction, and his treatment of the anatomy, as well as the other forms of prose fiction, has been one of the most influential aspects of his critical theory, spawning numerous works of practical criticism. What eventually appeared in the *Anatomy* had its genesis in an essay that Frye wrote more than twenty years before, "An Enquiry into the Art Forms of Prose Fiction." This paper, which may have been written for one of the honour English courses Frye took during his final two years at Emmanuel College, or perhaps for Edmund Blunden in 1937,[28] is typical of Frye's allusive method, ranging far and wide over the literary tradition from the Bible and Homer to Joyce and Eliot. Frye refers to 103 separate works in the paper, and to more than 100 writers and composers. It is difficult to imagine how a student in his early twenties who had taken but four English courses as an undergraduate could have encountered, much less read, even the major works in the canon, not to mention such relatively minor writers as Thomas Fuller, Richard Brome, and John Earle. But whatever doubts we have about Frye's actual knowledge of all of the primary texts he mentions, the piling up of examples to fill out his taxonomic schemes was to become one of his signatures; this essay, which prefigures the efficient cause in many sections of *Anatomy of Criticism*, turns out to be, in its intellectualized approach and its display of erudition, an anatomy itself.

This we might call the *dianoia* of Frye's early work—its rational, spatializing, Aristotelian tendency. But, as Frye learned from Whitehead, space and time interpenetrate, and in these early papers there is as well a highly developed sense of *mythos*. In fact, Frye tends to privilege the latter half of the dialectic, with its emphasis on the flux of time, the rhythms of history, the experience of religion, and the intuitive life. He often suggests that time, along with everything he associates with the temporal, holds veto power over space, with its own cluster of associated ideas. Plato, Frye writes in the essay on Orphism (no. 9),

> had the artist's mind: no other philosopher has ever had a tenth of his influence on creative artists of all kinds, despite the hostility and Philistinism he displays toward them in the *Republic* and the *Laws*. He realized that the highest knowledge is intuitive rather than intellectual, or, more exactly, that there are two kinds of intellectual perception, understanding and intelligence. The former is the passive recipient and organizer of information: the latter the actively synthesizing mind, which perceives relationships hidden to others and infers a complete pattern from small data: the mind which comprehends the outline of a body from seeing a fossilized knucklebone. Such a mind is essentially a symbolic mind: it is continually selecting outward experiences significant for inward ones. So the myth in Plato does duty for the presentation of this ultimate, symbolic form of truth.

Frye's mind was also essentially symbolic, and his lifelong quest to find verbal formulas for the symbolic forms of truth, culminating in *The Double Vision* (1991), begins, not simply with his discovery of Blake in the early 1930s, but also with the writing of these student essays.

IV

The final two papers—on Chaucer and Eliot—come from Frye's first year at Merton College. In Frye's published work there are very few references to Chaucer, and he never wrote an essay, or even part of an essay, on Chaucer's poetry. *Anatomy of Criticism* has occasional references to *The Canterbury Tales*, but they usually occur at those places where Frye needs an example to fill in one of the slots in his modal, archetypal, or generic taxonomies. "A Reconsideration of Chaucer" (no. 22), then, represents the most extensive attention he ever gave Chaucer, and what he reconsiders is not *The Canterbury Tales*, but Chaucer's other works, devoting almost half of the paper to *Troilus and Criseyde*. Frye places Chaucer in the context of both English and European culture, examines Chaucer's religious impulse, studies the comic vision in the minor poems, and gives a detailed reading of *Troilus and Criseyde*. The essay is a sophisticated piece of criticism, though it is difficult to imagine the paper as having been written by one who had become a freshman all over again, this time at Oxford. Frye says in connection with Chaucer that the greatness of a poet can be determined in part "by the very general argument which presents the range and scope of his thought and his constructive ability." That is an attribute of the great critic as well, and while it would be hyperbole to call Frye a great critic at this stage, the seeds of greatness are clearly present.

The introduction to the Eliot paper is somewhat inflated, as Frye is trying to impress his fellow students in the Bodley Club, but once he has gotten past this gambit, the talk settles into an exceptionally sensitive and mature reading of Eliot. Here we have an Oxford undergraduate who, in tracing the shape of Eliot's work through 1935, provides what became the orthodox interpretation of Eliot's poetry. Frye's critical development was very much influenced by Eliot, both positively and negatively: he absorbed a number of Eliot's new critical principles, but at the same time he set himself in conscious opposition to Eliot's classical, royalist, and Anglo-Catholic sympathies. In spite of their very different predispositions, Frye believed that Eliot was a poet, playwright, and critic who had to be read, and this essay is actually an early version of the introductory book on Eliot he would write twenty-five years later.[29]

There are literally scores of places in these papers where Frye's ideas will be seen as interpenetrating his later work. Interpenetration itself was to become an important philosophical, theological, and literary term for Frye, and the word, or some form of it, appears in four of the present essays (nos. 2, 6, 17, and 20). As Frye said in the interview quoted above, the idea developed from his reading of Spengler and became articulated when he encountered Whitehead's *Science and the Modern World*, the first book of philosophy that he read solely for pleasure.[30] While the word itself does not actually appear in Whitehead's book, the passage that struck Frye with such force comes from Whitehead's chapter on "The Romantic Reaction": "In a certain sense, everything is everywhere at all times. For every location involves an aspect of itself in every other location. Thus every spatio-temporal standpoint mirrors the world."[31] This, Frye says, was his "initiation into what Christianity meant by spiritual vision."[32] Interpenetration is, metaphorically, Blake's seeing the world in a grain of sand. Philosophically, it is the identification of the one and the many, which Frye intended to make the motto of the third book he planned to write.[33] Theologically, it lies at the heart of Frye's understanding of the Incarnation. At the end of his paper on Calvin (no. 20) Frye says:

> we are coming to the end of a cultural development, and our historical perspective is steadily approaching that of Augustine, who stood at the end of his. In that perspective the rise and fall of civilizations is the pattern of the fortunes of the world; the clinging to the one event in history which hints of something better than an endless dreary record of cruelty and stupidity is the function of the Church. When these two aspects of human life interpenetrate and focus into one, we shall have a theology which can accommodate itself to twentieth-century requirements.

Interpenetration, then, is another of those topoi in Frye's early papers about which we can say, in his beginning was his end.

Victoria College Essays

1

The Basis of Primitivism

This essay was written for Professor Pelham Edgar during the first semester of Frye's final year at Victoria College. It was submitted for English 3e, "Restoration and Eighteenth-Century Literature." The title page of the essay is dated 29 November 1932. Frye received a grade of 86 for the paper, the typescript of which is in the NFF, 1991, box 37, file 10.

Primitivism is the name given to a literary movement following in the wake of the rococo or eighteenth-century tradition and anticipatory of the romantic revival. Positively considered in itself, it is merely a passing aberration of judgment; relatively, to the two great periods which sandwiched it, an episode of the highest significance. The comparatively unimportant formulation of the myth of the noble savage takes on a more dignified aspect when its roots are seen embedded in that profound change of thought, the most complete and far-reaching the world had yet seen, which the transition in question signifies.

The prevailing note of primitivism is dissatisfaction, in any sphere in which it makes its appearance. And the expression of dissatisfaction in literature is usually in terms of revolt against the prevailing style. English poetry had worn a fashion ever since the Restoration, when the rhymed couplet came clanking in like the Spectre of the Haunted Grange, and a fashion which was as limited in scope as it was exclusive in appeal. For the preceding century the idea of poetry was a peculiarly plastic one. Criticism, under the leadership of Samuel Johnson of the pachydermatous ear, accepted the maxim that poets, like children, should be seen and not heard.[1] "Form" in a *tangible* sense was the chief desideratum—Johnson himself, though he could not hear poetry, could

at least feel it, and, hence, preferred the hard enamelled surfaces of Pope
and Dryden to the rough-hewn masses of Shakespeare or Milton. Now
Dryden and Pope, to be appreciated, certainly do have to be judged
from a plastic point of view—their neatness, smoothness, finish, preci-
sion, dexterity—all plastic terms—are what we see in them. Similarly,
Edmund Burke's rococo theory of aesthetics, though intended as a general survey of the field, is couched throughout in plastic metaphors—
rough, smooth, hard, soft, are the words he works with.[2] Blake, too,
clung to the hard, carven line, abhorring the Titian–Correggio–
Rembrandt technique. Even such a "nature poem" as *The Tyger* expresses the joy of a sculptor in creation:

> And what shoulder, & what art
> Could twist the sinews of thy heart? [lines 9–10]

—lines hardly the work of a *paysagiste*.[3] The romantic movement was a
revolt in favour of the pictorial. In my freshman days I was told to evaluate all the poets I encountered in terms of their "feeling for nature,"
and soon had a collection ranging from Pope, who was not supposed to
have any, to Wordsworth and Keats, who were supposed to have a
good deal, and it gradually dawned on me that a feeling for nature was
an essential concomitant of romanticism. Now this pictorial attitude—
which implies a landscape—was woven into the very fabric of the
poems—Coleridge's mastery of alliteration, Keats's exquisite vowel-
play, are static and literally picturesque sound patterns. The very
rhythms seem caught up and arrested, as they are in a painting. And
when we compare the cameos in the *Songs of Innocence* with the brush-
work of the *Book of Thel* it is obvious that a change has taken place.[4] In
such a case it is inevitable that primitivism should bridge the gap.
Rococo poetry dealt with civilization, romantic with the landscape;
primitivism was the transitional, thetical, argumentative period which
compared them to the advantage of the newer.

The philosophical change underlying this is too immense to deal with
in detail, but it may be possible to indicate a few leading principles. The
French Revolution, the Industrial Revolution, the sudden growth of cities, the decay of old privileges, the rise of nationality and democracy, all
point to the unifying fact that the centre of gravity in life was no longer
the small culture-town, with its guild conceptions of workmanship,
but the new metropolis. Aristocratic patronage gave way to popular

approval. Now the old towns had their roots very definitely in the land; they drew from it life and power. Creativeness, which up to this time had been a necessary stamp of greatness, means a living strength pressing the intellect into the service of blood and being. But the new soul in the big city floats free in space; he has no roots anywhere. Now in the first place this pulling up of roots leads to a sense of freedom.[5]

This freedom is that of primitivism, and of irresponsibility. Other great poets refused to be bound by conventions, but in being original they were quite conscious of origins. Spenser in his archaic medievalism, Shakespeare in his plot derivativeness, Donne in his scholasticism, Milton in his Christianity, all supported a great tradition, but primitivists were the first instance of a literary movement dissatisfied with its traditions. They did not want to return to but to constitute origins—the aboriginal rather than the original was their aim. They referred vaguely to Homer and Ossian as poets who were great because they had no traditions. Their position was, of course, a hopelessly false one, modern scholarship having proved that they were quite as wrong about Homer as they were about Ossian. But there is good reason for its falsity. To be dissatisfied with things as they are and to "return," to put back the clock, is always a fallacy, for the simple reason that the movement of time permits of no alteration. To react is to be suspended, and primitivism, therefore, created no new style in itself, remaining eighteenth century through and through, as with Warton and his contemporaries, until the romantic attitude became definitely established.

It will be apparent that the change above-mentioned can be expressed in terms of the collapse of creativeness and the rise of criticism. As long as art is drawn from the soil it is living; when separated from it into a metropolitan product, it no longer is life, but looks at life. That is the obvious reason for the pictorial nature of romanticism. In philosophy the eighteenth century saw the final expression of the great creative period when Leibnitz, in his poetic pregnancy of language and extraordinary penetration of mind, brought into existence the ultimate convictions of Western thought, to be followed by Kant, who compressed that thought itself into its final categories. Following the creativeness of metaphysics comes the criticism of ethics, of politics, of aesthetics, of a philosophy of history and a history of philosophy.

Similarly primitivism is also a criticism of life as it had up to that time been lived. Its forward bias pushes it into the pessimism of the great romantics and the fatalism of Hardy. It may be a foolish and futile criticism, but it was a pioneering one, and it implied more than it realized.

But if primitivism is a transitional phase, it must, like all transitional phases, carry implicit a contradiction which leads to its extinction, as it of necessity brings into sharp conflict the differing ideas of the two ages it separates. Primitivism split on several such contradictions. In the first place, it abjured a pessimistic view of human nature as such, resenting such a view as emanating from materialists, like Hobbes, who regarded man as essentially an animal and only incidentally a human being. The whole primitivistic thesis rests on the assumption that man is by nature good. Now this in itself is a mark of the rising tide of democracy and the rule of the "people." The diction of the common man was quite good enough for Wordsworth.[6] Even earlier the common man was set above the artificial gentleman suspected of hypocrisy, as shown in the antitheses of Charles and Joseph Surface, Tom Jones and Blifil.[7] The same idea is carried out later in Dickens ad nauseam. The attack on privilege, on the infringement of rights, in the name of liberty, equality, and fraternity, the economists' superposition of individual happiness over the common good, all focus the attention on the dignity and worth of the individual in the abstract. The old land–town connection implied a felt if never rationalized consensus: being all parts of an organism, individuals felt themselves integrated into a living unity. But the loss of that inward unity forced the individual himself to become the centre of the world, and in this primitivistic conception the romantic egoism and the egoistic romantic theory of imagination alike had their origins.

The greatest poetry, according to this theory, was the spontaneous outpourings of the bard. Hence, a search began to find other poetry which was equally the work of the common men, therefore natural and unforced, therefore good.[8] Although literary fingers got rather badly burned occasionally by Ossian, by Rowley, even by the "Shakespearean" forgery of *Vortigern*,[9] a great deal was done, and Gray's Icelandic researches, Percy's *Reliques*, Scott's antiquarianism, all brought out much valuable work.[10] But this influx resulted in a more eclectic survey of poetry than had hitherto been possible, paving the way for greater tolerance and appreciation—for popular approval, in short, as opposed to the judgment of a clique. Thus, in accomplishing its mission primitivism did something it did not altogether intend to do. It got the freedom it wanted, but it brought a more adequate appreciation of traditions with it.

The theory of imagination was partly fostered by dearth of intelligent criticism. Eighteenth-century critics became more and more at a loss in dealing with the new poetry, and later, in the time of Shelley and Keats, when *Century* and *Blackwood's* presided over English literature like a couple of Carthaginian idols,[11] the average critic of the time was a pompous ass, with no brains or ears.[12] To call Keats a cockney is, properly and sympathetically analysed, a most profound remark to make about him, but when this is found in connection with wholesale condemnations of his poetry by "critics" who had not read it, it does not inspire confidence.[13] But such a collapse was inevitable in view of the fact that, since the poet himself was becoming a critic, he had to arrogate the function of criticism, as with Byron, Coleridge, and Poe's dissection of his *Raven*.[14] The primitivistic theory, thus, works through historically to its direct opposite, for if poets or poet-natures can alone evaluate poetry, it follows that the appeal of poetry is an esoteric one, and this idea is developed by Arnold, Pater, Swinburne, and others until it reaches its extreme statement in Wilde: "Man has two duties in life. The first duty is to be as artificial as possible. What the second duty is no one has yet discovered."[15]

A similar metamorphosis of rococo into romanticism through primitivism may be worth noticing here. The primitivistic ideas developed from the movement that marked the collapse of the old order in the first place—the cult of sensibility. The strength of the great baroque tradition breaks down into a decadence of femininity. The fussy intricacies of the later architecture, the powerful influence of the economic factor of the woman reader—which helped to develop the Richardson novel— the outpouring of sentiment in the form of confessions, diaries, and letters, all mark the female character of the period. Poets like Klopstock, Mackenzie's men of feeling, and many other instances of the vague emotionalism of thought, apparent alike in the deism and the scepticism of the time, testify that the sopping handkerchief was the order of the day. This tendency produced Rousseau's *Confessions*—it is hardly necessary to condemn it in stronger terms—and Rousseau was the immediate ancestor of primitivism. When primitivism itself came, it was largely a feminine admiration of the strong man—Rousseau's philosophy is of the type best adapted to be discussed at gatherings of women—and if not invariably feminine, certainly often effeminate. The economic change described above, which forced the whole of life down into the distaff side, is accompanied by many complaints about the loss of masculinity. There is then a very evident development from here to the swashbuckling romantic tradition of Hugo, Dumas, Schiller, Echegaray, perhaps even Byron, which springs up as a narcotic to the sedentary. Here again there is a final and extreme formulation at the opposite end in Strindberg.

Primitivism was more successful in its ideas on diction, which with Wordsworth start a development the closing scenes of which are now being enacted. As long as poetry is a living language it is natural and sacrosanct. Prose expresses something conceptually rather than imaginatively and is a style subordinate to matter—what is said is something over and above the manner of saying it. When poetry, too, begins to "say something," in the conceptual sense, the barrier between prose and poetry disappears. The gradual interabsorption is a long and complex question, but its existence is apparent enough. Ossian made the first assault; Blake followed. The *vers libre* form was then popularized by Whitman and the spade work was finished with him. The criticisms hurled at this poet on technical grounds all revert to the one complaint eventually, that prose and poetry were merging. Bad free verse is not only bad poetry but also bad prose. With the advent of the prose poem (e.g. Giovannitti's *The Walker*)[16] the boundary is well on the way to dissolution. So many hairline cases exist at present—Marianne Moore, for instance—that to refuse a writer the title of poet on the ground that he writes prose has long been regarded as pedantic. The connection is probably that free verse tends to equate the line with the idea, and prose the sentence with the idea. It is an open question if any better free verse is written today than the prose of Bernard Shaw, whose long sentences are obviously intended to be spoken in a breath, like the lines in a poem of Sandburg's, or than the antiphonal chant of G.K. Chesterton.

The approach in manner as well as technique starts with primitivism. Gray's theory, built as it was on a classical training, had to give way before a tendency toward what we can only call colloquialism. Wordsworth did not get very far along this line; here Blake is the pioneer, with his direct and forceful speaking style. The leader in this field is Browning, corresponding to Whitman on the technical side. The spiritual informalization of poetry by Browning (together with Meredith, Hood, and even Gilbert) played a great part in shaking up the idea of "elegance," and perhaps the violent reaction produced by the work of Tennyson was an even greater negative influence. Today the language of poetry approximates more closely than ever before to speech, the great goal of the primitivists. Inversions, extended similes, expedients like "o'er," "th' expanding," etc., the use of words—"ere," e.g.—not found in conversation, are excluded from modern poetry to an extent which even so rigid a formalist as Pope would probably find incomprehensible.

The objectifying of art into the realm of the sense world brings with it an immensely widened scope. The idea of absolute freedom in choice of subject, taking its rise from pioneers like Thomson in the country, Blake and the child, Wordsworth in his wide but coherent world which included even idiots, and followed by the great romantics whose subjects were essentially exotic, brought poetry into every sphere. This point is evidenced in Stevenson's discussion of Whitman and his use of the word "hatter." You can't bring a hatter into a serious poem, said Tusitala; it's not literary tact.[17] Primitivism and its successors deny the existence of literary tact. But this depends again on the validity of the egoistic theory, for infinite subjects imply infinite methods of treating them. Primitivism aims at breaking down the old strict forms one by one—the development of the ode is a symptom that a new spirit was striving for the mastery, not of form, but over form itself. Primitivism never gets away from impressionistic implications. And as impressionism is a highly artificial and sophisticated form of art, we are back in the vicious circle we noted above.

Primitivism created no new style, for it was not a new idea but the first of literary fads. It is, in fact, *the* literary fad, for all crazes are primitivistic, the feverish desire to find something new being itself the result of an artificial and disillusioned weariness, through ready recognition, of further complications of old practices. Unless something genuinely new does come, however, the fad has no support in reality and what is ascribed to the primitive is a cheap product of the *status quo*. Space utterly precludes discussion of the many false alarms which have since been raised. The development of national consciousness in America built up a primitivistic complex there, as it was considered that Whitman and others would form the basis of a brand new literature. Says Edgar Lee Masters of his earlier, undistinguished poetry:

> Tick, tick, tick, what little iambics,
> While Homer and Whitman roared in the pines!
>
> [*Petit, the Poet*, lines 17–18]

The association of Homer with Whitman has a familiar ring. Now Whitman certainly had this idea himself, but, being the anticipation, not of a

new culture, but of the advancing mature civilization of the United
States he proved to be a born poet but not a born prophet. It is true that
the United States itself never woke up to the possibility of such a poetic
mantle being cast upon it until its renaissance just before the war, when
it was far too late. Whitman, for instance, wrote some superb poetry, but
in attempting to formulate the conceptions of a dawning future age, of
democracy, liberty, individualism, and so forth, he was simply repro-
ducing the ideas of a belated Patrick Henry. Mark Twain's pitiful failure
to deal with the teeming life in which he moved is more striking. The
old country, however, not being so close, was more ready to revive the
primitivistic idea, and between London's reception of Otaheite and that
of Joaquin Miller there is hardly an atom of difference.[18]

Other fashions, such as the "Squirearchy" in Georgian poetry,[19] the
entry of the sea into English literature, and countless attempts in America, must here be passed over. Perhaps the best example in contemporary literature—though it has passed its meridian—is the cult of the
Negro in the United States admiring thoroughly Yankee work produced
by coloured people. It is believed by many that jazz originated in Africa,
that Negro spirituals are Negroid folk music, and I understand it to be a
current impression in Europe that the songs of Stephen Collins Foster
are Negro folk tunes.

But the primitivism which helped to destroy the eighteenth century
and make the nineteenth century possible, being the first of these fads,
signified far more by its appearance, and whatever we may think of its
inherent quality, much of the finest English poetry is not fully comprehensible unless we recognize the inevitability and historical fitness of
the noble savage.

2

Romanticism

This paper was written in 1933 for Professor George S. Brett of the philosophy department at the University of Toronto. It was submitted for Philosophy 4g, "Modern Philosophy," one topic of which was the romantic movement. On the title-page Frye wrote, "The first part of this essay deals with the general definition, concepts, and features of romanticism, the second part with romantic philosophy, the third with romantic music, the fourth romanticism in English literature, and the conclusion indicates the general trend in politics. I have not had time to deal with the painting or with Continental literature. I hope that the inordinate length of the essay will prove to be as necessary an evil as it is an unmitigated one. Romanticism being a cultural phenomenon, the centre of gravity of this essay lies in the realm of aesthetics." The asterisks Frye used to mark footnotes have been changed to numbered superscripts. The typescript is in the NFF, 1991, box 37, file 8.

The essay is broadly organized as follows:

Part One. Introduction
  I. Romanticism as a Cultural Term
  II. Romanticism in Terms of Space and Time
  III. The Organization of the Critical and Creative Arts
  IV. The Four Periods of Romanticism
  V. Romantic Conflicts: Youth versus Age, Male versus Female

Part Two. Romantic Philosophy
  I. Rousseau
  II. Kant
  III. Fichte
  IV. Schelling

Part One

I

What is born must live; what lives must die. The consideration of any problem in history belongs to life. Hence, it is essential in examining any historical phenomenon to keep in mind the unit of life, so to speak, to which it belongs, and the larger the scope of the phenomenon, the more essential this is, and the nearer the ultimate background approaches. With a purely cultural question to deal with, such as romanticism certainly is, we are at once implicated in the larger one. Our initial survey, then, takes in the duofold question: What unit of life is implicated in romanticism? and, Where and how does romanticism come into that life?

The word *culture* in itself helps to define our unit. There is no satisfactory adjective in common use which does so, but the nearest is the term

"Western." Romanticism is neither a national movement nor a universal one. It springs up at the same time in England, France, Germany, Italy, and even in America, but there is no Oriental and not even a true Russian romanticism. We altogether misunderstand the term in its strict sense as a cultural phenomenon (i.e., as distinct from the merely general use of the words *romance* and *romantic*) unless we regard it as definitely a phase in the organic life of that culture-soul which arose in Western Europe at the beginning of the "medieval" period and has confined its range if not its influence to Western Europe, spreading later into virgin territories like the Americas. Romanticism, then, is a cross-section of Western culture. There is no necessity other than an abstractly logical one to bring the whole history of that culture into its ramifications, but it should be advisable to outline the general form in order to show romanticism in its proper context. To give an exposition of romantic philosophy and a criticism of romantic literature, music, and painting without at least attempting to deal with the how and the why, as well as the what, might be exhaustive and painstaking, but would remain two-dimensional, superficial, and, in the last analysis, meaningless.

Romanticism signifies the second cultural change in the Western world since the great migrations, the other being the Renaissance-Reformation. Now a change in a living form is inevitable and not accidental or adventitious; the fully developed plant is implicit in the seed. The "starting point" of the Renaissance is so elusive that it baffles all attempts to grasp it, though some persevering scholars have chased it halfway through the Dark Ages before giving up and declaring that there is no starting point and, consequently, no Renaissance. We do not propose a similar pursuit, believing that such an attempt is based upon a false conception of the problem involved. We shall attack first, not the question of what originates romanticism, but of what underlies it.

The great medieval civilization is essentially a culture of the land and soil. The economic system is feudal, the central art form architecture, the philosophy bound up with religion and directed toward a complete cosmogonic synthesis. All these are land symbols; the village is a market place and the town a nexus or focal point around which all the land systems centre. Necessarily, the activity being directed toward the town, there comes a time when the town suddenly takes on a change of status. It becomes something in itself, something distinctive and opposed to the land. That change underlies the Renaissance and Reformation. The burgher and guilds appear; the arts separate out and are practised by a school of great masters. The old religious land-synthesis is shattered: the instinctive communal affinity of the earlier period changes to an appeal to reason centred in the individual. The town, now become alien, becomes fascinating as well, and eventually tears itself up by the roots from the countryside and becomes, no longer the culture-town, but the metropolis. That change occurred at the close of the eighteenth century, and romanticism is to the metropolis what the Renaissance was to the culture-town—its philosophical and artistic product.

We should clearly understand that this metropolitan growth represents a new idea, a new form of life, and not simply an expansion of the smaller centre. Even older cities which had been central points of their respective national units, like London, Paris, or Vienna, did not simply grow faster: they swelled up and burst. Paris was in 1900 five times as large as it was in 1800. In England Liverpool, Glasgow, Birmingham, Manchester, appear as suddenly as fungi. In Germany the culture-towns like Nuremberg, Leipzig, Munich, either change into the metropolis form or disappear, and the new spirit rears its head in the gigantic symbol of Berlin, which gradually absorbs the whole of Germany and a great deal of Austria and Scandinavia. In America the change is clearest when we see how utterly different the spirit of colonial revolt in Boston and Philadelphia is from the immense energy which annihilated the Southern culture and incarnated itself in New York and Chicago. New colonies with small populations, like Canada or Australia, immediately have all their energy sucked dry in evolving two or more unnatural and tumorous city-growths. Japan, with no culture-soul of her own, takes on the Western form and produces Tokyo; China and India reached the megalopolitan stage centuries ago and do not change. In Russia we can see the radical difference between precultural centres like Moscow or Kiev and the Western impositions of Leningrad and Odessa, as thoroughly exotic as a rubber plant in a New England homestead. Of course, it is conventional to say that this change was "caused" by the Industrial Revolution; let us suspend this question for a moment and examine the nature of this new cosmopolis.

The Western metropolis is a general Western phenomenon. The great cities are not national centres, in spite of their being so often used as nation-symbols by jingoists and reactionaries. Even the accidental differences of language are almost obliterated in extreme forms like New York. Travellers returning from Tokyo or Buenos Aires are never tired of repeating that they are "just like any big city over here."

The metropolis, then, is a formless and chaotic floating mass, and is essentially an inorganic form. If we compare the culture-towns of any culture with its later metropolis-forms, we can easily see this difference between the city developing out of the soil like a plant with an organic self-contained growth and the dead confusion of its gigantic successor. Tyre as against Carthage, Republican as against Caesarian Rome, Athens as against Alexandria, Mecca as against Baghdad, all show the same opposition of, say, Florence as against Berlin. What is more, this sudden tearing up of the metropolis out of the land must of necessity represent the final stage of a culture. We have seen that the life of a culture is commensurate with its urban development; therefore, when the city becomes inorganic and limitless, the culture dies. Now in every case of which we have any record this movement has always been associated with a cultural development corresponding in every essential respect to our romanticism.

It is possible to reduce this basis of romanticism to lower terms. As any culture, unlike the metropolis, must have some kind of a root, it follows that it must have that root in only one of the big cities over which it spreads when in that stage. Classical civilization in its last stage had Rome, Antioch, Alexandria, and Constantinople, but the romanticism of the classical world centred in Alexandria. Similarly Mohammedan romanticism emanates from Baghdad rather than Cairo or even Cordoba. And although Western civilization has dozens of big cities, the supreme symbol of romanticism is Paris, not the Paris of Louis Quatorze or Louis Quinze, but modern Paris, which was born on the Fourteenth of July.[1] We shall find that the subversive approach of romanticism to what precedes it centres in Paris in every instance. Its irresistible attraction for sophisticates and artistic novices, and its reputation among the unsophisticated as very gorgeous and splendid but very wicked, mark it out as the focal point of the last effort of Western cultural activity. Instinctively feeling its significance, provincials of other countries revolt from it just as the Hebrews did from Nineveh and Babylon, two sinister names which ring through all subsequent prophecy with the same meaning as the classical *delenda est Carthago*.[2] In spite of Shakespeare, Rabelais, Cervantes, the Renaissance centres in and radiates from the Italian culture-town. In spite of Calvin and Knox, the Reformation was produced by German burghers. And similarly, in spite of the easy supremacy of England and Germany in literature, philosophy, and music, romanticism centres in and radiates from Paris.[3]

II

Now that Buckle and Mommsen[4] have finally been embalmed in their unreadable opuses[5] and responsible historians are taking the organic view of history for granted, more and more use has been made of cultural terms like Renaissance, baroque, rococo. Not only do we speak of the art, literature, or philosophy of these periods, but we are also beginning to talk of Renaissance science, baroque mathematics, rococo economics, and so on, including all departments of life under a *Zeitgeist* terminology. But romanticism obviously does not apply to a culture period having the same universal connotation. Everyone knows in a general way what is meant by a romanticist in art, literature, philosophy, or politics, but what romanticism in mathematics or science could be, other than a term of contempt, is hard to imagine. We shall see later that there are romantic approaches to both, such as that of Fechner to physics,[6] but we feel that these have overstepped their boundaries. Similarly, the economic, scientific, mathematical, and engineering activity contemporary with it rests on a basis which might be called, for want of a better term, positivistic. There is a positivistic philosophy, of course; we can see traces of positivist influence in literature—Zola, for instance—but the question of what kind of music, let us say, that a positivist composer would produce has never, so far as I know, come up for detailed consideration. It would appear that there is a fundamental and irreconcilable opposition here which we do not find in the earlier periods.[7]

Obviously all cultural activity, in fact all activity of any kind, is comprehended through the two ultimate data of time and space. It therefore follows that the organic development of a culture would be fundamentally an organic synthesis of temporal and spatial concepts. In mankind the two great temporal symbols are the blood and the reproductive faculty: the senses and reasoning are spatial. The former is, thus, implicated in being, the second in thought. Thought is plainly an abstraction of which the concrete entity is being, so that a creative activity, in the strict sense of the word, is one in which thought is subservient to the demands of being. Hence, in the climax of a creative period, mathematics, the purest form of thought, would be worked out in ontological implications, and the completion of the organic number-world would bring with it a statement of the ultimate convictions which emanate from the blood.[8] The derivation of the word *religion* from *religare*, to bind together, suggests that religion is the name given to that activity which forces the world comprehended by sense and reason into line with the inner intuitive urge of the throbbing temporal propulsion. Consequently, we should expect to find that the greatest creative mathematicians, such as Descartes, Newton, Pascal, and Leibnitz, were all men of a profoundly religious nature. Opposed to these figures are Bacon with his rigid program of inductive empiricism, and Hobbes with a thoroughgoing scientific materialism,[9] both thoroughly sceptical natures, one ignoring the importance of mathematics and the other a mathematical dilettante. The first thing that strikes us about romanticism, then, is that philosophy becomes unmathematical and the great romantic philosophers uniformly carry on without it. Mathematics separates out from philosophy and goes over to the camp of its old enemy, empirical science. This leaves philosophy shorn of a good deal of its metaphysics. With the advent of the Kantian critical philosophy that field begins to narrow. The ultimate questions it pursues change from the ontological to the ethical. A new and dominant activity moves up beside this—the philosophy of history and the history of philosophy. Now a concentration on the historical and moral aspects of speculation is a concentration on the temporal element. Similarly science parts from its moorings and shifts over to a purely spatial ground of empiric positivism. Now if religion be the binding and linking force holding together temporal and spatial outlooks, the force which separates them can logically be called *skepsis*.[10] This, then, is the second great underlying fact of romanticism.

It is not difficult to see the essential connection of *skepsis* with the metropolis. There is something plantlike about the growth of a culture, and it takes root in a certain place just as any vegetable colony does. This taking root is always accompanied by a religious spirit which dominates every activity. Precultural or nomadic peoples, who have not yet taken root, make no attempt to turn their vital powers in the direction of an organized spatial thought-conquest of the world. "Taking root" as a matter of course suggests the development of agriculture. It follows that a religious spirit has a close affinity with the soil,[11] and when the metropolis arises and culture becomes an epiphyte, this connection disappears. A metropolitan, thus, floats free in space, with his senses and reasoning powers no longer bound to arrange his world for him in accordance with what he feels to be right. He is in a position to look at life, but not to feel its upthrust inwardly.

There is an integral connection between atomism and chaos (atomism in the old-fashioned sense of constitution by indivisible units), the conception usually being associated with atheism. The structure of a metropolis is atomic, each individual existing by himself with no essential connection with anyone else. Friends are friends of elective affinities,[12] attracted by the senses and reason. In a metropolis it is impossible that a group as varied as the Canterbury pilgrims could all travel together to the same place with the same object. There is not the same religious or linking force present. Consequently, it is necessary that in a metropolitan existence there should be implicit an idea of absolute relativity. Each individual must constitute himself the centre of the world. Subjective nominalistic idealism must be taken for granted. Now in the soul there are will, an outward-directed faculty with a social connotation, reason, an ego-effacing faculty with a universal one, and feeling, the differentiating and peculiar aspect. An egocentric approach to the world must, therefore, subordinate will and reason to feeling.

If the temporal and spatial concepts begin to separate, it follows that time and space pose separate problems. Having already traced out the fundamental opposition of romanticism and positivism, it would seem logical that, as positivism is obviously associated with spatial problems, romanticism represents the temporal side. Evidently the egocentric contemplation of time as a sense datum, which replaces the inward feeling of its propulsion, is a space-approach, and reduces time to a kind of fourth dimension. In other words, it is a paradoxical, antitemporal attack on the mystery of time-movement, and so rests on a sceptical basis, whatever religious doctrines it may carry over from an earlier tradition.

It is not difficult to see what a sceptical approach to time would implicate.[13] It is plainly its business to look at time, and, hence, to classify and work out the formal ordering of temporal manifestations. This means that what is interesting in philosophy, for instance, is not the attempt to formulate an impregnable system, but to show and explain the growth of all the impregnable systems that have already been formulated. The history of philosophy is only part of the universal aim of a philosophy of history.[14] Philosophy is a spatial fixation, history a time-movement. Similarly when we examine the work of writers and composers whom the world has agreed to call romantic, we shall find them attacking a temporal dynamic art statically and pictorially.

III

There are three compulsions of activity. The first is the time-compulsion to action, or morals. The second is the space-compulsion to thought, or logic. The third is the feeling-compulsion of aesthetics. Justice, truth, and beauty is a triad as old as Plato. Let us consider the time-space opposition in this light for a moment. Obviously the religious approach would be from time, to implicate truth in morality. This is just as true of Leibnitz as it is of the patristic tradition, or any thinking done in a creative period. If truth is moral, then there is implicit an optimistic basis for thought. The classical soul is different from ours, and when Plato, who corresponds to the Leibnitzian period in his culture, attacked this problem, he did so from the typical classical viewpoint, which is the opposite of ours, starting from the spatial side and attempting to enmesh justice by logic. Now this is just what a critical approach to Leibnitz in Western philosophy, such as that of Kant, would do. Plato was as little satisfied with the result of his investigations as Kant was. The separating out of justice and truth under pressure of *skepsis* destroys this optimistic basis of thinking and results eventually in pessimism—romantic pessimism. This is implicit in Kant, who reached essentially the same solution as Plato—conviction of God's existence, or any working hypostasis of optimism, resides in the blood and not the brain. But the Western mind differs from the classical in its possession of an historical sense. Such a sense precludes scepticism from being a mere denial or suspension of judgment. The proposition that we know nothing is dismissed, and the proposition that we know only phenomena replaces it. And, as we have shown, to treat time-manifestations as phenomena is to treat them spatially. But now let us take this third compulsion—the aesthetic, which belongs to feeling. If romanticism subordinates to feeling will and reason, then correspondingly it would subordinate to aesthetics morals and logic, and we shall find that it does this very definitely. It would be expected, too, that romantic pessimism would turn to beauty and away from both life and science for solace, and we shall find that this, too, is so. But as time and space are ultimate data, feeling cannot be outside them, nor can it belong only to one, which would absorb it in will or understanding. There is only one thing left for it to be—an interfusion of time in space.

There is, therefore, an opposition in aesthetics between art regarded as a spatial abstraction from a temporal force and art regarded in the other direction as a living time-phenomenon frozen into a space-dimension.

The temporal approach belongs to the religious period, spatial to the sceptical. As the word *creative* has been so frequently used in connection with the former, the latter suggests the antithesis—"critical." This opposition runs parallel with all the others previously mentioned. Creation is realistic, in the *universalia sunt realia*[15] connotation, and deals with the abstracting of types and patterns in space and time. Criticism rests on egocentricity and subjective idealism; the world remains exactly as it is, and the faculty of artistry is spatial, one of selection and arrangement.

In the prereligious stage of culture the central art form is, of course, a more or less chaotic interpenetration of time and space feelings. The subject matter is a mixture of creation and criticism, or legend; the presentation a similar mixture, or poetic narrative. The basic art is in short the epic. With the religious sense comes, necessarily, the sense of objective form, and out of the womb of the Church are born the great time-creation of music and the space-creation of drama. As a sense of form depends upon a power of forming, it follows that the plastic arts last as long as the religious period does. Architecture is the great plastic time-form which goes along with music, sculpture the space-form associated with drama. With the rise of *skepsis*, architecture disappears as an art form, the last true style being the Empire, and there is no typically romantic architecture, but only a romantic approach to architecture, that is, taking what styles already exist and selecting and arranging them. The same is true of sculpture. It should be noted here that, as the approach is in Western culture from the temporal side, a great deal of Western sculpture is absorbed in architectural detail, and drama has a tendency to approach a musical form in some cases.[16]

Running along with these four is the art of painting. Now painting differs from the others in being a sort of commentary art, an individualist approach and reaction to the world. That is why it became most prominent when the Italian Renaissance brought individualism into prominence. It is, in short, a critical art, a religious time-space criticism. It definitely emphasizes selection and arrangement rather than abstraction and is the only art requiring versatility in the artist. It bears a personal signature and has nothing of the anonymity of a Gothic cathedral or the abstract completeness of a fugue. As a running commentary on the others, it absorbs some power from each—architectural in Giotto, sculptural in the Renaissance carven line, musical in the technique of evolving an outline by flecks and dots of colour, and dramatic with the narrative painters.

But we have shown that the criticism of organic life forms is the chief business of the romantics, so that their whole aesthetic ideal must be concentrated on the pictorial. The shift in painting psychology from a succubic to an incubic status is the prime feature of romanticism in the arts. We shall trace this idea out in more detail later on. Now out of painting come a time and a space criticism, the one descending from music, the other from drama. The abstract tonal presentation of the accented rhythm of life becomes a subjective reaction to it, giving us an art form which I am unable to find a name for and for the present will call the lyric-essay. The critical analogue of the drama is more evidently fiction.

To illustrate by a diagram:

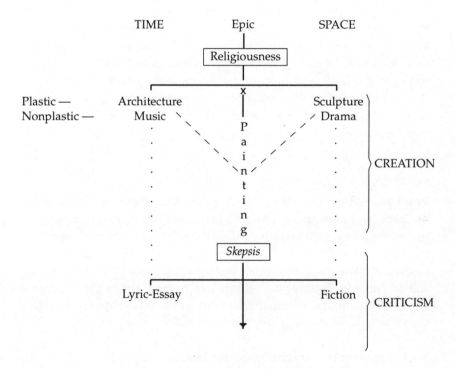

We have said that the difference between creation and criticism is the difference between abstraction and arrangement. The rhythms, patterns, and symmetries implicit in nature underlie the first, nature itself the second; hence, the question of form is external in the former instance and relative to the artist in the latter. Here is the chief cause of the popular antithesis of classic and romantic, the one imitative of form and depending on the artist for content, the other reversing the process. Impressionistic implications in romanticism are not hard to find, as we shall see. This means that with the rise of *skepsis* the spatial activity of science will depend upon arrangement, or experiment, and the temporal activity of life similarly upon arrangement of time-phenomena, or philosophy of history. But the point is that in the latter case we are not really dealing with phenomena, which are spatial, and, hence, historical thought cannot, if it works from its own premises and not those of science, found its case on historical facts as they are, but on the significance and meaning of their appearance. Every time-phenomenon is a symbol. Hence, the form of the philosophy of history is that of the picture, and this extends itself over every ramification of romanticism.

So at last we arrive at a working definition of romanticism as the cultural manifestation of an activity directed toward a critical and symbolic time-synthesis. As such, it remains in opposition to positivism, which is similarly a critical and factual space-synthesis. The distinction is, of course, only an emphasis difference—there are few things more romantic, for example, than some aspects of the thought of Comte. But the distinction is there.

IV

In arriving at our definition we have ignored the implications of some of the steps, and have so far considered romanticism in its negative aspect as an opposition to the spirit of the precedent age. The movement we have just defined as romantic, however, shows in itself a development extending from the middle of the eighteenth century to the present day, and to gain a perspective it might be well to trace out its general course before following it out in more detail in its various fields. In general, it shows four periods which defy strict chronology:

   I. The period of sensibility and the primitivist thesis.
   II. Systematic period.
   III. Postromanticism and decadence—rise and domination of positivism.
   IV. Rehabilitation in a synthesis of exhaustion.

The opposition of romanticism to rococo is preceded by a transitional, thetical, argumentative period which compared them to the advantage of the newer. This is first of all an attempt to justify the shift to feeling as the centre of the individual. The dying rococo age is characterized by a remarkable phenomenon called the cult of "sensibility," where the man of fine feeling was regarded as the highest type. Sensibility as practised was almost equivalent to sentimentality, but the word has its uses for our thesis. What men like Richardson, Klopstock, Rousseau were really getting at was not so much sensibility as sensitivity. The refined man was the man most open to emotional impressions from every side. Here is the birth of romanticism: a swing out to the senses and divorcing them from every other part of the soul. The emphasis on the emotional response to sensations, rather than mere observational power, shows that they were regarded, not as facts to be examined, but as symbolic of the observing activity. The chief result was, therefore, not an immediate expansion of knowledge but a flood of egocentric and highly self-conscious letters, diaries, confessions, which by their very nature were marked for sudden death. In our day the man who is awed by every-thing he sees and writes great stretches of letters and diaries is the pro-vincial finding himself in the big city for the first time, and enthusiastic about it.[17] (The fact that this cult antedates the Industrial Revolution and its metropolis by about fifty years proves nothing except that a consis-tent economic determinist has on his hands an enormous mass of recal-citrant facts to explain away.)

This was followed by the primitivist postulate. It should be noted that while the thought of an organic period rests on the optimism brought out by Leibnitz and shown by Kant to be the product of the blood rather than the brain, such optimism is unintelligible without the doctrine of original sin. Optimism in thought requires to balance it a sort of work-ing pessimism as the basis of action. But with the collapse of the former imminent, it was necessary to bolster it up by carrying the exaltation of feeling a stage further. The man of feeling, that is, the individual and peculiar man, is by nature good. The whole organic development of the religious period has conspired to make him bad. Religion itself is an invention of self-seeking priests, and mankind was far happier before it came, back in the nomadic days. In this is concentrated the whole extent of romantic pessimism in thought and positivistic optimism in action. The noble savage arises to symbolize the new sceptical revolt arising from suddenly turning around and looking at the propelling force of life. The new metropolitan eyes the soil from which he has been cut off, and when he thinks of having lived in connection with it he grows bitter. But as a new form of sense experience, he is delighted with it. The idea of a country vacation for a city worker springs up, and Marie Antoinette goes forth to milk cows.[18] The noble savage represents the joys of living in the country without the responsibilities attached to a peasant cultivation of the ground.

On the other hand, the sudden consciousness by the Western world of its own cultural traditions brings the latter into the limelight for consideration as well. The organic period had taken it more or less for granted that the Middle Ages were a nightmare of horror and stupidity and that civilization was developing away from them into a Utopian promised land governed by pure reason. But the earlier romantics who had the courage to look back upon this Sodom and Gomorrah found that it would bear more sustained investigation. Here is another source of the classic–romantic opposition. An organically developing period must, broadly speaking, ignore the whole of its earlier traditions, because its face is set in the other direction. But if it can see another culture which has been completed and can model and discipline itself upon what it has seen done, it gains a tremendous impetus, just as any poet finds the work of others more valuable to him for imitation than his own earlier productions. The whole of Western culture up to this time had been modelled upon the work of the classical civilization, so potently from the Renaissance on that it got from it a momentum that often propelled it through decades of sterility. However, this practice is bound to make for pedantry eventually, and revolt is as natural to pedantry as a recoil to a gun. It should be noted that a creative activity, which requires a model, usually looks at the later and more critical period for it. Hence, the classical influence on this period is, largely speaking, more Roman than Greek—the Hellenic nature of the Renaissance movement is now recognized as greatly overestimated. The critical period of Western culture takes in a more sympathetic appreciation of the Greek and tends to swing toward Euripides and Pindar and away from Ovid and Seneca. On the other hand, the proportion of classical influence as a whole dwindles appreciably. This formula is confirmed in a negative way by the political movements which signified the growth of the romantic spirit. A change in history is duofold—ideal and material.[19] A period of ideal change must for stability be worked out in a static environment, as with Kant and Hegel. Conversely, a material change such as a revolution must consolidate the *status quo* in thought—a revolution engineered by a theorist being foredoomed to failure. The ideal change collateral with the French Revolution was the exaltation of feeling over will and logic—but the Revolution itself ended up in the worship of the goddess of reason. Similarly, the classical influence upon the French and American revolutions was overwhelmingly Latin.[20] The new critical spirit could understand its own culture as well, and a revival of interest in medievalism was the result. Heine, who is certainly a romantic, defined romanticism as an enthusiasm for the Middle Ages.[21] Hence, we find romanticism associated with extreme liberalism or extreme conservatism according as the viewpoint is focused on the noble savage and the natural man or on the period of Gothic feudalism. Heine's definition taken together with the curt but profound remark of Goethe—"Classicism is health; romanticism is disease"[22]—will give us a basis for approaching what are now seen to be the two leading features of romanticism, which we may call the exotic tendency and the esoteric tendency. When these two tendencies are held together the result is romanticism; when they separate, we have positivism and postromanticism. Let us trace this movement out.

The romantic theory of imagination, which says that the intuition of the critical artist is more to be respected in matters of form than any external dicta, implies that the greater the artist, the wider his range of sensation will be. Hence, it is necessary for him to study more and receive a great deal of purely second-hand artistic or philosophical inspiration. Of course, everything he perceives has to be thoroughly absorbed into his mind in order to rank among the egocentric ideas which form his world. But the ideas are transplanted from outside, and in a sense every artistic idea in a critical period is exotic. Originality, which consists in selection, depends, thus, to some extent upon the novelty of that selection, and it is necessary for the artist or philosopher to have a wide range of subjects at his command. The poets turn to the landscape and from the landscape, after that novelty has worn off, into the strangest and remotest countries. Many scenes from romantic plays, novels, and poems are enacted in places that are little more than geographical concepts. Indian, Arabian, Chinese influences are brought wholesale into philosophy. Painting includes some of heaven and nearly all of hell in its range. In the case of an art, the influence of other arts filters in. Literary and pictorial programs for music, social problems for literature, and so on, become commonplaces.

All this is quite in keeping with the viewpoint of the wide-ranging watcher which the artist or philosopher has become. We have shown, however, that mere ranging is not done for its own sake, but the external sensations are exploited purely with reference to the perceiving soul. As they are not in the last analysis fully comprehensible by anyone else, the implication of the esoteric in the exotic is, thus, seen as essential. Now we have noted that romanticism is a factor of the approach which depends on the selection of phenomena. But, of course, the selective process, though fundamental, cannot be the whole of activity, and in, say, an artist, there must be a struggle with an abstracting and creative tendency. The result of this battle is that artistic work tends continually toward making some kind of abstracting pattern out of the subjectively arranged ideas, and, of course, a subjective abstraction arises. Here we see the source of that recondite turning away from life and "literature of escape" motif which is so closely associated with romanticism. Hence comes with romanticism the dominant symbol of the narcotic. The fumes of alcohol, tobacco, and opium rise in clouds from the work of the greatest romantics—Coleridge, Poe, De Quincey, Carlyle, Berlioz, Doré. Art and literature in many instances become opiates, romantic politics possessed of an unmistakably alcoholic stimulus—augmented to heroin in some cases—and philosophy itself, in its tendency to broad and occasionally lazy generalizations, reminds one of the quiescent reflectiveness of tobacco smoking.

This means, of course, that a subjective, individual critic must for his work abstract himself from life. What connections he has with life are as a matter of course sense connections and his reconditeness is the result of the romantic repudiation of the organic life preceding it. Philosophy, too, must go through a similar repudiation. The man of feeling looks back on a period of temporal propulsion as under the domination of will. Looking at it pictorially, the philosopher sees it as dreary and miserable. To go back into the world-as-will would be as undesirable as impossible; all that is possible is a retreat into the abstracted idea, or egocentric idea-group, the world-as-idea.

Man is by nature good: the world-as-will has made him bad. Hence, self-expression must be right. We cannot prove that God exists or that he ever incarnated himself in man; but we can feel those things. Proof henceforth can only be given by the agreement of individuals. Activity of some sort is necessary, and the only satisfactory form under this new condition is not the elaboration of a religious world-synthesis, but simply the acquisition of a large stock of ideas and comparing them with those of others to see which ones will work. This gives us the beginning of positivism. Work is necessary; this kind of work is the only possible one.

So thought turns from the contemplation of the time-world-as-will into the conquest of the space-world-as-idea. The new gospel becomes, therefore, a gospel of reform in analytic action. With the rise of positivism non-Euclidean mathematics appears, replacing the old intellectualized concept of abstract space, and empiric science begins to work out its development, acquiring the time-provinces of biology and economics. Metaphysical foundations of this structure are not present, because this science is not a structure at all, but an excavation, a search for hidden secrets in the world, with a vague unexpressed hope of finding a rock-bottom formula somewhere. Now an activity like this must of necessity either slight the time-problem or reduce it to a space-dimension. In the latter case the great romantic philosophies of history are replaced by the pseudoscientific banalities of materialism, and in the former romanticism becomes decadent. The narcotic art and literature noted above change from the wine of Shelley or Heine to anodynes and chloroforms. The abstraction from reality becomes a sentimental glossing of it. The exotic tendency is carried to the most tasteless limits, for instance in architecture. Positivism hates romanticism because of the latter's insistence on the former's lack of foundations and its predictions that science will break its shins eventually on the mystery of time-movement. In this period romanticism acquires a bad name. It becomes associated with large loose generalizations and the most presumptuous question begging in philosophy, with wild-eyed and exceedingly cloudy liberalism and radicalism in politics, with sentimentality in music, with flamboyance in painting, with gaudy but futile daydreams in literature. Romanticism, in short, is equated with the faults of romanticism. And, as we are still in the backwash of positivism, this attitude persists in many quarters. When I announced my choice of a thesis to a Toronto-Oxford graduate of recent standing, a fanatical and in this post-pragmatic era a somewhat belated empiricist and sceptic, he said: "You'll find it interesting if you don't get the idea that there is anything in it." However, a movement which finds philosophical expression in Fichte, Schelling, Schleiermacher, Schopenhauer, and strikes its roots deep into Kant and Hegel, may be repudiated, but cannot very well be dismissed with a gesture.

Under the domination of positivism romanticism turns into post-romanticism. This has the same attitude to the world-as-will, and cannot content itself with a retreat into the idea and turn into pure positivism because its dislike for the world-as-will is too strong, and positivism looks like a compromise with it. Neither can it hang back in the pictorial stage of romanticism proper, because that is out of harmony with the tendency of the age. The exotic has been lost to positivism; there is nothing to do but continue with the esoteric. Some conception must be evolved whereby the action-program of positivism can be gathered into the individual and not referred to a majority vote. This conception is the will to power, and, as that is doomed to frustration in practice from the start, it manifests itself largely in crankiness, freakishness, and the baiting of humanity in general, whereby it continues the tradition of the supremacy of the feeling-compulsion of aesthetics. Consequently, it is practised by abnormal intellects which are either partly insane, as Strindberg, Baudelaire, perhaps even Wagner, or function normally for a time and then go to pieces—Nietzsche, Schumann, MacDowell, Hugo Wolf, and Van Gogh. This merges insensibly into a somewhat rancid decadence of extreme disillusionment, supercilious erudition, and a contempt of convention.

But at the same time it becomes increasingly clear that the reduction of everything to a space-dimension is equally decadent. Pure materialism, economic determinism of history, linear adaptive evolution, are found unsatisfactory because they are time-problems worked out from an entirely spatial bias, and the only way to deal with the problems arising from the outgrowing of these primitive conceptions is to turn back to time. A reaction sets in against decadence which is really a renovation of romanticism. With the scientific recognition of entropy as a continually increasing random element, a creative or emergent (from this particular point of view it does not matter much which) factor is postulated, first in evolution with Bergson, then in history with Spengler, and the tentative systems of the epigones of Darwin and Marx, as they stand, collapse before a reincarnation of Fichte and Hegel. Pragmatism springs up to show that spatial truth, however abstract or eternal, is in the last analysis relative to the temporal conditioning.

This is the final stage of romanticism. The new era is not one of combining romanticism and positivism in a supreme synthesis, but simply a recognition that each is equally valid and that there is a great and impassable gulf between. Romanticism itself had shattered the great attempt at a synthesis from time; it had returned to shatter its descendant attempt at a synthesis from space. Civilization is a continual abstraction of the city from the soil, materially considered. Considered ideally, it is equally a continually increasing development and abstraction of thought from being. The former is a space-conquest, and when it finally breaks off from time it can only revolve around it like the moon around the earth, brilliant but completed, systematized, and inorganic.[23]

V

In life, that is, in time-movement, there are two great conflicts and contrasts. The first is the conflict of youth immersed in time with age abstracted from it. The second is the clash between male and female as opponent spatial and temporal tendencies.

First, then, romanticism falls almost entirely into the hands of young men. The symbolism of the rise of youth seems to emanate from Mozart, just as the rise of the woman seems to emanate from Goethe. But we feel Mozart's early death as something abnormal and monstrous: the insensate exploitation of Mozart the child burns out too quickly Mozart the man. We get the same idea of early exhaustion in the romantics, but it cannot fairly be said to be premature in any case that I have reviewed. An artist with an urge to create is bound to die young; a philosopher who gains his viewpoint in youth has no further continuous compelling urge and may live on, like Schopenhauer.[24] A romantic politician, too, may live on after finishing his work, though there is marked danger, due to change in conditions, that he will become an infernal nuisance if he does—Mazzini being the best example.[25] The reason for this dominance of youthfulness is not hard to see. Romanticism is an attempt to work out a philosophy or art by dealing with temporal factors from what must necessarily be a spatial standpoint. Youth is that period of life in which the time-urge is most evident. Hence, in general in the organic period, youth undergoes a continual subjection similar to that of woman, because a spatial abstraction can only be the work of a man arrived at an abstracted and spatial viewpoint—that is, a mature man, in whom the various time-surges of enthusiasm and exuberance, notably the sex instinct, do not run away with the attempt to impose a spatial discipline. In other words, a youthful approach would be one preoccupied with temporal considerations, which is what developing art or philosophy cannot be and what romanticism must be. Youth is the period, too, of feeling and imagination, and the supremacy of these is helped along by the fact that the great roman-

tics so often reach their true style almost with their first attempts. The
result is a sharp clash with age—Schopenhauer versus Hegel, for
instance, or Mazzini versus Cavour[26]—the revolt of romantic genius
against academic pedantry being largely the dislike of a young fool for
an old fool. Unfortunately, the public for artistic and philosophical
attempts contains an overwhelming majority of mature people—the
very strength of the temporal force in youth makes them as a rule interested in other things. Besides, all the power and prestige belongs to
maturity. The great romantics, thus, usually lead lonely, unrecognized,
and poverty-stricken lives. Our conception of a young genius starving
in a garret probably dates from this period. Not that lack of recognition
is peculiar to romanticism, but we do not get quite the same phenomenon of ignoring a young artist or philosopher completely and then suddenly recognizing him at a time when, if he were still alive, he would
be in his old age. Usually he has starved to death long ago, Schopenhauer being an isolated exception.

The sexual implications of romanticism are more elusive. The romantic movement, broadly speaking, changes the status of woman from
primarily mother to primarily wife—that is, from a time- into a space-
symbol. In the creative period woman is the great reproductive force,
and she fights a silent battle with time while man evolves his religious,
scientific, and artistic space-conquests and abstractions. When she is cut
off from the soil she becomes, not so much the evolutionary force which
produces man and makes possible his work, as a complement and
rounding out of his nature. This as a matter of course causes the sexes to
approach steadily in costume,[27] build, and environmental opportunity.
A gradual interabsorption of sex characteristics in temperament results,
the female assuming those of the male, the male losing those which distinguish him sharply from the female. The historical development
through mother and son, the one continually pulling away from the
other, shifts to a settling down into marriage as the fundamental basis
for activity. The economic system of the market place and culture-town
was a constant copulation of the masculine city and the feminine soil—
industry and agriculture. Now agricultural development becomes a
source of raw material for industry, and economics is worked out on a
purely industrial and masculine basis in which recurrent depressions of
ever increasing intensity and vicious annihilation wars which sweep
along millions helpless in its grip are inevitable features. These bear an
obvious relation to auto-eroticism, and the hope that they will eventu-

ally effect the complete sterility of a nationless and classless society is not an unnatural one.

Hence, when the great romantics came they were brought face to face with the mystery of sex as a symbol of time. The springing up of a large number of priapic romantic artists and the great mythological figure of Don Juan go along with the romantic struggle with the time-problem. The positivistic turning away from time brings with it, therefore, a nervous prudery, anticipated by Schopenhauer's misogynistic absorption in sex.[28] The romantic rehabilitation cancels this and returns to the romantic attitude under changed conditions.

As long as the sexes are separate, the one is seen to be the great time-symbol of will, the other the great space-symbol of understanding. When they intermingle, the organic thrust and parry is metamorphosed into an endless static conflict in the one soul, of primarily sexual significance—the conflict of libido and ego. Hence, the theory of artistic and philosophical production as the result of suppression and sublimation of the libido falls down by its inexactness of perspective when applied to the organic period, but becomes far more plausible in connection with romanticism. We can see a good deal of suppressed libido in the great romantics and a good deal of suppressed self-expression and frustrated will to power in the postromantics, for instance in Tschaikowsky and the English poet James Thomson.

The recognition of woman as wife and rejection of her as mother is, thus, essential to the metropolitan break-off. The romantic period is the period of the mistress, with Byron, Chopin, Shelley, Burns, Goethe, and many others. The positivist period establishes her as wife. The great romantics often fight with their mothers—Byron, Schumann, Schopenhauer, Fichte are examples—and a deep-rooted hatred of the old woman past the desirable age begins to appear, chiefly, of course, in the records of humour. The most celebrated humorous productions of the positivistic era—the Gilbert and Sullivan operas—in almost every instance have their plots based on the ridiculing of an old woman, which impresses the next generation as unspeakably caddish.[29] The positivistic attitude is worked out theoretically by Weininger and in drama by Strindberg.[30] With the rehabilitation of romanticism women are recognized as a symbol of the dominant time-force which is at last admitted to absorb everything finally in its movement. Humour, from Bernard Shaw to the comic strips, makes the supremacy of woman its central theme. Tragedy consists in watching with a fascinated horror the ego going down before the libido. . . .[31]

Those periods in which the time-problem is squarely faced or at least recognized as valid are, consequently, feminine periods. The cult of sensibility is unmistakably the first feminine entry into culture. The order of the sopping handkerchief rules supreme, from the literary "confession" to the fussy intricacies of architecture. Philosophy takes a similar trend. What is silly and amusing about the noble savage myth results chiefly from its being largely a feminine admiration for the strong man, and Rousseau's doctrines seem to be as fully intended for feminine digestions as Richardson's novels. Obscenity in the grand style immediately collapses in literature, particularly in England. The organic period dominated by the male is necessarily associated with obscenity, because the sexual impulse in man is what holds him down to time, and his spatial abstractions in literature must contain a good many shrugs, winks, and guffaws at the force which so potently pulls him back. On the other hand, the sexual characteristics are the essential part of femininity, and to a woman flippancy in connection with them is unbearable. In the positivistic period this is supported by the masculine desire for purity of spatial abstraction from time, and as sex remains a relentless and unyielding time-force, it is impure. With our romantic rehabilitation, feminine dislike and masculine love of obscenity are combined to form a constant but in the main serious and frequently morbid preoccupation with the theme.

For my personal point of view I have always found it convenient to illustrate historical vistas in colours, and I usually think of Western culture, with its continually lowering vital force and advancing maturity, as a descending spectrum. The gorgeous fierce terror of violet is in the Romanesque; deep mystical indigo ecstasy in the great Catholic period; cold blue abstraction in late scholasticism; lush and often rank naturalism of green in the Renaissance; yellow, with its pomp and its blinding illuminating intensity, is in the logic and state-form of the baroque; orange, the colour of gold, for the romantic-positivistic era; and red, the colour of sex, irritation, and restlessness, for our own day. If we are not afraid of symbolism, we may find it a help to visualize the rise of romanticism as an introduction of a red colour scheme into culture. Red is the colour of sexuality, as any animal knows,[32] and is, consequently, the great time-colour which underlies all the rest and which eventually succeeds them, the other two primary colours being both abstractions into space, the one religious and mystical, the other religious and logical. We shall see later how romanticism in politics works through to a movement of irritation and force, symbolized by communistic red and the red of British imperialism alike. We have seen the rise of a tremendous sexual force in life which the early religious period recognized when it associated the red arising from orange—scarlet—as the colour of adultery, and we have seen that romanticism signifies it.

And so, having endeavoured to make clear the general concept of romanticism even to the point of visualization, let us proceed to our analysis.

Part Two

I

After what has been said, we should expect romantic philosophy to show a development corresponding to the general outline we have given. First, a period in which the attention was turned from thought-conquest to the edifices already built by civilization, the reaction of the feeling-man rather than the thought-man. Then a systematic period of development in which the distinction between the world as it is and the world as we see it gradually grew to be, not one of greater spatial homogeneity, but one of time and space. After this, a strenuous egocentric struggle to power and transvaluation of values, and finally, the working out of the final implications of the romantic position.

The first period is usually regarded as synonymous with Rousseau, according to the principle that the destructive attack of romanticism is always French. Rousseau was the first dissentient voice in the chorus of tranquil placidity which prevailed throughout the rococo. As such, he brought the "enlightenment" down to earth by a historical retrospect—a fictitious one, certainly, but still an appeal to history. Like Schopenhauer after him, life as represented in history is evil, and, consequently, civilization as we have it now is bad. It really is bad, in spite of its being the "best of all possible worlds,"[33] and that fact, the natural reaction of the man of feeling, contains the seed of the great romantic *skepsis*. Rousseau had learned from experience that most of our elaborated theories are merely justifications for our feelings. No matter how compelled we may be to think logically, still all our thought aims at vindication of our original bias of mind, which is embodied in prejudices. This fact is amply verified in experience.

Now we must digress for a moment to show the implications of Rousseau's position. All organized thought, up to this time, was based in large upon reason. But mere reason does not come into existence of itself; it must be formulated by a will to reason. The will is the time-force, reason a spatial conquest, and, hence, the organic thought of a culture is an impregnation of nature by the force of spirit. It is this force which abstracts forms from matter, which are the tools of knowledge and art. But the great nominalistic space-conquest from the Renaissance to Leibnitz had concentrated on reason so much that the will had become unconscious and instinctive, or, as Schopenhauer would say, blind.[34] Thought, space-conquest, is good, but too much dwelling on action is paralysing and evil. Now feeling is also an interfusion of time- and space-concepts, but it is not a living or organic synthesis of them. It is the spatial reaction which looks at the "religious" one. Feeling, criticism, *skepsis*—these three words are all closely interrelated. Hence, feeling must reverse the presupposition of religion that thought is good and will bad until it recognizes that the latter is separate and unknowable. The thought-conquests actualized in civilization are bad, and men who have produced them are bad. What is good comes from nature. If we ask what this nature is, we discover that it is the world beneath our spatial abstractions of it. It is, with Kant, the thing-in-itself, and with Schopenhauer, the will. Thus, the "nature" of Rousseau turns out to be more on the side of what the Germans would call *Geist*.

The reason for this is that Rousseau symbolizes the new metropolitan, who has turned to look at the soil, but has not yet turned on the force propelling him out of the soil. But it should be noted that even here there is no complete surrender to a "state of nature." The point is significant that Rousseau approved of the state of nature because in it wants and the capacity to satisfy them are equivalent, and the will cancels out. What Rousseau wanted to recapture was that rare moment of culture-birth which combined the pleasures of nomad and culture-man; civilization had spoiled this by making a temporal attack on space. *Amour propre* is a sign of the struggling will, and struggle, or useless energy, is bad. This must be reversed. We must return to a life which is fundamentally contemplation—that is, the natural expression of our feelings or reactions. Positive education, which annihilates the child and regards him as an imperfect adult, must be replaced by negative education, in which the validity of the child's time-absorption is recognized. The political outlook is, of course, focused on romantic sympathy—the atomic attraction of the metropolis.

Will is not good, nor is it in itself bad. Reason is similarly irrelevant to moral values. It is the use made of them that is significant. The only moral value lies in the picture-blend and criticism of them, which is feeling and is organized by conscience. That is fundamentally good. Rousseau's thought, as we have seen, is self-contradictory. The organizing will is bad, certainly, but nature, in which the good of man lies, is also will when the concept is pressed hard enough. But as the contradiction is a historical necessity, we cannot dismiss it by discovering it.

II

It is, however, in Kant that the matrix of romanticism lies. This is true, not because Kant was a romanticist, but because it was Kant who definitely ended the organic period and thereby gave romanticism its *raison d'être*. Romanticism and positivism represent a contradiction, and it was Kant who pointed out the contradiction while laying down the program for both. In discussing Kant's relation to romanticism, therefore, it is necessary only to indicate his general historical importance for philosophy.

We have shown how all romantic artistic activity is subjective and critical; we should expect romantic philosophy to exhibit the same characteristics. It was Kant who destroyed both dogmatism and scepticism, which are obverse and reverse of organic philosophy, and made necessary for all future philosophers the critical approach. Now dogmatism, for Kant, is an attempt to build a philosophical structure from first principles. But the fact that none of these systems have stood the ultimate test of universal and unfailing application in any period of time suggests that those first principles are in every case insufficiently analysed. The general characteristic of these principles is that they refer to a fundamental distinction between the sensible world and the intelligible world—the world as sense impression and the world as evolved from understanding. Philosophy, which explains the one from the other, ends up in scepticism or scholasticism respectively. But when we come to analyse the origin of these first principles, we find, first, that they all depend upon our two ultimate forms of perception for their existence—space and time.

Now it is peculiar that the great tradition which comes down to us from the Greeks, differentiating the worlds of thought and of experience, postulates the former as higher and more truly real, no matter which it starts from. And if we ask in what the difference consists, we find that the one is always true, unchanging, and eternal, while the other is constantly shifting and dissolving—one is always there and the other perplexes by its constant change and instability. The world of sense perception is a world of extension in which extended objects are continually getting messed up, as it were, by the relentless time-force of succession. The ultimate goal of knowledge, then, is toward complete space-abstraction. The existence of God is the hope held out that there is a pure being who forms within himself a cohesion and immortality independent of becoming.

The higher our knowledge, the more independent of time it is, and the more it tends to spatial abstraction. Thought is fundamentally a space-conquest. But, says Kant, there is no difference in the last analysis between what we think and what we see—everything that is an object of knowledge originates in experience, and everything we can know is phenomenal. The sensible world we find difficulty in conquering, because there is something in it that we cannot ultimately know—time. Knowledge strives to get at the essence of the world by throwing out this element, but the result is no more real than the other in the sense of being any less dependent on experience. No knowledge can get beyond the spatial world. This is the ultimate *skepsis* which ended the creative period of philosophy.

Now if even a world of pure forms is just as phenomenal as the ordinary world of mixed objects, it is fully as pictorial. All knowledge is a synthesis, and the totality of concepts is a world-picture and nothing more. In this world-picture space in its essence exists, but time in its essence certainly does not. Succession has to be necessary—that is, phenomena following in time have to be thought of together as bound in a relationship which excludes the time-element. Any dogmatic philosophy must proceed from a spatial grasp of time—the axiom of causality. The ultimate in organic *skepsis*, similarly, has been reached, when this principle is attacked. The same is true for the relationship of potentiality to actuality. All twelve categories are space-concepts.[35]

The next step is, what evolves this world-picture? The perceiving subject, obviously. But the subject is a time-entity, who does everything in time. His world-picture is similarly a temporal product, though it represents a temporal negation. We perceive in time—hence, a world of pure space we do not perceive. But knowledge is an activity, and we perceive actively an outer world. A picture is two-dimensional, and what an eye passively receives must similarly be two-dimensional. What gives us activity must be a depth-experience producing form. But this must proceed from the nature of living, which is a temporal force. Form, then, must be the impregnation of the sensible world with a time-force of being (being with a small b; living, the concrete of which thought is an abstraction). The more formal, that is, the more purely spatial, knowledge becomes, the greater the temporal force required to condition it. All organic knowledge results from an interfusion of time in space. We have seen that this points to feeling, and so all creative knowledge rests, not on reason, but on faith—the underlying feeling-compulsion. Religious philosophy is an artistic product.

Critical philosophy, then, must recognize that if dogmatism, or creative philosophy, is a living form, it can live only as long as the temporal-spatial interfusion force lasts. Once time is recognized as *there*, as unbeaten and the real baffling force behind the phenomenal world, we have two problems confronting philosophy. One, positivism, deals with the exploring and exploiting of the universal picture. The other, romanticism, with the examination of the time-problem by its spatial deposit of history. Do not invent universal formulas—they must be hidden somewhere. Romanticism says, can we by seeing what lies back of the organic development of history discover the nature of the force which pushed it on? The reason why the case of romanticism is so much weaker than that of positivism is that it could not examine facts, which are space-phenomena, except insofar as they symbolized a time-force. Out of the fossilized remains of a dinosaur one may evolve a skeleton and infer a picture of what the animal was like. Both results are purely spatial and phenomenal. Romanticism tried to produce a living dinosaur, on a false basis—that time is phenomenal. Only its spatial manifestations are phenomenal, and that is all we can know of time.

III

Hence, romanticism has to be revolt against Kant. Had Kant been universally accepted, or, rather, had the implications of his teaching been recognized, we should have expected that the whole subsequent philosophical activity would have been positivistic, or simply repetitive. Romanticism is under the influence of the great systematic tradition, and its philosophy is just as much of an art form as that of the preceding age, its very name being a metaphor derived from the arts. It is a sort of

appoggiatura,[36] or suspension, of positivism. We therefore find two
stages in its development—one the idealistic stage of enthusiasm, the
other the weary disillusioned stage which turns to positivism. Fichte,
Schelling, Hegel, and Schleiermacher represent the first stage, in
approximately that order; Schopenhauer is the supreme example of the
second.

The systematic stage is committed to idealism for two reasons. First,
the thing is a pure spatial fact, the idea is symbol of it; and we have seen
that romanticism is fundamentally a symbolic activity. Second, the time-
problem refers to the percipient who evolves the idea out of the thing.
Fichte rejected materialism on the ground that, while each approach was
self-contained and consistent, the material one cannot start from the
beginning (this is a time-word, and, consequently, begs the question)
because it does not explain the possibility of ideas, nor does it recognize
that being can do without consciousness of being.[37] Time is fundamentally stronger than space, and all spatial ideas are subservient to time.
Our approach must be egocentric and critical throughout, and subjectively idealistic. Everything outside us is non-ego, against us and a
counterconcept to us. We are saved from solipsism by the obvious independence of the non-ego from our purely temporal activity—that is, our
will. But if our idealism is to be consistent, then, if our world-picture is
the product of a limited ego, the world itself is evidently the product of
an absolute ego. The basis for scientific activity, then, which a solipsistic
interpretation of idealism would paralyse, lies in this recognition of our
limitation. This is the negative way of stating the Kantian idea of
forms—for form, negatively considered, is a limitation with a meaning.
We have seen that form springs from feeling, so here again is a basic
romantic conception. Feeling is obviously identified with conscience.
Here, out of Fichte's thought there begins to shape an idea which was to
bring about the eventual destruction of systematic romanticism. If all
activity is formal, one has only to bring in its obverse statement that
activity consists in working within limitations to arrive at the concept
that life is all struggle and effort. This was grasped as early as Lessing,
and is explicitly recognized in Fichte and many other romantics. Now
give this statement again its antithesis, and we say, first, that because life
is all struggle and will, it is all dissolution and change and is, therefore,
chaotic, and because life is all effort, it is a great weariness and hopeless-
ness and is, therefore, evil. Recognition of the inevitability of a time-
force implies recognition of its irresistible power. But we anticipate.

In Fichte we first find the romantic application of the great law of the three stages upon which the present thesis is based. Kant had named dogmatic, sceptical, and critical as his three. Applied generally to history, this would coincide with the one which actually took place and which can instantly be seen once we postulate the culture as the unit of history, if we understand that here scepticism means simply an empiric and nominalistic approach to the dogmatic point of view. But with Fichte the second period drops out as merely transitional, and his three are the so-called "normal nation" of barbarism, the age of authority, the age of reasonable knowledge.[38] This is the first and the primitivist one of the several romantic interpretations which found their essence in Hegel. The wide-ranging nomad of the steppes is rehabilitated by the wide-ranging uprooted nomadic metropolitan critic. Both are antitemporal existences separated by a temporal-to-spatial age of authority of chiefly a disciplinary value.

In Fichte, too, come the storm troops of the conflict of contraries. A limited ego, compelled by its nature (Fichte names no other source) to struggle with its limited non-egoistic world-picture, finds its activity composed of a mutual interaction of limitations. The egoistic acts are identified with time, the non-egoistic phenomena with space. These two forms of perception are antithetical, and one cannot be deduced from the other. But, Fichte says, a synthesis results from these two, and that is why we can have organized thinking, which could not proceed out of a flat opposition. But, of course, as we can only "know" time spatially, there is no doubt about the synthesis, except that it does not signify anything more than the romantic pictorial attack on time.[39]

IV

In Schelling we are deeper into romanticism and more conscious of some of its difficulties. Fichte's interest in philosophy was largely of ethical orientation—the problem of time brings in the regulation of time-compulsion. But to Schelling philosophy starts with the untrammelled freedom of the ego, instead of regarding that as a final ideal. As he recognizes no adequate distinction between consciousness and content, or even mind and matter, ethics has little importance in his work. We might summarize the leading theme of his philosophy by calling it a world-as-time idea. As the ego exists in time, the world is its idea. Here Schelling breaks with Fichte. With the more critical philosopher *Natur* and *Geist* are antithetical. Schelling attacks Fichte on what is definitely a weak point—if this is true, no knowledge can result from mere opposition, which cancels both parties to it, and how can a synthesis be formed if we do not start with some basis of essential understanding of nature by spirit? Fichte had given no satisfactory answer on this point. If time and space are antithetical, one of them we do not know, unless one be included in the other. If we "start" with the ego, space is included in time, and the world must be explained in terms of forces. Nature then is an "Odyssey of the Spirit," and exists as in a measure symbolic of it— the actuality of nature is the potentiality of spirit.[40]

Therefore, the intelligible world, the world of reality, is the world of symbols. Schelling rejects empirical science, not referring even to it for verification, because it deals only with facts as facts, and, consequently, rests on a hypothetical basis. Science is not rejected, however, as it was with Parmenides, for the sake of a motionless and timeless world of pure being. The reciprocal interconnection of phenomena is all right in itself; we cannot understand anything without it. But space is contained in time, and all science is a surface ripple behind which lies the time-force. It does not go deep enough. Science must deal with dead or deadened material—the fact is dead, the symbolic interpretation of the fact points to life. All thought consists in comparing and analysing, as Kant had shown. Facts in space may be compared ad nauseam. But is there not some underlying principle by which we can arrive at a comprehension of living forms? It may be assumed that the time-force is uniform; hence, whatever is uniform in nature is significant. The way to understand living forms, in short, is by analogy. But the sense of analogy is from an external impression which makes an immediate appeal to us independent of reasoning analysis, so that our comprehension of the world is intuitive.

But in Schelling, too, we find that when time is approached it becomes a space-dimension, and so his world-view is just as motionless and pictorial as that of any positivist, except that in him the foreground is comprehended in the background, while with the opponent philosophy the reverse is the case. With Schelling the world is a world of forces, or powers, of constantly rising purity from absolute nature to absolute spirit, or ego. Underneath all there is a peculiar animism—forces and motions in nature form approximations to conscious life. This is evolution, certainly, and it is the first romantic evolution. Conscious life is the ego, and the ego is implicit in the approximations to consciousness. As *Natur* is contained in *Geist*, what is apparently its independent development is the result of the world becoming idea. In Schelling absolute idealism begins to lift its head, and as long as that expression makes sense we can have romanticism. When the world-as-idea begins to separate out from the working through of the force which is recognized as will, romanticism is doomed. In any case, the ascending scale of powers means that everything is transitional between *Natur* and *Geist*, and whatever is transitional must contain an inner contradiction which connects it to both its neighbours. This contradiction, or polarity, in Schelling corresponds to the subject-object distinction, so that here again is the conception that the essential reality of everything is form, and form to a romantic, as we have so often seen, implies the creative force of time. As any scale is quantitative, Schelling is quite right in calling his scheme "dynamic atomism."[41]

Schelling is far more advanced than Fichte, to say nothing of Hegel, and is far closer to Schopenhauer, in that the synthesis in connection with the opposition of *Natur* and *Geist* in his philosophy underlies the latter and remains hidden, thus making thought-activity fundamentally an excavation. One needs only to draw an inference from this to arrive at the differentiated conceptions of will and idea. Schelling did not arrive at any explanation of this underlying blend, except to name it "indifference,"[42] but later, when he turned to the religious problem, having once established his position in his youth, he could only get as far as calling the antithesis fundamental and saying that evil is as necessary to God as good. Like practically all subjective idealists and egocentrics, he develops his position in early youth and turns to mysticism with maturity.

V

The connection of Hegel with romanticism rests chiefly on Hegel's own conception of the *Zeitgeist* as symbolic of the inner unity of the time-problem. He disliked romanticism because its idealism did not press forward into reality. His own chief interest, as well as his interest for posterity, centres on the strong impulse to unify and cohere the spiritual side of life into a conception sufficiently clear to be recognized as the driving force of material. He wanted the idea to penetrate the innermost interstices of reality; and in this he revolted against romanticism because he attempted what they desired but shirked. He started out with Schelling, attacking earlier critical philosophers, notably Kant and Fichte, because their approach had destroyed the systematization result-ant from the matching of subject with object. Like the romantics, he was necessarily a subjectivist critic, yet he hated subjectivity because he faced out to the world-as-idea and was bent on its idealistic conquest, a process easily ruined by introspection. Then he broke with Schelling because of the arbitrary and formalized schemata of that philosopher, which represented to him an immature and hasty jumping at conclu-sions. He wanted to *realize* idealism and to idealize reality, and no one can attempt this without in some measure being answerable to the charge, when the approach is made from the ideal side, of having butch-ered facts to make a theorist's holiday.

It should now be clear what we meant earlier by saying that the ulti-mate aim of a romanticist was a philosophy of history. History is simply the space-manifestations of time, and, hence, the approach to the time-problem is gradually forced down to a purely historical basis. If the ear-lier romantics did not recognize this, it was because they had a static, pictorial goal ahead of them and wished to capture the whole of time, instead of a section of it bearing some semblance of spatial order, which Hegel called the *Zeitgeist*, in a visible presentation. Hence, Hegel is the stage intermediate between Schelling's thermometer diagram of cre-ation and the positivistic dislike of all history. There is still an attempt to rein in the conception of a universally evolving world, toward which precipice romanticism was rushing, for in Hegel's world of absolute idea there is little allowance made for organic growth in time or an inner integration directed toward development. To allow a causative force in the world was a step of great boldness; to consider the force homoge-neous and invariable was one of shrinking authoritarianism. Both these characteristics are evident in Hegel.

In Hegel's dialectic lies, of course, the sine qua non of Hegelianism. The dialectic of a thesis carried over into an antithesis and resolving upon a synthesis is another romantic approach to Kant's law of three stages. It breathes as well the very essence of that optimism in action which was to become the keynote of positivism. From the three stages of Comte's[43] historical outlook to the three-volume novels with happy endings, the positivist era was dominated by a belief that it constituted a third and final section of development leading to Utopia.[44] But with Hegel there is no more development in this than there is in a syllogism. The thesis becomes a synthesis, not because it is outmoded, but because it is limited, and by bursting out into the empty receptacle of its antithesis it is simply breaking down a barrier in a homogeneous, constantly preserved mass of knowledge. This dialectic is Hegel's world-process. Pessimism underlies this, as it underlies all romantic thought, because when closely examined the negation of an antithesis takes us to a region suspiciously resembling the purlieus of the original thesis. But it was not conceived pessimistically—on the contrary, it gave the romantics what seemed a powerful bludgeon to wield on the proposition that we know only (space) phenomena. If reason or the idea is the causative factor of experience, the development of pure reason could still take in all existence. And there is necessarily no "creative evolution" in this type of thinking. Romanticism was to find, however, that the greatest of all theses—space—had for its antithesis time, and that one, as Fichte under the influence of the critical philosophy had pointed out, was not deducible from the other.

Hegel concludes the romantic assault on the time-problem by his complete all-embracing spirituality. There is no development in nature, but only metamorphosis, and a constant refinement of externality into spirit. His theory of the state is almost Hobbes's leviathan seen in reverse. Similarly the mind-thesis embodied in psychology unites with the material antithesis embodied in sociology to form the universal mind embodied in the great synthetic structures of art, religion, and speculative philosophy. This is the peculiarly human stage, and with Hegel the romantic *skepsis* herewith receives its antinomian confirmation.

VI

In Schleiermacher we are brought face to face with the religious problem, freed from the ethical and social overemphasis with which Fichte and Hegel had charged it. Here we have the antithesis of temporal religious synthesis and spatial feeling-grasp directly presented. The lack of emphasis on social ethics thus results from Schleiermacher's denial of a universal compulsive synthesis. In application to ethics this destroys the idea of a valid moral law. The break-up of a religious or linking force among humanity has left "feeling" a purely individual affair. Protestantism, then, is reduced with Schleiermacher to its lowest terms—any doctrine, or ism, is a personal contribution to and an individual slant on knowledge. Evangelism presupposes the individual as unit; the only permanent, lasting good is obtained by personal example and reciprocal exchanging of influences. Let each intellectually honest or decent person take his own way, and he will not go far wrong. Here is the systematic working through of the primitivist postulate that man is by nature good. His nature, according to the romantics, is fundamentally feeling.

When the feeling-critic is brought up against and opposed to religion, or a feeling-creativeness, he makes a pictorial reproduction of it which converts religion into something very like aesthetics. The attempt to show that the good is good because it is beautiful is at least as old as Shaftesbury,[45] and with Schleiermacher the influence of the spirit of God comes to man through the attunement of his feeling. The romantic esoteric draws himself in to the very essence of his own soul, and there he can, if a sensitive aesthete, detect for an instant the mysterious moving time-force of the will of God. This sounds like mysticism, but it is nothing of the kind. With a thinker who summed up the creative period, like Blake, it easily becomes so, but mysticism is impossible to a romantic. A mystic works, not only with a *psyche*, or subjectively idealistic soul, but with a *pneuma*, or universal spirit in which individuality is completely absorbed. Schleiermacher has the soul, but the spirit of God is revealed only in that, and between the peculiar soul and the entelechic *pneuma* there is fixed the great gulf between creation and criticism. The romantic *skepsis* pushes God out of the actual world and positivism digs a scientific mine under the gulf to try to find his materialistic incarnation.

Thus, in this system dogmas are to religious thought, or rather contemplation, what the ordinary conventions of society are to the thinker—they have no deep-rooted immutable foundations in reality, but they save time and trouble in exchanging ideas in social intercourse. Religion, once for all, does not trust to proof, whether cosmological or ontological. Reason has, it is true, a connotation of universal mind-compulsion, but reason can take us no further than phenomena, as Kant had shown. The underlying opposition of *Natur* and *Geist* remains, for Schleiermacher. Reason may conquer *Natur*, but that is all. The way out is to recognize that man's nature is not by any means exhausted in his reasoning faculty, and there is something in him which lies deeper, which is far older, and constitutes his real essence. This faculty of feeling gives us ideas which transcend experience. It is true that these ideas have only a symbolic value. But if symbolism is present, there must be a reality outside all possible experience of which it forms a mirage. This is, of course, that unknowable force which is called God, will, or time, depending on the attitude. There is infinite variety in humanity because of the infinite potency of the differentiating feeling. Hence, feeling alone can deal in any way with infinity—knowledge works through form, or limitation. Similarly, what gives the reason-structure vitality, what dynamizes it and connects it with the time-force, is the original, personal thesis expressive of common nature.

If feeling underlies reason, faith knowledge, our idea of God, which implies the unity of thinking and being, must be taken as a starting point, and also as unknowable. The goal is the completed world-idea, which is unrealizable. The activity in between is the understanding, organizing, positivistic space-construction based on a blood-feeling of God, and works with limits, or force-engendered forms. Criticism, in the world of living conscience, checks up on this activity and compares it with the inaccessible terminus. Only religious feeling can go back to the starting point, God, for strength and solace. Its feeling is real, but its meaning and expression are symbolic. God-consciousness is the highest thought-activity; yet it is not knowledge, but only a grasp at the root of knowledge. Christ was a transmitter of God-consciousness.

This romantic religion is the logical working out of Kant's ethics and marks the beginning of romantic disillusionment. Thoughts correspond to being, and a totality of concepts to a causal relation. Here we are very close to Schopenhauer. The miraculous in religion is abolished, and the way cleared for positivism. God as unity to world as totality is an infinite series, but still a series. Schleiermacher represents the last attempt of the romantics to hold together *Natur* and *Geist*, space and time, world and God. With him they hang together by a feeling which is opposed to the organizing activity of science. There is real opposition, then, implicit, and the next step would be to separate them and, in giving supreme expression to romanticism, destroy it as it stood.

VII

This step was taken by Schopenhauer. Romanticism, as we have seen, resolves itself into positivism as inevitably as positivism itself resolves into neoromanticism, the total progression reminding one of a six-four cadence—in fact, probably symbolized by it. Thus, Schopenhauer, because he is the last systematic romantic, is the first positivist. Romanticism struggles to approach the time-problem and is, thus, a kind of reversed systematic philosophy; positivism turns to space. Schopenhauer, in finally making the division, marks in himself the turn. Near the end of systematic romanticism we find in every field a group of essentially bourgeois minds bringing out the positivist implications in it. The exotic tendency in romanticism is, thus, seen to be the bourgeois tendency, as the contiguous neighbours of a metropolitan are so infinitely varied, his friends being the result of sense selection. The esoteric romantic, on the other hand, conceives it his duty to *épater le bourgeois*.[46] Schopenhauer speaks very definitely with the voice of the middle class and is, like Schumann, a typically German phenomenon. His intense originality among philosophers is largely one of style and expression. I am given to understand that he was practically the first philosopher of his race to write readable German.[47] Thus, Schopenhauer is a genuine world-historical phenomenon, appearing with the same inevitability of necessity as any other figure. The smug self-complacency which ascribes Schopenhauer's pessimism to environmental or even physiological factors and then dismisses it is taking a totally unwarranted step. To say that pessimism generally is mainly faulty elimination, and Schopenhauer's in particular only the complaint of a dissatisfied soul, and, therefore, something of an accidental irruption into philosophy, is like saying that Schleiermacher's religion is merely the self-justification of a liberal-minded preacher, or Fichte's hard and rigorous ethical doctrines the dogmatic self-assertiveness of a stern and unyielding fighter. These statements are all quite true, no doubt, but they mean very little, and they do not prove anything at all. What the man is, per se, is of no importance; why that type of man should have become prominent in that age is another matter.

In Schopenhauer the full implications of romanticism stand out. We know only phenomena. Sensation is all that is immediately given, and as all space-phenomena exist in the unknowable time, the underlying law of knowledge is the spatial grasp on time, or the causal law. Outside this causal law is the thing in us, the thing propelling us through time. That is totally separate from what we can know, and is, consequently, the world-as-will. The latter is the world-as-idea. The world-as-will lies outside knowledge and, hence, the noumena, or things in themselves, are symbolic of the will, and phenomena, including our own bodies, are their material projections. The content of this world-as-idea is, thus, material. The world-as-will can be *known* only as an idea, and its existence must be implied from its manifestations. The will, though a blind unconscious thing, is pure energy, because it is time, and, hence, there is a sort of animism recurring all through the world-as-idea which the understanding dehydrates, so to speak, when it builds up the purely spatial structures we have dealt with above. This living power is signified by force. Here Schopenhauer makes a clean break with all systematics. For a complete system, everything must be accessible to our knowledge, and Schopenhauer, by showing once for all that the will-force was inaccessible, reversed the procedure of earlier thinkers, who made will a product of force, and, hence, got their cognitive distinction of matter and motion.

We have seen that romantic *skepsis* is the complete reversal of organic religiousness because it overturns the optimism in thought and pessimism in action of the earlier period. Romantic thought is pessimistic through and through, because the growing conception of something unknowable against which knowledge will beat its wings in vain comes gradually to be recognized as the dominant force in the world. With Schopenhauer, the will struggles to incorporate itself more and more completely in phenomena—the doctrine that works through to be creative evolution. It progresses up from mechanical interaction to the spatial incarnation of causality, and from that up to consciousness and conquest of the world-as-idea. Systematic organic growth is a product of the will, and the optimism of thought it results in is the will's instinct for self-preservation. The development suddenly snaps when the consciousness is discovered to be will—the opposition of *Natur* and *Geist*, always a real opposition, now becomes final and irrevocable. The force of the will is existence. Existence is struggle, and struggle is mainly suffering. But to say that life is worth the struggle is a totally unproved hypothesis, and it is, of course, again suggested by the will. Death is less evil than life; hence, the death of a culture, which romanticism signifies, is a higher development because of its break-off from the will. Schopenhauer's philosophy breathes a dislike for everything connected with the time-problem. In the first place, he disliked all the romantic philosophers, Fichte, Schelling, Hegel, all being stuffed shirts and windbags. Secondly, he made a most indelicate remark about history, calling it a tissue of lies, which it certainly is when its data are examined as facts instead of as parts of an embracing synthesis.[48] Third, he hated women, the great symbols of the time-force of will.

Now no romantic in the systematic period believed in a real development of nature in time. The reason for this is that their time-view was held static and pictorial. Schopenhauer has no faith in progress, which can only mean a progress of the will—the individual grown self-conscious is the only possible unit of deliverance. There are two avenues of escape. In the first place, the great static abstractions which have signified the conquest of the idea over the will in the religious period are the masterpieces of art, which, when will interferes, become philosophy. This kind of art is no longer possible, but the critical arts leading to self-absorbence and subjectivity are far better adapted to this new age, the greatest of all arts being, of course, music, the epitome of life. Struggle, again, can be ironed out in that romantic sympathy as engendered by sense connections of which the saint is the corresponding ideal in the religious period. In the metropolis the only true friendship possible is a communion of interests—hence, though I do not know that Schopenhauer draws this inference, there is possible an excavation activity on a large scale in the world-as-idea in which the only interest taken is the scientific one and no clash of individual wills can result. These two avenues of deliverance are obviously connected with the esoteric and exotic tendencies mentioned above. Romanticism had held them together; Schopenhauer rent them apart, and, hence, postromanticism separates out from positivism.

VIII

In postromanticism the typical figure is easily seen to be Nietzsche. There is no systematic philosopher who seems to have much in common with this period, for the will to power instinct is implicated more in the realm of politics than systematic philosophy. Nietzsche is, of course, more of a poet than a philosopher, but still what is noisy and arresting about him seems to have eclipsed the deeper aspects of his thinking. Unsystematic philosophers have a peculiar way of being justified by events, however, and the rise of Hitlerism in Germany should provide a favourable opportunity for a reconsideration of the author of *Also Sprach Zarathustra*, who happened to be right when so many apparently sounder contemporaries went wrong.

Rousseau wanted to recapture the birth-ecstasy of culture; Heine had admired the Middle Ages; Nietzsche is most enthusiastic about the Renaissance. He wants a new Renaissance in Western culture; that is the whole nexus of his position. The Renaissance had brought to life the great constructive possibilities of formal Western art and logic, and what the romantic revival signified had killed it. It must be reborn. The corresponding period in Greek culture was the Dionysian cult, whose infusion upon the Apollonian religion had liberated tragedy and sculpture, just as the Renaissance had liberated music and drama from the Church. Apollo, Dionysus, and Socrates; these represent the three stages of every culture—in our culture the medieval, the baroque, and the contemporary scenes—dogmatism, nominalistic *skepsis*, and the criticism which represents the ultimate *skepsis*. His attitude is impossible thoroughly to disentangle until we realize the fact, and take it as a starting point, that he cries out for a resurrection of culture and a return to an organic development, and if his work is full of contradictions, they cannot be entirely unexpected in a philosophy based on such a quixotic impulse. With this motive in mind, it is inevitable that he should begin by acclaiming figures such as Schopenhauer and Wagner, who in their novelty bewildered and dazzled, and, by closer inspection finding that they were inevitable to their time, end by despising them eventually as decadents. The point is that Nietzsche himself, born in a positivist era, wants action, and the action turns out to be a liberation of the strongest passions of his own age. Hence, the pessimism in thought and optimism in action characteristic generally of romanticism is augmented to a titanic conflict which results in a blind worship of strength, and a furious yea-saying combined with a bitter aversion to mankind and emphasis upon the loneliness of the thinker and a desire to wipe out the human race and bring to birth another and better. We must have a new Renaissance, but it is not for us.

The main importance of Nietzsche as intermediate between systematic and rehabilitated romanticism lies in his having put the former on a dynamic basis. The pictorial attack on time was motionless but gradually worked out to be an emphasis upon the evolution of the idea. Nietzsche aims at an obvious practical application of Hegel's doctrine of the idea controlling reality—development out of imperfection in a creative evolution. Nietzsche is on this side of the pessimism which recognizes the world as evil and imperfect. The old hierarchy of angels, men, and beasts appears in a new light. If men once were little better than beasts, why should they not deliberately labour even in pain to produce an *Übermensch* which could carry on the torch of life falling from our dying hands? Something cannot very well come out of nothing, so that this creature must come from the best we have now. An extreme aristocracy results. As this is a gospel of action, the aristocrats are the forcemen, who transcend morality. There is, in fact, very little morality

except slave morality, which was engineered by Christianity, against
which Nietzsche is bitterly opposed, and is perpetuated by the great
slave race, the Jews. The aristocrats must remove themselves to a paradise of their own—it is in this where the esoteric quality of postromanticism comes out—those social virtues, such as pity (the scavenger of
misery, as Shaw calls it),[49] which aims at a general eugenics among
helots, are to be abhorred. The aristocrats despise the weak; they will
not harm them, but they will not help them. The whole value of history
is concentrated, or at least embodied, in great men; for those great men
to have absolute sway is, therefore, the highest duty. Just how those not
of the elect are to be persuaded of this does not worry Nietzsche. His
outlook seems to be practically Karl Marx turned inside out—the opposition of German against Jew goes very deep—the same class war
between exploiter and proletariat, growing more and more acute until
the weaker class—with Nietzsche the slaves—are exterminated. This
political opposition will appear more clearly later on. We need only say
here that slaves like peace, masters want war, because it is so much fun
for them and is part of their self-expression. Nietzsche, like most sissies,
had an inordinate admiration for strength, and was immensely
impressed by the efficiency of Prussian militarism.

   The central impulses underlying Nietzsche's thought are so obviously
a *reductio ad absurdum* of the romantic narcotic that they have about
them the atmosphere of a Freudian dream with the emphasis shifted
from sex to desire for power—the typical day or waking dream. We
have seen earlier why it is so likely that a postromanticist should be of
rather abnormal mental development. In Nietzsche the fact that a dead
civilization coming to life again implies the nonpermanence of death
may have led him, psychologically if not logically, to the hideous cyclic
theory which preluded his insanity.

IX

A complete survey of romantic philosophy would take in many names
of minor importance, such as Schlegel, Schiller, Novalis, Hamann, and
other figures of the systematic period who all added their more or less
digressive comments to the general stream of thought, would analyse
the concepts of those poets who held all the ideas of romanticism in
their grasp intuitively, notably Blake and Goethe, would include
English Hegelian reverberations such as Coleridge and Carlyle, would

estimate the value of the work of Lotze in putting the idealistic claim into a better working harmony with reality, and would do many other things beyond our present scope or grasp. As, however, there does not seem to be a great deal of intelligent writing on romanticism, much less any attempt at synthesizing its total activity, we shall probably have to wait some time for an adequate appraisal of its various manifestations in the history of culture. In our contemporary field there are many figures illustrating the exhaustive stage of romanticism, notably Bertrand Russell, whose religious opinions I have characterized in another essay as a mixture of Schopenhauer, Satan and Superstition[50]—all integral elements of romanticism. The contemporary attitude in its more entelechic exponents such as Freud, Shaw, or even Einstein would have its connection as well. But the romantic synthesis of exhaustion proper is actualized in two great stages which call for a brief indication before we close this part.

The first stage is Henri Bergson, a Frenchman leading the destructive attack again. The implications of his position are precisely what would be inevitable for anyone immediately succeeding the positivist period. In him, the time-world finally assumes supremacy. A detailed exposition of Bergson's philosophy is, of course, out of place here: all that concerns us is his work in making time achieve its ultimate conquest. First of all, he definitely shows that the positivistic attack on time which makes it a space-time or space-dimension does nothing toward solving the mystery of time at all. This phenomenal time is not duration. The whole world behind our spatial abstractions, the sum of noumena, is pure becoming or time, and this does not imply a mass of dead matter vitalized but simply a reflection of universal becoming upon a particular intellect. For the intellect can know only space-phenomena. It perceives because it limits as much as it takes in; in other words, as we have seen as far back as Kant, knowledge is formal, and form implies limitation. But as we know only phenomena, we can never know reality. The intellect busies itself with space-worlds, and as Bergson's innovation in philosophy consists chiefly of his having explicitly recognized the universal noumenon or world-as-will as temporal, due to his having come after the evolutionary development, becoming is reality, and so all science does not close with reality. Romantic *skepsis* can hardly go further. There is, however, the faculty of intuition, which is practically putting oneself in tune, or rather in rhythm, with the temporal force. The romantic descent of this intuition is evident enough in Schelling; it was what music represented to Schopenhauer and practically what Schleiermacher meant by a religious experience.

The romantic pictorial concept of the world was motionless; there was little evolution in it except the complete liberation of the idea from reality. When romanticism became esoteric postromanticism, this meant that the idea turned from reality. Evolution, in the Darwinian sense, is pure positivism, the survival of the fit, fitter, or fittest and adaptation to environment are both purely spatial attacks on time which reduce it to a space-dimension, because it postulates an unbroken chain of causality through life, and causality, as we have seen, is the primal space hold on time. Neoromanticism shows time as noumenal and baffling—the *élan vital* is there, but it is there for intuition and not the knowledge of scientific analysis.

The second stage is Oswald Spengler—the final one because we have seen the ultimate aim of romanticism to be, consciously or subconsciously, the philosophy of history, or the actualization of conscious life—the time-force aware of itself. The working through of the absolute idea in Hegel was as far as romanticism proper could get in this direction, and be consistent with its pictorial outlook. Positivism brought the counterparts of Darwin to postulate a similar unbroken causal chain in history springing from environment. The most important protagonist of this view is, of course, Marx, though Buckle and, more by implication than by direct statement, Mommsen, were better known at the time.[51] But with Spengler the time-element becomes supreme in conscious as well as unconscious life. In about ten pages he explodes the linear conception of history and builds up his thesis on all the final implications of the factors in romanticism.[52] "The causal sequence of social phenomena" is a bizarre and monstrous conception of life, as we find trivial causes for disproportionately huge effects; the Great War being "caused" by the murder of an imbecile prince. History is incarnated in culture-growths, the secret of life in them being unanalysable, because it belongs to time. With Spengler time, the cosmic, is finally separated from space, the microcosmic, and can be comprehended only by intuition of the type whereby we size up a stranger, a man who exists previously unknown to us in time, at a glance. Hence, the fundamental opposition between history and science is seen to be the working through of Schelling's scale of polarity. Hegel's concept of the absolute idea in history becomes, after evolution, an idea of a culture forcing the world into subjection by the energy of a living growth. In the *Decline of the West* neoromanticism receives its final word, and it is not easy to see how its concepts can be developed any further, except by criticism and commentary. The "decline" is merely the particular historical context of the principle that time is a force that eventually overmasters space. It is unfortunate that this same context has led to an overemphasis of the pessimism inherent in the word *decline* and has led to the book being regarded as the work of a calamity howler of the Max Nordau genre.[53] But we have seen that pessimistic inferences can be drawn from any romantic.

Part Three

The romantic attitude of the critic contemplating time cannot be unmusical, but it may in a very definite sense be antimusical. Life, as a Western mind conceives it, is a dynamic accented force, the accent residing in the catastrophe, the hero, the renaissance, in any foreground event, but the force moving with it and producing it. In consequence our civilization formulates its supreme artistry in a dynamic accented art, moving, like life, in time, devoid of the resisting material tending to make for a static effect. This is as a matter of course music. To us, music is the epitome of life, and comprehension of it brings a quicker and more intuitive comprehension of life than any other approach can possibly do.

Hence, the pictorial synthesis of history brings with it a recognition of music as the art par excellence, as we can see in Schopenhauer. At the same time a creative faculty means a power of entering into the preromantic attitude which is out of the question for those not born in it. The prime art of romanticism is painting, and painting, a visual, spatial, static, and intensely subjective art, is the direct antithesis of living music. The romantic approach to music would, thus, in tending to make a pictorial concept out of it, destroy its essence.

Music is essentially dynamic and its essence is rhythmic counterpoint. Melody is the pure temporal element in it; harmony the pure spatial. There is no idea of body in a bare tune unharmonized, no idea of vitality in harmony. The word *harmony* implies a static, quiescent, satisfied unity, which will not do for music. Music usually ends on a harmonic chord, but harmony always implies a pause: music even harmonically conceived must move in discords, as we shall see later. The "religious" element in music is, therefore, counterpoint, melody and harmony mingled. Rhythm is its distinguishing temporal force. So a pictorial approach to music would be a "sceptical" one; we should expect to see rhythm overcome and melody and harmony to fall apart. Again, music is the most abstract of all the arts and is, therefore, the most intensely personalized; the more objective an art, the greater effort of genius it takes to tear it up bodily by the roots, as it were, out of life. In consequence music is dependent on the effort of great musicians for its life to a far greater extent than, say, the lyric is dependent on the supremely great lyricist, there not being the same room for a minor composer that there is for a minor poet. Similarly its performance must be an ensemble; this is due not only to its contrapuntal construction but to the fact that an objective art is too many-sided for a soloist, which latter might as well be the author himself. Lastly, the audience for an objective, abstract, creative art must be a select, to some extent esoteric, group of patrons and sympathizers, such as might be found, for instance, in a church. Hence, we should expect to find in romantic music a tendency pursued as far as possible toward democracy in composition, solo performance, and a large and more undiscriminating audience, patronage being replaced by popularity. Conformably to the general principles laid down above, we should also expect a basis of religious optimism replaced by one of atheistic pessimism, a change to an egocentric and subjective approach, and the commencement of a definite winding up of the possibilities inherent in the art. Let us see how this works out.

I

The initial romantic attack is, of course, French. Contemporary with Bach, Handel, and Scarlatti, the Frenchmen Couperin and Rameau were definitely attempting the visualized tone poem, writing pieces habitually with imaginative (visual, that is) titles—*La Poule, Le Coucou, Les Barricades Mystérieuses*, etc. The first treatise on harmony (1722) was that of Rameau,[54] and in it he prophesied the speedy extinction of music due to the ultimate exhaustion of melodies. Now this is as pure primitivism as Rousseau. Only a man who thought of melody and harmony as disparate could say that. The fact that so great a musician could think of music as fundamentally a succession of harmonized tunes forebodes an attack on music as thoroughgoing as Rousseau's attack on philosophy. Again, the French, particularly Couperin, overcame rhythm by smothering their pieces in ornaments—reminding us acutely of Empire architecture. This was their way of dealing with the short sustaining power of the harpsichord, in opposition to, say, Scarlatti and the other Italians, who overcame it rhythmically, by increasing the speed. When romanticism itself came, the same tendencies were in evidence.

The rhythmic force of music is incarnated and symbolized in the dance. Hence, men like Bach, Handel, Haydn, Mozart, were all dance composers. The suite or collection of dances in one key was a standard art form, and later, when the sonata sublimated the dance rhythm of the suite into a stricter form, the minuet, in many ways *the* typical dance, was very often retained. With romanticism the dance was overthrown, and idealized dance replaced it—the dance in which the rhythmic propulsion is subordinated and does not stand out in its pure energy. Weber's *Invitation to the Dance* starts the attack on the waltz. With Beethoven, and generally from him onward, the minuet is replaced by the scherzo. Scherzo means joke, and the Beethoven scherzi are definitely parodies of the minuet—they retain the rhythm but burlesque the spirit by rushing the speed and thumping the accents.[55] From romanticism on the popular dances—polka, schottische, and so on—drop out of music. Chopin is usually considered a master of dance forms; let us see what forms he used. First, and most frequently, the mazurka, which is a syncopated dance, and syncopation is a fight against rhythm. Older composers used syncopation almost altogether for slow movements, in order to bring attention to the rhythm and prevent the music from lagging, and its use in faster music is generally characteristic of romanticism. Secondly, the waltz, the most fundamental and persistent of dances, and, consequently, the one to be conquered at all costs. We are not surprised that Chopin loves the mazurka and turns out some fine gems in that form, and that he often degrades the waltz to a salon show piece. Third, the polonaise. This is very similar to the march (♩♪♫♫) and a march is not a dance; it moves by mechanical propulsion. The march is never seriously treated in music until the rise of romanticism, because it is not a vitalizing dance but a dance of death. Schumann, and after him many postromantics, was the first to be fascinated by it, taking his cue from Beethoven. The funeral march is not, so far as I know, ever

even attempted until the romantic period,[56] and the mere fact that with
Beethoven, Chopin, and Berlioz music, the epitome of life, can symbolize death as well, reveals the depth of the romantic opposition to the art.

Now if the dance is the typical rhythmic form, it follows that in rhythmic music it must have a close affinity with a life-rhythm. The whole
being of a listener can enter into the light easy swinging balance of Bach
or Mozart. But a composer who does not feel but who can see this life-
rhythm makes it necessarily into a picture and handles the qualitative
differences in time fearlessly. Rush and hurry, on the one hand, and
dragging and shuffling, on the other, are not rhythmic, but they are
temporal. Rhythm can only be felt. Hence, romantic music tends to
extremes of speed. The slow as distinct from the merely slower movement appears in music with romanticism. The great Italians all yawned
over slow movements, and Haydn or Mozart rarely go slower than
andante (walking). Even the magnificent slow arias of Bach usually
have an insistent beating rhythmic figure under them. To listen to ada-
gios, largos, lentos, and so on brings in an outside stimulus to the
listener, a sort of philosophical contemplative attitude being necessary.
On the other hand, the pounding, driving allegros and prestos of
Beethoven's finales are things to be watched, as we watch a race. And
when these are written for a soloist, the latter usually takes care that the
main interest is centred on his technical agility.

II

Coincident with the overthrow of rhythm, and far more important,
comes the break-up of counterpoint. The first thing that strikes us is that
the song is brought into music by a romanticist. In the song the melody
is more or less a conventionalized and harmonized tune, and for this
reason it accompanies a breakdown of organic development in music. In
the very early period, when music was being organized by abstract
scholars in cathedrals and monasteries, the people developed of themselves the folk song. Consequently, it is an approximate rule that a
nation's contribution to systematic music is in inverse ratio to the wealth
of its folk-song material. Germany, the nexus of Western music, has a far
poorer folk song than France or England; Ireland and Wales are richer
than all three but have done little of importance for music. We said
above that we should expect a tendency toward democracy in composition. There is a revival of folk-song interest, which increases all through

the nineteenth century and is now a dominant musical activity, especially in Great Britain. This tendency is, of course, common to the primitivistic stage of romanticism, being associated with the poetry of the "natural man" and contemporary attempts to show that Homer's uncommon poetry resulted from an aggregation of common men. Inevitably in romanticism, however, comes up the art song and Schubert.

Schubert perhaps did more than anyone else to smash counterpoint, not because he lacked contrapuntal skill, but because what contrapuntal skill he has consists largely in melodic combination, and viewed from a harmonic point of view much of his work is little short of infantile. He lacks the restraining disciplinary sense which would prevent his larger works from spilling over at the expense of the plasticity of the form. As a result, even his instrumental works are largely vocally conceived; they often consist of a pleasant but well-nigh interminable succession of melodies. The ensemble performance breaks down into a solo one. It need hardly be said in passing that the solo song is the most typical form of the pictorial approach to music. The dependence of *Der Erlkönig* or *Am Meer* (to mention only two) upon the picture need not detain us here.

In Chopin the pictorial inspiration is obvious enough, though never definitely stated in a title; we learn from biographers of the effect produced on him by pictures, and there is hardly a composition of his that does not irresistibly suggest a visualized scene. It was Chopin who developed the nocturne—obviously a pictorial metaphor—and all through his work the harmonized tune excludes counterpoint. In this, Chopin is typical of the French school. He developed as well the separate prelude, which is so obviously a picture-form that he could not find a musical name for it, and, conformably to the traditions of romanticism, made a good deal of the ballade—a form which dominates his sonatas as well. Schumann's inspiration is also thoroughly pictorial—the titles of his pieces state that more definitely than in the case of Chopin. The "novelette" could by its very name hardly have any other effect. Schumann, too, was a great song writer, and his visual imagination is made evident in his love for the carnival. Schumann is one of the first to introduce visual effects into music. Former touches of program music, except the French school, gather up sound into music: if we listen with a divided attention, it is because we hear something behind the music. Thus, in the *St. Matthew Passion* we can hear the cock crowing in the tenor recitative, the dropping of tears in Peter's aria, and the hideous creaking of chains in the night wind in the Golgotha solo. But with romanticism the program music is visual—thus, in the Schumann Papillons (op. 2) we can "see" in the music the various figures in the carnival, the guests departing at the end, the clock striking, the blowing out of the candles, and the exit of the janitor. Anyone who has ever read Liszt's interpretations of the Chopin Preludes will be amazed at the lengths to which this sort of the thing can go in romantic music. As for Liszt himself, the subject of his program music is a painful one and utterly obvious to any listener, so we shall let it go at that.

Now, what has all this pictorial element to do with the overthrowing of counterpoint? Well, a picture being a statically conceived art, it follows that pictorial music will treat counterpoint statically, that is, harmonically. The way to do this is just to isolate one part of the counterpoint and subordinate all the others to it—only in this way can we have a "perspective" necessary for visualization. This is the reason for the development of the song in Schubert, the song-form in Chopin, and the square-cut conventionalized tunes in Schumann. A similar tendency is found in Berlioz, and, of course, it could only be a matter of time until the advent of Mendelssohn and the "song without words." Now it is interesting to note that harmonically conceived music throws the discord into prominence. The discord gives an effect of pain and the impulse to proceed to a smooth concord, which never comes until the end of the piece. It is not too fanciful to see how the contrapuntal interval of Bach or Mozart is creative and at its basis "optimistic"—it throws the emphasis ahead. The discord perpetually seeking resolution in romantic music is its direct antithesis—music, the microcosm of life, is an uneasy stumbling toward peace and rest. Hence, the rise of positivism brings with it a conception of music, not as harmonic but as "harmonious," that is, dead. With the romantic rehabilitation the discord idea is renewed, with the final concord sometimes granted and sometimes not.

But if romanticism, by bringing the discord into music, is antimusical, the nervous dread of discord which is engendered in the positivistic era is not antimusical, but simply nonmusical. One has only to glance at Victorian England to assure oneself that they were as tone-deaf as the petrified city in the Arabian Nights. All through Tennyson and Coleridge is evidenced a total and often ludicrous ignorance of poetry's most powerful ally. The culture theorists all ignore music. The exception is Browning, who, as the interpreter and voice of his age, as Shakespeare and Milton were of theirs, could not get along without it, but in him the music is eighteenth-century and is based on the harpsichord as thoroughly as Milton's is based on the organ. The music of the time was as concordant as possible, discords only being brought in in order that they might melt into sweet sounds again. The affinity of Tennyson, Mendelssohn, and Dickens,[57] who all produced the same effect in their respective spheres, is evident, and the story of Mendelssohn's rushing downstairs half-dressed to resolve a dominant seventh a friend had played on the piano is full of profound significance for the student.[58]

With neoromanticism the conception of the single chord (a discord, of course) as a splash of colour is ushered in. Scriabin, for example, starts out on a thoroughly romantic basis, his earlier work being almost indistinguishable from Chopin. He carries the harmonic-stiffening ideas of the romantics to their logical conclusion. He overthrows the contrapuntal modes of music (major and minor), substituting a purely harmonic one—the scale of overtones. His last five piano sonatas are based on an initial single but quite sufficiently hideous discord—an idea foreshadowed as far back as the *Eroica* symphony, one of the first great apologias of romanticism. Romantic pessimism receives its ultimate justification when a series of sensuous chords—that is, a delight in discord—comes in to overthrow the rhythmic propulsion.

As we shall see later, colour is a predominant feature of romantic painting; hence, we should expect a similar effect in music. The tendency to regard the chord as a splash of colour has been noted; but in the early stages of romanticism the affinity of colour with timbre was first taken into account, and there arises the great massed colour-orchestra of which Berlioz is the progenitor. Berlioz, a Provençal, wrote a classic treatise on orchestration[59] (the parallel with Delacroix is striking) and remains the supreme apologist of orchestral colour. His attack on counterpoint is, thus, even more open than that of his contemporaries. In *Le Damnation de Faust* a company at an inn are singing a short and rather shaky fugue, whereupon Mephistopheles remarks, "Here we find bestiality in all its frankness."[60] The journalistic articles of Berlioz contain many attacks on the Palestrina and Bach traditions. But if colour is not music, we are not surprised that Berlioz is not the steadiest of musicians. The dynamic difficulty must be overcome, first, by constant variety in orchestration, which means an immense orchestra and a loud noise. "Ah," said the King of Prussia to Berlioz, "you are the composer who writes for five hundred performers." "Wrong, sire," said Berlioz, "sometimes I write for four hundred and fifty."[61] Second, music must lean heavily and creakingly on a nonmusical program for support, which culminates (perhaps) in Richard Strauss.

Of course, we can learn more about romanticism in music by popular compositions than in any other way. We should expect a pretty tune gently harmonized on arpeggios, like the *Spring Song*,[62] to be the most hackneyed work of the positivistic era. If the modern trend is toward the conquest of harmony over counterpoint, we should expect that a piece like the Prelude in C# Minor,[63] in which dead harmonic chords trample on the bleeding and unresisting body of counterpoint with a fiendish collocation of howls and bellows, would be greeted with much glee. Similarly, at the close of negative romanticism, we should expect some vicious outburst of Philistinism of a precisely similar nature, and when Gounod takes a Bach Prelude, forces it into an accompaniment and writes a tune over it, calling the result *Ave Maria*,[64] we bow our heads in the presence of destiny. With jazz the harmonized tune has completely conquered, and the relentless syncopation of the upper register and the equally relentless thumping out of a lifeless beat in the lower grinds all the rhythmic vitality of music to atoms in its jaws.

III

The attack on strict form follows as a corollary. Every art form, whether associated with time or space, contains within itself two specific strict forms, one embodying the temporal and the other the spatial tendency in the art in question. In music the supreme pure instrumental form which seems almost to have evolved out of architecture and contains the whole time-force of music is the fugue, and the form which tends more to a spatial and dramatic presentation is the sonata. These two forms were carried to their height by Bach and Mozart respectively. The vocal forms associated with them are obviously the oratorio and opera, which were similarly treated by the same composers. The romanticists had no sympathy with either fugue or sonata, particularly the fugue. Couperin and Rameau had, of course, ignored both. Berlioz's opinion of the fugue has been recorded,[65] and earlier another Frenchman, Grétry, had attacked the sonata form as tiresome and tautological, concentrating his fire on the repeating of the exposition.[66] The fugue is most peremptorily dismissed. For all their admiration of Bach, the romanticists did not revive this form. Schubert avoided it, Chopin and Weber ignored it,

Schumann played with it a bit and developed the "fughetta." Beethoven
starts the attack on the great classic form of the variation, which in the
Bach or temporal period appears as the passacaglia and in the Mozart
period as the theme with variations. At the very outset Beethoven made
what was practically a suite out of the form. Later, after he had torn it to
pieces in the Diabelli waltz variations,[67] the variation form disappeared,
to be replaced by the Liszt "metamorphosis of themes" and the Wagner
"leitmotif"—both adjuncts of program music and essentially nonfor-
mal.[68] (The fugue is merged in these as well.)

The oratorio is a tragic form of art, and the opera similarly comic. The
drama is divided into tragedy and comedy just as the two musical forms
are, tragedy tending to the temporal and comedy to the spatial, and the
musical forms correspond. Hence, when Mozart brought the opera to its
highest stage of development, it would have to be the comic opera. We
have dealt earlier with the principle that a spatial abstraction from a felt
time-force rests on a basis of religious optimism. Romanticism, in denying this, would have to evolve in revolt the tragic opera. This represents
a shift to the pictorial, and, hence, takes on a continually increasing
trend toward the theatrical, which culminates in Wagner, perhaps the
greatest theatrical genius of all time.

Beethoven's attack on the sonata form is more subtle. Broadly speaking, it centres around the pictorial approach, and, hence, the compression and economy of the Mozartian sonata disappears, and the sonata
takes on a greatly enlarged aspect. The speed no longer swings about a
balance, but the various movements (Beethoven expanded the three-
movement form to a four-movement one) are rhythmically contrasted.
The middle theme of Mozart is expanded to a tremendous development
section—a purely pictorial idea which analyses every implication of the
given themes and holds them up to the light, as it were. A similar
impulse leads Beethoven to develop the coda. The egocentricity of his
later forms is, if often exaggerated, nonetheless present, and it can
hardly be altogether an accident that the greatest of romantic musicians
became deaf in his later years, whereby the individual concentration
power would be so much augmented. There is in Beethoven, however, a
good deal of the will-to-power spirit as well. In his later works he is no
longer content merely with a spatial attack on the sonata form; he must
probe deeper and analyse the fundamental secrets of the time-problems
in his art form. In consequence, the two works of his last period which
are on perhaps the largest scale deal first of all with an exhaustive and

distinctly pessimistic and despairing analysis of the sonata form, ending
in a slow movement, and followed by a terrific burst of energy which
tears to pieces, in the one case the fugue, in the other the oratorio. The
two works in question are *Hammerclavier Sonata*, op. 106, and the *Choral
Symphony* (see note [at end of pt. 3, sec. V]).

IV

The harmonic basis of Western music is the chromatic scale, that is, an
octave arbitrarily and compromisingly divided into twelve semitones,
on which are based a system of interlocking major and minor scales.
This "equal temperament" system, though not formally recognized
until the time of Bach, is more or less implicit since Byrd at least. The
major scale is evolved with the concept of rhythm, and may, therefore,
be presumed to have an integral connection with it. The major and
minor concords are the only "points of repose" yet discovered in Western music. Now it is evident that the creative period of music from Byrd
to Mozart felt the major scale as the essential foundation of music and
the minor only as a modification of it. The usual classical theme with
variations contains one minor variation sensibly regarded as a contrib-
uting and essential but subordinate element. In the great apologia of
equal temperament, *The Well-Tempered Clavichord*, fully half the preludes
and fugues in minor keys end on the *tierce de Picardie* or parallel major
chord, in the first volume, though in the second, published two decades
later, this decreases. All of the composers before Beethoven show a
marked preference for a major key, and when they use a minor they
tend constantly to modulate into the major. Now while there is only the
one major scale, there are three minors. First, the natural minor scale,
which has always impressed the writer as rhythmless; it is used as a
basis for much pre-Elizabethan strict counterpoint and for the folk songs
of unmusical countries (which would be richest in them, as see above
[pt. 3, sec. II]). The major scale, on the other hand, seems powerfully and
irresistibly rhythmic. Now when the major scale emerged as the leading
mode of music, the minor was brought into line with it. This attempt
disclosed the fact that in a major-scale music the minor was unconquer-
ably "sceptical" or duofold, possessing a separate melodic and harmonic form. It is, thus, more pliable and subjective than the major. In
short, the major is the fundamental scale of metaphysical optimism, the
minor that of romantic pessimism, and anyone with a pair of ears knows

that the minor sounds sadder and more adaptable to tragedy than the major.

The preference of Chopin for the minor is so marked that it is distinctly cloying. To anyone who feels an atmospheric difference in keys, as Berlioz did, C# minor seems the most thoroughly romantic of all, and is Chopin's obvious favourite.[69] It is interesting that in a similar conflict which runs through Beethoven the antithesis is usually presented as relative (i.e., one of key-signature, as E-flat major and C minor (three flats)). On the other hand, Mendelssohn, in trying to blend them, habitually thinks of the contrast as parallel (i.e., one of pitch, as E major and E minor). In the former the minor is breaking away to independence, in the latter feeling its way back to classical spontaneity. And as we should expect, the early Frenchmen are particularly fond of minor keys, and often their dances are in ternary form enclosed in a minor theme. The contrast here is also usually parallel.

Antiromantic music, therefore, avoided the minor mode. But any exploitation of a minor scale must imply a recognition of the major scale as essential if not basic, and two notes more bring in the entire chromatic scale. Neoromanticism, thus, begins with the exploitation of the chromatic resources in their entirety. The romantics were the first to acclaim Bach. It was Bach who foreshadowed contrapuntally the full resources of music and thereby implied its eventual termination. But he expressed himself in terms of the great contrapuntal tradition he summed up, and so to follow Bach at that time was death. His successors, who had to develop the sonata form, turned their backs on him, and it was not until the time of Mendelssohn that he was rehabilitated. Now Bach is about as romantic as Spinoza, and he was revered for the same reason—that in the abstract completeness of his music is incarnated the universal grasp which is the great romantic desideratum. Now the exploitation of the chromatic scale as such begins with César Franck and Wagner, and their followers, who were, of course, mainly Frenchmen. The chromatic scale is the half-tone scale, and abstractions made from it lean, not to major or minor, but to simple chromatic multiples—the whole-tone scale (Debussy) or the quarter-tone scale (Schoenberg).

If there is such a thing as a third-dimensional element in music, it is probably the question of key-relationship. Thickness, solidity, support, all derive from the modulation, and it is the balance of these modulations that sustains the music. To reduce this to a pictorial or two-dimensional concept would require that the idea of key-relationship be replaced by the idea of key-contrast. Tracing out this factor through Beethoven is easy enough, and in general the sudden modulation may be considered typical of romanticism. Again, we find in pre-Beethoven music, apart from the propagandic *Well-Tempered Clavichord*, an extreme conservatism in regard to the use of keys—those remote from C major are almost altogether avoided. With the romantics comes a fairly impartial use of the whole twenty-four. The keys more remote from C major are esoteric, tertiary, and typically romantic.[70] Besides, it is evident that in the period of major-scale dominance C major, whatever its sound, symbolizes the architectural stability of music, and the prodigality of the romanticist is a symbol of the uprooting of this.

V

Romanticism saw the harpsichord replaced by the pianoforte, which latter is the basic instrument of the romantic period. There are several reasons for this. In the first place, the pianoforte lends itself to a harmonic concept of music better than any other instrument. The damper pedal is its chief auxiliary, and this is essential to a harmonic concept and utterly meaningless in connection with a contrapuntal one. Again, the question of dynamics is brought under control of the performer. The "shading" of dynamics, another pictorial concept, comes into romantic music. The harpsichord and pre-Beethoven music generally recognized loud and soft, but the performer's control of all nuances of shading was as meaningless as any similar control over rhythm. The whole tendency in the performance of romantic music, conformably to the basic idea of romantic egoism, is to make the performer a soloist and give him as much critical power as possible. Improvising as a fine art begins to vanish and composers of concertos give up the practice of leaving the cadenza bar blank. But in order to produce a pictorial effect it was necessary to have an instrument that could outline a melody and subordinate the rest, and this the pianoforte could do better than the harpsichord. Again, harmonically conceived melodies are bound closely together. An instrument that could produce a legato effect was, thus, necessary. In harpsichord music the notes appear from nowhere; in pianoforte phrasing they are drawn, in groups. There was, therefore, an effort to make the piano as legato an instrument as possible. It was to be an Aeolian harp, not a kettledrum. But all this power given to the performer naturally resulted in a rise of virtuosity of effort in the will-to-power period. Anyone comparing, say, Mozart with Liszt cannot fail to see the change from technic to pyrotechnics, from cleanness to brilliance. That factor, which the Germans call *Zopf*, is an inevitable outcome, too, of the romantic shift from patronage to popularity, necessitating the larger audience and the big concert grand pianos and massed orchestras, providing for executant strugglers and romantic heroes like Paganini, Rubinstein, and conductors through to Toscanini. The positivist contempt and dislike for music was similarly reflected in the endless procession of tasteless arpeggio artists on the piano or violin, who regarded music as dramatic elocution and played through a stock of regulation warhorses by Beethoven, Chopin, or Liszt until music practically ossified under their iron grip. With the rehabilitation of romanticism, there is a tendency, corresponding to several others, to atomize the notes of a piano and make it frankly an instrument of percussion. Stravinsky is perhaps the leader in this field.

Note

After dealing with Beethoven's attack on the sonata form, its subsequent development was inadvertently omitted. There is not much to say about it, except that it practically disappears, as in its enlarged form no one can handle it except Brahms, who bears about the same relation to romantic music that Lotze does to romantic philosophy. The subjective pictorial form of the symphonic poem replaces the symphony. This is almost invariably program music, and, being allied with postromanticism, deals extensively with a twisting and manipulation of themes (metamorphosis) rather than with developing them. The symphonies of Tschaikowsky require for their propulsion a force almost approaching hysteria, and the treatment of the Frenchmen succeeding Franck leans more to the suite than the sonata. As for Franck's Symphony in D Minor, it should be noted how even in that work there is a tendency to bind the whole symphony together thematically, and that in the first movement particularly an idea suggestive of neoromanticism appears, it being in a way a "creative evolution" of a three-note motive.[71]

Part Four

The problem of romanticism in England is complicated a little by the

fact that the material and ideal changes which produced it really started
in that country with the Puritan Revolution. The same victory of London over the land, of the moneyed merchant over aristocracy, of democratic constitutionalism over despotism, of colonial enterprise over
insularity, which romanticism brought to other countries, all begin early
in the seventeenth century in England. If there is such a thing as a
national bias, we may say that that of England has been in the main
directed toward that condition of life in which romanticism finds
itself—urban and mercantile, but held culturally by a compact atomic
idealism. Romanticism proper brought a recrudescence of poetic energy
into England which no other country approached, not even Germany,
whose romanticism was preceded by Goethe. There is also a sort of
romantic stream running through English literature from Chaucer
down, which is most strikingly brought out in Spenser.

Let us look back at our diagram of the arts for a moment. We should
expect that music and drama would give place to a group of pictorial
arts marked off into the lyric-essay and fiction. Music and drama collapsed after the Elizabethans under the rise of the Puritans, who waged
a fierce war upon both, and the lyric-essay and fiction traditions date
from Milton and Bunyan respectively. However, the Puritans were not
only critical, but positivistic, and the change they brought about was
far too sudden to be permanent. The Restoration consolidated a shift
which stopped halfway between creation and criticism. The central art
forms become a blend of music and drama on the one hand, and of
architecture and sculpture on the other. The former, which brings a
dramatic situation directly into the accented rhythm of life, is actualized in the comedy of manners; the latter is more obviously furniture.
The trend is, however, toward the spatial: thus, the comedy of manners becomes far more effective and powerful the nearer it approaches
the spatial or pessimistic side of satire, as with Swift and Hogarth, and
the psychology of artistry is more concentrated on furniture than on
the comedy. When we speak of the poetry of Dryden or Pope, we judge
it in furniture terms—polish, elegance, symmetry, finish, smoothness,
and so forth.[72]

I

Dealing first with the poetry, we find romanticism centring around
what I have called the "lyric-essay," the critical pictorial art form which

descends from music. Music is, as we have seen, the great time-creation which epitomizes life; its critical analogue would, therefore, be the subjective reaction to life which sees life as a picture, and goes along with the romantic musician's attack on music. The lyric-essay cannot be equated with lyric poetry generally, because lyric poetry does not always mirror the individual personality; a great deal of it, the Elizabethan lyric, for instance, is pure singing, and singing, being under the influence of music, is more abstract. (This sounds inconsistent with what we said of the vocal solo as a relapse into criticism with Schubert, but the question is, as we have seen so often, one of orientation and a contrast of a lyric form pulled over into music and a musical form pulled over into lyricism.) Nor is the expression invariably poetic—the "purple passages" of the prose writers, such as Ruskin, De Quincey, Pater, Meredith, Hardy, belong here too. The term "purple passage" is vulgarly used to denote a passage of prose which is written for the purpose of giving the writer's reaction as emotionally as possible, and with this the distinction between prose and poetic utterance becomes accidental. Now we have seen that every general division of art carries within itself two specific strict forms, one embodying the temporal tendency and the other the spatial tendency. In the lyric-essay the former, a time-reaction representing the thrill and rush of the temporal urge through the egocentric artist, is the ode; the other, representing a mirror of his reflection, is the sonnet.[73]

Romantic poetry and poetic prose, then, must centre on a pictorial eye-synthesis. Being critical, the poet has to arrogate the function of criticism. The pseudo-Aristotelian pedantries of the type of critic who was supposed to have murdered Keats are replaced by poet-critics, of whom Byron, Coleridge, and Poe are outstanding examples. The new idea that the poet is the centre of his own world is heralded by many extreme and often absurd examples of romantic egoism. According to Blake, all art consists in pure self-expression, and the imitation resulting from long education is a sin against genius.[74] Earlier we have primitive stirrings of this in Goldsmith's writing airily at great length on subjects he knew nothing about, which for sheer "cheek" can be equalled only by Rousseau's contemporary experiments in music.[75]

A picture, however, is an optical art, and poetry appeals to the ear; hence, the dominant feature of romantic poetry is a sound pattern. In English literature this means a careful and exact choice of words and balance of phrases, combined with a practically motionless rhythm.

There is almost no suggestion of speed in romantic poetry—the words are intended to be looked at and lovingly dwelt upon:

> Thou still-unravish'd bride of quietness,
> Thou foster-child of silence and slow time. [*Ode on a Grecian Urn*, lines 1–2]

The exquisite static balance and variety of vowel-sound in Keats is counterbalanced by Coleridge's more Teutonic preoccupation with consonants and his use of alliteration. In more extreme forms of romantic poetry this pattern becomes a motionless dream haze, like *Kubla Khan*, an effect imitated in Tennyson's *Lotos-Eaters*. (*Kubla Khan*, of course, is actually of dream origin.) Alliteration and vowel assonance are all part of a general echolalia scheme developed most typically by Poe, which makes for repetition of words and a sort of suppressed refrain:

> He holds him with his skinny *hand*,
> "There was a ship," quoth he.
> "Hold off! *unhand* me, gray-beard loon!"
> Eftsoons his *hand* dropt he.[76]

It therefore follows that rhyme is essential to romanticism in poetry. Blank verse drops out, and free verse is a later development. The heroic couplet, which is the smoothest form of verse, clinches a balanced antithetical form of expression which has nothing to do with the subjectivist's peculiar world-picture and, therefore, seldom appears except in its more pliable octosyllabic form. A favourite stanza is the Spenserian, with its close-knit rhyme scheme and its dreamy Alexandrine chiming in like the undersea bell in Debussy's tone poem. Rhyme is the great external musical symbol in poetry, because it draws attention to the word as pure sound. Looking again at our diagram, poetry which looks across at music is rhymed; poetry which definitely approaches it drops it out, as it has in a measure a tendency to become "wordless" and shrinks from calling attention to the word. We can see this progression in Shakespeare. Romantic verse is attached to rhyme because it is almost altogether unmusical—the "lonely flute" of Coleridge [*The Rime of the Ancient Mariner*, line 364] being a random shot at a sympathetic approach. Except for Browning[77] the postromantics carry this still farther.

Stylistically, then, romanticism represents the epitome of the synthetic and subjective world-picture of which the philosophy of history forms

the macrocosmos. It is quite rigid and formalized—a prosodist, no matter how pedantic, will take more examples from Keats than from Pope
or Dryden. Positivism, therefore, brings an attack on this. It is dangerous to generalize, but, broadly speaking, positivism in English literature is represented by Browning; postromanticism by Swinburne. With
Swinburne rhyme and a choice of words go hand in hand with a tremendous surging rush. Comparison of any alliterative passage in Coleridge with one in Swinburne should be enough to show that the one
deals with the contemplation of the world-as-idea and the other with
the will to power:

> Five miles meandering with a mazy motion
> Through wood and dale the sacred river ran,
> Then reached the caverns measureless to man,
> And sank in tumult to a lifeless ocean. [*Kubla Khan*, lines 25–8]

> From the depth of the dreamy decline of the dawn through a notable nim-
>   bus of nebulous moonshine,
> Pallid and pink as the palm of the flag-flower that flickers with fear of the
>   flies as they float
> Are the looks of our lovers that lustrously lean from a marvel of mystic
>   miraculous moonshine
> These that we feel in the blood of our blushes that thicken and threaten
>   with throbs through the throat? [*Nephelidia*, lines 1–4]

The latter is admitted to be a vicious and unfair example, but it
emphasizes the point. Similarly the romantics had held their rhythms
tightly together in a static, arrested pattern, which was not disturbed by
any pounding rhythmic propulsion:

> When the lamp is shattered
> The light in the dust lies dead—
> When the cloud is scattered
> The rainbow's glory is shed.[78]

The above is a skilful reining in of two rather restive metres. But with
Swinburne the iambic norm of English poetry, which the romantics in
the main clung to, is torn to pieces, and a galloping procession of dac-
tyls, choriambs, and anapests symbolizes the postromantic activity.

We have seen that postromanticism is a sort of running commentary on positivism, so we should expect there similar tendencies but less compromise. Browning's poetry is markedly spatial—Oscar Wilde in reacting from him called him a prosaic fiction writer,[79] and that way he certainly tends. His plays are not successful, not because they are bad, but because they are imperfectly dramatized novels. He launches an energetic attack on the romantic picture. He revives blank verse, and his choice of words is nonexistent, except insofar as his brusque guttural diction makes for a discordant destruction of colour blending. His attack on rhyme is even more uncompromising:

> While, treading down rose and ranunculus
> You *Tommy-make-room-for-your-uncle* us!
> Troop, all of you—man or homunculus
> Quick march! for Xanthippe, my housemaid,
> If once on your pates she a souse made
> With what, pan or pot, bowl or *skoramis*
> First comes to her hand—things were more amiss!
> I would not for worlds be your place in—
> Recipient of slops for the basin!
>   [*Of Pacchiarotto, and How He Worked in Distemper*, lines 518–26]

There is a marked tendency among many of the positivistic poets to fight rhyme by reducing it to a like absurdity in trying to rhyme the most impossible words, and, thus, getting rhyme out of the literature for good and all. The whole of the positivistic attack on rhyme and rhythm is concentrated in Hood's *Bridge of Sighs*. Browning's chief model was Shelley, who anticipates the positivistic era, his position being somewhat analogous to that of Beethoven. There is a sort of bourgeois philosophy and an interest in spatial facts, a cheerful recognition of atheistic materialism, and a tendency to let his verse move faster, to be far-flung and spacious, which distinguishes him from other romantics.

Antitheses between romantic and postromantic go far deeper, however, than stylistic evidence alone. We have spoken of Don Juan as a great romantic myth which stands, cynical and smiling, to represent the time-force, victorious and baffling all spatial conquests. Similarly, we should expect another figure less purely sexual in symbolism to represent the romantic shift to feeling, the romantic egotistic recognition of a

relentless temporal revolt against spatial abstraction, which was dominant in the religious period. Now the latter, being religious, is obviously
associated with God, and romantic *skepsis*, therefore, evolves the opponent time-symbol of the Devil. There is no Goethe in English poetry,
because of the suspension of the century between the creative period
and the critical, and what that poet signified had to be actualized in
three stages—Milton, Blake, and Shelley. With Milton Satan was baffled
just as was the Puritan positivism, and the dauntless warrior of the first
part of *Paradise Lost* gradually wastes away and degenerates, until in
Paradise Regained he has become a sniggering little imp. In Blake the Mil-
tonic plan is reversed; all moral values are explicitly inverted, putting
evil where good formerly was. Blake starts out as a diabolist and worshipper of evil, or time, "the active springing from energy" [*The Marriage of Heaven and Hell*, pl. 3]. God, or Urizen, is a tyrant who invented
law and logic, spatial inhibitions both. Hence, the Satanic time-power is
expressed as revolt—Satan becomes a Messiah and engineers the French
and American struggles for liberty. The clearest symbol of the revolt
stage is Orc. Later, as Blake developed, he turned to deeper fundamen-
tals, and the great myths of the Prophetic Books are dominated by the
mighty Los, the God of time out of whom space (Enitharmon) proceeds
as an emanation struggling to free herself. Finally she does free herself and runs shrieking from Los, only to be pursued, caught and reab-
sorbed. . . .[80] Shelley is no prophet, but he is an anticipation of the new
empiric attack on space, and Prometheus is the great figure who, armed
with the new fire of time-energy, stands unbound and triumphant
before the Zeus of religion, who does not possess it, because it possesses
him. Positivistic poetry, therefore, turned its back on the time-force. It
becomes as sexless as possible and attacks the time-problem only from
the point of view of the spatial conquest of it—in other words from the
moral side. In Browning love becomes the highest form of morality and
God is reinstated as the rock-bottom formula of the excavating scientist,[81] being always just one step away:

> We find great things are made of little things,
> And little things go lessening till at last
> Comes God behind them. Talk of mountains now?
> We talk of mould that heaps the mountain, mites
> That throng the mould, and God that makes the mites.
> The Name comes close behind a stomach-cyst,

> The simplest of creations, just a sac
> That's mouth, heart, legs and belly at once, yet lives
> And feels, and could do neither, we conclude,
> If simplified still further one degree:
> The small becomes the dreadful and immense!
>
> [*Mr. Sludge, "The Medium,"* lines 1112–22]

Tennyson and Swinburne are less committed to this orientation and relapse into pantheism.

Similarly the approach to medieval culture is external and unsympathetic. With primitivism the interest in it was mainly directed toward the ballad, just as, and for the same reason that, the romantics in music revived the folk song. The most powerful formative influence on romantic poetry was Spenser, the pictorial critic of medievalism, and a glance at the poems of Coleridge or Keats which deal with this period is sufficient to show that they were far more attracted by the colour of illuminated missals than edified by their contents. The great Christian romances deal with a definite search for something, like the Holy Grail, and opposed to these is the horror of the atheism of an older civilization incarnate in the wandering Jew, who travels blindly under a curse. Romanticism brings back the weary and aimless wanderer in two well-known but opposed figures: the Ancient Mariner and the Flying Dutchman. In the latter, as almost everywhere in Wagner outside of Tannhäuser, the wanderer symbolizes the endless revolution of space-abstraction around the time-force, into which latter he is finally drawn by his sexual attachment to it—in other words, he is "redeemed by love." The Ancient Mariner arrives at a positivistic solution, losing his esoteric haughtiness in a purely exotic impulse to take every spatial concept into his soul. Positivistic poetry revives the search for the Grail, at least four major poets becoming absorbed in Arthurian legends (Tennyson, Swinburne, Masefield, and E.A. Robinson)—chiefly the Tristram and Isolt story, where the love-redemption theme centres.[82]

II

If romanticism is typified by the lyric-essay, we should expect positivism to centre in the novel, and romanticism to tend to the destruction of that form. The novel is, of course, the critical successor to the drama, the arrangement and selection of life by a watching narrator replacing the purely objective abstraction presented on the stage. Now just as music and drama are ensemble performances for audiences, so the critical arts are written by and addressed to individuals, and this applies as much to a novel as it does to the lyric-essay. We altogether misunderstand the idea of the novel if we think of it as objective. In its essence the novel is the subjective presentation of an ordered picture of life as an idea in the mind of the author. It is not a cross-section of reality, but it typifies one. There must then be a kind of localization, whether one of place or one of social stratification. The centre of an idea, being the ego, is unapproachable; therefore, the novel consists essentially in variety of characters grouped around a hero and heroine whose psychology is not examined but who are left alone to symbolize the abstract normality of the mind of their creator. The marriage of hero and heroine symbolizes the closing up of the lacuna in the said mind through which came the novel, and, hence, signifies the end. The central theme is, consequently, love and the treatment comic, with a happy ending. These are not rules for novel-writing; they are merely principles which underlie the actual historical fact of the art form, which flourished—that is, lived and died—entirely within the era of positivistic dominance. They are not satisfactory to contemporary novelists, but neither is the novel.

The positivist novel corresponds, of course, to the contemporary experiment in science—given certain factors with certain conditions, let us see what will happen to them. A novel without a happy ending in which all difficulties are smoothed out and explained away would be as meaningless as an experiment without a calculable result. But it is evident that an art form in which love culminates in marriage and forms the central theme has affiliations with the sexual point of view of the positivist period.[83] We should expect that romanticism, which made several onslaughts on the novel and finally destroyed it, would be associated primarily with the long-ignored but irresistible time, and to some extent, therefore, with the masculine reaction which reaches such bitter depths in Weininger and Strindberg.

In the first place, the great aim of the romantics we have seen to be a philosophy of history, and positivism, starting with Schopenhauer, turns its back on history. The typically romantic attack is, therefore, the historical novel of Scott, which bears with it all the political implications attacked by Borrow that we shall endeavour to trace in part five.[84] Scott halted the development of the novel for several years, because he was a great artist in his own line and had behind him all the force of romanticism, whose historical imagination was focused on the Middle Ages and the Stuarts.[85] But a force allied with him lay even deeper. We have seen in music how romanticism, by first recognizing time and space as separate concepts, brought about the separation of melody and harmony in counterpoint, these being respectively time and space elements. Music being propelled by a temporal force, its exhaustion would be accompanied by a victory of harmony. Conversely, the life of the novel residing in its spatial abstracting power, we should expect the time-element to destroy it. The "harmony" of a novel is what sustains it, and that is obviously its balance of characterization. The "melody" is the story, or the plot. The story, like the folk tune, is the popular element, and in the creative period of masculine domination it entirely runs away with the characterization which goes to make a novel. The Catholic period was that of the knight errant, but the Renaissance destroyed it in *Don Quixote* and replaced it by the picaresque tradition. In England the picaresque novel reigned supreme from Bunyan to Smollet as the masculine form of the novel. The women, whose demand was as yet chaotic, read instead the chaotic Scudéry type of romance.[86] In the eighteenth century Richardson brought into existence the modern novel on a feminine basis (developing it out of the letter, the prime symbol of individual communication) and Fielding annihilated the picaresque in *Jonathan Wild*. The novel was now firmly established, and the first protest of romanticism proper was a flood of cheap horror tales. These were not effective and were shipwrecked on the iceberg of Jane Austen, who shaped the novel into its ultimate positivist form. Scott's historical attack followed, but that could only last as long as romanticism did, and then came Poe, who isolated the time-skeleton of the novel, or pure plot, and produced the detective story. This centres around a crime and is, thus, the direct descendant of the rogue-romance. Both are concentrated on the antisocial because the novel is an experiment in life and demands controlled conditions—that is, a static society. What attacks this would have to be antisocial. The novel demands a certain smug self-satisfaction in the novelist, because of this fact and because it tends naturally to a happy ending.

The critic contemplating life, or the set of symbols he has evolved out of life, is, of course, a romanticist, and the novelist shrinks from the full implications of the "view of life." Characterization in the novel proper is purely external, and society is postulated as static, because the novelist is turned away from the attitude which would recognize the time-implications in life. He does not consider either the macrocosm of the world or the microcosm of the individual. He must abstract a section from the former and group the latter, dealing with both as spatial. The romanticist, then, when he finally comes up to rehabilitate himself, destroys the plan of the novel by his insistence that there is something wrong with the world. The detective story is the strict objective form embodying this conception. Several novelists in the positivistic era, headed by Charles Reade, bring in the social problem. This destroys the novel as an art form, because it replaces it with a propagandic type sub-servient to a thesis. It is significant of the complete overthrow of the novel that the usual reaction to this approach urges the other: "it is the business of a novelist just to tell a plain story."

There is naturally a strong pull upon the novelist to draw him into the sweeping time-sequence of life and make a reformer out of him. This pull is almost inevitable, in fact, and I do not really know of any pure novelist, in the formal sense, except Jane Austen, who first defined that form. George Eliot, Zola, Balzac, Thackeray, even Flaubert, all kept ulterior motives in the background. The clearest example of this difficulty is found in Dickens. From a purely technical point of view Dickens is not only the world's greatest novelist, but one of the supreme artists of all time: the ease with which he manipulates an immense host of characters around his two central figures, intertwining them with a superb sense of pictorial contrast, is little short of miraculous. But the pull of the plot is too strong. He did not seem to consider his technical faculty as evidence of real technique at all, and laboured much over the composition and working out of an alien and absurd plot. As a novelist, he could not very well go in for straight detective stories, but compromised with the mystery, to which he gradually sacrificed his greater talents, culminating in his last unfinished work,[87] and even in his great novels the long impossible subterfuges of some of the characters, which reveal the so-called mystery at the end, are very miserable affairs. He suffered precisely similar inhibitions with social reform, though he handled this better than did George Eliot, for example.

So even in the greatest practitioners of novel-writing the time-element overrides. But romanticism has not yet altogether shot its bolt. We have said that a novelist draws his characters externally, because they exist only as ideas in his mind. A novel moves by the shifting interplay of characters, and a prolonged examination of one figure destroys its spirit.

Hence, we have a movement precisely analogous to the chord-as-colour concept attack on harmonic music, which isolates one portrait and studies it—the biographical novel, which is developed through to the huge tomes of *Jean-Christophe* and *Ulysses*. This reverts to a temporal consideration. It is the romantic view of time made individual instead of synthetic and symbolic. There is infinite variety in individuals, just as there is infinite variety in the world as a whole, and infinity is too big to be contained in a defined art form.

III

We have avoided giving the same exposition of romantic English literature that we did of philosophy and music, because the field has been so frequently covered, and to reinterpret it all in terms of our thesis would be at this stage tautological. The illustration of the working through of the romantic force is certainly more interesting and probably more significant. When the reign of positivism is over, rehabilitated romanticism sets in. As we have seen, positivism posits an optimism in action and a sort of suspended judgment in thought that makes it inseparable from a peculiar set, posed quality we usually call smugness. When the cocksureness of material science begins to break up, the time-element is recognized as beyond our apprehension, and "space-time," or the manifestation of time in space-phenomena, becomes separated out from it. In literature this has a similar repercussion in that the question of the will is no longer approached from the point of view of the compulsions binding it to space. In other words, literature from now on does not aim so constantly at the moral and respectable point of view. The decadence of postromanticism, which culminated in the trial of Wilde, produced a reaction, certainly, but the literary reaction was a swing toward health. Romanticism had come into its own.

The subversive attack for this era is again French. But a little later than the positivists come the *symbolistes*, who turned romanticism into impressionism. These two latter terms are connected as are reality and truth—the one is the product of the other and is begotten by the critical mind. Impressionism is to romanticism as romanticism itself is to the creative period. It aims at the photograph, not the painting. Consequently, it depends upon a single effect. But the effect must be an instantaneous reproduction of reality. Its art is too swift to permit of its being filtered through a working mind. The camera sums up reality at a glance; the painter interprets it by prolonged watching and communion with it. The opposition of "realism" to "romanticism" implies that the latter, in its flight from the world-as-will and its absorption in the world as subjective idea, is to the latter as seashell pink to dirty drab (this figure occurs somewhere in Meredith)[88] and, consequently, takes that view of life. But we should remember that the idea that prettiness is unreal and that the "real" depicted in realism is ugly (journalists usually replace this word by "stark") spring from the same postulate—the romantic pessimistic rejection of the world-as-will. When romanticism is rehabilitated, the world-as-will is finally and squarely recognized without any emotional reactions. But we cannot know this world-as-will—that we have finally discovered—hence, it can only be lit up by a lightning flash, held spatially for an instant, and symbolized by an instantaneous appeal to feeling.

Now this sudden comprehension of the world-as-will must be pictorial, but must use some force powerful enough, as the lyric-essay and the novel certainly are not, to bring about an immediate response. Hence, the neoromantic period brings a revival of music and drama in this new flashlight form. Music has been dealt with, and we have seen that its unit is fundamentally the single chord. The reason, of course, is that the chord signifies the isolation of a single impression of the underlying evanescent unity. Atmosphere represents the same thing in painting. In exactly the same way the dramatic and fictional arts tend. The grasp of form in the drama is centred on the scena or one-act play in Yeats, Synge, Shaw, and O'Neill. The longer works of the latter two are scenas strung together. The novel gives way to the short story, which exhibits a constant tendency to approach the dramatic scene, a tendency running through Poe and de Maupassant to Hemingway and Katherine Mansfield. Poetry centres on the presentation of one theme, long poems being generally the work of minor poets. These are very general statements, because of the experimental complex of the age which results in trying everything at least several times, but it is hardly possible to escape from the conclusion that this impressionist technic is the dominant note of the artistic activity of the whole of the contemporary neoromantic period and generally characteristic of and inevitable to it.

In literature this ultimate exhaustion is made possible by the break-up of poetry into prose. The essential distinction between these two forms is chiefly that in prose the idea is microcosmic and exists independently, while in poetry it is cosmic, the rhythmic beat of its formulation being its essence. Now as the microcosm is reflected in the atomic individualism of the prose, a new "naturalness" comes into poetry which starts with Blake, perhaps the first great poet to keep a natural speaking rhythm enclosed in a line of metrical verse. As the speech became more forceful, free verse was developed by Whitman and strict verse exploded by Browning. The great bulk of poetry today is in free verse, and after puzzling over its *raison d'être* for some time, the writer has finally been forced to the conclusion that if a generalization can be made about it, it would be that in the case of those major poets who obviously know best what they are doing, free verse tends constantly in its technique toward bringing out and emphasizing the rhythmic implications of the sentence. The sentence is evidently the unit of modern prose. The prose of the creative period is forced into a quasi-poetic mould in which the rhythm is too subtle to be detected and the period is more a caesura than a full stop. Comparison between the prose style of Berkeley, Hume, or Gibbon with the echoless thumping of Macaulay or Mill should show that in the latter the writing is more "natural," that is, more colloquial and with a mechanizing tendency to equate the sentence with the idea. In prose stylists, like Ruskin or De Quincey, the sentence is exploited to a degree unparalleled since the naive attempts of euphuism. Romanticism, then, brings English literature down to the sentence, and the sentence is the pictorial representation, completed and balanced, of a temporal art. The mechanizing tendency of the sentence is far more obvious in music than in literature, because there it is made up in a regular progression of beats. A measure is a single rhythmic pattern, two measures a phrase, four a section, eight a period, and sixteen a typical conventionalized tune. The whole of popular music is centred on the last-named unit—some time ago I glanced through several volumes of popular songs in an endeavour to find one that was either more or less than sixteen measures in length, being finally rewarded by discovering one with thirty-two. In the closing stages of music we find this preoccupation with the precise, clipped, two-or-four-bar rhythmic unit to an irritating extent in Grieg and Scriabin.

The snobbishness of erudition, starting from the romantic "escape from life," is, of course, easy enough to trace, through Baudelaire and Browning to the decadents, and through the decadents to Pound, Eliot,

and Joyce. The metropolitan spirit finds an antithetical provincial protest in the regionalism of France, the United States, and the English pastoral poetry which has a marked primitivistic bent. The two tendencies
in romanticism, the exotic and the esoteric, are, as we have seen,
opposed, one turning to space and positivism, the other to time and
postromanticism. Hence, the one is allied with the metropolitan looking
at the countryside, the other with the metropolitan looking in upon
himself.[89]

The French origin of the neoromantic period gives it a strong appeal
to those English-speaking countries which in their revolt against the literary supremacy of England have turned to France and have sided in
with the French destructive attack on Western culture. The growth of
English literature in England becomes repetitive and self-commentating
after the close of the last century, its contemporary development being
in the hands of Ireland and America. The intense nationalistic self-
containedness of the smaller country has given it a more organic grasp
and has swung it further toward the drama and mysticism in the lyric-
essay, while the Americans, representing in the main the protest of individualism, have tended more to the lyric. Both countries went through a
cultural renaissance heralded by a movement of expatriation to
England—Moore, Shaw, and Wilde from Ireland, Pound and Henry
James from our neighbour. One reason for their greater susceptibility to
the Parisian *déraciné* attack is their own orchidaceous position with
regard to Western culture, both countries lacking the systematic cultural
growth of England and any musical or architectural traditions of their
own—architecture as a creative time-art and not a product of applied
science, and music as an art form and not as a folk song.

A closing word should be said concerning the romantic attack on the
drama. We have seen in music how the opera became tragic with
romanticism, so it seems natural that the tragedy should become operatic. As the romantic drama belongs more to German literature, with
Schiller, Kleist, Grillparzer, and others, than to English, this does not at
the moment concern us. The most notable operatic tendencies in our
own tradition are the dramatic scenes in Byron. Plays of English romanticism, even so powerful a work as the *Cenci*, belong more to the lyric-
essay than to the drama. It was not until the positivist period that
sufficient sympathy with a spatial art could be attained to formulate a
definite attitude toward the drama, albeit from a subjective point of

view. An objective, spatial, dynamic art form would naturally be symbolized by a sphere, while a subjective, spatial, static art form would be better represented by a ring. Hence, Browning's great drama (it has nothing to do with epics), which the Roman gold ring so symbolizes, as the poet expressly tells us [*The Ring and the Book*, lines 1–31], presents modern literature with the technique of the modern drama worked out in full. The characters illuminate the subjectively conceived theme like floodlights—that is all they exist for—and a perfect modelled drama would have the complete balance of the ring. This secondary contribution of characters to theme is most plainly evident in Shaw. The theme of *The Ring and the Book* also has obvious affinities with the detective story, because the strict form of the theme of the novel[90] is similarly the detective story.

We have shown above that impressionism restores the dramatic sphere in its microcosmic seed-coat. We might note in this connection that an experimentally produced sphere, blown up until it burst, would represent the whole essence of the pessimistic approach to the age. Hence, the ghastliest short story in literature, Henry James's *Turn of the Screw*, employs this technique: an embryonic dramatic scene becomes more and more unendurable until it reaches the breaking point, and then vanishes exactly like a soap bubble. Ravel's *Boléro* does the same thing in music, and the fact that this piece has been called the musical description of an orgasm is not at all inconsistent with the sexual implications of neoromanticism discussed in part 1. In art this psychology underlies the advertisement, which reflects in epitome a neoromantic world continually inflating economically to the breaking point and then vanishing in the depths of depression or war.

Conclusion

There is room for only the briefest mention of the movement of romanticism through politics.

The period of systematic romanticism is usually associated with an eager-eyed liberalism of the type of Shelley: of a bitter resentment of all forms of tyranny and a post-Rousseau insistence on the rights of man and of the individual's liberty. This is the first and primitivist stage: the after-echo or feeling reaction to the French Revolution. The rights of the common man were lauded by all romantics, though many, including most of the English poets, repudiated the revolution because of its guillotine, and because it had not brought either the liberty it promised or an immediate progress in ideas. However, this peculiar vague and sentimental love of humanity represents much of both romantic and positivist ideals. The overthrow of creative religion meant the annihilation of the God transcendent; the God immanent, or rather pantheistic, was the conception replacing it, and he could be perceived only in humanity. Worship of humanity is, then, the romanticist's religion as well as Comte's. The difference is that a time-synthesis from a spatial viewpoint will recognize a unity in succession more clearly, and will, consequently, postulate a present one which is incorporated in Hegel's conception of the *Zeitgeist*. This word was practically a shibboleth of young German romantic liberals, and considering Hegel's own viewpoint, it is obvious that the conception is too deep and broad to be identified with either liberalism or conservatism, which indicate the wings and not the centre of the social development. The worship of the *Zeitgeist* was the romantic religion. It was not Schleiermacher's religion, but Schleiermacher signified its dissection into the individual and is, thus, midway between Hegel and Schopenhauer, the latter of whom saw in it a cross-section of the hated will. In England a somewhat similar movement took place through the humanitarianism of Shaftesbury to the individualism of Methodism, by far the greatest and most powerful product of romantic religion, becoming insensibly and subtly an ally of capitalism. Schleiermacher's thought, therefore, has a double aspect. The romantic political worship of the *Zeitgeist* meant practically that God exists in the world of men, because where men are gathered a consensus results which evolves a new factor greater than the sum of individuals, which is the highest thing we can know. We worship in society. Schleiermacher represents a feeling-reaction to this—look inside, not outside, into your own soul for God-consciousness. This leads alike into the esoteric narcotic ecstasy of the postromantic and the spatial conquest of the world-as-idea.

All of which is by way of introduction to the fact that a *Zeitgeist* must have some defined form. In the world there are two such forms: the nation and the race-language group. One could imagine on the one hand an English, German, or south Slavic racial and cultural *Zeitgeist*, and on the other a British, Austrian, or American national one. But the former alone has its roots in time and partakes of the mysterious time-force. The latter is a space-symbol and space-conquest. The political activity of romanticism, then, centred on attempting to make national

units identical with racial and cultural ones. The most prominent exponent of this school, both in theory and practice, is Mazzini.[91]

Positivism is a logical development of this, for a space-conquest has
geographical as well as scientific connotations, and positivistic politics
is incarnated in imperialism. Romanticism is not imperialistic, except
where the will to power enters into it, for imperialism is sustained
only by a continual and purely spatial production of goods supported
by exploitation, a continually increasing one, of raw-material markets.
Postromantic political thinking, then, develops in opposition to this
the conception of class. If the nation is the unit of romanticism, it is
because it holds together the exotic and esoteric tendencies, whose
cohesion is essential to it, as no other unit will; there is room both for
the sense connections of the metropolis and the facility of intercourse
of language which binds them together. The class represents the carrying through of the divorced esoteric element, just as the empire carries
through the nation divorced from language-entity. There are two pro-
tagonists of the conception of society as divided, not into nations, but
into classes—Nietzsche and Marx. But Marx cannot be called a postromantic, because his whole thesis rests on an inversion of Hegel's
romantic approach to history, and is rather far gone into positivism.
As a result, there is a class struggle, but no class distinction: the difference in class is one of economic or spatial position; if the proletariat
win out, it is a purely quantitative victory of numbers. This theory is
almost postpositivistic, being an inference drawn from the positivistic
politics of laissez-faire and capitalism. Nietzsche's master class, on the
contrary, are qualitatively superior to the slaves, and it is their ideal
and blood-supremacy which results in the extermination of the latter.
The metropolitan upheaval brought into existence the bourgeois class
as we now understand the term; systematic romanticism was a bourgeois product. Postromanticism, an abstraction from the bourgeoisie,
has nothing to do with millionaires or proletarians in themselves; they
are not opposed to the bourgeoisie in the restricted sense of the middle class, but to the bourgeoisie in the larger sense of the whole of society, differentiated only by the accidental position of wealth. *Épater le
bourgeois*, however, is not political action; the cranks by their very
nature are not an organized class. So while many, like Baudelaire,
deliberately cultivate a taste for homosexuality or something else
objectionable enough to exasperate society, this political action is
incorporated mainly in anarchism, which, like every other subversive

approach, centres in France and descends from Proudhon to Sorel and syndicalism.

The rehabilitation of romanticism brings in a new idea. We have seen that in thought the romantic broadening of the idea was over-turned by the positivist idea of evolution, with its continually increas-ing differentiation and wider spatial activity. Romanticism came back to shatter the linear evolution by showing that the idea had to be there as a creative factor. A precisely analogous change takes place in poli-tics. The concept of nationality as synonymous with cultural affinity was replaced by the expanding state. The return of romanticism brings with it the fact that the essence of imperialism is still the nuclear nation. Hence, it could only arise after imperialisms had clashed. Socialism, or state control of industry, is a general statement of which imperialism, shorn of its laissez-faire connotations, is a particular application. Neoromanticism, therefore, following the war, is actual-ized politically in National Socialism. In Italy Mazzini's controversy with Marx[92] shows the connection of romanticism with Fascism easily enough; and Mussolini's own thinking, we learn from his biographers, was largely dominated by two postromantics, Nietzsche and Sorel.[93] Hitlerism is practically the working through of Nietzsche, even to its anti-Semitism. It seems a pity that brave and generous spirits such as Byron, Mazzini, Heine, and Fichte should find a remorselessly logical outcome in the development of a Philistine Italy and in the vicious cul-tural suicide of Germany. But "classicism is health; romanticism is dis-ease," and what we have called rather clumsily the rehabilitation of romanticism in a synthesis of final exhaustion can only be the return of that disease in a chronic form.

3

Robert Browning: An Abstract Study

Frye wrote this paper during his fourth year at Victoria College (1932–33) for Professor Pelham Edgar. Frye's transcript does not identify the particular English course in which he was enrolled, but it was almost certainly English 4f, "English Poetry of the Nineteenth Century." Some of what Frye says about both Browning and romanticism is identical with material in his paper on romanticism (no. 2): it is not clear which paper was written first. Edgar's marginal comments are recorded in the notes. Edgar occasionally put an "X" in the margin, representing perhaps points he wanted to discuss with Frye. The texts of NF's quotations from Browning, including the punctuation, have been reconciled with those in Browning's The Poems, *ed. John Pettigrew, 2 vols. (Harmondsworth: Penguin, 1981), and the line numbers are to the poems in that edition. The typescript is in the NFF, 1991, box 37, file 9.*

The effect of the romantic revival on English literature was so powerful and widespread that no subsequent poet can be considered without some reference to it, so that all the poetry of the last century or so is to that extent postromantic.[1] It is especially in dealing with the great names of the Victorian era that we cannot be too explicit in insisting that the social change, the most important since the great migrations, of which romanticism was merely one symbol, signified something more than merely the advent of the nineteenth century. The French Revolution was catastrophic evidence of a universal process which resulted in the final uprooting of the great city, the metropolis as distinct from the culture-town like Florence or Nuremberg, from its surroundings, the countryside. The outcome of this process is, of course, the establishment of a purely civic outlook in thought, which means, in philosophy, that intellect can no longer be pressed into the service of being,[2] and, in the arts, that the great creative period of Western culture was over and the critical one had commenced. Along with the final exploitation of the major scale in music by Mozart, with the final overthrow of the Rembrandt "brown sauce" tradition in painting, comes the final expression of systematic philosophy in Kant, and the great name in the thought of the romantic era which followed him, Schopenhauer, bases his whole thesis on the concept of an intellect divorced from being or willing and grimly regarding it.[3] Kant himself had shown that an intellectual proof of God's existence was impossible and that conviction of it resided in the blood, not the brain. The nineteenth century, therefore, meant something entirely different by philosophy, religion, and creativeness in art than any previous age had meant.

We have to grasp this idea in its implications before we can see any underlying unity in Victorian culture similar to that of the precedent era of development. The preromantic period contains a number of lines of thought held together in coherence by a unifying religious spirit, bound by ontological lashings. Hence, a poet in such a time can, if he be great enough, feel that unity in the life he deals with, and can by attuning himself to the beat of his language attain to an instinct for giving it expression. But the view of the romantic is indirect and pictorial; he is a subjective idealist, not an objective one, and the divorce of the creative faculty from the creative spirit gives us that "art for art's sake" conception which makes of the artist a watching critic, whose whole *raison d'être*, and, consequently, whose whole religion, consists in viewing the world from his standpoint, an attitude which extends itself to every department of life. In a systematic pursuit unity is, thus, given by consensus; it is not something which exists *ab initio*. The majority vote, which arose with romanticism and democracy, which replaced patronage by popularity and made the growth of science possible, was a sign that every aspect of thought was separating itself out from the rest, linked and not bound to them, that, consequently, every point of view was peculiar, and that the broad divisions of culture, arts included, were being shifted over to specific grounds of empiric positivism. Romantic pessimism, by finding solace in physical beauty, takes this attitude. Would you find out what God is? asks Wordsworth in effect. Then look around you. Do you wish to find truth? asks Keats. You can find it in beauty:

—that is all

Ye know on earth, and all ye need to know,

[*Ode on a Grecian Urn*, lines 49–50]

which is merely an application of Kant's doctrine. Blake, holding fast to the thought of an earlier age, fought a dogged, hopeless battle against the "vegetable kingdom"[4] and was ignored; the other romantics all outdid one another in their "treatment of nature." Their whole view of poetry was as a matter of course pictorial—the view of the static and abstracted artist. Even the inner unity given by mystic introspection went by the boards—Shelley championed atheism, and all the attempts of the past to bring together the compulsions of logic, morals, and aesthetics fell to pieces. The fact that the age did not wish to recognize a necessary alliance of art with morals, for instance, was made manifest by popularity of the cheap cynicism of Byron,[5] and the similar vogue of Scott reflected an impulse to widen the scope of history and see the past as pictorially as the present. With the great romantic poets even the technique was picturesque; the gorgeous sound patterns, Coleridge's alliteration theories, Keats's vowel arrangement, the caught-up, arrested rhythms, the revival of picture-forms like the sonnet and the Spenserian stanza, all testify to the idea of isolating for an instant and making visible the thrusting force and pulse of poetry. Exactly the same tendencies are shown in thought. Developments in German idealism, which worked out the romantic position systematically, were brought into England through the media of Coleridge and Carlyle, but the true inwardness of the English spirit is best shown in utilitarianism. Bentham, in consigning all previous philosophy to the ashcan,[6] on the ground that it was not useful, simply means by doing so: Would you find the field of philosophy? Then look around you. Utilitarianism, as Bentham conceived it, is an empiric, not a systematic, ordering. It collapses at the first touch of the a priori any attempt to rationalize it, such as that of Mill, merely succeeding only[7] in hedonizing and, thus, entirely destroying it. It faced, not inward to spiritual unity, but outward to reform. Would you find inward peace of soul and intellectual security? bellowed Carlyle. Then Work! Do Something! Newman expressed the Catholic contribution in similar terms, stressing the liberal and wide-ranging education.[8] The greatest novelists, notably Dickens, took the same position, writing novels illustrative of a kind of naive delight in watching the endlessly varied forms taken by humanity.

Thackeray alone, with his eighteenth-century complex, tried a more symbolic view,[9] and brilliant sketching interspersed with irritating bursts of sermonizing are the result. The affinity of all this with the political, social, and economic make-up of the time is too obvious for comment.

When we take two statements, one on each side of the cleavage, which seem to express similar attitudes, we find that, properly examined in their contexts, there is this same difference between them. The similarity of Browning's "God's in His Heaven—All's right with the world!" to Pope's "Whatever is, is right"[10] has usually been put down to a smug optimism in both resolutely denying the importance or even existence of evil, pain, or sorrow. This attempt to make Pope and Browning a couple of addle-pated fools is not one that will commend itself to any qualified critic, the less so if it can be shown that the two epigrams do not even mean the same thing. Now when a great eighteenth-century intellect said anything like "Whatever is, is right," he expressed that philosophical optimism which is the germ of Leibnitz, which dances and lilts all through Mozart, which lies at the immense still depths of the second part of *Faust*, and which even in Blake, with the grim two-handed engine of the guillotine already at the door, hangs like a curtain-drop behind the petty[11] tyranny of Urizen. This was the last culminating effort of Western thought to overcome the blind life-force, to implicate the unique fact in the universal truth, to postulate a moral goodness as the controlling factor in the universe. Evil is not unreal, it is incidental, even necessary, to a higher good, and all things flow, in an inexorable rightness, from the goodness of God. It is hardly too much to say that "Whatever is, is right" is the kernel of all Western metaphysics, and certainly it is at any rate a positive, intelligible metaphysical proposition. Now let us look at Browning. "God's in His Heaven—All's right with the world." And how does Pippa lead up to this conclusion? By watching the day in the springtime, the lark, the snail on the thorn. Here is again the great romantic doctrine—truth is beauty, that is, truth can be tested and made manifest by beauty. Browning is here denying and negating the whole of metaphysics.

It will be objected, of course, that we have no right to wrench this couplet from its powerful dramatic context and hold it up as unadulterated Robert Browning. But it is so frequently the focal point of attacks on the poet that it is obviously regarded as such, and it may be as well for us to digress for a moment and show that the couplet is the clearest expression of an assumption underlying the whole of Browning's poetry. That Browning meant precisely what he said here I think indubitable, not only from its repetition in so many other places, but from the context itself. Browning showed himself all through his life as one of the greatest lovers who ever lived and still remains unexcelled as a portrayer of love from the standpoint that love is a moral good and that the passions which pretend to override morality, therefore, end by trampling real love itself under foot. The opposed type of lover, who regards his love as something transcendent, sweeping aside everything in its path, is perhaps best represented in Antony and Cleopatra. Browning and Antony both have a tremendous reservoir of strength the other does not suspect, and so each looks on his opponent as fundamentally weak. Antony might despise Browning as a fearful prig, afraid to take the consequences of his love; Browning might point to the collapse of Antony's empire as a sign of Antony's weakness and lack of self-control. In any case, Ottima is Browning's Cleopatra, a woman whose whole energy is centred in a passionate infatuation. Sebald, however, is not Antony, but a stolid German with a conscience. He cannot persuade himself that his action is right, and Pippa's song strikes a responsive chord of feeling in him. He tests truth by beauty as he knows it, and under that test Ottima shrivels into a hag. Now this is logical enough, but it is Browning's treatment of Ottima that reveals his attitude. When she hears Sebald turn on her, she breaks out into passionate reproaches. She is, in truth, a creature of passion, that is, as Browning sees it, fundamentally weak. She cannot bear to be despised: —"Speak to me, —not of me!"—and finally breaks down wailing helplessly, "You hate me then? You hate me then?" [*Pippa Passes*, pt. 1, lines 245, 257]. When Sebald goes, in the great sorrow and anguish of her soul she rises to her supreme crisis, which proves to be one of self-sacrifice: "Not me—to him, O God, be merciful!" [*Pippa Passes*, pt. 1, line 282]. Now it is at least probable that here Browning has underestimated her strength. Women of Ottima's type care nothing for masculine courage in the conventional sense; they judge their lover in terms of how far he measures up to the love they bear him, and it is not easy to regard the Ottima-Cleopatra she-panther as otherwise than a creature of the most boundless egoism. When such a woman has to meet a crisis, she assembles together what is strongest in her—the fervour of her love transmuted to hate. One can imagine Cleopatra rising in a cold white fury to tell a quivering Antony what she thought of a poltroon who developed a conscience and deserted her like a prostitute because he had suddenly discovered the existence of God. Ottima might be capable of self-destruction, like Cleopatra ("I always meant to kill myself" [*Pippa Passes*, pt. 1, line 273]); hardly of self-abnegation. It is the awful finality of Pippa's innocent song, first paralysing, then purging and transfiguring, the lovers, which makes it apparent that Browning sees a self-evident and powerful truth in it, striking Ottima and Sebald with all the force of its obvious rightness, like oxygen on a man gasping under chloroform. The ironic expression of the same idea gives us *Porphyria's Lover*, and the searing contempt of the last line of this poem is enough in itself to define Browning's position.[12]

Voltaire, the great opponent of Leibnitz, who did so much to destroy the eighteenth century, once said: "If God did not exist it would be necessary to invent Him."[13] This is the cynical formulation of an idea which lies back of[14] the vital impulses of the nineteenth. God's in his heaven— that is not a reasoned conviction but an instinctive one rising from the necessity for a working hypothesis. Thought and action alike need a centre of gravity, and, that once established, the evils of the world do not appear as unreal, but neither do they appear inevitable or irremediable. All's right with the world—it is on a sound basis fundamentally, and, if we work hard, we may arrive at a solution. In this is seen the cause of that smugness for which the Victorians have been so unsparingly attacked, arising in their[15] turning around from intellectual doubts and forward to action—they prided themselves on being practical men, not dreamers. We are in perspective with regard to them; we have gone through the scepticism to which a concentration on the empiric invariably leads; we can see that positivism of this type bears the seeds of the pragmatism, toward which, as the final negation of the absolute, the thought of the whole time tended. Above all, we know where the economic and political side of this outlook has landed us. But we should not be blinded by the immaturity of the Victorians as compared to us. The immense strength and self-discipline of the age affords ample evidence that their gospel of action is worthy of a respectful approach.

In Browning we find a refined statement of their position.[16] Browning is a poet of action and his view is fundamentally subjective, the world around and about him being his theme. Love, with Browning, is again the democratic consensus of romanticism mentioned above; love is focused on humanity with him, as with all the Victorians and their contemporary Comte. That is why he thought sexual love should culminate in marriage and why he was so opposed to any aspect of human passion which travestied or negatived this deep underlying love of mankind. Anyone with this feeling in him might override the law, which addresses itself to men negatively—an idea implied in *The Statue and the Bust*, but love itself cannot be unmoral; it is itself the highest form of morality. This consensus, which Whitman in one place sees as underlying all the philosophies and teachings of history, Christ, Buddha, and Socrates included, makes Browning an apologist of "common sense," in every aspect of its meaning, who is bitterly opposed to the two static and quasi-misanthropic theories of life, the hedonistic and the mystical. We have said above that Mill's neo-Epicureanism destroys the spirit of the utilitarians. In the same way the Grammarian would have forfeited his claim to true greatness had he adopted the more rationalized procedure, while the tired and disillusioned Bishop of St. Praxed's, who quotes from the Book of Ecclesiastes and might well have written it, shows in his pathetic, broken death-song the utter barrenness and emptiness of his soul. To the epicure, as distinct from the Epicurean, Browning extended nothing but contempt, Rabbi Ben Ezra refusing to regard him as anything else but a fool. Again, the mystical introspectionist who shuts his eyes to his social existence Browning was inclined to regard with suspicion. He had no inherent sympathy with mysticism, paying very occasionally the perfunctory respect which poets tender it, but by no means ready to embrace its attitude. The purest mystic in Browning's portrait gallery is Johannes Agricola, who gibbers in a madhouse.[17] A mystic proper, as Plotinus saw, really works with a double mechanism; he has a *soul* which unifies the world into an idealistic pattern for himself, but he must also have a *spirit* which integrates that pattern into the absolute and universal.[18] Consequently, he can exist only in an age in which the intellect is a mere creature of being, the important thing being the vital blood-feeling rather than the abstract vision. When these two factors fall apart, as they did with the romantic revival, mysticism disappears, along with the spirit, leaving the soul with its subjective idealism. The albatross is brought in by the Ancient Mariner, not altogether without a protesting squawk, to illustrate to the Wedding Guest that the post-romantic consensus extends itself to every sentient being,[19] and that is about as near as any romantic gets to mysticism. Browning, with his contemporaries, conceived of the fact, the small thing, as something in itself.[20] Symbolism vanished, and the men of his time, from the Gradgrinds to Carlyle, from the utilitarians to Shelley, possessed a voracious appetite for facts. Obviously the logical result of romantic egoism, or

subjectivity, is antinomianism, and so the whole position rests, unconsciously as a rule, on an atheistic basis. Thus, does Browning, again
unconsciously, push God out of his world. The symbolism of a small
thing does not exist in it,[21] but in its proximity to the God who is behind
it. Sludge says, in an inspired moment:

> We find great things are made of little things,
> And little things go lessening till at last
> Comes God behind them. Talk of mountains now?
> We talk of mould that heaps the mountain, mites
> That throng the mould, and God that makes the mites,
> The Name comes close behind a stomach-cyst,
> The simplest of creations, just a sac
> That's mouth, heart, legs and belly at once, yet lives
> And feels, and could do neither, we conclude,
> If simplified still further one degree:
> The small becomes the dreadful and immense!
>
> [*Mr. Sludge, "The Medium,"* lines 1112–22]

God is always just one step away. Again, if it be asked why we should
insist on a working, active life, the answer is that God will find a use for
it somehow. The reward, if it comes at all, will come after death, and
some passages imply the idea of a continuous series of lives with the
reward still in the middle distance. Life is a limit, and living consists in
working within limitations. God, the infinite, is outside. The blinding
light of heaven is too much for our view on earth[22]—Lazarus, having
glimpsed it, is thereby permanently dead and cannot be brought to life
again [John 11:1–46]—that, I think, is the meaning of the *Epistle*.[23] With
St. John the Evangelist death and the "universal prick of light" are synonymous.[24] Victorian poetry is highly valetudinarian in spirit—a glance
over the titles of Mrs. Hemans's poems[25] would give Peter Pan himself
some uncomfortable moments—but Browning is diametrically opposed
to the point of view presented in most of it. *Death* is to Browning too
negative a word to have any meaning, and he can see nothing beyond
death but more life. Here he is, of course, not opposing the Victorian
spirit, but giving it clear expression. Browning, therefore, is an optimist
in believing that imperfection of life implies perfection beyond it. The
view is the same as that of Kent, which, being founded on an emotion,
faces forward to his immediate successors [*King Lear*, 5.3.319b–22]. The

end of the poem called *Time's Revenges* gives it the negative statement: "There may be heaven; there must be hell" [line 65].

We must pass over the rest of this question, as the thesis that Browning is a poet of Victorianism is too trite to need further elaboration. It is equally easy, but much more significant, to take another step and say that he is *the* poet of Victorianism, a title often accorded to Tennyson, but not to anyone else. With the latter this holds good for external qualities rather than for the true inwardness of his poetry. Tennyson has probably not been given sufficient credit for his intellectual honesty; in any case he remained, if not actually a sceptic, certainly very dubious about the solidity of the Victorian position. As a result, his work has not the completeness of Browning; it changes and alters, as is natural with a poet who kept himself so keenly alive to all the movements of his time. His mind was not so large or comprehensive as Browning's, perhaps, but what he had he held with clarity and restraint. The essence of Tennyson is his taste, and as far as viewing life is concerned, taste is a strictly personal, hence, a negative, quality. Tennyson, in short, is the abstract of Victorianism: Browning is the Victorian abstract of English literature. Now in every age there is one supreme[26] poet who, in remaining strictly a product of his era, expresses the whole inwardness and force of it, he having gathered it up into a serene and catholic soul. His greatness as a poet, thus, depends on the greatness of his age. Such were Chaucer to the Middle Ages, Shakespeare to the Elizabethans, Dryden to the Restoration, Pope to the Age of Anne, Crabbe to the Georgians, and Browning to the Victorians. Similarly there is an opponent figure each time, a voice crying, lonely and desperate, more mature and vigorous, perhaps, but more bitter and partial. Thus, we have the protestant Langland (I use the word in a general sense) opposed to Chaucer. Even against Shakespeare, writing in the supreme hour of England's creative triumph, a powerful force lay undercurrent which was to find expression in Milton. Bunyan stands opposite Dryden, Swift opposite Pope, Blake opposite Crabbe. And as against Browning I think we could, knowing both the poet and his time, construct even out of pure theory a figure which would very closely resemble that of Thomas Carlyle.

Because the cleavage of romanticism draws a hard and fast line separating Browning from his predecessors and making him a figure homologous but not analogous to them, a critic among creators, so Carlyle, the protestant figure of the nineteenth century, is alone in looking back rather than forward. Hence, there is curious affinity between Carlyle and Browning. The poet was almost the only contemporary man of letters the philosopher had a good word for,[27] and Carlyle was one of the two cranks (we shall come to the other later) whom Browning cultivated that[28] the rest of the world had given up in despair.[29] Now Carlyle is anything but a systematic philosopher; he is, primarily, a stylist. That is, his contribution to the thought of his time derives its value from the manner in which it is expressed. That is why I class him as a poet. He detested his own time and advocated a return to that religious grasp,[30] binding all subordinate branches of knowledge together by its unity and comprehension of feeling, which the romantic revival and the greater change it signified had irrecoverably lost to humanity. And if we ask how his style, or manner, expresses this difference from his age, we shall find two curious facts. First, his view of history, that is, of life, is far more vivid than most other men's, and his *French Revolution* remains unique among histories because it retains so powerful a grip on the *drama* of the situation. Secondly, his hero thesis is the only one of his time which shows a recurrent beat, or rhythm, in life; years of inertia punctuated by the energy of a hero, the spirit of a time accented by the great man. "All things are song," says *Sartor Resartus*, and this is truly a *musical* picture of history.[31]

Carlyle, then, stands out from his time as one who wished it to recapture the creative spirit of the preromantic age by showing that that spirit was associated explicitly with a religious sense, implicitly with music and the drama. Now even a casual survey soon shows that the Victorians had no sympathy with either music or the drama, and that Browning is the exception proving the rule. The reason is obvious. The drama is the province of the creator; it is so purely objective an art that it takes a creative personality to abstract a symbolic order and unity from life, as a geometrical pattern is abstracted from space, and it takes something very like a mystic to give a picture in which each part falls into its right, its foreordained, its inevitable place. Tragedy of the Shakespearean sort, thus, belongs to preromanticism; we have instead the externalized tragedy of Hardy and the problematic tragedy of Ibsen, both of which are theoretical. The novel, on the other hand, is the province of the critic, for it stresses variety, held together by the projected personality of the novelist. Life here remains as it is, and the author moves through it watching. Similarly music is so objective and abstract an art that it is an intensely personalized one, and correspondingly the essay belongs to criticism.[32] Thus, the Elizabethans, in an

intensely creative age, left the essay in the Baconian stage of extended
aphorism and the novel in a similarly primitive condition, reaching
their heights in music and the drama, while the Victorians developed
the novel and essay to the complete exclusion of the creative arts, which
Browning alone held out for. This is why he has been called an Elizabethan figure among the men of his time. The Victorian theatre was in a
disgraceful condition, dominated by proletarian mawkishness in its
worst form; it was the heyday of cheap melodrama and of diaphragm-
thumping Hamlets. Those who were interested in the drama as a living
art had to subsist as best they could on mechanical toys imported from
France. Robert Browning is the only literate[33] playwright we possess
between Sheridan and the school which arose with Shaw, Jones, and
Wilde. The Victorians, again, were almost uncannily tone-deaf. At least
one of the choicest spirits of the century—Charles Lamb—had a positive distaste for music,[34] a dislike we find repeated later in two of the
most popular foreign authors—Dumas *père*, who is said to have
"detested even bad music," and Mark Twain, who hated it like a Philistine and an ignoramus.[35] None of the novelists ever bring music in
except Thackeray, who had an infallible instinct for liking the wrong
things. You will find[36] gypsies in Borrow, but no gypsy music. Even the
poets, always excepting Browning, seem to think that to have music in
one's soul and to be moved with a concord of sweet sounds are the
same thing, and nowhere, so far as I know, even in Tennyson or Coleridge, does music really become vital and alive. The great culture-men,
from Ruskin and Arnold to Pater and Morris, never dream of placing
music on a level with art, literature, or architecture, much less above
them, where it belongs. What is even more important, the musical idols
of the Victorians were Handel and Mendelssohn. Now Handel stands
like a rock in a stream which has cut through the great contrapuntal
gorge ending in Bach and is flowing past the meadows of the
Augustans. Mendelssohn, too, is a point of repose in the development
from classic to romantic. They are the only definitely static composers
in music, and both have a peculiar quality of conservatism, even dogmatism, in them, which make them the only two figures which have
really exerted a retarding and stultifying influence upon music.[37] To
prefer Handel to Bach, or Mendelssohn to Mozart, then, means something more than merely preferring an inferior man. It works out, in the
long run, to extolling the antimusical over music.[38]

"He has plenty of music in him," said Tennyson of Browning, "but he can't get it out."[39] This remark is, as we have shown, profoundly true in one sense, but is liable to a gross misunderstanding, which, as a matter of fact, Tennyson probably fell into in making it. The connection between poetry and music has usually been approached from a literary angle, which makes for mere gush as far as the music is concerned. It is, of course, not very difficult for an intelligent person to get over the crude idea that a vowel is musical and a consonant not, nor will he long maintain that Italian is musical because it is full of vowels, or German harsh because it is full of consonants, in the face of the fact that the Germans have produced greater word-artists than the Italians, and more of them, to say nothing of musicians.[40] What is more difficult to establish is that each art owes its individuality to its own inner organic construction; what particular sense it addresses itself to is incidental: the psychological and not the physical appeal defines it. Keats is said to be musical because of his mastery of sound, but his lines are sound patterns, and a pattern belongs to the arts of design. Pope has been called musical because he is smooth, but "smooth" is a metaphor derived from a tangible art, like sculpture. Neither quality has any reference to music; what is evidence of music in poetry is evidence of musical thought and organization. This is what we find in Browning, who thought musically as no other poet had done before him.

Music contains two clashing elements, the rhythmic dance and the antirhythmic song. Our conception of it is so strongly rhythmic that composers do not find it difficult to bind the most lyrical idea into a metric unit, and there is always the discordant movement of the harmony to prevent any falling apart into chaos. The conflict is present even here, however, as we can see by the immense length of a Schubert symphony or the insistently beating figure recurrent under a Bach aria. But a poet, with only a single melodic movement to go on, is faced, if he naturally thinks rhythmically, with a prodigious difficulty. With the Elizabethans the rhythmic problem was just being enunciated in music itself by Byrd,[41] and did not enter much into the poetry, which was mainly singing. This is the case even in Shakespeare. *Hamlet* marks the turn from the dramatic proper to the musical in his work. *Julius Caesar* is a drama; *Coriolanus* (the supreme example from this point of view) a secular oratorio. Plot and underplot are antithetical and contrasting in the histories; in *King Lear* they are contrapuntal. *Romeo and Juliet* moves to a dramatic climax; *Macbeth* sweeps to a point of repose. But the whole musical idea is vocal, as is natural in a drama, and the movement is even and flowing, not pounding or driving. In this, Shakespeare is a true contemporary of Palestrina. In Donne, the first "musician" of the Browning type, the rhythmic drive is pushed down and sublimated, just as the dancing man of the world was forced into the singing preacher. Hence, the fierce strugglings and conflicts in his poetry, the conceit spun out and elaborated through variation after variation, the song suddenly caught up short and pushed into a conclusion, passages of clanging cacophony suddenly punctured with a long slow line of crushing beauty. With Milton, the connection with the organ is too obvious to dwell upon, but the organ is a vocalized instrument and Milton remains what the organ is—the supreme master of dynamics, with a statically contrapuntal conception of music:

> Untwisting all the chains that tie
> The hidden soul of harmony. [*L'Allegro*, lines 143–4]

With the Restoration the Puritan iron finally entered the English soul, and a century of criticism followed which preferred the elephantine clump of a *Davideis* or a *Cato* to the whirling dissonances of Donne. The next "musician" is Burns, in whom the rhythmic impulse which produced *Tam O'Shanter* and the *Jolly Beggars* was brought into the sharpest possible conflict with the songs. Some day a sympathetic critic may arise who will show us that the contention of these forces had at least as much as any whore to do with the poet's tragic destruction, but, as Burns's commentators are, of course, mainly Scotch Calvinists, the contingency seems remote.[42]

Browning's whole concept of music is Handelian, he having been trained in that tradition and that of the vigorous and sprightly contemporaries of Handel, Scarlatti, for instance, or, more evidently, Galuppi. Like all frustrated musicians, he was afraid of Bach, and *Hugues of Saxe-Gotha* seems to me a polemic aimed not so much at contrapuntal pedantry as at the great contrapuntal tradition itself.[43] And he does not seem to have the faintest idea where the music of his own time was going. As a result the musical impulse in him is almost purely rhythmic and instrumental. He finds Avison's sturdy little march more appealing because of its rhythmic vitality than all the colour concepts of Wagner or Dvořák.[44] Once we realize that his whole poetry, at least up to *The Ring and the Book*, contains a psychology really indigenous to this kind of music, nearly every feature, in fact nearly every mannerism, of his style can be brought into line with it.

With Browning poetry is not to be heard, still less looked at, in the sense of being lovingly dwelt upon. To read any poem of his in the same way one would read a Keats ode would be nonsense. Except for an occasional short lyric (which is often a recitative, like *My Star*) it is usually possible to affix a definite metronome mark, and if not, we are apt to feel that he has not a clear grip on his subject matter. Hence, his rhythmic originality—there is no question, with him, of elaboration inside a conventional form, and when he uses one he often hurries it into a most indecorous gait.[45] Not only does he send the funeral cortège of the Grammarian scrambling up a steep hillside, but makes the heroic couplets of *Sordello* gallop through the blackness that envelops them at a speed far greater than anything in Dryden or Pope, who are admittedly "smoother." *Abt Vogler* and *Ixion* are almost alone as examples of blank Alexandrines that really move. He never shrinks from writing vast quantities of doggerel—with a great poet the sign of vigour and impatience, and many of his mannerisms, such as the omission of the third person singular pronoun in *Caliban upon Setebos*, and his awe-inspiring contractions:

> Monstr'-inform'-ingens-horrend-ous
> Demoniaco-seraphic [*Waring*, lines 54–5]

make for speed. Poem after poem is written for the sheer exuberant love of rhythm—the Ghent to Aix Ride, the *Cavalier Tunes*, *Through the Metidja* all exhibit what Shaw has called "the naïve delight of pure oscillation,"[46] and this delight is probably the inner meaning of the much quarrelled-over *Last Ride Together*.

Here can, I think, be found the key to Browning's peculiar use of rhyme which Oscar Wilde found so inexplicable.[47] Rhyme is the binding and linking rhythmic force which prevents the energy of movement from relapsing into chaos. In Browning's music-poetry it is his bar line. Just as in music an increase of speed is counterbalanced by an increase of accent emphasis, so the rhymes get worse proportionately as the movement tends to run away with itself:

> I could favour you with sundry touches
> Of the paint-smutches with which the Duchess

Heightened the mellowness of her cheek's yellowness
(To get on faster) until at last her
Cheek grew to be one master-plaster
Of mucus and fucus from mere use of ceruse:
In short, she grew from scalp to udder
Just the object to make you shudder.

(*The Flight of the Duchess*, [lines 825–32])

It is not difficult to shudder, but it is easy to see how the increase of rhyme shows how the speaker is holding in his exasperation and forcing himself not to break out. Similarly the upward strain and fatigue of the Grammarian's procession is shown in an alternating series of single and double rhymes. The reverse use is shown to better advantage in one of the slowest and most reflective of Browning's poems, *Love Among the Ruins*. I have spoken above of the uniform figure underlying a Bach aria, and I do not think it too fanciful to compare this method of treatment to that of the poem in question, in which the dreamlike haze of the subject matter is regularly brought up standing, as it were, by the beat of the rhyme scheme.[48] Sometimes, as with the monstrosity called *Pacchiarotto* or *The Glove*, the rhyme is something in itself to listen to,[49] just as we tap our feet to jazz or a light opera when the musical idea bores us—a use found more clearly in Swinburne's work than here. But it should be noted as well how many of the Victorians, such as Hood and Gilbert, support a tendency to get the rhymes over with and out of the language for good and all. Whitman may ignore rhyme, but a poem like the *Bridge of Sighs* reduces it to absurdity.[50]

This pulsing musical quality obviously leads to an outstanding virtue and vice, the virtue concentration, the vice obscurity. The terrific condensation of the whole Renaissance into the dying Bishop of St. Praxed's, the whole of Hellenism into Cleon, are large examples of close packing of thought, and, long-winded as Browning is, he is not so diffuse or prolix as is often imagined, and it is by no means easy to cut him intelligently. In miniature, we often come upon sudden flashes of inspiration in which an epic is compressed into a terse phrase or two. A long and dreary tragedy is implicit in the climax of *My Last Duchess*:

. . . This grew; I gave commands;
Then all smiles stopped together. There she stands
As if alive. [lines 45–7]

A whole Dutch painting is in this:

> An hour they sat in council,
>   At length the Mayor broke silence. (*The Pied Piper of Hamelin*, [lines 35–6])

Obscurity arises in several ways. First, and most evidently, from an overconcentration. A musically thinking poet is hampered by the comparative slowness of the monodic form of poetry, and much of Browning's most inscrutable work bears distinct evidence of his having tried to say four or five things at once. Frequently it is when he is most earnest, even most vociferous, that he is least intelligible. Again, it certainly cannot be denied that his preoccupation with rhyme occasionally goes far to extinguish the reason:

> And after, for pastime,
>   If June be refulgent
> With flowers in completeness,
>   All petals, no prickles,
>   Delicious as trickles
> Of wine poured at mass-time,—
>   And choose One indulgent
>   To redness and sweetness:
> Or if, with experience of man and of spider,
> June use my June-lightning, the strong insect-ridder,
> And stop the fresh film-work,—why, June will consider.
>   (*Another Way of Love*, [lines 23–33])

Obscurity through allusiveness is not so often met with. Browning may be said to have started the tendency toward immense curious erudition continued through Swinburne and Morris to Eliot, Joyce, Pound, the French post-Baudelaire school, and others—a sort of recrudescence of the spirits of Donne and Rabelais, to both of whom Browning was extensively indebted. With Browning allusions are caught up and swept forward so fast that they are often lost in transit, so to speak, if hardly to an extent which would justify a glossary similar to that of *The Waste Land*.[51] Here belongs, too, the violence and flash of his figures, of which examples are well known. Thus, all his obscurity (the amount of it has been greatly exaggerated, and in any case Browning himself is crystalline compared to most of his commentators) results from the welding together of a musical style and a poetic mould. The irritation of Browning at requests of earnest devotees for "explanations" is easily understood. The unit of his thought was not the concept in the abstract—if it were, he would have written prose, and I sincerely hope it is obvious from what has preceded that his literary expression would have to be poetic.[52] Oscar Wilde's clever-clever epigram in this connection[53] will not bear sustained investigation any longer than the rest of Wilde's epigrams, or a soap bubble. In prose the idea, or subject, is microcosmic; it exists in itself and forces everything else into line with it. In poetry it is cosmic, the rhythmic beat of its formulation being its essence. So it obviously was to Browning, and prosaic minds who inquired, just as Philistines always do, with a nervous and excited eagerness, "Yes, but what does it *mean*?" thereby achieving an easy conquest of it, could hardly be regarded as spirits kindred to the poet.

But the motive force in music is not purely rhythmic. Modern music is motivated as well by a progression of discords perpetually moving toward a point of repose, or resolution in a final concord. This is what lies back of[54] much of Browning's cacophony. For legitimate discord does often become cacophonous in poetry, due to the resistant force of words. Not that Browning deliberately chooses sharp piercing words as Milton chooses resounding mellow ones, but he often produces that effect:

> While, look but once from your farthest bound
>   At me so deep in the dust and dark,
> No sooner the old hope goes to ground
>   Than a new one, straight to the self-same mark,
> I shape me—
> Ever
> Removed! (*Life in a Love*, [lines 16–22])

A diction like this naturally conspires to aid rhythm and speed. This discordance (the above is not quoted as an example of ugliness but of sharp, incisive, staccato diction) extends itself to subject matter. If I were asked to name the two poems in English which were most clearly triumphs of rhythmic music, I should probably name the *Jolly Beggars* and the *Heretic's Tragedy*, and it would be difficult to find grimmer or more repellent subjects.[55] Much of the *grotesquerie* in Browning, the occasional touch of vigorous coarseness, which in a less squeamish age would have resembled more closely that of Chaucer, Rabelais, Shakespeare, or Swift, and much of his love for the strange and recondite, which gives him his modulations, can be traced back here,[56] and, once arrived at this position, it will seem the less fantastic to recognize an element of suspended resolution into a full close in his defence of the ultimately indefensible—Bishop Blougram, Sludge, Prince Hohenstiel-Schwangau,[57] and the rest. His fondness for the theme with variations, from his boyish plan of which *Pauline* was (and fortunately remains) a fragment to *The Ring and the Book*, is clearer.[58] *Paracelsus* is developed in a kind of sonata form, and *A Soul's Tragedy* reminds one rather of a sonatina. Chesterton, in his essay on Browning, complains of Pippa being suddenly thrust as a participant into one of the intrigues she should visit as an impersonal, even a disembodied, spirit.[59] The criticism would hold good were it not that the impingement of Pippa upon the final scene constitutes the stretto of a fugue which—but we had better return to more solid ground.

It is a curious fact that while the main exotic influence on Coleridge was German, his poetry is remarkably Italian, what with his prepossession with broad, open vowels, his dexterous lulling of consonants to sleep, as it were, by alliteration, his Latin locutions and inversions. Conversely, while Browning's inspiration is largely Italian, his diction is unmistakably Germanic. Germany and Italy seem to be complementary as far as England is concerned, the reason possibly being that the German genius is musical, the Italian pictorial. German is, as hinted above, a musically rhythmic language, Italian lazy and full of vowels—melodious. Italy's most characteristic contribution to music is melody and song—the antirhythmic characteristics. The melody is the static quality in music, the element which gives it the caught-up, arrested quality of rhythm in painting. Italian poetry is picturesque, evolving the sonnet, the frame of a picture, and the *terza rima*, the web of a pageanted tapestry, which Browning used only twice, in the *Statue and the Bust* and *Jochanan Hakkadosh*.[60] German art, on the other hand, is shown at its best in the hard-bitten and intensely musical etchings of Dürer. Hence, Browning's style is forced into a hard guttural sweeping succession of consonants, just as Burns was forced back into the Scotch dialect, finding eighteenth-century English too ponderous a vehicle. The Germanic influence in English poetry makes for a straightforward, colloquial utterance, German syntax being very similar to ours in its abrupt forcefulness, which with us has to be toned down by the quieter Latin strain. This gives us the bite and grip of concrete nouns and transitive verbs, a rapid staccato speaking style, and the other characteristics of Browning which are too well known to need detailed discussion. The German tendency in writers whose style most reminds us of Browning, such as Carlyle and Meredith, is more evident.

The centre of gravity in the music which formed Browning's background is the harpsichord, and that is to Browning what the organ is to Milton. There is no more shading to be gotten[61] out of him than out of that instrument—there is little beyond the piano of *Andrea del Sarto* and the forte of Caponsacchi. A rhythmic sense is not conducive to a careful choice of words—hence, there are few, if any, gradations of tone in Browning, apart, of course, from the natural gathering together of the dramatic subject matter. Milton knows that a vowel produces sound while a consonant merely modifies it, and can, consequently, get a thunderous crescendo by simply moving a few consonants out of the way:

> Hitherto, lords, what your commands impos'd
> I have perform'd, as reason was, obeying,
> Not without wonder or delight beheld:
> Now of my own accord such other trial
> I mean to show you of my strength, yet greater;
> *ff* As with amaze shall strike all who behold.[62]

But Browning is not an organist, nor has he the resources of orchestration we find in Shakespeare, who gives us everything from the husky insidious breathings of Caliban to the wild screaming wails of the ghost in *Hamlet*. Browning's uniformity of tempo and close unity of thought are eighteenth-century characteristics in music—there are no sudden breaks or contrasts beyond a natural change from loud to soft (e.g., in *The Bishop Orders His Tomb*), no extremes of slowness, andante usually being about the limit both in Browning and the music we refer to, but there is an intense concentration and economy of structure in each. Nor should be overlooked the connection between the vigorous full closes in the music and the last lines of Browning's poems, which usually contain a distinct quality of "resolution," ranging from the lilting pathetic piquancy of "But then, how it was sweet!" in the poem called *Confessions* [line 36] to the magnificent coda of Guido's death-speech.[63]

After *The Ring and the Book* Browning lapses into pure criticism, and the musical impulse largely subsides. The immense translations and narratives owe their vitality to a sort of mechanical propulsion. The force of the colloquial utterance persists, the metric and rhyming technique still holds, but the exuberance is gone, and the last half of his poetry, from this point of view, largely subsists on the momentum supplied from the first half. All through this later part of his work he is feeling his way toward conventionality, toward the oracular pronouncement, toward the subjectivity for which he so admired Shelley, toward a facility in narrative which does not appear in his prime, unless in a subordinate position, because it means that the poet has to draw on some other source of motive energy. There is no doubt a biographical significance in this, with which we are not concerned, but it is certain that while the volumes from *Balaustion's Adventure* to the *Asolando* lyrics contain some of the finest gems of poetry, they are for the average educated man of today mainly uncut gems. This is a great mistake, of course, for many other qualities given by maturity help to atone for the loss of buoyancy, but that peculiar tang about Browning which makes him Browning is not found with the same pungency, and to deal with this part of his work is to deal with more abstract poetry. The more he strives toward the subjective viewpoint, in fact, the less important his personality becomes.

For music is itself intensely personal and creative, as any objective or abstract art, lifted bodily as it were from life, must needs be. It is not for nothing that the professional musician is the most conceited of men, and if Schubert was the "only modest musician on record," it is surely because in him alone, due to lack of systematic training, is there marked evidence of the conflict of instrumental rhythm and song.[64] Therefore, if one thinks musically, one had better write music, because the medium of words is inseparable from a garrulity and didacticism of idea which detracts from the dignity and profundity of the artist. Or, to put it in English, a poet who thinks like a rhythmic musician must talk very fast and must always be saying something. Music and metaphysics go hand in hand, and the two poets of this type in our language, Donne and Browning, are alike full of conceptual aridness. The egoist talks faster and more musically—that is, more rhythmically and energetically— than anyone else. Shaw, the individualist, writes prose which is precipitous compared to that of, say, Pater, the retiring scholar. Swinburne is swifter than Arnold, Anatole France than Sainte-Beuve or Renan, and so on. It is usually assumed that because Browning had a message and a definite body of teaching, he adopted a vigorous and staccato utterance to give it clear expression. Obviously it would be just as easy to say that because he was inherently a stylist of vigorous and staccato tendencies, he adopted a definite philosophical attitude to preach in terms of that style. And, obviously again, it would be much too easy to prove a causal connection either way, and it is apparent that assuming the priority of matter over manner, or vice versa, reflects only an individual preference. Victorian criticism, of course, which made even Shakespeare a super-Polonius, was strongly on the side of sententiousness—hence, the Browning Society.[65] The contemporary attitude would probably be that a man who is a prophet or preacher very seldom writes anything, let alone cryptograms like *Sordello* or *Numpholeptos* for the exercising of an esoteric brain.[66] If the most valuable thing in Browning were his "teachings" or, worse still, "message," he would disappear from literature as completely as Savonarola has disappeared from theology.

Music is a creative art, which if the creation be excluded becomes the essay, and Browning did indubitably, in his style, confound the creativeness of a musical sense with its counterpart, treating music, in short, like an essayist. Similarly, if creation be extracted from the drama and criticism substituted, we have the novel, and it is even more obvious how he treated the drama like a novelist. Chesterton, with a flash of insight rare in a writer on Browning, has remarked that if Browning's plays were not failures, at any rate they should have been, as he seems to have been born to dramatic failure.[67] Music and the[68] drama are ensemble performances (even if it is only an ensemble of ten fingers) for audiences; they belong to organic growth. The novel and the essay (note the necessity for the definite article!) are solo performances for an audience considered as of separate units; they are written by critics for critics. Browning's music is not the music of the bard, to be heard and applauded; it must be studied and carefully thought out, and Browning's plays are not for the stage, but for the study.

A curious likeness has been shown to exist between Browning and Brahms, and certainly Brahms remains supreme as the critical composer of the time; in him as in no one else is the music made essay. Wagner, the postromantic subjectivist, achieved a tremendous reputation by his attempt to show that music and the drama are, after all, the highest forms of art, and the greatest artist is he who synthesizes them. But he succeeded only in mixing them, and Brahms remains the leading interpreter of his time. With Brahms stands Browning as the dramatist made novelist, and *The Ring and the Book* is from this point of view his most significant work.

In Browning the dramatic emphasis is on variety. Every character he
created is a thing in himself considered without essential relation to
anyone else. This is why the natural form of dramatic expression for
Browning is the monologue. *The Ring and the Book* has been spoken of
above as a colossal theme with variations. Obviously it is a drama in its
essence; it has nothing to do with epics, and its having a theme foreshadows the difference between the postromantic and preromantic
drama. The former is a diatribe balanced by the differing attitudes of the
characters; in the latter the balance exists between the characters themselves. The true historical significance of the work now becomes a little
clearer. It really sums up Browning's career and everything he signifies;
what came after was pure repetition; one reason, no doubt, for the slackening of vitality. A Shakespearean drama, or the *Canterbury Tales*,[69] is
shaped like this: ⬭, the dots representing characters; *The Ring and the
Book*, or a Shaw play, is shaped thus: ✳, the circle in the centre being
the theme, which, of course, exists only in relation to its author. A little
imagination soon shows that the circle is the symbol of objectivity, the
radiating figure subjectivity. *The Ring and the Book* stands at the head of
modern drama, and the evolutionary problem belongs to Darwin, How
did these characters arrive at their present attitudes? not to Leibnitz,
whose type of approach would be, How do these characters develop
through time as organic units? Hence, the logical complete form of one
is the sphere, held together dynamically, and of the other the ring, held
statically. This is, therefore, the source of Browning's symbolization. His
"Ring" is Rome-work, modern, made to match "Etrurian circlets" [*The
Ring and the Book*, 1:3].

Robert Browning was thoroughly a man of his time, and he never
thought of the poet as anything else than that critical subjective
observer, which he certainly was in that time. The essay on Shelley,
Browning's only important prose work, states quite definitely that this
is the bard's function.[70] One of his chief admirations was for Landor,
who, as no one else, made subjectivity dogmatic.[71] The artist who sees
life whole, in the catch phrase, the great dramatist, is, philosophically,
a mystic turned inside out. When the nineteenth century came, the
unity in life necessary for this attitude disappeared, and its various
aspects fell apart into their several constituents. Hence, when the poets
turned to life, they were thrown on their own resources, so to speak,
and could give only a personal impression of the world. Here is the
cause of the romantic escape from life. Wordsworth, for instance,

never attained that instinct of comprehension which the great dramatists Chaucer and Shakespeare possess. He tells what he sees and what
he thinks, but he does not show us the pulse of the world beating; he
does not even feel the world of nature as an entity. Whitman, again, a
pioneer in his own tradition in which aggressiveness, not to say vulgarity, is implicit, accepts his position gladly. In this he is considerably
further away than his English contemporaries from the preromantic
attitude. He may say that a mouse is miracle enough to stagger sextil-
lions of infidels [*Song of Myself*, st. 31, line 669], but take this earth-
quake and fire and set it beside the still small voice in the *Auguries of
Innocence*, and it becomes evident that, while Blake is not necessarily a
"greater" poet than Whitman, he arrives much more easily at this position. Even lesser men like Cowper and Gray, puny figures certainly
compared to the American, can show by the delicate shading of a line
or two a readier sense of coherence. Tennyson, gazing at the flower in
the crannied wall and realizing that if he could see the symbolism
implicit in it he could have that sense, has too much self-respect to try
to persuade himself that he can.[72] Now I am not claiming that every
minor poet up to the romantic revival had something that no major
poet beyond it possessed, but I do say that, taking the greatest names
from each side, the earlier have an objective (or projective) sense of idealism which in the later is subjectified. This does not imply that there
need be any deterioration in quality as between Blake, the mystic, say,
and Whitman, the "answerer."[73] But a poet like Browning, who by his
dramatic-musical nature was impelled to the same universal portrai-
ture as Shakespeare, will find himself at a disadvantage if he is a contemporary of Tennyson.

This, then, is the source of the conflict in Browning's soul. He did not
reach the heights, first of Chaucer or Shakespeare, because his whole
view and comprehension of poetry was focused on the subjectivists, like
Shelley and Keats. Nor, secondly, did he reach the heights of the latter
two, because his whole poetic instinct was that of the earlier. The
humour of the man who gave us Falstaff does not reappear in English
poetry until the time of the man who gave us Dominus Hyacinthus.[74]
No other poet since Shakespeare had so comprehensive a grasp of life;
no other poet since Milton had such immense powers of technique and
intellectual construction. He had it "in him" to rank with the greatest,
but the necessity for expressing and giving voice to his own age baffled
him. Hamlet exists; he is not a mask over Shakespeare, but strip the dis-

guise from any portrait in Browning and the poet is there, the emperor descending into the arena.

It is probable that critical opinion of Browning will steadily rise. An age which does not need to react against Victorianism because they are not so unfortunate as to have been caught in its backwash is due to come up eventually. Self-conscious criticism, from which Browning has always suffered, must sometime disappear, when he will be subjected to a rigorous and dispassionate test, which there is no doubt of his ability to endure. The further time moves away from the Victorians, the greener and fresher they will appear, and new values and new pleasures are sure continually to develop. At the end, when English becomes a long-dead language, it is not difficult to imagine a professor in the remote future, who does not altogether understand the true genius of our tongue, saying: "This man was the greatest of all, for the qualities of the other great ones are combined and blended in him."

Emmanuel College Essays

4

The Concept of Sacrifice

This essay was written for Professor Richard Davidson's Old Testament course at Emmanuel College. At the end of the essay Frye wrote, "for bibliography see next essay," the next essay being "The Fertility Cults." In a letter to Helen Kemp, dated 1 January 1935, Frye reported, "I am doing some work in Old Testament for Davidson that should knock his eye out—connecting it with Frazer's Golden Bough." In addition to these two essays Frye may also be referring to "The Jewish Background of the New Testament," which he wrote for Davidson as well and which draws on Frazer. In any case, both this and the following essay were written for Old Testament 2, which, like other courses at Emmanuel, ran for the entire academic year. Ordinarily, papers were submitted at the end of each term. During this time Frye, who had been appointed a reader in the English department at Victoria College, was teaching two courses, English 1b and 2b. Because of his teaching load, he received permission to submit papers late.[1] This dispensation, along with the note on the bibliography and the information in his letter to Helen Kemp, means that Frye almost certainly submitted "The Concept of Sacrifice" and "The Fertility Cults" at the end of the second term of his first year. Frye received an "A" for the paper, the typescript for which is in the NFF, 1991, box 37, file 13.

The fundamental problem of experience is the problem of the good life: how best self-development may be integrated with the social relationship. The religious attitude to this claims that by communion with God man achieves the highest possible synthesis of the separate and sometimes conflicting claims of the individual and the group; that in the perfect life the highest freedom coincides with absolute subjection to necessity. All human progress, as a dynamic religion conceives it, is bound up in the enunciation and actualization of this ideal. Christianity specifically claims that the enunciation commenced with the dawn of the reasoning faculty in the history of mankind, whenever that occurred, and became finally and fully stated by Jesus. The force which made this development possible was that of the Holy Spirit working in man, becoming articulate with the prophets, identical with Jesus, and associated with the tradition emanating from Jesus. This dogma formerly had to be stated in abstract theological terms, but since the rise of science, and in particular since the growth of the evolutionary concept ushered in by science, it is now possible to fill it out with the concrete verifications afforded by a scientific approach to it.

We at the present day see human history as a thin slice of organic biological development, a slow, long, painful ascent from beast or near beast to man. The Old Testament we see recording part of this process, tracing the growth of a race of people from savagery to civilization. Religion has, of course, developed with mankind; or, more accurately, it has developed mankind. In its earliest forms religion necessarily takes on many naive, crude, disgusting, and bestial forms, just as the general pattern of history does. That it is now a compulsion on the highest ideals of twentieth-century man is a truth not affected by scientific discoveries about its primitive forms, of course; which is an error a good many fall into even yet.

Religion is primarily concerned with establishing communion between man and God. Now it is evident that, while man is naturally a gregarious animal, the herd instinct is far more fundamental a one in the lower levels of culture. The horror of isolation for the savage, the absolute and irrevocable doom of anyone cut off from the protection of the tribe, is more immediately obvious than for us, with whom the social environment is infinitely more complex and tenuous. And if in our discovery of God we owe an especial debt to the Hebrews, that has much to do with the fact that the desert nomad has an even more ineradicable sense of communal obligation than any other type of primitive. It is this which makes the virtue of hospitality so prominent among desert tribes, and even their proverbial restlessness and love of war is to some extent at least an outcome of the feeling of the sharp discrimination of the tribe from anything possibly hostile to it. Consequently, religion at this stage is a social phenomenon. The whole moral aspect of religion is only implicit, not explicit, morality being relevant to a more individualized and differentiated social development. All religion in the primitive community can, therefore, be subsumed under the heading of sacrifice, the action in which man establishes communion with God insofar as he conceives him as immanent, and gives something to him insofar as he conceives him as transcendent.

Communion and gift: these are the primary concepts of sacrifice. It seems most logical, however, to adopt Robertson Smith's hypothesis, that sacrifice begins in communion. The savage is a thoroughgoing materialist, and God is a purely material life-force sustaining the solidarity of the group and ensuring its continuance. For the nomad in particular the god is a tribal god, a patriarchal god, the essence of solidarity, the superkinsman. As this life-force is material, it must be manifested in some concrete living object, whether man, animal, or vegetable (or, of course, even a stone, which is thought to have some life in it because of some curious shape).[2] The most materialistic way of establishing communion with such an object is to absorb its body into the worshipper's body: in short, as Mr. Micawber would say, to eat it.[3] Most primitives believe that by eating an animal one acquires the qualities of that animal. It is, of course, true that the savage feels himself surrounded by vague impersonal forces, some of which are without doubt hostile and malicious. The Old Testament contains many references to demons, though we are more apt to find an elaborated demonology in a period of later syncretism. There is the mysterious Lilith of Isaiah 34 [v. 14], the succuba or night-hag that will haunt the ruined Edom; there is Azazel or the demon of the waste, the Minotaur who devoured the scapegoats;[4] there are terrifying and repulsive animals, like he-goats, ostriches, jackals, and hawks, that become theriomorphic demons. But these are evil spirits: it is the demon who is bribed with offers of food, who is cajoled and bamboozled with charms and spells. *There* the leading idea is that of separation, of warding off. This contrast is brought out very clearly in the Passover, in which the god is eaten at the paschal meal and the evil spirits warded off with the blood sprinkled over the door. The sign of the cross and the holy water serve the same apotropaic purpose in the Catholic Eucharist. This is, however, a purely negative and defensive reaction to a mysterious mana, and the primitive is more courageous than that. He wants to make some positive use of an energy obviously stronger than he to reinforce his own powers. To assume, as was done by E.B. Tylor, an early writer on this subject, that sacrifice begins in gift rather than communion, the gift being essentially a bribe, is to ignore this whole point.[5] We have said that both ideas, of communion and of gift, are inherent in sacrifice. But logically this would only arise at a time

when the god was conceived as a mysterious transcendent force which
was only partly incarnate in the object sacrificed, and continued living
after its death, so that the sacrifice could be both a meal of the god and a
meal with the god. Such a conception seems to be a later development
than the pure animism which thinks of the soul of the god as resident
entirely within the body of the victim.

What is the most fitting object to sacrifice? With most primitives the
logical victim would be the king—the man who holds together the tribe.
He who is the incarnation of the solidarity of the group is necessarily its
god. The tribe can last only as long as the divine force in the king which
makes him king can last. Hence, the king is hedged about by taboos; he
begets a son and transmits his virility to him. The fortunes of the tribe
are bound up with him: if his virility wanes, then, by the most elementary principles of sympathetic magic, the energy of the tribe declines. So,
as soon as the king begins to show signs of failing, he is killed, his flesh
is eaten to permeate the tribe with his effluence, his blood and ashes, if
the tribe be an agricultural one, sown over the land to ensure fertility.
But the slaying of the divine king has left little if any trace on Hebrew
culture: perhaps because their early nomadic life made the preservation
of fertility a less insistent problem. The god is then conceived to be manifest in what sustains existence, that is, food. Hence, the staple food of
the tribe contains or is intimately associated with the god of the tribe.
With a hunting people, animals such as the boar or deer are apt to be,
thus, canonized; with a pastoral people, sheep, cattle, or goats; with an
agricultural people, corn, vines, or trees. This embodiment of the god in
theriomorphic forms is a genuine cultural advance on cannibalism, and
it entails an increase of conscious awareness of the outer world on the
part of the primitive. The Hebrews begin with the dividing of a common
object of food among the worshippers, with some of it restored to the
god who embodied himself in it. The complete assimilation of the god-
animal and the divine king ideas, in the social organization we know as
totemism, may or may not have existed among the Israelites: Robertson
Smith thinks so,[6] later writers are not so sure.

There are many motives in primitive sacrifice: communion, propitia-
tion, bribery, feeding of the god, establishment of a blood bond, reinforcing the efficacy of a curse, obtaining of an oracle, transferring of a
disease to an animal, preserving a newly built house, and so on: but all
of these fall under the two fundamental categories of communion and
gift, or an application of either idea. Probably sacrifice starts simply

with man's fondness for company and for a feast, the feast being the only occasion on which the idea of group cohesion becomes evident, through relaxation of activity. Refreshments are the mainstay of social activity, as such, in any level of civilization, and there is no reason to suppose that primitives at the very beginning of conscious life had any loftier spiritual attitude than, say, we evidence toward Thanksgiving. Even when the idea evolves of the critically important ritual feast with overtones of a larger significance, the meal is retained. It does not occur to the primitive that the god does not necessarily eat or drink. He leaves food for the god, who eats it up in the form of a jackal, vulture, or hyena. The Old Testament records an era in which the god was thought of smelling the food of the sacrifice with relish: perhaps the transfer from the appeal to the sense of taste to that of smell represents an access of spirituality. When the idea of an etherealized and transcendent god has fairly well set in, the offering is burned, being sent up to the deity in the form of smoke. When the ritual is brought indoors, the burnt offering becomes sublimated into the burning of incense. The Hebrews distinguished two forms of sacrifice: the *zebah* or communion sacrifice, and the *'olan* or burnt offering gift. But there were several ways of establishing a communion with the god beside the communal meal. According to primitive physiology, power or energy is resident in the flesh in a more or less quiescent form, but the liquid or running parts, the blood and fat, represent the essential life. The fact that a tribe lives together means that it exists as a blood brotherhood. Hence, the god is bound to the tribe sometimes through the ritual of blood brotherhood. The god-animal is slain and the flesh eaten, but the blood and fat are reverently preserved, as in the Passover. The victim is usually slain on an altar, or some stone which will hold the blood: occasionally we find stones with holes bored in them to let the blood seep through, back to the earth mother, perhaps, or the spirit in the stone. This may be reason, too, for the curious little cup-shaped marks found in rocks, at Gezer, for example.[7] The life, that is, the blood and fat, is reverently preserved when the victim is slain, wildly paradoxical as that may sound. Sometimes the idea of the blood brotherhood is completed by sprinkling some of the blood on the worshippers: in even more logical cases the worshippers drink the blood, a practice most notoriously associated with the Mithraic cult. The fat of a sacrificial victim is frequently rubbed on the king at his succession (originally, of course, the fat of his unfortunate predecessor) or on an adolescent undergoing the rite of admission to adulthood at puberty.

Again, the blood brotherhood compact with the god might be made from the blood of the worshippers rather than by that of a victim, and of this practice the mutilations of the priests of the Baal mocked by Elijah [1 Kings 18:27] may be a reminiscence. But the distinction between the body and blood, one divided and broken and the other poured out, goes back to the mistiest regions of antiquity, though historically the libation of pouring blood is later than the offering of food.

It sounds like special pleading to me to call this rite at any stage purely magical. The ascription of a Benthamite self-interest philosophy to the savage may be natural enough to a Benthamite anthropologist, but does not make for catholicity. Surely the first datum of intelligent consciousness is the perception of some cosmic mana in the environment. The moment man becomes critically aware of the world, he is aware of a rhythmic recurrence of seasons and heavenly bodies, an organic living world independent of his will which augurs a larger control of forces than he himself has. The breaking of a taboo might disrupt the workings of an inconceivably huge and delicately adjusted machine. No matter how anthropomorphic a god may be, his power must be literally incalculable. All calamities, whether earthquakes, famine, storms, or war, are the result of an angry god. The feeling of helplessness, the sense of guilt, and the necessity to make amends, can hardly ever be totally absent from the concept of sacrifice. No doubt this is at first a matter of experience rather than remorse: in fact if it were not so the prophets would have never overthrown sacrifice, and we should be sacrificing yet. But the germ of religious development is there. Inequalities are present in the world. Consequently, mankind, according to the great hypothesis of Loisy which has been accepted by the majority of reputable scientists, reaches monotheism by a process of induction, rising from polydaemonism to polytheism, from polytheism to monolatry, and from monolatry to the dogma pronouncing God the Father Almighty.[8] There appears to be no instinctive monotheism among primitives; the only thing that looks like it is the worshipper's desire to flatter the god he is addressing by telling him that he is the greatest of all gods, which is the approach we call henotheism. In most of the Old Testament Yahweh is subject to all the weaknesses of man: anger, forgetfulness, repentance, short-sightedness, sacrifice of means to the end, and so forth. He has apparently a purely arbitrary dislike of Cain and like of Abel; he is apt to overlook sin unless it is brought to his attention; he will, in order to carry out his aim, cause people to sin; he will be sorry for overhasty action and make amends. God the Father, of Christianity, is implicit in the very dawn of the moral sense, and Jesus' conception owes not a little of its dignity and subtlety to the fact that it recaptures the freshness of an original religion not yet disillusioned by civilization. God is far more human and understandable in the J narrative[9] than in Amos, who, though extolling nomadic virtues, is dealing with an overcivilized and decadent people. The fussy, scolding, irascible, benevolent deity who put his trespassing children out of his garden but makes coats of skin for them, who checks his bullying son Cain but forbids the others to take advantage of him, is nearer Jesus in spirit than the anachronistic God who creates the sun, moon, and stars chiefly to provide a calendar for Jewish ritualistic observance.[10] This point is perhaps important in restoring a balance to our perspective of the psychological basis of atonement. We are too apt to think of the piaculative offering in terms of the unrelieved grimness we adopt today in giving money to foreign missions. The ordinary healthy human being cannot permanently think of himself as crushed and prostrate before a tyrant god. The naivety of some of the attempts recorded in the Old Testament to conceal a somewhat childlike sense of guilt and appease an angry but soft-hearted and indulgent Yahweh can be better appreciated by those who are not troubled with an *écrasez l'infâme*[11] complex.

At first, no doubt, the sacrifice, being a special rite, was adopted on a special occasion. But for any idea of permanence to be retained, which, of course, was necessary to the basic postulate of the sacrificial act, the haphazard and occasional sacrifice had to be subordinated to a regular one. Something had to control it to make it repeated and recurrent. Now the whole religious aspect of the idea of entering into the god is basically an impulse to achieve a larger unity or balance in life, if on a subconscious level, and this attempt obviously carries with it the incipient perception of the fundamental rhythms of nature. The elaboration of a calendar is a very early and purely religious proceeding: the rhythm of the sun which forms the day, the rhythm of the moon which forms the month, the rhythm of the seasons which forms the year, are bound up with festivals and ceremonies. In particular the continually waxing and waning moon is thought to be a leading principle of growth and decay: man should, therefore, work when the moon is in rhythm and stop work when it is in repose: in other words, on its phases. Thus, the week grows out of the month, and the Sabbath, which originally was a full-moon festival, became the consecrated day. It has been conjectured by some that the alphabet, the symbolic structure of communication, owes its origin to a lunar calendar.[12]

It is, as we have said, the mode of life that determines the attitude to religion, as far as the primitive, whose thought is so strongly conditioned by his environment, is concerned. In considering the development of the Hebrew cultus we have to take account of the impact an agricultural religion, as practised by the Canaanite peasants, made upon the invading nomadic tribes from Kadesh and Sinai. Now for nomads the moon is the primary object of adoration, as their lives do not especially depend upon the ripening of crops: the sun-god and the storm-god are alike deities indifferent when they are not merely destructive and blighting. Hence, the lunar feasts constitute the starting point of nomadic sacrifice, which explains why the Sabbath was so deeply ingrained a custom.

The most important nomadic sacrifice, however, is the Passover, which, though it suffered an eclipse of some centuries after the settlement in Canaan, gradually emerged as the central sacrifice upon which everything else converged. The nomads depend upon sheep and goats for their existence, and they think of the year as revolving, not around the seeding and harvesting of crops, but around the lambing and shearing of ewes. At the spring equinox, therefore, the firstling of a pastoral flock would be sacrificed to ensure increase throughout the year. For the firstling of the flock, in representing the advent of life and fertility, would according to primitive ideas be the incarnation of fertility, or the divine spirit of life. The lamb was, therefore, eaten in communion, probably with the moon, whose waxing and waning make it an obvious symbol of organic growth. This would explain why the Passover was held at night on full-moon day, though after the settlement in Canaan, when the family replaced the tribe as the social unit, it becomes a purely household feast. There was also a sheep-shearing festival in the agricultural period which probably goes back to nomadic times, although the nomads tore the wool off with their hands. It is easy to see that in nomadic times there would be comparatively little of the piaculative element in sacrifice. One thinks of these festivals as entirely unconnected with the terrified, cringing worship of the arbitrary and capricious god of the harvest, as comparatively free from the masochistic obscenities of an appeal to nature rather than to a protector of the tribe. One thinks of them as free and easy festivals in which the members of the tribe drew together with a warm sense of comradeship, secure in a mutual trust of the Yahweh who held them together. Our word *hallelujah* seems to be etymologically a synthesis of the ideas of the appearance of the new moon, the shout of joy raised to greet it, and the praise of Yahweh.

In the Canaanites the Hebrews found an agricultural peasantry and an agricultural religion. Now where the nomad leads a roaming life, the peasant is rooted in the soil; and where the nomad's social unit is the unit of the tribe, the agricultural social unit is the family or household, so that Yahweh, the great tribal god of the Hebrews, found a formidable rival in the household god Baal. Again, where the nomadic god watches over the raising of sheep and goats, the agricultural god is invoked to provide a fertile soil and a good crop. These two aspects of Canaanite religion, the household god and the fertility cult, exerted a powerful disintegrating influence upon the worship of Yahweh, and the vivid and dramatic story of the conflict between these two deities is the pre-exilic history of Israel. Obviously the fertility cult represents the more communal side of religion, and the household worship the more localized side. Consequently, the former would be less important than the latter in pre-Hebraic Palestine, where social organization was so tenuous, and by the time the Hebrews arrived, worship had centred on Baal as a local spirit, the dying-god myth always having something exotic about it.

We have seen that the necessity for regulating sacrifice implies an observance of the procession of the heavenly bodies and the seasons. Of course, the agricultural year revolves around the seeding and harvesting of crops. To the primitive anything alive has a spirit; the crop, therefore, has a spirit, and the soil which produces it must have a spirit too. As the soil bears the crop, the crop-spirit exists to the soil-spirit in the relation of son or daughter to mother. And as the crop (the crop here is only used for a more specific illustration: the concept includes all deciduous vegetation) disappears in the autumn and reappears in the spring, in all agricultural primitive communities there arose the myth of the young god or goddess dying every year and reviving in the spring. In Syria the dying god's name was Adonis (which means lord; the cognate form is Dan); in Babylonia it was Tammuz; in Phrygia Attis; in Egypt Osiris; in Attica Dionysus. Sometimes the vegetation spirit was a goddess, as with the Greek Kore or Persephone. And as the mother or earth spirit was thought of as bewailing the loss of her son or daughter, as Venus did of Adonis, Cybele of Attis, Isis of Osiris, Demeter of Kore, then according to sympathetic magic women were set to bewail the death as well. The wailing for Adonis is a stock literary allusion; and the weeping of the women for Tammuz, in the very gates of the Temple, brought a curt and contemptuous reference from Ezekiel [8:14]. Similarly, doubtless Baal, and certainly Dagon, go back to some such similar myth in prehistoric times, Baal being originally a god of fertility and Dagon always being a corn-god.

Now, again according to sympathetic magic, something which represents the spirit of the dying god has to be slain when the god dies. This would originally be, as we have seen, the divine king; later this fierce rule was sufficiently relaxed to allow the king to substitute a son, preferably a first-born son, or, still later, a captive, someone chosen by lot, or even a volunteer. Some think that the Old Testament records the change from child sacrifice to animal sacrifice, particularly in the story of the origin of the Passover [Exodus 12] and in the story of Abraham's substituting a ram for Isaac on Mount Moriah [Genesis 22:13]. Certainly child sacrifice was prevalent among the Canaanites. The hideous and nightmarish orgies associated with the worship of Moloch are familiar to everyone, and skeletons have been found of children, sometimes cut in two and sometimes buried alive, in pre-Hebraic Palestine. The Hebrews, naturally, abhorred child sacrifice; but there are enough references to it in the Bible to show that it was deeply implanted in the peasant soul of the Canaanite, and transmitted to the Israelites. Not till the exile, if then, did the people get away from the idea that to sacrifice a child was the supreme, the exceptional sacrifice, to be used only as a last resort, but certain to be powerfully efficacious if used. The animal sacrifice they considered adequate ordinarily, but in the last analysis a makeshift, and they felt that in times of stress such as a siege, or as a result of an extraordinary crime, only the sacrifice of a child would answer. Thus, the King of Moab sacrificed his eldest son when his capital was besieged [2 Kings 3:27], and the practice is attacked as a contemporary scandal by Micah [6:7]. The sacrifice of Jephthah's daughter belongs, ostensibly, to this category of superlative bribe, being the fulfilment of a monstrous bargain with the god [Judges 11:34–40], such as was all too frequent in the ancient world (the Middle Ages were sufficiently advanced to confine such compacts to the devil); though the reference to the unfortunate girl as "bewailing her virginity" [Judges 11:37] suggests that she may have been sacrificed in the role of a Kore or an Iphigenia.

The Israelites were almost unique, however, in that they did not adopt the practice of the annual fertility sacrifice and seem to have reduced it to this haphazard and extraordinary status among the

Canaanites. In other countries the advance of civilization caused the sacrifice festival gradually to soften down into some comparatively harmless clowning such as we find in the contemporary carnivals of Latin Europe. The Roman festival of the Saturnalia was of this nature, as was a parallel Sacaea festival at Babylon. When the Jews returned from Babylon, they brought this custom with them in the feast of Purim, myth attached, and worked it into the aetiological-historical form of Esther, a form very frequent in the Pentateuch. Esther and Mordecai are the Babylonian Ishtar and Marduk; Vashti and Haman are two Elamite gods. Frazer has thrown out the suggestion that Jesus may have been crucified in the role of Haman, or in that of the victim of the Roman Saturnalia, which was not the good-humoured carnival in the provinces that it was in Rome, or as a result of the coincidence of both, depending on what can be deduced from the calendar.[13] If this is true, the symbolism of the crucifixion as the last act of the old world and the first of the new, the end of the pagan world and the commencement of the Christian, takes on an even more vivid and powerful significance.

A far more dangerous opponent to Yahwism was the cult of the household god. "Baal" is a general term meaning the presiding spirit, something like our "genius." The baal of the household corresponded to the lares and penates of the Romans,[14] and, with the growth of an Israelite peasantry, the tendency to a localized image worship was very strong. The main attribute of Baal was his authority as a corn-god; Hosea has to insist that the corn comes from Yahweh and not Baal [2:8]. The necessity for the Israelites to unite in a common bond against outside aggression gave Yahweh the victory over Baal. Among the Phoenicians the baals grew into eponymous ancestors of tribes or cities. Moloch means judge, Adonis, lord. The importance of this for sacrifice is the growth of a tendency to regard a building as an abode of a spirit, which resulted in a widespread custom of burying the body of a child or captive under the threshold, or, sometimes, under the gate of a city.

When Israelite civilization got fairly well under way, the only important sacrifices became the ritual or calendar sacrifices. There were many subordinate motives in sacrifice superseded by the development of the cultus, and we can hardly do more here than to record the fact that they existed. Sacrifices in the various forms of bribery were extremely varied. In war, the enemy and all his possessions were sacrificed to the tribal god in advance, and after a victory to destroy everything belonging to the enemy was only fair play. This is, of course, the reason for the bewildering ferocity ascribed to the Israelites in the wars of Joshua and Saul. Again, the criminal in primitive society was primarily a man who had broken a taboo, the moral code of early societies, so that his execution was considered as to some extent a sacrifice and was accompanied by the usual rituals. Sacrifice as the fulfilment of a vow was very frequent; in time of stress man is likely to offer his god anything in return for help. Some special sacrifices were, of course, piaculative, either intended to avert the wrath of the deity or express genuine contrition. Of course, the great weakness of gift-sacrifice is its assumption that the god needs and can use what his petitioner can use. Otherwise there is little point in offering food, clothing, weapons, or something containing a life-force which will supplement the god's. The prophets pointed out that no god at all worthy of worship could possibly use anything of this, and thereupon the gift-sacrifice became an exploded superstition.

But if the Hebrews did not adopt the fertility sacrifices of the Canaanites officially, they borrowed many festivals from them. They learned to leave part of the crop (the abode of the corn spirit) unharvested. The harvest and vintage festivals now took the place of the nomadic Passover; and the materials of the communion meal became less flesh, blood, and fat and more bread, wine, and oil. The vintage festival was morally perhaps the most reprehensible of all; its Bacchanalian and orgiastic features, its exploiting of sacred prostitution, brought it under fire in the prophetic period, so that wine came to be forbidden in sacrifice. There were three harvest festivals: the feast of unleavened bread at the beginning, the feast of first-fruits at the height of the season, the later Pentecost, and the feast of ingathering or tabernacles at the end. All these feasts had legends which assigned a historical origin to them. The feast of unleavened bread absorbed the Passover for a time. When the postexilic cultus was firmly established, we have a feast of dedication, apparently originally a solstitial festival like our Christmas, the New Year festival, and the Day of Atonement which came to be more or less fused with the New Year, after the Hebrews moved the latter back from the feast of ingathering or booths. The New Year festival was originally accompanied by the blowing of horns, presumably to drive away evil spirits, as is done today in China, who may be supposed to be especially numerous on that day. The high ethical and piaculative tone of the contemporary Day of Atonement is, of course, a later development.

One very important result of sacrifice in the primitive world remains to be noted: unfortunately it is probably less true of the Hebrews than of other peoples. We have seen that sacrifice is the embryo of all religious development, which must mean that it contains approaches to all forms of the good. Plato divided the good into the just, the beautiful, and the true, which give us three systematic developments, morals, art, and science. We have dealt briefly with the moral and the scientific (i.e. magical) aspects of sacrifice; it remains to consider the artistic. Now art is concerned with presenting a selected unity of experience; the work of art is an entity in which each detail is significant and relevant to the whole. Therefore, art is the static individual expression of a religious impulse, or a criticism of religion; for religion is concerned with the achievement of this unity in life itself. Art, dealing as it does with the imposition of a pattern upon experience, is ultimately based upon patterns of the ultimate data of experience, space and time. Hence, the arts may be divided into the temporal arts based on rhythm, and the spatial or plastic arts based on symmetry or proportion.

The plastic arts begin in attempts to reproduce the image of the god, hoping to gain some power over him or from him by possessing his picture, which according to primitive thought is a part of him, just as his name is. Painting and sculpture are basically iconic arts, beginning in cave drawings and totem carvings. The Hebrews made little contribution here; Yahwism had no iconic tradition in the desert, and idolatry, though widespread, was never taken very seriously. Yahweh might be occasionally represented as a bull; theriomorphic images were common enough in the eighth century for Hosea to resent them [8:4–6], but for the most part images were merely little household statuettes, or such personal ornaments as earrings, amulets, and so forth, which probably had a common apotropaic origin.

Sympathetic magic, however, holds that the god can be compelled or approached, not only through possession of part of him, but by some act in rhythmic rapport with him. Hence, the sacrifice is usually accompanied by appropriate gestures and movements, which latter eventually develop into a procession around the sacrificial object to help impregnate it with the divine affluence. Only when we understand this impulse toward a rhythmic expression of worship can we grasp the extensive use of swinging as a sacrificial rite, such as we have today in the Catholic censer, or the Jewish practice of waving a sheaf in the air at Pentecost. From spasmodic and rudimentary gestures of sympathetic magic, such as leaping into the air to promote the growth of crops, there gradually develops the dance, which frequently consists in re-enacting the adventures of the god invoked. The dance is both musical and dramatic; musical originally because of the need for noise against the powers of darkness, and later because it is the most ultimately symbolic of all arts. The Chronicler's sole cultural interest is in music, and it seems to have been the only art to which the Jews were much addicted. With the Greeks Orpheus was both the supreme musician and the supreme theologian. The Jews did not develop the drama out of the dance, but the Greeks did. The word *tragedy* means a goat-song, and was originally a goat sacrifice like the scapegoat offering to Azazel among the Hebrews [Leviticus 16:8]. The tragic drama is a spiritual sublimation of the inward essence of all sacrifice. For sacrifice, like all religion, is concerned with the reintegration of individual and social imperatives in God. In communion the worshipper projects his soul into the divine being of the sacrificial object, just as the spectator projects his soul into the tragic hero, who is, at any rate in Greek tragedy and Shakespeare, a figure of superhuman proportions. In the ritual slaying the worshipper is conscious of the communal solidarity of his religion, just as in the fall of the tragic hero into his environment the spectator experiences a catharsis or purgation of spirit in his self-abnegation. The development of comedy out of the festival or carnival is just as logical, but too intricate and irrelevant for further discussion. Music and drama are the two great religious arts, the communal performances of an ensemble for an audience, which in our own culture have been born from the womb of the Christian Church. The greatest works of art the human race has ever seen or is ever likely to see are the two colossal musical and dramatic structures of Bach—the B Minor Mass and the *St. Matthew Passion*. It can hardly be altogether an accident that the latter of these is the artistic presentation of the supreme sacrifice, and the former that of the supreme symbol of it.

With the coming of the prophets the literal and physical imagination of the primitive becomes impossible in an advancing society, and a more spiritual conception takes its place. Instead of the mere desire to placate an angry god, there comes the conception of contrition, humility, and atonement. Instead of a god demanding food and strength, there arises a God requiring complete spiritual surrender. Instead of the god of the tribe, there comes the Creator of the world. Instead of a communion designed to ensure a renewal of physical strength, there comes a communion leading to a spiritual rebirth, or salvation. Instead of seeking promises or succor for the adventures of the tribe, there comes a seeking after the redemption of the soul.

There are many subsidiary features of sacrifice in connection with the establishment of the postexilic cultus with which we hardly have space to deal; among them the very complicated question of the development of the priest from a sort of guide to a holy place to the sole possible communicant between God and his worshippers. In general, it may be said that the trend of religious thought goes through the prophets, that what is organically important and permanent about sacrifice was absorbed by them, and that the official Jerusalem religion was a conservative consolidation of traditions which were spiritually obsolescent. In particular, the typically ritualistic idea of transferring sins in a corporeal form to an animal, or the almost insensate orgy of commentary on the law, designed to make the tradition as complete—and, therefore, as dead—as possible, lacks so much of the fearlessness and subtlety of prophetic thought that we may well leave it for the curious scholar. What the prophets did, finally, was to establish that the sole reality of the religious life lay in the realm of the spirit. This left the way open for the inference that all physical acts in sacrifice have a value not inherent but symbolic of the real inner religion of the soul. Therefore, the literally physical religious act—the sacrifice—was replaced by the symbolically physical religious act—the sacrament.

It is, of course, a fundamental point of Christian theology that sacrifice broke down because it was useless: God does not require food or drink, and if we are to get any good out of the sacrifice of God, God will have to sacrifice himself. We are bound to a cycle of life and death; we can kill, but we cannot bring to life again; and any sacrifice founded on the idea of preserving life is impossible for us. Negatively, therefore, we reach Jesus as the supreme sacrifice by a process of breakdown and collapse of human effort. But we can also approach it positively. The change from the literal sacrifice to the symbolic sacrament is an inevitable stage in the development of mankind, but it can hardly take place if there is nothing for the sacrament to symbolize. The conception implicit in all sacrifice, of the paradox of the god who cannot die because he is eternal and the god who does die because he is incarnate, has to be worked out in history, not only in philosophy; in experience, not only in thought. With this conception our next essay will be chiefly concerned.

(for bibliography see next essay)

5

The Fertility Cults

For the provenance of this paper, see the headnote to the previous essay, "The Concept of Sacrifice." Frye received an "A" for the paper, the typescript of which is in the NFF, 1991, box 37, file 13.

The discovery by anthropology of the fertility cult rite among agricultural primitives is a comparatively recent one, but fraught with the highest importance for future developments in religion, art, and in general the symbolic aspects of culture. The term "fertility cult" is usually held to designate whatever religious practices are specifically associated with the sympathetic magic which aims at promoting the fertility of the soil, and, consequently, exists only among agriculturalists or among dwellers in the forest, where the lives of the people are bound up with the fate of the vegetation.

Our problem is to trace the influence of fertility cults on the Hebrews. The Hebrews proper being nomads, we should not expect to find anything germane to our problem there; but the Canaanites and the other peasant dwellers of the land conquered by the Hebrews would be subject to the same organic laws as other agricultural peoples. Thus, the program of Hebrew religious history is that of the conflict between Yahweh, the nomadic god of the tribe, and Baal, the generic name of the agricultural or fertility gods of the surrounding nations; a struggle of unity and monotheism against localization and polytheism, of ethics against magic, love against fear, the devotional against the orgiastic.

Plato in his *Symposium* states that the primary force of coherence, the Eros, is driven to reproduction through its necessity for self-preservation and self-perpetuation.[1] In the same way among primitives the gregarious instinct for social cohesion finds immediate and instinctive expression in some act designed to secure the perpetuation of the social cohesion. Now to the primitive the social "life" cannot be an abstraction, but a concrete embodiment with a virility of its own, resident obviously in the man who is himself the incarnation of social unity—the king. The primary rite, then, is to keep the king's power undiminished and permanent, in the only way in which that can be done—by handing on the succession to his eldest son as soon as his strength begins to fail him. For with his strength is bound up that of the tribe, and if a young and vigorous man is not always head of the tribe, the tribe suffers decay in consequence. Hence, the king is surrounded with the most elaborate precautions and taboos, for, should he make a single false step, untold disaster will befall the tribe.

But, of course, the king has to die eventually, and it would be a sinful waste of divine energy for the tribe not to absorb the strength in him which is the strength of the tribe. So the king, as soon as his powers fail, is promptly killed and eaten among the most rudimentary of primitives; his body is divided among his ex-subjects and worshippers, his blood drunk among them to establish a blood brotherhood, his fat rubbed over his successor doubly to reassure a transmission of virility. It is easy to see how with the rise of civilization among agriculturalists these crude and disgusting materials of a cannibalistic repast would be sublimated into bread for flesh, wine for blood, anointed oil for rubbed fat, with the symbolic basis retained.[2]

The slaying of the divine king, however, is apparently a universal practice among primitives, not confined to agriculturalists, and we are here concerned with the fertility aspect of it. For with these peoples we have the special problem added, not only to maintain social solidarity, but to ensure the fertility of the soil and an abundant crop.

Now the primary instinct for self-preservation and perpetuation of life brings with it a perception of recurrence. No one lives for ever; but life is transmitted from father to son and is, thus, recurrent. What is true of the human world is just as true of the natural world: the heavenly bodies and the seasons are recurrent. And with vegetation we have, of course, the annual death at the beginning of winter and revival in the spring. With agricultural primitives the perception of seasonal rhythm synchronizes with the instinct to eat the divine king in a ritual sacrifice, so that the latter rite becomes either a harvest or vintage festival or a spring festival—generally the former. But this correspondence between the human and natural worlds does not extend only to this, but to its reverse—the humanizing of the natural. "Vegetation," like "society," is too abstract a conception for the primitive: there must be a spirit of vegetation, a divine and dying god of natural as of human life.

Thus, all agricultural primitives develop much the same myth of a young (because flourishing and vigorous) god of vegetation slain annually in the fall and reviving in the spring. This spirit, being nourished by the soil, exists to that soil in the relation of son or daughter to mother. Each fall the god is conceived as slain by emasculation (the thigh wound of Adonis is a later euphemism), his sterility in death being bewailed by the women, representing the earth mother, along with certain charms of sympathetic magic, such as throwing pots of flowers into the water. Sometimes, in sympathy with the rhythm of the seasons, the divine king is slain in the fall when the god dies, and his successor does not take control until the spring: a peculiar feature of government preserved by the Romans and written into the American Constitution. In any case, the god or goddess dies and is mourned in all countries, only the names being changed. The most famous of all such fertility gods is the Syrian Adonis, whose mother-lover was Aphrodite. The god was called Tammuz in Babylonia, Osiris, beloved by Isis, in Egypt, Dionysus in some parts of Greece, Hyacinthus in Sparta, Attis, son of Cybele, in Phrygia; but the myths were so similar, and the rites so identical, that under the theocrasia of Roman imperialism they became inextricably confused. Adonis gradually extended his sway over Greece, and Attis over Rome, but with the rise of Christianity they disappeared, leaving only Adonis as a purely literary memory, until science began to unravel the symbolism latent in the art which developed from the fertility cults. In Greek mythology there are dying goddesses as well, of whom Proserpine or Persephone, beloved by Demeter (whose name, earth mother, shows most clearly her origin), Iphigenia, and Kore are the best known. The idea has also left its traces on the figures of Orpheus and Pan.[3]

Any bright red vegetation was associated with the spilt blood of the god: the red anemone with that of Adonis, and the red silt brought down by the Adonis river; the pomegranate with that of Dionysus; and the hyacinth, "that sanguine flower inscrib'd with woe,"[4] with that of the spirit whose name it bears. To understand how natural and unforced such an idea would be we have only to think of the spontaneous growth of the symbolism of the "poppies" in the Great War. Some of the gods, among which the Philistine Dagon must be included, were explicitly corn-gods; others, like Dionysus, were wine-gods; still others, like the Teutonic Balder the Beautiful, were tree-gods. According to the principles of sympathetic magic, in order to ensure fertility of soil, unrestrained sexual licence on the part of the tribe should prevail during the ritual period of harvest and vintage, and, sometimes, a period of abstention was observed in the spring, which latter, being far more encouraged by Christianity, has survived in Lent. Of the essentially orgiastic nature of the fertility cult ritual there seems no reasonable doubt. The god who controls the rains on which depends the life of the people is essentially a god of caprice and haphazard, only too likely to be indifferent. With most agricultural peoples there grows a pernicious tendency to compel the attention of the god by some action which, by virtue of its sensational horror and wickedness, will be certain to stimulate action. Hence, mutilation and murder, both ritual and spasmodic, form a large and sinister part of the ceremonies.

The barbaric ferocity of the slaying of the divine king could naturally not survive the first impact of civilization, and the king at first provided a substitute in his eldest son, then, as the rule relaxed, an annual victim of some kind, captive, slave, youth chosen by lot, even sometimes a volunteer. From slaying this mock-king civilization advanced eventually to holding a carnival, with the sham king as the presiding clown, or, as he was called in England, the "lord of misrule." The clown would be given a triumphal procession, and sometimes some rough treatment afterwards, but the general atmosphere would be one of good humour and horseplay.

With this softening down on human sacrifice the sacrificial victim becomes an animal. The tendency to associate the corn-spirit with some animal lurking near it is very strong, and the particular animal chosen is largely a matter of accident. Thus, the myth that Adonis was killed by a boar means that Adonis was frequently worshipped in the form of a boar, the opposition between animal and god being paralleled by a transition in the attitude toward the animal itself; from being sacred it comes to be regarded as unclean. These ideas of sacredness and uncleanliness are the obverse and reverse of the same thing, connected by the idea of taboo. Scientists tend to believe that all the "unclean" animals in Judaism, Mohammedanism, and Hinduism were originally sacred. The association of Dionysus and Pan with the goat is also well known.

This was the type of religion rampant in Palestine, in all probability, before the advent of the Hebrews. There is no reason to suppose that the dying-god myth was not in Canaan when it was everywhere else. But just to what extent the rites permeated into the life of the Hebrews the redaction of the Old Testament records, chiefly by P,[5] has prevented us from knowing. That an extensive permeation did take place is evident, and is symbolized by a curious piece of irony: the name Jehovah, which is a synthesis of the consonants of Yahweh and the vowels of Adonai, lord, which is only another form of Adonis. Dan, one of the twelve tribes, is a name also cognate with Adonis. We have, however, to read a bit between the lines if we are to obtain what we are looking for.

It is possible that we have blurred, refracted, and distorted forms of many fertility rites. The extremely unpleasant story with which the Book of Judges closes, which related how the tribe of Benjamin was replenished, may describe a fertility festival.[6] Something of the search for the lost spirit in the darkness of the underworld which we find in the story of Orpheus and Eurydice may have crept into the story of Lot's wife.[7] There are strong traces of a sun mythology attached to a culture hero in the Samson cycle,[8] and solar and chthonic rites are never, as we shall presently show, to be clearly separated. Possibly the hanging of the five Gibeonite kings on trees in Joshua 10 may be, like all hanging, a reminiscence of sacrifice in tree worship.[9] The wanderings of the children of Israel are perhaps collateral with the initiatory search for Kore in imitation of Demeter, a prominent feature in the Greek mysteries. Certainly there were sacred trees, which the Phoenicians called *asherim*; these were usually evergreens, which preserve the life spirit of vegetation through the winter and are invoked at the winter solstice as harbingers of fertility, as in our Christmas festival. Abraham's oaks at Mamre were presumably sacred. But there is one fairly clear instance of a fertility sacrifice: the story of Jephthah's daughter. The redactor has made this look as much as possible like a simple story of fufilment of a vow, but the crucial passage in Judges 11:38–40 makes it clear that the unfortunate girl was sacrificed in the role of a Hebrew equivalent of Iphigenia.[10]

The orthodox Yahwist party never relaxed its opposition to all fertility cults. The ascetic stern virtues of the nomadic Hebrews were cited by innumerable Cato censors[11] as proof of the moral degeneracy and effeminacy of the exotic customs. Those with higher moral standards set by the more rigorous life were outraged at Canaanite licentiousness, from our point of view with considerable justification. The tendency toward the worst possible gesture in sacrifice which we have mentioned was

expressed in child sacrifice. Some investigators think that the Old Testament records an era in which child sacrifice was gradually giving way to
animal sacrifice, and that the story of the origin of the Passover [Exodus
12:1–36] and Abraham's substitution sacrifice of his son Isaac on Mount
Moriah [Genesis 22:1–18] illustrate for the Hebrews that animal sacrifice
was more desirable to Yahweh than child sacrifice, the implication being
that child sacrifice was the ultimate rite, so powerful as to be sure of
efficacy when used as a last resort. The vehement assurances of the
prophets that Yahweh does not want the blood of murdered children
undoubtedly reflect a popular superstition that the animal sacrifice was
a makeshift for the god's supreme demand. The influence of the
Canaanites is obvious, whose obscenities are too notorious to dwell on
here. Again, the sexual licence of the ritual orgies was shunned by the
Yahwists as something dirty and disgusting both physically and morally. Westermarck and Edward Carpenter have both shown that among
many peoples this sexual licence and sacred prostitution are balanced
by a tendency to set apart homosexuals for special offices such as the
priesthood, and the extensive development of homosexuality among all
people who have concentrated strongly on the purely reproductive
aspect of normal intercourse is very frequent.[12] Moral delinquency,
effeminacy, child sacrifice, whoredom, sodomy: this is a formidable
indictment to bring against any religion, and the prophets of monotheism, from Elijah to St. Paul, made the most of it.

   The Yahwist reaction gathers strength, of course, with the division of
the kingdom and the revolt of Israel against the syncretizing tendencies
of Solomon.[13] It seems fairly certain that Yahweh was worshipped
as a bull, a stock symbol of fertility and strength, and that the well-
developed Egyptian and Mesopotamian pantheons were represented in
the Temple. But Yahweh's prestige as the tribal god gave him a powerful advantage in the struggle for national unity against the Philistines, as
opposed to the localizing tendencies of Baal worship. The Canaanites
were peasants, which meant that their worship, besides being agricultural, was largely an affair of the household. The "baal" was in nearly
every case simply a local genius or presiding spirit of any given house,
tree, river, mountain, or other natural object. The disintegrating influence such a worship would exert on the spirit of national unity is obvious, and the prophets carried on a bitter and unceasing fight against it,
the great saga recording Elijah's contest with the Baal worshippers [1
Kings 18:1–40] being the theme of an epic struggle completed only by

Christianity. More and more the prophets struggled to make the issue a clear-cut one between the acceptance of morality and the rejection of obscenity. It is largely the heat of such a struggle that engenders the asceticism characteristic of so much monotheism in its earlier developments.

With the Exile, however, the fight, so far from gaining success, actually lost, owing to the increment of exotic influences. From the indignant descriptions in Isaiah 57 and Ezekiel 6 it is evident that the fertility cult had become unrestrained in Palestine during its Captivity. Ezekiel (8:14) sees the women bewailing Tammuz in the very gates of Jerusalem. And in postexilic times a development of the fertility cult had become settled into the Judaistic ritual in the inauguration of the feast of Purim, with its quasi-historical aetiological myth, the Book of Esther.[14]

We have said that with the advance of civilization the slaying of the divine king had become sublimated into the slaying of a captive substituting for the king. Mexico in Aztec times never got beyond this stage. But in Mesopotamia and Rome the captive became simply a temporary clown, brought in to inaugurate a period of carnival in which, as symbolic of his mock kingship, servants ordered around their masters, and a general air of substitution prevailed. In this event, so far from slaughtering a wretched captive, a condemned criminal would actually be released to serve as clown. This festival was called the Saturnalia with the Romans and the Sacaea with Babylonians, and the Jewish Purim is essentially the same thing. Esther may or may not be a historical reminiscence, but in any case Esther and Mordecai are in all probability Ishtar and Marduk, the great Isis and Osiris of Babylon. The Haman who wanted to hang Mordecai and got hanged himself is the luckless sham king, with his triumphal procession frustrated and given to the real king. The Purim feast was acknowledged to be one of relaxation of emotions, and even as late as the Middle Ages Jews on Purim day would kidnap and hang or crucify a Christian child in the character of Haman.

Now we have enough evidence for an exceedingly plausible and interesting hypothesis: was Jesus crucified in the character of Haman? There is nothing shocking in the idea, except insofar as it illustrates the symbolic in addition to the historical mockery of the Christ and his rejection of men. Here was a captive, charged with proclaiming himself King of the Jews. He had had a triumphal procession through Jerusalem, like the clown-king; he had overthrown the seats of the money-changers in the Temple, quite in character with a Saturnalia. What more obvious than to crucify him in the same role? Hence, the crown of thorns and the mock-ing salutation of "Hail! King of the Jews!"; hence, the inscription over his head on the Cross; hence, the custom of releasing a prisoner. Frazer sug-gests that Barabbas was released as the clown-king;[15] had Jesus been released he would have been compelled to undergo a gauntlet of undig-nified but fairly harmless horseplay. An objection is, of course, that Jesus was mocked by the Roman soldiers; but the Roman soldiers may have been provincial Syrians, and, if not, the Romans themselves knew all about the Saturnalia, which in the Danube frontier provinces was fre-quently a human sacrifice and not a carnival. In the Passion stories per-haps the cursing of the barren fig tree is an unobtrusive underscoring of the fertility motive. It also seems logical to associate, as Chesterton sug-gests, the slaughter of the innocents with the passing of the old world as a last despairingly ferocious gesture.[16] More and more one becomes con-vinced that the establishing of an integration of the historical and sym-bolic implications of the supreme sacrifice is a task of imminent and overwhelming importance for the Christian apologist today.

Long before this, however, the world of the eastern Mediterranean had become sufficiently advanced culturally to grasp the idea, for its religious life, of abstract recurrence rather than simply the recurrence of concrete experiential data. Consequently, the various myths of recur-rence begin to coincide in a single idea. The periodically disappearing fertility god is parallelled with the periodically vanquished but perenni-ally arising sun-god. Sun worship is a study by itself, with which we are not concerned except when it joins with the fertility cults in the abstract conception of a temporary descent into the world of darkness or death and arrival again into light or life, whichever the protagonist is. But with fertility worship sun worship establishes a double relationship: it estab-lishes a common factor and a relation of tension or antithesis.

First, for the common factor: religion develops the doctrine that the human soul, like the forces of nature, has to disappear into darkness and be reborn. This is the central idea behind all Greek religion, which, as inward life rather than as purely superficial cultus, was essentially a religion of initiation or purgatorial progression through difficulties and dangers to the full awakening of the spirit. The Orphic and Eleusinian mysteries are based on this idea, and the fact that the purgatorial pro-gression consists in a search for the lost Kore and culminates with the symbolic act of sowing an ear of corn shows its fertility origin. In the same way the rise of purgatorial literature among the Jews, the growth of eschatology and apocalyptic, the various symbols of the katabasis such as we find in Jonah and Daniel, the developments of the ideas of the Suffering Servant and the Son of Man, illustrate the same process.

Now for the antithesis: the sun is a purely transcendent force; the fertility of the earth an essentially immanent one. Even when the gods of the classical pantheon had yielded place to Mithra and Attis, the complete fusion did not take place because of the tension between solar and chthonic ideas. Pantheism is the religious heresy resulting from an overemphasis on either a transcendent or an immanent God, without attempting to maintain the eternal tension between them, and paganism is essentially pantheistic. The Christian doctrine of the Trinity not only retains the paradox, but supplies the missing link in Jesus, the God-man who was at once hanged on a tree as the god of the trees incarnate, and stretched on the Cross in the radiating posture of the sun-god. Christ is the chasmogamous opening of Judaism from history into symbol, and the focusing, looking at him the other way, of all symbolic religious and artistic aspirations in historical actuality.

In the above I have implicitly identified the God immanent with the Holy Spirit. This conception is said to be in genesis a female principle, as Isis was to the son-god Horus and the father-god Osiris. Catholicism replaced the abstract doctrine with the poetically far apter idea of the brooding Mother of God, the Madonna, like the earth mother maternal but inviolate.

I have spoken of the fertility and solar cults as bound up with the symbolic rather than the historical expression of religion. This means that what it may lack in the moral approach to the good it makes up in the aesthetic, for the unit of art is the symbol. It is now rapidly becoming a commonplace of literary criticism that out of the pagan rites—chiefly the chthonic ones—were born the great rhythmic and communal art forms, music and drama, the essence of all objective art, forming a sort of corolla of the liturgy. The cultus begins with the spasmodic actions of sympathetic magic, leaping in the air to make the crops grow higher, walking in a processional circle to isolate a sacred area in enchantment, inarticulate ecstatic cries, and so on, gradually developing into a ritual dance, generally intended to re-enact the adventures of the god invoked. Out of this ritual dance grows a disciplined and mature drama. Tragedy was originally a goat sacrifice, like the Jewish scapegoat offering to Azazel,[17] the goat being an incarnation of Dionysus, and Dionysiac ecstasy being the primary impetus of Greek creative activity. The fall of the tragic hero is in essence the death of the sacrificial victim. For the hero is the incarnation of the aspiring ego, the desire of man for self-apotheosis, and his fall brings the profound cathartic reaction of a reabsorption into society, like Samson (an important but frequently overlooked example of a sacrificial victim) justified by death. Maud Bodkin says in her entertaining book:

> If, as I suggest, the spiritual power, which the philosopher analysing his poetic experience is constrained to represent, be conceived psychologically as the awakened sense of our common nature in its active emotional phase, then our exultation in the death of Hamlet is related in direct line of descent to the religious exultation felt by the primitive group that made sacrifice of the divine king or sacred animal, the representative of the tribal life, and, by the communion of its shed blood, felt that life strengthened and renewed. Hamlet, though he dies, is immortal, because he is the representative and creature of the immortal life of the race. He lives, as he desired to live, in the story with which he charged Horatio—and us who, having participated in that story, descend from the poetic ecstasy to draw breath again in the harsh world of our straitened separate personalities.[18]

But if tragedy develops from the sacrifice, should not comedy develop from the idea of the mock or substituted king, with its archetype the carnival? Dr. Richards says in his *Principles of Literary Criticism*: "The breaking-down of undesirable attitudes is normally part of the total response to a comedy."[19] This is a very cautious generalization, but I believe that a theory of comedy to be at all adequate would have to presuppose as the comic essence the exposure of a sham, the unreal deliberately but deliberately unsuccessfully substituted for the real.

In the same way the plastic arts, basically iconic, develop: from images and cave drawings which attempt to control the god by making an image of him, sculpture and painting take their origin.

This, of course, explains why the Hebrews gave so unique a contribution to culture and yet ignored the specifically cultural: the development of the arts. Job is too late and cosmopolitan a production to pass as representative Hebrew drama; the Yahwists abhorred the plastic arts; all the prophets attacked idols and Amos at least attacked architecture ("the great houses" [3:15]) as well. It preserved, however, through the Chronicler, an unusually strong interest in music, and so enabled Christianity, when music and drama were reborn in the womb of the Church, to develop the only systematic tradition of music the world has ever seen.

The pagan rites were a matrix of art, and of science as well, for science, as I have suggested in opposition to Frazer, develops from magic and occultism. The magical element in the rites is obvious enough; but not so occultism, as that development can take place only when paganism has finally reduced itself to its ultimate antithesis of earth worship and sky worship. Yet what is astrology but the forcing of the sun-gods to serve human speculations, or alchemy but the wresting of the quintessence of earth for man's use? But the fertility rites, important as they were, by themselves, unaided by Judaism, would have failed. To progress, to save his soul or ameliorate his condition, man must live in time and must have an intuitive grasp of the meaning of time-existence. A religion focused on an historical Incarnation, thus, automatically distinguishes itself, as a religion of progress and challenge to life, from all others. And fertility religions are focused on the pure present; they move from season to season without advance in right living. By their periodic stimulation of the appetites and their value as an exhaust valve of energy they can continue indefinitely, but their ultimate futility can bring nothing but the unutterable weariness we find settling down on the late pagan world.

"Thou wast wearied with the length of thy way; yet saidst thou not, It is in vain: thou didst find a quickening of thy strength; therefore thou wast not faint."

Bibliography

Frazer, Sir James: *The Golden Bough*, 12 vols., esp. *The Dying God* and *Adonis, Attis, Osiris.* [London: Macmillan, 1907–15]

Frazer, Sir James: *Folklore in the Old Testament*, 3 vols. [New York: Macmillan, 1923]

Chesterton, G.K.: *The Everlasting Man.* [London: Hodder and Stoughton, 1925]

James, E.O.: *Primitive Ritual and Sacrifice.*[20]

Bodkin, Maud: *Archetypal Patterns in Poetry.* [London: Oxford University Press, 1934]

Cornford, [Francis M.]: *Origins of Attic Comedy.* [Cambridge: Cambridge University Press, 1914]

Nietzsche, F.: *The Birth of Tragedy.* [3rd ed. New York: Macmillan, 1923]

Calverton, V.F. (ed.): *The Making of Man.* [New York: Modern Library, 1931]

Harrison, Jane: *Themis*. [Cambridge: Cambridge University Press, 1912]

Weston, Jessie L.: *From Ritual to Romance*. [Cambridge: Cambridge University Press, 1920]

Tylor, E.B.: *Primitive Culture*[: *Researches into the Development of Mythology, Philosophy, Religion, Language, Art, and Custom*. 5th ed. 2 vols. London: John Murray, 1913]

Driver, [S.R.]: *Introduction to the* [*Literature of the*] *Old Testament*. [New York: Scribner, 1913]

Oesterley, [W.O.E.] and [Theodore Henry] Robinson: *Hebrew Religion*. [New York: Macmillan, 1931]

Lods, Adolphe: *Israel*. [London: Routledge and Kegan Paul, 1932]

6

The Jewish Background
of the New Testament:
An Essay in Historical Apocalyptic

Determining the course for which Frye wrote this paper is complicated by the fact that on the cover sheet Frye entitled the paper "The Jewish Background of the Old Testament." (The "New Testament" title appears on the first page.) What is certain is that the paper was written for Professor Richard Davidson, who taught Old Testament literature and exegesis at Emmanuel College and served as principal of Emmanuel, 1932–44. Emmanuel required all students to take two general courses in Old Testament, 1a and 2a, "The History, Literature, and Religion of the Old Testament in Outline"—courses in which Frye enrolled during his first and second years at Emmanuel. Although "The Jewish Background" was written for Professor Davidson, it could have been, as the title suggests, submitted for a New Testament course. In this case Professor Davidson would have read the paper for one of his colleagues, which was an occasional practice. The subject of the paper would not, of course, preclude its having been written for Old Testament 1a, 2a, or 4d, the last a special topics course in the Old Testament Frye took during his second year. But the best evidence for situating the essay comes from a statement in the essay itself: "it is no accident," Frye says, "that a philosophy of history did not enter the world until Christianity did. This problem can be worked out only by thinkers in the tradition of a true religion, a proposition we have shown in some detail elsewhere." The "elsewhere" is almost certainly in his paper on Augustine, which Frye wrote during his final year at Emmanuel (1935–36). The best inference, then, appears to be that he wrote two papers for New Testament 4g, "Early Christianity": "An Augustinian Interpretation of History" and the present paper. Frye received an "A" for the paper, the typescript of which is in the NFF, 1991, box 37, file 13.

The *Golden Bough* is admitted on all sides to be a magnificent piece of scientific research and perhaps the most important and influential book written by an Englishman since the *The Origin of Species*. Certainly Frazer has, aided by what must be something very like a regiment of assisting field workers, compiled a huge nineteenth-century *Anatomy of Melancholy* for which all lovers of *quidquid agunt homines*[1] will be grateful. But, as one bores his way along the shelf of books, one is conscious of the Macaulay-like tone of the supercilious middle-class Victorian contemplating the wasteful and gloomy pageant of history, which cuts under the majestic piling up of details and illustrations with the cheap sarcasms of a second-hand Voltaire. It may perhaps be said, without undue presumption, that Frazer in establishing his thesis has been far more aware of its extent than of its depth. We are dealing with forces which, while they appear outwardly in absurd and generally repulsive antics of savages, constitute inwardly a powerful evolutionary impulse which has given us everything we hold valuable today. Consequently, it is very disappointing to come to the twelfth volume and find that Frazer's inferences from his investigations toward a philosophy of history are only a rehash of that incorrigible sentimentalist among philosophers, Auguste Comte. It appears that history moves through three stages.[2] First, the magical era, when man tries to control nature by forces of attraction and sympathetic response. Second, the religious, when he gives this up and throws himself on the mercy of an imaginary supernatural deity. (Frazer does not say in so many words that the latter is purely imaginary, but one is irresistibly reminded of Spinoza's aside to God as recorded by Voltaire: "Mais je crois, entre nous, que vous n'existez pas.")[3] Third, the scientific, when man advances from superstition and tyranny to fashion for himself, through his knowledge of what natural forces actually are, a Utopia or Golden Age, to start approximately from the time of writing. This scheme reminds one of Chesterton's remark about the Victorians who turned all human records into one of their own three-volume novels, sure that it would end happily because it was ending with the Victorians.[4] I take the liberty of saying that Frazer's philosophy of history seems to me a bourgeois shibboleth quite as obsolete as any magical formula discussed in his book. Granted the advance from magic to science, the transition could take place only through some form of activity, psychologically identical with both (which by Frazer's own confession religion is not), which could actually represent a consolidation of magic into a matrix for science. This I should take to be, not religion or any form of it, but occultism, the development of alchemy and astrology, which extends from those mysterious centuries preceding the birth of Christ to the breakdown of the medieval world. This activity, the attempt to control the forces of nature, is a constant and unbroken one from primitive times to our own. Religion is another matter altogether: it is not correctly defined as a negative and passive submission to an overmastering will. Religion is the definite and organized attempt to gain an integration of all the faculties of the soul, including the knowledge of the outer world afforded by science, but where science deals with phenomena, religion struggles with the noumena lying behind them, the forces of absolute reality which we cannot know, but can experience. The religious impulse is as perennial and unbroken as the scientific, and the two run parallel in all ages. Perhaps if we continue to juggle these wide generalizations about history, we may think of religion, too, as advancing in three stages, suggesting that the religious attitude called pagan is a necessary background to magic, providing as it does a sort of pantheistic naturalism; that the religious attitude called Catholic is a necessary background to occultism, and that the religious attitude called Protestant is a necessary background to science.

We still have our three-volume novel, however, though perhaps in better proportions. History cannot be viewed purely as a linear progression of indefinite advance, and we have to postulate another factor before our evidence can be laid down. Human life is a biological growth, and it is subject to certain definite life-rhythms. The organic unit of history is the culture, just as the species is in biology, and all cultures go through definite biological stages of growth, maturation, and decay. From a childhood in which its population is thoroughly communal in spirit, rooted in the soil and naive and buoyant in outlook, the culture advances through a development of cities to a late metropolitan period of civilization, with a completely discriminated individuality, an imperialism allied to a technical and industrial society, a disillusioned and sophisticated critical intelligence. Thus, if we take our own culture and compare with it the other we know best—the classical—a parallel growth is obvious. The *Iliad* and the Norse sagas, the *Odyssey* and Dante, the Dionysian revival and our Renaissance, the city states like Athens and the culture-towns like Florence or Nuremberg, Aristotle and Kant, Alexandrine and Napoleonic imperialism, the shift of power westward from Greece to Rome, and from Europe to America, the disaffection of the Roman proletariat and the modern labourer, the rise of Caesarism and of Fascism: there are literally thousands of illustrations to show the morphological nature of civilization.[5]

This long preamble is neither padding, digression, nor the riding of a hobby: it is a necessary and basic postulate for the twentieth-century Christian who wishes to justify his religion. Christianity presupposes, in claiming what it does for Jesus, that human life is bound to a cyclic rhythm of organic movement from birth to death. Christian philosophy of history is based on Augustine's distinction between the *civitas Dei* and the *civitas terrena,* and Augustine was enabled to understand the nature of the latter only by the realization that the Roman empire which was at that time its basis had fallen to pieces in decay and that all history, viewed in retrospect, is the rise and fall of empires. It is only after we have grasped this principle that we are in a position to see the unique contribution made by Christianity. For the whole point about the Incarnation, from the purely historical point of view, is that it came at the first genuine interpenetration of cultures of which history had up to that time given evidence.[6]

It is, of course, manifest, from what we have said, that at that time classical culture was in a very late stage of development: much later than anything we have reached in our own. The *pax Romana*, which had began to coalesce by the time of the first triumvirate, was achieved not so much by the strength of Roman arms as by the weakness and exhaustion of a dying Mediterranean world. The Roman legions could conquer disorganized tribes, but they did not win many pitched battles. Except for the Jews, they met with little resistance throughout Asia and Africa: the King of Pergamos left his kingdom to Rome in his will. When they encountered people of more virility, such as the Germans or the Parthians, they were cut to pieces. Now Judaism itself was contemporary with classical culture. The Hebrews had settled Palestine probably about the time that the great Doric migrations took place in Greece, a movement which directly caused the influx of Philistines from the Aegean. Thus considered, Israel was in many respects an outlying flange of the Mediterranean world. The association of Caiaphas and Pilate was a perfectly natural one. The intellectual life of the Jews was absorbed into the general diffusion of Hellenistic culture over the Mediterranean from Alexandria. Alexandria and Jerusalem were politically subject to Rome: Rome and Jerusalem were culturally subject to Alexandria. For this fusion of Jewish and Mediterranean traditions the Sadducees seem most clearly to have stood. The Sadducees were aristocrats and intellectuals with a wide cosmopolitan view: Jews like Philo in Alexandria are to be more closely aligned with them than with any other party.[7] They read and studied Greek: the note of Pyrrhonic and Epicurean scepticism which we find in Ecclesiastes we find in their quizzing of Jesus, obviously a provincial attempt to imitate the wit and brilliance of the Athenian agora: though possibly it would appear to better advantage against a less formidable antagonist. On the other hand, the national consciousness of Judaea, the sense of discrimination against foreigners, we find represented in the Pharisees, the middle class who followed the Jewish law, ritual, and tradition. The antithesis of Sadducee and Pharisee is one to which the opposition of Anglican and Puritan in English history may perhaps offer a rough analogy. The Sadducees supported the ruling classes and took their ritual more or less for granted; the Pharisees represented the earnest, zealous patriotism of the bourgeoisie, an unimaginative but powerful conviction of the necessity of salvation in obeying the Word of God. The left wing of such a class would be the revolutionaries or Jacobins (this last word has an interesting overtone)[8] of the time, anxious for political independence and national unity, such as we find in the Zealots. Now both Sadducees and Pharisees agreed in the fact that they represented an ancient and achieved tradition. They drew different inferences from the same premise: arguments for a Jewish contribution to Hellenism or for Jewish exclusiveness both rested on the postulate that Judaea had as long, honourable, and disciplined a culture as any in the world.

Jesus plunged himself into this late, weary, ultrasophisticated world, fought it, destroyed it by his death as Samson destroyed the Philistines. He was steeped in its culture: better than the Sadducees he knew that the rule of Rome was to be preferred to revolt; better than the Pharisees he knew the law and the prophets. But this is the world of Jerusalem, a metropolitan world, and Jesus' roots were in Galilee, in the country, close to the soil. Undoubtedly the Zealots must have presented a powerful and subtle temptation to him, just as Communism presents a powerful and subtle temptation today to any Christian with a passionate sense of social justice. But he did not join the Zealots; and though he was in Jerusalem he was not of it: he went there expressly to carry out the inexorable opposition between the Roman-Judaean civilization and what he stood for to its logical extreme of martyrdom. We have to look for some other force to explain his victory, and that brings us straight to the heart of our problem.

In the life of the time we have carefully to distinguish another rhythm of cultural development. The Books of Samuel and Kings give us a steady and logical progression from the primitive warfare under Saul to the decadent prosperity under Jeroboam II;[9] but as soon as we strike Amos, Hosea, Isaiah, we are conscious of a new strength, not an old civilization turning uneasily in its sleep, but a young, powerful, original life-unity, which becomes more evident when we collate this movement with the rise of Chaldea and Persia on the ruins of the Assyrian empire and the monotheistic tendency of Amos and Hosea with Nebuchadnezzar's passionate adoration of Marduk, and the rise of Zoroastrianism in Persia. Monotheism is, in fact, the keynote of this development, the dawning of full and conscious belief in one principle of good in the world. The Behistun inscription of Darius[10] recalls the loftiest sentiments of the prophets, if we could imagine a prophet living in a proud and victorious empire, stretching from the Danube to the Red Sea, rather than a crushed and humiliated province. In this new movement there was little place for older civilizations: Nineveh was wiped out, Jerusalem followed; and within the walls of Jerusalem Jeremiah was urging submission to Chaldea, the agent of God. Later Judaea's greatest prophet, Deutero-Isaiah, hails Cyrus as a messiah. Possibly the friendly relations between Persia and Judaea resulted from religious affinities.

This young culture was necessarily a culture of the country rather than of the city. Israel recoiled from the decadent splendours and tolerant theocrasia of Solomon's court through popular prejudice, and the mere fact that this prejudice could be exploited by a brigand like Jehu[11] with such complete success shows how strong it was. The prophets were the spokesmen of the popular sentiment, and an opposition grew up between the older tradition at Jerusalem and the more powerful feeling outside it which is reflected in the bitter antagonism of the priestly to the prophetic utterances, which increases all through the postexilic period and culminates in the treacherous murders of the prophets or any spokesmen of religious feeling not in direct sympathy with vested interests. Even a canonical prophet like Zechariah was murdered, Jesus tells us [Luke 11:51]; Malachi had to write anonymously;[12] John the Baptist was murdered [Matthew 14:6–11]; and the Crucifixion scene brings to us more vividly than anything else the deep-rooted hatred and bitterness between Jerusalem, with its history founded on Moses, Samuel, and David, its metropolitan mob, its monopoly of learning and priestcraft, its catholic claim to be the religious centre of all Jewry, and the rising peasant culture of Galilee and Samaria, the devout religion of the Essenes and the Mandeans, the habit of thinking in the future rather than in the past tense, which was capitalized by apostolic Christianity.

After, or along with, the prophetic sagas came an outburst of folklore and legend. What is genuinely ancient in Genesis, what goes back to the cultural origins of the Hebrews, is here re-echoed. The stories of Judith, Tobit, Susanna, Bel and the Dragon,[13] are as genuine and unmistakable folklore as we find anywhere, and it is evident that a new organic unity of thought and feeling is taking root. Compare Judith with Jael,[14] Susanna with Tamar,[15] the culture-hero Joseph ruling Egypt, divining Pharaoh's dreams, and tempted with adultery, with the culture-hero Daniel ruling Chaldea, divining Nebuchadnezzar's dreams, and tempted with loose living,[16] the origin of the Passover with the origin of Purim,[17] the traces of solar myth in Samson with the journey through the underworld of Jonah,[18] the fall of the angels in Genesis 4 and a more elaborate version in Enoch,[19] the forty years' desert wanderings of Israel and the forty days' desert wanderings of Christ [Exodus 16:35, Matthew 4:1–2]. Of course, it is impossible to say how much of this is a symbolic reworking of the earlier myths, or how much of the earlier legends has been by recension adapted to later forms of thinking: some interpenetration is certain, but the new growth is original and not a commentary.

But the new culture, young as it was, was, of course, far less naive and crude than the earlier: where the Pentateuch is superstitious and magical the Apocrypha is symbolic and esoteric. The outcropping of peasant superstition and legend, which is so remarkable a phenomenon, recalls a similar growth in medieval Europe during the Dark Ages: those immemorial myths of the gods of fertility and the heavenly bodies, of creation and the elements, of love and war, which spring up from the very bedrock of the human brain, all appear, but in a disguised and elaborated form. For this culture is, like the Western one, raised on the ruins of several ancient empires. Egypt and Mesopotamia were already shrouded in antiquity: Jews and Chaldeans alike treated the Babylonian records as classics. Genesis quotes as freely from the *Gilgamesh*[20] as Virgil does from Homer. The larger, more powerful, better disciplined traditions of Hellenism and Judaism caught many of these floating tales and gave them a form better in accord with their older spirit, just as Christianity caught the folklore of Europe and absorbed it into legends of saints, and varnished the immensely ancient romances of the Holy Grail cycle, which go back to the dawn of human intelligence, with a coating of Eucharistic and paschal symbolism. Even its earliest beginnings were cast, not in the form of epic or saga, but in the rhapsodic prophetic denunciations of society, which have an ethical interest imposed upon them by a restricting environment.

Now this complicated problem, of an old and moribund culture with a new fertile cycle in humanity pushing up through it, makes this period of history at once the most baffling and mysterious, and the most critically important, in the life of mankind. As a result of this crossing of rhythms, the Asiatic mind became aware of a movement in history, of a tide in the affairs of men,[21] of a curve of maturity and decadence. The seven centuries or so between Zoroaster and Jesus represent the coming of our historical tradition, that is, that of the occidental world, to full awareness, an advance from consciousness to self-consciousness, from a knowledge of the outer space-world of appearance to an experience of the inner time-world of reality. The transference of a tradition from one culture to another resulted in a genuine evolutionary "lift," which is as important to us as the access of intelligence itself at the close of the Tertiary age,[22] and is the only one that man has had in historic times. And it does not take the auto-suggestion of our system of chronology to see how it revolves around the figure of Jesus.

To prove this assertion would obviously be a colossal task, entailing a full treatment of the most complicated and difficult questions of history, philosophy, and theology. Yet I believe it to be the task Christian apologetics has to face in the coming century. Whole libraries have already been written on the development of religious thought through the prophets to Jesus, from the inflexible righteousness of Amos's God, through the long-suffering forbearance of Hosea's, the paternal solicitude of Isaiah's, and the lofty spirituality of Micah's, to the divergence at exilic times into Jeremiah's conception of a universal covenant transcending the nation, which is the fountainhead of apostolic Christianity, and Ezekiel's ideal nation state under Yahweh, which is the fountainhead of rabbinical Judaism. With Deutero-Isaiah we find the idea of the transcendent creator God in the text, and the suffering of the servant of God as the only possible sacrifice in the Ebed-Jahwe Songs,[23] which together give us the first unified statement of the Christian program. Then throughout the Apocrypha, and more particularly in the Book of Enoch, the conception of the redeeming Son of Man takes on a more definite form.[24] By the time Jesus came to the world all the intellectual preparation necessary to receive him had been achieved. This general evolution has been traced too often for me to scrape its outlines any further here. It remains to view it in its proper historical perspective, and that implies a careful investigation of the two great rhythms in history, the culture-growth and the evolutionary development of the species.

Montefiore, after a thorough analysis of Jesus' teaching in relation to the thought of his time, claims that our Lord taught no new doctrines, and that he was intellectually a fine but quite typical product of Judaism, all his sayings being as clearly or as loftily stated elsewhere.[25] I cannot see why any Christian should be concerned to deny this: had Jesus taught any new doctrines, he would have represented an irruption into his environment, an accidental anachronism as little connected with the scheme of things in the world as a shooting star. The greatest man is not the man who runs out of step with his time, but the man who most completely sums it up in himself: which is why the conception of the prophet as an oracle who foretells future events is so vulgar. The Christian's point about Jesus is not that he advanced a new theory, but that he brought a new strength: it is not by virtue of what was said about the regeneration of mankind through belief in God, but by virtue of what was actually done about it, that Christianity claims to be a fulfilment rather than a divagation from the Jewish tradition. Because of the actual historical outcome of the situation, the critical and crucial position of Jesus in this development remains unshaken. But we can never arrive at any rational comprehension of how Jesus was enabled to work the miracle he did if we assume that he lived purely in the dying Judaistic world. The culture he represented was a vigorous pullulating culture in the springtime of its development, analogous in many respects to our own medieval period. We find an intense communal and mystical spirit of piety and devotion in the Essenes,[26] or in the primitive Christian Church which resembles the Essene movement in many ways, who belong to a genuine religious order such as we find in the Middle Ages. St. John the Baptist is a sort of St. Dominic of this rising spirit; Jesus, as far as his Galilean period is concerned, is its St. Francis.[27] The Galileans who followed Jesus, the crowds of Mandeans[28] and other sects who heard John the Baptist, were moving in an utterly different time-rhythm from the Judaeans. Jerusalem culture was engaged in winding up its long tradition of creative literature in a shroud of criticism and commentary; it is learned, sophisticated, and complex, like our literature today. Outside there were growing up such bewilderingly and hauntingly beautiful stories, such as the Matthew and Luke accounts of Jesus' birth; and to find a parallel to this we have again to go back to the Middle Ages. It was this sprouting energy that fostered apostolic Christianity; without it its incredibly rapid spread in the first century is incomprehensible.

It is, of course, impossible in practice always to distinguish a phenomenon belonging to the younger culture from one belonging to the older, when the former is based on its predecessor and derives many of its modes of expression from it. Our general thesis is, we have said, that the transfer of energy from the culture that starts from Moses to the culture that starts from the prophets brought about a saltation in human experience. The advance from primitive religion to monotheism is, we have also said, inductive and gradual. Man works with a double world: the outer world of appearance and the inner world of reality. The former is the world of perception; the latter the world of existence. Man can realize this inner world in his own subjective experience; and he can infer it from the moving of forces in the world of perception which change it independently of his will. Religion is concerned with piercing through the picture-world of sense experience to the transcendent energy which underlies it: this is the whole psychological basis of communion, whether conscious or subconscious. In western Asia man had slowly advanced from purely materialistic communion, in which through a feast two kinds of material energy, subject and object, are interfused, to the realization that the outer world is a cosmos and that the creative force behind it a unity. He is led to infer the cosmos through his observation of the phenomenon of recurrence. Man lives and dies, and when he dies there is an end to him. He can originate another life, but that life is not his. The universe, however, transcends man because it is continually dying and being reborn. The sun dies every day and is reborn; vegetable life dies every year and is reborn; the moon dies every month and is reborn; rivers flow continually into the sea but are continually replenished at their source. All art, we have seen, originates in man's attempt to express this rhythm of recurrence. Now the world of perception is a space-world; we cannot perceive anything that dissolves or alters during perception: all forms of knowledge are timeless. The inner world of existence, on the other hand, is the time-world of experience, so that the comprehension of the unity of energy which motivates the cosmos implies a consciousness of a temporal force in the world.

The Hebrew prophets were intellectually aware of the fact that God was eternal and immutable; but they worshipped him primarily as the source or principle of continuous dynamic energy. For monotheism is, after all, only a prelude to theism. God for them was fundamentally a God of power. It is important to recognize here the difference between the reaction a young and vigorous culture would naturally make to the discovery of a unified force actuating the world and the reaction of an old and tired one. The writer of Ecclesiastes thinks of the phenomenon of recurrence negatively, as a cyclic repetition of activities without a creative faculty implied.[29] The spirit of this book is not far removed from the Pharisaic doctrine of the immutability of the divine law. Differ as they may in dogmatic details, the monotheists of the priestly code of Judaism saw little if anything of Jesus' point that the stability given us through our belief in one God enables us to conceive the present as continuous; we look at the lilies and realize that every moment there is something new under the sun. That is why the conception of monotheism had to be transferred to a newer culture to come down to us as it has.

If God is the creative energy of the cosmos, then he is revealed in our own experience, which is part of that energy. It was the realization of this fact that brought about the transference in prophetic thought of the religious act from the physical to the spiritual. In the days of the sacrificial rite, men achieved communion with a god by literally taking the life of a victim in whom the god was conceived to be incarnate. According to the monotheist discovery, there is one God who is a factor in our life; consequently, religion is bound to become a sacrifice and rebirth of the soul. This, of course, fits in with the awakening apprehension of recurrence: God as a purely transcendent force is superior to us because his works die and are reborn; but if he exists in us spiritually, then it is necessary for us spiritually to die and be reborn in order to achieve communion with him.

All this is exceedingly elementary theology; but I am not so sure how far as yet it is the elementary datum of historical interpretation and art criticism that it ought to be. That it is the only possible explanation of the fact that tragedy produces a catharsis in the spectator seems to me obvious. It implies, of course, that in the death of the soul man passes through suffering; and it is in the discovery of the purgative and redeeming nature of that suffering that the prophetic tradition fulfilled its mission.

The literature of the pre-Christian period is basically a literature of purgation and katabasis. The dark night of the soul, as the mystics call it; the entry into a lower state of existence in order to free the higher nature and leave the baser behind: the passage through some sort of physical ordeal: this is the keynote of the imaginative work of the time. Jonah's descent into the fish's belly; Daniel's descent into the lion's den; the three men in the fiery furnace; the lycanthropy of Nebuchadnez-zar;[30] all these are well-known initiation symbols. It does not require any especial pro-Christian hypostatizing to see how all this feeling converges upon the logical necessity for the death and resurrection of a Christ. For the fact of death in the world, even if it lead directly to a rebirth, shows that this purgatorial progression of spirit is as true of the spirit of God as of man. That is the basis of Zoroastrianism; the necessity for God to struggle with and overcome a principle of death and suffering. The theme of ethical dualism, of an adversary of God, runs through much apocryphal thought: Asmodeus in Tobit, Abaddon and Apollyon in Revelation,[31] Lucifer and Satan in the Gospels, are instances: historically it works through to the Gnostic and Manichean heresies. Christianity being steeped in such conceptions, it took to Europe a somewhat adventitious personal devil, who was much exploited by folklore but never really absorbed into Christian thought. The far subtler conception really at the heart of Christianity, which we can trace in Enoch and the Servant Songs of Isaiah, starts by drawing a clear distinction between the human and the divine natures; the former being subject to death but the latter not, a distinction resolved by the Incarnation.

But this development of the idea of purgative suffering, necessary as it is to make the historical transilience we postulate, is not yet the central focus of our problem. We have not yet accounted for the unique contribution of the Judaistic background of Jesus. Orphism[32] in Greece had, albeit aided considerably by Asiatic influences, reached essentially the same idea. The fact remains throughout that the rising culture of western Asia arose on a basis of a consolidated and disciplined older tradition of Judaism. Now with Judaism religion was essentially monolatrous, and the importance of this fact just at this point is that, as Yahweh was primarily the god of the Jewish nation, he was deeply and intimately concerned with the fortunes of the people. We have spoken of the prophetic culture as representing the advent of a time-consciousness, making experience self-conscious, or aware of its own progression. And if we add to this increment the older belief in the care and solicitude of Yahweh for his people, the result is the growth of a *historical* sense.

In the codification of Judaistic traditions humanity learns for the first time to view the present as a moving point between the past and the future. The literature of the period discussed is marked, first, by an extraordinary concentration on the past, which gives us our earliest philosophy of history; second, by an equally intense interest in the future, which gives it its eschatological and apocalyptic aspect: prophecy in the secondary sense of the word.

In a philosophy of history there are necessary the two postulates we have laid down: the human and the divine progressions. The former we have declared to be the growth and decay of a cultural unit, more familiarly phrased as the rise and fall of empires. The latter is the inexplicable progress from one plane of living to a higher which postulates an eternally creative activity transcending our own powers. All this is implicit in the prophetic philosophy, though at first it took a necessarily crude form, in the proposition inevitable to monolatry: all the other nations would be destroyed, but Israel would advance indefinitely. To this period belong Amos's denunciations of the nations [Amos 1–6], and, on a much more extended scale, the "burdens" of Isaiah, which culminate in the terrible but magnificent pandemonium scene in which the demons of the waste are dancing on the ruins of Babylon, while below them the departed spirits mock the city's conquered king [Isaiah 13–14]. To this stage of thought must be assigned the nationalistic Messiah, the invincible Jew who was to reestablish the prestige of the kingdom of David. All three Maccabees were hailed as Messiah in turn;[33] Jesus' lineage had to be traced back to David; various fanatics fomented national uprisings against Rome. The supporters of this theory argued that Israel's eventual success was assured because of a covenant made between God and his people. But even in Amos the inference is drawn that it takes two to keep a covenant, and that if God could not break it Israel could; and after the Exile a new culture which was more cosmopolitan than Judaism developed a better idea.

Naturally, though the historical argument rested on the past, the emphasis was thrown on the future. The development from the naive jingoism of the Jewish patriots tended to see the establishment of a universal kingdom on the ruins of empires. Thus, in Daniel we have the superb vision of the passing away of the successive attempts at world unification, and the advent of an eternal kingdom of God on earth. This gradually focused on the eschatological conception proper, which expanded to their widest limits the two data of a philosophy of history we have mentioned: the culture-unit and the evolutionary advance. The apocalyptic writers were able to grasp the tremendous panorama of a world passing through the purgatorial progression: the Satanic millennium in Revelation means this. Out of the complete collapse of world empires, symbolized by the author, following Isaiah, as Babylon, the Last Judgment, the purging of all the time-world, would take place.

This movement is too complicated for us to do more than mention it here; but so far we have dealt only with the expansion of the idea of the dying and reborn world. The concreteness and definiteness of outlook which would carry eschatology into the realm of reality was afforded, again, by the historical consciousness of the time. More or less unconsciously, as a result of the impact of the prophetic culture on the Judaistic, the apocalyptic conception of the Last Judgment and the nationalistic conception of the historical destiny of the people of Israel fused into a sense of something imminent and tremendous about to take place in history.

Man cannot live ultimately without some sort of ideals; and all deliberately chosen good actions rest on the postulate that nothing tending toward the good is wasted, and that, therefore, a good action is a positive contribution toward the actualizing of an ideal. Now with a historical consciousness this implies a sense of a development or evolutionary progression in history transcending the cycle of fertility. But this progression is not a gradual ascent; otherwise it would be the only rhythm in history. It is necessary to think of it as proceeding by creative discontinuous efforts to break away from the fertility cycle. And as soon as man became historically conscious, the necessity for such a "lift" became self-evident, and for the conscious idea to result in a program of action the Incarnation was necessary. But a philosophy of history is the ultimate or metamorphic theoretical activity of the human race as it exists today. All organized knowledge, or science, no matter in what field, is of value only when it is coordinated into a philosophical system. Thus, philosophy is admittedly deeper and more fundamental than science. But no system is infallible, because it has simply gathered up the achievements and attitude of its own time. In its last essence it is a historical phenomenon; thus, the history of philosophy underlies abstract philosophy as the latter does science. But the history of philosophy is only a part of a universal history, which cannot be theoretically examined unless it contain certain fixed principles which will yield to analysis. This gives us the philosophy of history, and behind that we cannot go. Our first data of perception are time and space. But all knowledge is essentially space-knowledge, as it works with forms which, to be true, have to be independent of time, and all existence is in time, so that the most fundamental activity of knowledge is its relation to existence. And from what we have said, it is apparent that the doctrine of the Incarnation is the only datum which makes sense of the problem. For no one until the nineteenth century had any idea of the biological doctrine of evolution, and up to that time the Incarnation was the only point of reference to confirm men in their faith that, though life entails more suffering than happiness as a rule, it is still worthwhile. It is necessary for the intelligent Christian today to see the Incarnation as the coping stone of all development in life, biological as well as historical.

Immediately after the Incarnation, therefore, the new Christian philosophy of history arose, and in the New Testament the Pauline Epistles, the Epistle to the Hebrews, the Gospel of Matthew, and, with a reversion to an earlier mannerism, the Apocalypse, all see in the historical figure of Jesus the keystone of religion and philosophy, thus concentrating the crux of all thought in the world of time. And if this is what we have claimed it to be, the ultimate theoretical activity of the human race, it is no accident that a philosophy of history did not enter the world until Christianity did. This problem can be worked out only by thinkers in the tradition of a true religion, a proposition we have shown in some detail elsewhere.[34] The classical world had no philosophy of history. To Herodotus, history was essentially a saga; to Thucydides, a drama. The sense of a profound meaning or teleological purpose in the past, which we have inherited from the Jewish and Christian thinkers, was entirely lacking. Consequently, the Greek and Roman point of view was focused on the present as an absolute, not as a moving point in time. Thus, when St. Paul plunged into this static world, steeped in both Jewish and classical traditions, he brought the energy of his passionate conviction of Christ to the moulding and disciplining form of the world in which he moved. He had nothing to do with the prophetic culture of Asia; he worked in cities, not in villages as Jesus had.[35] The impact of the dynamic message of the Incarnation had the effect of galvanizing the Mediterranean world, so that the steady and unbroken advance of Christianity to conquer that world was inevitable from the beginning. Now that we again have reached a late stage of civilization, let us hope that we will be as fortunate, either in revitalizing our present tradition or in gaining a new one, through the awakened consciousness of the coming in glory of the Son of God.

Bibliography

James, E.O.: *Primitive Ritual and Sacrifice*.[36]

Frazer, Sir James: *The Golden Bough*, 12 vols., esp. *The Dying God* and *Adonis, Attis, Osiris*. [London: Macmillan, 1907–15]

Frazer, Sir James: *Folklore in the Old Testament*, 3 vols. [New York: Macmillan, 1923]

Gray, S. Buchanan: *Sacrifice in the Old Testament*. [Oxford: Clarendon Press, 1925]

Lods, Adolphe: *Israel*. [London: Routledge and Kegan Paul, 1932]

Lightley, [John William]: *Jewish Sects and Parties in the Time of Christ*. [*Jewish Sects and Parties in the Time of Jesus* (London: Epworth Press, 1925)]

Fairweather, [William]: *Jesus and the Greeks*. [Edinburgh: T. and T. Clark, 1924]

Charles, [R.H.]: *Religious Development between the Old and New Testaments*. [New York: Henry Holt, 1914]

Montefiore, C.E.: *The Old Testament and After*. [London: Macmillan, 1923]

Fairweather, [William]: *The Background of the Gospels*. [Edinburgh: T. and T. Clark, 1908]

Oesterley, [W.O.E.]: *Studies in Isaiah 40–66*. [London: Robert Scott, 1916]

Calverton, [V.F.] (ed.): *The Making of Man*. [New York: Modern Library, 1931]

Tylor, E.B.: *Primitive Culture*[: *Researches into the Development of Mythology, Philosophy, Religion, Language, Art, and Custom*. 5th ed. 2 vols. London: John Murray, 1913]

Robertson Smith, [William]: *Religion of the Semites*. [London: A. and C. Black, 1894]

Reinach, [Salomon]: *Orpheus: A History of Religions*. [New York: Liveright, 1932]

Oesterley, [W.O.E.] and [Theodore Henry] Robinson: *Hebrew Religion*. [New York: Macmillan, 1931]

Various articles in the *Encyclopaedia of Religion and Ethics*, *Encyclopaedia Britannica*, *Catholic Encyclopedia*.

7

The Age and Type of Christianity
in the Epistle of James

This paper was most likely written for Professor John Dow's New Testament 1 course, "Introduction to Textual Criticism and the Literature of the New Testament," which Frye took during the 1933–34 academic year. Frye received an "A" for the paper, the typescript of which is in the NFF, 1991, box 37, file 9.

The weight of modern scholarship seems to be on the side of a view which states that the Epistle of James dates approximately from the middle of the second century A.D., and, thus, was not written by James the brother of our Lord, but by someone else, either of the same name or pseudonymous. The readers of the Epistle are the "Twelve Tribes in the Dispersion," which has a Jewish sound, and the various expressions such as "Abraham our father" (2:21), and "Lord of sabaoth" (5:4), the references to the Old Testament traditions and scriptures (to Job in 5:11; to Elijah in 5:17; to Rahab in 2:25, etc.), the mention of a synagogue (2:2), and a Jewish respect for law (2:10) are positive arguments for a Jewish Christian public. Negative arguments stress the complete absence of the usual Christian dialectic concerning the Messianic claims of Christ, the glory of his Resurrection and the atoning power of his death, the zeal for expansion and evangelism of the primitive Christians, a cautionary and conservative note rather than the buoyant courage and optimism we should expect if the Epistle were really an echo of Pentecost. This is sometimes accounted for on the assumption that James was reticent and unwilling to insist too much on what he was afraid would merely antagonize and arouse ridicule in his hearers. Such appearance of compromise and shamefacedness with regard to the Christian gospel does not

compare James too favourably with Peter or Paul, and against the
Judaistic theory may be urged the lack of any explicit reference to the
Mosaic code or any Ebionite leanings[1] on the part of the author, and
the complete ignoring of the tremendous import of the Jewish–Gentile
controversy in the primitive Church. If the Epistle were really written
after the destruction of Jerusalem by Titus in 70 A.D., the notion that
James was addressing Jewish communities collapses at once. It seems
probable, then, that the type of Christianity reflected and presupposed
in the Epistle is not specifically Judaistic. The reference to Jewish traditions implies a fairly late and well-organized Christian community
which was aware of the background of Christianity and would be quite
reconciled to being addressed in terms which implied them to be the
ideal Israel, the elect of God, rather than the chosen race. Such a relationship is worked out by Matthew, and as that appears to be James's
favourite gospel (cf. reference in 5:12),[2] its tenets would be instinctive
with him.

We have spoken of the comparative lack of buoyant zeal and the general emphasis on the sententious and moralistic. James seems to be
addressing a community which had indefinitely postponed the hope of
an immediate second coming, such as we would expect to find in the
second century: people who still accepted the doctrine, but would not
allow it unduly to disarrange their affairs. James's reference to it (5:7–9)
gives it precisely the minatory emphasis which a fairly conservative
adjudicator of that time would be expected to advance. The people
addressed are advised with respect to their lives, on the assumption of
their indefinite continuance. The moral and social virtues are stressed
and moral and social vices condemned. Avarice is especially attacked,
and in words distinctly reminiscent of the great prophets Isaiah and
Amos (2:1 ff.; 5:1 ff.) James points out the dangers of encrusting the spiritual life with material possessions. There is no definite reference to the
communism of primitive Christianity; it is assumed that there are rich
and poor in Christian communities, and the attack is rather on the abuse
and idolatry of riches. It is rather unkind to suppose avarice a specifically Jewish vice; it is probable that James's words are as much as anything a literary convention borrowed from the prophets and the sayings
of Christ. Apparently, then, Christianity had gained some hold among
fairly solid and respectable citizens, and there was a growing belief in
the permanence and stability of a Church, which we would hardly get
till the eschatological fervour had subsided and the work of Paul had

been accomplished. This seems to be reflected in James's attack on the tendency to substitute the routine and ritual of Church work and membership for inward Christian living. Hence, the argument on the inefficacy of faith without works (2:14–26), and, on the other hand, the recognition of charity and generosity as important virtues of Christian society gradually becoming clerical (1:27; 2:15–16).

This leads to the larger criticism implicit in the distinction of James between the Church and the world. With the earlier apostolic writers the distinction was a positive one: by an act of faith men rose out of the world into a community of believers. With James and his second-century contemporaries it is negative, the Church being conceived as more a withdrawal from the world; not in an eremitical sense altogether, but a separation in which evangelism is conducted more by example than persuasion (1:27). It is really this change of attitude which underlies James's view of works as the test of faith. The era of argument, of the justification of the divinity of Jesus, the upward theological development of Paul, the note of apologetic and appeal to tradition, has waned. James is addressing Christians and Christians alone: people who take the ecumenical doctrines of the faith as they were at that time for granted and who need to be urged only to live up to that faith. Prayer, even, the private and individual nature of which had been insisted on by Christ himself, is judged purely with reference to its immediate and practical value (5:13 ff.).

Not that James lacks anything of subtlety or erudition. In fact, it is largely this that militates so strongly against the possibility of the authorship of our Lord's brother. References to the gospels, particularly the one in 5:12 to Matthew, are more obvious than actual references to the words of our Lord, and the utter lack of any personal knowledge of the historical Jesus or the note of reminiscence which could not possibly be kept out of anyone's advocacy of his own brother's religion, shows clearly enough that the kind of Christianity James is talking about has already lost the immediacy of Jesus' personal appeal. The book is of an unusual literary sophistication. The adoption of the epistolary form itself is in all probability a literary pose, as was common at that time. References have been traced which show James's familiarity, not only with the Old Testament, but even more, from a literary point of view, with the Old Testament Apocrypha, notably the Wisdom of Solomon and the book of Jesus ben Sirach, with Philo and with the development of New Testament thought.[3] Those who regard James's Epistle as early will consider that Paul in Romans, I Corinthians, and Galatians (cf. the argument in James 2:14–26, referred to above), Peter (I Peter), and the author of Hebrews (*vide* James 2:21 ff.) are referring to or quoting from James, but the general tone of literary allusiveness in the latter supports other evidence for a second-century date in assuming that James quoted from and referred to them. On the other hand, it does not seem to be quoted by anyone else before Origen, except by Hermas, ca. 150. (This is what Moffatt says, p. l;[4] apparently the long list of ante-Nicene quotations given by Mayor, p. cxxi,[5] do not bear examination.) The Epistle is the work of a man who had an easy command of Greek language and literature, who was acquainted with much of the best Greek thought, probably through Hellenistic commentary, and who preferred the Septuagint to the Massoretic text of the Old Testament. He can hardly, therefore, be addressing simple-minded or uneducated people, yet he does not sustain an argument. He is, thus, neither a theologian nor an evangelist, but a bishop of souls.

We have said that the conception of a permanent Church was beginning to take hold of the minds of Christians in the second century. James's Church would be, therefore, the central fact of Christian society, but not yet an elaborate organization. There are no bishops yet, only a distinction between elders, or men of approved experience and piety, and the rest of the congregation.

The history of the Epistle has been fitful. It has not had the high and undisputed rank equal to any of the Gospels, which it surely would have possessed from the first if it had been what Mayor claims it to be.[6] It narrowly missed an undeserved oblivion, along with the Epistles of Clement,[7] but a weight of tradition gradually accumulated behind it and propelled it into the canon. The high authority of James, deliberately invoked by the author (whether his name was James or not, the connection with Acts 15:13–32 is probably an argument for pseudonymity) at last bore fruit, and gave us the finest example of the sententious, pietistic, didactic literature of the second century, typically represented by the *Shepherd of Hermas* and the *Didache*,[8] the lull between St. John and Origen, a period of adjustment between the early hope of a second coming and the later ideal of the Catholic and apostolic Church.

See Commentaries by Ropes, Mayor, Knowling, Moffatt, and Hort.[9]

8

Doctrine of Salvation
in John, Paul, and James

This essay was written for Dr. John Dow, professor of New Testament at Emmanuel College. Frye enrolled in New Testament 2, "The Religion and Theology of Paul," during his second year (1934–35). At the end of the paper, Dow wrote, "v. interesting but suffers from the half truth of generalization." His other marks are recorded in the notes. Frye received an "A-" for the paper, the typescript of which is in the NFF, 1991, box 37, file 9.

The vitality of apostolic literature is almost entirely owing to the impetus given by Paul to a synthesis of philosophy and tradition to sustain the preaching of the new gospel. Without Paul, it is hardly too much to say that the message of Jesus might have been distorted, or lost altogether, through the indifference of Christians expecting a Parousia. As it was, however, Christian literature takes a sudden upward sweep through the Epistles and the Gospels, culminating in the Gospel of John, to subside for a time in the tracts, homilies, and pious discourses of a Church by that time settled, respectable, and already a bit smug, a literature of which James is the finest example. (The question of the date of the Epistle is, thus, begged at the outset.)

We have, therefore, Paul and James at opposed ends of a curve, and we should expect to find them more or less antithetical. McNeile calls James the most completely non-Pauline book in the canon—this though he inclines to the apostolic authorship theory.[1] The two writers are connected, as Christians, by the double qualification of Hellenistic and Jewish background. But there is a marked contrast between the societies they address. Paul is socially unconscious, wishing to preserve the status quo in the world, and regarding classes as abolished in the body of

Christ. The majority of his adherents were poor people, but that fact is a social accident as far as he is concerned. But with James Christianity has spread over the entire community, rich and poor, and the extreme difficulty of being both rich and religious, noted by all the Hebrew prophets and by Jesus, is a living problem to him. Consequently, we are faced at once with the essential factor in the James–Paul opposition. Paul's whole theory of salvation transcends the social order altogether: in other words it is individual. But James, whose Christianity is centred in a social milieu, bases his soteriology, of necessity, on the problem of the relationship of the worshipper to the community.

Hence, it will seem the less surprising to find James's emphasis on "works" as the test of the Christian, opposed to Paul's emphasis on "faith," though for us, at any rate, the opposition supplements rather than contradicts. James takes what is literally a common-sense view— the sense of the community; a social approach and a worldly criterion of "results." He points out that to a community of Christians, the test of moral conduct is bound to be pragmatic; if the Parousia, though eventually certain, may perhaps be a long way off as yet, then the only advantage of the Christian life over any other is the fact that it works better. From the world's perspective, justification by faith is difficult to distinguish always from self-justification. If faith is valid, it will reveal itself: if my life is right, my belief cannot be wrong, and any faith that is not strong enough to permeate reality and social conduct is merely intellectual lumber. This socialist approach is initially, from the point of view of theology, agnostic; it suspends judgment on all creeds until it sees them in practice. James is very much the liberal fashionable preacher, full of graceful literary allusiveness, full of helpful advice and never at a loss for a platitude, but no man to insist on any of the great theological disciplines of the Church—the Incarnation and death of our Lord, his Resurrection, his presence among believers. He assumes all this on the part of his hearers, or would say he did if challenged. He has precisely the social conscience, the tendency to idealize the poor and inveigh against the rich, the armchair sympathy with the slave class,[2] we should expect to find in such a man. The novelty of Christianity as an experience he does not understand. He is inherently a ritualist,[3] for there is no more obvious way of "showing" one's faith than to engage in church work and services. Prayer, instead of being a private communication with God, is a social obligation, and the cautions against swearing probably reflect a preoccupation with the spoken word and its influence.

To some extent this attitude of assumed acceptance of doctrine and emphasis on a central Church might be described as a Catholic attitude, where Paul's tremendous upsurge of the individual soul through divine grace is Protestant. The words are used in a very general sense, of course; though the influence of James in moulding the Catholic sacraments, the confessional, and the Church disciplines is not irrelevant, any more than the Pauline impress on the thought of Luther and Calvin. In any case, Paul's message can be best appreciated by a rare and exceptional specialist in religious experience, James's by an ordinary man of affairs. It should be noted how antithetical were the religious backgrounds of the two great thinkers. James reflects the social conscience of Judaism, the Pharisaic sense of the majesty of ritual,[4] the almost inhuman respect for law, and the complete subjugation of the individual to society's superstitious belief in the cosmic effect of punctilious observance of routine. Paul was also a Jew, but the background of his religious experience was probably largely Greek. Now Greek religion—religious experience as distinct from convention—was as overwhelmingly and excessively individualistic as Judaism was the reverse. It was above everything else a mystery and an initiation into an esoteric cult. The visionary raptures of the Orphic votaries left their mark on Paul,[5] who combined their influence with the social emphasis of his Jewish training by means of his Hellenistic sophistication and common sense. But the sense of the transcending, supernatural quality of religious emotion is fundamental to Paul's thought.

This leads us at once to the opposition of Paul's and James's attitudes on the rhythmic adjustments to be made by the individual toward God. Where Paul's adjustment is revolutionary, James's is evolutionary; where Paul stresses the miraculous undeserved grace of the transcendent God the Father in leading the soul to Christ, James emphasizes the sustaining power of the immanent Holy Spirit[6] to perform the same office. To James, a Christian born in an already Christian environment has the ethical ideal to start with. The process of the Christian life is, therefore, one of perfectibility, a constant struggle to reach the ideal, victory being the sign of salvation. But what is positive development to James is a negative purgation to Paul. The individual thrown back upon himself gains a terrible conviction of sin and a realization of his own helplessness. Society can do nothing for him: the only thing that will be able to transcend his own state is the voluntary help or divine grace of an infinite God.

It has been said, by those who like such epigrams, that Paul's is a gospel of faith, Peter's of hope, John's of love, James's of wisdom. Now faith is obviously the side of religious activity most directly concerned with God, and wisdom that most concerned with society. Love is intermediate, connecting both social and mystical impulses. That is roughly John's general position, midway between[7] Paul and James in point of development, synthesizing and reconciling the two approaches at times, emphasizing the cleavage at other times.

The transcendent experience of the Christian soul was not, we have seen, directly connected with its present life. It can be concerned chiefly, therefore, only with a future life; hence, Paul's teaching on salvation is permeated with eschatology. John combines the mystical illumination of Paul with the self-conscious social awareness of James, emphasizing the transcendent nature of Christian experience in this life. His interest is predominantly in the illuminated life: in the Incarnation of God in the life of Jesus rather than the dying God which held Paul's allegiance, and in the constant irradiation of earthly life by divine intervention in miracles. Paul stresses the necessity of illumination, James of example; John combines them: it is the love of man as revealed in the teachings and life of Christ, the teachings of the Logos and the atonement of Jesus' death,[8] which provides inspiration for the good life. Paul stressed self-surrender, James self-development: John takes a middle course again, showing that the latter comes from the former—knowledge and wisdom from a will to believe. Similarly, with Paul faith is trust, with James action: John regards it as an intellectual assent resulting in both. That is, belief for Paul is a prerequisite of salvation; in James it is merely assumed as a postulate, while with John it is taken for granted that belief will necessarily follow from salvation,[9] again mediating between the opposition we have treated above. There is, consequently, a strongly dualistic, almost a Gnostic, tendency in John, to set the illuminated world inhabited by the elect of Paul's theology over against the mundane world which is the background of James. We ascend from the latter to the former by a process of regeneration and rebirth, passing, as in birth, from darkness to light.

Perhaps we have limited Paul too much in our anxiety to differentiate him from James. James builds on the preceding work of Paul: Paul anticipates James. As stated above, they supplement rather than contradict; it is not disagreement or antithesis, but an opposition of context and environment, that we are dealing with. Still less do we imagine John to be a synthesis of James and Paul; though he is the ripest fruit of apostolic culture, a fruit containing the seeds of decadence. Biblical scholarship is concerned, neither with the reconciling of apparent divergence among inspired writers, nor with the rejection of some in favour of others, but with the progressive development of their thought from age to age.

9

St. Paul and Orphism

This paper was written for Dr. John Dow, professor of New Testament at Emmanuel College. It was the second of two essays Frye submitted for New Testament 2, "The Religion and Theology of Paul," which he took during the 1934–35 academic year. Frye received an "A" for the paper, the typescript of which is in the NFF, 1991, box 37, file 13.

This paper is chiefly an investigation of the Greek religion known as Orphism, with a note on the similarity of its tenets to those of St. Paul. It does not raise the issue, except by implication, of how far St. Paul could safely be said to have been "influenced" by Orphism. It may be advisable, therefore, to defend this position at the outset, as it apparently shirks what is generally regarded as the most important question in connection with their relationship.

In the first place, there is the obvious point that any examination of "influence" is mainly a groping in the dark. We do not know what influenced Paul, or in what proportions, or at what times, or in what ways he was influenced by other people's opinions. And nothing short of actually discovering his diary could throw any light on the matter. Even then, the question could not be regarded settled: no thinker is ever perfectly aware of the influences acting upon him. All the writings of Paul we possess are indisputably works of his maturity, when all influences have been melted down in the crucible of his own experience. A personality is not a compound but a complex: it is not a rope of intertwining strands but something infinitely varied, shifting, elusive, and subtle. That Paul was in himself partly Jew, partly Greek, and partly Roman, no one will deny, any more than they will deny that in the course of his ministry he worked with Jews, Greeks, and Romans. But that these three elements in him are all quantitative, that they are solid and discrete entities which scholarship can separate like strata in a rock, is another matter.

When scholars approach Paul as a sort of intellectual Cerberus, with three distinct heads on his shoulders, they are really working with stereotypes, all of them false. We think of the Jew, specifically the Pharisaic Jew, as a legal, almost mercantile, thinker, and whenever we come upon something in Paul that reminds us of the stereotype we call it "Jewish influence." Similarly, his wide culture suggests the stereotype of the Greek philosopher and is promptly assigned to "Greek influence"; while his talent for organization brings up the image of the Roman consul and is transformed into "Roman influence." Both Romans and Pharisees were legally minded, and if most Jews were devout monotheists, so were a good many Greeks: there was Jewish culture as humanistic and rational as the Athenian; and Paul's age was one very like our own, in which the great cities were almost indistinguishable from one another, constituting a pantheon of races and nationalities quite as syncretic as the contemporary religious one. Just as Jerusalem today is a less Jewish city than New York, so the Jewish cities of Paul's day were as much Rome and Alexandria as Jerusalem, and the nationalism of the Pharisee was, like German and Italian nationalism now, purely a political bluff, without any meaning in culture or in economics. Nineteenth-century Europe hypnotized itself into a belief that nationality and race were real things instead of myths, and nineteenth-century Biblical scholars saw meanings in Paul's cultural mixture that had probably long ceased to have any meaning for Paul. Protestantism, again, arose with nationalism, the two phenomena always having been closely associated. Consequently, the Protestant prefers to see in Christianity the product of a national consciousness, the growth of which is traced in the Old Testament. This is less true of Calvinists, perhaps, than of nineteenth-century liberals; but just as Jesus becomes the culmination of the Jewish prophetic tradition, so Paul is, in all his thinking, considered to be the logical continuation of the Old Testament tradition. The antithetical position, which sees Paul as essentially a Greek phenomenon, does not escape the same racial and nationalistic preconceptions. Many of the earlier thinkers were rather shocked at the proposition that there could be any extra-Biblical background for Paul. And even some of those who have overcome this prejudice maintain another closely related to it: that even if Paul did live and teach in a world gone completely cosmopolitan, nevertheless he either preserved or ought to have preserved a nationalistic integrity in his teaching, the assumption being, of course, that there is something very bad about a syncretic religion. Professor H.A.A. Kennedy believes that he did preserve it; Professor G.H. Gilbert believes that he ought to have preserved it. The latter says:

> When the Jesus of the Gospel was transformed into the Alexandrian Christ, what was achieved was not the gathering of the Gentile world into the Kingdom of Heaven, not an acceptance by that world of the religion of Jesus, but an overthrow of the very basis of that religion. (*Greek Thought in the New Testament*, 100)[1]

And the former, by tracing similarities between the mystery cults and the Septuagint, and then asserting the very obvious fact that Christianity was a unique religious product, leaves us with the assumption that Paul *could* have derived his mystery conception from the Old Testament, and the reflection that if religious developments in Judaea and Greece were so strikingly alike, the differences between them are less important than their similarities.[2] The logical outcome of all such disputes is finally that we have on the one hand the conception developing from the researches of Loisy, Reinach, and Reitzenstein,[3] which tends in the direction of explaining Paul completely in Greek terms, and on the other hand the reaction from this, which sees him with equal plausibility as entirely Jewish. Surely it is unnecessary to go beyond certain elementary facts. Tarsus was a centre of Greek culture. The people addressed by Paul were many of them converts from mystery religions. Paul talked to them in their own terms; he used the language of initiates, probably not in any very technical sense, but as a courtesy to hearers coming to him from religious traditions, some of which he was bound to respect. The question of Paul's personal initiation into a mystery cult is purely a matter of guesswork, and is likely to remain so.

Of all the varied and conflicting religions alive in Paul's time we select Orphism for discussion. It is in many respects the most interesting, as it is perhaps the closest approach of the Western world to a religion as Christians understand the term. With the exception of Judaism, it possessed the only body of theological writing extant before Paul's first Epistle: it had not been watered down into pure philosophy, like Stoicism or even Neoplatonism, nor had it been entirely absorbed in popular superstition. It was perhaps, with Judaism, the only religion which had succeeded in lifting its doctrines from anthropology into ethics on any extensive scale.

So far from syncretism being a bad thing, it seems to us an indispensable factor in the rise of Christianity. Christianity succeeded, not as a brand new invention, but as a synthesis evoking, in an intelligible form, the real *meaning* toward which the symbolism in rival faiths was tending. In investigating the "influence" of one of these contemporary religions on St. Paul, we have drawn a complete blank; and in trying to investigate uniformities in their doctrines, we have reached largely negative conclusions. But still we feel that an examination of Orphism from several points of view has some value in isolating a very significant element in the intellectual background of Paul's time.

I

The orthodox religion of Greece was Olympian, or, as Nietzsche called it in *Birth of Tragedy*, Apollonian.[4] This religion was one which wavered between polydaemonism and polytheism. Its Bible is largely Homeric epic, and its myths were transmitted by poets. Originally, it seems to have combined a cult of heroes with a general animism which deified every phase of experience. The gods were magnified humans, which meant that they were mostly liars, cowards, bullies, and lechers. Zeus had committed every crime in the calendar; Hermes, the patron of thieves, was not far behind him; Aphrodite was an adulteress of incredible appetite; Poseidon a petulant bureaucrat of the high seas. Yet they were endowed with a strange power, and their worship became largely a matter of rites. Public religion was almost altogether apotropaic and prophylactic.[5] Each sacrifice safeguarded the state against some thin-skinned and short-tempered deity: conversely, all disasters were the result of some divine anger or jealousy. Such a religion could not attract the more sensitive minds indefinitely, and Olympian religion and Greek philosophy consistently ignored each other. The majority of the people passed from indifference to open mockery. But a habit confirmed by tradition is hard to break off, and even after all interest in the rites had vanished, there remained the feeling that failure to observe them was dangerous on political if not religious grounds. This feeling lasted all through the early centuries of Christianity: the Christian martyrs were executed for sedition and treason, not for their religious beliefs.

True, Olympian religion did gradually become more refined; its later period abounds in such attractive conceptions as Graces, nymphs, and Muses. But the earlier strata remained. Later on, the conservatives, faced with the challenge of more advanced religions, tried to infuse an ethical and moral spirit into the ancient savage myths by allegorizing them. Plutarch is the most conspicuous example of this process, which lasted until the torrent of ridicule in *The City of God* swept it away.[6] The theocrasia of the Hellenistic world encouraged the belief that the gods of all nations were more or less alike, because all nations formulated their religious experiences in similar ways, and that, consequently, the more important gods represented abstract principles. According to Plutarch, war is evil, and, therefore, cannot be a god: war relates only to humanity in this sense.[7] The good qualities engendered in war, courage, cooperation, self-sacrifice, energy, and so on: this is what must be deified. So there becomes a divine war which is the god Ares, and an evil war which is only the result of the folly of mankind. This Platonizing tendency on the part of the timid and vacillating pagans of the era of decadence is largely a shrinking back from the uncompromising ferocity of the Christian zealots, and being so transparently a rationalizing of its own weakness, its ineffectiveness hardly causes much surprise.

The theology of the Olympian cult was as rudimentary as its mythology was complicated. Its ideas of the afterlife advanced very little from the primitive conception of the dead as "shades," weak and ineffectual like the shadow of a living man. Homeric treatments of this are very similar to such scenes as the King of Babylon in Hell passage in Isaiah [14:4–9]. The gods being so completely amoral, there was little idea of reward or punishment in the future life, other than a few savage stories of divine vengeance which supported the unethical rather than the ethical approach.

This religion was official and aristocratic, imposed on Greece originally by its Dorian conquerors after the Trojan War, and never far away from association with caste and race privilege. Its impact on the populace had been largely in the form of festivals. Pushing up, however, more and more strongly, was a new popular religion, all the more new for being immemorially old.

II

All primitive peoples who are agricultural and, therefore, dependent on the fertility of the soil for their existence develop a myth which regards the spirit of fertility as a deity necessarily young and vigorous, but either masculine or feminine. This deity, when the former, bears a double relation to the soil which nourishes him, a relation at once that of son to mother and of lover to beloved. As the fertile life of the world disappears every autumn and reappears every spring, the god is conceived as dying in the fall and reviving in the spring. Usually a sacrifice, frequently human, symbolizes his death. An orgiastic drunken frenzy in which sexual excitement reaches its highest pitch is, according to the conceptions of sympathetic magic, which assumes that all phenomena of fertility are interdependent, the appropriate expression of the revival of his potency. Around these two ideas of death and resurrection all the fertility cults revolve. They are usually but by no means invariably associated with the periodic harvest, vintage, sowing, shearing, new and full moon, equinoctial, and solstitial festivals of the ordinary calendar. The dying of the god is bewailed by the women, in the role of earth mother: he is conceived as being slain by emasculation or loss of fertility (the thigh wound of Adonis is a later euphemism), and is often worshipped in the form of some animal which is conceived as having some influence on the crops because of living near them.[8]

Adonis, the youth beloved of Aphrodite, slain by a boar (which means that he was originally worshipped in the form of a boar), is the most famous of the fertility gods. His cult was originally Syrian, and the red clay brought down by the Adonis river was taken as containing his blood. The Babylonians had their Tammuz, the Phrygians their Attis, beloved of Cybele, the Egyptians their Osiris and his loved one Isis. Most of the purely Greek fertility deities were female (Iphigenia, Kore, Persephone or Proserpine), but they had two important male ones: Hyacinthus of Sparta, and Dionysus of Thrace.[9]

The fertility cult was widespread among the Canaanites, and came into sharp conflict with the nomadic monolatry of the Hebrews. It undoubtedly permeated the Jahwist cult: its influence is symbolized by a curious piece of irony: the name Jehovah, which is a synthesis of the consonants of Jahweh and the vowels of Adonis. The redaction of the Old Testament records has no doubt erased much evidence to this effect. What remains is slight but significant. Jephthah's daughter, whose women "bewailed her virginity" [Judges 11:40], was obviously sacrificed in the role of a local Iphigenia or Kore. Joseph's coat of many colours is an evident vegetation symbol [Genesis 37:3]. After the Exile

the monotheist conscience of the Jews began to sharpen. Ezekiel complains of the women weeping for Tammuz in the very gates of Jerusalem [Ezekiel 8:14], and Trito-Isaiah attacks the fertility cults violently.[10]
But that did not prevent Antiochus Epiphanes from introducing the cult
of Dionysus into Judaea,[11] and by the time of Christ the Jews, educated
and uneducated, were thoroughly well acquainted with the dying and
rising god. There was a sect of Jews which worshipped Dionysus under
his name of Sabazius (which, like most of that god's surnames, relates to
some kind of intoxicating liquor), confounding it with the Lord God of
Sabaoth.[12]

Of all these fertility cults, that of Dionysus has been most notorious
for the ecstatic and orgiastic nature of its rites. It was introduced into
Greece from Thrace and had a long struggle for Olympian recognition.
Dionysus is not a god in Homer; but he eventually became admitted to
the Olympian hierarchy: there are several no doubt aetiological stories
recounting his dispute with Apollo. The reasons for his popular acceptance are shrouded in obscurity. Possibly he evoked the remembrance to
fertility rites held before the Dorians came; no doubt he brought a
revived hope of immortality, and undoubtedly his emblematic wine cup
was irresistible. Popular tradition, connecting him with Attis and Adonis, assigned an Asiatic origin to him. He is usually pictured as attended
by male followers called satyrs, and women followers called maenads.
The latter were, of course, the women who bewailed the death of the
god and worked themselves into orgiastic frenzies during his revival.
Dionysus was always a god of the vintage rather than the harvest, and
the worship of fertility gods was largely in the hands of women. Plutarch has an interesting suggestion to the effect that Olympias, the
mother of Alexander the Great, was an overenthusiastic maenad, and
that the well-known strained relationship between her and her husband
Philip of Macedon was due to this fact.[13] The mother of Dionysus was,
of course, the earth mother, Semele (the Slavonic Nova Zembla, "new
land," exemplifies a cognate form). His father was Zeus—that is, after
his cult had spread widely enough in Greece to compel his adoption.
Essentially a god of intoxication, his fertility origin caused him to be
worshipped in the form of trees and various animals, usually a bull, a
well-known symbol of fertility.

All music grows out of a synthesis of dance and song, rhythm and
melody. In the Middle Ages this double origin of music is clearly
marked, the dance being popular and the song (the plainchant) monas-

tic and academic. This affords an instructive parallel to the rise of music and drama in Greece. From the beginning there was the contrast between the Olympian devotional song or paean, associated with Apollo, and the ecstatic dance or dithyramb, which belonged to Dionysus. The latter, probably in its ultimate origin a leaping into the air to promote the growth of crops by sympathetic magic, eventually became a ritual song of the winter solstice festival (the modern Christmas).[14] On the dramatic side the τράγος or goat-song (the word means both goat and a kind of barley, and may refer back to a time when the fertility spirit of the barley crop was considered to be incarnate in a goat) in honour of Dionysus, chanted by his male attendants the satyrs at a goat sacrifice, eventually developed into the satyric drama, and from the satyric drama into the tragedy.[15]

The purpose of the wild revel of intoxication in the worship of Dionysus was not simply to let off steam or find an excuse for getting drunk. The original sacrifice which accompanied the rite of the dying god was the king of the tribe, in whom the spirit of the god was conceived as incarnate. He was, in other words, *the* fertility or virility of the tribe. Hence, his sacrifice was consummated as soon as he showed signs of weakening, and his vitality thereby passed to his successor. The king is dead, long live the king;[16] there must be no break in between. But the sacrifice was more than a ritual murder: the king was divided among his tribe and eaten. This communion distributed the king's vitality and it reinforced the solidarity of the tribe. Later on, of course, human sacrifice was commuted to animal sacrifice. The climax of the Dionysiac revel was the tearing apart of some animal as a sacrifice and the dividing of it among the worshippers. A still further development was in the direction of offering the fertility god, the lord of the harvest and the vintage, some of the fruits of his work, and making that offering a communion as well, so that the body is replaced by bread, blood by wine. Some dim idea of this seems to have penetrated the Dionysiac cult: in any case intoxication was enthusiasm, possession by the god. At the moment of ecstasy the communion became complete, and the worshipper became one with his god.

When we say that we see frost forming a design on a window pane, we do not imagine the frost to be conscious of any design, but that it unconsciously goes through a process we can interpret in terms of design. Similarly, the unconsciousness of primitive ritual does not preclude its predictable laws of behaviour, its uniformities where no transmission is possible, its use of an essentially invariable symbolism so that its development takes on what to us is a coherent and logical outline. In the crudest ritual of cannibals there is always a meaning which the trained observer can interpret, just as our dreams are built up involuntarily but quite logically out of the symbols our unconscious works with. Hence, in every phenomenon of anthropology, there is something which can be restated in ethical, philosophical, or even scientific terms. The history of religion records a process of development in which physical and material acts come to be increasingly regarded as mental, spiritual, psychological, symbolic—whatever our vocabulary is accustomed to.

Now in the cult of Dionysus there are certain genuinely religious ideas implicit, which need only a more discerning and conscious mentality to be brought out. Such an access of capacity for abstraction is most likely to be the result of an increased self-consciousness and, therefore, the product of individual reformers. One thinks of the strong individuality of the Hebrew prophets, which infused the old Jahwistic monolatry with ethical and moral ideas and reformed it into a genuine monotheism. One thinks of the arrogant dictatorships established by the Protestant reformers when they wiped out the worship of saints, the veneration of relics, the traditional mythologies absorbed by the earlier Church, and the idea of mechanical efficacy in sacrament. And the relation of the Hebrew prophets to the old priesthood, of the Protestant reformers to the Catholic Church, is, *mutatis mutandis*, the relation of Orphism to the traditional Olympian religion of Greece.

III

The cult of Dionysus, we have said, was absorbed, after a considerable struggle, into the official religion of Greece. Delphi became a seat of worship for Dionysus as well as Apollo. But the maturing Hellenic civilization could not tolerate indefinitely the frantic orgies of the Bacchic ritual, its intoxication and sexual license. The extraordinary grip such a ritual held on the imagination is preserved for us in the *Bacchae* of Euripides. A reform, however, in the interests of refinement was inevitable, and about the name of Orpheus that reform centres. Orphism is, like Christianity, Islam, and Buddhism, a religion with a personal founder. It was never a national religion: it was esoteric rather than communal, and its ritual was one of secret and private initiation rather than public festival or sacrifice. It is a sophisticated religion depending on theology rather than myth, doctrinal and revealed rather than spontaneous and symbolic, working from sacred texts rather than from a traditional observance. In other words, it has all the characteristics of organized religion, and is, we have seen, the first such religion to appear in Europe.

Orpheus himself is a figure somewhat like Jesus in many respects. That there was a historical Orpheus seems almost beyond dispute. The Greeks reverenced him as a hero, with supernatural attributes, but never as an actual god. The most common story of his death is that he was torn to pieces by Thracian women maddened by the intoxication of the Dionysiac revels, which may well point to a real martyrdom. As the tearing of an animal was, we have seen, part of that ritual, it appears that Orpheus, like Jesus, was martyred in the role of sacrificial victim or Lamb of God. Again, like Jesus, he is associated with sweetness and gentleness. There is no trace whatever of the war-god about him. He is represented as a magical musician of irresistible power, charming even the inanimate world with his lyre, just as Jesus is the teacher whose healing personality draws all men to him. Orpheus evaded the sirens by outdoing them at their own art of singing, just as Jesus overcame the temptations of the devil by turning his arguments back on him. The famous story of his love for Eurydice (the original version was a long way from a love story), his visit to Hades to reclaim her, and the tragic failure of his mission, has no direct parallel with Jesus, but surely Jesus' descent from heaven to the world to reclaim the world and his rejection by a recalcitrant humanity is suggested by it, and in Orpheus' descent into Hades and his rescuing of Eurydice we have a genuine katabasis and, perhaps, an early form of a harrowing of hell. These parallels are suggested to show that the Orphic religion followed a really Christlike founder, and that Paul may very well have come in contact with Orphics as devout and pious as any Christian could wish to be. Besides, the earliest Christian art, particularly that of the catacomb period, represents Orpheus in place of Jesus, and the transition from the master musician to the Good Shepherd is an almost insensible one. At the same time, the essentially magical attributes of Orpheus made him a shaman as well as a reformer. We cannot afford to overlook the degenerate and superstitious side of Orphism in our admiration for it, any more than we can ignore that side of Christianity. In Euripides' play of the *Cyclops* a lazy and cowardly sailor proposes to use a charm of Orpheus to compel Ulysses' flaming torch to propel itself into the eye of Polyphemus.[17]

Nietzsche's *The Birth of Tragedy* is built around a thesis developed from Plutarch, and may well go back from there to the very heart of Orphic theology itself. In Greek culture, says Nietzsche, there are two opposed outlooks, the Apollonian and the Dionysiac. The former is the conservative, orthodox element. It is civilized and intellectual and corresponds to the Greek love of unity in all things, moderation in conduct, proportion in art, strict bounds and reasonable limits to everything. The latter is incorrigibly primitive and subconscious; it delights in breaking out of restrictions, it exults in life and energy for their own sakes, it is anarchic and disruptive of all forms of stability. Where the Apollonian tendency is toward unity, toward the typical, the catalogued and classified, the Dionysiac accepts the variety of the actual world and explodes the idea of unity. Dionysus, the fertility god, wears a coat of many colours; he is life in a million forms: he is the driving, plunging rhythm of activity. The assimilation of these religions to one another had, therefore, brought about a tension which it was the business of more reflective and philosophical minds to solve. The religious consciousness moves from polytheism to monotheism, because it is trying to get away from the transient and shifting to the stable and permanent. Consequently, it has to deal with the paradox of the one and the many: why so much complexity in experience, if God is one?

A partial resolution of this tension, of course, is afforded by the symbol of communion. Here the united god is dismembered and divided among his worshippers, whereupon a new integration takes place: he reunites and the worshippers become one with him. But another factor is suggested by the nature of the fertility god. It should not be forgotten that the quarrel between the two religions of Greece is a quarrel between Dionysus and Apollo. Apollo stands out as the representative of Olympian religion, which is called Apollonian after him. He is the master musician who resents Orpheus' rivalry and cannot tolerate his singing head which, tradition says, was preserved at Lesbos after his martyrdom. There are vases depicting Apollo scowling at the head (which gave further offence by uttering oracles like those of Apollo himself at Delphi) and saying: "Leave that which belongs to me." If they later became friends they must have had something in common.[18] Apollo was originally a sun-god, and Dionysus was a fertility god. Orpheus, the reformer of the Dionysiac cult, was himself not strictly a god, but his descent into the underworld in search of Eurydice is evidently a fertility myth, Eurydice probably representing the earth mother. Now both the

sun and vegetation are transient, but they recur: and that fact of recurrence brings in an element of permanence and a feeling of stability. So
the paradox is overcome by observation: the sun dies every day, but is
deathless; vegetation dies every year, but every year revives. Communion and the idea of a dying and reviving god are inseparably part of the
symbolism which works out this tension of one and many. The sun-god
and the fertility-god blend into the abstract idea of recurrence.

  The archetypal myth of Orphism presents this problem in symbolic
terms. Zagreus (Dionysus in a chthonic form) is as an infant torn to
pieces by the Titans or giants; his heart is miraculously preserved, and
by means of it he comes to life again in the form of a new Dionysus.
There are dozens of variants of the story: sometimes the heart is placed
in a gypsum statue and reanimates it; sometimes Zeus swallows the
heart; sometimes the god is conceived as having been dismembered in
the form of a bull or goat, which probably means that an original child
sacrifice later became an animal sacrifice. What is essential is the combination of two ideas: the dividing of the god and his resurrection. It is
this that constitutes the fundamental theogony of Orphism.

  The idea of recurrence was extended by the Orphics to human life.
Most of the Orphics accepted some form of the doctrine of the transmigration of souls, and in Plato's conception of anamnesis, the identification of knowledge with recollection, we have the Orphic tendency to
think of things in terms of recurrence. But the idea of recurrence, by
itself, can lead only to a pessimistic and despairing fatalism. From being
a conservative idea, an assurance of stability, it soon becomes a monotonous turning of a wheel, and to this wheel all living things are bound.
The theological interest of Orphism was largely directed to the problem
of how to escape from this wheel. In Plato's myth in the *Republic* the universe turns on a spindle held on the knees of Necessity [bk. 10, 616d]. In
its essentials Orphism is very like Brahmanism: everything is bound to
fate, karma, for ever and ever, unless some remedy be found.

  Plainly the next step is to regard some form of recurrence as a potentially moral experience. Thus, Orphism develops the idea of reward and
punishment in the afterlife. This we shall consider in a moment. But for
this to be completely achieved it is necessary to discover some symbol of
death and resurrection in life itself. So the dying and reviving sun, the
dying and reviving vegetation, come to impose a pattern on human
experience. Gradually there develops the idea of moral progression in
physical recurrence. The descent into the world of darkness and death,

and the re-emergence into life, which both sun and vegetation undergo: does not this correspond to the struggle of humanity, which is bound by all the fetters of sin and flesh, to gain a new strength and vitality? There is probably more of the spirit of Orphism than is generally recognized in Plato's profound allegory of the cave [*Republic*, bk. 7, 514a–520e]. So Orphism develops a technique of palingenesis, or new birth, as an essential element in its religion.

We are not concerned here so much with the Orphic ritual (assuming that there was a ritual uniquely Orphic) as with the moral aspect of its religion. A religion depending essentially on new birth, on purification, is bound to work with some idea of dualism implicit: the starting point and the goal of the worshipper's progress must be opposed. Let us glance back at the myth. The infant Zagreus, we saw, was torn to pieces by the Titans. The Titans, then, must be evil spirits, and as such they were, according to the myth, slain by Zeus with his thunderbolts. But the evil they personified lives on. Man's nature inherits, as a result of the original murder of Zagreus, an evil and a good side. The titanic, savage element represents the evil side; the Dionysiac the good side. It is the duty of Orphic worshippers to purge themselves of the original sin of the Titans by imitating Dionysus in his death and new birth. This kind of dualism is certain to draw a sharp distinction between flesh and spirit, body and soul. Orphic thought was dominated throughout by the idea of the sinfulness of the flesh. The soul (of course, the soul and body were distinct entities for the Orphics) was imprisoned in the body, and was struggling to be set free. Plato says in the *Cratylus*:

> I think this (i.e., the word σῶμα), admits of many explanations, if a little, even very little, change is made; for some say it is the tomb (σῆμα) of the soul. . . . I think it most likely that the Orphic poets gave it this name, with the idea that the soul is undergoing punishment for something; they think it has the body as an enclosure to keep it safe, like a prison.[19]

Along with the idea of palingenesis grew the idea of catharsis, the cathartic experience being the deliverance, however temporary, of the soul from the body. All the practices usually associated with this were encouraged by the Orphics: asceticism of all kinds, Orpheus himself having been a good deal of a misogynist; vegetarianism, the eating of meat being an absorption of more flesh, and in a reincarnation theology amounting to cannibalism in any case; abstinence from alcoholic beverages (we are getting further and further away from Dionysus); and cremation, or the annihilation of the earthly body at death. This sounds like a repudiation rather than a reformation of the Dionysiac cult, but it was designed for the same end, communion with the god, although it revolted against the materialistic practices of the earlier sect and replaced them with spiritual ones. For physical intoxication the Orphics substituted mystical ecstasy and the hallucinations resulting from the self-tortures of the ascetic; for the physical absorption of the god's body, a spiritual union. In doing this they eliminated an important element in the Dionysiac religion, and brought about their own eventual destruction. The Dionysiac religion spread over Greece with something of a missionary fervour, because it was itself genuinely catholic and communal: its orgies, crude and even repulsive as they seem to us now, were at any rate social gatherings; the feast united the worshippers. The Orphics, in spiritualizing this process, made it individual and, consequently, esoteric. Its unit was the brotherhood, the small group or thiasos. Like all religions depending on secret initiation, Orphism was never very far from intellectual snobbery.

This last trait is amply revealed in the Orphic doctrine of election. The development of the concept of original sin reached almost the point of Samuel Butler's caricature of it in *Erewhon* with the Orphics.[20] The soul is indestructible and immortal, the body transient and corrupt. The pure soul is a god: by purifying our soul we unite with the gods. All living men are souls who have been compelled for some fault to become united to a body. Hence, the body is the prison of the soul in a very literal sense: all our souls are convicts. At the end of ten thousand years or thereabouts the soul has served its term, in various forms, and then returns to the other world, awaiting its final judgment. According to Plato the only people who get their sentences shortened for good behaviour are virtuous philosophers and homosexual school teachers. He says in the *Phaedrus*:

> The soul must be a thing both uncreate and immortal. . . . All that is soul presides over all that is without soul, and patrols all heaven. . . . When it is perfect and fully feathered it roams in upper air, and regulates the entire universe; but the soul that has lost its feathers is carried down . . . and when it has settled there . . . the name of animal is given to the whole, to this compound, I mean, of soul and body, with the addition of the epithet mortal. . . . [246a–c]

Those who have lived justly receive afterwards a better lot, those who have lived unjustly, a worse. For to that same place from which each soul set out, it does not return for ten thousand years . . . unless it has belonged to a guileless lover of philosophy, or a philosophic lover of boys. [248e–249a; trans. J. Wright]

These get away with about three thousand years.

Dionysus had conquered Greece partly because he brought the irresistible hope of immortality: through communion with an immortal god one partakes of his immortal nature. Orphism preserved this concept and worked out an elaborate eschatology. In its crudest form the eventual release from the karma of material life was, of course, simply the Mohammedan houri-paradise for the good, eternal torture for the bad. As to the latter, their punishments in the main reflected the same pattern of recurrence. Sisyphus, who rolls a stone eternally uphill and has it come rattling and bumping back down again—$\alpha\hat{v}\tau\iota\varsigma$ $\check{\epsilon}\pi\epsilon\iota\tau\alpha$ $\pi\acute{\epsilon}\delta ov\delta\epsilon$ $\kappa\upsilon\lambda\acute{\iota}v\delta\epsilon\tau o$ $\lambda\hat{a}\alpha\varsigma$ $\grave{a}v\alpha\iota\delta\acute{\eta}\varsigma^{21}$—is a typical figure. Tantalus is another favourite denizen of Hades, and the Danaides, whose story recalls Jesus' parable of the wise and foolish virgins—the connecting link being Plato's comparison in the *Gorgias* of the foolish soul to a leaky jar [493b]—also appear on the Orphic vases and paintings, the most famous of which is the great underworld scene of Polygnotus described by Pausanias.[22] This materialistic conception of the afterlife has been well caricatured by Plato in the *Republic*:

Still grander are the gifts of heaven which Musaeus and his son vouchsafe to the just; they take them down into the world below, where they have the saints lying on couches at a feast, everlastingly drunk, crowned with garlands; their idea seems to be that an immortality of drunkenness is the highest meed of virtue. . . . But about the wicked there is another strain; they bury them in a slough in Hades, and make them carry water in a sieve. [bk. 2, 363c–d; trans. Benjamin Jowett]

Gradually, of course, the idea eventually consolidated that only those initiated into Orphism would be saved. All others, not having gone through any palingenesis or catharsis, were necessarily impure according to the doctrine of original sin, and the stock phrase to describe them was "lying in the mire," to which Plato refers [363d]. One of the most striking relics of Orphism are the little gold leaf inscriptions of what the soul is to see in the underworld, and what he is to say to the spirits who approach him.

Some authorities prefer a Cretan origin for Orpheus, others a Mycenean: there seems something exotic about him in Greece. It would be interesting to know if he were part of the vast spiritual and intellectual revolution in western Asia which brought about the monotheism evident in the great progression of Hebrew prophets, in Zoroaster, in the Babylonian worship of Marduk and Nebuchadnezzar's passionate adoration of him, in the Behistun inscription of Darius.[23] Christianity and its contemporary rivals resulted from the aging of the great classical civilization: they arose in its last phase, the phase of imperialism, of great cities, of a disaffected proletariat, of a dried-up agrarian economy, of decadent, sophisticated culture. In such times the proletariat forms a church, or new religious consciousness, and consolidates a cultural tradition which survives the shock of nomadic invasion and destruction.[24] This process is going on today; it went on two thousand years ago, when Christianity became the religious faith of the proletariat of the classical world and conquered the barbarians who destroyed the Roman Empire. Is there not a possibility that the growth of early Asiatic culture, which reached its late imperialistic stage in the time of Zoroaster and Amos, produced a parallel phenomenon, and that Deutero-Isaiah bears to Cyrus a relation somewhat like that of the Christian Pope Leo the Great to the Christian Alaric?[25] There is the same proletarian consciousness in the Hebrew prophets, the same internationalism, the same dream of eventual peace, the same hatred of the rich and exaltation of the poor, the same acute sense of economic realities, that we find in apostolic Christianity. Is Orpheus part of this consciousness?

This, of course, is pure guesswork: we cannot be sure whether Orpheus is earlier or later than Homer. The famous Orphic poetry, of which Orpheus himself, with his disciples Musaeus and Linus, were said to be the greatest composers, has not survived, beyond a few lines quoted by Plato and others, and a number of pseudonymous works. In the sixth and fifth centuries before Christ there seems to have grown up an extensive sacred Orphic literature, now also lost. But whatever Orpheus' own origin, Orphism became at once a big-city religion, like early Christianity. It centred in Athens and in the great cities of south Italy, notably Kroton, famous for destroying the notorious Sybaris,[26] perhaps in a fit of Orphic prudery. At Athens Orphism probably absorbed a good deal of the official agrarian mysteries of Eleusis. In the fifth century B.C. the tyrant Pisistratus at Athens favoured Orphism and set an Orphic called Onomacritus to edit the Orphic texts, which he seems to have done rather unscrupulously. At the same time the poems of Homer were edited. There would naturally be a sharp opposition between the Orphics and the poems that formulated the religion they were attacking, of the sort reflected so uncompromisingly in Plato's *Republic*. That they made interpolations into the sacred Homeric text seems certain. The most plausible suggestion in this connection is that the great underworld scene in *Odyssey* XI is Orphic, as it points to a conception of the afterlife unknown to the Homeric Odysseus. The original was apparently somewhat like the Witch of Endor scene in the Old Testament [1 Samuel 28:7]: Odysseus seeks advice from the shade of Tiresias, and calls him up. This is expanded into the great canvas which includes Sisyphus, Tantalus, and the other stock criminals of Hades. In general, it may be said that the great contribution to art made by the Orphics was the art form of the katabasis, or descent to the underworld. This theme, which in painting develops into the *danse macabre* in the Middle Ages, is developed from *Odyssey* XI by Virgil in the great sixth book of the *Aeneid*, and from him by Dante. Probably Shakespeare's *Tempest* belongs to the same tradition.[27] The Old Testament, no doubt as a result of Hellenistic as well as Mesopotamian influence, has one genuine katabasis, the King of Babylon in Hell [Isaiah 14:4–9], and there are a number of other symbols of initiation and the descent of the soul. The three children go through the purgatory of Nebuchadnezzar's furnace, and emerge unscathed. Daniel descends into the lion's den, but comes out miraculously preserved. In Jonah's descent into the fish's belly the moral and purgatorial nature of the experience is more clearly marked. Yet all three experiences are genuine initiations.

As Orphism grew and spread over Greece, it developed, like all religions, in two directions, up and down. Downward, it absorbed all the mechanical ritual formulae of the earlier nature cults, and the initiatory rites became a solemnly ridiculous hocus-pocus to anyone with a well-developed sense of humour. Orphism was an individualistic religion, and thereby in danger of priggishness; to its relation to the established Eleusinian cult that of Puritan and Anglican may perhaps offer a rough analogy. Aristophanes' play *The Clouds* has a long scene which is nothing short of an intricate and detailed parody of the Orphic rites.[28] His attitude may be compared to Ben Jonson's attitude to the Puritans in *Bartholomew Fair*.[29] On the other hand, an involved theology sprang up

from the Zagreus myth, and without this theology much of the development of Greek philosophy from Thales to Plato is as unintelligible as the
development of Western philosophy from Descartes to Leibnitz would
be without some knowledge of the doctrines of the Catholic Church.

The theology that developed from the Zagreus myth added little to
the essential symbolic structure of Orphism. Cosmological and theo-
gonic guesswork, the main material of pre-Socratic thinkers, worked its
way in. In Orphism the most influential documents were the *Theogony* of
Hesiod and a *Rhapsodic Theogony*[30] ascribed to Orpheus himself. The
central doctrine of this is, of course, the problem of the existence of variety and the demand of metaphysical and theological thinking for unity.
We have considered this intellectual situation in some detail. The epigram assigned to Musaeus, Orpheus' disciple, sums it up: ἐξ ἑνὸς τὰ
πάντα γίνεσθαι, καὶ εἰς ταὐτὸν ἀναλύεσθαι.[31]

The theogony resulting from this follows a stock pattern. Creation
started as a result of the dividing and discriminating of objects from an
original unity. In the beginning was time (Chronos) or duration. Out of
time appears a cosmic principle (the aether) and a chaotic one (Chaos or
Erebus). The collision of time and the cosmos results in the creation of
an egg, symbol of potential and created life. From the egg is hatched the
first-born of the gods, Phanes, the source of life as associated with light
and energy, who is also Dionysus and Eros. He has a daughter-wife
Night, who bears to him Earth and Heaven (Ge and Uranus). Apparently there are two strains of the myth, one beginning with night and
the other with light, just as there is a water-chaos and a drought-chaos
version of the story of creation in the Genesis cosmogony.

Then comes the race of giant gods and the well-known myths about
Cronus, his swallowing of his children and the miraculous preservation
of Zeus, and the eventual supremacy of Zeus. Zeus becomes the creator
and unifying principle of the world by swallowing Phanes. (This
extraordinary myth perhaps relates to a historical quarrel in which the
Orphics were unwillingly compelled, out of deference to popular feeling, to accept their arch enemy Zeus as the creator-god. In any case, it
was no doubt useful to have in the sacred text the example of a god who
could swallow everything.) Zeus in turn has a daughter-wife, the earth
goddess Kore-Persephone, who bears to him Dionysus-Zagreus. This
latter becomes a third universal god, Zeus abdicating in his favour.
Then follows the myth of the rending of Zagreus by the Titans, already
considered. Zagreus is the reborn Phanes: his relation to Zeus is very

similar in many ways to the Christian relationship of divine Father and Son. As we have seen, he is redeemer as well as god, the opponent of the evil or titanic element in man and champion of humanity.

In this complicated myth one discerns certain recognizable traits. Simplified somewhat, it is not greatly unlike the Christian doctrine of Incarnation, at least in its later stages. The involved and exceedingly incestuous genealogy reflects the logical difficulty of getting a plausible line of descent from elemental ideas of order, chaos, and creation to the world of man and nature; from the perfect to the imperfect, from the infinite to the finite. The same thing no doubt is responsible for the endless lists of eons and emanations in Gnosticism. There is the repetition of the theme of death—usually through being eaten—and rebirth, of division and reunification of all things. According to Guthrie the original element in this theogony is the notion of a creator-god.[32] In the story of the infant Zagreus, lured away from his guardians by the Titans with gifts of toys and playthings, we have a genuine cult of a divine child. Eros (love) is here attraction, in both the ordinary-sense relation to sexual love, and in the physicist's sense of the gathering together of matter. Cohesion is the stability of the world of space; procreation and reproduction, the stability of the world of time: both depend on "love." This is the basic principle of the philosophy of Empedocles, and its significance for future Christian thought needs no comment. Further implications of the doctrine are worked out in the *Symposium*, where beauty is interpreted as the attempt to make love permanent. Later theologians added various abstractions as deities, such as Ananke (necessity), whom Er saw in the *Republic* [bk. 10, 616c], Dike (justice), and Adikia (injustice). There is an amusing vase on which a rather shrewish-looking Dike is depicted as vigorously beating an ugly and speckled Adikia with an implement that looks somewhat like a crowbar.[33]

The philosophical developments of Orphism are still largely a matter of dispute. On the whole, the religion seemed to attract speculation by the pungency and vividness of its imagery and symbolic language, but remained confined throughout its history to small groups: one is again reminded of Puritanism in England. Apparently the Pythagorean cult of southern Italy was to some extent a development of it: it worshipped Apollo, but followed the Orphic way of life, though it replaced the mythical theogony with a quasi-mathematical and occult one. The cosmological guesses of the Ionians, particularly Anaximander, remind us of the Orphic myths in their general outlines, but there is little need to attach too much significance to that fact. That two a priori speculators working on insufficient data arrive at similarly shaped conclusions is probably about as significant as the fact that they would both describe approximately perfect circles if they were lost in the woods. It seems fairly certain that Heraclitus and Empedocles were Orphics.[34] But, of course, the real philosophical spokesman of Orphism is Plato. Sharply critical of its vulgarities, devoutly appreciative of its purer qualities, Plato is as undoubtedly an Orphic as Leibnitz or Pascal were undoubtedly Christians. Most of Plato's more important dialogues contain myths giving what are apparently authoritative statements of Orphic doctrines. The *Republic*, the *Phaedo*, and the *Gorgias* end with magnificent myths of Orphic eschatology and visions of the afterlife; the *Phaedrus* deals with the myth of transmigration; the *Timaeus*, with the myth of creation. An Orphic dogma is frequently as valid for Plato in refuting arguments as Socrates' dialectic. Plato had the artist's mind: no other philosopher has ever had a tenth of his influence on creative artists of all kinds, despite the hostility and Philistinism he displays toward them in the *Republic* [bk. 10, 595–607] and the *Laws* [bk. 7, 817]. He realized that the highest knowledge is intuitive rather than intellectual, or, more exactly, that there are two kinds of intellectual perception, understanding and intelligence. The former is the passive recipient and organizer of information: the latter the actively synthesizing mind, which perceives relationships hidden to others and infers a complete pattern from small data: the mind which comprehends the outline of a body from seeing a fossilized knuckle-bone. Such a mind is essentially a symbolic mind: it is continually selecting outward experiences significant for inward ones. So the myth in Plato does duty for the presentation of this ultimate, symbolic form of truth.

The appeal of Orphism was peculiarly Platonic in its philosophical implications. It dealt with the world in terms of an antithesis: evil was positive and actual; good, ideal and potential. Logically, therefore, it was a religion depending on the rejection of the world. It tended to see the world as Heraclitus saw it, a seething mass of dissolving unrealities, without stability, order, or recognizable purpose behind it. The real, the permanent, to the Orphic lay elsewhere. If the world was to be rejected and the flesh cast off and despised, only the mind could arrive at truth, so that truth and reality were purely mental phenomena. This does not mean that they are purely subjective: what is subjective about us is only the bodily, sensible part of us. Our prisoned souls, which alone can apprehend truth, know it really and objectively. This is at once Platonic philosophy and Orphic theology, and it is evident that Plato was peculiarly fitted to be the interpreter of Orphism. To the inductive, empiric mind of Aristotle, who identified myth with art, art with fiction, and distinguished them all from facts, Orphism made no appeal. He saw no sharp dualism of soul and body: to him the soul was the form of the body. He saw no sharp cleavage, therefore, between truth of the soul, which was formal and ideal, and truth of the body, which according to Plato was relative and uncertain. His great authority may be said to have destroyed the prestige of Orphism as an intellectualized, theological religion.

By Paul's time Orphism becomes as elusive as Proteus. It formed, necessarily, the religious basis of Neoplatonism, but the fertile minds of the Neoplatonic commentators read what they liked into the Orphic tradition. The three centuries between Paul and Alexander the Great had seen the Greek and Oriental world come into contact and produce the Graeco-Asiatic mixture we call the Hellenistic civilization. An enormous number of identifications of gods took place. The Hellenic Olympian worship, like the Baal worship of the Phoenicians, was thoroughly localized: it tended to assume that the gods worshipped in any locality were powerful in and for that locality. This developed into a bureaucratic conception of divinity, and many of the better-educated Romans paid homage to whatever deities they considered most powerful, often including Jehovah and Christ in their worship. At the same time, the striking similarities of different pantheons soon led to rapid assimilation. The wholesale identification of Greek and Roman gods is familiar to everyone. The fertility gods, Attis, Adonis, Osiris, Dionysus, soon blended: Adonis gradually extended his sway over Greece, Attis over Rome.

Orphism had always had something syncretic about it: it was never thoroughly assimilated to Greece, and the similarities between it and Hinduism almost preclude the possibility of entirely independent development. In Palestine the Essenes were perhaps the leading exponents of Orphic and semi-Orphic views.

IV

In Paul's time mystery religions were everywhere, but it is probably safer to lay emphasis on Paul's differences from them rather than his connections with them. Paul never accepted any doctrine of the mechanical or magical efficacy of rites, and Messrs. Kennedy and Anderson Scott have fairly well exploded the theory that his use of initiate terminology was really technical.[35] But most of these and other doctrines of the mystery religions were as much bad Orphism as they would have been bad Paulinism. Orphism had accompanied the great cultural achievements of Greece: its great moment had come with Plato. Aristotle had destroyed it intellectually, and Aristotle's contemporary Alexander the Great had started a theocrasia which had long before Paul's time inundated its finer elements. Its esoteric character had disappeared: its rites were casually mentioned and discussed rather than vaguely hinted at, as in Plato and even in the dramatists contemporary with him. The philosophers of the day were on the whole, even the Neoplatonists, closer to the philosophy of Stoicism than the religion of Orphism. The Orphic way of life, whatever popular appeal it still had, was not the religion of the "best people" in Paul's time. At first sight it might seem that to talk of any connection of Paul with Orphism would be like talking of the influence of Franciscan nominalism on a contemporary evangelist: that whatever connections we might find we could put down to pure coincidence. To a large extent this is undoubtedly true. One of the most important questions in connection with Paul's affiliations with the mystery religions is that of his view of sacrament, more particularly of the communal meal; and it is highly probable that the Orphics gave this up: their prohibitions against meat-eating and wine-drinking strike at it in its two possible forms of sacrifice and sacrament. The extent to which Orphism retained its hold on the people after it had lost its hold on the philosophers is a matter of hypothesis, not certainty. The point has been made that allusions to Orphic rites in Aristophanes and his successors would depend on a widespread popular knowledge of them.[36] Religion is inherently conservative, and the Greeks were the most conservative of peoples. Some transmission of tradition from the Orphic devout contemporary with Plato to the cultural milieu of Paul is a long way from impossibility.

Let us review, as briefly as possible, the obvious comparisons and contrasts between Orphism and Christianity as a whole. Both religions centred around the ideas of new birth, regeneration, conversion. Both regarded religion as essentially a way of life. And while the founder and the god of Orphism were not united into one figure, as with Christianity, still the story of the martyred infant Zagreus undoubtedly does illustrate the fact, if it illustrates nothing more, that the symbolism of the story of Christ went home to all men, for all nations had been struggling to formulate something like it in their own religions from the earliest times.

The purpose of conversion in each religion was deliverance from evil. In Orphism there was no clear idea of sin, because their moral ideas had not yet become separated from magical ones and because there was in Orphism no definitely personal god. Purification for the Orphic always had something hygienic, something purely physical, about it. Between the moral sin of injustice and the breaking of a magical taboo of vegetarianism they made no distinction. Of course, this distinction should not be pressed too far, as Christianity probably escaped very little further, in practice whatever its theory was, from the same thing. And broadly speaking, both religions accepted, from their own points of view and interpretations of the concepts, the doctrine of original sin and the feeling that ordinary experience provided a dissatisfaction religious experience could overcome.

We have mentioned the connections between Orpheus and Jesus and the fact that a link between the religions was preserved by the Christians themselves, who in their paintings passed from the delineation of Orpheus the musician to Jesus the Good Shepherd. David in most cases serves as the link. Frequently Orpheus is represented as crucified, and there was a tradition of the crucifixion of Orpheus. And, of course, there is a large element of the dying fertility god symbolism about Jesus (cf. John 12:24), and the Orphic's theology was definitely in the direction of making out of Dionysus and Zeus a son-god and a father-god, just as their idea of communion with the god after initiation tended toward monotheism. In eschatology, no doubt, there was more assimilation. The Christians, of course, dispensed with all the paraphernalia of reincarnation, transmigration of souls, the wheel of birth, the ten-thousand-year gaol sentence, and the rest of it. But probably the Orphic idea that there was some intermediate stage between the earthly life and final bliss, some underworld place of judgment, eventually developed, with some help from Virgil, into the Christian purgatory. On the other hand, the Christians believed in bodily resurrection, while the Orphics cremated the body.

These resemblances are too striking to be overlooked: the development of Christology in Greece from Paul to the Nicene Council did not grow out of the air; there must have been a strong theological tradition already present which the dogmas of Christianity summed up. The idea of separating the creative and redemptive principles in the Godhead is surely one peculiar to Greece rather than Judaea: the Jewish tradition postulated more of a gap between human and divine natures. Of course, the early Church Fathers, notably Justin Martyr and Clement of Alexandria, explained these resemblances by falling back on the stock argument that the devil had invented false religions as parodies of the true, so as to confuse the faithful.[37]

But certainly both Orphism and Paulinism have a very similar scaffolding, however different the completed buildings are. The emphasis of both is overwhelmingly eschatological, and they both stress the significance of the ecstatic state. The ecstatic experience of the Orphic initiate is largely magical and, thereby, is far cruder than Paul's; but in both cases the ecstasy is involuntary, something ultimately not related to the human will. For both Paul and the Orphics this points to the unsatisfactory nature of life in the unecstatic state. Both assigned the origin of this to a strain of evil (Paul and the Orphics had, of course, as already explained, very different ideas about evil) inherent in man. The Orphics called this titanic; Paul connected it with Adam. This original sin was in both religions inescapable for the uninitiated. For the Orphics man is bound to an endless wheel of existence: for Paul he lives under the curse of the Law. The penalty of the unregenerate life is in each case associated with fatalism. For the Orphics all living beings are convicted souls: for Paul all of us are judged by the wrath of God. Both connected the antithesis between the life of sin and the life of regeneration with a further antithesis of flesh and spirit. For both, the highest life was ascetic and contemptuous of the body. Both worshipped a sacrificed and reborn god, and both believed that imitation of the god's death and resurrection was connected with conversion. Both tended to feel that the reborn god at the centre of the religion was not the whole of the Godhead: that his work was to save rather than to judge, and that the best image to describe his relation to the creator-god was that of son and father. Paul, of course, and the Orphics probably, accepted the historical reality of the reborn god: the grave of Dionysus was pointed out at Delphi. Both were in any case convinced of his ubiquity and his power to unite all his worshippers in their communion with him. The Pauline church and the Orphic thiasos were both brotherhoods. Both spoke of the religious experience as conversion to a new life: both found in this a regeneration and an escape from the horror of ordinary life. Both believed (cf. Plato in the *Republic*) [bk. 10, 614e–616a] that the sufferings endured by the faithful were of no account beside the rewards of the afterlife. Both were conservative in politics, but uncompromising to the last degree in religion. Both were essentially missionary faiths, working by the founding of brotherhoods rather than by emotional mass appeals.

None of this, of course, touches the climacteric aspect of Paul's teaching. The important things about Paul are things which cannot possibly be wedged into Orphism. Had Paul been just one more Orphic, he would have been, by that time at least, a nonentity. The moral emphasis of Paul, his complete lack of any reliance on mechanical rites, save as a memorial or symbol, his ethical challenge that what was free to one was free to all, shattered the exclusive, selfish, esoteric priggishness of Orphism and thereby destroyed its whole structure. Again, his historical consciousness, his sense of the actuality and the recency of Jesus' life and his sense of the imminence of world catastrophe, gave his message a concrete reference and an urgency the speculations of the Greek sect lacked. He thrust in front of his hearers the time-world they were living in, the world that the Orphics turned away from. Without this, Paul would have been ineffective, just as Orphism was. We can set down his moral and historical senses to his "Jewish influence," if we like; certainly he would never have had them had he not been a Jew. But he was not a mere crossing of Jew and Greek: he was a Christian, something qualitatively different from either, and an individual genius of the type occasionally permitted to appear and change the shape of human history.

Bibliography

Angus[, Samuel]: [The] Mystery-Religions and Christianity[: A Study in the Religious Background of Early Christianity]. New York[: Charles Scribner's Sons], 1925.

Angus[, Samuel]: The Religious Quests of the Graeco-Roman World[: A Study in the Historical Background of Early Christianity]. New York[: Scribner's], 1929.

Deissmann, A. [Gustave Adolf]: St. Paul: A Study in Social and Religious History. London[: Hodder and Stoughton], 1912.

Dodd, C.H.: The Bible and the Greeks. London[: Hodder and Stoughton], 1935.

Frazer, Sir James: The Golden Bough, esp. The Dying God and Adonis, Attis, Osiris. London: Macmillan, 1907–15.

Gilbert, G.H.: Greek Thought in the New Testament. New York[: Macmillan], 1928.

Glover, T.R.: [The] Conflict of Religions in the Early Roman Empire. [London: Methuen, 1909.]

Guthrie, W.K.C.: Orpheus and Greek Religion. London[: Methuen], 1935.

Harrison, Jane: Prolegomena to the Study of Greek Religion[, 3rd ed.]. Cambridge[: Cambridge University Press], 1922.

Harrison, Jane: Themis[: A Study of the Social Origins of Greek Religion, 2nd ed]. Cambridge[: Cambridge University Press], 1927.

Kennedy, H.A.A.: St. Paul and the Mystery-Religions. [London: Hodder and Stoughton, 1913.]

Macchioro, V[ittorio].: From Orpheus to Paul[: A History of Orphism]. New York[: Holt], 1930.

Machen, J.G.: The Origin of Paul's Religion. New York[: Macmillan], 1921.

Murray, Gilbert: Five Stages of Greek Religion. Oxford[: Oxford University Press], 1925.

Nilsson[, Martin P.]: History of Greek Religion. Oxford[: Oxford University Press], 1925.

Plato: Dialogues, esp. those referred to in the text.

Plutarch: Of Superstition.

Nietzsche: The Birth of Tragedy.

Rohde[, Erwin]: Psyche[:The Cult of Souls and Belief in Immortality among the Greeks]. London[: Kegan Paul, Trench, Trubner], 1925.

Schweitzer[, Albert]: Paul and His Interpreters[: A Critical History]. London[: Albert and Charles Black], 1912.

Schweitzer[, Albert]: The Mysticism of Paul the Apostle. London[: Albert and Charles Black], 1931.

Scott, E.F.: The Gospel and Its Tributaries. Edinburgh[: T. and T. Clark], 1928.

Scott, [Charles A.] Anderson: Christianity according to St. Paul. Cambridge[: Cambridge University Press], 1927.

Encyclopaedia of Religion and Ethics: art. "Greek Religion," by L.R. Farnell.

10

The Augustinian Interpretation of History

This paper was written for Kenneth H. Cousland, professor of Church history at Emmanuel College, probably for Church History 5, "Selections from the Christian Fathers and Other Source Readings," which Frye took during his final year at Emmanuel (1935–36). Frye received an "A+" for the paper, and on the last page Cousland wrote: "This is so good that it's worth considering a development of it into a thesis and publishing it. A good book on the subject is needed." The essay is divided into three sections, marked by two spaces Frye left in the typescript, which is in the NFF, 1991, box 37, file 11.

It is generally admitted, with regard to St. Augustine's *De Civitate Dei*, that a book of such enormous influence and power contains a great many things deliberately intended by its author and a great many hints seized upon by a later generation. These latter, being adapted to the needs or at least the desires of a different time, can hardly with justice be assigned to the authority claimed for them, so out of proportion are they to the definite intent of the original. Just which class the element of a philosophy of history belongs to has been variously estimated. Some have been unwilling to see one in the work at all, beyond what is accidental and the result of a reverent but badly strained modern reading. Augustine, these say, did not set out to compose a philosophy of history, but a Christian apologetic, a defence of the Church and an estimate of its place in a crashing civilization. What review there is of world history is cursory and haphazard. Assyria and Rome serve vaguely as examples of the *civitas terrena*;[1] Greece and Egypt are ignored.[2] The attitude to Hebrew culture is purely didactic, consisting of glosses on the Biblical narrative. Augustine is not interested in history, but in morals, and moral standards are too small a yardstick by which to measure the course of actual events. Thus, the superimposing of the theory of the two cities on the history of the ancient world grossly oversimplifies the problem. It may possess some value as a religious symbol, a poetic metaphor, or a weapon of dialectic, but to call it a serious interpretation of history commits a grave injustice against a book having another emphasis altogether. Its only political relevance is to the medieval quarrel of pope and emperor; and as this problem did not exist for Augustine, it is not surprising if both sides could appeal to his work, which deals only with an ideal relationship.[3]

Thus far, and much farther, the devil's advocate; but others adopt a different bias. They claim much for Augustine in this field, even going so far as to assert his unqualified priority. The classical world, they argue, gave us no philosophy of history at all. Only a world religion could do that, one which had worked out its own attitude toward the relationship of man to God, and which had absorbed most of the sacred and profane thought of the age. In Augustine for the first time the program was laid down, and it is his interpretation of history, and that alone, which emerges from the pages of a vast, digressive, and chaotic book to give it vital and searching significance for us today. He may be obsolete, riddled with superstition and prejudice, or he may contain an outlook which the thought of our time must absorb to reach a finally valid position. But of his originality there can be no question.[4]

What does appear evident is that everything in Augustine's day seems to converge on exactly this problem. Practically everything of importance in the thought of the last three centuries was irresistibly tending to it as the last question to be reached by speculation and the first to be solved for constructive advance. All the political events similarly seemed to make the first task of a thinker of primary importance the working out of some intelligible view of a world which seemed to be crashing around the ears of a perplexed generation standing between paganism and Christianity, wondering which was safer. If St. Augustine had no philosophy of history, he certainly missed his calling as a philosopher. If there is any truth in a fairly obvious maxim that the great man is he who brings to fullest expression the intellectual attitude of his time, he would not be likely to have attained much eminence, except through a misunderstanding. Let us briefly review, then, the elements in the culture of the fifth century which made a philosophy of history imperative, before trying to decide whether one was contributed by St. Augustine.

We shall first have to see whether there is anything in the thought of the ancient world corresponding to it.

It has been repeatedly remarked that the great philosophical and artistic structure of Greek culture was reared quite without reference to the course of history, which is less true of the still earlier Egyptian and Mesopotamian ones. The Egyptians in particular preserved the records of the past strictly and accurately. But that profoundly religious sense of a purpose in the world, of some shape and meaning to the course of history, was lacking, apparently, and with good reason. A philosophy of history is a mature and comparatively late thought-product, because of its emphasis on perspective and a catholicity of thought. We can hardly be conscious of any large meaning to the past, over and above the mere interest of its records, or the occasional moral lessons it may teach (it was this latter kind of meaning Hegel had in mind when he said: "We learn from history that men never learn anything from history")[5] without at least one of two prerequisites. The first we shall deal with more fully later—the religious awe which sees in the progression of human activities the working out of a divine plan. We shall here only notice that such a religion has to be strongly allied to abstract thought in order to examine the problem, and monotheistic, giving a supreme deity enough power and knowledge for the task. The complete divorce of the religions of the ancient world from their philosophies, coupled with the chaotic god-families inherited from centuries of superstition and barbarity, partly caused and partly resulted from the lack of historical understanding. The second is the knowledge that the course of world events has recently turned in a perplexing, distressing way which forces the men implicated in it to turn their attention to the currents propelling them, to find out where they are going, and what has brought them to where they are.[6]

Any thinker is primarily and essentially a member of the age which produced him. Now as long as he belongs to a civilization which is normally expanding and prosperous, he reflects something of its buoyancy and energy. The problems that exist for him are the problems of the universe. For the only possible objects of knowledge are those which change, so as to attract attention, and yet remain more or less constant, so as to be subject to analysis. A certain amount of regularity or recurrence belongs to everything worked into a system of speculation or experiment. But a philosopher deceived by the ease with which his society bears him along, will, according to his bias, think of human society as a fact too assured and requisite to go behind, or a phenomenon too fleeting and evanescent to be worth investigating. Often he will say the latter when he means the former. The first event in history likely to give one pause, to divert the attention of thinkers to mankind and his fortunes, is the rise and fall of a civilization. The perception of a great rhythmic beat in history is the first step in the direction of trying to understand it, and such an idea hardly suggests itself until a great empire collapses. It is, thus, apparent that the primal civilizations, Egyptian, Babylonian, or even Greek, had little to go on in the way of precedent. On the other hand, the crash of Rome before the barbarians, preceded as it had been by the downfall of so many tentative world empires, was more than enough, considering the prestige of the city, to wake up the most ecstatic Neoplatonist to the affairs going on around him. The one supreme effort at world dominion and world unification, begun by Alexander and ended by Hadrian,[7] had completely and signally failed.

Another aspect of the problem, bound up with this one, is more obvious if less important. The necessity for an impartial survey, already indicated, implies a cosmopolitanism which is so broad as to include the whole world, or as much of it as is known. Any philosophy which attempts to include history in its survey, emanating as it must from a religious force, has to find in that religious force universal applicability. It must be able to analyse the various characteristics of each race and the causes of their divergent fortunes. This is the leading reason for the failure of the Greeks to get very far in this field. Athenian philosophers could hardly learn much from the fate of Nineveh or Sardis,[8] besides platitudes about the instability of human interests, when they regarded all non-Greeks as equally barbarous. There is no such thing as Greek history in the modern sense of the word. To Herodotus, history was a saga; to Thucydides, a drama.[9] Both writers owe their extraordinary vividness simply to their tendency to wipe out the past by making it one with the present.[10] The ideal of the historian was the ideal of the poet—to delight and instruct. Greek history derives entirely from the tradition of its greatest poet—Homer. Even with the maturest developments of Greek thought no attempt is made to evaluate the non-Hellenic, even to think in terms of a larger political unit than the city state. The difference in reference between Plato's πόλις [polis] and Augustine's civitas is enormous. The natural unit of historical thought is not the city, in itself an artificial and extremely haphazard form of society, but the race and the civilization produced by the race. Not that there was any native inability on the part of the Greeks to investigate problems of human origins; the argument of Glaucon in the *Republic* of Plato sounds like an early Thomas Hobbes,[11] and the wonderful eighth book is an analysis of civic degeneration unparalleled in philosophy.[12] Aristotle, too, taking all knowledge for his province, made a study of the various forms of government and their interrelation. But political theory is not a philosophy of history. The explanation for this hiatus in Greek civilization can only be of the broadest. Christianity has given the world a religious synthesis of all the faculties of the soul—will, feeling, and reason—in which none need predominate. Any culture lacking this is forced to lean mainly on reason for constructive development—reason in Plato, as with Greek philosophers generally, being assigned the mastery of the civilized man. But reason works with static, timeless forms—for nothing is true unless it is eternally true—and the whole Greek view of life was formal. The infinite was simply the chaotic. The aesthetic ideal was perfect form; all nature, in Aristotle, tended upwards to pure form. But form, in a world of time and space, is purely spatial; the analysis of the time-problem belongs to the Christian tradition alone. Even in Heraclitus, impermanence and becoming, as characteristic of the universe, so thoroughly permeated it that analysis was given up as hopeless. In Greece there was a conspiracy of silence between the cosmological and the ethical thinkers against history, just as today there is a conspiracy of silence between the evolutionists and the physicists against history, as a factor in philosophy. So in classical history fact and legend are hopelessly entangled. A hero is deified as soon as dead; and when tradition was obscure or not sufficiently picturesque the creative imagination had full sway. The sense of sacredness or potency in the past was entirely lacking. With Thucydides, no events of importance had occurred before the Persian Wars; that is, before the time which could still be associated with the present. Nor was there much idea of a teleology; Greek history, with its interminable city-state wars, not giving any overwhelming conviction in any case of an intelligent purpose at work over all the world.[13]

What is true of Greek history is true in part of Roman history. But Sallust, Tacitus, Suetonius, are far nearer the modern attitude, because of the greater maturity of their position. Where the Greeks had looked out upon Greece, the Romans looked out upon the world, and the access of cosmopolitanism brought them far more closely into touch with the historical problem. Besides, the more legalistic, politically minded Romans turned their attention, far more than the Greeks, to the problem of human interests. The administrative faculty largely replacing the artistic one, they gradually developed some idea of what is necessary to a world outlook. The Roman tradition is a strong and necessary ingredient in Augustine's thought, for it runs almost without a break, through Tyconius, Varro, and Seneca, into the pages of *De Civitate Dei*. But the necessary preoccupation of the Romans with the *pax Romana*, the attempt to keep the world as it was, subject to Rome, still precluded a fearless handling of the theme of eternal change in the life of man, as contrasted with the true peace, to be found nowhere on this earth. One sign of a great historian is his complete scepticism with regard to the indefinite continuance of any human institution.[14]

A strong and prosperous nation does not take kindly to a philosophy of history. It needs no great white hope in the future, nor promise in the past; it lives in the pure present as a causal agent, not as an actor in a larger drama. Augustine had available the whole Jewish tradition of a nation as proud and self-sufficient as any of the Greeks, yet constantly subject to overlordship. The Old Testament canon is entirely unique, in the literature of the ancient world, in its historical outlook, distributed as it was between the past and the future. It was necessarily the textbook for any early Christian philosophy, as it is throughout conceived in terms of the relationship of man to God, as illustrated by the history of one nation.

The decline and collapse of the one great world empire, removing the only apparently eternal principle from history, first brought men's minds sharply around to the problems of immediate existence. Whatever the motive, this was certainly the immediate occasion for Augustine's book. But this political disaster was accompanied, necessarily, by a similar weakening in philosophy. The systematic development of Greek thought culminates and concludes with Aristotle, along with the fall of the city state at the hands of the Macedonians. The conquest of Asia loosed a torrent of exotic philosophies into Greece, and to these influences the Greek thinkers lay open, the various cities having all murdered each other and having exhausted their creative vitality. The intellectual strength, the naive confidence in the power of logic, the self-sufficiency of the solutions, which characterized the vigorous upward development of Greek thought, waned and finally faded out, as academic pedantry succeeded it. But pedantry means, first and last, a reliance on some authority, preferably ancient, necessarily reputable.

Hence, the rise of sects of commentators, of the Neo-Pythagoreans and the great Neoplatonists. But that the authority should be as high as possible, philosophical sterility becomes increasingly religious in its bias, partly because of the impulse to make the authority divine, partly through the exhaustion of the unsupported reason. Here is where the Oriental religions came in. Most were old, some were wise, and those that were neither were at least esoteric, thus possessing an equal appeal. The instinct of the commentator and critic broadened out into some idea of a history of philosophy, the development and mutation of forms of thought, which is merely the other side of a philosophy of history. Just how broad this grasp was the destruction of Alexandrian literature has prevented us from knowing. Another Alexandrian tendency developing from this, that runs from Philo into Christianity at least as far as Clement, is the large attempt to give Greek logic as a whole its place in a synthesis with the religious traditions of the Orient. This is the farthest that the pre-Christian world could go in the direction of historical interpretation.

The development of Christianity brought into the limelight the definite problem. The doctrine of the Incarnation is in itself a philosophy of history, as was recognized by the New Testament writers.[15] The Pauline Epistles, the Epistle to the Hebrews, the Gospel of Matthew, and, with a reversion to an earlier mannerism, the Apocalypse, see in the historical figure of Jesus the keystone of religion and philosophy, thus concentrating the crux of all thought in the world of time. In the first place, ethics received a tremendous stimulus in the discovery of human personality. The entry of God into the world of men, the ideas of sacrifice and atonement, had necessarily placed supreme value on the individual soul. Almost immediately Christianity was freed from its Jewish affiliations and made representative of the entire world, thus synthesizing the historical bias of the Jews and the cosmopolitan outlook of the empire. If Christianity seems in its earlier stages to underemphasize the intellectual side, it is only because it is busied in giving knowledge a new approach. With the Greeks, the metaphysical basis of thought had reference primarily to eternal forms. Reality subsists, with Plato, in universals. Consequently, all events in the world of time are the mere flickering of shadows, the incessant aberrations of the material copies of truth. Truth itself lies in eternity, and can only be inferred from history. And this, as before pointed out, is the farthest that philosophy, in itself, can go. The *Timaeus* hesitates on the borderland, not knowing its way

in.[16] The swing to religion integrates the personality, so that the macrocosm is no longer abstract essence, the reflection of the reasoning power
alone, but becomes a correspondingly infinite personality—a personal
God. This conception can hardly be held without peculiar reference to
the world of personalities, so that the creation of the world of time and
space becomes polar to an Incarnation, like foci of a great ellipse round
which all knowledge revolves as its two primary data.[17]

No doubt much of this was purely eschatological, but the permanent
and abiding part of it was not. The new approach, however, had to work
out some relationship of the world to God, and this task the Gnostics set
themselves. It is largely to this heresy that we owe the beginnings of the
Christian philosophy of history. The synthesis to be made was, of
course, the ever present one of the Greek philosophy and the Christian
religion. Now the Greeks had rested their case, with regard to God and
the world, on a dualism in which the eternal form was real and the
material only an idolatrous manifestation of the real. From the Orient
came the interest in the working of God in history. As all human history
must be considered in relation to God, and as human history has been a
heart-breaking record of aspiration and defeat, evidently God must be
struggling against another power, this one evil. Zoroaster represents the
ultimate position of the East in regard to the philosophy of history.
What more natural, then, than that, as a basis for combining two traditions, the Platonic distinction of the idea and the object, the Aristotelian
division of form and matter, should be identified with the ethical distinction of good and evil as the driving force in history?

Unfortunately this identification forced the Gnostics to regard the
God of the Old Testament, who created the world of matter, as an evil
being. To the extent that this world was full of unredeemed pagans, they
were no doubt in line with the orthodox, but the doctrine of the original
sin of Adam shelved that difficulty. The attempt soon broke down of its
own accord. If matter, being evil, is not reality, neither is evil. The difference between superstition and enlightenment in religion, in fact, is
exactly this; that in the former evil is positive, and in the latter negative,
merely a defection from the good. The enormous complexities of the
Gnostic eons and emanations illustrate the difficulty of deriving a positive evil from a more positive good. God the Father and God the Son, if
they are flatly incompatible, hardly deserve their names.

The religious dualism found its clearest expression in the Manicheans,
and, whatever his final position, St. Augustine is irrevocably stamped

with the seals both of Mani and Plato.[18] Thus, he stands for us in the fifth century, heir to the complete will and testament of the ancient world. The question whether Augustine was essentially the last thinker of ancient history or the first of medieval answers itself by being asked. He had absorbed the essence, for his purpose, of Plato, he had outgrown the Manicheans, he knew of the Gnostics, and he understood why they had failed. He lived through the fall of the Roman Empire and a very early period of official Christianity. Philosophically and politically he was "on the spot," or, in a more dignified phrase, the man of the hour.[19]

So far we have spoken of the philosophy of history as one of the ultimate secrets or inner mysteries of Christianity. And this we believe to be the case. It is no accident that this factor did not enter philosophy until Christianity did. No matter how we approach the problem, the philosophy of history is the ultimate theoretical activity of the human race, and can only be worked out by thinkers in the tradition of a true religion. In the foregoing prolegomenon we have tried to show why theology, not philosophy alone, can cope with the problem. All science, no matter in what field, is of value only when it is coordinated into a philosophical system. Thus, philosophy is admittedly deeper and more fundamental than science. But no system is infallible, the reason being that it has simply gathered up the achievements and attitude of its own time. In its last essence it is a historical phenomenon; thus, the history of philosophy underlies abstract philosophy as the latter does science. But the history of philosophy is only a part of a universal history, which cannot be theoretically examined unless it contain certain fixed principles which will yield to analysis. This gives us the philosophy of history, and behind that we cannot go. Our first data of perception are time and space. But all knowledge is essentially space-knowledge, as it works with forms which, to be true, have to be independent of time, and all existence is in time, so that the most fundamental activity of knowledge is its relation to existence. The coordinated form of knowledge is philosophy, and the coordinated form of existence, history. Or, to take it the other way, existing in time, we must grasp knowledge as a temporal progression, and as we know nothing of the future and understand nothing of the present, except by what we infer from the past, it is upon the past we have to turn. We have tried to show why men were not ready for that activity until a great civilization had collapsed and until a sufficiently powerful religious force had gripped them. It would appear, then, that there are two factors necessary to grasp in order to make sense of the problem.

The first is the civilization as the organic unit of history; the second is the Incarnation.

First, then, for Augustine, the political problem, the collapse of the Roman Empire. It was easy to accuse the upstart religion to which Augustine belonged of having caused the downfall, and the first ten books are taken up with defending the Christians and attacking the pagans. For our present thesis this is important in clearing the ground for the doctrine of the two cities. The immediate, obvious opposition Augustine had to contend with was that of paganism and Christianity; not until that was outlined could the theory of the two cities follow. The latter is an abstract conception of some difficulty, and to introduce it at the outset would upset what balance the book still retains. Although it is not deliberately a philosophy of history, but an apologetic, the germ is there.[20] Almost at once Augustine outlines the essential change that the coming of Christianity has made in the world. Christianity is not responsible for the fall of Rome (I, i), in the sense that the Romans have failed through deserting the gods that could have helped her. These same gods lost Troy (I, iii); how should they preserve Rome? On the other hand, Christianity has brought an entirely new note of gentleness: Rome's Christian conquerors spared her to an extent which Rome herself never practised toward her foes (I, ii). In the ancient world there was no idea of anything else than the most brutal revenge in warfare (I, iv). No, the cause of the Roman defeat lay in herself (II), in her essential weakness and wickedness. Her empire, allotted to her as a reward for certain terrestrial virtues (V), such as justice, temperance, courage, and so on—on which Augustine dwells with much enthusiasm—has been forfeited by her vice.

Several important inferences for a philosophy of history, thus, emerge at the outset. In the first place, the Roman Empire, the strongest and finest of man-made institutions, is passing; therefore, no man-made institution can indefinitely endure. On the one hand, the Romans have been gradually struggling upward toward the light (IV)—Varro, among many others, has recently condemned image worship and commended the monotheism of the Jews. On the other, they have been steadily going downhill morally and have collapsed on account of it (II). The process illustrates the helplessness of man without divine grace (III). Rendered into modern terminology, but without any essential change of meaning, this means that the curve described was inevitable; that is, it was the normal process of growth, maturation, and decay through which a civilization, like the individual, like all organic life, must go. The only thing that can overcome this is a sudden evolutionary upthrust by which a new form of energy, mysteriously but definitely, enters and moves on to a higher development.

The Incarnation proves God at work in the world (V); God must have some purpose in the world. But his purpose overrides all individual fortunes—we can never gain material prosperity or security simply by following the true God (I). God does not bribe or reward. Here at a touch falls a lingering superstition which is inevitable to a philosophy of history attempted from a parochial point of view. In this Augustine abandons the Hebrew tradition in favour of the cosmopolitanism of the Empire. We have tried to show that no philosophy of history can be complete if worked out through a nationalistic bias; for with this, God, or the historical process, or whatever ultimate is taken, exists only to justify the philosopher's immediate hopes and patriotisms. The German tradition we usually associate with the philosophy of history fails, as with Fichte, Goethe, Hegel, Nietzsche, Leibnitz, Spengler, exactly here, in its attempt to identify God with the driving force of German development. Mazzini sees world history as justifying nineteenth-century Italy; Macaulay sees little of importance which does not lead up to the English Whig; even Comte's humanism, a parasitic growth on Christianity, is a purely French ideal.[21] But Augustine sweeps all the sons of Adam into one category and assumes at once the natural gregariousness of the species—two necessary postulates.

Rome, the highest constructive effort of unaided man, is passing, and justifies the omnipotence of God by doing so (II, III). Hence, the whole idea of a world empire is a mirage. It would be better for man to formulate his political existence in a smaller and more manageable unit—a state which is neither aggressively militaristic, like an empire, nor defensively so, like a city state (IV, xv). This note of anti-imperialism caused much quarrelling in the Middle Ages.

Another highly significant contribution is the famous tag (IV, iv): *Remota justitia, quid regna nisi magna latrocinia?*[22] Substitute a more materialistic meaning of Justitia than it possesses here, with its Platonic overtones, and we have the germ of Karl Marx. It sounds like a strange alignment at first, but let us look more closely. "Justice" is that spontaneous social cooperation which man has through his native constitution as a political animal. Without this, the state is purely material: the essence of the *civitas terrena*. Such a state can be held together only by the force of men who maintain order for their own sakes. This is organized brigandage, nothing short of the exploitation of the subject-class of society for the benefit of the rulers. Now any thinker who holds that materialistic forces are the main conditioning impulses of history is bound in consistency to extend Augustine's epigram to the whole of history, calling the latter a record of class struggles.[23]

In these first five books comes a hint as well of Augustine's conception of history as a fundamentally aesthetic product, fashioned by God the supreme artist. The question may be raised if the omnipotence and omniscience of God do not lead to regarding history as the working out of the divine plan, artistic or otherwise, and so deprive it of any inherent reality at all. It is this conception which Augustine is at pains to deny. Despite the power of divine grace, man's will is free, and he exists in the world as a causal agent (V, ix). God can foresee the effects of the cause, necessarily, but does not manipulate the historical process without reference to mankind: the spasmodic intervention of miracles shows us that the plan is not a prearranged or mechanical one. The life of mankind has a supreme intrinsic importance; thus, Augustine preserves the central essence of Christianity, avoiding the pitfalls of solipsism which beset a great deal of speculative Christian thought.

The next five books cut deeper into the contrast of Christian and pagan. Augustine brings up the best that he can find in paganism in order to weigh it and find it wanting. No intelligible shape can be assumed by history as long as the deities are conceived as partial, as good only for special departments (VI). An intelligible view of the world must reflect a dominant intelligence. But what is true of God in relation to the gods is true of the city of God in relation to the *civitas terrena*. The state is established on religion, not religion on the state (VI, iv) as the classical thinkers had said. The latter conception can hold only as long as religion is a matter entirely separate from the other activities of man. Two characteristics mark Christianity sharply off from paganism— really two sides of the one. In the first place, Christianity is faithful to the highest ideals of the soul. Augustine's incessant ridiculing of the puerilities of the various pagan cults, together with his lengthy denunciations of their obscenities, merely serves to emphasize the fact that he does not believe it is possible to detach paganism from its darker side (VI). These are inextricably entangled, so much so that pagan religious thought, as is admitted openly by Varro and Seneca, shows a vicious tendency to fashion its gods out of the worst elements in the human soul (VI, VII). Even with the great Neoplatonists, the same sadistic streak is reflected in their assigning demons a higher role in the universe than man (VIII). Augustine, thus, brings out into the limelight his essential insistence on the supreme importance of humanity. Nothing intervenes between man and God; the Incarnation, God becoming man, settled that once for all (VIII). Hence, there is necessary the theistic relationship between God and man, as only a personal God could become a personality. Augustine attacks pantheism on the one hand (VII, xxix), thereby separating the world from God so as to allow for his antithetical distinction of the two cities, the one existing in time, the other in eternity. On the other hand, he attacks Plato's doctrine, or what he considered to be Plato's doctrine, that God holds no intercourse with men (VIII, xviii). It goes without saying, of course, that the antinomianism of the classical world, the tendency to deify heroes, was another result of slurring over the time-problem (VIII, xxvi). The Christian historical attitude, which is focused on a critical historical event, makes that event unique of necessity. Christianity's God became man, but no Christian man becomes a deity. We respect our saints, says Augustine, but we do not worship them (VIII, xxvii). A corollary of this tendency is the insistence on heroic and pompous gods. Augustine glories in the supreme humiliation of Jesus and mocks those too proud to stomach the idea (X).

The wonderful tenth book, largely a panegyric on the worship of one all-powerful God, brings out the second unique contribution of Christianity, which develops from the first. With the Greeks, religion was one thing and philosophy another. Christianity had synthesized them. The split had entailed a similar division between the will and the reason, the conative tendency to faith and worship having nothing to do with the logical processes of the intellect. The result was that the union of soul and body was imperfectly attained. The body expressed itself in religion, the spirit in abstract speculation. That was why it was impossible to separate the pagan religions from the orgiastic and obscene elements. And on the other hand, Greek philosophers despised the body, a tendency Augustine attacks (X, xxix). Here Augustine puts his finger on the focal weakness of Greek thought. In VI he draws out very clearly the difference between the Christian concept of the practice of religion as the whole of life and the perfunctory ritualism of the pagans. The one is the religion of an integrated personality, the other not.

There is a sharp antithesis between a religion of Incarnation and a religion of reincarnation. The first postulates the possibility of indefinite development towards an ideal. The second excludes this in its doctrine of an eternal recurrence of life. The idea of the soul as something fixed and immortal, and the body as the accidental house of the soul, also implies a lack of comprehending soul and body as complementary to the individual and each vitally necessary. Hence, reincarnation, the refuge of an exhausted religious force, is unsparingly ridiculed (X, xxx).

Broadly speaking, the first five books abolish the efficacy of the pagan gods in the *civitas terrena*; the second five banish them from the *civitas Dei*. It is true that the work, consciously, is an apologetic rather than a Christian philosophy of history, but we entirely miss the point by not realizing that Augustine fully grasps the possibility of the latter and the factors which make it possible. In fact, he understands it so well that he practically takes it for granted; that is why it is necessary to approach him through his historical and philosophical background. We have said that for a valid philosophy of history the two factors necessary are the concept of the culture or civilization as the unit of history and the concept of an historical Incarnation which, by its uniqueness, gives history a direction as the other idea gives it its shape. The first is the spatial or pictorial aspect; the second, the temporal or dramatic. The first five books give us what Augustine understood of the first; the next five are an apology for the second.

In the rest of the work the two ideas are combined in the concept of the two cities. The fact that no one has been able to say precisely what Augustine meant by the word *civitas* should at least hint that he was trying to express something to which his time offered no concrete illustration. At times the city of God is apparently the Church, yet it is not quite the Church. Sometimes the city of the world is the Roman Empire, yet it is not altogether that either. It is apparent that the cities symbolize the relation of God to man, in that the former exists in eternity and is changeless, the latter in time and is transient.[24] The *civitas terrena* is of the world, the *civitas Dei*, being made up of men, is perforce in it. A further idea they symbolize is, consequently, the material and the form of Plato's distinction. The two cities are both fundamentally theological ideas rather than historical generalizations. That is, they derive from philosophy and are only metaphors when applied to history. Hence, they are strait waistcoats confining a specific historical survey—the long view of world history is largely rather sterile allegory. Though they express a profound idea underlying history, they contain the suggestion that, no matter how important the temporal existence of man may be, the historical process itself is something abrogated by the Resurrection. But if this is true, it is only because Augustine's attitude places supreme emphasis upon the ideal in history. The ideal, however, is a concretion, not an abstraction—it is in this that the profundity of his thought lies. Had Augustine remained a Manichean, he would have run the antithesis of good form against evil matter into history. Then the solution would probably have been ascetic, entailing a flight from the world and a denial of the body. But in refusing to regard evil as anything positive, Augustine keeps both cities in the world. The Greek ethical solution, arrived at by reason alone, was the golden mean, negatively stated as the avoidance of extremes. The Christian one, reached by the entire soul, takes the same course, but positively, regarding the mean as the synthesis of the extremes. A completely spiritualized existence being impossible in this world, the true course is neither flight from the world nor absorption into it, but a working harmony which does both at once, seeing always the ideal through the reality.

Augustine was heir to a tradition which separated the idea from the object, but he saw, with his historical insight, that there was a deeper distinction underlying that, the relationship of eternity to time. He accordingly begins (XI, ii) with the moment of separation of time from eternity—the creation of the world. All objects are in the mind of man, all forms in that of God. The city of God begins with the creation of light (XI, vii), the means by which man is able to comprehend his maker's works, while the *civitas terrena* is correlated with the duration of time. Thus, time is bound up with the historical process; it is essentially to be considered in relation to changes in the external world, and is not simply a subjective form of perception (XI, v). But time necessitates imperfection, in order to be distinct from eternity, and, therefore, evil arose, not created by God, but an essential element in his creation (XI, xvii). That is one reason why for Augustine there is no hope for the *civitas terrena* in itself; all time proceeds by a synthesis of good and evil (XI, xviii), which means everlasting struggle and war as its leading characteristics (XII, iv).

Augustine is, consequently, most ruthlessly realistic, in the most approved modern way, when dealing with the earthly city (XII). The essence of material life is a struggle for existence (XII, iv), so that all nature takes on the form of the predominant types, the fittest surviving. Pride is the beginning of all sin (XII, vi); this is symbolized at the creation by Lucifer's revolt and is continued throughout history in the form of exploitation and class struggle. (Augustine partly ameliorates his pessimism on this score by his denial of the longevity of the world (XII, iv) and his conception of it as an artistic product of God, the beauty of which serves to glorify him.)

Pride is the assertion of will, declaring itself independent of reason, and breaking the religious grip which alone holds the soul together. The essential distinction between the two cities, he says later (XIV, xxviii), is that the earthly glorifies the self at the expense of God, the righteous one reversing the process. The only evil is the evil will (XII, vi) taking the wrong course deliberately, as a deficient rather than an efficient cause (XII, vii), out of a desire for the assertion of the ego (XII, viii). There is no definite source for evil except in the will (XII, ix): it does not come from flesh, which is not evil in itself, nor from temptation, for pride antedates temptations (XIV, xiii). The subordination of the flesh means merely that pride prefers the flesh to the spirit (XIV, iii).

The emphasis on original sin (XIII, xi–xx), the doctrine that men are necessarily in themselves evil, is an integral factor of Augustine's position. The philosopher wants a unity of soul and body, but the personal presence of the spirit of God makes it necessary that in order to advance in what we should now call the evolutionary scale the human spirit should control the human body, the body being still associated with the lower, more animal side of life. To postulate the whole of the human soul as good, to admit no hierarchy over our impulses and desires, is to revert to the animal stage. The cry of the man who considers man constitutionally good is, back to nature! and, whatever he means, he is revolting against the social instinct of mankind, which is based on subordination of self-assertive elements.

Augustine now proceeds to a review of history in the light of the two cities thesis (XV–XVIII). This need not detain us very long, as, though logically necessary to the completion of his scheme, it adds nothing to and detracts much from the force of his preceding argument. He divides history more or less unconsciously into its various civilizations (XVIII): Assyrian, Greek, Egyptian, Hebrew, and Roman. Of these, Greece and Egypt are ignored, largely for artistic reasons. The contrast of Rome and Christian Church affords an effective antithesis roughly corresponding to that of the two cities; though the inhabitants of the city of God are not the members of the Church, necessarily, but the truly elect (XIX), some of whom are outside the Church. The inhabitants of the city of God cannot be definitely equated with any earthly institution. Before the coming of Christianity another contrast, more approximate than the later, can be found in the Hebrew and Assyrian civilizations (XVIII, xxiv). The latter is pure *civitas terrena*; the former was the sole abode of those in the higher city on the earth, but still not that city: otherwise the promises of permanence in the Bible would refer to the Jewish state, which they obviously do not. As it is, however, Hebrew culture in its prophecies is more ancient, more uniform, more consistent, than anything in Greece (XVIII). The city proper, life concentrated in the world, is the symbol of the *civitas terrena* (XV, i); the inhabitants of the heavenly city, in the world though not of it, are symbolized as wanderers and pilgrims on the earth. The contrast begins with Cain and Abel (XV, i). Cain built the first city; Abel was a pilgrim. The Tower of Babel is the supreme example of an earthly city (XVI), the largest instance of pride and self-esteem exalted in contempt of God. And so on, with a general antithetical scheme running all through, sometimes ingenious, sometimes striking, sometimes rather forced. It is difficult to see why Sarah and Hagar (XV) line up so definitely as respective types of the cities.

After reiterating the nature of the change which the coming of Christianity has made in the world, Augustine passes on (XIX) to a more exhaustive analysis of Greek ethics. He finds their failure to reside in the fact that the great ethical desideratum, the summum bonum, was placed in this life, the Greeks not having any clear conception of an afterlife. With this emphasis on the hereafter as the supreme reality of existence, to which our temporal life is only a prelude and all created time an episode, Augustine's case winds up. This insistence on something otherworldly is necessary to keep an ideal in the world at all, as it is the very essence of an ideal that it does not correspond to anything we can see. Hence, the ethical solution for this life is negatively stated as peace (XIX, xi), the cessation of struggle. This is precisely the reverse of the goal of those who do not go outside the earthly city, which is in most cases positively given as freedom. All war—and material existence is essentially a death struggle—aims at peace (XIX, xii), and peace is conceived as a harmony (XIX, xiii, xxvii), a balance of the three loves enjoined by Jesus, of self, neighbour, and God (xiv). But a perfect harmony is static and unchanging: it too is an ideal, unrealizable in a world of time, which means change, and perfect peace can be attained only in the next world. Peace in this sense is equated with justice, and no non-Christian state can have justice, but only the approximation to it necessary to maintain

social equilibrium. Augustine's complete distrust of the power of
human civilization to work out its own salvation leads him to regard
punishment, in practice, as retributive rather than corrective, and,
hence, to develop the ferocious doctrine of hell which disfigures the
twenty-first book. The insistence that hell is purely a physical torment,
the attack on Origen (xvii) as more kind than God, repel us now, though
it is a question how far Christianity would have consolidated its hold on
superstitious and bloodthirsty savages without some such weapon. The
extremes of pessimism with regard to one city, and of ecstasy with
regard to the other, are brought together at the conclusion (XXII), in
which all evil and suffering are treated as means to an end, the universe
being the handiwork of God. No miracle, in the sense of anything supernatural, ever occurs. All natural effects have spiritual causes, and what
looks unnatural, that is, miraculous, is just as much a manifestation of
God's will in the world as anything else, except that we have not thoroughly understood it. After repeating the essential break Christianity
makes with Greek philosophy, in making God personal, speculation
subordinate to conduct, and a historical redemption the crisis of all
thought, Augustine concludes.

Our present estimate of Augustine is perhaps too strongly coloured
with his relationship to the medieval Church. Superficial thinkers with
an anticlerical bias pass him by with a reference to his endorsation of
slavery.[25] But Augustine was here perfectly consistent and perfectly
right. As long as the ideal is not approached in the world, as long as the
civitas terrena is the organized reality, all growths of culture and civilization are artificial and, consequently, to some extent parasitic. All human
history is a record of class struggles, says Marx, and so says Augustine
in XII. This means continual exploitation and slavery. True, the whole
tendency of the Christian Church has been away from slavery, but that
is because it is gradually coming to realize that an ideal such as the city
of God represents is strong enough to mould reality. Hence, we can see
a genuine advance in the feudal system, tyrannical as it was, over the
classical idea of absolute ownership of the body and soul of another
human being. Hence, we can also hope that the machine is an evolutionary step in the direction of the abolition of slavery, though there are
more slaves today than there ever were in Augustine's time. But that
slavery and everything that Augustine means by the civitas terrena are
inseparable is amply justified. All Augustine held out for was a personal
relationship which accorded the slave some measure of human dignity,

such as the industrial revolution has spent its energy in trying to extinguish. The initial alignment of the earthly city with time, the heavenly with eternity, implying that the former would last as long as time did, gives Augustine the strain of social pessimism and conservatism we have noted.[26]

Even more serious students of Augustine, such as A.J. Carlyle, seem to consider him purely in relation to the Middle Ages, and have concentrated attention on one of his vaguest problems: the extent to which the two cities can be identified with Church and state.[27] We have tried to show that either a Guelph or a Ghibelline answer[28] to this is a misinterpretation; that for Augustine the Church's importance did not lie in its power as an instrument of temporal reform. The inhabitants of the city of God were wanderers and pilgrims on the earth; the Church was a place of refuge for them and a bulwark to preserve something like an assured continuance of a divine tradition in the world. As a matter of fact it might be maintained that the true inward spirit of Augustine was too mature and sophisticated to be grasped in its entirety by the medieval thinkers, not because of any lack of subtlety or insight on the part of the latter, but simply through failure to understand the point of view of a man in Augustine's historical position. Hence, it might be shown that the sudden accession of maturity typified by the Renaissance represented in some aspects a revival of Augustinianism, beginning with Vico's monumental commentary.[29] The Protestant theologies of Luther and Calvin, undoubtedly a break with Thomism, owed much to the earlier thinker in their views of predestination. Within the Church, it might be maintained that the whole activity of the Counter-Reformation was Augustinian in spirit. The Jesuits, for instance, in their combination of education and organization (the famous *perinde ac cadaver*[30] is said to derive from Augustine) represent an application of Augustine's ideal of the duties of the inhabitants of the city of God far more closely than the medieval papacy. And it was the Jesuits who taught Descartes, father of modern philosophy, whose *cogito ergo sum* goes back to the great Roman[31] and whose rigid dualism is largely a philosophical abstract of the conception of the two cities.[32]

Time and space, whose function is to limit, will not permit any detailed investigation, at present, of these provocative and stimulating suggestions. But it does seem as though it were high time for a revaluation of Augustine's central thesis in terms of contemporary thought. Assuming that that central thesis is his philosophy of history, as we

have attempted to prove, let us in the short space remaining try to outline the general position of the time in regard to this question and see
how it compares with Augustine in depth and range. We hope that our
estimate of the importance of the problem is convincing enough to make
such an attempt seem justifiable.

The chief reason for the disjunction of the Augustinian philosophy of
history from the scholasticism of the Middle Ages is to be found, as
hinted above, in the difference of historical point of view. The expanding and consolidating Western world had not its immediate attention
focused on a cultural decline, but rather the reverse. We have spoken of
the way in which a developing civilization tends to ignore the historical
problem, which an apologetic, like Augustine's work, has in the foreground. Aquinas is concerned, not with analysis, but with synthesis. He
does not emphasize the distinction between the spiritual and the temporal, but their organic relationship to each other. He is interested, not in
reaching the substructure of thought, but the end of it. The value of the
philosophy of history to be found, or read into, the *Summa Theologica* is
as nearly negligible as anything connected with so great a work can be.
The only organic unit present to scholasticism was that of the individual. In the Middle Ages the only contributions to a philosophy of history
could come from thinkers addicted to mysticism, to reflection rather
than systematization; that is, with sympathies not altogether given up to
the development of systematic philosophy, yet enough influenced by it
to work it into their thought. Such a figure, quasi-mystical and almost
Oriental, was Joachim of Floris (1145–1202), whose interpretation was
threefold. Augustine's view of the temporal progression (not the most
important element of his philosophy of history) was flat, balanced, antithetical, and hinged on the Incarnation. The world of time, after its creation, was the scene of a dramatic change from comparative darkness to
comparative light. This was the only essential alteration possible to the
civitas terrena. The great medieval abbot visioned an organic development in which the age of the Father, or the reign of law, before Christianity, advanced to the age of the Son, or reign of the Gospel, to be
finally fused in the age of the Spirit, a sort of Kantian kingdom of ends
in which all hierarchical distinctions were to be abolished. The general
progression was that of the liberation of the life of contemplation from
that of action—the eternal struggle to make thought independent of
being.[33]

The bankruptcy of scholasticism at the time of the Renaissance turned the attention again to the immediate problems of life, and the collapse of the great medieval cosmopolis of Christendom forced men to reconsider the question of government. Machiavelli, Aretino, Vico, More, are only a few names symptomatic of the new interest, or at least a new attitude.[34] Their problems, however, were not our problems, and it was not until the collapse of this phase of civilization before the Industrial Revolution that the specifically modern era sets in. At the source of this stands Hegel, with an (unconscious) adaptation of the Joachimite heresy.

For the philosophy of history is an examination of the problem of time, and the logical development of it beyond Augustine would be to include the ideal, which he had placed in eternity, in with the time-progression, necessarily the future. This would mean regarding the Incarnation as not so much the unique manifestation of the connection of time with eternity as a necessary stage in the development of mankind. Now any actualized Utopia is a static society. The static is spatial and the dynamic temporal, and we have tried to show earlier how reason is connected with space-forms, and how will is existence in time. Hence, a Utopia is an ideal of pure reason. Joachim of Floris is intermediate between Augustine and Hegel. Augustine's view was religious, in which ideal and material run parallel, connected by the Incarnation. Joachim, partly religious and partly philosophical, superimposes one on the other in time, connecting them by the era ushered in by the Incarnation. Hegel's view, religious but dominated by abstract reason, sees the ideal as permeating and transforming the reality, in which the Incarnation is neither unique nor transitional, but eternal and omnipresent. The essential reality, with Hegel, is the static absolute idea. Consequently, any dynamic process, to be valid, must be neutralized by its opposite. The initial process is called the thesis, the opposite the antithesis, and the result of the balancing of them the synthesis. All history is, thus, the constant broadening out of dynamic thrusts in time, which represent imperfection, into a final absolute idea, which is God.

All the stock criticisms of Hegel focus fairly well on the point that history is not quite so painless or automatic a process; that Hegel's philosophy of history is good philosophy and bad history. For obviously, if Hegel's theory applied to history as a whole, the idea would in his day have achieved a substantial conquest of reality. Hegel recognized this and attempted to justify the absolutism of the Prussian state of his time on precisely this ground.[35] No more pointed attack on Hegel is necessary than merely to point out this fact. We have said that history is unintelligible unless it takes something like a shape, and the only thing giving it an *objective* shape, up to this time, was a crisis which essentially alters its character. This crisis we have assigned to the Incarnation. Without this, history, viewed at first retrogressively from the standpoint of the thinker, becomes at length, to his eyes, entirely existent in relation to his own perspective: all history leads up to him and to what he stands for. Now obviously this is to some extent justified, as he does stand on the shoulders of his predecessors, but in proportion as his own outlook is limited by his environment his value to posterity decreases. Pride, with Augustine, is the sole source of evil, because, being the assertion of the will, it breaks the synthesis of will and reason which religion attains. It is a denial of the objective element in the personality. A corollary of this is that the sole source of intellectual heresy is self-justification. All the great heretics of the philosophy of history have been vitiated by this element. To the strength and originality of Joachim is attached an obsolete ideal of monasticism. Hegel, one of the great seminal minds of the past century, was also the author of the spiteful attack on Fries prefacing the *Philosophy of Rights*.[36] To Spengler's *Decline of the West*, perhaps the most important book yet produced by the twentieth century, succeeds the imbecile balderdash of the *Hour of Decision*.[37] Hegel looks like the most sentimental of romantics, at times, beside the hard-headed realism of Augustine, the difference being, as above, the result of the greater subjectivity of the later thinker.

Yet Hegel does represent a genuine advance on Augustine in his metaphysics, though there the credit is more due to Kant. Kant had identified the objects of knowledge with phenomena, space-forms. Time and space were the two ultimate data of perception, and nothing we have any knowledge of goes outside them. Hence, the eternal form of Augustine's city of God is really a space-form, and what is timeless is not eternal, but simply spatial, as far as our knowledge of it is concerned. This means that the ideal of Augustine is a human ideal after all, and Hegel, in bringing it into the actual historical process, laid down the program for the modern approach.[38] An inference from this is that, if Hegel is right in assuming that humanity tends toward an absolute ideal, yet life is a dynamic process, and the tendency may be, not dialectical in nature but characterized by the dynamic forces of struggle and development. This idea is the germ underlying the various philosophies of evolution which necessarily come next in the philosophical agenda.

A good many of the more unreadable books of the past century were written under the impression that the evolutionary and the historical processes were the same. This meant that the city of God, however it was interpreted, lay very definitely at the end of the temporal road, but the conceptions of the development leading to it were still mechanical. It cannot be too often urged that without one definite, unique, historical event, devoid of all symbolical and subjective distortions, history can be conceived only in relation to the thinker regarding it. This means, for one thing, that the Utopia, or close of the struggle, was very definitely mundane. Augustine did not so conceive it, and his temporal ideal, as before stated, was a negative one—peace, the positive formulation of which is freedom. This is the core of the doctrine of Marx, an acute analysis of the *civitas terrena*, worked out entirely without reference to its complementary city. The relation of this to Augustine's conception has been earlier indicated. It soon became manifest, however, that the unbroken progression of life from amoeba to philosopher was as impossible a conception as a steady progression of individuality. Evolutionary development must have proceeded by organic stages, each stage representing a new lease on life.

Thus, the advance made on Augustine's theory by the nineteenth century was finally defined, as the postulating of an evolutionary unit in history with the implication that the goal of human effort belongs in life, that the *civitas terrena* perpetually tends toward realization of the ideal *civitas Dei*. This leads to a modern restatement of the doctrine of grace as understood by Augustine. Up to the time of the nineteenth century only one organic unit in history had been generally recognized: that of the individual. This had started with Christianity's doctrine of personality, the whole impulse to worship arising from the consciousness of the mortality of the body and the consequent impotence of the soul. Now the new evolutionary unit of the species adds to that religious conception the doctrine of God as organic and dynamic force, which removes the element of externality from Augustine's working out of the problem of the entry of God into the human soul.

So far we have neglected one of our postulated essentials: the concept of the civilization as the unit of history. The relation of the individual to his evolutionary status is microcosmic and complementary; the two units lie at the extremes of philosophy of history. The larger takes in the record of the whole of life; the smaller, the record of an individual consciousness. Between them lies the synthesis, fundamental to under-

standing them, the philosophy of history. Now, as all knowledge works
with forms, the cognizance of a form or limit underlying any problem is
the first step in understanding it. Hence, there is necessary an organic
unit in history intermediate to the other two.

This we have called the civilization, and Oswald Spengler, in the
Decline of the West, published after the war, though written earlier, culminates the "heretical" tradition of the philosophy of history;[39] that is,
the attempt to work one out without the aid of an Incarnation. We have
shown how Hegel was injured by levelling the Incarnation to the rank of
a symbol of indefinite recurrence and thereby losing his objective grip
on history. The evolutionary philosophies developing from him made a
similar error, and their bankruptcy could hardly be better illustrated
than by the work of Nietzsche and Shaw, with whom, standing as they
do, like Augustine, at the turn of a civilization, the only solution does
not lie in mankind at all, who is an outmoded species, but in a superman, the advent of whom would exemplify the manifestation of a vital
force in the world.[40] What this practically amounts to is a call for
another Incarnation. But Spengler saved himself by discovering in history the organic unit of the civilization, which he calls the culture,
becoming a civilization proper in its later stages. History according to
this view appears as a succession of culture-growths, which pass
through certain inevitable stages of birth, maturation, and decay, just
like any other organic process. They grow out of the soil, like plants,
concentrating in towns. The early period is a soil-growth, such as Western culture, which arose about the year 1000 in the Gothic period. The
passing of the time develops the towns, at first only focal points in the
surrounding district, into culture-units, and this gives us our Renaissance period and the classical domination of the city states. Finally the
town tears itself loose from the soil and becomes a metropolis, a stage
we entered a century and a half ago and which is represented in the
classical world by the advent of Rome. With this, the culture enters the
civilization stage and dries up, inhabited only by floating inorganic
masses of city dwellers, its creative vitality in the arts and sciences gone,
replaced by technical and engineering feats.[41]

Without wishing to dwell on this thesis in too great detail, it should be
noticed that Spengler has, by his postulation of the culture-unit in history, made a substantial and welcome contribution to our problem. It is
curious that his treatment of St. Augustine should symbolize his deficiency.[42] He sees nothing in history beyond the flourishing of culture-

groups. His final unit is a multiple one. He has no teleology, of course, and no sense of an evolutionary development upward which overrides and breaks through the progression of organic growths. Hence, when one culture grows up after another, it learns nothing essential from it, carries nothing on into a higher synthesis. The classical civilization and ours work out two separate destinies. The Greek Dionysiac revival corresponds to our Renaissance; Aristotle corresponds to Kant; Alexander to Napoleon; the Roman Empire to the imperialistic engineering civilizations of our day. In between was a third intermediate culture-growth, the Arabian culture. In this, early Christianity corresponds to our early Gothic; Augustine, say, to our Cusanus; Averroës, to Aristotle and Kant; Mohammedanism, to our Puritanism.[43] But it is obvious that this, though very largely true, is not all the truth. Augustine is *not* "essentially a Manichean thinker," and no amount of theoretical straitjacketing can make him one. There is, over and above the indisputable development of culture-growths, something of a tradition absorbed and carried on: in addition to the various risings of cultures something symbolizes an irrevocable push forward. Things like the abolition of slavery, the gradual growth of altruism and tolerance, the spread of pacifism and liberalism, all products of Christianity, are realities, and true of mankind as a whole. When a civilization declines, those who can stand contemplating its decline, like Varro, Seneca, and Augustine, are the great men of the day.[44] But he who can feel that mankind, as opposed to races of men, is not an abstraction, as Goethe, Spengler's master, claims,[45] and that this larger unit brings about, gradually but surely, a definite and continual advance, is the great genius of the age. Such a man was Augustine, who "corresponds," not to a figure in our Early Renaissance, but to the supreme philosopher of the twentieth century, if we are so fortunate as to have one.

For Augustine, let it be said bluntly, is the critical figure of any history of philosophy, and the greatest *transitional* thinker who ever lived. The Mediterranean world in his time saw the only example of a civilization growing up over and inheriting the tradition of an earlier. Classical culture, whether in art, science, or philosophy, had worked out its vein. What Augustine carried over into the future development was the larger integration of a philosophy of history. A corresponding task lies ahead of us. The great synthesis made by Augustine was that embodying a recognition of the historical position of decline and the larger perception that no decline could be absolute. Hence, he combined the description of eternally rising and falling civilizations with the great assurance of progress implied in the Incarnation. We have added something to Augustine's problem; we have reinforced the idea of the essential connection of God with mankind as a whole by the idea of the essential development of the species. We know that the decline of civilizations is fundamentally a biological rather than a moral phenomenon. But however we may approach the problem, that problem itself, of making our own larger integration to be carried on into a later development, remains the same as Augustine's.

Bibliography

With regard to a bibliography, apart from the text of *De Civitate Dei* itself, a few of the Epistles, and some hints from the *Confessions*, there seems little on which to go. Figgis, *Political Aspects of S. Augustine's City of God*, was the main commentary used. Carlyle and Carlyle, *Mediaeval Political Theory in the West*, vol. 1; Gierke, *Social and Political Theories of the Middle Age*; Hearnshaw (ed.), *Political Thinkers of the Middle Ages*; and Dunning, *Political Theories*, vol. 1, were consulted for the development of Augustine's thought during the medieval period. Also, of course, the various texts referred to: Hegel, *Philosophy of History*; Marx, *Das Kapital*, vol. 1; Spengler, *The Decline of the West*, and the books referred to in the footnotes.

No book that I could locate has been written specifically on Augustine's philosophy of history.[46]

11

The Life and Thought of Ramon Lull

This paper was written for a course in Christian missions, which Frye took during his final year at Emmanuel College (1935–36). The following note by Edward Wilson Wallace, professor of missions, appears at the end of the essay: "A thorough piece of work, on which I congratulate you. Fuller reference to Lull's missionary activities would have rounded out the story." Frye's chief sources were Allison Peers, Ramon Lull: A Biography *and Peers's edition of Lull's* The Book of the Lover and the Beloved, *both of which are listed in the bibliography at the end of the paper. Frye used the 1923 edition of* The Book of the Lover and the Beloved. *The page references in the text of the paper as published here, however, are to the more readily accessible revised edition (New York: Macmillan, 1945), which differs in a few particulars from the one Frye had at hand. These references are given in square brackets following* BL. *Frye's discussion of Lull's life and works comes almost exclusively from Peers's biography. I have not noted the places in this book where Frye draws upon Peers, except those instances when he reproduces Peers's own quotations from Lull: Frye's use of the biography is easy enough to trace by using the headings in the table of contents and the index of* Ramon Lull: A Biography; *this book is cited in the notes as "Peers." No grade is recorded on the typescript, which is in the NFF, 1991, box 37, file 13.*

Ramon Lull was born in Majorca, sometime between 1232 and 1236. The Balearic Isles had been taken from the Moors by King James of Aragon some years previously, and those who had fought on the conquering side had been suitably rewarded with gifts of land. Among these was Ramon Lull's father, of the same name. The boy grew up in what appears to have been the class of minor nobility who followed a king and who, largely through their prowess in arms, were forming an avant-garde of the new social order which eventually destroyed the feudal system. At the age of twelve Lull was sent to the court of the King of Aragon and brought up there as a page. As a result, he became steeped in the troubadour culture of the northwest Mediterranean world which centred in Provence and branched out through Catalonia and Italy: a culture of a highly conventionalized etiquette of love and war. In this atmosphere grew the ideals of chivalry in warfare and the amorous intrigue in love we usually associate with the name of Petrarch. The obvious importance and influence of these traditions on Lull are easy to underestimate, as we are so seldom inclined to associate anything like the court of love or the knight errant with medieval piety. But the chivalric knighthoods of the Templar and St. John orders were settled in the Majorca they had helped to conquer, and the idea of a union of all orders, chivalric, missionary, and monastic, into a single weapon for a united and catholic Church never left Lull. Nor is it possible thoroughly to understand the process of Lull's conversion without recognizing the influence on him of medieval love conventions. He seems to have first attracted attention as a fashionable courtier, writing light verses and making love to women according to troubadour models. His early life is usually called profligate, but we should beware of the tendency of hagiography to stereotype its subjects. The gay young noble shocked into an intense loathing of his life by a sudden glimpse of its falseness and converted by a divine vision is a fairly standard form which covers a large number of biographies of holy men. One thing seems clear: the young Lull was thoroughly a man of the world and never lost hold of his understanding of it. His love affairs were no doubt carried on according to rule: the lover courts some lady whose virtue is assured by the fact that she is married; the lady is properly cold and coy, the lover is importunate, bemoans his fate, threatens suicide or a crusade, and the lady finally yields. The lady's honour was affected only if the intrigue became known. The husband was frequently the lover's best friend and aided the affair in every way he could.

The superb tableau which depicts Lull suddenly halted in the consummation of one of these intrigues by the lady's exposure of her cancerous breast to him in the presence of her husband is one of those scenes which seems to give us a focus for the spirit of the entire age. The story may be historical or it may be symbolic, but it is not in either case fictitious. If it did not happen to Lull, it certainly represents something that did happen to him and to dozens of others in his time. The whole Middle Ages is in that picture: the haughty idealist's contempt of the body, the sharp contrast between eternal and temporal love, the dramatic intervention of the grace of God in the soul, the respect for woman and the clear recognition of the dangers she provides for the genius or the saint. Anything so nearly concerned with the conversion of a saint cannot very well be of only incidental importance.

There followed, of course, the usual repentance, then, all the lover's importunity being transferred to religious devotion, the appearance of Christ urging the surrender of Ramon's soul; for the conventions of mysticism are almost as stereotyped as those of Petrarchan love. This epiphany naturally convinced Lull that he was destined for the service of Christ, and to a mind brought up on chivalry the missionary enterprise, the adventuring of God's knight errant, was the first idea that suggested itself. And as the knight errant was supposed to fight the enemies of Christendom, and as the enemies of Christendom at that time meant Mohammedans, Lull prepared at once for his life's mission, the rationalist crusade for the conversion of the Moors.

After a pilgrimage, Lull settled down to study Arabic, giving up a career at the University of Paris and returning from Aragon to Majorca. He was married before his conversion and seems to have had one son. As an exercise in Arabic, he wrote his immense *Book of Contemplation*,[1] a work of overwhelming size, complexity, and variety, which is basically a repudiation of the delights of the world of sense, a satire on the folly of mankind, and a call to the study of religion with a view to spreading the Christian faith among all the heathen. This was followed by the *Book of the Gentile and the Three Wise Men*, one of the finest dialogues of the Middle Ages.[2] In it, a Gentile meets a Jew, a Christian, and a Mohammedan, who expound their respective faiths, the Christian, of course, winning the day.

It is in this work that we notice two of the characteristics of Lull that make him so appealing and vital a personality. In the first place, he is as much a scholar and a gentleman as any humanist of the Renaissance. He lets the Jew and the Muslim speak for themselves as well as he can; he has taken pains to acquaint himself with their creeds and, though he obviously prefers the Mohammedan to the Jew, he puts both cases with a moderation almost incredible for that age. His Saracen is given a fine peroration:

"Thou hast heard and understood my words, O Gentile, and the proofs which I have given of the articles of our law; and thou hast heard what bliss there is in Paradise, which shall be thine for ever and eternally if thou believe in our law which is given of God." And, when the sage had thus spoken, he closed his book, and ended his words, and saluted the two sages according to his custom. [Peers, 95]

Living in one of the most cosmopolitan districts in Europe, Lull is at the crossroads of Jewish, Christian, and Mohammedan cultures, and he is well aware that the Christian civilization is less mature in many respects to[3] the other two. In the second place, he feels he can afford to be tolerant, because of his absolute confidence that, as Christianity is true, it is bound to withstand the most searching critical investigation, while, as the other religions are false, they are bound to collapse under it. Lull has complete confidence that the end of rational discussion and logical argument is conversion. The truth of Christianity can be demonstrated as clearly as the proposition that two and two make four and not five, and as no one will be obstinate enough to claim that two and two make five, so the force of logic will convert the world to Christ, if the gospel is preached. The crusades have tried to conquer by force of arms; they have failed, and the way of persuasion is left. Lull says in the *Book of the Lover and the Beloved*:

The Lover asked the Understanding and the Will which of them was the nearer to his Beloved. And the two ran, and the Understanding came nearer to the Beloved than did the Will. [*BL*, 22]

and he never forsook his faith in the possibility of a completely rational approach to God.

And as long as he retains this naive but noble belief in the infallibility of reason (which, as far as missionary activity is concerned, fails chiefly because it overlooks the fact of original sin and adopts the heresy of the perfectibility of man), Lull is extraordinarily gentle, patient, and tolerant. One magnificent flash of Christian charity is in the *Book of Contemplation*:

Many Jews would become Christians if they had the wherewithal to live, and likewise many Saracens, if the Christians did them not dishonour. [Peers, 74]

He realizes that the Christians have to achieve peace with themselves and their neighbours, and that their religion cannot be propagated by a crusade, whether a crusade with the quixotic courage of the first or the abominable treachery of the fourth. He says in the *Book of Contemplation*:

> Since the Christians are not at peace with the Saracens, O Lord, they dare not hold discussions upon the faith with them when they are among them. But were they at peace together, they could dispute with each other peacefully concerning the faith, and then it would be possible for the Christians to direct and enlighten the Saracens in the way of truth, through the grace of the Holy Spirit and the true reasons that are signified in the perfection of Thy attributes. [Peers, 73]

Later on he modified this view, as tolerance was too frequently, in the thirteenth century, the same thing as indifference. In 1290 he presented Pope Nicholas IV with a plan for conquering the Holy Land; by one of the grim ironies of history, the following year saw the disaster of Acre and the complete and final defeat of Christian arms in the East.[4]

After the completion of his Arabic studies, Lull retired to Mount Randa, temporarily suspending his missionary projects till he felt himself spiritually mature. Here he received a mystic illumination which provided him, as he claimed, with the formula for his *Ars Magna*, his system of dialectic, which he completed in 1274.

Then he returned from solitary contemplation to the world of men. He went to Montpellier, one of the greatest cities of Aragon, submitted his books to the king, and wrote his educational treatises, the *Book of the Order of Chivalry* and the *Doctrine for Boys*. The former is the only work of Lull which found its way into our literature before the twentieth century: it was translated into English by Caxton and into Scotch by Sir Gilbert Hay.[5] The latter is the usual book of didactic educational treatise common in the Middle Ages, dominated by the general idea that childhood is a dangerous and rather repulsive state of imperfection, to be discouraged as much as possible.

On the accession of James II, who was friendly to Lull, to the throne of Majorca, Lull was encouraged to push forward a project he had long entertained of founding a number of training schools for missionaries. James founded one at Miramar in 1276. The project proved fruitless in the end, and, though Miramar struggled along for about ten years, it never seems to have sent out any missionaries. At Miramar Lull wrote the *Book of the Holy Spirit*, a rather arid dialogue explaining the *filioque* controversy from the Roman point of view.[6]

It is obvious that Lull, with his dream of a great chivalric and missionary Christian order trained in the discipline of Christian theology, was trying to do what Loyola did two centuries later. His failure can be explained, I think, by the fact that an established Church is committed to conservatism and, therefore, to retrenchment and smugness. When Christianity, or any form of Christianity, is associated with an established social order and made respectable, it loses its enthusiasm, which is continually expanding, antisocial, and revolutionary. The more powerful the papacy grew and the more complete the scholastic theology became, the more the missionary enterprise suffered. The Catholic Church, shocked out of its complacency by the Reformation, produced the Jesuits; but the Church of Lull's time was shocked only by threats to its political or economic interests. Around the turn of the century Europe saw the world order of Christendom visibly cracking apart into national units, and such programs of spiritual conquest and expansion as Lull's fitted in better with the rising material ambitions of princes than with those of the papacy, which was engrossed in holding on to its declining power. So the remainder of Lull's life is a disheartening record of interviews with sympathetic but selfish kings, humiliating rebuffs from Rome, and spasmodic missionary journeys. His output of books, of course, never abated.

Lull's first visit to Rome (1277) was to the friendly Pope John XXI, who had approved the founding of Miramar, but the latter died before his arrival. Nothing much is known of Lull's life between 1277 and 1282, a period perhaps spent in travel. It was probably in 1283, and at Montpellier, that Lull completed his most celebrated work, the prose romance *Blanquerna*.[7] Blanquerna is a man who leaves his parents to become a hermit and persuades a girl his parents wanted him to marry to become a nun. The heroine rises to be abbess of her convent, and her regimen is fully described. Blanquerna wanders through the world going through a number of highly allegorized adventures, is finally made pope, converts and reforms the world, and retires from the papal chair to become a hermit again—the celebrated abdication of Celestine V is foreshadowed here. As a hermit Blanquerna writes the *Art of Contemplation* and the lovely *Book of the Lover and the Beloved*, which are inserted at the end. In the framework of medieval allegory and knight-errant romance Lull has put an intellectual and cultural synthesis of ideas which make *Blan-*

querna a worthy connecting link between Joachim of Floris and the Grail legends of the Middle Ages and the great Utopian writers of the Renaissance—Campanella, More, Rabelais (who ridiculed the *Ars Magna*) in prose, Ariosto, Tasso, and Spenser in poetry.

Honorius IV, who succeeded to the papacy in 1285, seems to have been well disposed toward Lull, and it was perhaps at his suggestion that Lull went to the University of Paris, the intellectual capital of Europe, headquarters of the Dominicans, upholders of orthodoxy and the papacy. There he lectured on his *Ars Magna* and tried to gain Dominican support for his projects, completely without success. He had appealed to this order before, and, discouraged, began to turn toward the Franciscans. Philip the Fair, King of France, gave him the customary support of royalty—good wishes and promises. At Paris, too, Lull wrote his romance *Felix, or the Book of Marvels*, a description of the wonders of the natural and supernatural worlds to a schoolboy, which is not yet available in English. One of its sections, the *Book of the Beasts*, is said to be a lively treatment of the medieval beast fable, with occasional Oriental touches.

Returning from Paris to Montpellier, Lull began to commence his appeals to the Franciscans, and with the accession of the first Franciscan pope, Nicholas IV, his hopes ran high. But the disaster at Acre in 1291 discouraged the pontiff, though, as it was largely due to rivalries between Templar and St. John Knights, it established Lull's point about a unified order. Finally Lull determined to go to Africa, and, though he shrank back the first time, remorse at his cowardice strengthened him still further, and he set sail for Tunis. He attempted, as always, rational discussion, arguing that the monotheism of the Mohammedans would tend to make God purely transcendent, and that the doctrines of the Trinity and the divinity of Christ were necessary to postulate a divine activity at work in the world. The mob stoned him, and Lull, realizing that they had won the argument, returned to Italy. He lived at Naples, continuing to pour out treatises from his unbelievably prolific pen and making petitions for a program of missionary activity to Nicholas IV, to the wretched Celestine V, and finally, to Boniface VIII.

This notorious scoundrel, whom Dante consigned to the very bowels of hell, was the first of the long discreditable line of poisoners, intriguers, and tyrants at Rome who eventually provoked the Reformation. His infamous bull, *Unam Sanctam*,[8] the most arrogant of papal pretensions, was quickly followed by his humiliation at the hands of Philip the Fair of France, an event leading directly to the Avignon separation. Such a man would have little sympathy with Lull. Lull, in despair, joined the Franciscans about 1295. The move has a certain historical importance, for, as the thirteenth century, the culmination of the Middle Ages, was intellectually a Dominican century, so the fourteenth, the beginning of the end, was intellectually a Franciscan one, and Lull, like Scotus and Occam, anticipates the later age where Aquinas and Dante sum up the earlier. St. Francis is one of the greatest emancipators of Western culture, not because of what he was, but because of what he represented. He was a mystic with all the limitations of a mystic, and was culturally and intellectually an obscurantist—literal observance of his precepts would have been pernicious. But he had the strength of the mystic too, the strength of the unanswerable seer of God, the individual to whom has been revealed a truth far higher than any reached by dogma or clerical hierarchy. The influence of such a man, when properly canalized, developed a philosophy which pushed theology into pure revelation— the Franciscan nominalism—released a torrent of self-expression in religion through creative art, specifically the painting of Florence, Assisi, and Siena, and by its popular preaching in the vernacular helped immeasurably in bringing to the middle and lower classes an awakened consciousness of their religion, and in fostering the growth of national literatures, as Lull fostered Catalan. Not only internally but externally the Franciscans were undermining the walls of medieval Christendom, and a Franciscan missionary spent forty years in China.

Lull solaced himself for his defeat at Rome by composing his immense and monstrous allegory of the *Tree of Science*, along with numerous other works. In 1297 he again went to Paris, and, meeting more rebuffs, wrote the *Tree of the Philosophy of Love*,[9] another didactic allegory and one greatly superior to its fellow, being more completely a literary art form than anything else he wrote, owing to its concentration on the theme of the contemplative life. A rumour that the Tartars had overrun Syria took him to Cyprus in 1301, where he preached against heretics. Boniface died, but his successors were still desperately holding their temporal prerogatives against the French king, and Lull made little headway. In 1306, being again in Paris, he met the greatest living Franciscan, Duns Scotus, then a young prodigy. The meeting brought together the two greatest thinkers of the time and joined the left and right wings of the attack on Thomism, but seems to have had no other than a symbolic importance. The next year Lull went to Africa the second time, was mobbed, imprisoned for a year, holding debates with Moslem savants the while, and banished, being shipwrecked on his way home. He landed at Pisa, where he wrote more books and endeavoured to organize a new military order, the Templars being on their last legs and Lull's faith in the irresistible persuasion of truth having waned. He journeyed to Avignon (the captivity had commenced) with the proposition that a crusade should be undertaken, starting with a naval attack on Mohammedan ports, in which he was, of course, entirely unsuccessful. Then he went to Paris for the last time.

Here his lecturing proved more popular than ever before; his treatises were examined and highly commended, and his prestige began to grow into something like real fame. Alarmed at the continued spread of the doctrines of Averroës, he put himself at the head of an intellectual crusade against them, and wrote a series of didactic treatises against them. In 1311 a general council of the Church met at Vienne, and Lull went to it to propose for the last time his projects of missionary colleges, chairs at universities for the teaching of heathen tongues, a united military order to carry on the crusades, and the furtherance of scholastic opposition to Averroës. The council adopted most of his suggestions, and that they came largely to nothing is hardly the fault of anything but the fact that the time was out of joint. Lull returned to Majorca, drew up his last will and testament, and, after a visit to Sicily, arrived in Tunis for the third time. The Christian and Moslem worlds were on fairly good terms at the time, and Lull for a while taught and wrote in safety. But a third mob gathered, and ended his long, heroic, unhappy fight for the Christian faith by stoning him to death (1315).

As the fifteenth century is one of the darkest periods in the history of the Christian Church, it is hardly surprising that by that time the rivalry between the followers of Dominic and Francis should have degenerated into squabbles all the more vicious for being petty and mean spirited. A Dominican, Nicholas de Eymeric, hounded the name of Lull all his life, accusing the great missionary of every conceivable heresy, forging (probably) a papal bull condemning his doctrines, and putting a blot on his memory never since erased, for even today Lull is Blessed, but not Saint, Ramon. The Franciscans have loyally defended him, and his influence was strong enough to cause riots in seventeenth-century Rome. He is still Majorca's greatest son and its patron saint, and he is perhaps the greatest name, both as a thinker and writer, in the history of Catalan literature. As the Catalans have always possessed a national conscious-

ness as ineradicable as that of Poland or Ireland, Lull is the spearhead of
the Catalan Renaissance provoked by the regionalist movement in nineteenth-century literature. Lull's output was tremendous, for there is
almost no period in the life sketched above which did not witness the
issue of voluminous treatises. But this capital has been increased in two
ways. In the first place, his cult has foisted on him an immense number
of works written by his followers, who wanted, or unwittingly gained,
the authority of his name. In the second place, his expansion into a legendary figure of superhuman intellectual powers and divine inspiration
(he had this reputation even in his lifetime, as his title of *Doctor Illumina-
tus* shows), together with the accusations of heresy and his Arabic connections, turned him into a magician and the author of innumerable
works on alchemy. His actual achievements as a writer are, of course,
uneven: undoubtedly he wrote too much and too fast, with a prolixity
truly scholastic. Like many others who have achieved literary fame in
spite of themselves, he was convinced of the superiority of didactic over
imaginative expression, and his more purely literary works, such as
Blanquerna, are continually straying off into sterile wastes of prosy and
tedious sermonizing. His achievements as a poet cannot be discussed
here: he is chiefly famous for his autobiographical poems *Desconort*
(Despair), his long lament at his rejection by Boniface, and the *Song of
Ramon*, and for his long, elaborate hymn on the *Hundred Names of God*,
the "names" being attributes of the divine nature. As a thinker he
deserves more extended mention.

Lull was all his life in the thick of the great struggle between Dominican and Franciscan philosophy which eventually ended in the victory of
the latter and the overthrow of the Catholic world. Lull, although a
Franciscan, cannot be aligned with the nominalists Scotus and Occam;
his attack on the Thomist synthesis came from the other side, but was
equally corrosive. Aquinas had developed the Aristotelian entelechy
into a colossal synthetic principle making for a universal process of
organic evolution. Matter is potential; form is actual, and all being tends
upward to the actualization of pure form. Now pure form must, of
course, be God, and as form is static, it is reached by the intelligence.
Consequently, the universe is the working out of a creation of infinite
reason. God exists because he is reason; we cannot deny his existence
without using reason and, therefore, affirming it. We live in the best of
all possible worlds, because it is potentially perfect. But as everything
tends toward the pure form of God, it follows that God is unalterable, an

intellect toward which all the activity of his will is directed. To the Franciscans this subordination of God's will was a reflection on his omnipotence. God could do what he liked, and, if so, then theology, the rational approach to God, could not be an inevitable development of philosophy, the rational approach to the world. Thus, after Scotus, philosophy tended more and more to rest on an empiric basis, whether, with the Baconian tradition, this was provided by the organic and applied sciences, or, with the Cartesian, by mathematics. Theology similarly tended to drop its distinction between natural and revealed religion and concentrate on the latter, specifically on the revelation of the Scriptures.[10]

With Thomism God became, if not exactly immanent, in a sense pantheistic; everything actualizes itself in the pure form which is God; thus, as an easy inference, everything partakes of the nature of God. Nominalism, by the breach it made in the Thomist subordination of will to intellect, established an explicit separation between the human and the divine natures. God's will is arbitrary and unpredictable, and, therefore, he is a transcendent God: this feeling of God's omnipotence and inscrutability is brought to its highest point by Calvin. The development of Aristotle made by Averroës, lacking the Christian tradition of the value of the individual personality, combined the faults of both Thomism and Calvinism by its naturalistic interpretation of the entelechic process, according to which truth was recognized as entirely impersonal and nonhuman, so that the process of life tending toward it was conceived as a fatalistic materialism.

Lull was not an Aristotelian, for he fought Averroës unremittingly, as we have seen; and he was persecuted for heresy by the Dominicans after his death. Nor was he a nominalist, for he was completely convinced of the possibility of a rational approach to God. It seems most logical, on the whole, to consider him as one of the great Christian mystics whose philosophical position is perhaps best described as Neoplatonic. Like most mystics, he tended to see religion as communication between the individual soul and the divine spirit. These two must be similar in essence; for the one is absorbed into the other: it is this doctrine which makes mysticism a heresy to Calvinists and, therefore, marks Lull off from the Scotists who anticipated Calvin:

> The Lover beat up on his Beloved's door with blows of love and hope. The
> Beloved heard His Lover's blows, with humility, piety, charity and

patience. Deity and Humanity opened the doors, and the Lover went in to his Beloved. [*BL*, 26]

Deity and Humanity met, and joined together to make concord between Lover and Beloved.[11]

and, even more explicitly:

Whether Lover and Beloved are near or far is all one; for their love mingles as water mingles with wine. They are linked as heat with light; they approach and are united as Essence and Being. [*BL*, 27]

Now this reaction to Scotism drove Lull back beyond Thomism. For with Aquinas God was perfect and man was part-way up on the scale of actualizing possibilities striving toward fulfilment in him. Man and God are not the same in essence; man is lifted to God through the agency of higher organizations, which include the Church, the sacraments, angels, and saints, and in general the redemptive work of Christ and the regenerative activity of the Holy Spirit. Lull saw man as essentially an intelligence, and as truth takes no account of individuality, the duty of the religious man is first to free his intelligence by cutting away the world and the flesh:

The Lover was all alone, in the shade of a great tree. Men passed by that place, and asked him why he was alone. And the Lover replied: "I am alone, now that I have seen you and heard you; until now, I was in the company of my Beloved." [*BL*, 27]

—and then to merge his human intellect into the divine:

Between Hope and Fear, Love made her home. She lives on thought and, when she is forgotten, dies. So unlike the pleasures of this world are her foundations. [*BL*, 22]

The religious life is eremitic and, therefore, ascetic: this is connected with the significant fact that Lull, like most ascetics, upheld the doctrine of the Immaculate Conception which Aquinas denied.

From the Thomist point of view, therefore, Lull erred, not on the anti-rational side of nominalism, but on the other extreme of identifying human and divine natures: the usual heresy of mysticism. Of course, men being imperfect and, therefore, driven to activity while God is perfect and changeless, it follows, if man and God are the same in kind, that man has the power of free will to take the initiative. Lull recognizes that this would have been impossible without the Incarnation, but as regards the religious life since it occurred he is a thoroughgoing Pelagian:

> Love gave himself to any who would receive him; and since he gave himself to few and inspired few with love, as he was free and had not been constrained, therefore the Lover cried out on Love, and accused him before the Beloved. But Love made his defence and said: "I strive not against free will, for I desire all lovers to have the greatest merit and glory." [BL, 58]

> The will of the Lover left him and flew to the Beloved. And the Beloved gave it into the captivity of the Lover, that he might use it to love and serve Him. [BL, 59]

Most mystics have a tendency to underemphasize the rational approach to God, but Lull's strong insistence on it led him to see the perplexing tangle of the world as an elaboration of very simple mathematical principles. He had the idea of the Pythagoreans and the whole occultist tradition that followed them that the world was basically mathematical rather than organic, complicated rather than complex. This feeling in Lull's case arose from his conviction of the absolute intelligibility, and, therefore, simplicity, of the nature of God, for as mathematics supplies the most irrefutable demonstrations in life, it has frequently appeared to various thinkers (Plato, Bruno, Descartes, Spinoza, Newton, Leibnitz, even Pascal) the best approach to the understanding of the divine nature. Such an approach usually fails by overlooking the continual reforming, regenerating activity of God in history: it has as a rule been more congenial to monotheists like the Jewish or Mohammedan thinkers than to those who genuinely believe in a Trinity or an Incarnation. Lull escaped some of these stumbling blocks, but, as he was not even a mathematician, he adopted the Pythagorean belief that cardinal numbers represented the ultimate formulae of the construction of the universe. Like them, he saw an infinite symbolism in numbers. In the *Book of Contemplation*, for example, the nine "distinctions" or divisions of book 1 represent the nine heavens; the thirteen of book 2, Christ and His apostles; the ten of book 3, the physical and spiritual senses, and so on, similar schemes being repeated in most of Lull's more elaborate works. This recalls, of course, the whole Pythagorean tendency of the Middle Ages: the endless threefold associations with the Trinity, the juggling with seven, and the kabbalistic fourfold symbolism based on the tetragrammaton. It is hardly surprising, therefore, if Lull should have believed in the possibility of reducing the world of concepts in a similar way. He was close enough to Thomism to believe in the real existence of universals, and so proceeded in his *Ars Magna* to expiscate the elements of thought. The gist of the scheme of the *Ars Magna* is as follows. All possible objects of knowledge are reduced to nine categories: God, angel, heaven, man, the imaginative, the sensitive, the negative, the elementary, the instrumental. All relations in which these objects exist are reduced to nine predicates: goodness, magnitude, duration, power, wisdom, will, virtue, truth, glory. All possible questions concerning them are reduced to nine: Whether? What? Whence? Why? How large? Of what kind? When? Where? How? Probably nine was chosen because it is the number of the universe, which is a ninefold sphere, and the complete twenty-sevenfold scheme is the cube of three, the divine nature being threefold. These are placed in concentric circles, one is fixed, the other two revolve, and so by permutation and combination we get a series first of all possible questions, then of all possible answers. This is a genuine dialectic, and if it does not work, it has yet to be proved that any dialectic will; we have not yet stopped evolving dialectic, and we probably never shall. Lull's attempt haunted men's minds for centuries, particularly the minds of Raymond Sebonde, the subject of Montaigne's great essay, and Giordano Bruno.[12] Humanity learns by trial and error, and anyone who makes a genuine trial is not wholly in error.

This belief in the elemental nature of numbers forms, we have said, an essential element in most occult thinking, in astrology, in numerology of all kinds, in kabbalism, in magic. Alchemy is the one branch of occult thinking which excludes it. It rests on the Aristotelian entelechy we have dealt with in connection with Aquinas: the mineral world is the most completely material, and, therefore, the least actualized; all earths are to metals as matter to form; the other metals bear the same relation to gold, and the transmutation of all metals into gold is symbolically connected with the regeneration of mankind. Thus, its premises are quite consistent with Thomism; too consistent to win the approval of Aristotle's great opponent. "Unam metallum in speciem alterius metalli converti non potest," says Lull. And again: "concluditur quod Alchymia non sit scientia, sed sit figmentum."[13] This definitely disposes of any attempt to prove Lull an alchemist.

The quality of mysticism in the *Book of the Lover and the Beloved* is rather difficult to define. It seems an extraordinarily airy and abstract mysticism: it continually soars upward without difficulty. The Lover and the Beloved have their lovers' quarrels, but there is almost nothing of the intense agony, the profound humiliation, the symbolism of a descent into hell and a rise through purgatory that we find in all the mystics who have gone through what is called the dark night of the soul. Only one passage hints of a katabasis, and that very lightly:

> The Lover set forth over hill and plain in search of true devotion, and to see if his Beloved was well served. But everywhere he found naught but indifference. And so he delved into the earth to see if there he could find the devotion which was lacking above ground. [*BL*, 25]

The symbolism of the two lovers is said to be Mohammedan in origin; but against this must be set the fact that with the Islamic thinkers the symbolism is usually more explicitly sexual: the soul of the Lover is feminine to the spirit of the Beloved, as we have it so frequently in the female mystics, Madame Guyon and Saint Teresa. There is a complete absence of sexual symbolism in Lull; all communication is on a purely contemplative plane. The only thing that seems to me to recall Sufi teachings is the sense that the beauty of the world is the most direct and central representation of the nature of God:

> The bird sang in the garden of the Beloved. The Lover came and he said to the bird: "If we understand not one another's speech, we may make ourselves understood by love; for in thy song I see my Beloved before mine eyes." [*BL*, 24]

> The Lover rose early and went to seek his Beloved. He found travellers on the road, and he asked if they had seen his Beloved. They answered him: "When did the eyes of thy mind lose thy Beloved?" The Lover replied: "Since I first saw my Beloved in my thoughts, He has never been absent from the eyes of my body, for all things that I see picture to me my Beloved." [*BL*, 26]

An extraordinary sympathy with the natural world runs all through the book. Sometimes the symbolism is more conventional:

> The Lover went into a far country seeking his Beloved, and in the way he met two lions. The Lover was afraid, even to death, for he desired to live and serve his Beloved. So he sent Memory to his Beloved, that Love might be present at his passing, for with Love he could better endure death. And while the Lover thought upon his Beloved, the two lions came humbly to the Lover, licked the tears from his eyes, and caressed his hands and feet. So the Lover went on his way in search of his Beloved. [BL, 39]

The theme of the harmless lion runs in mystic literature from the Book of Daniel to the *Pilgrim's Progress*.[14]

The three roads of mystic contemplation are those of the will, the understanding, and the memory:

> The Lover and the Beloved were bound in love with the bonds of memory, understanding and will, that they might never be parted; and the cord with which these two loves were bound was woven of thoughts and griefs, sighs and tears [BL, 42],

and the end of contemplation is achieved neither through suffering (though the disciplinary value of that is clearly recognized) nor in joy, as with a more conventional Christianity, but in that mystic *extasis* in which joy and sorrow are surpassed in a fervour of devotion too concentrated to permit of any emotional criticism:

> The Lover lay in the bed of love: his sheets were of joy, his coverlet of griefs, his pillow of tears. And none knew if the fabric of the pillow was that of the sheets or of the coverlet. [BL, 42]

Memory is, therefore, essential because it alone preserves the continuity of devotion. At times Lull seems almost to draw the Platonic inference of anamnesis: that all our contemplation is recollection, and that we exist as ideas of God:

> They asked the Lover: "Whereof is Love born, whereon does it live, and wherefore does it die?" The Lover answered: "Love is born of remem-

brance, it lives on understanding, it dies through forgetfulness." [*BL*, 43]

Lull is much more sure of the power of man to lift himself to the contemplation of God than any follower of Paul or Augustine would be, and it is easy to see that for him the test of the religious life is good works rather than faith, particularly the supremely voluntary gesture of martyrdom; for it is obvious that the decision to be a martyr for Christ was made long before even the first visit to Africa:

> They asked the Lover what sign the Beloved bore upon His banner. He replied: "The sign of One dead." They asked him why he bore such a sign. He answered: "Because He was once crucified, and was dead, and because those who glory in being His lovers must follow His steps." [*BL*, 37]

Perhaps by the tests of the world Lull is a failure. As a philosopher, his dialectic is not the divinely inspired instrument of truth he thought it. As a missionary, he failed to reclaim any part of the Islamic world, even the North Africa from whence Augustine had sprung. As the organizer of an order, his dreams were ignored and faded away; his project for missionary colleges came to nothing; the Christian world rushed forward to its great cataclysm unheeding. He saw his Aristotelian opponents given more authority than ever. He himself gained after death the reputation of a sorcerer, a dabbler in the black art, a disseminator of superstition, a charlatan, and a heretic. But for seventy years he fought without once giving up; when one project for the advancement of his faith came to nothing, he started another, and when he gave his life at the end, he did so with an unalterable conviction that those who fight for the true God are never defeated; that however futile and quixotic they may appear to the world, God is using them in the advancement of his purpose. It is much easier to be a great man if the age will respond to one's greatness: Luther always had powerful support behind him; Lull was almost as isolated as Athanasius for most of his long life.[15] Somehow or other, all good actions are conserved and carried on; all evil ones separated out. Such was Lull's faith.

> The birds hymned the dawn, and the Beloved, who is the dawn, awakened. And the birds ended their song, and the Lover died in the dawn for his Beloved. [*BL*, 23]

Bibliographical Note

1. *Ramon Lull.* By Allison Peers. London (Macmillan: S.P.C.K.), 1929.

This looks like the nearest thing to a definitive biography of Lull in any language. It has completely superseded the two following works and is a book of thorough and complete information, excellent writing, and broad sympathies.

2. *Raymond Lull, the Illuminated Doctor.* By W.T.A. Barber. London (Charles H. Kelly), 1903.

A minor work, of little importance now, said in the Peers bibliography to be inaccurate. Mr. Barber makes out a case for Lull the alchemist.

3. *Raymund Lull, First Missionary to the Moslems.* By Samuel M. Zwemer. New York (Funk and Wagnalls), 1902.

A fairly readable but somewhat antiquated account, disfigured by a violent antimedieval and antischolastic prejudice.

4. *Raymund Lully, Illuminated Doctor, Alchemist and Christian Mystic.* By A.E. Waite. London (W. Rider and Son), 1922.

Mr. Waite, perhaps the greatest living authority on occultism, makes out a good case for a pseudo-Lull who was one of the greatest alchemists between Geber and Cornelius Agrippa and lived in the fourteenth century somewhat later than the genuine Lull, spending much of his life in England. The author rather spoils this thesis by attempting to show that the pedant who wrote the *Ars Magna* cannot be the fervent mystic who wrote *Blanquerna*.

The *Cambridge Medieval History*, vols. 5, 6, and 7, provided the historical background for the essay, and Windelband, *History of Philosophy*, the intellectual and philosophical. The *Encyclopaedia of Religion and Ethics* has a useful article on Lullism, and the *Catholic Encyclopedia*, an irritating but somewhat amusing attack by Thomist orthodoxy standing on its dignity. The *Encyclopaedia Universal Illustrada* has separate entries for Raimundo Lullio and Ramon Lull, but my Spanish is not equal to deciphering either.

5. *The Book of the Lover and the Beloved.* Translated from the Catalan of Ramon Lull with an introductory essay by E. Allison Peers. London (Macmillan: S.P.C.K.), 1923.

All quotations from Lull in the essay are from this work, unless otherwise stated.

12

Robert Cowton to Thomas Rondel,
Lector at Balliol College, Oxford

In a letter to Frye, dated 22 April 1934, Helen Kemp refers to this paper. The paper was written, then, during the spring term of 1934, when Frye was enrolled in Professor Kenneth H. Cousland's Church History 1 course. Even though the description of the course indicates that it covers the period up through St. Hildebrand (eleventh century), Cousland set 1300, the year of the Roman jubilee, as the terminal date for the course material. A note at the end of the paper, written in Cousland's hand, reads as follows: "An informative and entertaining report. Written in excellent style and with understanding of conditions and aspirations of medieval life." The source of Frye's information about the Franciscans Cowton and Rondel, both of whom were members of the Oxford Convent, was Andrew G. Little's The Grey Friars in Oxford *(Oxford: Oxford Historical Society at the Clarendon Press, 1892), a work Frye lists in his bibliography.[1] Frye received an "A+" for the paper, the typescript of which is in the NFF, 1991, box 37, file 13.*

When this letter reaches you, dear brother,[2] you will know that I am now safely arrived in the Eternal City. A trading vessel leaves Ostia[3] for London in a few days, and will arrive there much sooner than I can return. The captain, who is a very worthy man, is commissioned to deliver this letter to our brethren in Southwark, and from thence I have no fears of its safety. I also commend to your care an Italian brother, Guido of Perugia,[4] who should arrive not long after this does, if God has prospered his journey. I encountered him in Assisi, and he gave me to understand that, having seen what there was to see in Rome, he would undertake a pilgrimage either to Canterbury or to Compostela.[5] I strongly urged upon him the veneration and sanctity of Canterbury, pointing out that it was second only to Rome in approved merit, as is admitted by all. He goes through Germany, and should now be not far from Cologne, if no mishap befell him.

I write to you now, my dear brother, as one whose view of the world has been so enlarged, that in the past six months he has learned more than years of the most unremitting toil over books would have afforded. For which reason I write to my tutor and preceptor, that when I myself arrive you may understand my present mood and will be able to frame to it your wisdom and counsel which I so eagerly attend. For when I first set out on my pilgrimage, I was amazed to observe the wondrous variety and strangeness of what I saw, and thought for a time that this was the only thing to be learned from journeying into far countries, the manifold and infinite splendours of the works of God. But as I went farther and talked with wiser men, the ceaseless changes of scene failed so much to amuse and instruct me. For all God's creatures have under different apparels very similar souls, and what moves men in England moves men here in Rome. My wonder is now, not that the world should be so great, but that it should be so much one. I have talked with a man who has been, or claims to have been, in an ecstatic state approaching heaven; I have seen a man who has been, or, again, is said to have been, in hell. I have seen great piety and hideous cruelties; I have seen the centre of the world's glory and miles upon miles of its utter misery and desolation. Is it any wonder, then, that a simple monk should be so bemused?

Let me begin at the beginning, brother, when first I left your presence at Oxford. I received, what I later regretted, a pair of shoes from a brother, to ease my feet on the way. Passing through a ravine near Reading, striding along in great comfort and complacency, I was set upon by robbers, who threatened to kill me. "But you cannot rob me," I said, "I have nothing; I am a Friar Minor."[6] "You a friar!" said the chief of them, "look at your shoes!" I looked down and saw my boots with the greatest horror and uneasiness. After many strong assurances, I was suffered to proceed, and, now in a thoroughly chastened mood, gave the shoes to a beggar and proceeded barefoot, as is more seemly to one of our vows. The robbers, however, were more generous than a wicked baron living near Westminster, who, out of the greed and rapacity of his soul, has set up a toll gate on the king's highway wherewith to fleece poor travellers, to the great distress of the countryside.

King Edward held court at Westminster, being freed from the troublesome burden of wars. He is a very tall and handsome-looking man with
little of the haughtiness which disfigures the French king.[7] If I mistake
not, however, there will come evil days upon the land when reigns his
son, called Prince of Wales, as he is a weak and slothful-looking youth,
loving idleness above all virtue.[8] I talked to a pardoner who had come,
he said, from Jerusalem, but as I had ample proof of his villainy, I much
doubt his having ventured further than Rochester. His wallet was full of
what passed as holy relics of venerable saints, nail parings of St.
Ambrose, hair of St. Augustine, an ear of St. Gregory, and other such
stuff. He told me with much glee that simple parsons and even some
gentlefolk would pay him more than they could well afford for a sight
of one of these trumperies, especially since Pope Boniface's proclama-
tions naming these as Doctors of the Church.[9] I must own, being but a
simple friar, that with his ready tongue he imposed upon me, until he
displayed a tooth of St. Jerome's, as he said, which would have been
more suitable to that Father's mule.[10] This rogue pleased me better by
telling me of the plans of our great Edward for uniting our island under
his sovereignty. Wales, he said, was already subdued, and Scotland,
there remaining nothing more than the hanging of a few rebels in the
northern country. And yet, if the Scots are as stubborn in battle as our
brother Duns in argument, I much question that they will be conquered
so easily.[11]

London itself, like many cities, stinks in the nostrils of men. I was glad
to seek refuge from importunate shopkeepers and insolent young noble-
men riding poor people down in dark narrow streets with my brethren
in Grey Friars.[12] They are full of talk about their new church, which they
affirm will be splendid. They were very kind to me, but I confess I did
not relish an air of worldliness unusual in our order. We of Oxford have
our studies to distract our attention from vanities, but the London brethren are not so fortunate. Now God bear witness I am no innovator, nor
fomenter of trouble, but it is our duty to help the poor by being of them.
Kings, nobles, princes take money from the people to build themselves
great palaces; shall we do the same, we who take the rule of St. Francis?
Let us hope that no one will arise to point the finger of scorn at us,[13] as
full of pomp and vainglory, but I much fear some such outcome from
our London church.[14] I liked better the fine bridge over the Thames, the
like of which I have not seen in my journey, built on piles sunk in the
river, and of an enormous size, that would allow people to live on it.[15]

From London to Canterbury the road was well travelled with pilgrims, and, after resting at the Tabard Inn at Southwark, I too set forth
on a pilgrimage to the great shrine.[16] At Gravesend I found bodies of
malefactors swinging from gibbets, and though I shuddered and prayed
for their souls, I shuddered still more at a crowd of people tearing flesh
from their bodies, not in fury, but in devotion. I asked one man what he
was doing, and he said: "This man died as a thief, though he robbed
only the rich and was a friend to all the poor. It is the pride and cruelty
of the great who have brought him to this; therefore, we reverence him
as a martyr." Filled with horror, I preached to them then and there upon
the folly and wickedness of their ways, and albeit they were somewhat
abashed, yet they desisted not from their dreadful practices. We friars
can sometimes see further than those greater and more powerful than
we. I mark with dismay increasing oppression among the rich, and
greater sullenness among the poor. I fell in on the way with an abbot, to
whom I recounted my day's experience, and he replied, "They are only
discontented now because there is peace. Give them war to kill some of
them off and provide the rest with something to do." At which I held
my tongue, though I doubted his charity.

Though I lingered long in Canterbury, I need not weary you with my
delight in a place you have seen a dozen times. Nor was there much of
moment in the journey to Dover, which occupied four days. I came
away from Canterbury with a merchant who had been cured there of a
gouty inflammation, and on the road we stopped to look at one of the
travelling mysteries, depicting the birth of Jesus as recorded in the Gospel of St. Luke. The people were much diverted, and I confess that I took
great pleasure in seeing the rustics enter so into the divine story. I was
less pleased, perhaps, at the long complaints of the shepherds about the
oppressions and exactions of the rich and noble, inserted by them in
defiance of Holy Writ.[17]

From Dover, which is a channel port, we crossed to France. The distance over the Channel is not so great as I had expected, being only
about twenty miles—a strong man might swim it if the water were not
so cold. The little sailboat pitched and tossed in the sea, making me
grievously sick, though when I recovered, I talked to my companion the
merchant, who lived at Dover, and had business in Calais. He was a
wool merchant, and said that some day England would have to capture
Calais. I was about to rebuke him for his enmity, but a traveller travels
to learn, and one does not learn by preaching. So I asked him his rea-

sons, and he told me that it was necessary for England to control both sides of the Channel, as a defence against invasion, and, besides, there would have to be a wool staple, or fixed market. We English produce more wool than anything else, he said, and we must have a market on the Continent of Europe which we own and will serve as a gateway to Flanders and France. "Were I king," said he, "I would give up a hundred Guiennes for a Calais,"[18] a remark which did not greatly please a Gascon who had joined us, whose father had been mayor both of Bordeaux and of London. This man said that wars were waged by kings for their own glory, not to please burghers, but the merchant told him that in future all wars would be fought cold-bloodedly, for the sake of gain, and that the day of fighting against infidels and Saracens was over. Already, he said, King Edward was summoning the burghers to help him govern the kingdom, and Philip of France was preparing to do the same thing.[19] I repeat all this, as it has become freshened in my mind by much of what I have seen and heard in Italy.

At Boulogne was a tournament, and as I knew too little French to speak in anything but English or Latin, I hurried on, as I could do nothing except protest to a French brother of the Dominicans I met by chance in the street. He agreed that the tournament was a shameful and bloody business, but the nobles, he said, were powerful and it paid them well to laugh at the warnings of God's servants. He had preached without avail against the tournament, though he said some things I should not have said, such as, that it was better for the nobles to be killing their enemies the English, or routing out heresies in the south, or going on another crusade to redeem the Holy City of Jerusalem, than to be endeavouring to slaughter one another. He spoke, as nearly as I could judge, very fluently and persuasively. The common people listened respectfully, but the younger nobles mocked him, and the older ones made a point of ignoring him.

At all events, we became companions by the way, as he was returning to Paris. We conversed, or rather should I say he discoursed, in Latin. Between Boulogne and Paris, through Amiens and Beauvais, I made more sure of what manner of country I was in, a country of which he seemed to be what we call in the schools a microcosm. For I could not help feeling, in the course of my journeyings, that our England is especially favoured of St. Francis and France of St. Dominic. The French love much talking and constant strife against an adversary, as do the Dominicans.[20] The French are not content to watch patiently or learn quietly,

but must ever be dictating to all about them, as with the Black Friars.
The French are very quick to seize upon a logical fallacy and will endlessly distinguish terms and definitions—they would subtly divide the
atom if they could, a thing said to be indivisible, and here the Dominicans are their spokesmen. We Franciscans at Oxford love knowledge as
scientia, the Dominicans as weapons for dialectic. Thus, the Dominicans
are not greatly original. They despise the mathematics, and contemn the
study of the works of God in nature. They are impatient of experiment
and interest themselves more in what ought to be than in what is. They
are content not only to take the dogmas of the apostolic Church as they
are now understood, but make no attempt to understand them more
deeply. Now God forgive me if I seem arrogant or presumptuous, but in
England knowledge is sought in peace and solitude of the soul, which
alone gives happiness. I cannot but revere the wisdom of the great St.
Francis, who enjoined us not to engage in the idle bickerings of the scho-
lastics. Of all things in England, I missed most our English ale. The
French drink a great deal of thin and sour wine, which no doubt
accounts for the feverish heat of their blood and their inward bitterness
of soul.

I own my Dominican brother was not greatly versed in our learning.
Of such Franciscans at Oxford as Duns and William of Occam,[21] whose
fame I thought had surely overspread the world, he knew nothing, and
he repeated to me an old wives' tale, which I have heard among the idle
in England, that the learned and unhappy friar, Roger Bacon, was a sorcerer who made brazen heads through which the devil spoke, shattered
by the Dominican Albert, whom he called Magnus.[22] I held my peace,
for I had always held the learning and intellect of Friar Bacon in great
reverence, though I own he did not well in speaking so maliciously of
your preceptor, Alexander of Hales.[23] He also discoursed at length on
what he was pleased to call the newfangled philosophy of Thomas of
Aquin.[24] Some of the Black Friars, he said, were much taken up with his
doctrines, and there was some talk of adopting them, but he was of the
opinion that they contained damnable heresies, and he was sure the
Dominicans would reject them. I marvelled greatly at such talk from a
Dominican and finally asked him wherein lay his opposition, but to this
he made vague answers, that it were better to stick to the old Fathers,
that we would gain nothing by trafficking with Aristotle, who was the
source of Saracen philosophy, not of ours, and much more to the same
effect.

Amiens and Beauvais, the first eighty, the second fifty, miles from Paris, were two of the towns at which we halted that I particularly noticed. The fame of the wonderful cathedral at Amiens has no doubt reached your ears but that of Beauvais was vain and pretentious, built, like the Tower of Babel, out of the levity and wickedness of pride, no doubt too in emulous rivalry of Amiens. Why grown men of one town should desire to have a cathedral merely bigger than that of the next town, I cannot tell. To punish those of Beauvais for their folly, God caused the choir roof to collapse some years ago, but even this chastening seems not to have humbled them.[25] Otherwise, the towns of Normandy seem to me to be full of dirt and impudence.

Paris in particular seems to hold within its walls—without them, too, as, having nearly thirty thousand people and nearly as large as London, it has outgrown them—all I have noted as belonging to the life of France. It is noisy, like the French everywhere—the shopkeepers and hawkers keep up an infernal din, shouting their cries, which, however, are sometimes musical and pleasing in themselves. The people are at once dishonest and polite—without my frugal and wary Dominican friend I should have been grossly swindled out of what money I had and without doubt should have been poisoned by their food.

We went from St. Denis through the Rue St. Martin, through the Ville and across the Pont Notre Dame, which bridges the Seine, to the université, where I parted from my friend, leaving him rather abruptly in the middle of a discourse on the universals, he holding strongly with the Platonic realists. This problem no longer greatly interests me, so I had few qualms in departing to join the Franciscans. The University of Paris is the greatest in Europe, much larger than Oxford, and it has a great influence, so they boast, over the decisions of the Pope of Rome. Moreover, they say, this is only the beginning of its career, and they believe that in future Paris will be the seat of all learning, the *caput mundi*[26] of thought. The students are more quarrelsome even than they are at Oxford, and, being in a larger town, spend a great deal more money. Incessant argument over the *Sentences* of the worthy Peter Lombard reveal to me such a gross perversion and misunderstanding of the whole problem that I propose myself to study here when I become licensed at Oxford, and clear up the great doubts that pervade the minds of men concerning this book.[27] I was somewhat homesick in Paris, as, though no heretic, I deplore the tendency of the Dominicans to tyrannize over the students and to stick too closely to the record of the

past. I also grieve that the Dominicans, by their excessive zeal for orthodoxy, are far better organized than the Franciscans, despite the fomenting of strife by the opponents of him of Aquin. The Franciscans here
know not whether to follow the philosophical paths of Alexander of
Hales or those of Bonaventura, the great general who was so bitter
against our Friar Bacon,[28] and they do not understand that both are
equally pleasing to God, if so be they would only pursue their studies
quietly, as we do at Oxford, and not try to condemn all as heretical who
do not think as they do. I distrust, however, a growth of Zealots in the
order, as they call themselves, men who pretend to approach more
nearly to the doctrine of St. Francis, in giving up all wealth, all knowledge, all understanding, retiring to huts and to the forests. This is a
gross perversion—a life such as they propose is surely no better than
that of a beast. They would rather preach to birds than to men, as
though they had misread the Scriptures, and thought God to care more
for sparrows than for those whom he made in his own likeness. It is not
likely, however, that this heresy will spread.[29]

The King of France is absent in Flanders, and I could not see him.[30] I
understand, however, that he is tall and fair, grave, courteous and at
times kindly,[31] but proud and in general more anxious for his own glory
than for the welfare of his subjects. The country is impoverished by war.
In England the classes of society seem to get along fairly well together,
though there is much social unrest between classes. In France, on the
contrary, the different ranks are rigidly set, and their duties to one
another, or, at least, to the higher, clearly defined, while among those of
one class are constant wrangling and strife. In both London and Paris I
much misdoubt the effect of the growing of towns upon the world. The
bourgeois, as they call them here[32] or burghers, are sturdy, and sometimes sturdy knaves. They are unwilling to own anyone but themselves
for their masters; they serve not in wars as the vassals do; they amass
much money in trade and are beginning to have a good deal of control,
in consequence, over the nobility and even the king himself, who is
always in debt for his wars and pleasurings. In England, when nobles
wanted money, they went to Jewish moneylenders, but as no Jew can
safely retain his ill-gotten fortunes in a Christian land, there was little
danger of this sort. There are still Jews in France,[33] but our present king
has banished them from England,[34] in misguided zeal for our faith, as I
think. I should not care to have such worldly fellows as these townsmen
become too powerful, but it may be difficult later to hold them in check.

I knew you were interested in the Knights Templar,[35] and I made a few inquiries. All I know about them is that, now that the crusades seem definitely to be given up, the king is at a loss to know what to do with them, as they are not nurses, like the Hospitallers,[36] and seem to be an encumbrance upon the land. Many of them are old, worn out with service, but the order has gathered great wealth and much land into its possession. There is some talk of uniting them to the Hospitallers, but their vows are not the St. John vows, and there seems nothing that can now be done with them except forcibly to suppress them. The king is known to be not only rapacious and greedy for gain, but withal in sore straits for money to carry on his wars, and I much fear that a sad end will befall the Knights of the Temple.[37] Some of their members are accused of heresy. I met their Grand Master, Jacques De Molay, whom I should not welcome as a brother in my own order, he being dour and sullen, with a most craven terror of innovation of all kinds.[38]

Nor is wanting a bitter dislike of all things English in the hearts of some of the less charitable brethren. In Paris I was talking to an abbot, a graduate of the university and in his way a learned man, who, as soon as he caught my name and nationality, turned to others that were present and commenced a long and slanderous discourse to the effect that Britain was the source of all atheism, which he was pleased to ascribe to the foggy mists which he asserted always hung over the island. "These noxious vapours," said he, "rise from below; they are the breath or effluvium of hell, and breed the most pestilential heresies: from Pelagius of accursed memory[39] to Friar Bacon the British have vomited forth a continuous stream of apostasy." At this I could no longer contain and broke forth into vehement protest. But he was not to be silenced and said furthermore: "The English have always tried to examine nature, as if, forsooth, there were secrets there not immediately revealed by God. In this last hundred years, not only your Bacon friar went into sorcery, but a fellow named Bartholomew tried to make a compendium of all knowledge,[40] as though he would be another Aristotle: always there is prying into forbidden mysteries. And not only this, but, in order to bolster up your vanity, you take it into the realm of philosophy itself, and talk, and have talked, since your patron saint Pelagius, about the primacy of the will as against the orthodox ideas of divine grace.[41] The whole tendency of English thought is toward the destruction of all philosophy tending to reconcile reason and faith and toward elaboration of natural science by observations and experiments made in the pride of the soul." He would have gone on, but was interrupted by a man also present of some consequence in France, named Pierre Dubois, who spoke bitterly of Pope Boniface's opposition to the French king.[42] He announced that the French king was truly, and not the German emperor, the temporal lord of the world, that the English were French vassals. He wanted the Templars destroyed and rooted out. "The heresies you mention," said he to the abbot, "will last as long as England does; they will ever plague and confuse the world till they are conquered by France."

I was glad to leave the company, for I do not understand and do not like what I do understand of a new spirit, rife even in England and rampant in France, of setting up the king to be supreme lord and ruler over all. Men like DuBois seem to want to break down all the social barriers between the king and his people, destroy the aristocracy, leave nothing but king and subjects. They do not say this, but I believe they would rejoice to see it done. And, therefore, they pay homage, in their pride, to their own nation, to contemn the Vicar of Christ and despise the unity of Christendom. Truly the world will be in great distress when the Christian nations undertake crusades, not against the infidel, but against each other. I do not like this nationalism, yet it seems to be growing steadily.

After I left Paris, I set out for Troyes, congratulating myself on having learned something of the Aquinian philosophy without becoming involved in dispute of my own accord; though in Rome I was compelled to defend the doctrines of my brother Duns at some length, as you shall presently hear, I was not anxious, feeling unprepared and very ignorant, to match my wits against those trained in the greatest university in the world. Barely had I left Paris behind, when a thin and shabby-looking man approached, who, seeing my cloth, flung a taunt in my face. I responded meekly enough, when, immediately relenting, he came up to me: "I see you are not one of those greedy ones," he said, "who wax fat on the sweat of the poor." I held some discourse with him and found him witty and entertaining, albeit too profane in his utterance. His name, he said, was Jean Clopinel (he walked with a slight limp), and he came from the town of Meun on the Loire, near Orleans.[43] He was a poet, and read me some verses of his, which sounded agreeably in my ears, though I winced at their freedom and the viciousness of his spite, of which the poor Franciscans received an ample share. In fine, we parted on good terms. He asked me when my own country would start writing poetry, and I hesitated, somewhat abashed, finally saying that the English language was a polyglot mixture of English and French, not as ripened or as disciplined in its numbers as the French. "Non-sense," said he, "your language is as good as any." And in truth I have often felt, preaching in England in the vulgar tongue, that there was a strong and supple strength in it that needed only the touch of a poet to make us see it. And I know other Franciscans, too, who have felt a thrill of pleasure from the same source.

In Troyes I encountered one Villani, a young Florentine, journeying to Paris.[44] He had just been in Rome and was on his way to Paris through the great trade road that leads from Italy into France through Champagne. He told me much of what I was to see at Rome and Florence, but especially the latter. He was glowing with enthusiasm and said that the jubilee celebration there had fired him with zeal to commemorate the glories of his own birthplace as those of Rome had been so frequently celebrated.[45] I liked him much better than DuBois; though he has only one idea, the splendour and greatness of Florence, yet he is a Guelph, for so they term adherents of the pope in Italy, and he has a rich store of information. Everything bears on his city, however; the Creation of the world was only the necessary prelude to its founding. Troyes has also a fine cathedral of St. Peter,[46] but a townsman with whom I talked told me he feared the king of France, for Troyes is the centre of Champagne and holds many prosperous fairs attended by the Flemings, but should Champagne ever be united to France, as Philip was moving heaven and earth to do, the Flemings would stop coming, and the town would be ruined.

I pushed on to Dijon in another three days, a splendid town where lives the Duke of Burgundy with a brilliant court.[47] A cathedral is going up, of course, beside the one of St. Bénigne, in which was a boys' school I visited.[48] This I liked not: their masters keep close watch over them, armed with rods which they hardly ever put down. Each master sleeps between two boys at night, and never lets them go where he cannot be spying upon them. Telling tales is encouraged, and all the masters are feverishly anxious to beat their charges on the least provocation. They call their cruelty and love of torture by such names as discipline and protection, which is all the more loathsome. One lad was being beaten when I was there, and, on my inquiring the cause, I was informed that, having been instructed in the doctrines of the Church regarding the future life, he had innocently asked whether he were now in purgatory or in hell. I wondered what our gentle St.

Anselm would say to such a place,[49] a school no better than a prison or a madhouse.

Here I met a Black Friar whom I greatly admired and respected, as much as anyone of that cloth I have encountered, despite his numerous faults. He was a German, Johannes Eckhart by name, and was on his way to Paris: indeed I had heard something of him there. He is truly a deep and noble spirit, a sort of thinker we call mystical, like Porphyry and his school. We talked as we walked through the streets of Dijon, and quietly, but, so as to command respect, in Latin with a rather heavy German accent, he led me into paths of philosophy I had never traversed. He was anxious to bring to his native Germany, as he said, some of the measure of learning with which Paris had astonished the world. He had no wearisome system of doctrines to expound all in a breath, but he spoke from such profound wisdom and insight that I marvelled, although some of his opinions sounded rather harshly in my ears. I had been startled to hear God called nothing, when he explained that a God of simplicity could not be predicated with complexities. He, too, is something of a Thomist, as they call the adherents of that renowned Black Friar, though from what I know of him I doubt his approval of such doctrines as that God is all existence, which smacks of a dangerous kind of pantheism, a fault I have noted as pervading very much of this kind of ecstasy-thinking. Nor was I better pleased at a mysterious Sabellian-sounding doctrine, that God's Creation and Incarnation must be the same, as in the former God entered the world of life, as his coeternal Son. I fear for the Germans, a lumpish race at best and totally unskilled in the subtleties of Paris or Oxford, that heretical mischances may beset them. But Meister Eckhart, for such they call him, is himself so much wiser than his doctrines, that the truth shines out through them, like a torch in a dark street.[50]

Being in a hurry to get to Rome, I chose to go through Geneva into the Piedmont country in Italy, passing through Florence, Siena, and Assisi to Rome. Not to visit Assisi for a Grey Friar would be a sin of omission;[51] to avoid Florence would be impossible after meeting Villani, and I was curious to learn the reason for his so earnestly conjuring me to avoid Siena as I would the devil. So I journeyed toward Geneva, which I found, as I have found many cities, in a state of unhappiness and turmoil. The city desires to be independent, like the Italian city states, and has revolted against its overlord, calling in a prince named Charles of Savoy, to aid them, and as the foreign prince assuredly does it not solely of his goodwill, I fear more bloodshed.[52] In addition, the tyrant house of Habsburg, which rules Austria and all the Alp country, presses the peasant in the neighbourhood of Geneva and far to the east, so that much sullen opposition arises.[53] I understand an alliance already has been formed. Formerly the peasants could appeal to the emperor, but now, with the Empire so weak, they may resist of themselves. They seem intent on forming yet another nation to disturb the rest of the people of God. At present all is quiet, a rebellion having been recently quelled, but the peace is outward only. The burghers, as is their custom, care more for themselves than for the fate of the peasants.

Outside an inn in the town, I heard a stream of the most scurrilous abuse, blasphemy, and obscenity coming from a voice I placed as that of a young boy, kicking and screaming in the grip of the innkeeper. I made inquiries, and found that the lad had been accused of stealing money from one of the guests. To prove his innocence, he was ordered to touch a red-hot poker extended to him, but by an agile twist, he wrenched himself free, the poker touching the innkeeper's thigh, to the latter's great discomfort. It transpired that the boy was a strolling German vagabond, full of tricks and merriment, but a thorough rogue. His name, they said, was Eulenspiegel, which in that tongue signifies Owl-Glass.[54]

I passed quickly out of Geneva and crossed the Alps over an old military road, built, it was said, by the Romans, like the road between Oxford and London. After about ten days I found myself in the plain of northern Italy and rested for a while at a town called Piacenza, which controls the trade route on the southern bank of the Po. You have no doubt heard that all the cities of Italy are torn by the factious strife between a party claiming to support the pope, called the Guelphs, and another the emperor, called the Ghibellines, the first wearing red roses, the second white ones. I cannot see why pope or emperor should be proud of either; they fight solely, it would seem, out of their own wicked perversity. For these Latins love nothing better than strife: the great nobles live only to hate one another and the people follow them gladly. The town of Piacenza is at the climax of a war with the ruler of Milan, Matteo Visconti; first submitting to him, one named Scotto is now in revolt.[55]

The Italians are very considerate with the pilgrims, and I reached Florence without difficulty, only to find that unhappy and beautiful city in an uproar. Not content with the Guelph and Ghibelline warfare, two separate parties have formed themselves, called the Blacks and the

Whites. Even while I was at Piacenza, the quarrel broke out in Pistoia, a town near here. Florence is a Guelphic city, and this brawling means that the Guelphs are fighting among themselves.[56] I spoke to a fellow-pilgrim from the south of France, lamenting much the folly and wickedness that compels men to take sides for the mere pleasure of slaughtering their fellow-creatures. "Oh," said he, "I have talked to some of the men here, and there is something behind it. You know, of course, that partisans of pope and emperor are the cause of the fighting between Guelph and Ghibelline. Now the emperor no longer rules the world, and the great pride and haughtiness of the present pope assuredly goes before his fall, if there is any truth in Scripture.[57] By his incessant warrings both in Sicily and in Tuscany, the pope has degraded himself to the rank of a mere prince. Hence, the nations afar off will shake his yoke from their shoulders, and wars will no longer be conducted for the sake of the dead cause of whether pope or emperor shall rule the world. Strong nations like Britain and France will arise and fight with each other; the emperor will have to fight his subjects at home. Italy can never be a nation: each city desires to rule itself. The city welcomes only those rulers who rule many other cities and are of no great strength anywhere, so that they may be the more easily overthrown. Hence, before Italy lies nothing but perpetual internecine strife and revolt."

I said that this was exceedingly clear, but I inquired how far the quarrel of White and Black had anything to do with this, as it seemed to have no purpose behind it. "That," said he, "is the sign of a new kind of war, a kind that will become more frequent later on. It is only the rich who fight, and they need money for wars. They take this money from the poor, and the poor will revolt. Hence, men will fight for gain." (I thought here of my merchant adventurer.) "But within the state itself will be a war of classes, of rich and of poor. The Blacks wear that colour to signify that they are tyrants: they desire to hold all things in subjection to their own pride. They are the great, rich, noble families, whose minds are ever dwelling on the past—their past—who have no faith in anything but force, and no confidence in any state not an oligarchy. The Whites are more liberal: they stand for reform and greater administration of justice, for patronage of the new art, of gradual growth of a freer spirit." I marvelled somewhat at this, suspecting him to have talked with one of White sympathies and, therefore, to read into the struggle, as heretics do with the Scriptures and Fathers, more than was there, as both sides seemed to me exceedingly cruel and greedy. I asked him if there were any hope for eventual peace and received the amazing answer that good and evil were equally strong in the world, that they would always contend with one another, being opposites in the body as well as in the state, for the spirit was good, but the flesh evil. At this I looked narrowly at him, and thought I could detect a deep circular scar winding up his arm; wherefore I concluded that he was of the so-called Cathari, one who had been questioned by our Dominican brethren and was going to Rome to seek absolution.[58] I can hardly yet understand how he escaped a worse fate than the rack, though, as this heresy is practically extinguished, vigilance may have been relaxed. I was told that King Philip of France was preparing for a campaign in the south which would unite Provence to that kingdom. I think he was afraid to acquaint me further with his heresies, fearing no doubt that he had already said too much.

I met another Provençal in Florence as well; indeed most of the pilgrims I have met came from there. He assured me he was not a heretic, but spoiled his protestations by telling me what the other man had, that the pope was too proud to hold dominion over the world long. "Other men are strong enough to destroy him," said he: "the King of France, perhaps, not the emperor, who has no Empire, but only a ghost of one. It is the nation which will arise, and among the greatest of those nations will be the Provençal, which has had a civilization and literature of its own already for centuries." In some ways this talk reminded me of that of a nominalist at Oxford, a friend of Master William of Occam, who asserted that "Christendom" was an abstraction, a *universalia post rem*, formed of nations, which had a *universalia in re*.[59] This newfangled nationalism, as I may call it, seems bound up with nominalism. This Provençal went so far as to say, being somewhat in his cups when I talked with him, that the Holy Apostolic Church was not universal, that each nation reshaped or translated religion in its own way. The so-called heresy of the Albigensians, he said, was only the Provençal way of worshipping God, quite right for the Provençals, wrong for anyone else.[60] Desire for dominion and power had led popes and kings against them. "Destroy the Cathari," he said, "and you destroy the troubadours," for such they call their poets and wandering minstrels, accounted the best in the world. I set down all these absurdities, dear brother, in the hope that you may be the less alarmed at the views expressed in Oxford by young students full of new wine.

Upon the many beauties of Florence I cannot dwell, nor on those of Siena, which is a Ghibelline city and a rival of Florence. I was eager for the end of my journey, and the strife and bloodshed of Italy blurred my happiness. The Florentines and Sienese each have schools of painting, full of a strange new beauty I cannot describe, as we have nothing like it in England, much as I should like to see it there. I do not claim to understand all the subtleties, as I am not acquainted with the art, but in the gorgeous colouring, the reds and greens and blues, the brilliant gold backgrounds, the loving care of decoration, in the haloes and framing of scenes, the majestic and yet easy balancing of figures, there is a piety and adoration all our learned doctors and theologians cannot express. The Florentines seem to me the stronger, more learned, more rich and various, the Sienese more light-hearted and winsome. Verily I believe, dear brother, that could our guide St. Francis have seen the works of the Sienese Duccio,[61] he would have counselled his order that here lay the true approach to God, not in striving to emulate the endless disputings and contendings of the Dominicans in logic and rhetoric. Perhaps, after all, that was what St. Francis meant.

Possibly I say too much, but at Assisi was all the labour and genius expended best fitting for our saintly founder. Assisi itself is a small and sullen town groaning under a tyrant, like all Italian cities, but in the cathedral of St. Francis I took my refuge. There were two men whose work I most admired. Cimabue, now an old man of sixty, has many pictures of a dignity and massiveness which do not lack grace, but, so I was told, reflect the Byzantine Greeks in severity and grandeur.[62] Somehow I missed the sweetness and gentleness of St. Francis. I caught it better by seeing the work of the famous di Bondone, who is here familiarly called Giotto, whom I caught a glimpse of in Florence, thin and refined of countenance, though with an expression so unaccountably droll and odd that it is apparent that he looks with much indulgence upon the capers of his brother ass.[63] I saw an artist working on a panel and was amazed at the skill and courage it takes to paint. He laid a coat of white lime on the wall and applied on it his paints with the greatest of skill and rapidity. Once his hand faulted, and to my astonishment, he did not correct his blunder, but erased everything he had done and started again with his lime coat. It would seem as though painting in this way would be apt to lead one into venial sins, as the cursing he did under his breath would have been sharply rebuked by a Dominican, but he talked with me later and said that, while alterations could be made with a smeary concoction of glue and eggs[64] which he showed me, no painter who valued his reputation ever used it.[65]

I paid my appropriate devotions at the shrine of our founder, and then set out for Rome, which I could hardly see, so crowded it was with pilgrims. A bridge leading to the great churches of St. Peter and St. Paul seems almost in danger of collapse, so vast is the number thronging it. At the shrines of the great churches money is tossed down in such quantities, gold, silver, baser metals, and the new Venetian paper, that the priests gather it in with rakes. The reproach is often levelled at the pope for holding this jubilee that he does it only to gain money for his wars, which are carried on to the north in Tuscany, where he sides with the Blacks, and to the south in Sicily, where he has temporal and dynastic ambitions unbefitting the Vicar of Christ. He extends indulgences to pilgrims who come to Rome, practically selling them in fact, which I do not like, nor do I care overmuch for the gambling tables which add so plentifully to his stores. I have heard strange rumours of his pride and contempt of his inferiors. Once he kicked a kneeling archbishop in the face; he has insulted all his cardinals, glorifies his family, and takes terrible revenges on his enemies. Though, like the English and French kings, he is handsome and of imposing presence, he inspires one with a feeling of fear for the apostolic Church. Men say on all sides that the world is too small to contain the pride of both the king of France and the pope of Rome, and that, when we see who is stronger, we shall no longer pay tribute to the latter. The pope, however, is mighty yet, and has powerful friends, though his enemies increase daily.

One pilgrim to whom I talked was a Franciscan brother from Illyria, who had a friend that had set out for the East. I supposed he meant Jerusalem, but he said that the brother went much further than that, further than the country of the Saracens or of Prester John,[66] out to a mighty and populous empire that lay to the west of a great ocean. The king of that country has a yellow face, slanting eyes, straight hair, and long nails, which, except for the last, I have seen in a strange-looking barbarian in Geneva, who was called a Magyar, and came from Hungary, the king of which land[67] is now in Rome. This Eastern monarch desires to learn something of our faith, the friar told me, and Franciscans and Dominicans had both been sent out.[68] "What think you," said the brother, "touching the opinion of Pythagoras, that the earth on which we live is spherical, and that the ocean which lies on the east of this kingdom beats on the west of France?" I had nothing to say to this, but was thrilled to the marrow at the thought of our faith thus encircling the world. He also told me that these people killed each other with something like Greek fire, which burst and destroyed everything around it. Armor, he said, was not proof against it, and it would soon become known in Europe.[69]

There was, too, a man from Catalonia, on the east of Spain, who was a pupil, as he said, of one Ramon Lull, a scholar deeply versed in the philosophy of the Arabs, one who had fearlessly faced martyrdom, preaching the gospel to the infidel in North Africa. He told me that his master had many schemes for the reform of education, in fact had written of a state administered according to good and sound laws, like the state of Plato, and though no one would listen to him in Rome or Paris, he was now on his way to Cyprus.[70] This pupil seemed learned, but I did not understand his bewildering Arab philosophic theories. The Moors, it would seem, labour more mightily even than the Dominicans over matters of logic. I understood much better why Master Lull had not been more attentively received in Europe. He has fallen in love with the Arab mathematic and would forsooth reduce the concepts of philosophy to symbols, as they use letters in their algebra. Hence, he may solve all problems possible to think of by the theory of numbers. This is called the "Great Art," and it would be a great art indeed, were concepts so simple affairs.[71]

Ever since I had left Paris, however, I had reflected much on what little I had heard of the Aquinian philosophy, and was eager to find someone of the darker cloth, to see if I had understood it correctly and if it would stand against attack. I had not long to seek, as a Dominican Florentine soon fell in with me and opened the question on which I had thought most keenly, that of whether the will or intellect were the stronger.

"You Dominicans," I said to try him out, "hold, as I conceive it, to a determinism on this matter which destroys the concept of free will."

"Absolutely wrong," said the Dominican. "The will is bound by lack of knowledge, and where it works as master, it is blind. Only the reason can free it from its bondage. Wherefore we hold that it is a matter of the plainest sense that the will not only cannot stir without knowledge, but that it is knowledge alone which shows it how to act. Knowledge alone can give ideas, including the idea of goodness. Therefore, when the will strives toward the goal of the good, that goal is marked by knowledge, and knowledge is the necessary determining cause of the activity of the will."

"I am not so sure," said I, "that the will in the mass of men makes such mighty strives toward the good; how could men not brutish do evil, if knowledge of the good necessitated good actions? But tell me. Where do we get our ideas? Are they not from nature?"

"Assuredly."

"But is nature determined or free?"

"She is determined."

"Nature obeys law, truly. But if ideas are from nature, they must be of nature; therefore, the will entangles itself, in its helplessness, with a mesh of determined natural causes. I protest I see nothing but determinism in this: if the will obeys intellect, intellect obeys nature."

"But where does will find its objects, if not from knowledge?" inquired the Dominican, somewhat abashed.

"From ideas, as you say; the servants of the will, the occasioning causes of its self-determined motion."

"But surely the will, even with this, chooses better ideas rather than worse ones?"

"It chooses, on the contrary, those sharper, clearer, more distinct, which stand out from a multitude of confusions. But never does an idea become clear unless we fasten our attention upon it, by which is signified the will."

"That may be true for empiric actions. But the intellect is still higher than the will, for its end, the truth, is higher than the end of the *bonum*, the good. What is true is always true; what is good is good only for a certain time and place. Truth is eternal; good is impregnated with the corruption of life and death."

"But do you assume so rigid a divorce between the good and the true?"

"What I mean," he said, "is, that good as such, *sub specie aeternitatis*,[72] is alone apprehended by intellect: the special transient forms it takes are achieved by will. Truth is eternal goodness."

"But if the will strives to achieve the good, and if it alone can so strive, it alone has the goal of the good in sight. Once reached, it may be asked, whether it be true or not that this is good. The good is, thus, an eternal principle, manifested empirically by the criterion of truth, which reverses your statement."

"How," demanded the Dominican, "could you attribute primacy of will to God? No one, I suppose, doubts the reality of the divine will, but we must assume that God creates only what he knows is good; that he works through self-determining necessity. The divine will is, thus, limited by the divine wisdom. Otherwise, if God were essentially a will, he would be an imperfect, desiring God, ever striving to achieve a goal, even as the human will."

"But the goal of good the divine wisdom postulates must either have been formulated by the divine will, or it must have arisen independently, in obedience to the mandates of a being greater than God, which is absurd. God is not infinite if he is not absolute arbitrary will: had he chosen to incarnate himself in a donkey instead of in a man, he could have done so.[73] One must not limit God to a necessary choice."

"Then is goodness not the essential nature of God; for if the moral law which is God's command issues from arbitrary will, there is nothing inherently good in it: for the will might have willed the opposite way."

"This I believe," I said. "For, though it may seem a hard statement that nothing is per se good except God, the complement is manifest, that nothing is per se evil except insofar as it violates the will or command of God, as we maintain against the Manichees."

"But if God is essentially will," said the Dominican, "then is our preaching and study vain, for we comprehend through reason, and if reason elaborates a philosophy, and theology is concerned with God, there can be no connection between philosophy and theology."

"There is none," I said. "I place the emphasis on their separation. Faith is faith, and reason is reason: we know what to believe, and our speculation may lead us into as many absurdities as it will without danger."

"If will is essentially strife and desire, how can we hope for immortal blessedness, which is surely nothing but the constant contemplation of the excellence of God?"

"Happiness can never be attained by reason; it is the result of directing the will towards God. Hence, the final state of blessedness is not mere passive contemplation, but active love, and action is willing."

But all my arguments on the Continent led eventually to reflections on my nationality, in conformity with the new fashion of thinking, and my Dominican was no exception. "Did Pelagius then found Oxford?" he asked. "For here is again the view that the wonderful human will does as it pleases with the poor divine grace."

By this time we had reached the Angel Bridge,[74] when I noticed a tall and thin man intently regarding the crowd, with an expression on his face of such bitter sorrow and yet such piercing wisdom that I was filled with horror and awe at once and whispered to my companion, asking him what manner of man he could be. "His name is Alighieri," said he, "a Florentine: they say he has been in hell."[75]

Verily I believe it to be a short and easy road thither from Italy, dear brother, and I cannot get that face out of my mind. Incessant warfare, unheard of cruelties, are the accompaniment of such splendour and magnificence as I should never have believed possible. Our great St. Francis would not despise the body, and in this he differed from many, who have despised it so long that in fury and resentment it seems even now to be rising up to destroy the spirit. The pride of the nobles has robbed the peasants so that the feudal tenure is falling to pieces. The towns are growing and puffing themselves up with pride and vain-glory. There is, consequently, more money, and the world is greedier for gain. The Church still stands, but corrupted at its source. Something is creeping over Italy, a pride and resurrection of the body, which is on one side glorious, strong, and with a terrible beauty, and on the other unimaginably cruel, lecherous, and evil. I am impatient to return, dear brother, to what seems to me now a tranquil and peaceful country, the England especially favoured of St. Francis.

Bibliography

History of the Middle Ages, 300–1400, Thompson. [James W. Thompson, History of the Middle Ages, 300–1500. London: K. Paul, Trench, Trubner, 1931]

Little: Studies in English Franciscan History. [Andrew G. Little, Studies in English Franciscan History. Manchester: The University Press, 1917]

Little: The Grey Friars in Oxford. [Andrew G. Little, The Grey Friars in Oxford. Oxford: Oxford Historical Society at the Clarendon Press, 1892]

Vida Scudder: The Franciscan Adventure. [Vida D. Scudder, The Franciscan Adventure: A Study of the First Hundred Years of St. Francis of Assisi. London: Dent, 1931]

Coulton: Five Centuries of Religion, vol. 2. [G.G. Coulton, Five Centuries of Religion. 2nd ed. Cambridge: University Press, 1929]

Gregorovius: Rome in the Middle Ages, vol. 5, pt. 2. [Ferdinand Gregorovius, History of the City of Rome in the Middle Ages. London: G. Bell, 1894]

Coulton: A Medieval Garner. [G.G. Coulton, A Medieval Garner: Human Documents from the Four Centuries Preceding the Reformation. London: Constable, 1910]

Taylor: The Mediaeval Mind. [Henry Osborn Taylor, The Mediaeval Mind. 2 vols. London: Macmillan, 1914]

Randall: The Making of the Modern Mind. [John H. Randall, The Making of the Modern Mind: A Survey of the Intellectual Background of the Present Age. London: Allen and Unwin, 1926]

Boase: *Boniface VIII, 1294–1303*. [T.S.R. Boase, *Boniface VIII, 1294–1303*. London: Constable, 1933]

Cambridge Medieval History, vol. 7. [Cambridge: Cambridge University Press, 1911]

Joan Evans: *Medieval France*. [Joan Evans, *Life in Medieval France*. London: Phaidon, 1925]

Ashley: *The Economic Organization of England*. [Sir William James Ashley, *The Economic Organization of England: An Outline History*. London: Longmans, Green, 1928]

Chaucer: Prologue to the *Canterbury Tales*.

Langland: *Piers the Plowman*.

Histories of philosophy by Windelband [Wilhelm Windelband, *A History of Philosophy*. 2nd ed. New York: Macmillan, 1921], Ueberweg [Friedrich Ueberweg, *A History of Philosophy from Thales to the Present*. 2nd ed. London: Hodder and Stoughton, 1875], and Erdmann [Johann Erdmann, *A History of Philosophy*. 2nd ed. 3 vols. New York: Macmillan, 1892].

General Reference Works: *Encyclopaedia Britannica*, *Encyclopaedia of Religion and Ethics*, *Catholic Encyclopedia*, *Dictionary of National Biography*.

13

Relative Importance of the Causes
of the Reformation

On the title page of this paper, submitted to Professor Kenneth Cousland, Frye wrote "Church History Essay I." It was the first of two papers he submitted for Church History 2, "History of the Christian Church from the Reformation Era to the Present Day." At the end of the paper, Cousland wrote, "An excellent interpretation," and he gave the paper an "A." The typescript is in the NFF, 1991, box 37, file 9.

The chronicler differs from the historian in that he sees history in two dimensions, as a series of pictures. Every movement or occurrence, regardless of size or importance, can be understood only with reference to whatever precedes it, so that the chronicler has no standard by which he may avoid confusing a "cause" with the precipitating event. According to him history is a grotesque series of accidents arising from the whims of court favourites, the sudden resolves of heroes, or the vanity of princes. Responsible historians, from Voltaire on, have summarily rejected this approach, but as school textbooks and popular romances continue its tradition, it remains accepted by the rank and file, though perhaps the Great War has brought a saner attitude. There cannot be more in the effect than in the cause; and the contrast between the murder of an imbecile noble and a world bent on suicide is too glaring even for the careless or unthinking.

True, the educated have a deeper view of causation;[1] but in dealing with a movement like the Reformation it is as well to be on our guard, in a world overrun with prejudice. All prejudices are either religious or antireligious, and history, past or present, is the only sphere in which they may be worked out. Hence, those who on religious grounds are utterly opposed to Protestantism have a definite interest in making the Reformation which gave it birth appear as superficial a movement as possible.[2] A glib-tongued fakir sells spiritual patent medicines to credulous rustics, and the greatest political and cultural ideal in human history is overthrown! A tempting gesture, even if it is rather melodramatic and perhaps a little fatuous. It tempts, however, not only the apologists of an older church, but those opposed to religion in general, who also have an interest in tracing the growth of a Christian ideal to the exploiting of the discontent of the ignorant and superstitious by greedy nobles.[3] But at the same time the Protestant himself is by no means likely to err too far on the other side.[4] For he would tend to think of the Reformation as a movement so natural, so inevitable and automatic a reaction from a system of intolerable abuse, that he too would see nothing incongruous in the indulgences controversy being its inception. For him the precipitating event is a genuine causal agent, by no means merely a catalyser.[5]

But with a great and wide movement like the Reformation, which brought about such momentous results in both the religious and the social fields, we have to look for underlying causes much deeper, and we must treat the indulgences controversy as merely an emblem of them. At the same time, we cannot altogether treat the transubstantiation and other theological debates too exclusively as merely symptoms of social unrest or regard the whole question of religion as the façade of an economic change. The economic determinist finds little difficulty in separating the economic motive for any great event; it is invariably present, and it is quite plausible to regard it, therefore, as the only essential one. But no historical movement is an unmixed effect, and if it spring from a number of forces then its cause is not any one of them, in itself passive, but the fact or occasion of several coming together. Thus, economic dissatisfaction results from injustice, and injustice is a moral issue. The moral decay of the papacy would not have been responsible for an organized attempt to throw off its power; a few of the sensitive would protest, the vast majority would remain apathetic.[6] The ambitions of princes and the exactions of Rome, though more obvious evils, would have stirred the masses, but would not have provided dynamic leadership as long as the pope retained his spiritual ascendancy. But both material and spiritual needs, insofar as they are expressed in revolt, are in themselves significant of the unrest of a gradual and general feeling of the necessity for and compulsion to a change of state.

Only with this basis is a harmony of mental and physical revolution possible. The realization of this ultimate basis is an intellectual formulation of new ideas. The Middle Ages were essentially a religious era, and the Protestant revolt was basically a new religious idea. Hence, the purely religious aspect of the Reformation is really the essential part of it, and not a mere carapace of a social and political compulsion.[7] A religious change does not mean a new set of theological doctrines, but an alteration in the view men take of their relation to God and their fellow-man.[8] The only thing that will bring about so far-reaching a change is not a class struggle, but a larger movement in which the class struggle is implicated—an organic change in the development and maturation of a culture.

Movements allied with the Reformation, the Renaissance, the rise of capitalism, the middle class and a money economy, inventions and discoveries, usually treated by historians of the Reformation in their introductory chapters, show clearly enough that the birth of Protestantism is inseparable from its general cultural *Urgrund*, which we can hardly define, but can only describe, like a colour. Whether we call it the birth of the modern age, or simply an awakening, it is a subtle, pervasive, and decisive change. The growth of a culture is analogous to the development of an individual, with this difference: that in the individual maturity brings with it a steady linear growth and perfecting of intellect, creative ability, and moral responsibility, while in the culture, which is the work of mature men in every age, those values are preserved, maturity being reflected only in the growth of self-conscious awareness in space and time. Art, systematic philosophy, and ethical ideals cannot advance or improve, but history and science do. It is impossible to improve on Aquinas or Shakespeare, but it is possible to supplement Froissart and the Bacons. The general principle of this contrast is that religion, in the cultural sense, the religion in which philosophy and art are embodied, is an organic growth; while the social order, in which history and science are compounded, is a gradual advance.

With this proviso, it will seem more acceptable to consider the growth from childhood to adolescence as the most valid symbol we can obtain of the movement we are examining.[9] In its historical unconsciousness and its utter lack of curiosity concerning the world beyond Christendom, in its egocentric preoccupation with the problem of individual salvation, in its ready acceptance of temporal and spiritual authority, in its tendency to argue endlessly from unexamined premises, in the self-contained, complete, and secure view of the universe, in the preoccupation of its painters with the theme of God as an infant in the arms of his mother, in its melodic and rhythmless chanted music, in its interest in commodities rather than money, in its sudden fits of irrational barbarity, in its literature of interminably wandering and adventuring knights, the Middle Ages, with all their subtlety and mysticism, form the childhood stage of Western culture. Similarly, in its contemptuous sceptical revolt, in its sudden awareness of the body and its pari-sexual eroticism, in its tendency to hero-worship, in its gradual consciousness of its actual place in the scheme of things, in its transformation of static ecstasy of perception to a subjective search for reality, in its substitution of a calculated sadism for instinctive cruelty, the Renaissance-Reformation is to that childhood stage the adolescent succession.

This movement is, therefore, the beginning of self-reliance. The child's consciousness and his environment are shaped for him by intermediaries; and the underlying pattern of the new awakening was the throwing off of those aids by which medieval man comprehended his position. From a static consciousness and a static environment man emerges into a new responsibility, more troublesome and insecure, but more intellectually satisfying. From this point of view, the Reformation is simply the articulated religious expression of a general movement of which another aspect is the Renaissance, and still another the rise of capitalism.[10]

First, then, the revolt against intervention, against aids to thought, creation, and action, which sustained the medieval civilization. Religion under Protestantism became a direct relation between God and worshipper. The intercession of saints, the supreme authority of the Church tradition, the automatic and irrevocable force of the sacraments, including holy orders which gave the priest his exalted powers of absolution, were thrown to one side. Government in the new age became a direct relation between the leader and his people. Monarchies were consolidated on the ruin of the old intervening class, the nobility, and the Machiavellian prince took control. Philosophy became a direct and empirical search for reality. The medieval realism postulated two helps which the Renaissance banished: faith and the universal, which enabled reality to become accessible to reason. The new philosophy, nominalistic in inception, pushed theology out of the field of speculation altogether; and by getting rid of this element of faith, it also abandoned the idea of a general concept's being the concretion of its manifestations. Henceforth the mind would deal directly with the fact, the object, as in itself an entity, without prepossessions of any kind and without interposing abstractions made solid by prejudice. The arts followed the same course. Where realistic philosophy had relied on faith, painting relied on religious symbolism; and where the realists had trusted the universal concept, the painters treated decoration, the geometric ordering of the aberrations of nature, as an end in itself. The Renaissance introduced a style more vital and flowing, dealing, again, directly with the model or subject.

Secondly came the overthrow of the static suspension or balance which medievalism had assumed to be the end of knowledge and had come so near to achieving in Aquinas. As a necessary corollary of this achievement of poise, the universe, that is, the environment as a whole, or space, was conceived as having an absolute centre in the world. Copernicus stripped away the onion-skin layers of the Ptolemaic cosmos, tore off the embroidered garment of sun, moon, and stars, and flung the earth into an infinite space. This was the central and focal expression of a growth of self-conscious awareness which also woke up to the discovery of other continents, other civilizations, other religions, and of a new realization of tradition and a new perspective of history.

All this was a reinforcement and strengthening of the individual. It was, therefore, a step in breaking down the social order into smaller units. The growth of self-consciousness brings with it an awareness of others as entities, and the consequent emergence of smaller and more concrete loyalties. The basic feature of this was the development of the town from a market town into a culture-town. By a market place I mean a nexus for a fundamentally agricultural, landed society; a centre for the exchange of goods and of ideas. The culture-town is a separate, self-contained unit, autonomous alike in government and ideology. Hence, the great age of architecture, the communal and anonymous art, ended, and gave place to the development of specialized arts in the hands of the "great masters," a purely urban and sophisticated development. Hence, too, of course, the city republics of Italy and the Hanse towns[11] of the North Sea, without which the Renaissance and Reformation respectively would have been abortive.

It is undoubtedly true that both Renaissance and Reformation were conditioned by the growth of nationality and the rise to absolute power of the prince. But the problem has usually been approached from the wrong end. What caused the rise of the nation was the emergence of the culture-town. The new nations were not groups of cities; they consisted of one culture-town,[12] arrogating to itself as much of the countryside as possible to feed it materially and spiritually.[13]

Therefore, the essential individual with whom we have now to deal is the burgher, or the inhabitant of the town, of whose individuality the prince is a symbol.[14] As a townsman he is committed to living in a society; hence, the summary close, particularly in England, of the monastic tradition. His whole life is one of social exchange on equal terms; the burgher is a trader through and through. He can trade in two commodities—materials and ideas—and to provide for a free circulation of both he develops a money economy and the printing press. His religion is fundamentally ethical: he knows little of saints or mystics.

The factors which bind the Reformation to the birth of the modern age generally seem to comprehend it entirely, save for the one differentiating factor that makes it the Reformation and not the Renaissance. The opposition between Renaissance pope and German reformer is a real one and has to be accounted for. What is the source of the opposition? The birth of the modern age was a movement towards the breakup of the rather vague cosmopolitanism of the Middle Ages. Now, if the great medieval civilization held together in tension any large antithesis, political or speculative, one would expect the new era to break along the boundaries of that antithesis, like a cell separating from its parent.

One thinks at once of the quarrel of pope and emperor. The Reformation was not the outcome of that quarrel, but of the deeper cleavage it signified. The Roman Empire had been politically destroyed by the Germans and spiritually annihilated by Christianity. These two movements, being fresh and vital and having a common cause, had met and fused. Whether it was the Lombards, the Franks, or the union of German states under the Hohenstaufens which took the lead, Western civilization was definitely consolidated on a synthesis of Latin and German traditions. With the Renaissance and Reformation these elements separated. The Reformation was the assertion of Teutonic independence against the pretensions of an Italian prince, and the Renaissance was the reinforcement of the Latin tradition by the realization of its pre-Christian achievements. The Renaissance proper, then, works toward the Council of Trent and the Counter-Reformation; its much-heralded paganism is simply an accretion of Latinism.[15] This may broadly be said to be the only important factor distinguishing the Reformation, and only by reference to it can we account for the utter collapse of Catholicism in Scandinavian countries or that of Protestantism in Italy. It is possible that the contemporary race-consciousness of Germany and Italy, obviously descendant from Luther and Machiavelli respectively, represents a catharsis preliminary to a new and more permanent cosmopolitanism.

14

Gains and Losses
of the Reformation

This paper was written for Professor Kenneth H. Cousland, who taught Church history at Emmanuel College. Frye submitted it for Church History 2, "History of the Christian Church from the Reformation Era to the Present Day," which was one of two required courses in Church history for all Emmanuel students. Cousland wrote this note at the end of the paper: "A penetrating and comprehensive piece of work though it does not seem to me to be up to your best standard either in construction or treatment." Frye received an "A-" for the paper, the typescript of which is in the NFF, 1991, box 37, file 9.

The gains and losses of the Reformation are, of course, inextricably bound up with gains and losses more directly brought about by other movements contemporary with it. The Renaissance brought tremendous gains and losses in art, science, philosophy, and scholarship, which were not altogether the work of the Reformation: so did the rise of nations and of the middle class: so did inventions and discoveries. Many of the greatest men of the time—Machiavelli, Erasmus, Copernicus—either remained aloof from the Catholic versus[1] Protestant struggle or refused to commit themselves to it. We owe incalculable debts to Gutenberg, Columbus, Magellan, and other neutrals that we can hardly be said to owe to religious reformers or reactionaries. Let us consider only such gains and losses, then, as we can definitely associate either with the birth of Protestantism, or its corollary, the overthrow[2] of the Catholic world.

In the first place, it can hardly be denied that Protestantism was, far more than Catholicism, on the side of liberalism and tolerance, imbued more than its adversary with the spirit of free enquiry and the use of critical intelligence in religious matters. Its record, particularly that of the Calvinist branches, is not snow white in this respect, but any rational comparison between Protestant rule in England under Elizabeth or even Edward and Catholic rule under Mary, or between the treatment of Catholic minorities in Scotland and Protestant minorities in Spain, should establish the point. There is probably no more inherent cruelty in one tradition than in the other, nor more sadism in Latins than in Nordics, but Protestant[3] emphasis on the direct responsibility of the soul to God made heresy far less an outrage on society, and its punishment, consequently, less a venting of popular fury on its victims. The Catholic tradition of apostolic infallibility once denied, the enormity of the crime took on far less cosmic proportions. Another reason for the somewhat cleaner Protestant record is without doubt the influence of its intellectual and sensitive progenitors among the mystics and humanists. Protestantism contains, at its finest, the refusal of a fine mind to be bullied by inferior interpreters of tradition. Erasmus is a great Protestant in this sense; so more obviously is Zwingli; and so is Luther when we admire him most.

The overthrow of a tradition alleged infallible and divinely inspired was an immense advance toward the assumption of individual responsibility in thought and action. Hence, the influence of Protestantism on the growth of empirical science was very considerable, despite the obscurantist tendencies of some of its leaders. It also provided for a greater variety of opinion and directly advanced the development of a reading public for the new printing press. It fostered, generally, a spirit of critical analysis, often among minds not purely Protestant, which eventually bore rich fruit. Consequently, the complexity of philosophical and social questions was better realized. Naivety, as a quality of first-rate minds, largely disappeared, and a more numerous class of people may be perhaps said to have become more intelligent, if we understand what we mean by that.[4]

The shift in authority from Church to Scripture may not have been a gain in consistency, necessarily, but it did bring the Bible, which remains the quintessence of the written word, into the vulgar tongues and into the possession of the commoners. The rise of nations, and, consequently, of modern languages, is a movement associated only with the Reformation and perhaps not directly caused by it. But of the great influence of the Bible in moulding our own tongue among others there can be no question. An even more significant gain was the advance in

historical consciousness it brought about. With all their respect for tradition, the Middle Ages were historically unconscious. The sense of the
organic development of an alien culture afforded Protestants a better
perspective and a wider tradition, and the vigour, power, and compression of Hebraic literature is by no means a negligible factor in the
growth and development of the poetry and philosophy of England or
Germany as compared with Spain or Italy in the centuries following
the Reformation. Sympathy with Jewish traditions probably helped a
decline of anti-Semitic pogroms and massacres, though again it is hard
to say how much of this was due to the rise of a middle class better able
to take care of itself.

The overthrow of the priesthood as a separate class of society took a
good deal of temporizing and half measures out of the practice of religion. The mechanical process of absolution and indulgence had tended,
by the time of Tetzel,[5] to put too much of religion on a commercial basis,
the indulgence scandal being more notorious, but hardly less grotesque,
than the treasury of merit concept[6] or the purchase of masses to liberate
souls in purgatory. That there was a general decline of superstition is
evidenced, too, by the disappearance of the "relics" swindle and alleged
miracles of priestcraft, such as the St. Januarius blood liquefaction,[7]
from Protestant countries. The general clearing out of spiritual intermediaries, such as the sacraments and the interminable catalogue of inter-
cessory saints, with their shrines and holy days, did much to pull the
practice of religion out of anthropology into ethics.

The secularization of the arts of music and drama is probably due in
large measure to the Renaissance. Of the drama this is obviously true,
but that the Protestants did give a tremendous impulse to music, and
that in a forward direction, can hardly be denied. The Middle Ages had
never made a working unity out of popular song and sacred chant, the
unity of the Lutheran hymnody, which combined the great rhythmic
and contrapuntal traditions in music. Luther stands directly at the head
of a procession of composers in Germany which culminates in Bach; Palestrina, great man as he was, sums up the sixteenth century without
being a pioneer for the seventeenth. The remainder of artistic developments are not specifically Protestant, though the rise of nations, which it
encouraged, gave art a possible advantage in more clear-cut national
units.

Even from a Catholic point of view it is difficult to believe that the
elevation of Catholic moral tone, the abolition of the scandals of papal

secularization, the doctrinal achievements of the Council of Trent, the consolidating and organizing power of the Jesuits, could have taken place purely as a result of internal reform.[8] For the rest, the more fluid society brought about by the rise of a capitalistic money economy and the abolition of the feudal hierarchy was certainly not hindered by Protestantism, though the political and economic nature of the Reformation itself is perhaps exaggerated.

It is by no means difficult to paint a very black picture of the Reformation, even when we are by no means[9] prepared to say that it would have been better for the Reformation never to have been born. In the first place, Protestantism cannot be entirely absolved from complicity with the self-seeking aggrandizement of princes as against the great cosmopolitan theory of the Middle Ages. We cannot answer the charges against the motives of Henry VIII,[10] nor refute altogether the Erastianism[11] of Luther, except by a *tu quoque* argument.[12] For on the question of the rise of tyranny honours are about even. If the English Reformation was the work of a selfish ruler, the Scottish Reformation was not; and if the Scotch and Dutch Reformations were national movements, so was the Catholic reaction in Ireland under O'Neill.[13] The Elector of Saxony can hardly be proved more of a jingoistic imperialist than Philip of Spain or any Valois,[14] and, after all, the petty princes who started the Reformation in the first place were not German, but the popes of Renaissance Rome; and the apologist of the petty prince was Machiavelli, whose hero was Cesare Borgia, son, or nephew by courtesy, of the worst of those popes.[15] The charges of such Catholic historians as Chesterton, Belloc, and Tawney, essentially that Protestantism broke the unity of Europe, should be made with more caution and fairness.[16]

The growth of responsibility of the individual, however, necessarily carried with it grave dangers. The abolition of the confessional, though perhaps an inevitable step under the circumstances, was no unmixed blessing. The confessional is psychologically one of the soundest of religious institutions, and psychoanalysis is beginning to realize it, along with its corollary theory of the terrific neuroses desire can form when repressed by a self-justifying ego. An unhealthy and morbid introspection disfigures too much of Protestant religious experience, the terror and gloom of many Calvinist traditions being proverbial. In the same way the awakened self-conscious awareness of religious life brought with it an overemphasis on Christian duties to one another, that is, a tendency to push the mystic and transcendent experience of Christianity away in favour of ethics. There can be little doubt that Protestantism did not produce enough saints or mystics. Too much energy was expended by covenanted congregations over doctrinal quibbles, instead of leaving such matters to schoolmen who had nothing better to do with their time. It is possible, of course, that we are now just completing an ante-Nicene period of Protestantism,[17] but a survey of the past, without regard to the future, does show a disproportionate stressing of good works.

That there was a gradual infiltration of tolerance into a distracted world at this time is a generalization which must be cautiously accepted. The split in the Christian camp forced both sides to defend themselves, nervously and self-consciously, against mental and physical attack. On the theological side this largely accounts for the comparative half measures of Protestantism, and its failure to become definitely a liberal and tolerant movement. Through what must be called sheer terror of going too far, Anglicans and Lutherans solidified into national sects, Calvinists into a tradition too rigid to deserve its name of Protestant. There are many ideas of the time which strike a responsive chord in our day, but which were sacrificed to the forces of reaction: the social theories of the more radical sects, the insistence of the Anabaptists on a continuing and vital tradition of Christian revelation, the sympathy with tolerance and free enquiry evinced by Erasmus and Zwingli, the demand of the peasants for social justice rather than theological subtleties, the obvious possibility of a new synthesis of religion and science, all ignored or subordinated to, so it seems to us, less worthy ends.

But if the Protestants were prevented by fear from attaining to the ideals implicit in their religion, the Catholics were driven back on a program of ferocious persecution and intolerance. The development of the Jesuit order, while achieving much in the way of education and missionary enterprise, also too often resorted to a policy of terrorism backed up in many cases by the abnegation of the most fundamental decencies of society in favour of dishonesty, intrigue, abuse of confidence, and cruelty, to advance what it thought to be the cause of its Church. The cold-blooded extinction of culture by the Jesuits in Bohemia[18] is one of the grimmest tragedies in history, and in priggishness, that is, the crime of belief in an inflexible moral code to be administered by man, the Jesuits compare unfavourably with John Calvin's Geneva at its worst. The development of the Inquisition brought in a regime of unspeakable horror and sadistic cruelty, which we cannot yet refer to without a shudder,

and the long intransigent policy of the Catholics, the stifling of innovation by the Index,[19] the bitter opposition to the scientific thought of Galileo and Bruno, and the general anachronistic tendency of the Church
ever since, accounts in no small measure for the cultural decline of Italy
and the stupefaction of Spain.

These evils are not, of course, purely Catholic: there was a general tendency toward the bloodless corporate aristocratic society of the baroque
in the north as well. The point is that the opposition of Catholic and
Protestant intensified the bitterness and suffering of the universal cultural transition. The same principle holds good for the overthrow of the
medieval cosmopolis and the rise of capitalism and monarchy. The association of Protestantism with the rising bourgeoisie forced the religion
to connive at many of the excesses of the class. Thus, the famous encour-
agement of private enterprise in Calvin's doctrine of material prosperity
as a sign of grace, a blunder committed by many Christians in defiance
of the New Testament.[20] What Calvin did for capitalism Lutheranism
did for the monarchy, playing directly into the hands of petty tyrants. In
the same way the religious motive was a powerful one in fomenting
imperialistic wars, a motive which remained a strong one till the eighteenth century, as evinced in the wars of England and Holland against
Spain.

The revolt against medieval culture and thought on the part of the
Protestants was perhaps carried too far. Granted that much unreadable
scholastic rubbish was cleared out of philosophy, the extreme and capital importance of synthetic thinking as we have it in Aquinas was overlooked, which led directly to the hopeless bankruptcy of Christian
theology in the nineteenth century, and its utter failure to assimilate scientific developments. In art, a gain in variety did not altogether atone
for a loss of depth and balance. The tendency was too much, in Protestant countries, to regard the Middle Ages as a nightmare of superstition and cruelty, and to consider all its products primitive, crude, and
distorted by its savage religious censorship. Hence, a contemporary
interest in things medieval is long overdue, for art, philosophy, and
economics.

Historic growth is a painful process, and much of its pain is caused by
those who are too convinced of the finality of their present stage. If it
were possible for humanity to learn anything from history, then one of
the greatest gains of the Reformation, from our point of view, would be
the singular applicability it bears to our own day. It was an age when

everyone thought that the religious struggle was the paramount one; an age when those who would not commit themselves to a definite religious attitude were deemed behind the times; an age when amateur prophets were prophesying a future struggle between Catholic and Protestant as the major issue of the next generation; an age rich in great religious personalities engaged in beating each other's brains out. The religious problem was finally solved, not by one party's having the correct solution and all the rest being wrong, but by the problems themselves becoming obsolete in the course of the struggle about them. The great artists and scientists worked on unheeding, leaving us to choose between the Copernican theory of the solar system and the Lutheran theory of consubstantiation, if we like, as representative of the best thought of the time. Substitute "economic" for "religious," and we have the contemporary scene.[21]

15

A Study of the Impact
of Cultural Movements
upon the Church in England
during the Nineteenth Century

This paper was written for Kenneth H. Cousland, professor of Church history at Emmanuel College. It was submitted to fulfil the requirements for Church History 3, "History of the Church from the Seventeenth Century to the Present Day," which Frye took during his final year at Emmanuel (1935–36). Frye received a grade of "A+" for the essay, the typescript of which is in the NFF, 1991, box 37, file 13.

So Christian turned out of his way to go to Mr. Legality's house for help; but, behold, when he was got now hard by the hill, it seemed so high, and also that side of it that was next the wayside did hang so much over, that Christian was afraid to venture further, lest the hill should fall on his head; wherefore there he stood still, and wotted not what to do. Also his burden now seemed heavier to him than while he was in his way. There came also flashes of fire out of the hill, that made Christian afraid that he should be burned. . . . Here, therefore, he sweat and did quake for fear. . . . And now he began to be sorry that he had taken Mr. Worldly Wiseman's counsel. And with that he saw Evangelist coming to meet him; at the sight also of whom he began to blush for shame.

Bunyan[1]

In this essay I propose to let a few of the more accredited representatives of the nineteenth century speak, as far as possible, for themselves. Whatever connective tissue I can supply will perhaps serve to form a pattern and a background. With the nineteenth century *cultural* means, when brought into any connection with the Church, literary and philosophical. Musically, the Victorian Age was as tone-deaf as the petrified city in the *Arabian Nights*, its sculpture being presumably much inferior. Architecture has a certain negative interest we shall touch on later; painting has a religious connotation only in the Pre-Raphaelite movement. In arranging this cento of quotations from the literature and philosophy of the age, I am not concerned to show, or to attempt to show, that there were any causal connections between the growth of culture and the development of the Church. There are no causal connections anywhere in history, other than the most superficial and haphazard. Literature, philosophy, and religion do not react on each other: they are reacted on by a definite group of people born in a certain age. In the nineteenth century we have an era as important and interesting as any of the three centuries preceding it, though in all branches of culture it marks an abrupt decline from them. It made up, to some extent, in variety what it lacked in intensity; and if it is a period of confusion rather than coherence, it is, for that very reason, one of analysis rather than growth, with a cultural pattern more explicit than civilization had yet seen. Culture, denied the height and depth of great inspiration, broke out and overflowed on all sides.

The nineteenth century was the offspring of the Industrial Revolution, of the movement towards national democracy which produced the French and American Revolutions, and in general the change described by Spengler as a change from culture to civilization, the entry into the last phase of growth possible to the Western world. Fundamentally, it represented a shift in social economy to the metropolis. Now the metropolis is the one completely individualized form of society. Everyone depends on his social environment in a completely impersonal way; his friends are not his neighbours, they are selected by his temperament.[2] The rise of technical and engineering developments brought about a sense of human sufficiency and power which made for a completely antinomian attitude to religion. Carlyle gives us both elements of the situation, looking at one objectively and presenting the other as his own belief:

This is not a Religious age. Only the material, the immediately practical, not the divine and spiritual, is important to us. . . . Our true Deity is Mechanism. It has subdued external Nature for us, and we think it will do all other things. We are Giants in physical power: in a deeper than metaphorical sense, we are Titans, that strive, by heaping mountain on mountain, to conquer Heaven also.[3]

To reform a world, to reform a nation, no wise man will undertake; and all
but foolish men know, that the only solid, though a far slower reformation,
is what each begins and perfects on *himself*. (*Signs of the Times*)[4]

Which gives us two of our leading motives: the idea of the inherent
power of humanity to achieve its own ends, and the sense that humanity is an aggregation of individuals.

As Kant was the only thinker who grasped the nature of this rise of
antinomianism, it is to Kant we must turn in order to understand what
is happening. Everything we know, said Kant, is the product of an
object and a subject: we operate by mental forms on everything we
perceive. Consequently, the world, as an object of understanding, is a
phenomenal world, not the real world. The real or purely objective
world eludes us. The difference between these worlds is a difference of
essence, or subjective apprehension of a thing, and existence, or the
thing-in-itself. All proofs of God's existence imply that his essence
involves it, which is impossible. We cannot rationalize our religion: it is
something we feel and experience.[5]

The romantic philosophers who followed Kant asserted that the
world of understanding was essentially a space-world; we cannot
understand the process of change. On the other hand, what we do not
understand, we feel and experience, and experience belongs to the
world of existence, which is similarly a time-world. This gives us the
key to our problem, for romanticism provides the general background
for all forms of nineteenth-century culture. The various religious
impulses of the period can be classified according to the attitude they
took to the pervading assumptions that time was existence or life and
that life was the ultimately real world. For the purposes of discussion,
we shall divide them into four. First, the negative attitude of pessimism
and scepticism, rising from the feeling that, as life entails more suffering
than happiness, it must be, because there is no higher reality, evil rather
than good. This we call the agnostic movement, or the identification of
religion with illusion. Second, the slightly less negative inference from
the doctrine that religion is inner feeling rather than reason, that one
should preserve the emotional kick of religion while repudiating its
dogma. This we call the aesthetic movement, or the identification of religion with art. Third, the more positive attempt to strive toward a higher
reality in the only possible way: by improving life. This we call the pragmatic movement, or the identification of religion with morality. Fourth,

the gathering together of these elements into a coherent religious point
of view. This, of course, is the synthetic movement, or identification of
religion with life.

It is quite impossible to identify any of these with the ordinary sectarian divisions of Christianity. The Catholic Church, standing out for a
genuine communal appeal in religion, gained the respect of those dissatisfied with the attempts of their own age, and, consequently, provided a
fifth movement we shall glance at later on. The Protestant sects were
less fortunate. Everyone took for granted, as a necessary axiom of civilization, the separation of Church and state; the idea, given currency by
Edmund Burke, of supporting the established Church because it was
established, was very widespread among the Tories, but made little
headway in culture. Coleridge is the one prominent name to be associated with the Protestant Anglican Church, and if he meant what he said
when he defined religion as "only reason, seen perspectively by a finite
intellect,"[6] he was standing for a rationalist tradition which goes beyond
Thomism itself and was a complete anachronism for the nineteenth
century. There is little to choose between Anglican and dissenting
Churches; they were seething in a curious hellbroth of morality and
respectability which owed something to Calvinism, something to
Arminianism, and much more to deism; which latter, by its withdrawal
of God from human experience, had cleared the ground for the immanent life-religions of the time. The separation of divine and human
activity in Calvinism was the remote source of this perhaps, but the
Industrial Revolution had knocked the underpinning from genuine Calvinism by its bolstering up of man's confidence in his own powers, as
we have seen in the quotation from Carlyle given above. Consequently,
religion came to be identified with various kinds of human activity. The
doctrines of justification by faith and the working of divine grace in the
human soul were almost unheard of during the nineteenth century.

The age was completely in the hands of the competitive, individualistic middle class. The aristocracy which had produced Chesterfield, Wal-
pole, Gibbon, Scott, Byron, and Shelley did not, after the Reform Bill of
1832, write down a single line worth rereading, such elevated bourgeois
parvenus as Disraeli and Tennyson being exceptions which go a long
way to prove the rule. Religion, however, is inexorably, in the end, a
community of believers; it can never be entirely individualized, and so
the various communities of artists, reformers, and human beings in general we have mentioned above became, for the majority of people, the

established social order, and religion a gesture towards its perpetuation. Methodism, by throwing in its lot with the expanding mercantile activity of the time, had prevented a no doubt premature revolution of the proletariat and had, in fact, been largely instrumental in enlisting the proletariat in the service of the capitalist system. Its doctrine of immanent and universal grace, contemporary with the German pietism which had nourished Kant, provided a nucleus for the life-religion developments of the time and a spearhead of reforming activity for both Dissenters and Anglicans. But for the most part, the really independent minds who did some original thinking on the subject of religion encountered an apathetic, maladjusted, usually openly hostile Church, and in studying the impact of one on the other, we must keep in mind the fact that the Church was for the most part very unwilling to suffer any impact at all, and what influence there is is indirect and largely posthumous.

The Agnostic Movement (Religion as Illusion)

One of the most important of the romantics who followed Kant was, of course, Schopenhauer. For him the thing-in-itself became a part of the world of experience, antithetical to the world of understanding. He called it the world-as-will. This, not being accessible to the intelligence, could not be conscious; it must be then a blind unconscious force, causing infinite pain with spasmodic flashes of happiness. Life is essentially evil; no conscious purpose in the world can be postulated, and the sole remedy, for most at any rate of Schopenhauer's followers, is spiritual isolation.

This doctrine, in most of the forms it takes, is too close to Buddhism, incomparably the greatest religion outside our own tradition, for us to deny that it is a positive religious attitude in itself. But no other age has ever sounded quite so despondent a note as the nineteenth. An age of bourgeois individualism isolates the genius, by shattering the implicit sense of a communal unity which the great artist evokes, and the constant bitter fight of artist and bourgeois produces some sinister results. The figure of the misunderstood, persecuted genius starving in a garret is a myth belonging to the nineteenth century. First there are the gloomy romantic heroes of the Byronic school: then, as the conflict sharpens, come the demoniacs or wilful eccentrics whose motto is *épater le bourgeois*,[7] the followers of Baudelaire in France; then the sadists with their association of beauty with pain; then the pathological cases of geniuses whose horror of society has driven them to lunacy or suicide, such as Laforgue, Strindberg, Nietzsche, or Van Gogh; then a dissolution in decadence as the hostile society breaks up, with Wilde and the Beardsley period in England, Zola and his followers in France. This development has been brilliantly traced by M. Praz in his book on *The Romantic Agony*.[8] It is a development which touches England chiefly at the points indicated, and, as it regards religion as a product of society, it repudiates religion by reversing it. For this kind of artist is merely a bourgeois turned inside out. Sadism produces a new black mass, a devil worship of the kind of Swinburne's blasphemous parody of a hymn to the Virgin:

> O garment not golden but gilded,
>   O garden where all men may dwell,
> O tower not of ivory, but builded
>   By hands that reach heaven from hell;
> O mystical rose of the mire,
>   O house not of gold but of gain;
> O house of unquenchable fire,
>   Our Lady of Pain!
>
> (*Dolores: Notre-Dame des Sept Douleurs*, [lines 17–24])

But we are more interested at the moment in tracing out the positive quasi-Buddhist religious attitude. In James Thomson's *City of Dreadful Night* we have the full horror of absolute pessimism, complete rejection of society and the forms it evolves, utter renunciation which moans to itself the refrain "No hope could have no fear" with a cumulative power to which no quotation can do justice.[9] John Davidson is more explicit:

> It has been said: Ye must be born again.
> I say to you: Men must be that they are. . . .
> Religion, Art, Philosophy—this God,
> This Beauty, this Idea men have filled
> The world with, study still, and still adore,
> Are only segments of the spirit's tail
> We must outgrow, if spirit would ascend . . .
> To reign untailed in heaven hereafter.
>
> (*Testament of a Man Forbid*, [lines 80–1, 97–101, 106])

Here, of course, is an English echo of Zarathustra on the mountain top. The answer of the artist to bourgeois civilization is couched in bourgeois terms, for the artist cannot avoid expressing his own age, however he may hate it. Individualism is the message both of despairing poet and confident economist. It may be objected that pessimists like Thomson and Davidson, however important in themselves, are not typical of the Victorian age. So let us storm the inner citadel of Victorian respectability and see what Tennyson says:

> The sun, the moon, the stars, the seas, the hills and the plains—
> Are not these, O Soul, the Vision of Him who reigns?
>
> Is not the Vision He, tho' He be not that which He seems?
> Dreams are true while they last, and do we not live in dreams? . . .
>
> And the ear of man cannot hear, and the eye of man cannot see;
> But if we could see and hear, this Vision—were it not He?
> (*The Higher Pantheism*, [lines 1–4, 17–18])

In this pleading wistfulness we catch what is assuredly the same feeling of profound distrust in the possibility of the existence of anything like a conscious or personal God. Tennyson's attitude is hardly dogmatic enough to be anything more than a tendency. Let us turn to the most representative philosopher of the age, who can hardly count lack of self-confidence among his weaknesses:

> We see that Atheism, Pantheism, and Theism, when rigorously analysed (i.e., after a discussion of twenty pages), severally prove to be absolutely unthinkable. . . . A religious creed is defined as an *a priori* theory of the Universe. . . . Religions diametrically opposed in their overt dogmas, are yet perfectly at one in the tacit conviction that the existence of the world with all it contains and all which surrounds it, is a mystery ever pressing for interpretation. On this point . . . there is entire unanimity. (*Synthetic Philosophy*)[10]

Herbert Spencer claims that the kernel of truth in religion is that God is unknowable. In him this agnosticism became the basis of an evolutionary philosophy we shall deal with later. A far greater philosopher, F.H. Bradley, voices a similar conviction, but with a more unified point of view:

The religious consciousness rests in the felt unity of unreduced opposites; and either to combine these consistently, or upon the other hand to transform them is impossible for religion. And hence self-contradiction in theory, and oscillation in sentiment, is inseparable from its essence. Its dogmas must end in one-sided error, or else in senseless compromise. (*Appearance and Reality*, 443)[11]

And in Bradley's scepticism we touch the very core of the nineteenth-century attitude. For it is associated with a spiritual isolation, a subjectivity of perception and thought, almost amounting to solipsism:

My external sensations are no less private to myself than are my thoughts or my feelings. In either case my experience falls within my own circle, a circle closed on the outside; and, with all its elements alike, every sphere is opaque to the others which surround it. . . . In brief, regarded as an existence which appears in a soul, the whole world for each is peculiar and private to that soul. (Ibid., 346)[12]

But the culmination of this sceptical pessimist agnosticism is in the work of Thomas Hardy. In his greatest production, *The Dynasts*, there, is significantly, the explicit influence of Schopenhauer; and there is the combination of the belief in an impersonal universe and in the isolation of the intelligent individual from an unconscious environment. Let us take a great tableau from the drama:

(S.D.): A new and penetrating light descends on the spectacle, enduing men and things with a seeming transparency, and exhibiting as one organism the anatomy of life and movement in all humanity and vitalized matter included in the display.

Spirit of the Pities (after a pause):

Amid this scene of bodies substantive
Strange waves I sight like wings grown visible,
Which bear men's forms on their innumerous coils,
Twining and serpentining round and through.
Also retracting threads like gossamers—
Except in being irresistible—
Which complicate with some, and balance all.

Spirit of the Years:

These are the Prime Volitions,—fibrils, veins,
Will-tissues, nerves and pulses of the Cause,
That heave throughout the Earth's compositure.
Their sum is like the lobule of a Brain
Evolving always that it wots not of;
A Brain whose whole connotes the Everywhere,
And whose procedure may but be discerned
By phantom eyes like ours; the while unguessed
Of those it stirs, who (even as ye do) dream
Their motions free, their orderings supreme;
Each life apart from each, with power to mete
Its own day's measures; balanced, self-complete;
Though they subsist but atoms of the One
Labouring through all, divisible from none;
But this no further now. Deem yet man's deeds self-done.

(S.D.): The anatomy of the Immanent Will disappears.[13]

We may regard this as a complete expression of the negative side of the time-religion evolved by the nineteenth century. Its Protestant ancestry is uncomfortably self-evident: Luther's justification by faith, Calvin's separation of divine and human activity, deism's separation of divine activity from the world; the descent to nineteenth-century pessimism is swift and inevitable.

The Aesthetic Movement (Religion as Art)

Just as the preceding development can be associated with Schopenhauer, so this one can to some extent be associated with Schleiermacher. For in Schleiermacher's theology the individual soul apprehends God through a synthesis of subjective factors in which feeling or emotion predominates; the same thing happens in art, and so the realities of religion and art become, by a ready inference, united in a basis of symbolism. This implies that all approaches to the good are united alike in religion and in art, as in Keats's identification of truth and beauty.[14] It also implies a historical basis for the consideration of religion, as so integral a connection with art implies that both are products of a culture,

and a culture is a historical phenomenon. In Ruskin, the greatest name
of the period associated with the philosophy of art, this point of view is
more or less taken for granted. He says in *The Crown of Wild Olive*:

> Next followed in Europe the great Christian faith, which was essentially
> the religion of Comfort. Its great doctrine is the remission of sins; for which
> cause it happens, too often, in certain phases of Christianity, that sin and
> sickness themselves are partly glorified. . . . The practical result of this doc-
> trine, in art, is a continual contemplation of sin and disease, and of imagi-
> nary states of purification from them; thus we have an architecture
> conceived in a mingled sentiment of melancholy and aspiration. (*Traffic*)[15]

There are several important inferences from this extract. In the first
place, Ruskin evidently believes that, as Christianity is a cultural product, it can be said essentially to exist only in that historical period in
which it explicitly dominated and unified men's lives, that is, in the
Middle Ages. Thus, Christianity is to a large extent identified, not with
the New Testament, but with the medieval world. The medieval world
has passed, and Christianity has passed with it; but the religion survives
in the works of art which remain, in the Gothic cathedrals, in the painting of Giotto and Cimabue, in the plain chants. Ruskin assumes without
discussion that works of art are expressions of a contemporary religious
impulse. Art is the permanent truth of religion.

Matthew Arnold carries a step further this approach to Christianity.
To him, Christianity is still essentially a cultural product. But he is less
interested in art than Ruskin and more interested in personality. Now
probably to anyone with a time-philosophy, and certainly to a Victorian,
the individual will appear as an organism struggling to achieve consolidation, order, balance, integration, while being pushed along at the end
of a propelling historical movement. The more cultured a man becomes,
the more he absorbs of his tradition, and the more his tradition becomes
internal, the less it becomes external, and the less, therefore, a propelling
force. Arnold, like most of the easygoing Hegelians of his time, saw the
historical process as a continuous thrust and counterthrust of an antithesis, which it was the business of the individual to resolve:

> Puritanism . . . was originally the reaction in the seventeenth century of the
> conscience and moral sense of our race, against the moral indifference and
> lax rule of conduct which in the sixteenth century came in with the Rena-

scence. It was a reaction of Hebraism against Hellenism. . . . Yet there is a very important difference between the defeat inflicted on Hellenism by Christianity eighteen hundred years ago, and the check given to the Renascence by Puritanism. . . . Eighteen hundred years ago it was altogether the hour of Hebraism. Primitive Christianity was legitimately and truly the ascendant force in the world at that time and the way of mankind's progress lay through its full development. Another hour in man's development began in the fifteenth century, and the main road of his progress then lay for a time through Hellenism. Puritanism was no longer the central current of the world's progress, it was a side stream crossing the central current and checking it. (*Culture and Anarchy*)[16]

This peculiar dislike of the antinomian Victorian for Calvinism will meet us again in Mill. Arnold makes it abundantly clear that for him the Puritans destroyed what elusive boundary line did exist between the Hebrews and the Philistines—this idea is found again in Shaw's *Quintessence of Ibsenism*.[17] There is also another Victorian stereotype in this extract: the belief that in the Greek pagan world all was dignity, self-expression, and culture, and that in the heyday of Christianity all was asceticism, humility, and masochism. We have already found this in Ruskin's rather silly remarks about medieval Christianity. It is not until William Morris that we find medievalism treated as something healthy and young rather than as material for decadents and amateurs of sadism such as Huysmans, who died in the bosom of the Church after a profound study of diabolism.[18]

Ruskin was the prophet of the Pre-Raphaelite movement in art, one of the rare associations of art and literature made in that century of anarchy and technical specialization. Nothing, however, in the poetry of Rossetti gives the quality of his painting, or of Beardsley's illustrations to Malory: the symbolic decorations of lilies, the waxen, languorous figures with corpselike skin and staring eyes, the saprophitic aroma of a ghoulish eroticism—all this testifies to what extent the Pre-Raphaelites carried out Ruskin's implications.[19] To anyone who tends to identify religion with human life and activity the supernatural world is only too likely to become very rapidly the world of the dead. In poetry, there are Rossetti's *Sister Helen* and John Davidson's *Ballad of a Nun*[20] to illustrate this curious perspective of Christianity as the Middle Ages in Madame Tussaud's.[21]

The humanism of Arnold was carried a step further by the thorough-

going aestheticism of Walter Pater. Arnold wanted merely to abolish
dogma and preserve artistic feeling; his definition of religion as "morality tinged with emotion" is a compromise with the Philistines.[22] Pater
was not interested in morality, but only in the tinge. In *Marius the Epicurean* Pater presents a conflict of pagan and Christian traditions for the
soul of Marius, the latter winning out, with a result well described by
his biographer:

> But the weakness of the case is, that instead of emphasizing the power of
> sympathy, the Christian conception of Love, which differentiates Christian-
> ity from all other religious systems, Marius is after all converted, or
> brought near to the threshold of the faith, more by its sensuous appeal, its
> liturgical solemnities; the element, that is to say, which Christianity has in
> common with all religions, and which is essentially human in character.
> And more than that, even the very peace which Marius discerns in Chris-
> tianity is the old philosophical peace over again.[23]

In *Gaston de Latour*, his last unfinished work, Pater describes another
conflict, this time with Renaissance humanism and scepticism as incarnate in Montaigne.[24] But there is in his work no appreciation of dogma
or of abstract thinking: he speaks constantly of "Christian sentiment" as
opposed to pagan philosophy. Reading his essay on *Pico della Mirandola*,
a typical product of his Renaissance studies, one becomes doubtful
whether he can distinguish Plato from Aristotle and certain that he does
not know what role either has played in Christian theology.[25] Pater, like
Newman, died a Catholic, but the contrast is cruel between Pater's haziness and Newman's crisp incisiveness on anything remotely connected
with Catholic thought. But give Pater a work of art like *La Gioconda*, and
he immediately expands it into a microcosm of the universe.[26] This is
obviously what helps Pater to make sense of the world; that is, in other
words, his religion: the emotional response to the beauty which the dignity and strength of a great religious tradition has evoked.

We have mentioned in the Pre-Raphaelite discussion the connection
of a sentimental, vaguely Catholic medievalism related to the other
movement mentioned earlier, the diabolism and sadism of the decadents who revolted against bourgeois society. The business of "uttering
platitudes in stained-glass attitudes" ridiculed by Gilbert in *Patience*[27]
was a prominent feature of the decadent period of the nineties dominated by Wilde. True, Wilde appealed more to Greek culture for histori-

cal justification of his personal life. After his conversion he talks in this vein:

> I see a far more intimate and immediate connection between the true life of
> Christ and the true life of the artist. . . . Christ was not merely the supreme
> individualist, but he was the first individualist in history. . . . To live for
> others as a definite self-conscious aim was not his creed. . . . But while
> Christ did not say to men, "Live for others," he pointed out that there was
> no difference at all between the lives of others and one's own life. By this
> means he gave to man an extended, a Titan personality. . . . Wherever there
> is a romantic movement in art there somehow, and under some form, is
> Christ, or the soul of Christ. (*De Profundis*, 68–93)[28]

We are not quoting these extraordinary statements for the purpose of ridiculing, or providing a *reductio ad absurdum* for the aesthetic movement. They form a genuine culmination of the various influences we have been dealing with. Out of a romantic philosophy comes a romantic religion, claiming Christ the prophet of the romantic movement. Out of the subjective idealism, which the individualism of the age necessitated, comes this microcosmic soul which, by absorbing the universe within itself, does indeed become a "Titan personality."

The germ of truth in this identification of religion and art had been provided by Blake, or would have been provided by him if anyone had listened to him. According to Blake, the artist is the man who selects experiences and welds them into a significant, that is, symbolic, unity. But this synthetic, consolidating activity is a necessary and fundamental impulse in every man, the artist proper merely being a man with specialized abilities. All the inner impulses of man towards self-improvement or betterment of society, toward communion with God, toward any creative or constructive activity whatever, are at bottom artistic impulses, and religion is only the social expression of this impulse. But Blake is not a mere aesthete; he does not infer that the essential good is beauty rather than justice or truth. He says that good is good only when these three approaches to it are held in synthesis. The arts, however, express and symbolize the central essence of this artistic-religious impulse which Blake calls the "Poetic Genius."[29]

This is a doctrine Christian theology will have to reckon with; has had to reckon with ever since the time of Schleiermacher. The critical attitude of the nineteenth century became possible only through the expiration of a good deal of creative energy, but it made possible a consciousness of cultural tradition, particularly as regards the Christian Church, which is a factor in contemporary thinking both permanent and comparatively new. It is only one aspect, however, of the entire contribution of the nineteenth century to religious development; we shall proceed to examine two others.

The Pragmatic Movement (Religion as Morality)

The antinomian development of the nineteenth century was, of course, like all overemphases on the human side of reality, optimistic. It believed in the worth of human activity, human activity being the only thing left to believe in; it believed in social reform and improvement of the material conditions of life. Cut off from anything like Christian humility or surrender of the will to God, it launched out on a program of conquest of the material world with immense energy and industry. The gospel of work, work for its own sake, was preached:

> I too could now say to myself: Be no longer a Chaos, but a World, or even Worldkin. Produce! Produce! Were it but the pitifullest infinitesimal fraction of a Product, produce it, in God's name! 'Tis the utmost thou hast in thee: out with it then. Up, up! Whatsoever thy hand findeth to do, do it with thy whole might. Work while it is called To-day; for the Night cometh, wherein no man can work. (*Sartor Resartus*)[30]

How all this production is to be distributed Carlyle does not say; that was a problem left for the twentieth century to worry about. Notice the doctrine of the microcosmic individual and the overtone of agnosticism. But why should one work? or, if that be too impertinent a question, what is work and what is misapplied energy?

The utilitarians first tried to answer this question. Starting from the premises of contemporary economists, that the sum of happiness in all individuals of a given social unit equalled the social good, Bentham evolved the well-known and well-worn criterion of the "greatest happiness of the greatest number."[31] This is, of course, a purely quantitative standard of happiness: to Bentham there was no real difference of kind between the pleasures of a philosopher and the pleasures of a fool. When Mill raised the qualitative issue the utilitarian thesis collapsed at once, the more readily through Bentham's own incredible ignorance and Philistinism. Mill said of Bentham in his essay on him: "Man is never recognised by him as a being capable of pursuing spiritual perfection as an end."[32] Religion has, therefore, no place whatever in the utilitarian scheme except as a source of self-satisfaction, which religion seldom is. There is no space here to deal with the philosophy of utilitarianism; theoretically the most fuddled system of thought ever evolved by man at a presumably high level of civilization, in practice it did a great deal of good, as it was never intended to be a philosophy but a program of social reform. Its childish idea of happiness is more easily explained when we remember what is too often forgotten, that it was an instinctive product of an antirevolutionary society, and was a program of reform *as opposed to* a program of revolution. Its whole case depended on whether all social evils could be cured by palliatives or not.

But while Mill broke with much in Bentham, he remained essentially Bentham's disciple, and retained the hedonistic standard of conduct in the name of a revived epicureanism. Naturally, therefore, he hated Calvinism, with its contempt of humanity, and he tended to see in Calvinism the essence of the whole Christian tradition. In his *Essay on Liberty* he says:

> Christian morality (so called) has all the characters of a reaction; it is, in great part, a protest against Paganism. Its ideal is negative rather than positive; passive rather than active; Innocence rather than Nobleness; Abstinence from Evil, rather than the energetic Pursuit of Good.... It is essentially a doctrine of passive obedience. ... What little recognition the idea of obligation to the public obtains in modern morality, is derived from Greek and Roman sources, not from Christian.... I much fear that by attempting to form the mind and feelings on an exclusively religious type ... there will result ... a low, abject, servile type of character, which, submit itself as it may to what it deems the Supreme Will, is incapable of rising to or sympathizing in the conception of Supreme Goodness.[33]

In this quotation, which reminds us to a considerable extent of Arnold, the pagan–Christian antithesis is put in its strongest terms. Many nineteenth-century thinkers exalted the pagan world and its civilization in the name of reason, their ignorance of Christian theology and scholastic philosophy being for the most part almost absolute. It became an axiom with the freethinkers that religion was a matter of the emotions, and their age being an intellectual one, religion was swiftly becoming identified with superstition and was being superseded by science. In Herbert Spencer, in Huxley, even in the cautious Darwin, we find the assumption that society will in the future mould its conduct on the absolutely valid rational processes furnished by scientific experiment, while moral criteria were vaguely supposed to be based on the instincts of normal people. The utilitarians, of course, have the same view. The most elaborate philosophical product of this attitude, developing itself into a new religion, was the system of Comte, who founded, or tried to found, a sect of worshippers of humanity and the sciences. Comte's interpretation of history as divided into periods of superstition, religion, and science finds an echo in Sir James Frazer's *Golden Bough*:

> Thus the keener minds, still pressing forward to a deeper solution of the mysteries of the universe, come to reject the religious theory of nature as inadequate, and to revert in a measure to the older standpoint of magic by postulating explicitly, what in magic had only been implicitly assumed, to wit, an inflexible regularity in the order of natural events, which, if carefully observed, enables us to foresee their course with certainty and to act accordingly. In short, religion, regarded as an explanation of nature, is displaced by science . . . the hope of progress—moral and intellectual as well as material—in the future is bound up with the fortunes of science . . . . magic, religion and science are nothing but theories of thought; and as science has supplanted its predecessors, so it may hereafter be itself superseded by some more perfect hypothesis. . . . The advance of knowledge is an infinite progression towards a goal that for ever recedes.[34]

The first of these reckless generalizations, if taken literally, would imply that Herbert Spencer (who might have written the above passage had he been a better stylist) had a keener mind than Newman—not a proposition which many would regard as self-evident. There is in Frazer's attitude the same Heraclitean gloom we have been meeting all along, the same belief that religion, which implies Christianity, was a cultural product passing with the culture. Carlyle was wise enough to see that the decline of religion brought disintegration and chaos along with a keener critical attitude, and those who followed Carlyle rather than Bentham were more chary of breaking with religion.

Browning, for instance, adopts what is essentially the moralistic emphasis we have been dealing with in this section. The Incarnation for him was not the will of a transcendent God, but the perfecting of an immanent one, and faith was a guide and a stimulus to moral action. Good works is Browning's justification; he does not understand mysticism. The purest mystic in his portrait gallery is Johannes Agricola, who gibbers in a madhouse. The Grammarian, on the other hand, is extolled because he denied himself the pleasures of life in a cause, trusting to God for his reward without inquiring into the nature of that reward:

> Earn the means first—God surely will contrive
> > Use for our earning.
> Others mistrust and say, "But time escapes:
> > Live now or never!"
> He said, "What's time? Leave Now for dogs and apes!
> > Man has Forever." . . .
> Was it not great? did not he throw on God,
> > (He loves the burthen)—
> God's task to make the heavenly period
> > Perfect the earthen?
> Did not he magnify the mind, show clear
> > Just what it all meant?
> He would not discount life, as fools do here,
> > Paid by instalment.
> He ventured neck or nothing—heaven's success
> > Found, or earth's failure:
> "Wilt thou trust death or not?" He answered "Yes:
> > Hence with life's pale lure!"
> > > (*A Grammarian's Funeral*, [lines 79–84, 101–12])

Rabbi Ben Ezra voices the same philosophy:

> Thoughts hardly to be packed
> Into a narrow act,
> Fancies that broke through language and escaped;
> > All I could never be,
> > All, men ignored in me,
> This, I was worth to God, whose wheel the pitcher shaped.[35]

Now when we combine Browning's moralized attitude to Christianity with a Christian treatment of the Greek–medieval antithesis we have

quoted so many examples of, we obtain one of the most significant pronouncements ever made in the nineteenth century about the Christian
faith, from Green's *Prolegomena to Ethics*:

> Now, when we compare the life of service to mankind, involving so much
> sacrifice of pure pleasure, which is lived by men whom in our consciences
> we think best, and which they reproach themselves for not making one of
> more complete self-denial, with the life of free activity in bodily and intel-
> lectual exercises, in friendly converse, in civil debate, in the enjoyment of
> beautiful sights and sounds, which we commonly ascribe to the Greeks . . .
> we might be apt, on the first view, to think that, even though measured
> not merely by the quantity of pleasure incidental to it but by the fullness of
> the realisation of human capabilities implied in it, the latter kind of life
> was the higher of the two. Man for man, the Greek . . . might seem to be
> intrinsically a nobler being—one of more fully-developed powers—than
> the self-mortifying Christian, upon whom the sense of duty to a suffering
> world weighs too heavily to allow of his giving free play to enjoyable
> activities.[36]

This annihilating refutation of Mill is given an extreme, paradoxical,
and in its expressed form obviously unacceptable formulation, but
never has the conception of Christianity as a religion bringing a
unique sense of the worth of every human soul under God, a religion
bent on the conquest and reform of the world, been more pungently
stated. Green was a philosopher of the revolutionary Hegelian school,
and, if he were alive today, might restate his position by saying that
apostolic Christianity was, in its relation to the Roman Empire, a proletariat religion, radical and uncompromising, wrecking and transforming the social structure to achieve an ideal. The Victorian age was an
age of reform, but emphatically not one of revolution—it, therefore,
had little conception of the power of primitive Christianity, nor did it
think that such a power should ever be released. The Greeks, who
took their social reform out in civil war and an occasional tyrannicide,
were more acceptable. But by the end of the century Bernard Shaw
could say:

> Christ is not the lifeless harmless image he has hitherto been to you, but a
> rallying centre for revolutionary influences which all established States and
> Churches fight. (Preface to *Androcles and the Lion*, lviii)[37]

Now just as the germ of truth in the aesthetic movement can be found in Schleiermacher in a genuinely new form, so the germ of truth in the pragmatic movement can be found in Ritschl, also in a genuinely new form, in the doctrine of the kingdom of God as taught by Jesus. The great expansion of missionary activity in the nineteenth century, and the Church's awakened social conscience today, are sure signs that as we move again into a period of metropolitan civilization paralleling that of the Roman Empire, we shall be forced more and more completely into the apostolic perspective.

William Morris provides an interesting fusion of aesthetic and pragmatic interests, for he was both medievalist and socialist, and in his *Dream of John Ball* he enunciates a social ideal which must have sounded curiously in the ears of the imperialists and neo-Darwinians of the time: "Fellowship is life, and lack of fellowship is death."[38] He goes on to describe his Utopia:

Ye shall not lack for the fields ye have tilled, nor the houses ye have built, nor the cloth ye have woven; all these shall be yours, and whatso ye will of all that the earth beareth; then shall no man mow the deep grass for another, while his own kine lack cow-meat; and he that soweth shall reap, and the reaper shall eat in fellowship the harvest that in fellowship he hath won; and he that buildeth a house shall dwell in it with those that he biddeth of his free will; and the tithe barn shall garner the wheat for all men to eat of when the seasons are untoward, and the rain-drift hideth the sheaves of August; and all shall be without money and without price. Faithfully and merrily then shall men keep the holidays of the Church in peace of body and joy of heart. And man shall help man, and the saints in heaven shall be glad, because men no more fear each other; and the churl shall be ashamed, and shall hide his churlishness till it be gone, and he be no more a churl; and fellowship shall be established in heaven and on the earth.[39]

The nineteenth century is, with one of its choicest spirits, waking up to the realization that the Middle Ages, when the Church ran things, was on the whole as progressive in its political and economic ideas as any period following it. The Church of John Ball's dream may be the carefully washed and exquisitely posed object painted by the Pre-Raphaelites, but it is a Church with a social consciousness and an equal awareness of the religious value of beauty.

The Synthetic Movement (Religion as Life)

We have been insisting all along that the nineteenth century was over-whelmingly an antinomian century: its rapid development in physical prowess caused it to reject the transcendent God of Calvin, in practice if not always in theory. The most pervading religious sentiment of the time, among the greater minds, was a kind of animism. If one's religious perspective is bounded by human experience, one naturally tends to identify a superior being with the life force that sweeps humanity along the time-progression. Besides, as Frazer pointed out in a passage imme-diately before the one quoted, magic and science are psychologically the same activity: magic postulates animism, religion develops out of the breakdown of magic, and science tinged by religion, therefore, becomes animistic too.[40] Let us first look at the poets for hymns to the life force, for there is hardly a major poet of the time who did not believe in it. Without going back as far as Shelley's *Triumph of Life*, we might first point out that Browning's metaphysics implies a purely immanent God working in Nature:

> I but open my eyes,—and perfection, no more and no less,
> In the kind I imagined, full-fronts me, and God is seen God
> In the star, in the stone, in the flesh, in the soul and the clod.
>
> (*Saul*, [lines 248–50])

or again, from a very different poem:

> We find great things are made of little things,
> And little things go lessening till at last
> Comes God behind them. Talk of mountains now?
> We talk of mould that heaps the mountain, mites
> That throng the mould, and God that makes the mites,
> The Name comes close behind a stomach-cyst,
> The simplest of creations, just a sac
> That's mouth, heart, legs and belly at once, yet lives
> And feels, and could do neither, we conclude,
> If simplified still further one degree:
> The small becomes the dreadful and immense! (*Sludge the Medium*)[41]

God is always just one step away. Or take something of Swinburne, from a "pagan" point of view:

> I am that which began;
>> Out of me the years roll;
> Out of me God and man;
>> I am equal and whole;
> God changes, and man, and the form of them bodily; I am the soul . . .

> Where dead ages hide under
>> The live roots of the tree,
> In my darkness the thunder
>> Make utterance of me:
> In the clash of my boughs with each other ye hear the waves sound of
> the sea.

> That noise is of Time,
>> As his feathers are spread
> And his feet set to climb
>> Through the boughs overhead,
> And my foliage rings round him and rustles, and branches are bent
> with his tread.

(Hertha, [lines 1–6, 133–44])

In Meredith the same worship of life and time is given a more explicitly chthonic twist:

> Cry we for permanence fast,
> Permanence hangs by the grave;
> Sits on the grave green-grassed,
> On the roll of the heaved grave-mound.
> By Death, as by Life, are we fed:
> The two are one spring; our bond
> With the numbers; with whom to unite
> Here feathers wings for beyond:
> Only they can waft us in flight.
> For they are Reality's flower. (*A Faith on Trial*, [lines 417–26])

Even Hardy, for all his agnosticism, sometimes tends to substitute a similar earth–life–time worship for Christianity or anything that assumes a transcendent God. The conflict is sharp at the conclusion of *Tess of the d'Urbervilles*, when Tess has been executed as a sacrifice to Christian morality:

"Justice" was done, and the President of the Immortals (in Aeschylean
phrase) had ended his sport with Tess. . . . The two speechless gazers bent
themselves down to the earth, as if in prayer, and remained thus a long
time, absolutely motionless: the flag continued to wave silently. As soon as
they had strength they arose, joined hands again, and went on.[42]

With this the prevailing religious attitude in poetry, it is hardly surprising that the science of the time should have developed, and the philosophy of the time elaborated, a theory of evolution. Evolution was no
new concept in theology, but it had previously been a hierarchic evolution: in Thomism a development from matter to form, outside the time-
process. In the conflict, alleged to be between religion and science,
which raged around the Book of Genesis, we have a very definite impact
of a cultural movement on the Church, but one so purely negative that
we are not anxious to spend much time on it. It looks, from this perspective, like a squabble between clergymen who knew nothing of science
and agnostic freethinkers who knew nothing of religion, the clergymen
defending an untenable, exploded, obsolete religion and the freethinkers an equally dubious, equally outworn, equally superseded scientific
attitude. The scientists undoubtedly shattered the prestige of the
Church, but the Church needed a good deal of shattering; its pitiful collapse was only an outward symbol of its intellectual bankruptcy, which
had been tacitly recognized all along. And yet, as we pass from Darwin's evidence to Spencer's speculations, thence to Seeley's political theories, thence to Kipling's poetry, thence to the Great War and the Great
Depression, one wonders if the warnings of discredited moralists
against substituting the law of the jungle animals for the law of love
proper to civilized human beings should have gone unheeded after all.

The philosophers who developed the implications of Darwin's theory,
Huxley and Spencer, were themselves agnostics, but towards the end of
the century the new scientific conception of the universe and the contemporary animistic attitude of the poets began to merge. A creative factor came into the evolutionary process, and God as life-force was finally
pinned down and identified. The great name associated with this is,
of course, Bergson; the first important figure in England was that of
Samuel Butler:

The memories which all living forms prove by their actions that they
possess—the memories of their common identity with a single person in

whom they meet—this is incontestable proof of their being animated by a common soul. It is certain, therefore, that all living forms, whether animal or vegetable, are in reality one animal; we and the mosses being part of the same vast person in no figurative sense, but with as much *bona fide* literal truth as when we say that a man's finger-nails and his eyes are parts of the same man. (*God the Known and Unknown*, 62)[43]

He goes on to say:

It is in this Person that we may see the Body of God—and in the evolution of this Person, the mystery of His Incarnation.[44]

After this it was an easy matter for Butler's disciple Bernard Shaw to declare:

Creative Evolution is already a religion, and is indeed unmistakably the religion of the twentieth century, newly arisen from the ashes of pseudo-Christianity, of mere scepticism, and of the soulless affirmations and blind negations of the Mechanists and Neo-Darwinians. (Preface to *Back to Methusaleh*, lxxvii)[45]

And there is little doubt that creative evolution, as it eventually became, does represent the peculiar and unique contribution of this very peculiar and unique age to religion. In adding to philosophy a new interpretation of the time-process, it added to religion a new sense of the importance of the religious impulse in history. The first great wave of Christian thought, culminating in Augustine, had concentrated on the philosophy of history implied by the Incarnation and was essentially critical and empiric in character: there followed, as the Church established itself politically, a dogmatic period of systematization, in which the historical basis of Christian thinking was to some extent lost sight of. This culminates in Aquinas; and the Protestant revolt against scholastic thought was part of a pervasive and corroding scepticism which separated theology from philosophy and brought the former to the sterility of the Victorian age. The downfall of the ideals of that age has forced us to go back to history for the source of Christian doctrine; and the theory of evolution, along with the philosophies of history that have accompanied it, Hegelian, Marxian, Spencerian, Spenglerian, provides a basis for this. In re-establishing a Christian philosophy of history, we shall give a

new shape and meaning to the activity of God in his immanent person,
the Holy Spirit, and we shall integrate into the body of Jesus' teaching
the conception, neglected until Ritschl, of the kingdom of God being
established on earth as it is in heaven. Thus, the nineteenth century has
supplied a matrix for the development of thought Christianity must
make if it is to survive. But it is here necessary to repeat what was said
earlier, that in the nineteenth century the Church of the time was apathetic, and the impact of cultural movements upon it for the most part
posthumous.

The Catholic Movement: Religion as Orthodoxy

The Oxford Movement, no matter what importance we may ascribe to it
in the history of the period, is logically outside our subject; as it was a
movement within the Church itself, and had no very definite cultural
connotations. It arose as the protest of the inner logic of religion itself, as
a reaction against the fourfold confusion we have been surveying. The
impulse that drove Newman to Rome was the conviction that religion
was religion and that, while art and morality and history were excellent
things in their ways, they were not religion, nor could they be substituted for it. Again, he felt the compulsion to unity on the part of true
believers, in opposition to the easygoing assumption of the time that the
more variety of opinions there were in society, the more interesting life
would be. Mill's *Essay on Liberty* is a typical product of this tendency to
make heresy orthodox. Newman fought against this disintegrating tendency, insisting on the synthetic, unifying function of the intellect and
the impersonal nature of truth:

> a truly great intellect ... is one which takes a connected view of old and
> new, past and present, near and far, and which has an insight into the influ-
> ence of all these one on another; without which there is no whole, and no
> centre. (*The Idea of a University*)[46]

He saw the utilitarian philosophy of his own day as a direct product of
English Protestantism, which evolved an empiric, epistemological mode
of thought with Francis Bacon that could end only in scepticism, intellectual paralysis, and social chaos:

> The Philosophy of Utility, you will say, gentlemen, has at least done its

work; it aimed low, but it has fulfilled its aim. If that man of great intellect who has been its Prophet in the conduct of life played false to his own professions, he was not bound by his philosophy to be true to his friend or faithful in his trust. . . . His mission was the increase of physical enjoyment and social comfort; and most wonderfully, most awfully has he fulfilled his conception and his design. (*Liberal Knowledge its Own End*)[47]

Newman does not deal with art, and remains, as a cultural force, a representative of a religious tradition chiefly in literature. But there he is orthodox. He realizes that religion, when most vital, is most completely the unifying force of culture; that its dogmatic superstructures are the product of an age sufficiently disciplined and self-conscious to establish its own cultural pattern. We have said that the nineteenth century marks an abrupt decline in all the major arts, especially the plastic ones. The reason for this is largely to be found, as even Ruskin could have pointed out, and did point out in regard to architecture, in the fact that in the wake of romanticism came the assumption that a work of art was a product of self-expression and that the individual artist was arbiter of form and content. The classical tradition, inseparable from a strong religious basis, had insisted on objective standards of both.

Newman recognizes all this, but, feeling himself in the oddly paradoxical situation of a Catholic representing a minority group, he speaks very frequently, when discussing culture, with the voice of a sectarian. In his rather miserable essay on English Catholic literature, in *The Idea of a University*, he first admits:

I repeat, then, whatever we be able or unable to effect in the great problem which lies before us, anyhow we cannot undo the past. English Literature will ever *have been* Protestant. Swift and Addison, the most native and natural of our writers, Hooker and Milton, the most elaborate, never can become our co-religionists.[48]

and then adds naively:

I would not indeed say a word to extenuate the calamity, under which we lie, of having a literature formed in Protestantism; still, other literatures have disadvantages of their own; and, though in such matters comparisons are impossible, I doubt whether we should be better pleased if our English

Classics were tainted with licentiousness, or defaced by infidelity or scepticism. I conceive we should not much mend matters if we were to exchange
literatures with the French, Italians, or Germans.[49]

He goes on to review the dismally Protestant scene, gaining encour-
agement from the fact that Shakespeare never tells us what his religion
is:

For instance, there surely is a call on us for thankfulness that the most illustrious amongst English writers has so little of a Protestant about him that
Catholics have been able, without extravagance, to claim him as their
own.[50]

He looks round for a champion:

A rival to Shakespeare, if not in genius, at least in copiousness and variety,
is found in Pope; and *he* was actually a Catholic, though personally an
unsatisfactory one.[51]

It is very obvious, from these quotations, that the one orthodox Christian movement of the nineteenth century which had definite cultural
implications did not contain many fertile seeds of future development.
With all respect to a great Church, Newman's position is reactionary,
stick-in-the mud. He says in praise of Shakespeare:

Often as he may offend against modesty, he is clear of a worse charge, sensuality, and hardly a passage can be instanced in all that he has written to
seduce the imagination or to excite the passions.[52]

One thinks of the critic who seriously praised Tennyson for never
having written a line that an English mother would wish unwritten or
an English daughter blush to have read. One thinks of the Podsnap in
Dickens's *Our Mutual Friend*, whose intellectual energy was so largely
absorbed in preventing blushes from coming to the cheeks of young
persons.[53] Newman was not a hypocrite, and Podsnap presumably was;
but they concur in the same shibboleth password of nineteenth-century
morality—aided, in Newman's case, by the Catholic association of religion and morality from which Protestantism has freed itself. If I have
been unfair to Newman in insisting on this unfortunate essay, it is only

to illustrate that the Catholic was no more free than the Anglican or Dissenter from the limitations of an age in which religion sunk to a low ebb. Surely no intelligent Catholic today, let alone any Catholic with Newman's intelligence, would repeat Newman's shrinking nervousness about the wickedness of Montaigne or Voltaire, or concur so completely in his acceptance of the official condemnation of Dante's *De Monarchia* or Machiavelli. Newman was a stout defender of religion, but in culture he was as sterile and Philistine as his contemporaries who defended other religious traditions, such as Carlyle or Wilberforce, and far more so than the sceptics, Arnold or Mill.

It appears evident, from a general survey of the century, that it was, from the point of view of the history of religion, a period of criticism, of testing and sifting. Its greatest asset was the rigorous intellectual honesty that appears both in the conservatism of Newman and the agnosticism of Huxley; and it worked out several lines of thought, in its effort to arrive at a new religion, all of which may gain a new religious significance as a result of its treatment of them, even if no one of them ranks as a substitute for religion. The nineteenth century showed the value of honest scepticism, and the urgent necessity for clearing away the debris of a dead religion which needed revitalizing and reinterpretation. It showed the religious significance of art, the connection of its symbolism with religion, and the possibility of a unification of Plato's three goods into a single religious consciousness, the just, the beautiful, and the true. It emphasized the importance of good works in religion, fought down a helpless quietism, got rid as far as it could of its own smugness and self-righteousness. It brought out a renewed sense of the activity of God in history, and began to develop a social ideal for Christianity which may yet make that religion an active and revolutionary historical force. It brought back something of the intellectual discipline and synthetic thinking of Catholic theology and philosophy. If we fail to make a unity out of these various contributions to our thinking, it is our fault, inherent in us and not our heritage.

Appendix

The dilemma of the Catholic poet is perhaps the most acute example of the cultural disintegration we have been treating. Coventry Patmore is a comfortable, domesticated instance of the way in which the Catholic could accommodate himself to the outlook of the Victorian time:

So when that night I pray'd
To God, I wept, and said:
Ah, when at last we lie with tranced breath,
Not vexing Thee in death,
And Thou rememberest of what toys
We made our joys,
How weakly understood
Thy great commanded good,
Then, fatherly not less
Than I whom Thou hast moulded from the clay,
Thou'lt leave Thy wrath, and say,
'I will be sorry for their childishness.' (*The Toys*, [lines 22–33])

The great spirits of the age we have been dealing with were all more or less, being geniuses, in revolt against their time: Patmore represents as perhaps no other name in the culture of the period represents (Christina Rossetti possibly excepted) the routine practice of Victorian religion. Nineteenth-century society was bourgeois, and that meant that it was organized on the basis of the family; the Fatherhood of God, and our own childlike relationship to him, was an extension from that perspective. It was far otherwise with the two Catholic poets who represent perhaps the most original poetic impetus of the period: Francis Thompson and Gerard Manley Hopkins. They had caught sight of a divine activity less benignant, not the household god, the lar or baal, of the "Providence" or "Lord" of contemporary parsons. Thompson brings into English poetry the first note of genuinely passionate mysticicsm, Blake excepted, heard since Crashaw. Compare the following with the Coventry Patmore extract:

How has thou merited—
Of all man's clotted clay the dingiest clot?
Alack, thou knowest not
How little worthy of any love thou art!
Whom wilt thou find to love ignoble thee,
Save Me, save only Me?
All which I took from thee I did but take,
Not for thy harms,
But just that thou might'st seek it in My arms.

> All which thy child's mistake
> Fancies as lost, I have stored for thee at home:
>> Rise, clasp My hand, and come! (*The Hound of Heaven*, [lines 165–76])

In Hopkins, the most profoundly original genius of the century, the feeling of separation between religion and culture is much sharper, for Thompson had in him a large amount of the sensuous ecstatic approach of the aesthetic movement, expressed sometimes almost in sadistic terms:

> Therefore, O tender Lady, Queen Mary,
>> Thou gentleness that dost enmoss and drape
> The Cross's rigorous austerity,
>> Wipe thou the blood from wounds that needs must gape. . . .
>
> Oh, this Medusa-pleasure with her stings!
>> This essence of all suffering, which is joy!
> I am not thankless for the spell it brings,
>> Though tears must be told down for the charmed toy.
>>> (*Ode to the Setting Sun: After-Strain*, [lines17–20,29–32])

But Hopkins, a Jesuit priest, having, on the one hand, the whole intellectual completeness of a scholastic view of the world, in which everything was pigeon-holed and explained, and, on the other, a powerful emotional feeling of the boundless inexplicable variety of the natural world, presents explicitly what is only implicit in Newman, the dissociation of poet and worshipper. As a theologian, he forsook Thomism for Scotism because of the greater emphasis the latter philosophy placed on the principle of individuation of form, which is the basis of creative activity. He has curious liking for the irregular and untamed in Nature:

> What would the world be, once bereft
> Of wet and of wildness? Let them be left,
> O let them be left, wildness and wet;
> Long live the weeds and the wilderness yet. (*Inversnaid*, [lines 13–16])

And the very vividness of his religious poetry derives in large measure from his sense of the inscrutable power of God: a sense more likely to be cultivated by Scotism than Thomism:

> Be adored among men
>   God, three-numberèd form;
>   Wring thy rebel, dogged in den,
>   Man's malice, with wrecking and storm.
> Beyond saying sweet, past telling of tongue,
>   Thou art lightning and love, I found it, a winter and warm;
>   Father and fondler of heart thou hast wrung:
> Hast thy dark descending and most art merciful then.
>
>   (*The Wreck of the Deutschland*, [lines 65–72])

Even here there is an unmistakable effort to break through the shackles of orthodoxy in search of a God immanent in experience, a God of the time-world. In his sonnet on St. Alphonsus Rodriguez, the door-keeper saint, the moral is practically that of Browning's *Grammarian's Funeral*:

> Yet God (that hews mountain and continent,
> Earth, all, out; who, with trickling increment,
> Veins violets and tall trees makes more and more)
> Could crowd career with conquest while there went
> Those years and years by of world without event
> That in Majorca Alfonso watched the door. [lines 9–14]

But everything great and fine in all the religious movements of the nineteenth century, the Catholic revival, the new worship of the Creator-God, the association of beauty with God, is caught up by Hopkins in one breathless sonnet with which we may close, as representing the purest concentration of the religious thought of the age, held for an instant in focus:

> I caught this morning morning's minion, king-
>   dom of daylight's dauphin, dapple-dawn-drawn Falcon, in his riding
>   Of the rolling level underneath him steady air, and striding
> High there, how he rung upon the rein of a wimpling wing
> In his ecstasy! then off, off forth on swing,
>   As a skate's heel sweeps smooth on a bow-bend: the hurl and gliding
>   Rebuffed the big wind. My heart in hiding
> Stirred for a bird,—the achieve of, the mastery of the thing!

Brute beauty and valour and act, oh, air, pride, plume, here
   Buckle! AND the fire that breaks from thee then, a billion
Times told lovelier, more dangerous, O my chevalier!

   No wonder of it: shéer plód makes plough down sillion
Shine, and blue-bleak embers, ah my dear,
   Fall, gall themselves, and gash gold-vermilion.

(*The Windhover*, dedicated "To Christ our Lord")

Bibliography

Carlyle:	*Sartor Resartus*
	Heroes and Hero-Worship
	Signs of the Times
Ruskin:	*The Crown of Wild Olive*
	Sesame and Lilies
Arnold:	*Literature and Dogma*
	God and the Bible
	Culture and Anarchy
Pater:	*Marius the Epicurean*
	The Renaissance
Wilde:	*De Profundis*
Butler:	*God the Known and Unknown*
	Life and Habit
	Luck or Cunning?
Bradley:	*Appearance and Reality*
Green:	*Prolegomena to Ethics*
Mill:	*Essay on Bentham*
	Essay on Liberty
	Utilitarianism
Newman:	*The Idea of a University*
	Apologia pro Vita Sua
	Liberal Knowledge in Relation to Learning
	Liberal Knowledge its Own End
	Discussion and Arguments
Spencer:	*Synthetic Philosophy*
Huxley:	*Administrative Nihilism*
Morley:	*Compromise*
Morris:	*Dream of John Ball*

Secondary Sources

Merz: *History of European Thought in the Nineteenth Century*, 3 vols.
Wingfield-Stratford: *Those Earnest Victorians*
                 The Victorian Tragedy
                 The Victorian Sunset
Chesterton: *The Victorian Age in Literature*
Benson: *Walter Pater*
Praz: *The Romantic Agony*
Ward: *The Oxford Movement*
de la Mare (ed.)   *The Eighteen-Eighties*. (esp. Eliot, Essay on Pater).[54]
Also, of course, the poetical works of the poets quoted (Thomson, Davidson,
Tennyson, Browning, Arnold, Swinburne, Hardy, Meredith, Hopkins, Morris,
etc.)
Prefaces of Bernard Shaw.

16

The Relation of Religion
to the Arts

This essay was written for presentation in Professor George A. McMullen's course in public speaking, which Frye took during his first year at Emmanuel College (1933–34). Portions of the paper present in a condensed and early form some of the material in "The Relation of Religion to the Art Forms of Music and Drama" (no. 17). Frye received a grade of "A+" for the paper, the typescript of which, entitled "Public Speaking Essay" on the cover sheet, is in the NFF, 1991, box 37, file 9.

> . . . Nature is made better by no mean
> But Nature makes that mean; so, over that art
> Which you say adds to Nature, is an art
> That Nature makes. You see, sweet maid, we marry
> A gentler scion to the wildest stock,
> And make conceive a bark of baser kind
> By bud of nobler race: this is an art
> Which does mend Nature, change it rather, but
> The art itself is nature.
>
> Shakespeare, *The Winter's Tale* [4.4.89–97]

Nearly all the deeper questions dealt with by modern philosophers bring us at once to the epistemological problem, the question of the theory of knowledge. In an age which prides itself both on its use of scientific methods and on the success with which it has used them, the presentation of a general metaphysical structure has become steadily more difficult. A tendency is now to regard this approach as naive; and the feeling does not decrease with the greater impressiveness of any individual attempt. To the extent that philosophy coordinates the sciences, it is busied necessarily with the question of the origin of knowledge; and this seems the only use the modern world has for speculation.

Now it remains a deep-rooted conviction to many thinkers that the axis of the knowledge problem does not strike through the centre either of religion or of art. No better empiric proof of this is needed, on the one hand, than the way in which modern preachers and artists avoid it; nor, on the other, than the number of utterly unsatisfactory attempts to approach religion or art from this bias, if it be a bias. Which means, of course, bearing in mind our above conclusion, that the science of religion, or theology, has today become a dead language, with the disciplinary value which seems to be inseparable from dead languages, and that aesthetic theory is in abeyance. But it should be noted that the incomplete solutions referred to have a curious tendency to equate the two problems. Anyone whose epistemology is sufficiently inadequate to allow him to regard art as a sublimation of the sex instinct is likely to attribute the same origin to religion. Anyone who regards the religious approach as a valid if perhaps untried route to reality is apt to consider it more or less sentimentally as having a purely artistic function. This would seem to indicate a relationship most peculiarly apposite, even if common sense should prevent its lapsing into identity; for if knowledge is comparison of ideas, how could thinkers fail to differentiate between two problems if two problems were present? Religion and art together merge, with Eddington, into the shadow-replica of the scientist's universe; with Freud, into the air-castle of the neurotic; with the materialist, into an indivisible *enfant terrible*. The problem of working out the relationship still remains, and while we do not propose to do this immediately, we might at least indicate the lines any future attempt could conceivably follow.

It is evident that the status of religion and art will have to be determined before twentieth-century thought presents anything like a coherent pattern, and I believe it to be a growing suspicion among contemporary thinkers that, for many reasons, this is actually the prerequisite of such a synthesis. In any case, it will surely be necessary to look behind their various systems to the large tendencies which underlie them. In other words, our approach must be a historical one, taking the traditional developments apart (if I am not mixing metaphors) and extracting from their components the great *Zeitgeist* characteristics which every age possesses. Our problem must be attacked from the standpoint of that profound constructive *skepsis* which views each individual philosophy, not as a thing isolated, but as a historical symbol. We begin to sense here the possibility of a historical approach to knowledge irreconcilably opposed to the scientific. For science is concerned with the fact in itself; history, with what it signifies by its appearance.

Going back to the enunciation of the knowledge problem, the Kantian distinction of the phenomenon from the thing-in-itself may suggest a further clue. All knowledge derives from sense, moulded by the mind with forms of perception and understanding. All knowledge is, therefore, phenomenal, concerned with the formal limiting of the thing-in-itself. Coherence is necessary to knowledge, form to coherence; and form means limitation. But what we must have abstracted from the thing-in-itself is its timeless, eternal quality, which alone we can apprehend. In other words, all knowledge is space-knowledge, and all phenomena spatial or pictorial. It seems reasonable to conclude that the residual noumenon is the time-existence which eludes knowledge, leading to the principle that time cannot be known, but inferred from the changes in space-forms.

As a man is a phenomenon, and as there is something in each one of us which we ourselves recognize but which escapes the knowledge of anyone else, it appears by analogy that our pure, peculiar ego, considered not in its negative but in its absolute time-existing aspect, is noumenal. Now if we inquire what element of the soul can be said to be the noumenal time-element, we shall find that we ordinarily call it the will; while the ego-effacing space side is even more clearly denominated the reason. But this disjunction is, of course, theoretical only; no one can live either in pure time or in pure space. The most complete life, then, would be the most complete merging of will and reason. But such a coincidence could take place only by finding a common factor and eliminating all actions which do not tend to be subsumed under it. That common factor, going back again to ordinary speech, is the good, the complete synthesis of will and reason, called by Kant the categorical imperative. It is obvious that to enter on a course of good action is to have each action implicated in a compulsion, and this gives us two more standard concepts, the system of compulsions affecting the will, or morality, and the system affecting reason, or logic.

Justice and truth irresistibly suggest the third member of the Platonic triad, beauty, as will and reason similarly suggest feeling. That beauty represents the good element in feeling, and that aesthetics is the system of compulsions controlling it, most would readily grant; but what is feeling? If it is not the same thing as will or reason, it cannot be purely temporal or purely spatial, and as it can hardly exist outside these forms of perception, the only thing left for it to be is a kind of interfusion of time in space. Now feeling is evidently the peculiar and differentiating element in the soul, the reaction of the ego considered as unique. It is, thus, a negative factor. Hence, it certainly cannot be the positive coincidence of will and reason: for reason transcends individuality and could hardly merge with will were the latter a thing essentially distinctive in each person. All wills, considered as pure time-elements, are the same in every man. Hence, feeling, being the negative expression of this synthesis, must be an interfusion of time and space in which the two elements are held together and reflected in the individuality. It is, thus, a reflection, or criticism, of the positive synthesis, which latter it is perhaps time we named. Obviously the will-reason coordination is simply the good life, and it must be all we can mean by any intelligible definition of religion. Religion is the imperative which brings together all souls around one concept, thus establishing the relationship of God to man. Now the individual criticism of this must be the same thing as the expression of it, for *expression* is a word meaningless apart from an individual. Art, then, is the expression of religion. It does not express either side of religion—that we shall deal with later—it expresses the central meaning of it. That is what so many thinkers mean when they claim that reality, in the last analysis, can be expressed only by a metaphor, myth, symbol, or work of art. For if art expresses religion, its whole appeal is symbolic. This will be later elaborated. We might note just here that while will and reason are democratic in equating personalities, feeling rests on an aristocracy of perceptiveness and sensitivity. This is the reason why the otherwise plausible Tolstoyan dictum, that great art must make an immediate appeal to the uncultivated,[1] fails completely on application. Art is essentially esoteric; religion open to all.

Another point must be mentioned for the sake of completeness, though not altogether relevant. If the good life synthesizes will and reason, expressing itself in feeling, it would seem likely that the evil life would reverse the process, exalting the feeling man, the unique ego, above his fellows and bending will and reason to the force we call desire, which aims at the complete satisfaction of the aggressive, assertive personality in happiness, appealing, thus, to a static principle as a goal where the other is creative and dynamic.

It is not suggested, of course, that art presents solely the religious point of view, which would make it as inflexible as the categorical imperative itself. There is and must be a distinction between the art which is creative and moves from religion through the individual and the art which is egocentric and springs from a feeling impulse. This would have to be traced out historically, and it would probably be found that the latter approach could be approximately equated with the romantic. But it is insisted that the truly greatest art is that which most clearly presents a symbolic picture of the deepest religious impulses of the age. No one will imagine that such a view is easy to defend; and I am only too sorry that exigencies of space compel me to leave it in its controversial form of enunciation. The position would become clearer under historical treatment.

Goodness is the whole of beauty, for the two words can be used interchangeably when beauty alone is under discussion; but beauty is not the whole of goodness. The religious good itself, apart from its separate constituents of justice and truth, may be expressed in two other ways. For the synthesis can be attempted one-sidedly; either in overwhelming the will by the reason or the reason by the will. In the first instance the underlying idea is evidently to make the will, the pure time-element, a pure spatial entity: in other words to abnegate the will and immerse the individual (for this is expression of religion, and, consequently, relates to the personality) into a timeless absolute. This is the religious approach we ordinarily call mysticism. Its goal is obviously not so much self-expression, therefore, as self-impression, and its subjugation of personality is united to a withdrawal so complete that communication, the essence of art, becomes difficult if not impossible. There is a long-standing contradiction between the mystic and the artist, and the attempts of the former to express himself (his desire for expression being the result of the comparative inadequacy of the approach) in terms of the latter rests on a compromise. A mystic poet, for example, must sacrifice to the poet the mystic's self-absorption to be able to become articulate, while he must surrender to the mystic the poet's love for a deceptive nature and his rapturous acceptance of the sense world.

In the opposite case the attempt is to erect a purely logical structure on the basis of will: that is, proceeding a priori from certain premises necessary to make the synthesis. This is the approach to religion termed the theological. It, like the mystical, is, though an essential factor, inadequate for the central final truth of religion, for a synthesis in which one element has absorbed the other cannot very well be entirely satisfactory. Hence, as one can hardly expect the theologian to yield precedence to the artist of his own accord, there arises an opposition between the two—the more narrow-minded and pedantic the theologian, the deeper his distrust of the artist and the stronger his desire to censor and strangle art. Naturally the artist has to mirror the desiring side of life as well as the religious side, and the most powerful driving force in the former is, of course, the sex impulse. A fearless and open handling of this question is a mark of the great literary artist. It is, therefore, on this that the theologian's attack is focused.

The root of this opposition lies in the difference between symbolic and explicit expression of religion. Just as art defeats its own ends as it approaches the mystical side and begins to lack communicative force so, too, it defeats its own ends by approaching the theological side and tending to explicit utterance of any teaching, no matter how lofty. It is, of course, very difficult for a great artist, who knows his business, to refrain from swinging over to didacticism. But even in the work of Dante, of Tasso, of Milton, of Spenser, that element is always recognized as antagonistic to true art. Shakespeare is the only figure of the first rank, perhaps, who has kept his own presentation symbolic, and even he, striving to penetrate the uttermost depths of the universe, drops from symbolism to allegory, the explicit statement of symbolism, in his last plays.

The relation that allegory bears to symbolism is paralleled by the relation borne by wit to humour, by pathos to tragedy. The first elements are recognized as less profound than the second, precisely because they suggest less and explain more. Wit is self-evident humour; pathos, self-evident tragedy. Therefore, they are brought into art to relieve the strain of pure suggestion.

Here we see again the necessity for esoteric appeal, the essential of arousing the interest of an adult mind. The appreciation of great art is a prerequisite—perhaps in the last analysis the only prerequisite—of maturity. Consequently, the transmitter of religion—the preacher— is faced with a purely artistic problem. He is most fully expressing religion, performing his greatest work, when his appeal is artistic. But if art is suggestive, it must suggest itself; hence, the explicit utterance leading to it is necessary. The sermon is brought in chiefly to ease the strain of artistic symbolism by establishing a common ground between religion and the worshipper, while music, prayer, architecture, and the rest of the arts subserve, in their turn, the awakening of aesthetic consciousness in the worshipper.

Thus, while the core of religious feeling is art, the whole of religion is not artistic; and a reasoned analysis of the other two approaches to the good, justice and truth, is necessary for completeness. It is the use of the word *theologian* in the thesis propounded that is unfortunate. For theology, based, necessarily, on the attempt of the will to enslave reason, can last only so long as the sources and derivations of the logic-structure are not examined. Whatever else the contemporary minister may do, he does not teach theology. If he be a philosopher, he has some idea of the systems of compulsions underlying justice and truth and can transmit those. If his appeal is largely theological, he soon ceases to be a vital force in a world which has gone through the investigation of the epistemological problem, which has arrived at a critical position for a century, and for which theology is, consequently, an anachronism. True, an anachronism necessary to culture, like all the contributions of the past, but not a creative force. More and more we are coming to realize that the evocation of response in a sympathetic soul is the primary appeal of religion, and it is to this end that the preaching of the Incarnation is directed.

It is evident that we cannot reach the "truth" of religion through art, because truth belongs to logic and to that alone. But the essential reality of religion is a different matter. If all art is creation, and if this creation is in its turn a criticism, a symbolization, of something else, would it not follow that the creative element was the essential factor in the religion it symbolized? So, at least, modern philosophy seems to believe in large measure. The parallels between the process of organic growth in the world and the rhythmic propulsion underlying art have never been satisfactorily investigated and never will be until a historical approach is made; one which will recognize a creative force in history as well as in biology. Aesthetics, like ethics, must come to realize that it is fundamentally history, not logic or biology. It is here alone that the possibilities for a new approach to religion lie.[2]

17

The Relation of Religion
to the Art Forms
of Music and Drama

Frye wrote "Theology Elective" on the cover sheet of this essay, meaning that he wrote the paper, not for a specialized course in systematic theology, but as a general Emmanuel College elective. The paper was written for Kenneth H. Cousland, professor of Church history at Emmanuel. Because Frye refers in the essay to his review of the Jooss Ballet, which appeared in the Canadian Forum *in April 1936, he apparently wrote the essay during the Easter term of his third year at Emmanuel, most likely for Church History 5. Frye received an "A+" for the paper, the typescript of which is in the NFF, 1991, box 37, file 13.*

1. The Three Goods

In attempting to examine the connection of religion and art in general, before passing on to a more specific application, the thing to be avoided at all costs is any attempt at a strict definition of the words *religion* and *art*. The only possibility is to indicate roughly where we believe their respective fields to lie in relation to this thesis. For the present writer, religion, true or false, adequate or inadequate, signifies a form or stereotype of activity certain individuals follow in order to bring them to what they consider a better way of living. If there is any question begging in this definition, it seems to the present writer to lie rather in the word *consider* than in the word *better*. Not all religious activity is considered or deliberate: perhaps none of it entirely so; and, of course, the individuals who pursue religious activity do not always do so as individuals. It is in fact necessary to religion that some communal factor be present. But all religious activity does aim at putting the worshipper, either as an individual or as a member of a group, in a more satisfactory relation to his environment, natural or supernatural. This does not mean that all such activities are religious: a man getting up to close a window when he is sitting in a draught is not necessarily performing a religious act, except indirectly through the observance of a taboo. But all religion aims at a goal, however vaguely or unconsciously, and that goal can be postulated, in a rationalized treatise like this, as "the good." If we came on a group of people sacrificing a child to an idol, and asked them why they did so, they might have no clear conception of "good" as an ethical abstraction, but would probably say that they thought they had "better" do it. If we came on a group of inquisitors torturing a heretic in a dungeon, they would no doubt postulate a "good" aim in more explicit and conscious terms.

Religion, then, is the practice of the "good" life. Now in a society that has struggled for a moment above a brutal sacrificial or persecuting stage (there are usually a few members in every society above that level) the "good" comes to be defined in more analytic terms. Western civilization from the time of the Greeks onward has made many attempts to express the nature of the good, and has not yet got very far away from the Platonic division of the *good* into the *just*, the *beautiful*, and the *true*.[1] If these words have a more sentimental connotation than *good*, it is only because the less earnest minds today prefer to use *good* as a euphemism with a more noncommittal meaning as a blanket term for the other three. But a little reflection will show us that these three words refer to different aspects of behaviour. *Just* relates to action: it is the compulsion the *good* exerts on the will. *Beautiful* relates to emotion: it is the compulsion the *good* exerts on feeling. *True* relates to thought: it is the compulsion the *good* exerts on reason. Each of these aspects of the *good* is systematic and constructive, as it leads toward an ideal. So we get three systems of compulsion of the *good* to a definite aim. From *just*, *beautiful*, and *true* we pass to *justice*, *beauty*, and *truth*. We now have morality, the system of justice; art, the system of beauty; and logic, the system of reason.

Further examination of our vocabulary will bear out this thesis of the interdependence of the just, beautiful, and true in the good. When we say that a work of art is *good* we mean that it is *beautiful*. Unfortunately the latter word has become so limited in its meaning that it is now practically synonymous with *loveliness*: around this pun, for it is nothing more, half the discussions about the beauty of modern art are waged. Loveliness is an important part of beauty, and should never be confused with sentimentality, but it is not the essential element in beauty: it presents the half of the world that attracts us, and it is the business of art to present the repellent half as well. *Beautiful* works of art in the broad sense of the word are often little more than morbid gloatings over the repulsive and grotesque. If, however, we speak of a point in an argument as a good point we mean primarily that it impresses us as true rather than beautiful. In short: goodness is the whole of beauty, and the two words can be used interchangeably when a work of art is in question. But beauty is not the whole of goodness.

2. Morality and Art

This analysis has been made only in the interests of clarity. Every good action has a just, a beautiful, and a true aspect. When we wish to justify the *raison d'être* of such goods as art or scholarship, we usually explain them in terms of one of the other goods, pointing out, for instance, that they may be beneficial to morality in some way. Morality is usually employed as the apologist for the other two, as it relates more directly to the concerns of the vast majority, who are incapable of scaling any very lofty altitudes in the latter. It was formerly fashionable to say that poetry should "delight and instruct"[2] and the poet, up to the end of the eighteenth century, was frequently regarded as a prophet or seer, someone with superior insight which could only be called religious.[3] The advent of the atheistic and blasphemous society ushered in by the Industrial Revolution naturally provoked a reaction. Truth stopped at the empiric stage; morality at the criterion of the useful; and art, under the aegis of the romantic movement, declared its independence and proclaimed its battle-cry of "art for art's sake."[4] The fact that the artists who believed this motto were usually bad artists made it doubly reassuring. There were, of course, some whose revolt took on the nature of replacing justice with either truth or beauty. One school, around the time of the French Revolution, contended that our actions were only good if they were rational, or, as the phrase went, obeyed the dictates of pure reason.[5] Pure reason got herself worshipped in Paris under Robespierre. The other school, with which even Schleiermacher might be associated, being more subtle, was less fashionable. Its point was that our good actions are carefully selected actions, and as art depends on this faculty of selecting the significant, the good life is a work of art. All that this means, of course, is simply the point we have just made, that as all good actions have three

316 Emmanuel College Essays

aspects, it is not difficult to explain goodness in terms of any one of the three simply by isolating it.

The most usual tendency during the last century, however, was toward the discrete. The three goods came to be conceived as separate. Art became impatient of moral restrictions. In this there was a good deal of justification, for the very word *restrictions* implies something negative and undesirable. Justice being one thing and truth another, it is impossible to make a science of ethics, a logic of activity. Law, the general name given to attempts in this direction, is a system of approximations, which when applied to anything so specific as a work of art becomes irrelevant. And, of course, any system of approximations is a reflection of mediocrity. So the moral restrictions imposed on art have usually veered between theological obscurantism and moral prudery, depending on whether the mediocre level of the society is inclined to be pedantic, as with the society contemporary with Tasso, or sensual, as with the society of our own day. But this protest of mediocrity against genius has nothing to do with the interrelation of art and morality. The real question is, When we say that a work of art is "good," do we ever, in any case, have in mind a goodness which has a moral as well as an aesthetic aspect?

It is apparent that all but the most bigoted of art critics do recognize as valid aesthetic criteria certain moral qualities. Sincerity is an obvious instance. It would be very difficult to prove that the kind of artistic sincerity that helps to redeem the works of Bunyan from prosy and tedious sermonizing is not fundamentally the same thing as moral sincerity. The revulsion which invariably sets in against a stuffy, cynical, niggling period of artistic decadence is usually both a moral and an aesthetic reaction. A perhaps more questionable example of a moral goodness necessary to good art is economy. When we say that Racine is economical and that Swinburne is extravagant we are using moral categories, but are implying that Racine is a better artist than Swinburne. (We do not raise the rather silly question, at this or any other point, of whether art is essentially communication or not. The alternative is to regard art as self-expression. But expression, as opposed to impression, means the putting of certain ideas or impressions into a communicative form.)

These are random examples: what we are really interested in at the moment is the difference between art and morals. The question has a peculiar importance today owing to the fact that the "art for art's sake" shibboleth is now out of fashion, and a reaction has set in which restates the moralist's approach to art in narrower and more bigoted terms than ever before. This reaction centres around the word *propaganda*, which is at present extending its meaning to include all forms of morally persuasive art. Our feverish political consciousness has imposed on us a concept of art as diatribe, as a weapon to be used in the interests of certain groups with certain philosophies and political ambitions. In Germany and Italy today, and in Soviet Russia until recently,[6] the intolerance and bigotry of the government has stifled artistic activity. Some of the propagandic school of thought even go so far as to maintain, with a combination of zeal and ignorance that would shame a Montanist,[7] that art and propaganda are the same thing: that class-conscious proletarians should avoid Shakespeare, whose art-propaganda was probourgeois, that any artist who reflects the class struggle is greater than any artist who does not, that agreement with certain political dogmas is a positive aesthetic quality, and the like. This is, of course, only the lunatic fringe of an important and intelligent body of thought, and the question it raises so uncompromisingly deserves some examination.

Morality, we have said, is the only good attached very firmly to mediocrity: both creative genius and high thinking are products of a privileged class, on the whole: the artist may starve in a garret; but if he does not get enough money for him to be able to spend all his time creating, he disappears as an artist. So a society, particularly a democratic society assuming that the dominance of the mediocre, or the majority, is equivalent to political justice, comes to feel that morality is the only "good" that really matters. This sentiment is exploited whenever any plea of political emergency can be raised. Then, the extremists tell us, we should forget everything else and concentrate on immediate social ends, revolutionary, reformatory, or repressive as the case may be. Art and learning are luxuries to be enjoyed after privileges have been distributed more evenly. This kind of challenge is inescapable from Christianity, and that it can be an extremely subtle attack will be obvious to any Christian, with his interest in the regeneration of humanity and his recognition of the claims made on him by the less fortunate.

But what about the artist? The assumption is that the artist's sympathies should be with a certain outlook; that he will illustrate those sympathies in his work, and will choose subjects lending themselves to that type of illustration. In other words, the artist should explain what his point of view is: the average swallower of propaganda feels himself cheated if the artist does not do so; he feels that he is being treated dishonestly. The early critical writings of Bernard Shaw, a typical propagandic artist, betray this feeling—or exploit a similar feeling in others—in regard to Shakespeare. And, of course, the nervous, itching attempt to find out "what Shakespeare really thought" lies behind a large proportion of critical work on that artist and remains the supreme Northwest Passage fallacy of literary criticism.[8]

It is here that we touch on the essential difference between art and morality. The moralist explains and argues; he wants his points made as clearly as possible, and he allows nothing to intervene between the presentation of his idea and the reader. The artist is equally interested in communication, but his method of communicating is somewhat different. Between himself and his audience he sets up something objective. The boundary line is impossible to draw, of course. The satirist, for instance, is an artist appealing to a moral sense on the part of the reader. Next to him comes the propagandist, preacher, orator, prophet, *vates*, or censor, as he has variously been called, who starts with a certain philosophy and applies it in his works of art to society. Swift was not himself a moralist, perhaps, but his work appealed to common sense, to the instinct to regard everything abnormal as ridiculous or disgusting. For this reason many satirists, from Aristophanes onward, have been conservatives and resisters of new ideas. The prophet or censor, of the Carlyle type, is more explicitly a man with a moral message. Yet the objective element in the specifically artistic presentation remains. Take the following:

Woe unto them that join house to house, that lay field to field, till there be no room, and ye be made to dwell alone in the midst of the land! In mine ears saith the Lord of hosts, Of a truth many houses shall be desolate, even great and fair, without inhabitant. [Isaiah 5:8–9]

The ground of a certain rich man brought forth plentifully: and he reasoned within himself, saying, What shall I do, because I have not where to bestow my fruits? And he said, This will I do: I will pull down my barns, and build greater; and there will I bestow all my grain and my goods. And I will say to my soul, Soul, thou hast much goods laid up for many years; take thine ease, eat, drink, be merry. But God said unto him, Thou fool, this night is thy soul required of thee; and the things which thou hast prepared, whose shall they be? [Luke 12:16–20]

There is no doubt about the artistic power of Isaiah, nor the moral passion of Jesus, yet the former gives us what is essentially propaganda, the latter a work of art. The story in the second extract is the objective element: we get a specific illustration instead of a general principle. In the first the moral lesson is explicit; in the latter, implicit. The one explains; the other suggests. In the former we are passively following another's line of thought; in the latter we are forced to make an active effort of response: the effort we call interpretation. Of course, this parable of Jesus is propagandic art, and we chose it deliberately as a borderline case: the objective material of the story is arranged in a certain way, so that we can hardly avoid its moral implications. But even there we have a certain latitude: we can interpret the story as tragedy or satire, or both. The story challenges our whole minds, for interpretation is largely intellectual and our appreciation of the power and concentration apparent chiefly emotional. The preaching of Isaiah appeals more to our instincts and prejudices: it is based on the assumption that in us is a chord which will vibrate automatically when touched with a certain stimulus.

From this example we can see that propagandic art is, when properly handled, more powerful *as propaganda* than straight preaching, which is, of course, the reason why propagandists always try to dragoon the artists, or turn to art themselves. But the essential element in the artistic presentation, we have seen, is the objective element which we found in Jesus but missed in Isaiah, not the propaganda itself. So it is obviously possible for art not to be propagandic at all. Propaganda, we have said, explains, art suggests, and propagandic art suggests in such a way as to compel a certain conclusion. But frequently the greatest art is arranged so objectively that it can be interpreted in all sorts of ways. Shakespeare was, no doubt, a member of the bourgeois class; but it would be extremely difficult to find a defence of the ideals of that class in his work. The class he belonged to was purely a matter of accident, having no relation whatever to his work. Music is another example of creative activity which can never do duty successfully for the propagandist.

3. The Kind of Thinking in Art

We have tried to distinguish art from morality: let us see how it compares with reason. Many have felt that between a logical activity like mathematics and an artistic one like music there is a very close connection. This feeling goes back, of course, to the Pythagoreans. With a mathematician, the whole personality goes into the working out of mathematical relationships, emotional as well as intellectual; and, to him, mathematics is beautiful as well as logical, and a mathematical demonstration takes on the proportions of a work of art. It is also possible to "interpret," though with what significance it is difficult to discover, a piece of highly concentrated music like a fugue in terms of mathematics. There have even been attempts made to reduce the rules of prosody, theoretical and practical, to mathematical formulae, or arrive at all possible kinds of dramatic situations by permutation. Similarly, the intellectual qualities obvious in all works of art have led some critics to exalt them as the only necessary ones, connecting emotion with subjective or lyrical expression, and lyrical expression with immaturity.[9]

What we are interested in here is the kind of intellect evident in works of art. Intellect works in two ways: it may be analytic or synthetic: it may work toward a meaning that denotes, or it may work toward a meaning that connotes. The former is typically the scientific intellect. It is interested in arriving at exact and invariable meanings, and for science to permit anything like latitude in interpreting its communications would be nonsense. It sticks to the concrete and avoids the generalized. On the other hand, the philosophical and theological intellects work with generalizations and, consequently, look for abstract concepts covering a wide variety of concrete data. Often this capacity for abstraction is pure verbalism, of course. Parmenides, starting from the fact that the verb "to be" meant existence and served as a copula, came to the conclusion that all things that existed were eternally linked together and that, consequently, motion and change were impossible. The speculations of Empedocles about attraction as a universal principle were based on the double meaning of "attraction" in the sense relating to sexual love and the sense relating to the law of gravitation.[10] These are purely metaphysical speculations: a scientist would sniff at them. But they are fairly close to artistic thinking. For the intellect of the creative genius is synthetic and connotative as well: he differs from the metaphysicians and resembles the scientists in working with concrete rather than abstract material; but he too looks for connections, snatches at the associative sets of meanings in words, instead of quarrelling with them, as a scientist is apt to do when they are not technical enough for him, and establishes unities where the ordinary man sees chaos. But his unities are very different from the uniformities the scientist tries to establish.

The relation of the artist to the scientist boils down to one very similar to his relation to the moralist or propagandist. The scientist explains, and his words and images denote; the artist suggests, and his words and images connote. No two people will look at a picture in the same way; and if I am looking at one, all the other possible reactions to it, which I may or may not share, form a sort of nimbus around my head, which I try to get away from. If I am looking at *Mona Lisa*, for instance, I withdraw into myself in order to escape from both Walter Pater[11] and the gum-chewing tourist beside me. This leads immediately to a very important principle. Morality we associated with the will; art, with feeling; logic, with reason. Now will and reason are alike in this, that they both are communal rather than individual aspects of the personality. In making a judgment we bow to an objective standard: everybody has to agree that two and two make four, and anyone arguing from that basis is appealing to reason rather than to individual intellects. He addresses "common sense," the sense all men hold in common. There can be no question of a private interpretation of mathematics, as there can be a private interpretation of Cézanne. The same quality holds good for the will. An individual's will is expressed in a social environment, and that environment is protected by rules which apply equally to all. The propagandist appeals to group consciousness and mass action, and to the individual as a factor in that larger unit. But feeling is the individual, discriminating side of the personality. In our emotional reactions to things we express our uniqueness. The artist, we have said, creates an objective situation for us to interpret in terms of our own experience. His work is a synthetic, coordinated unity. Our lives are mostly chaotic and meaningless: in our struggle toward the religious or "good" life we strive to make our experiences more significant and unified. The artist, by his creation of significant unities, imposes a pattern on experience. We absorb that pattern into our own experience and thereby advance a step in our own process of coordination.

Art is, thus, a peculiarly central and direct expression of religion as compared to morality and logic. Scientific activity may, and usually does, lose sight of a religious goal; and theology may become arid and abstracted from experience. Morality may be legalized into a passive routine. But art, in retaining this unique, discriminating factor of feeling as central, has a persistent vitality about it.[12]

4. Explicit and Implicit Religion in Art

Now as religion embraces all forms of the good life, it is dependent on communal as well as individual impulses. Its ultimate goal is ideal; and is never revealed in actual experience. Yet it is essentially the same goal as that of the artist: the selection of a significant unity of experiences in life. The work of art is, however, a concrete, specific, sharply outlined unity, or ought to be; where the work of religion is a small fragmentary phase of a vast and dimly conceived process. Consequently, the most obvious relation for art to bear to religion is that of illustration. A work of art is a formal expression of a religious impulse. The whole of religion is far too large for any one mind to grasp it; but in the work of art it is seen, if only through a glass darkly, as a kind of prismatic perspective. Hamlet called the drama a mirror of nature [3.2.24]; but a work of art is more active than that: it catches the light of nature selectively, like a carefully cut gem. In short, a work of art *symbolizes* the religious impulse. One might turn this around, as Blake did, and, putting the individual creative will at the centre, say that religion is a social form of this creative or artistic activity, which Blake called the "poetic genius" and identified with the "true man."[13] The work of art, either way we take it, is a microcosm, an epitome of all experience, the revelation of the universal in the particular. I once read a book on Joyce's *Ulysses* which said that as every great work of art was an epitome of the universe, a knowledge of the elementary principles of the universe would prove a valuable aid in the understanding of *Ulysses*.[14] It is not necessary to go that far in order to agree with the general principle implied, that the coordination of art helps us to coordinate our own lives, and thereby adjust them better to our environment, which is ultimately the universe.

But perhaps it is high time we began to limit our terms a bit. We have been proceeding on the assumption that all constructive or "good" activity is religious. Ultimately that is probably true. Science is an end in itself, but its accumulation, description, and arrangement of data seem to suggest general principles which are elaborated intellectually by philosophy and welded into other forms of activity by theology, so that all thinking, from this point of view, is ultimately theological. Recently a reporter on a local newspaper assaulted a Catholic priest and asked him if he "believed in evolution." "That," said the priest in effect, "is a scientific question. My field is in religion; I am not a scientist." Asked if he thought evolution was related to religion, he said: "Everything is related to religion."[15]

Here we have the word *religion* used in two senses. The second sense is the sense in which we have so far been using it, as a general word covering all forms of activity considered constructive or "good" by those performing them. The first sense is the ordinary sense, as a word relating to a specific stereotype of activity. We have said that the work of art symbolizes religion because it is hard and sharp where religion is incalculably extensive. A precisely similar demand for consolidating, clarifying, and making concrete the generalized religious impulse operates in religion itself. From the general idea of religion we pass to a clearly outlined body of doctrine with definite dogmas, organization, and historical tradition. The two conceptions are not contradictory, but supplementary: they are both necessary to avoid a vague and sentimental deism on the one hand and a narrow sectarianism on the other. We have said that the action of a man closing a window when he is sitting in a draught is not specifically a religious one. In the general sense of the word *religion* it would be, as it relates to the care of the body, and the body is the temple of God. But we do not ordinarily speak of religion in this absolute way. When Jesus spoke of the religious quality of the action of giving a cup of cold water in his name [Mark 9:41], he brought together these universal and specific aspects of religion, and incidentally showed how the more general aspect had to be corrected by the limitation of the other.

Similarly we must limit our three approaches to the good. There is a special type of religious reasoning, in our new sense of the term, we call theological, and a special type of moral activity we call—or used to call—pious. There is also an explicitly religious kind of art in addition to the general implication of all art. For example:

> Goe, and catche a falling starre,
> 　Get with child a mandrake roote,
> Tell me, where all past yeares are,
> 　Or who cleft the Divels foot,
> Teach me to heare Mermaides singing,
> 　Or to keep off envies stinging,
> 　　And finde
> 　　What winde
> Serves to advance an honest minde.[16]

At the round earths imagin'd corners, blow
Your trumpets, Angells, and arise, arise,
From death, you numberlesse infinities
Of soules, and to your scattred bodies goe,
All whom the flood did, and fire shall o'erthrow,
All whom warre, dearth, age, agues, tyrannies,
Despaire, law, chance, hath slaine, and you whose eyes,
Shall behold God, and never tast deaths woe.[17]

These passages are by the same author, though one is the voice of young Jack Donne, shiftless, flippant, cynical, always in trouble, and occasionally in gaol, and the other is the voice of the great Doctor Donne, Dean of St. Paul's. The second is explicitly a religious poem, the first is not; yet in the first, the extraordinary variety of things, most of them having religious connotations, unified in the pattern, the synthesis of emotions of disillusionment, cynicism, irony, and the hunger of the soul for an ideal go to make up an incisive, concrete outline in which religious impulses common to all men are suddenly caught and frozen. So the difference between an explicitly and an implicitly religious poem is largely one of convenience: the difference between a religious poem, in the general sense, and a nonreligious poem is the difference between a good poem and a bad poem.

The work of art symbolizes the religious impulse, we have said, and the inference is that the symbol is the unit of artistic creation. Explicitly religious art, therefore, would work with certain generally recognized symbols. Or, more exactly, there are certain archetypal patterns in general religious experience that are reflected both in the dogmas and myths of the historical religion and the artistic conventions which illustrate them.

One more consideration remains to be noted. For art to have any explicit connection with religion, religion itself must be sufficiently catholic and true to its communal nature to admit of all three approaches to the "good." As society becomes secularized, its various activities become discrete. We have already dealt very superficially with a late stage of this process in our own cultural tradition. This process began with the Renaissance-Reformation: since that event, religion as something binding all forms of activity disappeared. Since the sixteenth century, the possibility that in society a group so varied as the Canterbury pilgrims could all travel to the same place with the same object has become inconceivable. Hence, an individualizing tendency arises in religion itself, a tendency which with us reached its culmination in Calvinism, repudiating the "good" as a conscious goal of religion. According to Calvinism, no man can alter his moral status or perform a "good" action, except as God wills it, so that all religious activity is God's. From this point of view any discussion of "religion and art" becomes confined to the explicit illustration of one by the other. Our own approach is Arminian, via Schleiermacher, and anti-Calvinist:[18] in accepting the statement that "man's chief end is to glorify God," we leave room for deliberate and consciously controlled forms of adoration, as well as for vaguely emotional spasms. Not only that, but we believe, too, that Haydn's dedication of his music to the glory of God[19] (the result, incidentally, being that his masses are so cheerful that no church will perform them) is qualitatively superior to an uncontrolled, unskilled, and amorphous glorifying of God. We take our chances on whatever cultural snobbery that may lead to.

5. Symbolism

Art symbolizes religion, and, therefore, the symbol is the unit of art, we have said. A symbol is something which stands for something else, and symbolism in art means the bringing together of two or more ideas into one object. The symbolic units are words in literature, and images in the graphic arts. In music, though music is so highly concentrated and abstract an art that this point is rather difficult to establish, the fact that every note has a melodic, harmonic, contrapuntal, rhythmic, timbric, and tonal context makes it a symbolic point of reference. The meanings of all words are similarly complex: they contain a large number of associations which are both historical, relating to their etymology, and syntactical, relating to their place in a given passage.[20] The symbolic nature of imagery is more obvious. The aim of symbolism may be generally stated as an attempt to relate something in the outer environment to the inner experience by giving it a mental significance and reference which inner experience can grasp. We may see a tiger, and simply add it to the list of things we have seen; we may experience strength, beauty, terror, the splendour of sheer physical power even when destructive, or the effects of these emotions, without organizing them. But when the artist relates these factors of experience to the tiger:

Tyger! tyger! burning bright
In the forest of the night, [Blake, *The Tyger* lines 1–2]

he has given the tiger a mental significance for us, on the one hand, and
has given our chaotic and disordered sensations and emotions a concrete point of reference we can associate them with, on the other.

Now, of course, this is not purely a conscious process. The symbolism
appeals to us at a subconscious level: we instinctively grasp the association, and in a way it may be said to be innate, or at least potential, in us.
It follows that if the artist speaks, or otherwise expresses himself, in a
symbolic language, that language is, like ordinary language, evolved
unconsciously. As a matter of fact, of course, ordinary language itself is
pure symbolism: the relating of objective phenomena to inner experience by mentally significant patterns. Onomatopoeic words are the most
obviously symbolic, perhaps, but the difference between them and more
abstract words is only one of degree. Art is a further complication of languages of communication in general: languages proper remain for us,
with all their inflections and syntax, as impressive enough examples of
unconscious logic. The symbolic language of art is also fundamentally
an unconscious language. If it were not so, all connection with religion
would disappear, for religious activity demands a communal sense art
has to evoke.

The scientific investigation of the unconscious nature of symbolism
has only begun, and it would not have started at all without a cross-
fertilization of two otherwise separate fields of scientific activity. Psychology and anthropology both tend toward an examination of the
unconscious activities of man, and where they converge is generally on
this point of the unconscious language of symbolism and particularly on
the relation of religion and art. For their discoveries bear out our thesis
that art is the expressed form of religion and that, consequently, all religious rituals are matrices of artistic development. When we say that
frost forms a "design" on a window pane, we do not mean that the frost
is consciously an artist, but simply that it unconsciously builds up something we interpret in terms of logical pattern. In the same way the psychological examination of dreams, from Freud on, has shown that our
dreams are expressions of desires that fail to come to the surface and
have to be transmuted into symbols. These symbols are largely phallic,
but they follow coherent and regular lines of symbolic structure.
Anthropology, starting from the investigations of Mannhardt and

Frazer,[21] has similarly shown that there are certain archetypal patterns running through primitive myth: ideas of a universal deluge, of a dying and reviving god of vegetation, of an incarnation of a god in the form of a man, and that as a result primitive rituals take on the same symbolic significance as dreams, the same potentiality of logical interpretation. Freud interpreted art as the dreams of unsatisfied sex neurotics. But investigators with a wider point of view have felt convinced that there is a less negative approach to art possible, and from the work of Jung on, we shall probably turn more and more to this idea of archetypal pattern in art, following from a universal subconscious language of symbolism.

After this, it should not surprise us that many great artists evoke symbolic patterns that go back to matters of which they can have no direct knowledge. Just as a reader of Frazer becomes accustomed to realizing that peasants in tsarist Russia and Aztecs in Mexico perform similar harvest rites, and that the natives of Kamchatka and Basutoland have similar sets of taboos for similar superstitions,[22] so a student of literature should not wince if he comes across a remark like the following:

> The inspired prisoner who wove the *Pilgrim's Progress* (as he tells us) out of the substance of his dreams, has reproduced with marvelous fidelity the very incidents of the initiation ceremonies of ancient Egypt, almost in the language of the Book of the Dead. (Allen Upward, *The Divine Mystery*, 222)[23]

6. Music and Drama

In saying that the essential function of art is to "illustrate" the religious impulse, and in speaking of the symbolic structures common to both as "patterns," we are using metaphors derived from graphic art. Now there is no doubt that the stationary arts give the most direct and obvious interpretations of a religious tradition. Painting and sculpture seem to have been originally iconic: primitive people felt that by drawing a picture of some incarnation of mysterious power they could get control of it. More sophisticated developments of the religious treatment of the stationary arts are easy enough to trace. Most religions supply a set of ready-made symbols and conventions for the artist to treat. The Annunciation, the *pietà*, the *Theotokos*[24] are, it can be seen at a glance, products of Christian genius. Conventionalized symbols like the cross or the halo also belong to the iconic tradition of Christianity. But with the dynamic arts the relationship is not quite so obvious. Where the stationary arts depend on pattern, or the imposition of a mentally significant form on the space-world, the dynamic ones depend on a similar imposition of form on the time-world, which we call rhythm. Now rhythm is essentially regular recurrence. The movement of time is chaotic and lawless: in order to get into it the stability and permanence the artist needs, it is necessary to regulate it, and the only possible way of regulating it is by some form of predictable repetition.

The fundamental activity associated with dynamic art is the bodily expression of rhythm, which is, of course, only a clumsy periphrasis for the dance and the song. The former is the rhythmic control of movement, the latter the rhythmic control of sound, movement and sound being the two phenomena of sense experience that we receive in a temporal rather than a spatial order. Now there are all sorts of artistic developments of dance and song, but those explicitly religious are the ones that concern us here. Originally all art was explicitly religious, and the dance and song, consequently, were part of a religious ritual. As society develops, divides, and becomes increasingly secularized, the arts follow a similar process. But, bearing in mind that religion requires a communal basis and art an individualistic one, we should expect group arts to be more closely associated with religion than more subjective ones. Religion, is derived from *religare*, to bind together.

Music and drama are both group art forms: that is, they are ensemble performances for audiences. The ensemble performance in music may be only an ensemble of ten fingers, and the dramatic performance may be a monologue; but the group concept is there: both arts are presented rather than read, interpreted by some performer or group of performers intervening between the artist and his public. Both music and drama, therefore, flourish chiefly in an integrated society: if the drama is to flourish, for example, there must be a large number of interests common to the audience; otherwise, it will not "get across."

Examples of this are easy enough to find. In our own culture, for instance, music and drama were both born from the womb of the Church. The great Renaissance developments of music and drama in England, France, and Spain did not take place until after a religious settlement had been made, following the split of the Reformation. The great musical and dramatic achievement of the Elizabethans would have been impossible without the Anglican "middle way" established in religion. But the Anglican church in Elizabeth's time had to fight the new force of Puritanism, which was strongly individualized: that is, it dispensed with all cultural connections and facilitated the advance of secular art. Its one great dramatic artist, Bunyan, is well on the way to the novel, which was established by the Whigs, who carried on the Puritanic attack after it had changed from a religious to a political struggle. The novel is, of course, the individualized drama, addressed by the author directly to a single reader. But the Puritans themselves fought music and drama from start to finish, trying to transform their instinctive dislike of a communal art form into a moral principle. They closed the theatres as soon as they seized power in 1642; they attacked music in the church service as sinful. The Restoration, on the other hand, brought back a revived drama and Purcell in music. Shakespeare adds his final touch to the portrait of Cassius, the ruthless Puritanic revolutionary, when he makes Caesar say of him:

> he loves no plays
> As thou dost, Antony; he hears no music. [*Julius Caesar*, 1.1.203–4]

Music and drama, then, belong to an era of integrated cultural development, and their communal nature brings them into line with religion. Perhaps it will be most logical to approach them one at a time, from more or less a historical point of view, the historical approach being, in art criticism, the most empiric and concrete, showing what connection they have so far actually had with religion. We must keep in mind, however, the points established a little earlier. Music and drama are time-arts; they depend on rhythm, and rhythm depends on recurrence. Consequently, we should expect them to symbolize a time-element in religion, specifically, religious experiences in life, which take place in time, and to impose on those experiences a pattern of recurrence. Let us take the drama first.

7. The Dramatic Presentation of Recurrence

The elemental form imposed by the human mind on the time-world being rhythm, and rhythm depending on recurrence, it follows that the feeling of something regularly recurring in experience marks the first conquest of fear, the first assurance of permanence and stability in the scheme of things. Two recurrent phenomena in nature come at once to mind: the renewed progression of the sun across the sky and the death and revival of vegetation with the changing of the seasons. The primitive feeling for these phenomena is, of course, economic rather than metaphysical, in an agricultural community particularly.

Out of this feeling of regularity comes the artistic expression of it. The impulse to worship through certain ritual forms is an artistic one, ritual being, we have said, a matrix of art forms. This naturally takes the form of imitating, in a conventionalized form, the movements of the god worshipped. Along with this purely artistic impulse there is another mainly magical. Magic postulates the same kind of universe the artist works in: a universe in which like is connected with like. All forms of occultism, where magic impinges on science, are essentially products of artistic thinking and are frequently sources of inspiration for art, although they are bad science. The magician believes that by spilling water on the ground he can compel it to rain, just as a Persian actor can convey to his audience that a scene is in a desert by exhibiting a handful of chopped straw. So leaping in the air to promote the growth of crops comes to be an established form of ritual dance, which perhaps accounts for some of the energy traditionally associated with this rite. In any case, drama is associated with action; it means etymologically something done, just as poetry means etymologically something made.

All primitive peoples dependent on the growth of vegetation of any kind for their existence tend to evolve similar myths of a god of fertility dying in the fall and reviving in the spring. In Babylonia this god's name was Tammuz, in Egypt Osiris, in Syria Adonis, in Phrygia Attis, in Thrace Dionysus, in Sparta Hyacinthus. The annual death of the god was mourned, chiefly by the women of the tribe (cf. Ezekiel 8:14), and his revival in spring celebrated. As his death usually coincided approximately with the harvest season, it was accompanied by a sacrifice, originally human, later, of course, an animal.

It is in Greece that the particular development from fertility rite to drama took place. The worship of Dionysus the fertility god centred around a spring festival. It was instituted in Greece at a fairly late period, and was Thracian in origin. Beginning in rural districts, it was brought to Athens during the tyranny of Pisistratus.[25] Repetition of a rite (the Greeks called their rites *dromena*) gets rather monotonous for people who do not particularly believe in it: Pisistratus had superimposed on the rite mimetic presentations of stories from Homer, in much the same way that the Catholic rites in the Middle Ages eventually expanded into presentations of Bible stories, and so brought to birth

Western drama. Aeschylus, who remarked that all his plays were slices from the great banquet of Homer,[26] is, of course, the first great name in the evolution of the *drama* out of the *dromena*. But the tradition developing from him retained its sacerdotal connection with Dionysus: the performances of plays were attended by the chief priests, headed by the priest of Dionysus, and the poets preserved their connection with Greek religion. The transition from the cult of Dionysus to the illustration of Homeric stories merely evidences the fact that by the time of Pisistratus the official Olympian religion, for which the Homeric epics were sacred books, had become fused with the later, more popular Dionysiac cult. Even the sceptical Euripides has given in the *Bacchae* an unforgettable picture of Dionysiac rites.[27]

Originally, of course, the rites of Dionysus were the ordinary, crude leaping into the air and similar gesticulations to promote the growth of crops. Dionysus, however, was always a vintage-god rather than a harvest-god, and his rites gradually took on an orgiastic, frenzied character. The aim of the worshippers was to become united to the god by enthusiasm, or possession of themselves by the god (the original meaning of enthusiasm). The sacrifice associated with Dionysus was that of the goat (τράγος: the word means both goat and a kind of barley, and may go back to a time when the fertility spirit of the barley crop was conceived as incarnate in the form of an animal lurking near it). The attendants of Dionysus developed a characteristic ritual song, the dithyramb, noted for its rugged and irregular rhythmic energy, and a characteristic dance, noted for the same qualities, performed by the male attendants of Dionysus, the satyrs or goat-men, and called after them the satyric drama. In the dramatic period proper the satyric drama was retained as the final play of a tetralogy.[28]

The tragedy, then, developed out of the τράγος, or goat sacrifice. Our next step is to see why the ritual of sacrifice is a potential art form. Investigators have tended to move away from Tylor and his early conception of sacrifice as essentially the bribing of a god,[29] and have generally placed the emphasis on the desire for communion. This has two aspects: in the first place the savage depends on the coherence of his tribe—without it he is almost at once a lost man—and needs to be regularly assured of its coherence. In the second place, the savage tries to strengthen himself by absorbing into himself a power greater than he. Taking those two ideas together, it becomes inevitable that the thing of superior power to be absorbed is that which incarnates the unity of the tribe, that is, the king. And as the savage's ideas of absorption are appropriately primitive and materialistic, the ritual of regularly killing and eating the king of the tribe grows up. Usually this is done as soon as the king's virility (which means the virility of the tribe) shows signs of waning. The king is dead, long live the king:[30] his successor must be appointed the instant the old king dies. Eventually, as primitive man becomes more conscious, he comes to identify the spirit of fertility with the vegetation, as we have already mentioned; at the same time an animal sacrifice is substituted for a human one, and so grow up rites like the τράγος, sacrifices with the same idea of communion with the god— now considered either incarnate in or bound in some way to the animal—retained.

The purpose of communion is a renewal of strength. The king dies, but in being divided and eaten by his tribe he reunites in the bodies of his worshippers and creates a new spirit of unity among them. It is possible that, as the psychologists suggest,[31] the king is to each member of the tribe a father, a representative of the father complex of his youth, so that his death brings to the worshippers a freedom from a neurosis. In any case, the sacrifice, even on this level, is implicitly an art form. The archetypal pattern of tragedy is this slaying of a divine king, of a hero, usually represented as a monarch, with unusual if not supernatural powers. And in his fall the tragic hero creates in us a new sense of strength, of unity and renewal.

To explain this we should, of course, have to bring out the moral ideas implicit in the tragedy, and we can see these more clearly by turning to Hebrew culture. The Hebrews were originally desert nomads, and developed no fertility cult and no drama. But what they lost in cultural development as a result they made up in moral penetration, and the Old Testament brings out very clearly the moral implications of sacrifice from the beginning. The interpenetration with the Canaanites brought some elements of the fertility cult into Palestine, of course: in spite of the careful revision of the redactor, we can see a local Iphigenia in Jephthah's daughter, and a vegetation myth in Joseph's coat of many colours [Judges 11:34–40; Genesis 37:3]. Later, in the Hellenistic period, these symbols of recurrence are repeated in more sophisticated forms. The sun goes down into darkness and recurs the next day: the soul symbolizing that pattern of experience would go through a similar death and resurrection. This is what happens at the sacrifice: the worshipper dies in the sacrificial victim and is reborn in communion with the god incarnated in that victim. The Jews put a moral emphasis on the sacrifice: their goat was not the Dionysiac τράγος, but the scapegoat, who carried the *sins* of the people to the wilderness. Hence, for the Jewish worshipper sacrifice was purification, a freeing from sin. So the symbols of the death and resurrection of the soul are purgatorial symbols, symbols of initiation. Daniel goes into the lion's den in defence of his piety, emerging unscathed [Daniel 6]. The three children go through the purgatory of Nebuchadnezzar's fiery furnace for the same reason and come out unharmed [Daniel 3:19–30]. In Jonah's descent into the fish's belly the moral nature of the initiation symbol is even more clearly marked [Jonah 1–2].

This moral interpretation of the recurrent death and resurrection of the soul was present in Greek culture too, of course, and was especially associated with the religion of Orphism. In literature, it gives us the art form of the katabasis, the descent into the underworld, which meets us in *Odyssey* XI (probably an Orphic interpolation), in *Aeneid* VI, and in Dante, where it became part of the Christian tradition. But on the whole the Greek interpretation of the purgation or purification of the spirit in sacrifice took on a different form. Even to the Orphics, for example, who believed that this purification, or catharsis, was nothing less than the deliverance of the soul from the body, the process was largely physical and magical and was conceived as resulting automatically from the performance of certain rites. But to Aristotle the catharsis conception had a more naturalistic appearance as a purging or cleansing of the spirit by a powerful surcharge of emotions, which he specified as pity and terror [*Poetics*, chap. 6].

We have said enough to show the connection of tragedy and sacrifice; what about the origin of comedy?[32] To get at this we have to go back to our sacrifice of the divine king. As the society developed and the old cannibalistic feast disappeared, the idea of a *substitute* sacrifice for the divine king became very widespread. Sometimes this was the king's own son; but later it came to be someone selected by lot who was made a mock king for a year and then was stripped of his false glory and slain. The Aztecs of Mexico were still at this stage when their culture was destroyed by the Spaniards. Still later it became a condemned criminal who was made a mock king for a time and then executed. The festival of the Sacaea at Babylon was of this nature:[33] the criminal was even given access to the royal harem. In the end this sacrifice of the mock king developed into the Saturnalia, or periodic overturning of social distinctions, and the carnival accompanying it, presided over by some buffoon or lord of misrule.

Just as tragedy is an artistic development of the sacrifice, so comedy is an artistic development of the carnival. Fundamental to the whole idea of comedy is the idea of false values, of something unreal, of sham in high places, of pretensions taken seriously. When Falstaff and Prince Henry confront one another we have a typical presentation of a lord of misrule and the real king who dethrones him after his brief tyranny. Falstaff's exit marks the end of the saturnalia, and of the comedy with it.[34] But the point is that we are left with a very strong impression that there is something more real about the kingship of Falstaff than there is about the puppet gesticulations of Prince Henry, so that we get a double comedy, with implications so powerfully satiric as to be quite unmistakably tragic. We shall return to this in a moment.

8. Christianity and the Drama

In the supreme sacrifice we have, of course, the supreme drama, and in that drama are woven both tragic and comic elements. In Christ's death we are saved from sin: he provides a universal catharsis for mankind. Slain at the height of his virility, the divine king of all men, in the role of the sacrificial victim or Lamb of God, he represents the consolidation in fact of a universal religious impulse. That is, all mankind approximates the Christian religion: non-Christian myths all strive to approach the Passion, which is the nexus of all religious symbolism. Christianity could not claim to be a universal religion did not all religions, however primitive, adumbrate, in one way or another, what it provides. People have occasionally attacked Christianity on the ground that it contains nothing that cannot be found in other religions. The point is, of course, that there is nothing in other religions that cannot be found in Christianity, the difference being that Christianity alone provides a concrete basis of historical fact and thereby has a reference to the time-world of existence other religions lack. This connection with the time-world gives a peculiar significance in the dramatic quality of the tragedy of the Passion.

Sir James Frazer has shown that the story of Esther goes back to the idea of substitute sacrifice we have been treating. Haman is the unfortunate mock king, stripped of his glory and hanged at the end. Esther and Mordecai are Ishtar and Marduk, ancient gods of Babylon. The story is an etiological account of the rise of the feast of Purim, the Jewish Saturnalia.[35] Frazer's theory is that Christ was crucified in the role of the mock king Haman. His tormentors would be Syrians, or else Romans of the outpost camps, to whom the Saturnalia would be, not the good-humoured carnival of Rome, but an actual bloody sacrifice. Hence, the mockery of Christ, the crown of thorns and the sceptre, the salutation of "Hail, King of the Jews!" and the ironic (to them) inscription over the Cross. Barabbas, we are told, was probably released in the role of buffoon and lord of misrule for the popular carnival.[36] This is the only thing needed to complete our conception of the Passion as the matrix of all drama: it is the world's supreme comedy as well as its supreme tragedy. The magnificent irony of the Passion as a carnival is the ultimate treatment of the double comedy we noted in connection with Falstaff and Prince Henry.

Since the death of Christ the whole concept of drama, particularly of tragedy, has been revolutionized. In Greek tragedy the whole point of the catharsis was the complete irrationality of the force striking down the hero. The hero was usually faultless in himself, and he was attacked by a blind and purely external fate. Christian tragedy, on the other hand, sees the tragedy as emanating from the character of the hero. Hamlet and Othello are both invulnerable, like Achilles, except at one point, and on that point they are struck and killed. Interchange their roles and both tragedies become meaningless: Othello could have killed Claudius in no time; it would have been nothing for Hamlet to have trapped Iago in his own web of lies. The tragedy of Judas Iscariot is the first Christian tragedy: it is a tragedy of character where the tragedy of *Oedipus Rex* is a tragedy of incident. In other words, since Christianity the world has been faced with an ethical challenge, and drama reflects, as no other art could reflect, the critical nature of that challenge.

The medieval drama was, of course, a product of the Church, growing up in a way somewhat similar to the growth of Dionysiac drama in Greece, as we have indicated. The matrix of ritual from which it grew was, of course, the Mass. In the last century it became fashionable among some sentimental aesthetes who occasionally turned Roman Catholic to regard the Mass as the world's supreme work of art. But the Mass is not art; it is a religious rite, and, therefore, communal where art is individualistic. Art is ascetic in a way, that is, it works with one sense at a time; or, if it uses two senses, it avoids the more intimate ones. Taste, smell, and as a rule touch (sculpture being a dubious exception)

are excluded for works of art. But the Mass has something for the gratifi-
cation of every sense: taste in the Eucharist, smell in incense, hearing in
the chant, and so on, precisely because it is not art, but the expression of
the completeness of the religious life. As a general rule those who
admire the Mass solely as a work of art are decadents; and it was a contemporary sign of decadence when program music was followed by the
symphonies of Scriabin, with their colour-organs and perfume-engines.
If Scriabin had had his way, he would have plunged ahead into what
could only have been called a black mass.

The medieval drama developed in two directions. One, the presentation of Biblical legends which parallels the absorption of Homeric legends into the Greek drama, we have dealt with. The other, the morality
play, was concerned more with the moral and instructive element of
religion. There are in the main two kinds of partial symbolism which
help to bind the drama in its earlier stages to a religious tradition. One
of these is the allegory: this is peculiar to the Christian development,
with its increased moral interest. The other is the myth or presentation
of the actions of divine or otherwise supernatural or heroic beings: this
was, of course, the sole intermediate stage for Greek drama and was a
very important one for Christian drama, developing as it did the so-
called "mystery" plays.

In Elizabethan drama, of course, the greatest dramatic development of
the West, we have a purely secular drama. It was a Renaissance art form,
and the Renaissance was in at least one of its aspects a reincorporation of
much of the pagan spirit of the classical world into a Christian tradition.
But Shakespeare, by the intuition of transcendent genius, approached
nearer and nearer the sacerdotal drama as his genius developed. To
prove this assertion would be a colossal task obviously; but the main
outlines of the development are clear enough. With our thesis of the
development of the comedy from the carnival, it is surely significant that
Shakespeare called his greatest comedy after the Saturnalia of the Western world—Twelfth Night. His heroic figures were classical and national
rather than Biblical, as the taste of the time demanded, and, of course,
any explicit association of religion and drama would have been impossible in the rising tide of Puritanism. Even Milton, whose Christianity is
not in doubt, was compelled to turn to classical mythology for his only
dramatic work intended for performance.[37] But from the commencement
of Shakespeare's mature period onward, the themes of his plays become
more and more evidently folklore, and, hence, approach nearer to the

archetypal religious patterns of recurrence. It is possible to trace back the stories of *Hamlet* and *King Lear* till they dissolve in nature myths; and about the folklore nature of such comedies as *All's Well that Ends Well* there can be no question.[38] After this period comes the last group of plays, and in these, the fertility theme of *The Winter's Tale* is impossible to mistake. Fairly obvious even in *Cymbeline*, in the later play the ideas of the sudden fury of winter storms, the banishment and apparent death of the vegetation, the sullen self-absorption of the young plants covered over with snow, and the revival in spring, are too insistent to overlook. As for the last play of all, *The Tempest*, that has now been fairly proved to be an extraordinarily faithful presentation of the Greek ideas of initiation and of the ritual that accompanied them.[39] And, as we have seen, these initiation symbols are logical developments of fertility symbolism, with which they were, both in the Eleusinian rites and in Shakespeare's play, explicitly associated. There are five years of complete silence between *The Tempest* and the death of Shakespeare; and, from the standpoint of our thesis at any rate, the only possible development from the theme of *The Tempest* would have been the passion play itself.

9. Paean and Dithyramb

Let us now turn to music. Here we are dealing with an art so profoundly abstract, so utterly devoid of all naturalistic symbolism, so complete an artistic control over time-movement, that it has frequently been regarded as the most fundamental of arts. The first enunciation of this theory is in Plato's *Republic*, though it must have played an important part in Pythagorean conceptions even earlier; Schopenhauer is perhaps the most conspicuous modern exponent of it. "Tous les artes," says Baudelaire, "faisent *rejoindre* la musique."[40] Walter Pater's view is similar: "The arts may be represented as continually struggling after the law or principle of music, to a condition which music alone completely realizes; and one of the chief functions of aesthetic criticism, dealing with the products of art, new or old, is to estimate the degree in which each of those products approaches, in this sense, to the musical law."[41] The problem this envisages, a philosophy of history in which the arts symbolize culture and music the arts, has not yet been seriously attempted, owing, undoubtedly, to the extreme difficulty of being able to interpret the history of music in any but the most abstract, tenuous, and metaphorical cross-references.

Now beside this fundamental fact, that music is the central art, we place another. There has only been one systematic development of a musical tradition in the world, and that was produced by Western culture under the spiritual leadership of Christianity. There are great dramas in every great culture in the world today, but without belittling the loveliness of much Hindu, Mohammedan, or Chinese melody, there seems to be no one outside our own tradition we can point to as a great composer, as we can point to Bach, Mozart, or Beethoven as great composers.

In examining what we know of the history of Greek music the conviction breaks on us that it was precisely the sense of the mysterious, ultimate nature of music that paralysed the Hellenic development of the art. There are two tendencies traceable in Greek music, corresponding to the two branches of their religion. The first tendency, which belongs to the stately, orthodox, official Olympian religion, is best symbolized by the paean, or devotional hymn to the Olympian god of the arts, Apollo. The second tendency, associated with the passionate, orgiastic cult of Dionysus, is a development of the wild, ecstatic, irregularly constructed dithyramb we have mentioned. Now of these, the word *paean* appears in Homer as the name of a great physician,[42] and the connection between these two meanings of the word seems to be that the song came to be conceived as having a magical character. The same tendency is observable among American Indians, where each deity or totem has its own song, a development of its *numen*. The use of the song in curing melancholic disease is familiar to every reader of the Old Testament. As for the dithyramb, the magical nature of the music of Orpheus, the reformer of the Dionysiac cult, is too well known to dwell on. The master musician, who by his lyre could attract even inanimate objects to him, is a figure symbolic of the whole Greek conception of music, which was worked out in more rationalized terms by the Pythagoreans, who combined the worship of Apollo with the way of life prescribed by Orphism. Their interpretation of music was the rationalized development of magic we call occultism. If Orpheus could control the universe through music, that was only because the ultimate principles of the universe were connected with the elementary mathematical relationships of numbers, which again were expressed in the time-world by music. Hence, the "music of the spheres," the mysterious unheard music which only someone both musician and magician could evoke.

Similarly Plato, in the *Republic*, after remarking that all phenomena can be reduced to a priori relationships expressed spatially by mathematics and temporally by music, ascribes moral qualities to the various modes: those starting on too high a note are shrill and effeminate; those starting on too low a note are sullen and insubordinate [*Republic*, bk. 3, 411a–c]. In other words, the Greeks seem on the whole to have thought of music plastically, as a relation between tones. Their greatest cultural achievements were in the plastic arts, and in them they expressed their love of the finite, the easily bounded, the tangible. Music, which evoked such mysterious and fearful hints of infinity, they left in an abortive stage: perhaps the myth of the sirens, whose music was an irresistible but fatal lure, best expresses their opposition to the art.

Nevertheless, we have, in the paean and the dithyramb, the two essential elements in music. The Olympian religion, or, as Nietzsche called it, the Apollonian religion,[43] was the respectable religion of the processional, and the paean was accordingly a solemn devotional chant. The dithyramb, on the other hand, was fundamentally a dance; in it the bodily expression of rhythm came to the fore. Precisely the same development took place in the Middle Ages. There was the stately, academic plainchant, developed in a monastic tradition by retired scholars and devotees of the orthodox faith. Outside was the popular element: the ballad, the carol, the old festival dances absorbed by Christianity, all going to make up the folk song and the dance. Suddenly, just before the Renaissance, these two traditions fused. Sometimes the juncture was a bit unfortunate, as when a composer would make a Church anthem out of a contrapuntal setting of a bawdy army song, but nonetheless a systematic development of music started, which is now an essential part of our cultural tradition.

Where lay the difference between this development and that of the Greeks? The answer is fairly obvious. Music, to become an art form, needs three dimensions: it has to have a solid thickness of body or rhythm, length or melody, and breadth or harmony. And, of course, it was this harmonic development that Greek music, and all music except Western music, lacked. No other culture has ever had any idea of counterpoint, of the organic welding of melody and harmony into a rhythmic pattern. And it should be noted that the development of counterpoint is not "Western" in the sense of having been originated by the Teutonic tribes who destroyed the Roman Empire. The eddas and sagas of northern Europe give no hint of a future Bach. Counterpoint was a product of Christian genius through and through: the development from Greek mode to Western scale, which made counterpoint possible, was largely the work of two great Doctors of the Christian Church, St. Ambrose and St. Gregory, and as far as contrapuntal music goes, there is no relation between the quality of a nation's folk song and its contribution to systematic music, except perhaps an inverse one. Germany, the nexus of Western music, has a folk song far poorer than that of Ireland or Wales, which have done nothing for music.

When we turn to Christian theology, and the reasons for its conquest over Greek speculation, we are struck by the extraordinarily dynamic quality of the former. Where Greek virtues are all to some extent negative, expressed in terms of avoidance of extremes, Christianity rests on a vital unity of subjective factors. This dynamic quality and, in addition, the extraordinarily concrete nature of the Christian faith and its insistence on the historical nature of its God give evidence of an attitude to life much more congenial to a parallel cultural conquest of the time-world. Then again, the dynamic nature of Christianity works out, in theology, to the idea of a tension of opposites. This opposition finds perhaps its most direct theoretical formulation in the doctrine of the Trinity, in which the eternal creative activity of the Father and the temporal redemptive activity of the Holy Spirit are brought together by the impact of Jesus. The connection between this kind of thinking and the kind of artistic thinking that produced the tension-forms of Gothic cathedrals has been often noted.[44] Its connection with the development of contrapuntal music is perhaps even easier to trace, in view of the fact that the feeling of the magical power of music never entirely disappeared—even in the enlightened sixteenth century Orlando di Lasso was credited with the power of Orpheus.[45] It is perhaps less surprising that Paganini should, in a more superstitious age, have made half his fortune out of people who believed that his technique was literally diabolical in its skill. The same half-superstitious reverence for music was undoubtedly an influence on that very superstitious man Pope Gregory and helped to make the connection of music with the sacerdotal tradition more explicit. The unwillingness of the monks to experiment, out of respect for the Trinity, with any other than 3/4 rhythms is a random example.

To deal at all fully with this aspect of our thesis would extend its length to well over a hundred pages. As we propose making this extension later on[46] and are at present concerned only to unite music to the dramatic presentation of the concept of recurrence in religion, it may be considered sufficient if we present a few further suggestions in a summarized form.

10. Summary

A. The Jewish insistence on the importance of music in ritual must have played some part in the development of Christianity. The Chronicler's sole cultural interest is in music, and that seems to be true for Jewish culture generally. In early Christian art the figure of Orpheus, the master musician, insensibly melts, via David, into the Good Shepherd Jesus.

B. The Renaissance, when it came, was too much of a classical throwback to be of much help to music. The madrigal excepted, there seems to have been little in music we can explicitly call Renaissance; most of it stems from the Reformation and Counter-Reformation. The traditions which preserved music on the whole tended to mediate between extreme Catholic and extreme Protestant obscurantism. The Reformation, involving as it did the separation of Teutonic and Latin racial traditions, also brought the central development of music further north. Spain produced a dramatic but not a musical Renaissance: Germany produced a musical but not a dramatic one. The personal influence of Luther also played its part in establishing a cultural connection between religion and music, which the Calvinists were only too willing to destroy. In particular, the Protestant nations, as opposed to the Palestrina tradition in Italy, seem to have developed the concept of rhythm in music as a linear series of accents, a development which necessitated a conventionalizing of tonality. The maturation of the Elizabethan madrigal shows this transition from strict madrigal with vague tonality to the later airs based explicitly on a chromatic scale with major and minor chords as points of repose. The idea of equal temperament in music was, thus, implicit as early as Byrd.

C. This conventionalization made possible strict forms of musical drama, and, in consequence, the explicit illustration of the Christian tradition in independent art forms. From the Renaissance onward, music rather than the strict drama took over the task of the artistic presentation of the religious impulse already dealt with. First, we have the development of the opera, in the early seventeenth century, with Greek tragedy as a model. Out of this early opera grows the later opera and the oratorio. We have mentioned the fact that medieval drama began in the illustration of Christian doctrines by Bible stories, just as Greek drama had similarly treated Homeric stories. The supreme development of this belongs to the oratorio. At the climax of the oratorio comes Bach, who, working in music, was able, in a way that Shakespeare was not, to present, in his two greatest works, the *St. Matthew Passion* and the B Minor Mass, the supreme sacrifice and the supreme sacrament or symbol of it. The oratorio proper keeps the Greek tragedy form of recitativo or narration and chorus. The oratorio is, thus, an essentially tragic form. The opera, when similarly brought to its artistic culmination by Mozart, was established as a comedy or carnival-form. Along with these vocal forms go the strict instrumental forms of the fugue and the sonata, the development of each being also brought to its culmination by Bach and Mozart respectively. The fugue develops from the paean side of music: it is a very sophisticated product of the academic contrapuntal song. The sonata on the other hand is a development of the suite, and so is similarly connected with the dithyramb side. Both are, however, essentially forms in which a theme or group of themes go through a process of analytic development and are restated at the close in a more rigorously unified form. In other words, we are close to the archetypal pattern of recurrence we have already noted: the same disappearance and re-emergence pattern of the katabasis.

D. With the advent of romanticism these strict forms break up as art becomes more individualized. Beethoven, after tearing the sonata form to pieces in search of a complete subjective control of form, was forced to make a similar assault on the oratorio (Ninth Symphony) and the fugue in his final period. What he did for music Wagner did for music and drama, and in his gigantic Dionysiac mythology we have the climax of the antireligious art of the time. The tendencies of Scriabin toward a "Black Mass" we have already noted. Only César Franck preserved the forms of oratorio and fugue. The exhaustion of the possibilities of the chromatic scale in our own day makes it obvious that the rigidly conventionalized art forms of music based on this scale will break up and give place to something else. But as music is a group art form, this cannot be done theoretically: Schoenberg is a grim reminder of that fact. It cannot exist apart from a new and more co-operative form of society: and if we get that we shall assuredly get a new form of musical drama, as well as a renewed strength in religion, and the two things are bound to be associated. The ballet[47] is perhaps our nearest approach as yet to this form.

Bibliographical Note

The generalized and partly summarized nature of the argument has compelled me to refer to the general theses of books rather than to specific passages. Hence, the footnote references are mostly of a *passim* nature. The main ideas on which the essay is based are developed from Frazer, *The Golden Bough*, and Jung, *Psychology of the Unconscious*. The former work suggested in particular the "comedy" archetype in the Passion. I am indebted to Maud Bodkin, *Archetypal Patterns in Poetry*, for the phrase "archetypal pattern" and for some suggestions on the psychological connection between tragedy and sacrifice. The observations on the development from fertility cult to initiation and purgatorial symbols are based on previous work of my own.[48] I might also refer to the standard works on early Greek drama consulted: Cornford, *Origins of Attic Comedy*; Harrison, *Ancient Art and Ritual, Prolegomena to the Study of Greek Religion, Themis*; Norwood, *Greek Tragedy*. The comparisons suggested between Greek and Western conceptions of music and drama are based on Spengler, *Decline of the West*.[49] The more technical part of the music section is entirely my own, and adequate references would entail a much fuller treatment in the text than I have space for. The opening sections are also my own; the thesis of the three goods is developed from some suggestions of Dr. McCallum.[50]

18

The Diatribes of Wyndham Lewis:
A Study in Prose Satire

This paper, dated 1936, probably incorporates material from an essay on Lewis that Frye submitted for an honour English course which he took during his second year at Emmanuel College.[1] As part of the present essay found its way into "Wyndham Lewis: Anti-Spenglerian," Canadian Forum, *16 (June 1936), 21–2, it was apparently written during the early months of 1936.[2] Frye does not give page references for most of his quotations, but these are provided in the notes and in the citations within the text. It is not always clear which editions of Lewis Frye is citing. For* The Apes of God *he probably used the 1930 edition published in London by the Arthur Press, a book that is among the annotated copies in Frye's library, now in the Victoria University Library. The only other book by Lewis in the collection that he could have owned at the time he wrote the paper is* The Childermass, *section 1 (London: Chatto and Windus, 1928). No mark is recorded on the paper, but Frye earned a first for honour English during his second year at Emmanuel. The typescript is in the NFF, 1991, box 37, file 12.*

It is now generally recognized that the cult of sensibility preceding the French Revolution and a similar cult preceding the Russian Revolution were respectively the beginning and end of a fairly homogeneous development, the outlines of which become clearer as we move farther away from it. In its specifically artistic aspect this development produced what is usually called romanticism in its earlier stages, and Impressionism in its later, its most outstanding achievements being, appropriately enough, mainly French and Russian. The chaos of the Great War hastened its collapse and provoked a reaction, which, like most first reactions, contained a small number of genuinely new ideas in embryo, along with the clinging debris of the older ones. We seem to be witnessing the commencement of a new wave of cultural activity, steadily acquiring a shape and force of its own, though at present still largely backwash from its predecessor. In the plastic and graphic arts it has generally been described as "expressionism," to mark if off from the "Impressionism" it is attempting to replace. Whether it retains and extends this title or not, critics of the future will probably recognize in the two figures of T.S. Eliot and Wyndham Lewis the completion of the first stage of its literary development in England, in an era they will no doubt refer to as the Georgian sunset.

It seems fairly certain, even now, that Wyndham Lewis will live, to whatever extent he is to live, as much by virtue of his critical as his creative work. He is both painter and novelist, but neither his drawings nor his novels have attracted any more interest or discussion than his long treatises, here called diatribes, most important of which are *The Art of Being Ruled*, *The Lion and the Fox*, *Time and Western Man*, *Paleface*, *Hitler*, *The Diabolical Principle* and *The Dithyrambic Spectator*, and *Men without Art*. Lewis has never any doubts about his ability as an artist, but his attitude to these books is rather ambiguous. He says in *The Diabolical Principle*:

> Such an essay as *Time and Western Man* is not supposed to imitate in its form an attic temple. It is a sudden barrage of destructive criticism laid down about a spot where temples, it is hoped, may under its cover be erected.[3]

If any of these temples are his own, they would presumably be his two novels, *Tarr* and *The Apes of God*, his fantasias, *The Childermass* and *The Enemy of the Stars*, and the short stories in *The Wild Body*. In this paper we shall not be concerned with him as an "artist," but as the critical and apologetic author of the works mentioned, which we regard, for reasons given later, as essentially satires, and as constituting an art form quite as original and significant as any of the others. His drawings do not concern us, and his poetry I have not seen.[4]

Lewis derives his importance as a thinker from his attitude to the cultural development outlined above. Whatever strength or unity his diatribes possess they owe to the clarity of his perception of it in all its aspects, artistic, political, scientific, and philosophical. Each book lights up a different aspect of his criticism. *The Art of Being Ruled* gives the most complete presentation of the political side of his attack; *Time and Western Man*, of the literary and philosophical side: and from these two books the others radiate as more specialized applications of his attitude. *The Lion and the Fox* and *Men without Art* concern us chiefly in connection with Lewis's own view of art and its relation to satire.

The Industrial Revolution, says Lewis, ushered in a form of society far more fluid than anything that had preceded it. Industrial technique entails an incredibly rapid movement in society, of a kind unknown before it; methods of production are no sooner developed than they become old-fashioned, and society accustoms itself to incessant metamorphosis. This engenders in society a certain stereotype of thought, which Lewis calls "revolutionary," best symbolized by the advertisement. *The Art of Being Ruled* is devoted to showing that the imminent collapse of this form of society will result in something more stable and permanent, probably an economic world order governed by dictatorships, the ruler of the future being a closer approach to the philosopher-king than the world has yet seen. *Hitler* treats the Nazi movement in Germany as a symptom of this Caesarean birth; this book, it might be noted, was written in 1931, two years before Hitler came into power. In philosophy, similarly, since the Industrial Revolution society has been evolving a Heraclitean view of life, which identifies reality with motion and change. Most of the artists, philosophers, and politicians of the nineteenth and early twentieth centuries reflect this obsession with the ideas of movement and duration. When the doctrine of evolution appears, it is promptly transformed into a religion. God becomes a propelling life-force, and philosophy steadily tends toward a temporal explanation of reality, a process which reaches its logical culmination in Bergson's creative evolution. But Bergson is not the final step. For this time-obsession is of social origin, and its ultimate goal is political rather than metaphysical. Bergson's world-view was made concrete and consolidated by Spengler's philosophy, in which reality becomes, not a life-force, but history itself. The second part of *Time and Western Man* is devoted to an analysis of the time philosophies of our own day, emphasizing those of Alexander, Whitehead, Bertrand Russell, Einstein, Bergson, and Spengler, the last named singled out for a particularly slashing attack. This first part of the same book deals with cultural manifestations of this time-philosophy, as we have them in the work of Proust, Joyce, and Gertrude Stein. Art advances toward the presentation of the movement of time contemporaneously with philosophy: when we have

Bergson in philosophy, we have Proust's long record of life processes in
literature; and when philosophy reaches exhaustion and bankruptcy in
Spengler, literature reaches a similar point in the "prose-song" of Gertrude Stein and the wandering interior monologue of *Work in Progress*.[5]
Closely connected with this absorption in the theme of life-forces are, of
course, the ferocious and fortissimo assertions of the will to live, such as
we get in Nietzsche and Marinetti. Lewis opened his career, just before
the war, with a magazine called *Blast*, which was devoted to an attack
on futurism in its first issue (it produced only one more)[6] and was,
therefore, largely a blast against Marinetti. The vicious assault on
Nietzsche in *The Art of Being Ruled* is one of Lewis's best pieces of writing.[7] In literature, as a counterpoint to this, we have Hemingway and
Faulkner in the novel,[8] and, in a more subtle form, the tendency to glorify life as something in itself, to concentrate on the temporal force of
activity, to get down to what Lewis calls "the smoking-hot *inside* of
things" [*ABR*, 403], the preoccupation with the visceral, which charac-
terizes the work of D.H. Lawrence. This time-consciousness develops, of
course, a time-snobbery, a cultural parasitism living in the past and nib-
bling the fruits of tradition, the pedantry of Ezra Pound and the obscurantism of T.S. Eliot being examples. Time snobbery expands into space-
snobbery, a cult of the exotic and remote, which meets us in Gauguin
and the savage pilgrimage of Lawrence, a primitivist exalting of "dark"
or less civilized races at the expense of the whites. To this movement the
brilliant *Paleface*,[9] in many respects the best of all Lewis's books, is
devoted.

   The political inference from this "revolutionary" consciousness is, of
course, the liberal democracy, the forms of which we are vainly endeavouring to preserve. This form of society depends for its stability on the
creation of stereotypes of mass thinking, mass entertainment, mass
action. It depends, in other words, on a wholesale vulgarizing of the creative activity of art, the speculative activity of philosophy, the exploring
activity of science. Industry vulgarizes science; man believes himself to
be living in a scientific age because he can play with toys like radios and
automobiles, which he could not have acquired without science; and it is
only in this "popular mechanics" form that science really reaches him.
Politics vulgarizes philosophy: Darwin's thesis of the survival of the fit
becomes the excuse for massed murder. Spengler presses philosophical
concepts into a counsel of reactionary fatalism. So the ordinary man gets
hold of philosophy only in the forms of social stereotypes. Nietzsche,

Sorel, Spengler, and Freud are perhaps the most prominent vulgarizers of philosophical ideas. Lewis is, of course, even more interested in the vulgarizing of art, for a precisely similar process goes on there. Instead of the genuinely creative work of the rare and isolated genius, we find his techniques imitated by shrewd and clever craftsmen, who swarm together in schools, movements, tendencies, groups, and generally in what Lewis calls phalansteries. These cliques, who are naturally on their guard to see that no real genius is given a hearing, vulgarize art into movements which become, like vulgarized science and philosophy, essentially political phenomena. Lewis's two novels are satires on these herd-artists. *Tarr*, its scene laid in the cultural underworld of Paris, is built around the antithetical figures of *Tarr*, the genuine artist, and Kreisler, the typical parasite and charlatan. *The Apes of God* shifts the scene to London. A Greek with homosexual tendencies, called Zagreus, leads a vacuous moron, Daniel Boylen, through a kind of katabasis in which he is exposed to all sides of this vast interlocking arty "public," of the "bohemian" variety, of people with private incomes who make hobbies of art, music, literature, and revolutionary politics. Lewis's world is essentially that of *Antic Hay* and the biting London scenes of *Women in Love*.[10]

The complete individualizing of society resulting from democracy, and the decay of great art, combine to provide the arty charlatan with one of his favourite shibboleths, *épater le bourgeois*.[11] Lewis makes the most of all the antimoral antics indulged in by what he calls the "revolutionary simpleton."[12] There is the cultivation of homosexuality by those who have no special gift for it, but cherish it as something delightfully wicked. There are the quixotic floutings of the taboos placed on sex by those who, in rebelling against convention, have not escaped from it. The usual result of such revolts is merely a further preoccupation with sex. There is the increased probing of abnormal states of mind in search of new thrills, which gives us the cult of the child, the affectation of naivety in Gertrude Stein's prolonged babble, of the subnormal intelligence in the giants of Picasso and Epstein, of the neurotic in all the Freudian literature, and of the whole development of sadism and diabolism explored by Praz (whom Lewis claims as his disciple) in *The Romantic Agony*.[13] The entire movement, from Rousseau to D.H. Lawrence, is permeated with primitivism: the sentimental admiration, by a sterile and senile society, of the untamed, the unexplored, the uncultivated, the amorphous.[14]

Such is in very broad outlines Lewis's attitude to the bourgeois society we are now gradually outgrowing. It will be noted that it is altogether a critical, polemic attitude. I have defined satire as the examination of society from the standpoint of a moralist, and I have used the word *moralist* as meaning one who works with pragmatic rather than dogmatic standards, who appeals to common sense rather than doctrine or tradition. The mind of the satirist is antithetic; that is, it is in an attitude of antagonism to its subject, and it is on its guard against a thesis of any kind, quick to pounce on it when it becomes an overstatement. The satirist addresses the common-sense jury rather than the expert judge. Now the reason why I describe the diatribes of Lewis as satires is because they take essentially this point of view. He says:

> I have said to myself that I will fix my attention upon those things that have most meaning for me. All that seems to me to contradict or threaten those things I will do my best to modify or to defeat, and whatever I see that favours and agrees with those things I will support and do my best to strengthen. In consequence, I shall certainly be guilty of injustice, the heraclitean 'injustice of the opposites.' But how can we evade our destiny of being 'an opposite,' except by becoming some grey mixture, that is in reality just nothing at all?[15]

So such books as *Time and Western Man*, from which this quotation comes, are admitted to be polemics. Lewis could have evaded his destiny of being an opposite by taking any other point of view than the satirist's. No systematic philosopher and no creative artist unconcerned with the satiric attack would see everything lined up as black, white, and a sneaking cowardly grey. As a satirist, Lewis criticizes effectively enough the existing time-obsession in art and thought, from the standpoint of the common sense that recognizes space as well as time. Where artists, following the dicta of Baudelaire and Pater, try to approach the musical in literature, Lewis points out the integrity and independence of the plastic ideal; where relativity attacks even mathematics, Lewis the satirist is there to protest that two and two absolutely make four. But Lewis's attack on our Heraclitean stereotypes is not based on any intelligible dogmas of his own. The satirist has no dogmas. The difficulty with Lewis is that he is not perfectly conscious of his own position: he thinks he has a solid dogmatic foundation, with the result that his reaction develops into an ethical dualism, of the sort outlined in *Men without Art*, which will meet us in a moment. But the fact remains that whenever

Lewis is concerned with specific criticism of an artist's work he is usually brilliant, and whenever he relapses into dogma we are seldom far
from a platitude or from some dishonest polemical dodge. He has, it
cannot be insisted too strongly, a purely reactive mind, not at all a systematic or structural one. In the criticism of a specific text he becomes
witty, pungent, and incisive, his lumbering style (of which more later)
springs into life, crystallizes into epigrams, rounds out its rhythmic periods, and coins unforgettable phrases. In the constructive field he is dull,
pompous, incoherent, and almost unbelievably inconsistent. Here he is
on Gertrude Stein:

> It is in a thick, monotonous prose-song that Miss Stein characteristically
> expresses her fatigue, her energy, and the bitter fatalism of her nature. Her
> stories are very often long—all the longer, too, because everything has to be
> repeated half a dozen times over. In the end the most wearisome dirge it is
> possible to imagine results, as slab after slab of this heavy, insensitive, com-
> mon prose-song churns and lumbers by. . . . What is the matter with it is,
> probably, that it is so *dead*. Gertrude Stein's prose-song is a cold, black suet-
> pudding. We can represent it as a cold suet-roll of fabulously-reptilian
> length. Cut it at any point, it is the same thing; the same heavy, sticky,
> opaque mass all through, and all along. It is weighted, projected, with a
> sibylline urge. It is mournful and monstrous, composed of dead and inani-
> mate material. It is all fat, without nerve. Or the evident vitality that
> informs it is vegetable rather than animal. Its life is a low-grade, if tena-
> cious, one; of the sausage, by-the-yard, variety. . . . The monstrous, desper-
> ate, soggy *lengths* of primitive mass-life, chopped off and presented to us as
> a never-ending prose-song, are undoubtedly intended as an epic contribu-
> tion to the present mass-democracy. The texture of the language has to be
> jumbled, cheap, slangy and thick to suit. It must be written in a slovenly,
> straight-off fashion, so that it may appear to be more 'real'. . . . (she may be
> described as the reverse of Patience sitting on a monument—she appears,
> that is, as a Monument sitting upon patience). [*TWM*, 61, 62]

This is excellent writing, though it gets much of its effect from cumulative repetition of the sort attacked. But here is a constructive suggestion
in the field of social reform:

> I have somewhat modified my views since I wrote that book (*The Art of
> Being Ruled*) as to the best procedure for ensuring the true freedom of

which I have just spoken. I now believe, for instance, that people should be compelled to be freer and more 'individualistic' than they naturally desire to be, rather than that their native unfreedom and instinct towards slavery should be encouraged and organized. I believe they could with advantage be compelled to remain absolutely alone for several hours every day; and a week's solitary confinement, under pleasant conditions (say in mountain scenery), every two months, would be an excellent provision.[16]

It might be noted that the mountaintop cure is pure Nietzsche. Similarly, *Paleface*, after making some of the most memorable criticisms of Lawrence that are ever likely to be made, winds up at the end by suggesting a matrimonial bureau for marrying Finns to Spaniards and generally systematizing miscegenation, so as to usher in painlessly the racial melting pot of the future [*PF*, 285–6]. Whether these suggestions are made seriously or not does not affect my point. But the most striking contrast is in *Men without Art*, where Lewis follows the best hostile criticism of T.S. Eliot yet made with his own creed of art, which is perhaps the most transcendently asinine ever composed.[17]

Lewis regards art as formalized expression: it is essentially something plastic and static and, therefore, differing in kind from historical phenomena, with which Spengler would class it. Lewis started out as a painter, and for him art means the stationary arts. All through his pronouncements on the subject there runs a hazy paronomasia associating the general term *art*, which includes music and poetry, with the more restricted use of the word which relates only to painting. Sentences like this keep recurring:

Art is as much a 'timeless' thing as technical invention is a creature of time. Its values are more static, as physically it is more static. [*TWM*, 37]

There are amateur philosophers (I have met a few) who assume, because they know that all philosophy is a search for reality, that any brand of it which calls itself "realism" must be the true philosophy. Lewis similarly assumes that real art is that which explicitly calls itself "art." He regards Oriental painting as the highest of artistic developments: Western culture, never having been quite static enough, never approached the Asiatic rigidity of outline. He says:

The fact is that the best West European art has never been able to be 'classic,' in the sense of achieving a great formal perfection. The nature of our semi-barbaric cultures has precluded that. [*TWM*, 9]

It was no doubt that same semi-barbaric culture that was responsible for the phrase "best West" in the above quotation. The West's big moment came in the discovery of science by Renaissance Italy, a period which also saw what Lewis considers the highest development of Western art. The great cultural achievements of Europe are, Lewis thinks, a product of the Latin mind and tradition. In *The Lion and the Fox* he says, several times:

> The flower of european civilization—and the only portion of it that can hold its own for a moment against the productions of the East, or of asiatic or egyptian antiquity—is to be found in the italian renaissance. . . . It is very noticeable how healthy and physically successful the type represented in italian renaissance art is: probably, excepting the greek and the negro, the most normally balanced physical human type of which we have a record. . . . It would seem almost, to look at these pictures, as though all the animal health of Europe, too, has flowed up from the latin soil.[18]

With German development of contrapuntal music he has no sympathy, as he knows nothing about it: his attitude to music changes from the perfunctory lip-service of *Time and Western Man* to the overt hostility of *Men without Art*. Nor has he, of course, any sympathy with the prophetic or emotional appeal derived from the Hebraic culture.

There is a negative side to Lewis's attitude, of course, other than the mere negation of the bad to the good or the false to the true. There are such things as dynamic arts, arts that depend on movement, such as music and poetry, and these arts cannot be described in purely plastic terms; they are rhythmic in their organization. Lewis is aware of their existence, but the gestures he makes in their direction are rather nervous and spasmodic, as in the following quotation:

> I prefer . . . the prose-movement—easy, uncontrolled and large—to the insistent, hypnotic rhythm, favoured by most fashionable political thought in the West. For me, there should be no adventitiously imposed *rhythm* for life in the rough. . . . *Musical-politics*—as the uplift politics of millennial doctrinaires can be termed—are, without any disguise, the politics of hypnotism, enregimentation, the sleep of the dance. [*TWM*, 26]

This attitude is elaborated through the whole of his preposterous book called *The Dithyrambic Spectator*, which consists of a number of respectful comments on a book about the rise of plastic art in Egypt, and a number of derisive comments on a book about the rise of dynamic art in Greece.[19] It is evident from the quotation given above that to Lewis a rhythm means a march rhythm, just as pattern might, to anyone equally ignorant of the plastic arts, mean merely that pattern of a linoleum rug. Spengler notes a similar reaction on the part of the Chinese to Western music [*DW* 1:228].

It is obvious, of course, that all moving arts have plastic qualities implicit, and all stationary arts rhythmic ones. In order to ward off this elementary objection, Lewis brings up another antithesis, equally false, but more popular, to buttress the other. This, of course, is the antithesis of intellect and emotion. The side of man busied with conscious formulation is the intellectual side; therefore, the greatest art is intellectual, formalized, plastic, a product of deliberate consciousness. The closer literature gets to this the better; the progressive or temporal approach of Proust and Gertrude Stein is musical and, therefore, emotional. Lewis, in attacking Bergson and Spengler,[20] makes the most of the fact that they represent to some extent a reaction against pure intellect. Bergson's point is, of course, that activity is a homogeneous unit and that both intellect and emotion are critical reactions to activity, not sources of it. Lewis waves all this aside: for him there is only the rational and the nonrational.

Now, what about literature? This "prose-movement—easy, uncontrolled and large" [*TWM*, 26]: is it not, when read aloud, a succession of sounds in time like music? The other side of Lewis's one-sided and partial view of art, which becomes so painfully silly when elaborated into a dogma, comes out precisely here, in his own writing. Rhythm is at least as important a quality in prose as a sense of plastic form, however "easy, uncontrolled and large," and Lewis's aesthetic attitude seems to be largely a "barrage" designed to cover the fact that he possesses no sense of rhythm.

At the end of *Men without Art* Lewis quotes the opening pages of *The Ivory Tower* and *Point Counter Point* in order to demonstrate the not very soul-shaking fact that the former is a better novel than the latter [*MWA*, 300–4]. On examination, however, there appears to be nothing very much actually wrong with Huxley's writing: it is perfectly competent work on its own level of artistic ability. But turn to the opening page of *Tarr*:

Paris hints of sacrifice. But here we deal with that large dusty facet known to indulgent and congruous kind: it is in its capacity of delicious inn and majestic Baedeker, where western Venuses twang its responsive streets and hush to soft growl before its statues, that it is seen. It is not across its Thébaïde that the unscrupulous heroes chase each other's shadows: they are largely ignorant of all but their restless personal lives.

Inconceivably generous and naïve faces haunt the Vitelotte Quarter.—We are not, however, in a Hollywood camp of pseudo-cowpunchers (though 'guns' tap rhythmically the buttocks). Art is being studied.—But 'art' is not anything serious or exclusive: it is the smell of oil paint, Henri Murger's *Vie de Bohème*, corduroy trousers, the operatic Italian model: but the poetry, above all, of linseed oil and turpentine.[21]

One sees here, in the forced, strained vocabulary, the cacophonous sound, the broken-winded stumbling rhythm, the laborious effort at an originality that succeeds only in being bizarre, not competent mediocre writing but merely bad writing. In the more argumentative works the sentences tend to lengthen out to bewildering proportions. "Germanic" or "Teutonic" is a favourite term of abuse with Lewis; he applies it impartially to Frenchmen like Zola and Americans like Gertrude Stein.[22] But in this abusive sense it is surely the only possible epithet for such a sentence as the following, selected at random from *The Diabolical Principle*:

When english was only written in England, it is true, it flourished up into a literature, one bearing comparison with any; but I am not concerned about english especially, so much as pure speech: literatures in any event depend upon circumstances that do not exist now in England or in any country: if a universal tongue is being manufactured in Paris (at the sign of the transplanted *Swan of Avon* within cat-call of the Odéon or elsewhere) as the literary bagmen or big and little 'drummers' of Letters and Art announce—in the most up-and-coming stale journalese of somebody else's mother tongue that I have ever encountered—why has that volapuk the anglo-saxon tongue as a main component at this time of the day?—what a foolish accident, or really serious mistake! [*DPDS*, 4–5]

There is no doubt that in this megalith Lewis has got the prose movement he prefers—very easy, very uncontrolled, and very large. See how it looks in telegraphic form:

When english was only written in England comma it is true comma it flourished up into a literature comma one bearing comparison with any semico-
lon but I am not concerned about english especially comma so much as
pure speech colon literatures in any event depend upon circumstances that
do not exist now in England or in any country colon if a universal tongue is
being manufactured in Paris left bracket at the sign of the transplanted ital-
ics Swan of Avon roman within cat hyphen call of the Odéon or elsewhere
right bracket as the literary bagmen or big and little quote drummers
unquote of Letters and Art announce dash in the most up hyphen and
hyphen coming stale journalese of somebody else apostrophe s mother
tongue that I have ever encountered dash why has that volapuk the anglo
hyphen saxon tongue as a main component at this time of the day question
mark dash what a foolish accident comma or really serious mistake excla-
mation mark

And what applies to the construction of Lewis's alleged sentences
extends itself to the construction of his arguments. Taken in groups, the
sentences follow one another like elephants in a circus parade, the trunk
of each twisted in the tail of the one ahead of it. He drives home his
points only through the most infuriating prolixity. He is a good deal of a
pointilliste: step by step he gives a curious effect of provocative and
stimulating brilliance, but as soon as a general design becomes imperative, the outlines fade away and dissolve. At the end of a book one
becomes vaguely aware of having read a large discrete quantity of
worthwhile statements, but without any unified sense of what the book
is about. This frustrated feeling deepens to exasperation when the book
is reread and the same result occurs. I am speaking of readers who finish his books; but his books are unusually difficult to finish. One simply
cannot bore the whole way through the deafening unaccented clatter of
words. The same defect vitiates the novels, of course: *The Apes of God* is
full of big Rabelaisian ideas that misfire completely, such as the split-
man's litany and the symbolic costume scene,[23] because there is no
rhythmic organization, as in Rabelais, to carry them through. The
scheme of that novel, essentially, as we have said, a kind of katabasis or
descent into hell, requires a terrific sweep and swing to bring it off; what
we get is the confused rattle of a train going through a tunnel.

One of the most noticeable features of Lewis's style is his huge vocabulary. In this he is quite within his rights as a satirist: the use of a large
vocabulary gives an effect in prose similar to the use of double and tri-

ple rhymes in poetry; as he says: "It is in the long run bluff to use our vocabularies except for comic purposes."[24] This preoccupation with words, as well as the barking colloquial style which unites them, has caused Edgell Rickword, in his otherwise admirable essay on Lewis in *Scrutinies*, volume 2, to associate the style with Nashe.[25] But the most remarkable virtue of Nashe's style is its amazing continuity, and the most outstanding vice of Lewis's his complete lack of it. Nashe is difficult to lay down, Lewis difficult to get through; Nashe is linear, Lewis punctiliar. What makes the remark even more questionable is the fact that in *Time and Western Man* Lewis has shown, in a strikingly brilliant passage, the similarity of Nashe's style to Joyce's [*TWM*, 106–9], and has set himself firmly in opposition to both. Beside the broken phrases of Bloom's monologue in *Ulysses* Lewis puts those of Jingle in *The Pickwick Papers*.[26] But though opposed to Nashe and Joyce, Lewis suffers from the same excess of verbalism, and in avoiding the jingle he merely falls into the jangle. Parallels to his curiously muscle-bound prose are not easy to find; he is certainly closer to Carlyle than to Nashe, and perhaps closer to Nathaniel Ward[27] than to either. As has been said, this criticism applies particularly to those passages in which he is doing what he is not by nature fitted to do, that is, sustaining and developing an argument. In specific criticism, in abuse and invective of all kinds, his writing is admirable. Lewis's prose, in short, is rather like a brook, if one might use so linear a metaphor: clear, rapid, brilliant, and vigorous on the surface, but merely mud and rocks at any depth.

In his criticism of Galsworthy in *Scrutinies*, volume 1, D.H. Lawrence remarks that in *The Forsyte Saga* there are no genuine people, but only Forsytes and anti-Forsytes, the latter, including Irene and Bosinney, being as much parasites on the Forsytes as the Forsytes are parasites on society, equally bound by fetters of class and money, equally snobbish and herd-minded.[28] This is a distinction it is possible to apply to a good many situations. The relation of Bosinney to Soames Forsyte[29] seems to me exactly the relation of Lewis to Bloomsbury. Just as Bosinney believes himself an individual genius because he is an anti-Forsyte, so Lewis calls himself an "artist" because he is anti-Bloomsbury and exploits as far as possible the fact that the people he attacks are on the whole of minor importance. There are several kinds of charlatans in the world of art, and the swarming, jabbering throng of bohemians and superbohemians, all vigorously criticizing and satirizing each other's work, are easily identified. More complex are the anticharlatans, people who cultivate some special pose designed to mark themselves off from the others. There is the eremitic anticharlatan, personified in Robinson Jeffers, who renounces society, taking care however not to escape from the critics or the journalists. There is the pedantic anticharlatan of the Pound variety, who makes a front-window display of erudition. There is the portentous anticharlatan of the Thomas Wolfe type, whose method is the straightforward self-distention of the frog in Aesop, confident that someone will eventually mistake him for an ox if he blows long enough and hard enough.[30] Compared to these, Lewis is really a very simple type of anticharlatan. For bohemia, after all, is the only milieu of his novels; he escapes from it far less even than Aldous Huxley does. Lewis has pointed out that the sex rebels of modern society seldom canalize sex, but remain more preoccupied with it than ever.[31] In the same way he himself is completely preoccupied with bohemia, and Stephen Spender's contemptuous epithet of "public-school satire" applied to *The Apes of God*[32] is hardly too strong. Wyndham Lewis is the jester in the court of Bloomsbury. His early vorticist antics are pure bohemian advertisement, and all his attacks on Ezra Pound cannot disguise the parallelism of their careers. They began together, each has defended a right-wing political dictator, and the rather shrewish scolding of the latter half of *Men without Art* echoes the raucous cackle of the later *Cantos*.

In calling Lewis's art form a diatribe we made use of a conception of Spengler's. To quote from *The Decline of the West*:

> As to the living representatives of these new and purely intellectual creations, the men of the "New Order" upon whom every decline-time founds such hopes, we cannot be in any doubt. They are the fluid megalopolitan Populace, the rootless city-mass . . . that has replaced the People. . . . They are the market-place loungers of Alexandria and Rome, the newspaper-readers of our own corresponding time; the "educated" man who then and now makes a cult of intellectual mediocrity and a church of advertisement. . . . Correspondingly, there is a characteristic form of public effect, the *Diatribe*. First observed as a Hellenistic phenomenon, it is an efficient form in *all* Civilizations. Dialectical, practical and plebeian through and through, it replaces the old meaningful and far-ranging Creation of the great man by the unrestrained Agitation of the small and shrewd, ideas by aims, symbols by programs. . . . It appeals not to the best but to the most, and it values its means according to the number of successes obtained by them. [*DW*, 1:359–60].

Now this seems, at first sight, to be exactly the kind of document Lewis is most concerned to attack and expose, so that his own controversial works would seem to be antidiatribes, diatribes to end diatribes. But Spengler describes this form as essentially a vehicle of propaganda, and just as the best art conceals art, so the best propaganda conceals propaganda. Let us return to Lewis's own remark about his works:

> Such an essay as *Time and Western Man* is not supposed to imitate in its form an attic temple. It is a sudden barrage of destructive criticism laid down about a spot where temples, it is hoped, may under its cover be erected. [*DPDS*, 32]

This sounds like propaganda, at any rate. Let us return to another remark:

> But how can we evade our destiny of being 'an opposite,' except by becoming some grey mixture, that is in reality just nothing at all? [*TWM*, 136]

So there can be little doubt that these works are propaganda, and they may, therefore, be examined purely as such.

One of the most frequently used weapons of propaganda is the pun, by which I mean an illegitimate associating of a word and an idea. I have spoken of the amateur philosophers who call themselves realists because philosophy is admittedly a search for reality. Similarly, an agnostic attacking religion will probably make extensive use of the word *mystic*, not because he knows or cares what it means, but because it sounds something like *misty* and *mystery*, and can, therefore, do duty as an abusive epithet, for he knows that his readers will instinctively turn a technical word into a commonplace one whenever they get a chance to do so. This is only a random example: of course every newspaper is full of puns on such words as liberty, democracy, socialism, and so on. The honest writer, not concerned with propaganda, will define and explain his terms as he goes along.

The prose satires of Nashe and Milton, of course, are densely packed with puns, but as most of their work is explicitly invective, this kind of verbalism becomes an easily recognized literary device. But Lewis pretends to something more than invective; he claims to appeal to objective truth, and if he does the same thing, his works count as propaganda, that is, as interested, dishonest writing. Take the following from *Time and Western Man*:

> It (the time-philosophy) is the fruit, of course, of the puritan mind, born in the nineteenth century upon the desolate principles promoted by the too-rapidly mechanized life of the European.[33]

Now the purpose of what I call the pun is, of course, to arouse unfavourable feelings toward whatever is attacked by associating it with something else generally recognized as undesirable. Most people have a vague animus against Puritanism; so Lewis takes a word belonging to a seventeenth-century religious movement and attaches it to the nineteenth-century philosophy he is getting after. The sentence is so badly constructed that the natural way of reading it is to take "born" as modifying "puritan mind," thereby suggesting that Puritanism actually arose in the nineteenth century. This is not, of course, the first time that Puritanism and nineteenth-century bourgeois morality have been associated or confused, which makes it all the easier for Lewis to trade on the prejudice. The whole argument of *Time and Western Man*, however, turns on the word *romanticism*, the name generally given to the cultural accompaniment of the Industrial Revolution. On page 22 of this book Lewis says:

> In analysing 'romance' the first definition required, perhaps, is to this effect: *the 'romantic' is the opposite of the real*. Romance is a thing that is in some sense non-existent. For instance, 'romance' is the reality of yesterday, or of to-morrow; or it is the reality of somewhere else.
>
>   Romance is the great traditional enemy of the Present. And the reason for the contemporary enmity to the mind of Greek Antiquity is because that mind was an 'ahistorical' mind—without perspective. (Italics in the original. The reason that 'ahistorical' is in inverted commas is that the idea is taken from Spengler—an unusual concession.)[34]

On page 25 he says:

> In the modern 'classic–romantic' opposition, Romantic is the warm, popular, picturesque expression, as contrasted with the formal calm of the Classical. . . . If Racine is your 'classic,' and Shakespeare your 'romantic,' then 'romantic,' in that instance, wins the day. Between Pope and Marlowe the

same thing happens, in my opinion. . . . So in that connection the 'romantic' is the real thing, I believe, and not the imitation. [*TWM*, 9]

All that this means is, of course, that when we call a sixteen-year-old schoolgirl "romantic" and when we call Shakespeare "romantic," we are using the word in two absolutely different senses, which it is impossible honestly to confuse, or even associate except in a dictionary. What Lewis is ultimately attacking is nineteenth-century romanticism, and "romantic" in this sense means something else again, entirely distinct from the other two. But Lewis wishes to associate this "romanticism" with the abusive sense of the word in connection with the "romancing" of an imaginative child, and in order to quash any feeble protest against this brings together by brute strength the "romantic" idle dreamer and the "romantic" Shakespeare. There is actually an intervening association with the medieval "romance." Fortunately, Lewis spared us more than a hasty and glossed-over reference to the *romance* languages.

Of all the critical observations on Wyndham Lewis, two similarly phrased ones call for discussion. Mr. G.W. Stonier, in *Gog, Magog*, calls him the greatest natural satirist the English have produced since Hogarth,[35] and Humbert Wolfe calls him one of the best natural metaphysicians the English have ever produced. We shall have to divide through by "natural," as we do not know what a natural satirist is, still less what a natural metaphysician is. It seems a curiously ill-assorted pair of remarks about one author. We have shown how the satirist is everything that the metaphysician is not: pragmatic where the metaphysician is dogmatic, concerned with aberration where the metaphysician looks for the typical, concrete where the metaphysician is abstract. Many of the greatest satirists of English literature—Nashe, Swift, both Samuel Butlers—have taken a fling at the metaphysicians. Not that there is any great gulf fixed between them: in my opinion there is an intermediate type, the preacher, the prophet, the orator, the censor, or whatever one wishes to call him, who starts with a certain philosophy and applies it to society, becoming satiric whenever society falls short of his standards. This type is extremely varied: artists so completely different as Blake, Carlyle, Matthew Arnold, Bernard Shaw, and D.H. Lawrence belong to it; but of these, perhaps only Blake could be called philosophic in the narrower sense of metaphysical.

The association with Hogarth has this merit, that it does bring out the fact that Lewis's satire is essentially caricature. The praise of "greatest since Hogarth" is to my mind extravagant: Lewis's range of studies is exceedingly limited, and he has nothing of the universality of such intervening caricaturists as Rowlandson or Dickens. But take this from *Bestre*, a story in *The Wild Body*:

> His very large eyeballs, the small saffron ocellatin in their centre, the tiny spot through which light entered the obese wilderness of his body; his bronzed bovine arms, swollen handles for a variety of indolent little ingenuities; his inflated digestive case, lent their combined expressiveness to say these things; with every tart and biting condiment that eye-fluid, flaunting of fatness (the well-filled), the insult of the comic, implications of indecency, could provide. Every variety of bottom-tapping resounded from his dumb bulk. His tongue stuck out, his lips eructated with the incredible indecorum that appears to be the monopoly of liquids, his brown arms were for the moment genitals, snakes in one massive twist beneath his mamillary slabs, gently riding on a pancreatic swell, each hair on his oil-bearing skin contributing its message of porcine affront.[36]

This is Lewis at his best, and it is masterly caricature, even if does rather stick out as a conscious *tour de force* against the development of the story. Now of all the types of satire caricature is the most preoccupied with the abnormal. There seems some justification, therefore, for Lewis's associating himself, in *Paleface*, with Thomist realism, which holds that universals are real and that individuals are aberrations. One would think, then, that he would have at least some sympathy with Platonic dualism. But no; in *Men without Art* Plato becomes the granddaddy of all romantics [*MWA*, 188–90]; his ideas are not in any way norms, but shadows in dreamland, and dreamland, we have seen, is not the true world. But is it the world of artistic creation? Well, yes and no, depending on how Lewis is feeling. On page 19 of *Time and Western Man* he says:

> Romance and reality, these are the two terms we most often employ to contrast what we regard as dream and truth respectively. The 'romantic' approach to a thing is the unreal approach. [*TWM*, 3]

On page 50 he says:

> Artistic expression is a dream-condition, and its interpretation must be

kept clear of sex-analysis, or else the dreamer passes over immediately into waking life, and so we get no art, and are left with nothing but sex on our hands, and can no longer avail ourselves of the dream-condition. [*TWM*, 34]

Again, are the subjects of art supposed to be eternally plastic, or are they arrested movement? Blake defended the importance of outline even more vigorously than Lewis,[37] but he made it clear that to him form was always the incorporation of energy. But with Lewis the answer to all such tiresome questions seems to depend on his liver or the exigencies of polemic. In *The Dithyrambic Spectator* he says:

Into the egyptian *living death*, again, a good deal of the *rigor mortis* has passed. And that suits art admirably. It asks nothing better than a corpse, and it thrives upon bones. Did not Cezanne bellow at his sitter when he fell off the chair, 'You're *moving*! Les pommes, ça ne bouge pas!' He preferred apples, in short, not because he otherwise discriminated between men and apples, but because men moved, whereas apples did not. [*DPDS*, 181]

But we have seen his eagerness to seize on the "deadness" of Gertrude Stein's writing and Picasso's painting when he can thereby establish a debating point against them. And in criticizing such thinkers as Spengler or Nietzsche, Lewis comes off best when he criticizes, not their doctrines, but the social effects of their doctrines. This is the typically satiric approach; it is exactly the attitude of Voltaire to Leibnitz, of Swift to Descartes, of Shaw to Herbert Spencer. But to criticize them on their own ground would imply a coherent metaphysical basis of his own, and this Lewis has obviously not got. It is difficult to see how even Humbert Wolfe could have called him a metaphysician.

We are now in a better position to understand that Spengler's conception of the diatribe applies directly to the polemic works of Lewis. What Lewis claims to be defending, of course, is true art, distinguished from bastard art by its assimilation to politics and its commercialization. With regard to the latter he says:

The same glittering of discreetly hooded eye of the fanatical advertiser, exists in the region of art or social life as elsewhere—only in social life it is their own personalities that people are advertising, while in art it is their own personally manufactured goods only. . . . And these more blandly-lighted worlds are as full as the Business world, I believe fuller, of those people who seem especially built for such methods, so slickly does the glove fit. [*TWM*, 23]

He becomes very much annoyed with Diaghilev for making a good thing out of the ballet [*TWM*, 31–3]—that is enough, apparently, with some *sotto voce* grumbling about the "epicene" sexual organization of the dancers [*TWM*, 33], to consign the ballet to bohemia and perdition. Yet I question if anyone understands the commercial methods of selling one's personally manufactured goods better than Lewis. His habit of perpetually referring to his earlier books and quoting extensively from them is perhaps of small importance. But he uses all the stock commercial tricks. He flatters his readers by telling them that they must be exceptionally gifted or they would not be reading his book. He says in the introduction to *The Art of Being Ruled*:

> Most books have their *patients*, rather than their *readers*, no doubt. But some degree of health is postulated in the reader of this book. . . . A book of this description is not written for an audience already there, prepared to receive it, and whose minds it will fit like a glove. There must be a good deal of stretching of the receptacle, it is to be expected. [*ABR*, xi, xii]

What women's clubber could resist an invitation like that? "Have you read Wyndham Lewis?" she will say at the next meeting of her bridge club, in the intervals of munching salted peanuts and wondering whether to bid four spades or five hearts. "You know how D.H. Lawrence says everything is internal and talks so much about sex; well, this man says things should be external and we don't need to stress sex so much." If Lewis ever becomes as popular at such gatherings as Lawrence, it will be owing to his shrewd recognition of the fact that the writer who overstates one side of a case is easier to understand than one who tries to be impartial. And he has another trick, of befogging a platitude with portentous phrases signifying that it is a profound truth only very intelligent people like him can discover, and only very intelligent people like his reader appreciate. A remark like this is typical:

> So what we generally name 'the new' is the very old, or the fairly old. It is as well to point this out, and even to stress it, since it is an impressive fact not sufficiently recognized. [*TWM*, 36]

His most widely publicized trick is his puffing up of himself, which is, of course, an appeal to society's passive instinct to take a man at his own valuation. His cocksureness and calm assumption of immense intellect makes the most arrant bluffing of Shaw look like a naked nun. This again he turns on his opponents when it suits his argument to do so:

> I refer to the vulgarization of the authentic and lofty 'detachment' of the 'supermen'—of a Shakespeare, a Pascal, or a Machiavelli—and of the penetrating truth of their vision of life (which made matchwood of all human disguises and embellishments) for the use of a swarming 'intellectualist' and artistic tribe of subsupermen. This swarming and restless minority, I would argue, has no right whatever to these things. [*DPDS*, 93]

It has no right to them, apparently, because Lewis wants to play with them. He says, for instance:

> Since, then, in one form or another, the eventual success of 'radical' ideas seems to me assured, I do not see why, in books such as mine, and those in which I am interested, the 'transitional' pretences cannot be dropped. It is of far greater importance to influence a minority in an intelligent direction, quite outside the parrot-cries of 'Left' or of 'Right' altogether, than for any intelligent person to do the hack-work of 'revolution,' which can be performed by one man as well as another. It is a machine-minding job (the mob is here the machine): it is not an intelligent occupation. [*DPDS*, 147–8]

These quotations are both from *The Diabolical Principle*. He says in *Paleface*:

> I have been denounced as a 'champion' or 'saviour,' and that charge I must deal with once and for all, if only to be able to prosecute my function of 'impartial observer.' [*PF*, 3]

This, of course, is a stock satiric pose: it is the satirist's business to make himself invulnerable if he can. Milton, in his prose satire, assumed an invincible priggishness and incorruptible virtue, and Lewis makes the same assumptions about his intellect merely for the same reason. But it is precisely because he is not an "impartial spectator" that Lewis's satire weakens into dogmatism and tries to make a philosophical principle out of his reaction to the time-philosophy.

His place in English literature is obviously as the successor of Bernard Shaw. He is, like Shaw, a "personal appearance artist,"[38] perhaps more important as a critic, certainly a far worse writer, and about as much of a humbug and windbag. And no more than Shaw is he a philosopher. It would take too long to examine the frantic muddle of the second part of *Time and Western Man*, and would be irrelevant in any case. The question, however, does arise: What is the philosophic unity, if there be one, behind Lewis's work?

It is obviously something not quite clearly revealed to Lewis himself, for he keeps feeling around for all sorts of quasi-dualistic theories to rest on. And of course it is not beyond possibility that his "barrage" conceals it among other things. Now it is a commonplace of psychoanalysis that the thing troubling the neurotic is simply whatever he is most anxious to conceal. And as Lewis always starts to gibber like a chimpanzee whenever he touches on Spengler, that may give us a clue. We have seen that Spengler prophesied the advent of Lewis's art form. And it is noteworthy that Lewis is not primarily concerned with the objective truth or falseness of Spengler's theory of the organic growth of cultures. He says:

> To say that I disagree with Spengler would be absurd. You cannot agree or disagree with such people as that: you can merely point out a few of the probable reasons for the most eccentric of their spasms, and if you have patience—as I have—classify them. That, I think, I have done enough. [*TWM*, 297]

This is of considerable significance. How does one find out the reasons for other people's spasms, and on what principles does one classify them?

Lewis attacks Spengler, not as an individual, but as a symptom of a cultural consciousness. The whole strength of Lewis's position lies, we have said, precisely in his perception of the unity of that cultural consciousness (or, as Pareto calls it, a "psychic state").[39] The underlying postulate of Lewis's argument, which he takes so completely for granted that he does not bother to formulate it, is that a given society produces the philosophy, art, literature, politics, and religion appropriate to it. Lewis apparently denies this as general principle. But the whole first part of *Time and Western Man* assumes the interconnection of the time-philosophies of Bergson and Spengler, the will-to-power attitudes of Sorel, Marinetti, and Nietzsche, the stream of consciousness technique of Proust, Joyce, and Stein, the political development of imperialism and nationalism leading to fascism, and more superficial phenomena like Charlie Chaplin and Anita Loos. He *says*, of course:

> This essay is among other things the assertion of a belief in the finest type of mind, which lifts the creative impulse into an absolute region free of spenglerian 'history' or politics. [*TWM*, 148]

But Lewis has never treated a single great literary figure in this absolute way. In *Men without Art* Henry James and Flaubert, in *The Lion and the Fox* the Elizabethan dramatists, are examined from this cultural consciousness point of view. And of course it is precisely the thesis of a cultural consciousness, to which everything contemporaneous in a given society is related, that forms the basic doctrine of Spengler. Lewis might protest that his whole point is that the nineteenth century never produced any really great or "absolute" art; that it was because of the "vulgarization" engendered by democracy that art got mixed up with politics and so became a historical phenomenon. Tackled on the score of *The Lion and the Fox*, he might extend this principle to our "semi-barbaric cultures." But every one of Lewis's diatribes is in some way concerned with that very culture. So what price the following syllogism: All Lewis's critical books are concerned with the analysis of the cultural consciousness of the Western world, mainly during its last hundred years or so, which is treated as a unity; Spengler's work is a general view of history based on the same postulate; therefore, all of Lewis's critical work is a special application of the Spenglerian dialectic. What Epicurus was to Lucretius, what Aquinas was to Dante, what, perhaps, Montaigne was to Shakespeare, that Spengler is to Wyndham Lewis. Lewis's whole thinking is dominated by Spenglerian concepts. The introduction to *The Dithyrambic Spectator* is based on Spengler's theory of craft-art in late civilization. His references to the "roman brutality" of contemporary sport and the "adolescence" of the Elizabethans as compared with our senile child-cult echo Spengler. His denunciations of bohemia are pure Spengler: both novels are Spenglerian satires. His theory of the emergence of the philosopher-ruler, worked out in *The Art of Being Ruled*, is Spengler's theory of the rise of Caesarism. His book on Hitler is in octave counterpoint to *The Hour of Decision*. And so on. In *The Lion and the Fox* Lewis speaks of Frederick the Great, who, himself the most perfect disciple of Machiavelli in history, composed a bitter philippic against him, which was exactly what Machiavelli would have advised him to do [*LF*, 98–105]. Similarly, Lewis examines Spengler, in *Time and Western Man*, as a historical and political phenomenon evolved by the cultural consciousness which also produced Bergson in philosophy, Proust in literature, Einstein in science, Picasso in painting, which is precisely according to Spengler's own instructions. True, Lewis's foreshortened perspective and his parenthetic repudiations of the very thesis he is advancing give him an air of being more common sense and practical than Spengler, and of course he makes easy game of Spengler's bombastic and truculent jingoism, his turgid apocalyptic writing, his irascible retired-colonel Philistinism. But the fact remains, that the more completely Lewis is the Spenglerian satirist, in the same way that Shaw is a Fabian satirist and Auden a Marxian satirist, the better off he is as a writer. Let us go back to the passage in Spengler about the diatribe:

> As to the living representatives of these new and purely intellectual creations, the men of the "New Order" upon whom every decline-time founds such hopes, we cannot be in any doubt, etc. [*DW*, 1:359]

and set beside it this from *Paleface*:

> [We] are now in the position of local tribal chiefs brought within a wider system, which has gathered and closed in around us; and that the *law* or *tradition* of our race, which it is our function to interpret, is being superseded by another and more universal norm, and that a new tradition is being born. . . . I am perhaps the nearest approach to a priest of the new order. [*PF*, 81]

The *Lion and the Fox* is a book about Shakespeare, emphasizing the conflict in his plays of the superman and the ordinary man, symbolized by the lion and the fox. The ordinary man is personified in Iago, and, in *Time and Western Man*, in Charlie Chaplin [*LF*, 188–9; *TWM*, 66–8]. Elizabethan drama is aristocratic tragedy composed by bourgeois artists, which means that their attitude to their heroes is one of contempt, tempered by pity when the latter fall to something more like the social level of the dramatist. Elizabethan drama developed a curious villain-type, the Machiavellian, with which dramatists frequently identified their own attitude. Out of all the irrelevant digressions, false starts, and uncompleted points made in this book, the general point of view emerges that the fall of the tragic hero always has a tragic and a satiric aspect. But it is the satiric aspect that is really welded into the concept of the tragedy; the pity the dramatist feels for his hero and makes him communicate to the audience is the result of the fact that only in his misfortune can an overworked and underpaid dramatist have any fellow-feeling for a king. In Shakespeare's case this is reinforced by a "feminine" mind which made him treat some of his heroes like a lover.[40] On the relation of tragedy to satire Lewis says:

> It would be found, if great examples of satire were examined one by one, that satire aims its dart only at the fortunate. In the same way tragedy deals only with the fortunate. . . . Both tragedy and satire aim their blows at the fortunate. They are both occupied with *hubris*, whose representatives they execute. But whereas satire is essentially ethical, or it is difficult for it not to be, tragedy does not necessarily regard its victim with exultation, however much it shares in the general delight at his fall. [*LF*, 167, 168]

He claims that, as a corollary of this, it is impossible for satire to attack the unfortunate and be great satire. Shakespeare's plays are for Lewis essentially satires; he stresses, perhaps overstresses, the importance of the fact that in the more explicitly satiric plays, such as *Timon of Athens* and *Troilus and Cressida*, we seem to get closer to Shakespeare's personal attitude to life than elsewhere. The *pathos* of the tragic hero's fall, Lewis claims, is not inherent in the situation: it is merely thrown in to make it sound well:

> But *we* must be aware of several things undreamt of in Timon's philosophy. We agree more with Apemantus than we do with Timon. We know, for instance, that ninety-nine per cent. of human beings—however *high up* you may transport them, however much insolence they may deploy when they discover themselves so *high up*, and however far you drop them *down*, and however much despair they may feel as they strike the bottom—will never show the least tincture of philosophy. They will never, we know, make even a tenth-rate tragic hero; and will neither produce, automatically, an organ-music like Bach, nor a mournful and gigantic rhetoric like that of Timon. They will say, "Ah, this is too bad! This is cruel! What have I done to be treated in this way? Oh, I am miserable! I wish I were dead and out of it." A few would be a little more musical, but most would articulate something like that. At the best (and at the worst) they will speak with that terri-

ble cold vibration of self-conscious "emotion" that the typical english actress produces when, as St Joan, or some other distressed heroine, she gets the tragic drop. They will *boo*, in short, like a cultivated and self-conscious cow ... nourished in the matter of emotional expression on the anglican pulpit. [*LF*, 254–5]

And the reason for this is that the tragic hero appears, under the cold eye of the dramatist, a spoiled, stupid, and fretful child. Lewis has some brilliant passages uncovering the satiric elements in plays like *Coriolanus*. But there, he contends, the satiric element gets the upper hand; in most cases Shakespeare falls in love with his hero:

In *Antony and Cleopatra*, for example, it is evident that the author of the play, if in love with anybody, is in love with Antony. And his attitude generally to his "strong men" is one of romantic devotion. [*LF*, 154]

But in doing this Shakespeare is merely trying to find an excuse to write about something in his best blank-verse style. Shakespeare was essentially an executioner of the tragic hero. His job as a dramatist was brutal and bloody [*LF*, 145]. And that is in many cases the kind of job a satiric artist has. Look at Hogarth, says Lewis; he had a face like a bull-dog. Tarr says:

I am the panurgic-pessimist, drunken with the laughing-gas of the Abyss: I gaze upon squalor and idiocy, and the more I see them the more I like them. Flaubert built up his *Bouvard et Pécuchet* with maniacal and tireless hands, it took him ten years: that was a long draught of stodgy laughter from the gases that rise from the dung-heap. [*TR*, 8]

In *Men without Art* Lewis claims to stand for this aesthetic attitude. He regards the satiric attitude as essential to great art:

This book has, in fact, been written, to put it shortly, to defend Satire. But to 'Satire' I have given a meaning so wide as to confound it with 'Art.' So this book may be said to be nothing short of a defence of art—as art is understood in the most 'highbrow' quarters today. (How I have been able to identify 'Satire' and 'Art' I argue in Part II.) [*MWA*, 10]

He is able to do it, of course, by his old punning method of talking about art and calling it satire. He begins by attempting to establish the principle that "the greatest satire is non-moral," repudiating his remark in *The Lion and the Fox* that "satire is essentially ethical" [*LF*, 168]. He says:

> There is of course no question that satire of the highest order has been achieved in the name of the ethical will. Most satire, indeed, has got through upon the understanding that the satirist first and foremost was a moralist. And some of the best satirists have been that as well. But not all. [*MWA*, 107]

He goes on to mention what he considers nonmoral kinds of satire. In Swift, for instance, we find a contemplation of the grotesque which is, says Lewis, "very painful" [*MWA*, 100]. This very painful contemplation of the grotesque is to Lewis the essence of satire, and he says it is not moral. Then it occurs to him that after all there are some forms of the grotesque which we do not laugh at:

> Therefore there is no society that does not refrain from guffawing at the antics, however 'screamingly funny,' of its shell-shocked men and war-idiots, and its poison-gas morons, and its mutilated battle-wrecks. [*MWA*, 112]

So the artist has to select his kind of laughter. That this act of selection is moral through and through is something that only Lewis's prose style could conceal. And, as Stephen Spender points out in *The Destructive Element*, what reason, except prejudice, have we for attacking one kind of person rather than another, if no moral standard is implied?[41] The delineation of the grotesque appeals to the reader's sense of the normal. But the satirist is more active than Lewis suggests: the satirist *attacks*, and if he attacks he must appeal to the reader against the grotesque object, and how that can be done without raising a moral issue I do not see, and Lewis does not explain. However, at the end of all this, Lewis throws up the sponge completely and comes with an enthusiastic bounce back into the moralistic fold:

> But to return again to Satire: Satire is *cold*, and that is good! It is easier to achieve those polished and resistant surfaces of a great *externalist* art in Satire. . . . There is a stiffening of Satire in everything good, of 'the grotesque,' which is the same thing. . . . This cannot be gainsaid. Satire is *good*! [*MWA*, 121]

True, it does occur to him later that "good" implies a moral standard, so he says that his idea of "good" is something very profound indeed, and that the nearest vernacular approach to it is "real." He proceeds to write a chapter then on "Is Satire Real?" and has very little difficulty proving that it is. But it is perhaps time to wade through another bog of argument closely connected with this one.

Satire, morally regenerate or otherwise, belongs to a certain approach toward art, Lewis maintains. There are two antithetical ways of creating art. One is from the inside: it tries to evoke the inmost consciousness, it is subjective, romantic, lyrical, musical, depending on the ear, favoured by Henry James, James Joyce, D.H. Lawrence, and Marcel Proust. This way is bad. The other is from the outside: it depicts people as they appear to the eye; it is purely an ocular art, classical, graphic, objective. This way is good. It is the method of *The Apes of God*:

> For *The Apes of God* it could, I think quite safely, be claimed that no book has ever been written that has paid more attention to the *outside* of people. In it their shells or pelts, or the language of their bodily movements, come first, not last. [*MWA*, 118]

We have already dealt at some length with Lewis's conception of "romantic" and have shown that in order to attack romanticism more effectively he tied it up with entirely different ideas of "romance." The result of this was to attempt to dismiss romanticism as a specifically historical phenomenon and gradually develop a conception of literature presenting a mighty Manichean opposition of classic and romantic running all through it. As nearly as one can make out, they are overemphases on intellect and emotion respectively. One is "light" and the other "dark," in the best Manichean tradition. Anybody can see that the inside of an oyster is darker than the outside; that is apparently Lewis's excuse for associating the antithesis of light and darkness with the antithesis of inside and outside. This antithetical scheme, as in most dualistic systems, tends to absorb every other kind of opposite. The light outside is "masculine," the dark inside "feminine"; one is concrete, the other vaporous. He says:

> To put this matter in a nutshell, it is *the shell* of the animal that the plastically-minded artist will prefer. The ossature is my favourite part of a living animal organism, not its intestines. My objections to Mr. D.H.

Lawrence were chiefly concerned with that regrettable habit of his inces-
santly to refer to the intestinal billowing of 'dark' subterranean passion. In
his devotion to that romantic abdominal *Within* he abandoned the sunlit
pagan surface of the earth. [*MWA*, 120–1]

Directly following this comes the passage already quoted, that "satire
is good." The Manichean scheme is complete; the "plastically-minded
artist" becomes the good artist. We have Ormuz-Lewis, protagonist of
sweetness and light, and Ahriman-Lawrence, demon of the horror of
great darkness. The objections to the preposterous passage about the
shells are too automatic to be worth dwelling on. Human beings have no
shells: their "ossatures" are inside, all tangled up with their intestines: if
a man did have a shell, he would have to come out of it in order to make
a fool of himself and so become a subject for satire: no art can be abstract
enough to deal with only the external side of life: a man becomes a subject for the artist when he starts to move, and not before: caricature gets
its effects wholly by suggesting past movements. And so on. Lewis
flounders on, actually making a creed out of his position. He says:

For an understanding of the literature of today and of tomorrow it is very
necessary, I believe, to grasp the principles involved in his question;
namely, that of the respective merits of the method of *internal* and *external*
approach—that statement of mine, made just now, I will return to before
concluding the present chapter.
   My reasons for believing that the method of *external* approach is the
method which, more and more, will be adopted in the art of writing are as
follows: [*MWA*, 126]

He goes on to make a series of points, which we shall in concluding this
essay examine one by one. Our comments are to be regarded as notes
for a projected Ph.D. thesis, to be entitled: *Wyndham Lewis's Theory of
Satire and its Relation to Zoroaster and St. Athanasius.*

(1) The *external* approach to things belongs to the 'classical' manner of
apprehending; whereas the romantic outlook (though it may serve the turn
of the 'transitionists') will not, I believe, attract the best intelligences in the
coming years, and will not survive the period of 'transition.'[42]

Here, of course, are the hosts lined up for Armageddon. This first point of Lewis's creed is his battle-cry, his triumphant affirmation that the right will triumph, and that the forces of evil and darkness shall be vanquished, shall flee away and be utterly dismayed. It is perhaps true that "transition" is a rather colourless word for this apocalypse, but dry and clipped speech, when one is choking with emotion, is no doubt part of the "classical" technique. Two other points come to one's mind. The first is that throughout this book Lewis mentions Mario Praz's *Romantic Agony*, a book he says was written under the influence of his own *Diabolical Principle*, and uses it effectively enough as a sourcebook of the Bible of hell composed by the sadists and diabolists of the last century.[43] But Praz explicitly states that he regards romanticism as a definitely historical phenomenon centring in the nineteenth century, at which time, he says, arose a new aesthetic concept of the beauty of pain, and as nothing more than that.[44] He gives no support to Lewis's Manichean theory of literature. The second point is that the phrase "the romantic outlook . . . will not . . . attract the best intelligences in the coming years" is composed in exactly the idiom of the "revolutionary simpleton" attacked in *Time and Western Man*, the novelty-hunter obsessed with the idea of "keeping up with the times" or with time.

(2) The *external* approach to things (relying upon evidence of the *eye* rather than of the more emotional organs of sense) can make of 'the grotesque' a healthy and attractive companion. Other approaches cannot do this. The scarab can be accommodated—even a crocodile's tears can be relieved of some of their repulsiveness. For the requirements of the new world-order this is essential. And as for pure satire—there the eye is supreme. [*MWA*, 127]

If Lewis would wallow in emotionalism long enough to listen to himself talk, he might avoid at least a few of these howlers. What is an emotional organ of sense? What has emotion got to do with sense experience? A is for art, B is for brains, and C for the canon of aesthetics that says that the different arts are different forms of imaginative organization and that the particular sense they appeal to is incidental. When Lewis claims that *The Apes of God* appeals to the eye he obviously means the mind's eye, if he means anything; if somebody is reading the book aloud to me, which heaven forbid, I am taking in a series of sound impressions, just as I am when I am listening to Mozart. It does not matter that Mozart sounds like Mozart and Lewis's prose like an army tank falling into the Grand Canyon. If Lewis means in the above paragraph that Goya, say, merely because he was a painter, could put across the grotesque in a way that Beethoven, merely because he was a musician, could not, or that the village studies of Breughel are capable of revealing the grotesque in a way that the *Peasant's Cantata*[45] is not, the ignorance and Philistinism such a proposition implies puts it beyond discussion. If Lewis means that the grotesquerie of Falstaff is mainly due to his fat body and not to the way he talks, he is again out of my depth. One continually thinks, however, of a phrase in an essay of T.S. Eliot: "If Mr. Lewis means (I am not sure what he means)—."[46] The only other thing to notice in the above paragraph is the remark: "For the requirements of the new world-order this is essential," which is exactly the kind of statement that makes a target out of Spengler in *Time and Western Man*.

> (3) All our instinctive aesthetic reactions are, in the west of Europe, based upon Greek naturalist canons. Of the *internal* method of approach in literature, Joyce or James are highly representative. Their art (consisting in 'telling from the inside,' as it is described) has for its backgrounds the naturalism (the flowing lines, the absence of linear organization, and also the inveterate humanism) of the Hellenic pictorial culture. Stein is Teutonic music, *jazzed*—Stein is just the German musical soul leering at itself in a mirror, and sticking out at itself a stuttering welt of a swollen tongue, although perhaps, as she is not a pure Teuton, this is not quite fair to the Teuton either—it is the mirror that is at fault. [*MWA*, 127]

Until I can be sure whether Lewis is trying to say that Hellenic pictorial culture and Teutonic music are part of the same tradition or not, and, if so, what music can conceivably have to do with naturalism or inveterate humanism, I can hardly consider myself capable of dealing with this broadside. I do know that I cannot argue with anyone who regards, or pretends to regard, the development of contrapuntal music in the West as a mistake. The remark about Gertrude Stein shows a curious insensibility. If Stein is anything, she is demotic—the absolute lack of complication in her style, the hypnotic effect of her repetitions, produce a startlingly vivid effect of colloquial vigour, when properly handled (as it is sometimes, more often perhaps by her imitators than by her). I should think that her position in English literature, along with the school which is exploiting her ideas and techniques, would eventually be somewhat similar to the position of the New Testament in Greek literature. Certainly the New Testament produces the only examples I have been able to find of anything like Gertrude Stein. Here, for example, is Stein:

> A composition of a prolonged present is a natural composition in the world as it has been these thirty years it was more and more a prolonged present. I created then a prolonged present naturally I knew nothing of a continuous present but it came naturally to me to make one, it was simple it was clear to me and nobody knew why it was done like that, I did not myself although naturally to me it was natural. [qtd. in *TWM*, 59].

And here is the First Epistle of John:

> That which was from the beginning, that which we have heard, that which we have seen with our eyes, that which we beheld, and our hands handled, concerning the Word of life (and the life was manifested, and we have seen, and bear witness, and declare unto you the life, the eternal life, which was with the Father, and was manifested unto us); that which we have seen and heard declare we unto you also. [1 John 1:1–3]

But this kind of effect is not usually the one we have in mind when we use the word *Teutonic* abusively. We think of a confused, heavy, dull, pompous, incoherent style, lumbering along in polysyllables, trying to express abstract ideas and not succeeding. In other words, we think of a style very similar to that of Lewis. Lewis's real predecessors in English prose were the nineteenth-century Teutons, Carlyle and Meredith. Had Lewis modelled his prose on them, and learned from them where to place his accents, he would have been better off as a stylist. But he never did learn anything about accents, and so remains, vaguely Teutonic, but jazzed—jazzed until both the fundamental rhythmic beat and the superimposed rhythm of syncopation disappear in a clatter.

> (4) If you consider the naturalism of the Greek plastic as a phenomenon of decadence (contrasted with the masculine formalism of the Egyptian or the Chinese) then you will regard likewise the method of the 'internal monologue' (or the romantic snapshotting of the wandering stream of the Unconscious) as a phenomenon of decadence. [*MWA*, 127]

Here, apparently, the assimilation of Hellenic pictorial and Teutonic musical cultures has advanced a step. All I can dimly sense in this paragraph is the emergence of yet another kind of intellectual snobbery. By intellectual snobbery I mean the exaltation of a certain attitude or cultural tradition at the expense of all the rest in estimating works of art, such as we find in moralizing criticism, in jingoist criticism, in the narrower Marxist approach, in the Anglo-Catholic formulas of the post-Andrewes Eliot.[47] No sooner have we got accustomed to the "classicist in literature, royalist in politics, and anglo-catholic in religion" shibboleth than we get someone else, also claiming to be classical, talking about the "masculine formalism" of one culture and the "decadence" of another. I suspect that, because the Chinese are fallible human beings, there might be a good deal of slimy (romantic) chop suey about their less successful efforts which it would be fatal to overpraise. I know nothing about that, however. I know only that the strength of Oriental art is the result of an immensely long tradition and convention, and that Lewis shares the "romantic" idea of the artist or genius as arbiter of both form and content of his work and as a lonely isolated anarchic individualist who prefers the "prose-movement—easy, uncontrolled and large" to any form of "enregimentation."

(5) A tumultuous stream of evocative, spell-bearing, vocables, launched at your head—or poured into your Unconscious—is, finally, a dope only. It may be an auriferous mud, but it must remain mud—not a clear but a murky picture. As a literary medium it is barbaric. [MWA, 127]

This is rather better. But he is still not thinking clearly. He is talking as though the meaning of art were a meaning which denotes, like the meaning of science. Art is synthetic, and connotes; that is its big distinction from science or philosophy. Art is bound to work with symbols which unite varied aspects of experience and bring them into ordered groupings. There is a certain misty residue about all art, owing to the fact that art means different things to different people. When a man is contemplating a picture, for instance, he tries to isolate his own reaction, because the reactions of all possible types of people beside himself form a nimbus around his appreciation. If I am looking at *Mona Lisa*, I can no more get away from the gum-chewing tourist beside me than I can get away from Walter Pater, except by responding to a meaning in the picture essentially "evocative" and "spell-bearing." One might also quote a stray passage or two from Lewis's own work: here are a couple of sentences from *The Childermass*:

Is not your Space-Time for all practical purposes only the formula recently popularized to accommodate the empirical sensational chaos? Did not the human genius redeem us for a moment from that, building a world of human-divinity above that flux? Are not your kind betraying us again in the name of exact research to the savage and mechanical nature we had overcome; at the bidding, perhaps, of your maniacal and jealous God?[48]

This sounds to me rather like a tumultuous stream of vocables launched at my head—there is a lot more of it—perhaps I am being captious.

(6) If Henry James or if James Joyce were to paint pictures, it would be, you feel, a very *literary* sort of picture that would result. But also, in their *details*, these pictures would be lineal descendants of the Hellenic naturalism. Only, such details, all jumbled up and piled one against the other, would appear, at first sight, different, and for the Western Hellenic culture, exotic.—Nevertheless, as in the pictures of most Germans, all the plastic units would be suffused with a romantic coloration. They would be over-charged with a literary symbolism; their psyche would have got the better of their Gestalt—the result a sentiment, rather than an expressive form. [*MWA*, 127–8]

I do not see what an "expressive form" could express except its own inside. But what is one to do with a writer who happens to be a painter as well, and then bullies all the other writers because they can't paint, having spent more time learning to write; complains that if literary people were to paint, their paintings would be literary; and *then* proceeds to construct out of the air an elaborate description of the paintings they would paint if they could paint, and builds an argument on that?

(7) We know what sort of picture D.H. Lawrence would paint if he took to the brush instead of the pen. For he did so, luckily, and even held exhibitions. As one might have expected, it turned out to be incompetent Gauguin! A bit more practice, and Lawrence would have been indistinguishable from that Pacific-Parisian Pierre Loti of Paint. [*MWA*, 128]

Still, if one rejects all Western culture as semi-barbaric, and all Hellenic culture as decadent, as Lewis does in proposition 4, and turns to the Orient as the true home of great art or to the masculinely formal tradition of Egypt, one gets again a kind of romantic exoticism. For the man who made this estimate of European as compared with Oriental and Egyptian art before Lewis made it was, of course, Gauguin. Set beside the fourth paragraph already quoted the following from one of Gauguin's letters:

> Keep the Persians, the *Cambodgiens* and a bit of the Egyptians always in mind. The great error is the Greek, however beautiful it may be.[49]

> (8) To turn more to the renowned critic with whom we started, Hazlitt. In reading Shakespeare, he said "we are let into the minds of his characters, we see the play of their thoughts. . . . His humour (so to speak) bubbles, sparkles, and finds its way in all directions, like a natural spring."—And that natural-spring effect is the Greek *naturalism*, of course, as I have already indicated. That naturalism (whatever else may or may not happen) is bound to be superseded by something more akin to the classic of, say, the Chinese.
>
> Shakespeare is the summit of the romantic, naturalist, European tradition. And there is a great deal more of that Rousseauish, *natural-springishness*, in much recent work in literature than is generally recognized. But especially, in the nature of things, is this the case with the *tellers-from-the-inside*—with the masters of the 'interior monologue,' with those Columbuses who have set sail towards the El Dorados of the Unconscious, or of the Great Within.[50]

So Lewis is going to head for the goal of the conscious, or the Great Wall. Columbus also thought he was going to China, incidentally. "Is bound to be superseded by the Chinese"; "whatever else may or may not happen." "Oh, those mysterious *musts* of Spengler's!" says Lewis in *Time and Western Man* [287].

> (9) Dogmatically, then, I am for the Great Without, for the method of *external* approach—for the wisdom of the eye, rather than that of the ear. [*MWA*, 128]

What he is really for is a clanking, clattering, rhythmless, and deadened civilization, which has gazed on myriads of meaningless, trivial, concrete visions until it has developed more blind eyes than a peacock. But its main trouble is still its tone-deafness. An entertaining cinema has recently showed us that if we went back to the eighteenth century the first thing we would be conscious of would be the bad smell;[51] and not until we realize that the hideous noises surrounding us are equally obscene shall we make any genuine advance in culture. Art is energy incorporated in form: the energy rhythm, the form plasticity. Overemphasis of the one leads to a surging Heraclitean chaos, overemphasis of the other to a frozen Parmenidean one. Both these, however, are really the same thing: the source of all evil in art is this unfortunate tendency toward the abstract antithesis, toward the composing of cheap epigrams which minor critics revel in and serious artists avoid. There is no use saying, as some good-natured weakling might say: But, after all, if Joyce is for the ear and Lewis for the eye, Lawrence for the internal and Lewis for the external, Proust for the musical and Lewis for the graphic, Spengler for time and Lewis for space; well, there is a lot to be said on both sides, so why not combine them and get at the truth? Our point is, however, that Lewis's criticism would be effective if it were confined to satire, but frozen into a dogma of antithesis it is worthless. One cannot combine the convex and concave to get a new perspective. If one combines two qualitatively different substances, like hydrogen and oxygen, one gets a genuine compound: in place of two gases that will burn we get a liquid that won't. But if we mix oxygen with carbon dioxide, which is merely a reaction against oxygen, all we get is hot air. There is no wisdom of eye plus ear or eye multiplied by the ear, any more than there can be the wisdom of eye minus ear which Lewis recommends, or the wisdom of ear minus eye which he attacks. There is wisdom only of the conscious mind, which, though versatile, is in one piece.

Other Essays

19

An Enquiry into
the Art Forms of Prose Fiction

This essay appears to have been written for one of the English courses Frye took during his second and third years at Emmanuel College. His transcript for those two years indicates only that he received firsts for "Honor English." The present paper is filed in the Northrop Frye Fonds alongside the papers on Eliot (1937) and Chaucer (1938), so it is also possible that it was written after Frye left Emmanuel. The references to Wyndham Lewis and Ramon Lull, both of whom Frye wrote about in 1936, might be used to argue for a date of 1936 or later. Another possibility is that the paper was written for Frye's Oxford tutor, Edmund Blunden. On 9 February 1937 Frye says in a letter to Helen Kemp, "I read my anatomy paper to Blunden last night."[1] The prose fiction essay may have been the anatomy paper, or a later version of it. In early November of 1938 Frye read a paper to Blunden on the character book,[2] and the references to that genre in the present essay provide some evidence to argue for a later date. The papers Frye read to Blunden seem to have been handwritten,[3] and the prose fiction paper is typed. But this does not rule out its being an Oxford paper, since Frye typed his Blake manuscript, as well as his Eliot paper (no. 21), when he was at Merton College, borrowing a typewriter from classmate Joseph Reid.[4] The evidence, in short, is inconclusive, but the paper does appear to have been written between 1935 and 1939.[5] The typescript is in the NFF, 1991, box 37, file 4.

Prose fiction today seems to fall into a general negative antithesis of fiction and nonfiction, the former being about things admitted not to be true, and the latter about everything else. Fiction and facts are, thus, placed in opposition, and the distinction is between the imaginary and the real, the imaginary and the imaginative being, of course, identified. With the extraordinary vulgarity of this distinction we take immediate issue, for the word *fiction*, like the word *poetry*, means etymologically something made for its own sake. We, therefore, extend the term to include any form of prose writing which belongs to literature rather than to another subject. The distinction between the literary and the nonliterary is admittedly a very approximate one, but surely it does exist; and we have no hesitation in saying that the *Anatomy of Melancholy*, because it survives obviously in literature rather than in science or philosophy, is fiction, and that Gibbon's *Decline and Fall* or Doughty's *Arabia Deserta* are both fiction and nonfiction, depending on what one reads them for.

And even when one looks at the connotations of the ordinary use of the word, *fiction* seems to describe, not a group of art forms, but a commercial product: it is a trade name useful to booksellers, reviewers, and librarians, but quite meaningless to critics. Fiction, like books in general, rests on another antithesis of novel, which is long and has to be bound separately, and story, which is short and can go in a magazine. But length is not a very satisfactory criterion either, as fiction can obviously be of any length, and when we find, lumped together under the title of novel, works which go back to radically different literary traditions, we begin to consider the advisability of cleaning up our terms a bit. The present paper is an enquiry into the possibility of regarding modern fiction as a vast conglomerate, in which may be discerned certain structural principles, each manifesting itself in an art form, with a tradition of its own giving us examples sometimes fairly pure, sometimes mixed, sometimes only reached by a metaphor. To take an example from another field: is an epic the name of an art form, or is it simply literary jargon for a long poem? If it is an art form, we can assign certain characteristics to it, of which length will doubtless be one; and within those broad characteristics we can include the *Iliad*, *Odyssey*, and *Aeneid* as classical examples, and the *Divine Comedy* or *Paradise Lost* as Christian examples. Browning's *Ring and the Book*, on the other hand, has nothing whatever to do with this tradition, and if we call it an epic, we mean that an epic is simply a long poem. Similarly, it may be true that the novel is a long prose work and nothing more. But this is unsatisfactory, for surely we have an instinctive feeling which tells us that *Point Counter Point* is a novel and that *The Seven Pillars of Wisdom* is not one, and it is the duty of the critic to examine this instinct and see what is implied in it. Our initial attempt, then, will be to isolate the novel as an art form and as a literary tradition.

Let us take the literary tradition first. The novel we find developing in the eighteenth century as a middle-class literary product. Like everything else produced by bourgeois society, it is individualistic. It does not, like the drama, depend either on group production or group response, nor does it require, like music or the sermon, any personal contact between artist and connoisseur. We have to say "the novel," while we can speak of "drama" without the definite article. Apart from this, however, the novel more nearly resembles the drama than any other major art form, for it is, like the drama, composed of plot or narrative, character and setting, with a strong bias toward objectivity. Historically, therefore, it descends from the drama, rising as the drama declines, and is bound up with the fortunes of a middle-class society.

The bourgeois revolt against the aristocracy, which reached the height of its power under Elizabeth, came in two waves, the first the religious assault of Puritan against Anglican, the second the political attack of Whig mercantilism on Tory conservatism, waves which to some extent overlap. With the former we have a long-sustained attempt to dethrone the two greatest Elizabethan art forms, music and drama, trying to transform an instinctive dislike into a moral principle. The Puritans fought the theatres from start to finish, closing them whenever they had power; they fought music until they permanently weakened its prestige in England. Shakespeare adds his final touch to the portrait of Cassius, the ruthless Puritan revolutionary, when he makes Caesar say of him:

> He loves no plays
> As thou dost, Antony; he hears no music.
>
> [*Antony and Cleopatra*, 1.2.203–4]

The political attack, after the Restoration had brought back a revived drama, and Purcell in music, was renewed after 1688, reinforced by the attack of Collier on the stage. The Puritans themselves did not produce the novel, though their one great prose artist, Bunyan, is well on the way to it; but the Whigs undoubtedly did. Defoe, the Whig, is the ancestor of the novel; Swift, the Tory, ignored it. In the de Coverley papers a novelist's interest is at work breaking down and disrupting the essay. As the novel rose with the middle classes, the drama declined. Congreve abandoned the stage at the height of his powers; Fielding, running foul of Whig censorship, turned to the novel. With the rise of the eighteenth-century weeping comedy, the drama became extinct as an art form, and with the fresh impetus given the middle classes by the Industrial Revolution, Jane Austen established the form of the modern novel, and the drama disappeared even as entertainment, surviving only as literature.

It is apparent that, while the drama uses the well-worn apparatus of plot, character, and setting, the more artistic the drama becomes, the more completely do plot and setting follow as implications of character. In other words, we shall not be far wrong if we define the drama as an objective study of character, and, if we examine the novel, we find that the same definition holds. This is why we say that the novel historically descends from the drama rather than simply that it replaces it. But a study of character, which, like the drama, depends on the limitations of time and performance and, therefore, on speed and on the ability of actors, is bound to make a use of convention which is not necessary to the novel. When Iago works on Othello, the development is inevitable enough, but we are given that development summarized: it is presented in the form of a convention the audience is prepared to accept. The novelist, if he is equally aware of the possibilities of his art form, avoids taking anything of the sort for granted: his approach is analytic rather than synthetic, and he expands his material to the limit. When Roger Chillingworth works on the hero of the *Scarlet Letter*, we get a sense, not of a swift piling up to a climax, as in *Othello*, but of an immense accretion of details, extending over a long period of time. In practice this means that the drama is, like music, a time-art, depending on rhythm in a way in which the novel does not. It also means the psychological analysis of character in the drama is presented in a summarized form, while in the novel all the implications are worked out. Thus, in the nineteenth century Browning, the one poet who thought of his poetry dramatically and in whom, alone of Victorian poets, speed and rhythm become positive factors in the writing, fails on the stage through overdetailed analysis and then develops the one dramatic concession to psychology, the soliloquy, into the monologue, and the monologue into the scheme of *The Ring and the Book*, fundamentally a drama turned inside out. The action in the drama means that the form is held together dynamically, and the world of the stage becomes a replica of the actual world, that is, a sphere, where the analysis of Browning's poem, being two-dimensional, is best symbolized by a ring.

This is what happens to the drama in poetry; we are at present concerned with prose. When we speak of the tradition of the English novel and of those who have been most conscious of the novel as an art form, we think instinctively of Fielding, Jane Austen, Thackeray, Henry James, and perhaps Meredith. Now if one generalization about these various artists is safe, it is surely that their genius is more at home in the sphere of comedy than of tragedy. Hardy and Conrad being obvious exceptions, there are few novelists who have treated the novel as a vehicle of tragedy, and in considering the transition from Restoration drama to the eighteenth-century novel, it is apparent that the latter owes, as an art form, more to the comedy of manners in the former than to the tragedies of Dryden or Otway. The tendency of tragedy to verse and of comedy, particularly the comedy of manners, to prose, should not be overlooked either. The novel, being a bourgeois art form, tends to focus interest on the domestic, the concrete, and the immediate, the criteria of action being moral rather than religious, and the approach realistic, which fits in with Aristotle's definition of comedy as a study of ignoble characters.

Now, is this association of the novel with the comedy of manners purely accidental, or does it lead us a step further in our quest for the isolation of the art form? Tragedy surely entails the striking down of a hero by some external force he cannot control. We say external, because, although in most tragedies the external situation coincides with a defect in the character of the hero, still the emphasis in tragedy is on the misfortune of the hero, so that such studies of decadence as *Volpone* in drama or *Emma Bovary* in the novel have too satiric an undercurrent in them to be called tragedies. Therefore, the development of an external force in tragedy carries with it the development of an emphasis on narrative, of a sense of linear movement which sweeps the characters along in its progress. This development of narrative is not the same thing as the complication of plot, for plot, in the sense of intrigue, is more of a uniform pattern than the wider term *narrative* needs to be. And if we are to establish a distinction in fiction paralleling that of tragedy and comedy in drama, we should restrict the term novel to the extended, analytic development of the comedy of manners, the art form of the study of character followed by Jane Austen and Henry James, and distinguish it from prose fiction in which a narrative takes an active part in bringing tragedy to the characters, a form which we here call the tale.

This difference is only an emphasis difference, of course; but the distinction is there, just as there is real distinction between tragedy and comedy even when we find them inextricable in the same play, in *Troilus and Cressida*, for instance. The association of the tale with tragedy is evidenced by the way in which tragedy in its most concentrated forms tends to require a narrator and a responding chorus, as in Greek tragedy and in the *St. Matthew Passion*. Again, the necessity for a swiftly moving tale to depend on rhythm makes it a good form for poetry as well as prose, and the intense conservatism of tragic formulae, as opposed to those of comedy, which change with every new order of society, gives an extended meaning and tradition to the word *tale* lacking in the word *novel*.

The tale, therefore, we here treat as an art form of prose fiction distinct from the novel, with a bias toward tragedy rather than comedy, and with a tendency to make the narrative carry along the characters rather than the characters work out the narrative. It has other characteristics as well. In the first place, as it deals with forces external to the central characters which are, as far as they are concerned, irresistible, it is in far closer contact with the nonhuman and superhuman worlds than anything connected with the comedy of manners could be. In the second place, depending as it does on narrative, it also depends on speed and compression of events in a way the more agglutinative novel does not, so that an obvious advantage is gained, as compared with the novel, through brevity. The novel gains where the tale loses by the accretion of detail. The tale is not, of course, the short story; that is another commercial product, a hybrid consisting of a tale-form inherited from Poe, an anecdote-form inherited from O. Henry, and a sketch-form inherited from de Maupassant.

In the eighteenth century the realistic psychological analysis of Richardson, which is obviously part of the tradition of the novel, is at the opposite pole from the tales of the Gothic horror school, an antithesis which later developed into the antithesis of Scott's treatment of the tale and Jane Austen's treatment of the novel. Scott was obviously much less conscious of his art form than Jane Austen was of hers, but it is significant that the most tragic of his stories, *The Bride of Lammermoor*, is admittedly the one which shows him most conscious of it. In Dickens, where the interaction of character is so skilful and the alleged "plots," such as the long subterfuges of old Martin Chuzzlewit and the Boffins, so irritatingly stupid, the only book more narrative than character study, *A Tale of Two Cities*, is the one tragedy. Later on we have *Jekyll and Hyde*, *The Prussian Officer*, *Heart of Darkness*, and *The Turn of the Screw* as varying examples of the pure tale. The tragic tone of Conrad and Hardy, as opposed to the comedy of manners tradition in Meredith, James, and

Galsworthy, is largely owing to their use of various characteristics of the tale; the association with nonhuman and superhuman worlds previously mentioned, and the careful planning of events so that the destinies of the characters appear to hang on them rather than the reverse. It was no doubt the association of the tale with a narrator which accounts for Conrad's use of Marlow, whose introduction on grounds of technical expedience is surely a mistake. The tragedy of Tess is presented, like the tragedy of Othello, in the framework of a convention to be accepted by the reader, which gives evidence of the influence of other traditions than the novel at work.

But, of course, tale and novel together, with all their ramifications, do not exhaust the concept of fiction as we have defined it above. *Gulliver's Travels*, for instance, is certainly fiction, but it is just as certainly not a novel. It is, ostensibly, a development of the traveller's tale, and the connection of *A Tale of a Tub* with the form is indicated in the title. But this particular adoption of the tale form is in both cases a pretext; the tale itself is parodied, in one case by the unexpected application made of its machinery, in the other by the digressions which smother it. The satire twists everything into another shape, and that other shape must be a third form of prose fiction, unless we are prepared to say that the satire is incidental, which is a complete absurdity with Swift.

There are, of course, two great periods of bourgeois dominance in Western culture: the one commencing with the movement represented by the Renaissance and Reformation and the other with the development of mercantilism and the Industrial Revolution. The former is the period of the highest culture in our tradition, extending over the sixteenth, seventeenth, and eighteenth centuries, the period of "great masters" in all the arts. In it prose fiction will, of course, take on different forms. There would hardly be much place for the novel and the prose fiction form of the tale with a flourishing drama, and prose fiction would tend to avoid both the study of character and the development of narrative in search of more distinctive forms. Now owing to our ordinary restricted use of the term *fiction*, most histories of English fiction are faced with a prodigious hiatus when they arrive at the seventeenth century. Deloney, Nashe, and the rest are, perhaps, canonical; but the seventeenth century, although it is the age of Browne and Burton and Earle and Fuller and Bunyan and many other fine artists who wrote highly entertaining prose solely for its own sake, becomes, for these historians, the age of translations of Madame de Scudéry. If we can establish an art form for prose fiction between the sixteenth and eighteenth centuries, we might arrive at a better perspective.

Two forms closely allied to *fiction* in the restricted sense of the word are, of course, the picaresque novel and the character book. The latter, which is in most of its manifestations closely connected with the theory of humours, is frankly an attempt to study character through other units than those of the individual: in the *Microcosmography*, for example, the individuals exist only insofar as they are types. In the picaresque novel, too, the emphasis is directed, not toward the analysis of character, but to the building up of an attitude, almost invariably satiric, toward society: it is, like the drama, a synthetic rather than an analytic form. Now if we consider both of these forms as different species of one genus, we arrive at a prose fiction which is, like the novel, individualistic so far as the author is concerned, but inclined to leave the study of character and the telling of stories to the drama, to generalize both characters and narrative, and to direct the form toward the building up of a certain argument or attitude the author wishes to present. It is more subjective in presentation than the novel and is more obviously selective; but it deals with equally objective material. In short, it is essentially, in the broadest sense of the word, a thesis, a working out or ordered arrange- ment of a subject or point of view. This art form of prose fiction, which dominated its field in English literature from the sixteenth to the eight- eenth century, we here call the anatomy. Its relation to the essay, if the latter term be restricted to the literary art form which develops from Montaigne and Bacon, parallels the relation of the novel or tale to the short story; the anatomy is a synthesis or interweaving of ideas where the essay develops one.

The word *anatomy* is, of course, a literary term, but logically it can be applied to any presentation of history, philosophy, religion, economics, etc., which survives through its literary value. Gibbon's *Decline and Fall* could be regarded as an anatomy from the point of view of English liter- ature, and Locke's *Essay* or Hume's *Enquiry* are examples of the carrying over of the machinery of the anatomy form into another field, just as the philosophical dialogue carries over the machinery of the drama. *The Compleat Angler* is an anatomy of angling; Berkeley's *Siris* is an example of a philosophical treatise in which the material is arranged, not so much in accordance with the demands of the subject called philosophy as in accordance with the interests and outlook of its author, and, there- fore, ranks as a philosophical anatomy. These are examples of an objective interest of the author treated from a literary standpoint. But the author may be interested in building up his own attitude to a given question, in which case we have such anatomies as *Religio Medici* or *Areopagitica*. Or he may be interested in working out his attitude to society, which may result in a generalized satire, such as the *Anatomy of Abuses*, or in a Utopia such as that of More or Campanella: the Utopia, and the satire on the Utopia, belonging essentially to this form. The archetypal anatomy is, of course, the Bible, and the issuance of the Authorized Version greatly influenced the seventeenth-century development of the form and helped to colour its tone.[6] One essential characteristic of all these anatomies is the display of erudition, which is necessitated by the demands of the form.

Coming back to the picaresque novel, we find that that, too, is on the whole a development of the anatomy. Some picaresque novels are, of course, wholly irresponsible, devoid of the more intellectual interest necessary for such a classification, but the greater ones preserve the quality of presenting a certain attitude on the part of the author. *Don Quixote* is only incidentally a study of character: the whole point about Don Quixote's character is surely that it is not all there. He forms a focus for the author's satiric attitude to certain carefully selected aspects of contemporary Spanish life. The same satiric attitude is usually responsible for the choice of the picaro: certainly in Lesage and in Quevedo, and hardly less so in our own tradition from Jacke Wilton to *Jonathan Wild*. The essential point about any anatomy which does deal with human character is, we have seen, that it generalizes personality to a greater extent than would be possible to a novel; but, of course, the extent to which it does so in any particular book may be a matter of opinion. However, *Arcadia* and *Euphues*, which latter incidentally is subtitled *The Anatomy of Wit*, are surely anatomies, as they manifest much more obviously the author's generalized attitude to society than they do any profound objective psychological analysis. The character book more evidently comes under the head of anatomy; the very choice of such a title as *Microcosmography* shows the anatomist's conceptual and abstract approach to human personality. But the character books are rather sketchy designs; the genuine anatomy does not stop with summarizing people as types or humours; it regards those types as representative of the larger thesis it is putting across. So that on those very rare occasions when the extended allegory enters prose fiction, it, too, becomes a phase of the anatomy.

The anatomy began with the Renaissance. The most important forms of prose fiction in the Middle Ages were the romance and the novella or summarized tale established by Boccaccio. Both forms survived the sixteenth century, but the anatomy can hardly be said to have existed long before 1500, though it was well on the way in such occasional precocious developments as Ramon Lull's *Blanquerna*. The reason may be that in the Middle Ages erudition had a primarily objective value, and the theses advanced were judged by their relationship to the system of thought prevalent at the time. With the abandonment of the scholastic synthesis, this objective criterion disappeared, and learning became an aspect of self-culture. The books written which expressed the ideas germinated by that learning, thus, tended to become individualistic theses. The anatomy led the attack on scholasticism; one of the earliest and finest anatomies was Cornelius Agrippa's *Vanity of the Arts and Sciences*. Erasmus's *Encomium Moriae*, More's *Utopia*, Castiglione's anatomy of a courtier follow in quick succession, and in the vast anatomy of Rabelais we have perhaps the highest Renaissance development of the form. Rabelais has everything: the presentation of an unmistakably coherent attitude, immense erudition, a Utopian scheme—are all included. Gigantism, again, as a technique for summarizing human character, is as important as the theory of humours or any other form of allegory.

There should be no necessity now to say that the anatomy in England reached its culmination with Burton. The *Anatomy of Melancholy* is not a book of Burton: it is Burton's book; the complete expression of his personality. Needless to say, all the characteristics of the anatomy we have noted are in it: Utopian scheme, erudition, view of mankind through the generalized technique provided by the theory of humours, ordered presentation of a subject, and the rest, except that what we find partial in other anatomists we find complete in him. It is perhaps noteworthy that the anatomy in its largest and most highly developed and concentrated forms tends to become *the* book of its author rather than one of many; Burton, Rabelais, perhaps Sterne, being examples. The *Anatomy of Melancholy* is divided like a prelude and fugue; the prelude, the introduction of Democritus to the reader, being free in style, and the anatomy being capable of exhaustive analysis on a general threefold scheme. The metaphor is not altogether an irresponsible one, for both the anatomy and the contemporary fugue in music are, in different arts, the working out of the implications of a given subject and the organizing of them into a rhythmic unit.

With the rise of middle-class culture the anatomy began to merge into the novel. Bunyan is the first obvious transitional figure. *Grace Abounding*, as contrasted with *Religio Medici*, leans far over not only toward the picaresque novel, but to the complete psychological observation of character we get later in Richardson. Badman, again, is a type, and a very highly generalized one, but the fact that his career is narrated brings his life and death towards the tale form, and the fact that events and setting arise out of and take their form from his character makes it essentially the first English novel. *The Pilgrim's Progress* is still an allegory, but Talkative, Faithful, Ignorance, Greatheart, are extremely wide awake humours, straining toward the complete independence they would have in a novel. The rigorous common sense of Defoe, Fielding, and Smollett anchored and localized the picaresque novel, and Richardson's epistolary scheme, half narration and half revelation, provided a matrix for the development of tale and novel. The epistolary form is one which can be pressed into the service of the novel, as with *Pamela*, or the tale, as with *Redgauntlet*, or the anatomy, as with Howell's *Familiar Letters*, and, therefore, does not exist as an independent form. The tale and novel reached, as we have seen, comparative dissociation in Scott and Jane Austen.

The advantage the English lost by giving birth to Jane Austen lay in the exploitation of the anatomy in the interests of the novel. We have seen that the anatomy attempts the intellectual completion of its subject, either through immense accretions of prodigious erudition, as in Burton, or through the selection of data on an objective body of material, as in *The Compleat Angler*, or through the revelation of the personality of the writer, as in *Religio Medici*, or through the rounding off of the form by an allegory, as in *The Pilgrim's Progress*. Seldom do we find this in the nineteenth-century novel. We have one superb anatomy, *Sartor Resartus* (perhaps two if we count the *Biographia Literaria*), and occasional workings over of traditional forms—Landor's *Imaginary Conversations* and Newman's *Apologia*. But these remain apart from the novel. The more intellectualized novelists, Peacock, Disraeli, even Meredith, are by the very nature of their approach committed to the anatomic novel, but the first two hardly achieve masterpieces, and it is only in Sir Willoughby Patterne that we get a real fusion of analysis of character with an anatomy of egoism. The one really important anatomic novel of the century, *Moby Dick*, belongs to another development. George Borrow is an interesting figure: *Lavengro* and *The Romany Rye* are novels definitely aiming to present a coherent attitude to society on the part of the author, and *The Bible in Spain* and *Wild Wales* are early sketches of the geographical, even the cultural anatomy which will meet us in a moment. But he is an isolated and minor writer. Eliot speaks of England as a country that has produced many men of genius and few works of art,[7] and nothing in the literature deserves that stricture better than the novel. It has remained an incomplete, abstract form, at its best narrow, localized, and class-conscious, at its worst chaotic. Nowhere does it give us the completeness of outlook of a Dostoevsky or a Balzac; and the purer as an art form it becomes, the less able is it to deal with the dynamic organizing forces of life, the more it shrinks away from the unsafe, from the unconventional, from the destructive impact of passion and the sex instinct on the safeguards on an established order.

In our discussion of the relation of the drama to the novel we stated that in the drama, which has to be over in two hours, speed is a positive artistic quality, and that as speed does not evidence itself in the novel, the drama depends on rhythm in a way that the novel does not. Now the anatomy, though it is as much a written art form as the novel, depends far more on rhythmic integration; it is essentially a synthetic form of art, as the emphasis is thrown on construction rather than analysis. This is a difficult point to establish, but it is obvious that when we are reading the anatomies of Burton or Browne we are conscious of a style in a way that we are not conscious of style when we are reading George Eliot or Dickens, and this difference is ultimately a difference between a work that is rhythmically organized and a work that is not. Style is always essentially a question of rhythm. Rabelais is immortal chiefly because he comes off rhythmically: the *Anatomy of Melancholy* is a living book and not a monstrosity of genial pedantry because of the breathless speed of the writing: *Euphues* and *Arcadia* were beached because they moved with more dignity and deliberation. In *Tristram Shandy*, the most perfect fusion of anatomy and novel we possess in English, and one of our few completely successful works of art, the continuous easy lilt and swing of the rhythm almost suggests a deliberate musical program. The counterpoint of my Uncle Toby's ground bass, symbolized by *Lillabulero*, and Walter Shandy's florid ornamentation over it, the amazingly skilful devices to avoid a full close anywhere in the work, the digressive episodes, the stretto climax of the Widow Wadman affair: all this elusive and subtle material is arranged with the most hair-splitting delicacy.

Paul Valéry says that the essence of a classical period in literature is to come after, to consolidate and regulate an impulse that has preceded it.[8] But classicism does more than consolidate: when carried far enough, it exhausts the possibilities inherent in the impulse. Thus, in the classical backwater at the turn of the seventeenth and eighteenth centuries we feel that Pope has not only matured the heroic couplet, but destroyed it; poets who come after Pope cannot handle it further, but must do something else. Swift lived at a time when anatomy and novel were merging, and being a Tory, he ignored the novel and concentrated on the anatomy—and destroyed it in the same way. His attitude to it is contemporary with Congreve's attitude to the drama. The same sense of the inward destruction and exhaustion of possibilities of the form I find in *The Way of the World*, and it seems to me that Congreve's retirement from the stage and his retreat into the frigid pedantry of his Pindaric odes manifest a pessimism in regard to a changing cultural order far more corrosive than Swift's. For Swift's attack on the anatomy was sustained and energetic, like Beethoven's on the sonata, and left the way more open for newer developments.

Practically everything in the anatomy tradition was dissolved in the acid bath of Swift's satire. First, there is the annihilation of the allegory in *A Tale of a Tub*. In Laputa, even in *The Battle of the Books*, the anatomy of erudition descending from Rabelais and Burton receives the same treatment. With the Houyhnhnms the target of the Utopia is set up only to be riddled the more completely. And the whole of the satiric anatomy form which comes down from the Romans is swept up, along with the picaresque tradition, in Lilliput and Brobdingnag. The individual contemplating society disapprovingly and remaining himself invulnerable: this is the scheme of the satiric anatomy. In Swift both individual and society become unbearably ridiculous, but all the endless variety and distortion of perspective in caricature, the whole system of Rabelaisian gigantism, has been rigidly conventionalized to a scale of one to twelve, neatly balanced by another of twelve to one. Satire on satire could hardly go further.

As for the rhythmic organization of the anatomy, the analogy between Swift's attack on it and Beethoven's attack on the sonata is suggested again. The difference between the rhythm of Burton and the rhythm of Swift is similar in some ways to the difference in rhythm between Mozart and Beethoven. The actual words in Burton may be read faster, but Swift gives an effect of greater speed, because the rhyth-

mic basis of Burton is an easygoing, good-humoured lilt, and that of
Swift is a pounding, driving burst of directed energy. With Swift it
might be permissible to say that *le style, c'est le nom*.[9] In *A Tale of a Tub*,
for instance, the breaking up of the allegory by episodic digressions, as
though the work were a rondo, would destroy the unity of any literary
work which did not travel at the speed of music. As for *Gulliver's Travels*, it is surely obvious that the ferocity and vigour of the satire require a
style of great compression and swiftness, and that, on the other hand,
such a style demands that sharp and pungent things be said. I am not
concerned to attempt to prove that Swift's choice of subject matter was
conditioned by the demands of his form, but I am anxious to disprove
the sloppy assumption that the breathless ecstasy of repulsion and horror in *Gulliver's Travels* can be explained purely on subjective grounds. If
Swift were a completely disillusioned pessimist, his work would surely
be sluggish, lazy, and despondent, if it got itself written at all. When a
great man writes a great book, there are no causal connections between
matter and manner in either direction, but a focusing of all the factors
involved: the author's character, the requirements of his forms, and the
stage to which literary history has developed those forms. To speak of
any acknowledged masterpiece as the work of a man out of touch with
his time defines the speaker as an incompetent critic.

A corollary of this principle is that art forms are organic growths:
they go through certain well-defined stages of development, maturity,
decline, and exhaustion. Elizabethan drama is an excellent example of
this: the collapse of blank verse into loose rhetorical prose, the gradual
distillation and thinning out of tragic themes in Brome and Shirley, the
continued probing of the borderlands of consciousness in search of novelty, the Puritanic advance and the closing of the theatres all coincide at
the end. The novel is drawing to a close in precisely the same way, as
the society which produced it changes into a new social order, and it is
going through the same stages of decadence and winding up of its
inherent possibilities. If we get a new organization of society, we shall
assuredly get a new form of prose fiction. The analysis of individual
character will give place to something else. If our new social regime
depends on cooperation rather than competition, and it looks as though
it will be compelled to do so, we shall probably see a new growth of the
communal art form of the drama, which will no doubt absorb much of
the study of character. It would appear, then, that we are developing a
prose fiction opposed to the Jane Austen tradition and more in sympa-

thy with the seventeenth-century anatomy. It will not be a revival of the anatomy: nothing ever revives in art; but possibly an expansion of the novel to include anatomic features and provide us with the synthesis of the two forms we found lacking in the preceding century.

In general, the novel does show a gradual process of expansion as it develops into something that is not quite the novel. We have noted the merging of tale and novel in Conrad and Hardy, and around the turn of the century the exhaustion of possibilities in the character-analysis novel coincided, of course, with a growing sense of larger intellectual problems in human situations requiring more explicit treatment and with an increased sense of flux in the social order. Thus, the study of character steadily tends to expand its perspective until it sees individuals as types again, this time as types of a class, or civilization, or culture. Samuel Butler, typical of Victorian self-distrust, reverts to the anatomy, *Erewhon* and *Erewhon Revisited* belonging to the satiric side of the Utopian tradition—the Utopia positive reviving as well, of course, with Morris, Wells, Bellamy, and so on. The autobiographical novel was a further step in trying to gain for the dramatic novel the generalized social perspective of the picaresque novel, a movement completed in the stream of consciousness tradition, which has a seventeenth-century ancestor in Pepys's diary. This pull toward the anatomy has influenced even those temperamentally unsuited to the form: H.G. Wells is a good blackboard example of a growth from first-rate tale to second-rate novel, and from second-rate novel to third-rate anatomy.

The rise of class-consciousness and the habit of thinking of people in terms of class labels necessarily plays its part in the development of a literary form to anatomize the capitalist system in its various aspects, simple examples being the popularized technicalities of Bernard Shaw and Bertrand Russell, and that in its turn expands to what might be called the cultural anatomy, the treatment of character as the product of a certain cultural consciousness. Galsworthy's Forsyte studies tend toward this: even *The Ambassadors*, the ripest work of the most conscious artist among English novelists, expands into a study of the impact of two civilizations and cultural modes of thought of which the characters become symbolic. In our own day Briffault's *Europa* and the *Men of Good Will* series are random examples of what is likely to become the central medium of twentieth-century prose. The more exotic cultural anatomy will probably gain more ground as the Spenglerian dialectic begins to penetrate into English consciousness: at present *Arabia Deserta* is the most conspicuous example. In the novels of D.H. Lawrence there is a gradual progression toward the cultural anatomy of which *The Plumed Serpent* is the best instance; in those of Aldous Huxley, a similar culmination in the Utopian satire of *Brave New World*, which continues the tradition of Swift and Samuel Butler into the contemporary cultural anatomy period.

As individuals continue to be increasingly regarded as cultural products, there will necessarily follow a new emphasis on symbolism. In this connection the importance and influence of one of the greatest anatomies in the English language, Frazer's *Golden Bough*, in revealing as it does the symbolic basis of unconscious activity, will be difficult to overestimate. The treatment of symbolism by contemporary psychologists, Jung for example, will no doubt merge with this, but it has at present fewer purely literary connotations. *Joseph and His Brethren* is perhaps the leading descendant of Frazer at present. The stream of consciousness tradition, following out the subjective side of the contemporary anatomic development, is rapidly moving into symbolism, and in *Ulysses* the imposition of the *Odyssey* pattern on the characters brings in a double focus which provides endless opportunities for treating the symbolic implications of human thoughts and actions. *Ulysses*, again, is, if we except Blake's abortive, unfinished, and unpublished *Island in the Moon*, the first rhythmically organized novel since *Tristram Shandy*. The general tightening up of rhythm in novels influenced by Joyce and Proust and the awakening sense that style, which is a sense of rhythm, is the essential element in the writing of prose, and not simply something to be ladled into a purple passage (if I am not mixing metaphors), are also factors in bringing us nearer to twentieth-century prose fiction.

There remains a further question. Much of the material we have been dealing with is satiric, and satire in prose is obviously not an art form but the expression of an attitude. But does not the satire in prose, i.e., a work permeated by the satiric attitude, tend to approach some such form as the anatomy? For the pure novel is rather too objective a form for the satirist to make sure that his points are striking home: in spite of its association with the comedy of manners, surely the most artistic novels, those of Jane Austen or Henry James, are satires only by implication. The satire demands some form which permits of more subjective arrangement of material, however objective the material itself may be: in the novel the expression of direct satire brings the author on the stage, as we can see in Thackeray. The material of the satirist is human society, *quidquid agunt homines,*[10] which implies that the prose art form we are evolving now, which is to incorporate the subjective arrangement and systematized outlook of the anatomy with the character study of the novel, will establish the satire as an art form. Wyndham Lewis propounds somewhat similar principles in his *Men without Art,* and *The Apes of God* is both an anatomy of charlatanism and a satire, though Lewis is far too proud of the fact that he possesses no sense of rhythm to supply a complete example.

There is hardly space here to examine the influence of the anatomy form on poetry, as distinct from the epic. *Religio Laici* corresponds to *Religio Medici,* of course; and, in various periods, the very literal anatomy of *The Purple Island,* the *Essays* of Pope, *The Pleasures of the Imagination,* are random examples. To recapitulate: the conglomerate of contemporary fiction consists on the whole of varying admixtures of three main elements, anatomy, tale, and novel, using these words as names of art forms. The novel and the tale are bourgeois developments of an objective treatment of the interaction of narrative and character which in an earlier age was on the whole associated with the drama, and they bear to one another somewhat the relationship of comedy to tragedy. In the novel proper the characters tend to act out the events; in the tale the events tend actively to influence the characters, so that we get more sense of nonhuman or superhuman activity. The tale tends to be briefer than the novel and to depend more on factors of concentration, such as speed of narrative or rhythm of style. *Heart of Darkness* and *The Turn of the Screw* are fairly pure examples of the tale: *Pride and Prejudice* and *Portrait of a Lady,* fairly pure examples of the novel: *Lord Jim* and *Tess of the D'Urbervilles* represent a fairly complete merging of both elements. The tale continually recalls the idea of a narrator and tends to isolate the rhythmic side of drama; the novel approaches drama more by its objectivity. The anatomy is the art form which dominated prose fiction between *Utopia* and *Gulliver's Travels,* reaching its culmination in Burton, merging with the novel in *Tristram Shandy,* existing beside a novelistic tradition in *Sartor Resartus* and *Erewhon,* and tending to merge with both tale and novel as those forms become exhausted with the breakdown of middle-class society. It is essentially a thesis or ordered presentation of a subject, either to reveal a certain attitude on the part of the author, as with *Religio Medici,* or to present one of his objective interests, as in *The Compleat Angler.* When it deals with human character, it views it as consisting of general types rather than personalities, as in the character books or the *Anatomy of Melancholy*, or else the focus is on the author's attitude to society as represented by certain individuals, as in the more consciously artistic picaresque novels, in the generalized anatomic satire, or in the Utopia form. The treatment of character in the anatomy, thus, is closer to the allegorical or stereotyped than in the novel proper. The anatomy depends on the completion of a certain outlook, both intellectually and rhythmically, and is, therefore, at its best more integrated than the novel and is a form in which style is a positive quality. It is not being revived now, but the novel is expanding into a new development of it, owing chiefly to the rise of class and cultural consciousness and to the impending renaissance of drama. Marx's anatomy of capitalism may influence the growth of a class-conscious anatomy-novel; Spengler's anatomy of Western culture, the growth of a culturally conscious one. At present anatomy and novel, though merging, are not completely fused: *The Golden Bough* and *Arabia Deserta* are not novels, and *The Forsyte Saga, Jean Christophe, Europa*, and *Men of Good Will* are not anatomies. But the central lines of twentieth-century prose fiction run through a form which will consider individuals in relation to the cultural or class entities they spring from, and may, therefore, among other things, establish an art form for satire. The closest nineteenth-century approach to this form in the novel is perhaps *The Brothers Karamazov*. It is possible that the new anatomy of civilization may be divisible, like the seventeenth-century anatomy, into subjective and objective presentations of the author's attitude, in which case the Bergsonian stream of consciousness tradition culminating in Proust might represent the furthest development of the subjective side we have yet achieved. In conclusion, may I throw out the tentative suggestion that the culturally conscious novel, such as *The Plumed Serpent* or *Joseph and His Brethren*, is associated with a study of the working of religious impulses in society, and that the class-conscious novel, such as *Europa*, is associated with a study of class struggle, and that if we eventually see a class struggle transforming itself into a religion, as with Christianity in the Roman Empire, we will also see a merging of these two traditions into the great prose art form of the future?

20

The Importance of Calvin
for Philosophy

The date and provenance of this paper are uncertain, but its location in the Northrop Frye Fonds alongside the essays Frye wrote when he was at Emmanuel College (1933–36) suggests that it was written during those years. Frye's several references to his audience (e.g., "We are not concerned tonight" in paragraph 3) point to an oral presentation. On 23 April 1935 Frye wrote to Helen Kemp that he was going to "cross swords with" Norman Langford "at the Theological Society next fall—Arminius against Calvin."[1] The present paper could well be the text of the talk he gave in the debate with Langford, a fellow student at Emmanuel, at the Theological Society. Frye seems to be referring to the society when he says in paragraph 2 that it is not necessary to recall for "so initiated as group as this" certain elementary facts about Calvin.[2] The typescript is in the NFF, 1991, box 37, file 13.

To make one's mark in the contemporary world of scholarship one must be both erudite and eclectic: the present age has a vast number of intellectual interests, and the attainments of those who specialize in any one of them are looked upon with respect increasing in proportion as the field becomes more narrow and intense. The high priests of modern learning are expected to be able to talk unintelligibly about their particular subjects and to require a hair-splitting nicety of statement from their acolytes. As a result, laymen feel a certain hesitancy in handling the really important questions of those cultural disciplines with which they are unfamiliar and prefer to have the assurance of expert opinion before canonizing any prejudice which involves them.

Why theology should be so grotesque an exception to this rule it is by no means easy to say. Perhaps the safest working assumption is that people are anxious not to concede the validity of theology's claim to be a cultural discipline because, once theology is recognized, religion must be recognized too, and if religion be recognized, what would become of contemporary society? So the well-educated, enlightened man of today grows up with a superstitious awe of science, and a certain amount of respect for philosophy and the arts, but is quite prepared to group theology with alchemy or kabbalism and to talk of religious developments in terms which, by the standards set for any other intellectual pursuit, would disgrace a six-year-old. Probably most of us will spend a good deal of time explaining gently to otherwise well-informed people that mysticism is not the same thing as mistiness, that predestination is not fatalism, or that the ordinary priggish rule-of-thumb bourgeois morality of the nineteenth century, according to which, if one observed the fifth and seventh commandments, one could break the other eight with impunity, is not Puritanism. After doing that, we should not be too much shocked if we find that John Calvin, who has done more to influence our conception of God than any other man, should be for many people an incarnation of the devil. For the stock caricature of Calvin as a merciless and humourless sadist who really believed only in hell would make a very fair Satan for some aspiring Milton. There may be a few even in so initiated a group as this whom it might be expedient to remind that Calvin was not a Scotchman, that he was only indirectly responsible for Calvinism, and that he was not responsible at all for degradations and perversions of his teachings made by superstitious bigots.

We are not concerned tonight with the rehabilitation of Calvin's character, but with the investigation of a problem closely bound up with the contemporary abhorrence of him, which may prove, on analysis, to be less inexplicable than it is ignorant and ill-considered. The problem may be briefly stated thus. There is no clear line between theology and philosophy: the questions they respectively deal with cannot be disentangled. Both are rationalized accounts of the interrelation of soul, external world, and God. Both rest on axioms supplied by faith. The difference between them is a difference of emphasis. At some periods the theologian and the philosopher become merged into one thinker: thus, Aquinas was the greatest philosopher of his time because he was its greatest theologian, and vice versa. Schleiermacher in modern times provides a parallel synthesis. In Calvin we have a theologian with a first-class brain; posterity may prove him wrong, but it cannot prove him a fool: why, then, does he not at least touch on the problems of philosophy? A general history of philosophy is bound to mention Aquinas; it finds no occasion to mention Calvin. The questions which are implied in this include two of some importance: First, does Calvin's theology have any integral connection with the philosophical thought of Calvin's time, as is the case with Aquinas? Second, has Protestantism such a thing as a philosophical foundation at all? The former is the subject of our immediate enquiry.

It is admitted, of course, that to say that Calvin had a logical mind does not necessarily imply that he had a systematic one. The *Institutes* is not predominantly an apologetic or polemic, as the *City of God* is, nor is it essentially synthetic or dogmatic, as the *Summa* is. It is critical and analytic, systematic chiefly by implication, professedly a commentary on Scripture and, therefore, inductive in its reasoning, and an opponent of uncontrolled speculation. It is a guide to action in religion and, therefore, avoids raising the larger issues which reflection would call forth. But, nevertheless, theology is a rational approach to the problem of the relationship between God and man, and both it and philosophy, to become complete, must invade one another's territories. We are accustomed to think of philosophy as the presentation of the facts of experience in an intellectual pattern. Science brings in data from the outer world, classifies it and sorts it out, establishes the presence of laws which work the physical machinery of the universe, and provides a barrage of objective facts against our prejudices. Philosophy works out the implications of science and presents a still more coherent view of the world, and systematic philosophy is, thus, admittedly deeper and more fundamental an intellectual activity than science. Unfortunately, however, it is less satisfactory in getting results that are tangible and irrefutable; for it reflects the state of knowledge existent at its time, and, being subject to the limitations that imposes, is essentially a historical phenomenon. The history of philosophy, therefore, underlies systematic philosophy as the latter does science. But in its turn the history of philosophy cannot be content to be a mere record of changing tastes and endlessly refuted opinions: if it does not contain a shape and significant form, everything dissolves in scepticism. That significant form, however, must lie in history itself; in other words, the most fundamental intellectual activity of the human race is a philosophy of history, an attempt to find a pattern in existence. As the only knowledge we can have is knowledge of the past, life as an object of knowledge must be history, so that a philosophy of history and a philosophy of life, popularly regarded as the only practical goal of knowledge, are the same thing.

Now Christian theology rests on the doctrine of the Incarnation of God in Jesus Christ, which it regards as a historical event, however it may interpret the doctrine of Incarnation itself. All theology is bound to be, in our tradition, a philosophy of history in essence; and one Christian sect is distinguished from another largely through the view it takes of the historical context of the coming of Christ. We have at one extreme a Catholic interest in the salvation of the world as a whole, which sees a critical and unique change in the Advent, symbolized by the establishment of an infallible Church and tradition of doctrine. At the other we have a Protestant interest in the individual, which tends to deny the historical importance of it altogether, and to regard it as an eternal relationship between God and man. But whichever side we favour, the point at the moment is that theology forms a matrix of philosophy, as well as of culture generally. In any age, the deepest intellectual problems are always theological, which means that our understanding of the cultural pattern any age presents depends on our understanding of its theology.

This implies, of course, that theology is no less dependent than any other study on the social conditions and requirements of the time. Theology is the summation of our knowledge of God; and as that can obviously never be complete, it must always be subject to human limitations, the most important and ultimate of which, when a number of the greatest geniuses of an age are working on it, is the outlook of that age. This is not to say that an agnostic historical relativism is the last retreat of wisdom, for there are permanent truths carried on and reinterpreted from one period to another. But in considering the theology of so powerful a thinker as Calvin, the point we have just made, that the understanding of it brings a quicker and more intuitive comprehension of the general intellectual pattern of his time than any other approach could do, implies the complement, that it is ultimately a part, although a central part, of that pattern. Besides, the fact that Christian theology is so closely associated with a philosophy of history makes it essential that the historical perspective of any contribution to it be taken into consideration.

What we have said, of course, implies a unity and coherence to Christian tradition; if we cannot accept the postulate that Christendom has remained an intellectual entity when it is no longer a political one, our thesis at once collapses. But once the obvious fact is recognized that

Christian theology has always striven primarily to recreate a relationship with Jesus, it becomes a necessary inference that this involves the
problem we are considering. For the ideal is constant and eternal, and
the need for reinterpretation arises from the changes in human fortunes,
so that Protestantism, like other approaches in the Christian faith, is produced by the necessity of a new historical perspective.

This new historical perspective, with its requirements, results from a
general change in the cultural pattern; and if we regard the latter as an
organic unit, or rather as part of one, rather than as the dustheap of a
conflict of material interests, theology becomes, not a tangled skein of
thin-spun concepts, but a kind of nervous system which penetrates into
the remotest corners of contemporary art, philosophy, politics, and
economics. Calvin's immediate historical context was such a change: a
crisis in the organic growth of Western culture, an access of self-
consciousness, and a consequent development of individuality. The
results of this are familiar to everyone: an increase in technical power
resulting in the rise of the middle class, the development of credit capitalism and colonial expansion, the shift from market-town to culture-
town and the consequent growth of nationalism, the development and
specialization of the arts. Luther and Calvin represent two rhythms of
this movement. The former belongs to the period of revolt, the latter to
the period of consolidation. Renaissance and Reformation both were in
origin a surging up of the vitality and energy of the physical against the
dried-up abstraction of an outmoded scholasticism, an assertion of
awakened delight in the world of sense experience. The typical figures
of this rebellion—Luther, Rabelais, Skelton, Titian, Paracelsus, Henry
VIII—all have a Falstaffian bodily exuberance about them. At the same
time there was all the disillusionment of a long, indecisive, incredibly
brutal conflict, and the great men whose energies were directed toward
consolidation and the establishment of order were of a very different
type. A hard intellectual ruthlessness, arising from a disciplined grasp
of reality and an anything but enthusiastic view of the human race, is
the hallmark not only of Calvin in theology but of Machiavelli in politics, of Montaigne and Cervantes, perhaps even Shakespeare, in literature, of Galileo in science, of the devotees of form and imitation of
classical models in the arts. (Machiavelli, of course, has suffered far
more even than Calvin from misrepresentation and confusion with the
prince of darkness, the main influence at work there being Elizabethan
drama.) In spite of much scepticism and even cynicism about these men,

their extraordinary clarity of perception, their completely controlled knowledge of the sin and folly of mankind, makes it difficult for the most sentimental of us to ignore them. Calvin's intellectual environment was one of profound contempt for cloudy or prejudiced thinking and for any form of naive optimism in regard to a human society boiling over with cruelty and selfishness.

For the most general impression we have of the time is that of a tremendous centrifugal sense of dislocation. The discovery of America and the trade routes to India had brought a movement of expansion without any compensating feeling of unity. The balance of power had shifted to the oceanic countries, Rome was no longer the psychological centre of the world, and the cosmopolitan Christendom of the Middle Ages had been torn apart into national units, but the result was purely disruptive, and anything like a cooperative ideal for mankind as a whole looked impossible. The historical perspective had been dislocated by the discovery of classical culture; the Catholic theory of the infallibility of the Church rested on a philosophy of history attaching all importance to the Incarnation, which had of itself transformed the world from darkness to light, abolished the old dispensation, and proclaimed the new. Such a thesis was hard to maintain in the face of the great literary and sculptural masterpieces which proved classical civilization to have been a higher flowering of the human spirit than the so-called Christian Dark Ages which followed it. Cosmology had been dislocated as well; in place of the geocentric medieval system in which man's concerns had a central significance, Copernicus had flung away the spherical wrappings of Aquinas's universe and showed the earth as a speck of dust in infinite space, in which man looked very small and very accidental. (Copernicus is added here because he completes the pattern: his ideas were by no means undisputed, even by reputable scientists, until late in the seventeenth century.) The whole movement of colonial expansion, of course, was part of the same thing. But while loyalties in the temporal world became less subtle and refined, they became far more material and concrete. The process of atomism that the rise of the middle class was forcing on Europe, the splitting up of the feudal pyramid topped by pope and emperor, reinforced its rapid expansion and division by the consolidation and close organization of each unit. Absolute monarchy and unquestioned obedience to the prince became, with most of the Erastians,[3] even a part of religion, and were in fact largely a substitute for religion, for it is easy to overestimate the actual hold of Christianity on the sixteenth century. Certainly in England a good deal of the Catholic cult of the Virgin was absorbed into the Protestant cult of the Virgin Queen. Not that this implied the passive subjection of the new and dominant middle class, of course; the middle class exalted the prince because their economic interest demanded the protection of a strongly centralized national unit. Their economy was a town economy, and most of the nations growing up at the time consisted of a capital city and a surrounding territory for it to draw strength from. The dictator-prince was a projection of bourgeois competitive individualism. This, of course, is what distinguishes the bourgeois culture between the sixteenth and eighteenth centuries from the bourgeois culture produced by the Industrial Revolution. The former combines an intense feeling of communal national solidarity with an aggressive individualism; energy, for it, will necessarily incorporate itself in strict forms. When the culture-town disappeared at the end of the eighteenth century and the metropolis emerged, with its panoply of democracy, machine technique, and a social feeling of a mass rather than a group, civilization became completely individualized.[4] Calvin is the presiding theological mind of the former period; that of the later, as well as we can judge at present, is Kant.

The sense of dislocation is just as obvious in the history of thought as in the history of politics. In Aquinas, at the height of medieval culture, we have a conception of a God who is infinite energy operating in intellectual forms. God's will is conditioned by his intellect: he has created a universe in which two and two make four, and he will not go back on that. To Scotus and Occam this was a reflection of God's power: God can do what he likes; the universe is a projection of his will, and one must not limit God to a necessary choice. Occam is reputed to have argued that God could have incarnated Himself as well in a donkey as in a man if he had willed it.[5] This, of course, was part of the creed of nominalism, according to which the objects of experience were real, and the generic types employed in their classification had a value that was conceptual and instrumental rather than intrinsic. For Aquinas reality lay in those general or universal ideas: it was impersonal and objective and, therefore, intelligible; whereas with his opponents reality was ultimately bound up with experience, of which reason is, like its ideas, an abstraction.[6] Scotus was the first to say that man cannot reach God through the reason. But this feeling of the nominalist, that universals were abstractions and particulars real, had its political consequences as well. The

Thomist doctrine that reality existed in universals had as its political inference a politically and spiritually united Christendom. The nominalists by contrast tended to become nationalistic; and they were, of course, supported by the weak but rising middle class, who allied themselves with the king against the nobles, who propped up the feudal system. Therefore, Wycliffe succeeds to Scotus and Occam in England, and with him the patriotic alliance is established. The nobles in England seized power and held it all through the fifteenth century, but eventually they collapsed. The political struggle sharpened on the Continent with Wycliffe's disciple Huss, and was completed by Luther, who went back to Occam for philosophical guidance.

Calvin comes at the close of the nominalist tradition and completes its destruction of the Thomist synthesis. He follows the great Franciscans in his exaltation of the arbitrary and omnipotent will of God. Aquinas's conditioning factor of the intellect left the way open, of course, for a systematic interconnection of religion with morality; God's actions, if intelligible, can be judged by moral criteria. But if God's will be absolute, it cannot be restrained by moral ideas, and Calvin, as acutely aware as Machiavelli or Nietzsche of the essentially nonmoral nature of experience, sweeps this aside. The Catholic test of justification—good works—is a moral one. The Protestants, in steadily hammering out the doctrine of justification by faith, were emphasizing the fact that reality lies in experience rather than reflection, and that religion, the ultimate reality, therefore, is to be conceived in terms of will, which does not operate in moral categories. Faith is not a moral activity: religion is concerned with God, morals with society; and according to Protestants they are not basically the same thing.

Another important inference from nominalism supplies us with a key to our problem. If God's will is not conditioned by his intellect, and we cannot reach God through the unaided reason, the Thomist distinction between natural and revealed religion disappears: everything is revealed, and theology, the rational approach to God, becomes impossible except by way of revelation. This, of course, was the reason for the importance of the Scriptures in Protestant doctrine, for the translations of them by Wycliffe and Luther, and for Calvin's complete reliance on them as the only source of revelation. But that is not the whole point. With the rise of nominalism, the connection between the theology and philosophy disappears. The philosophical descendant of the nominalists, Francis Bacon, banishes theology from discussion on the ground that it deals with revealed truths which by hypothesis cannot encroach on philosophy or science.[7] On the other side, Calvin clings to the authority of Scripture and attacks philosophy whenever it crosses the border of theology.

The general pattern of disruption, then, separates philosophy from theology, and the two studies run separately until the next cultural crisis contemporary with the Industrial Revolution. But the lacuna itself is simply part of an expanded but still unified pattern; the explicit connection disappears, the implicit one remains. There is no cardinal doctrine of Calvin which is not an intellectual product inevitable to the Renaissance. In Calvin's insistence on the sovereignty of God we see reflected the intense Renaissance feeling for absolute order and cohesion, which exalted the prince to the verge of deification, which in the arts made a cult of strict form and strong outline, which in philosophy reared the dizzy mechanical and mathematical structures of Descartes and the Cartesians. We can see the new feeling for a centralized autocracy, of course, in the Erastian sects. But Calvin is far subtler. In his doctrine of election there is mirrored the immense energy and power of the expanding mercantile capitalism of his time, the activity of which had no moral responsibilities, but responded only to an overruling and irresistible driving force. This is not in Lutheranism, or at any rate not completely in Lutheranism; it is only in Calvin's doctrine of predestination that we can see the connection between the new self-conscious individualism of the Renaissance and the new autocracy, which at first sight seems such a paradox. In his exaltation of the transcendence of God we see the Renaissance contempt of human society that we find in Machiavelli and Montaigne; and in the individuality of Calvin's appeal, the isolation of the human soul in its relation to God, the Renaissance "complete man." I am not for a moment concerned to deny that Calvin's concepts are on a spiritual level and that the things I connect with them are on a temporal one. The patterns remain analogous: Calvin has grasped the inner form of Renaissance life and has worked it into a theological system. The Catholics carried on a parallel development: Loyola and the Jesuits brought a similar revival of Augustine's doctrines of grace and self-discipline, a similar separation of morality from the work of the will of God in the world, a similar feeling for complete cohesion of organization and subordination to authority. The authority was spiritual as well as material: just as the cult of the prince was associated with the following of classical models in art, so was Calvin's emphasis on the sovereignty of God associated with an absolute reliance on Scripture. But we have to look deeper than scriptural exegesis to get at the conditioning factors of Calvin's theology. As it is quixotic to look for literal coherence and absolute consistency in the Bible, a theologian seeking scriptural authority is bound to impose a preconceived form on the material provided by it. That form in Calvin's case was established by the requirements of his own time, which he, as a genius, could grasp as a unity.

If this thesis, that a great book owes its greatness to the fact that it makes explicit the intellectual outlook of its time, be conceded to have any validity, it will at once become apparent that our attitude to tradition is simplified. The one thing certain about the theology of the immediate future is that it will be a twentieth-century theology. However, contemporary thought expends a good deal of its energy in predicting the philosophy just around the corner in terms of the swing of a Hegelian pendulum. We have gone too far in this or that direction: there is bound to be a reaction in that or this direction: such is the monotonous argument of innumerable books written today. In making this reaction we will "go back to" some thinker we have neglected, or we will move further away from him and view with alarm, as a symptom of decadence, what he stood for. All this seems to me to be bosh. Whether the future be inevitable or not, there can be no doubt the past is, and the past extends to the present and conditions it at every point. We are not at liberty to free ourselves from the rhythm of history as it sweeps us along the moving dot we call the present: if we are born in a tradition, we have to do the best we can with that tradition. A good deal of Catholic thought today is greatly weakened by the fact that it feels itself bound in consistency to regard the Renaissance and Reformation as essentially a mistake, the development of individuality since that time having been on the wrong track, and to propose that we return to the ideals of the Middle Ages in politics, philosophy, and art.[8] Surely such a reaction to history is hopelessly quixotic. We move very quickly in a linear progression; we are dragged backward into the future, and are not free to stop and start again. Protestantism works with the unit of the individual, not a movement primarily nor the political or cultural manifestation of a movement. It, thus, gains an advantage in that it is not tied to a social group: it does not have to prove that society was happiest when it was most Protestant, nor does it have to whitewash all Protestant governments to show that there was a purity about them that others lacked. The fact actually is that the world has undergone a Protestant

Reformation, and we are living in a post-Reformation world and have no choice in the matter.

I shall not, therefore, wind up with the conventional peroration that Calvin's ideas, though they may be outmoded in many ways, yet contain much that is valuable for us, and that as we are moving away from facile humanism and prosperous liberalism, we will find a new value in discipline and humility, etc., by going back to Calvin. My point is throughout, paradoxical as it may sound, that Calvin's value for us is in direct proportion to his value for his own time: that the latter made him great, and his greatness makes him valuable. Truth, in spheres other than those that can be treated by exact science, depends on organic coherence. Calvin is a fact in our tradition: he is at work moulding and influencing us and countless others in all sorts of subtle and intangible ways, and he is not an isolated thinker we can accept or reject or pick and choose from. The same thing is true of Aquinas, of course; consequently, it is hardly possible for Christianity to preserve much longer the antithesis of Catholic and Protestant. The traditions of Catholics, which run through Loyola and Pascal instead of Luther and Calvin, are different from ours; but as Loyola and Calvin approximated similar cultural patterns, and Catholics and Protestants today do likewise, the difference is far less than we might imagine. Our immediate concern, then, is to review as briefly as possible what lies between Calvin and us.

The most important factor here is, of course, the emergence of a second crisis in the development of Western culture: the shift from culture-town to metropolis which brought about the Industrial Revolution in economics, the French and American Revolutions in politics, and romanticism in the arts. This crisis is all the more important for us, since before it those religious traditions which were not Calvinist can be clearly distinguished from Calvinism, but after it a transformation of religious thought took place which began breaking down these distinctions and shaping an entirely different outline of thought.

The first thing to be noticed is that the association of Calvinism with the psychological attitude of a social class resulted in the gradual casting of it off as a disguise for political and economic movements. Thus, the rise of the middle-class oligarchy in seventeenth-century England was primarily a religious movement in 1642, primarily political in 1688, and primarily economic in 1776. With this subsidence of the religious impulse, it became inevitable that activity should be increasingly regarded as an impersonal force and in origin autonomous with man.

Deism, the most prevalent religion of the eighteenth century, prepared
the way for the complete individualizing of bourgeois society and the
final disruption of belief in a creative consciousness.

The philosophers of German romanticism, who in the main followed
Kant in their epistemology, worked out the theory of impersonal overruling will in the world to its logical conclusion. The pessimistic fatalism
of Schopenhauer represents perhaps the ultimate reaction to Calvin. For
predestination implies a transcendent God, fatalism an immanent one.
A transcendent God, postulated as good, is necessarily a completely
conscious God: the working out of his purposes may be inscrutable, but
should not the less command our loyalty. But an immanent God, practically the same thing as organic nature, must be a blind irrational irresponsible force which causes endless suffering and fitful happiness, and
which is never likely to achieve its own self-realization and certainly is
unconscious of our own participation in it. This repudiation was balanced, partly even in Schopenhauer, by the doctrine of the perfectibility
of man through the destruction of evil institutions, a theme which
started with Rousseau and finally swept up the Darwinian discoveries
into the complete bourgeois synthesis of Herbert Spencer, in whom the
universe becomes one vast capitalistic system of competitive development, expansion, and progress, always refining and complicating its
technique to produce bigger and better forms of life. In somewhat more
appealing forms the philosophy of evolution postulated a Utopian goal
for humanity somewhere at the end of history. It is good for us to die
fighting to reach that goal, said these philosophers, though there may be
nothing to compensate us for our pains but the perfunctory and generalized gratitude of posterity: a view of life so monstrous and hopeless that
the most hardened Calvinist might shudder to contemplate it.

Eventually, with Bergson for example, the evolutionary philosophy
and the romantic doctrine of the organic, creative, unconscious will met
and merged. But this completion of the pattern has shown us very
clearly that the access of self-consciousness brought about during the
Industrial Revolution was basically an awareness of the movement of
the time. We have been evolving a time-philosophy for over a century
and are at present being paralysed through the introspection resulting
from the contemplation of motion, seeking more permanent and endur-
ing forms than those afforded by the processes of organic growth: forms
more easily accessible both to the intellect and the moral sense. Much of
the contemporary horror of Calvinism can be traced to the fact that his

predestination is regarded in the perspective of evolutionary fatalism; we take it for granted that the purpose of a transcendent God is the same thing as the "immanent Will and its designs" of Hardy's *Dynasts*. Again, it is not always realized how comparatively easy it is to see the essential value of Calvin's concept of sovereignty and detach from it his particular view of the future life. We have fully realized now, surely, that while rewards and punishments and eternal life may exist after death, all must be infinitely subtler a process than we imagine: that to project into eternity our three-dimensional ideas of earthly existence is an activity essential to symbolic art, but has no place in speculation.

Contemporary with Calvin, the thought of the transcendence, immutability, and permanence of God led philosophers to attempt to approach him in terms of the most static forms they could conceive, which they necessarily derived from mathematics and physics. Spinoza's conception of God, worked out in mathematical metaphors, was completely depersonalized, entirely dissociated from any process of organic development. Thus, the philosophy of Calvin's age, owing largely to its separation from theology and theism, led first, with Spinoza, to a dead Parmenidean space-universe, and then, with Bergson, to a surging Heraclitean temporal one. This means that we are now through with reactions: we must go on from Bergson, but we shall certainly not "go back" to Spinoza. The more we try to react from the time-philosophy we were born in, the more assuredly we shall be caught in its backwash. That is a necessary part of our cultural inheritance; the facts it presents are irrefutable, and our future development will depend on an increased absorption of tradition, not on a further selection from it. But that Calvin will be one of the factors absorbed is indubitable. For one thing, he provides, as we have already seen, the possibility for exactly the synthesis we are bound to make. The combination of the doctrine of the sovereign God with the doctrine of election gives us a working basis to establish the permanence and transcendence of form, on the one hand, and the reality of organic experience, on the other.

Whenever a movement in philosophy passes on to another, society passes out of one mould into another, and vice versa. The expanding time-philosophy of bourgeois society can last only as long as that society does. Apparently we are engaged in forming a social order dependent on cooperation and a group response rather than anarchic and chaotic individualism, but a group response which will more closely resemble, let us hope, Kant's kingdom of ends than the stampeding masses of frightened fanatics who seem to be shaping political events today. It seems highly probable that Christianity will become more what it was in apostolic times, a proletariat religion, as we move into a society of metropolitan culture such as was existing in imperial Rome. As our political units become more stable, our philosophy will become more so too. The inference bourgeois society made from the Copernican theory, for example, that the earth is a discrete unit in an infinite and meaningless space, is bound to give way to a sense of relativism which will recognize that the centre of the universe is wherever one happens to be.[9]

It is obvious that if we look at Calvin we can see in his view of God a Cartesian feeling for order and permanence, and that if we look at his view of man we see that for him human activity springs from sources deeper than the human will. The immense energy and uncompromising heroism of Calvinism, its tendency to consolidate in theocratic dictatorships, sufficiently refute the theory that according to it our relation with God should be one of helpless quietism. As a social force, Calvinism identified itself more explicitly with the bourgeois than with the royal side of the alliance of prince and middle class, in opposition to the Erastians, but as a doctrine both factors are present. But they are present in antithesis, not synthesis; God and man have too wide a gap between them. Just as Aquinas had extended the feudal society of his day into heaven and established a hierarchy of angels leading up to God, so in Luther we find an absolute monarch protecting the interests of a democratic body of the saved through their faith in and obedience to him. There is something of this in Calvin, but on the whole his scheme disregards the state and the organization of human society, resting on an Augustinian dualism between a city of God, or body of elect, and an excluded world.

As our civilization becomes more mature, it is bound to expand and take in more of its cultural heritage. A greater eclecticism will no doubt do much to rehabilitate Calvin, but the positive contribution of the thought between Calvin's time and ours cannot be ignored; nothing less than the full consciousness of the unity of our tradition will be satisfactory for us. And it seems that the time-philosophy of the last century has a real value in reinforcing Calvin's doctrine. Now that evolution has penetrated into our intellectual make-up, we are beginning to sense the working out of a purpose in the organic world, so that the Manichean dualism of a static principle of good existing beside an unregenerate nature, which came into Christian thought with Augustine, is no longer necessary for us. Of course, as we have said, the purely evolutionary doctrine, that the only truly elect are posterity, and that the ideal is actualized at the end of a historical progression, is full of contradictions and is, when pressed to its logical conclusion, unthinkably repulsive. But nevertheless we have inherited a feeling which expressed in Christian terminology might be said to be a perception of the creative, developing, redeeming power of the Holy Spirit in the affairs of men, conserving the good, progressing toward the better. To assume that this exhausts God's activity is to assume God an imperfect force striving to self-realization, such as we find in the creative evolution religions of such thinkers as Bernard Shaw. The weakness of such an attitude is that it recognizes no evolutionary lift in human history; it depends ultimately on geology for its religious dogmas and in most cases turns to the idea of the development of a "superman" which, expressed again in Christian terms, amounts practically to a call for an Incarnation, an identification of the evolutionary principle with an historical event. Nor has it a firm enough grasp of the permanence, pre-existence, and immutability of the phenomenal world, the world as an object of understanding, which the immediate successors of Calvin perhaps overemphasized.

Our conception of a dynamic world must surely arrive eventually at some idea of a tension of opposites as an underlying principle. On the one hand, there is the sphere of reality which we can in some measure understand but can never comprehend; the world of order, form, and permanence symbolized by mathematics, science, and in general the material worked on by the reason. On the other, there is the sphere of reality which we can in some measure experience but can never control; the world of development, process, and growth symbolized by political and economic movements and in general the material worked on by the will. But thought cannot stop with an antithesis; there must be tension, thrust, and counterthrust: and if there is tension there must be resolution, potential or actual. This resolution is symbolized by the arts, concerned with the incorporation of energy and inspiration in form, the deepest expression of the religious impulse. But symbols are not enough; the deepest powers of our nature drive us to find the resolution in history, and this the Christian sees in the Incarnation. In the Incarnation the redemption of the world and the infinite power of God become united in principle. Thus, Christianity is in every age a religion based on a Trinity, however that may be interpreted. For the Incarnation was not the achievement of a transient success: it was not an electric shock to the world that spent itself and passed away, but the actualizing of a principle as fundamental, as permanent, and as eternal as the love of the Father or the redeeming force of the Holy Spirit. Calvinism is not pantheism; it contains, potentially, the elements postulated above. But it has never completely freed itself from the charge of Arianism; it has not clearly differentiated the three persons of the Trinity in its insistence on the unity of God. Its doctrine of sovereignty brought it too close to the grim fighting monotheisms of Judah and Islam. For God's power is admittedly absolute, but hardly his sovereignty; *sovereign* is a word which implies subject as its complement, and complementary terms are relative to one another.

If the Incarnation was the resolution of a tension, however, it becomes a definite and unique focus in human experience, particularly if it can be related to a concept of the Holy Spirit as an evolutionary redemptive force in the organic world. Thus, the Incarnation was not arbitrary and a priori, but an event important through its historical context. What lies ahead of Christian theology is a philosophy of history less antihistorical than Calvinism. For we are coming to the end of a cultural development, and our historical perspective is steadily approaching that of Augustine, who stood at the end of his. In that perspective the rise and fall of civilizations is the pattern of the fortunes of the world; the clinging to the one event in history which hints of something better than an endless dreary record of cruelty and stupidity is the function of the Church. When these two aspects of human life interpenetrate and focus into one, we shall have a theology which can accommodate itself to twentieth-century requirements. It will not be Calvinism, but Calvin will be in its tradition.

21

T.S. Eliot and Other Observations

Frye's instructions to himself throughout this paper to "read" passages from Eliot indicate that it was prepared for an oral presentation. It is almost certainly a talk Frye gave to the Bodley Club in 1937 when he was at Oxford. It includes several references to Merton College, suggesting a local audience, but the best evidence for the time and place of the paper is in a letter to Helen Kemp (22 February 1937), where Frye says, "I'd spent most of the week trying to write a paper on T.S. Eliot, and for some reason, although I eventually wrote quite a good paper, I took an enormous time writing it—began to worry about the sentence rhythms and echoing vowels and things to the most morbid extent, so I don't think I shall try to write a paper for [Edmund] Blunden this week."[1] A bit later in the same letter he says, "I got through the paper and a very good discussion followed, although it was mostly a catechism of me. About six of them knew their Eliot well—one who knew him personally stayed and talked to me till midnight afterwards. Then I drank all the beer that was left—two bottles, apart from four left for the scout—and went to bed, still hungry. The Bodley Club means a lot of extra work for the scout, cleaning up and so on." The title of the paper mimics that of Eliot's first book of poetry, Prufrock and Other Observations. *Frye was working from this volume and from Eliot's* Poems, 1909–1925. *The poems Frye refers to will be found in the more accessible edition that includes these two early volumes,* The Complete Poems and Plays, 1909–1950 *(New York: Harcourt, Brace, 1952). The typescript is in the NFF, 1991, box 37, file 4.*

Modern literature seems at times to be animated by a spirit of practical communism: those who cannot write read the works of those who can and write an additional book about them. The twentieth century has

been well described as *l'âge des petits papiers*, and the number of books
about books is now of astronomical proportions, bound volumes being,
of course, only a small part of the total spate. Possibly one source of the
modern obscurity so frequently complained of may be the artist's feeling that, if his work is to support a swarm of scribbling parasites as well
as himself, the latter should not have too easy a time. In any case, highbrow journalism is not quite as painless as it was: the commentator in
search of a trend has now to grapple with Auden and MacLeish, where
formerly he could have got away with Aldous Huxley or Walter de la
Mare, but no slackening of output is yet perceptible. Since the war,
Lawrence, Joyce, and T.S. Eliot have been inevitable hosts, but as
Lawrence is dead and Joyce no longer has much news value, the novelty
of *Work in Progress* as well as that of *Ulysses* having worn off, Eliot, in
more than one sense, carries at present more weight than either. Two
slim volumes published by Faber & Faber, at 7/6 apiece, contain practically the whole of his poetry;[2] all his prose of any importance would
hardly fill a greater space;[3] yet the critical encrustation already on this
modest output would take a lifetime to examine completely. A few
months ago I set down the names of thirty-five books of the type
referred to which contained essays on Eliot, apart from three devoted
solely to him;[4] and as I made no attempt to draw up an exhaustive list, I
have no reason to suppose that I collected more than 10 per cent or 15
per cent of the whole. This is exclusive of magazine articles and book
reviews, which would run to several hundred, and of shorter references,
of which there are many, many thousands. The serious student of Eliot
would have to reckon with specialized treatises also, including such
exotic items as "T.S. Eliot et la fin de la poésie bourgeoise," by Prince
Mirsky in *Échanges*;[5] "T.S. Eliot and His Relation to T.E. Hulme," *University of Toronto Quarterly*;[6] *The Critical Ideas of T.S. Eliot*, by Ants Oras,
Tartu, Esthonia, 1932, and scores of others. There are the sociological
critics who assert that Eliot is not a revolutionary and ought to be one,
or that he is an Anglo-Catholic and ought not to be one; there are the
Zeitgeist critics, who point out that he is a modern poet and that, while
he is very difficult and very disillusioned, so are all modern poets; and
there are the source and influence critics, who establish his relationship
to everybody else from Hawthorne to Picasso. And this is not the worst.
Whatever the number of superfluous books on any classical poet, at any
rate he is dead: he has said all he is ever going to say, and nothing
remains but for critical vultures, scholarly hyenas, and pedantic bacteria

to annihilate the corpse. But Eliot is still very far from having written himself out. Every important poem he has published so far has been unexpectedly different from any preceding it, and, though his development has been perfectly logical throughout, it has to be reconsidered afresh in the light of every new production. All the tons of pulpwood which announced that Eliot, in *The Waste Land* and *The Hollow Men*, was voicing the disillusioned scepticism of the age, looked very silly after he turned Anglo-Catholic and wrote the fervently devotional *Ash-Wednesday*; and the hasty disgorging of tons more to show that he was a worn-out, decadent romantic, an ingrown lyricist spinning his cocoon among books, looked even sillier after he turned propagandic dramatist and wrote *The Rock* and *Murder in the Cathedral*. Fully nine-tenths of the critical writing on Eliot is, therefore, already out of date, as ephemeral as the flowers in May, and far less appropriately coloured. However, to write an essay on him, as I have just done, remains a recognized "blest office of the epicene,"[7] and one might as well be shameless about it. He provides an unbreakable anvil to hammer on, like Shakespeare and the Prelude in C# Minor. Besides, he has a special claim on our attention as the first poet of English literature to study at Merton College who ever became more notable for anything else. And he is not, of course, hack-neyed without good reason. The small volume of his writing keeps its head well above the flood of contemporary literature like an epigram among platitudes, and he has established himself as almost the only living poet whom it is safe to call permanent, which is as close as one can reasonably get to the word *immortal*. This is largely because he is so pre-eminently readable: of all poets since Keats, while there have been many bigger and bulkier than Eliot, there are none less likely to be left unread by posterity. That of itself would do nothing to establish his "greatness," whatever that means, but it does ensure his lasting significance and importance.

Until our own generation most of what can fairly be described as American culture was produced by New England. This culture was, of course, chiefly Puritanic in its inception and had become hardened and academic by the time of the Revolution, not because there was anything inherently sterile in Puritanism, but because America was no longer a small enclosed pale on the coast of a savage unexplored continent, but a growing nation whose energies were absorbed in pioneering. In New England an aristocracy developed from a number of families which accumulated wealth and prestige in the course of centuries, tolerant,

respectable, Nonconformist, Anglophile, and healthily interested in
education, and this aristocracy was the milieu of most of the established
writers of the nineteenth century. The bigoted prudery of New England
today has nothing to do with this class nor with Puritanism: that was
brought to it by Irish Catholics who flooded the country after the potato
famine. These immigrants seized all political power and left the aristocrats socially ineffective, though with their wealth and dignity unim-
paired. The famous epigram to the effect that

> The Lowells talk only to Cabots
> And the Cabots talk only to God[8]

expresses their general attitude well enough, though it is a slight exag-
geration: there were a few other families still capable of discoursing on
equal terms with all three, and of these the Eliots were one of the most
illustrious.

Thomas Stearns Eliot, though born in St. Louis, was educated as a
matter of course at Harvard, and from there went to the Sorbonne. He
read philosophy with Santayana and Josiah Royce, but among all contemporary thinkers his greatest admiration was for F.H. Bradley, of
whom he has written an appreciation based on the thesis that "Bradley,
like Aristotle, is distinguished by a scrupulous respect for words,"[9] and
ranking him higher than Matthew Arnold as a prose stylist.[10] It was no
doubt the name of Bradley that attracted him to Merton College, where
he came in 1914. He had been writing and occasionally appearing in
print since his Harvard days, and in 1917 his first book of poems, *Prufrock and Other Observations*, was published, which placed him at once
among the leading poets of his time.

About the year 1912 the United States, for no ascertainable reason,
had suddenly started to write poetry. Where formerly a genuine American poet was a rare and sporadic phenomenon, in the five years preceding the publication of Eliot's book E.A. Robinson, Frost, Millay,
Sandburg, Lindsay, Masters, Amy Lowell, H.D., Ezra Pound, and a
dozen minor writers had appeared and had put America on a level with
France and far ahead of England as a home of accomplished poets. The
main trouble with this poetry was that there was not enough of a tradition behind it. These writers could look back to no American predecessor except Whitman, who was far too intense an individualist to
constitute a tradition, and nineteenth-century English poetry was not

much help. As a result much of their work was garrulous and overasser-
tive, and much more failed to escape from a self-conscious complexity
and a kind of niggling cleverness. But France, for the past century, had
been producing a mature and controlled verse, and in this Eliot had
steeped himself, so that his book, not in spite of all its echoes from such
French symbolists as Laforgue but because of them, spoke with the
authority of technical assurance. It was not on the defensive and was not
afraid to be simple.

Prufrock and its companion poems are localized for the most part in
New England, but their prevailing mood is the sick melancholic nostal-
gia evoked by any grimy metropolis. The respectable class, with its
effete and bewildered culture, is presented as fighting a losing battle
against squalor and vulgarity because it has nothing to fight for but its
own decaying interests. This class is symbolized by Prufrock, a middle-
aged man of some education and culture, vaguely sensitive to beauty
but too self-centred to absorb it, and tormented by a desire to love but
paralysed by nervousness and his knowledge of his own mediocrity.
Prufrock is now one of the best-known characters of contemporary literature: in his ambiguous auto-erotic monologue the modern world finds
one of its most typical moods expressed. The other pieces are less uni-
versalized, but the picture they give of dingy poverty side by side with
equally dingy affluence is also typical of civilization as we have it everywhere: (Read *Morning at the Window* and *Aunt Helen*.)[11] The attitude is
satiric, of course; but Eliot's satire is not confined to direct portrayal of
degeneration: he sharpens and heightens the latter by contrasting it with
beauty. Thus, in *Rhapsody on a Windy Night* the romantic stirrings awakened by a glimpse of the moon are mingled with the dirty rubbish of the
city from which she is seen: (Read.) Again, the exciting mystery of the
world outside of Prufrock intensifies the morbid mystery of the world
inside him: (Read.)

Three years later came another volume of poems, in which Eliot
expanded his outlook.[12] His new characters are the dubious cosmopolitan rabble of all the great cities, the most prominent of them being
Sweeney, a character whom Eliot presents with the same trick of making
personal hygiene a symbol of animal sensuality, which Joyce uses with
such powerful effect in *Ulysses*. The tone of this collection is set by its
opening poem, the monologue of Gerontion, an older man than Prufrock and much more sophisticated, who has done all the things
Prufrock wanted to do and whose despair and disillusionment are calm

rather than irritable. The symbolism of this poem, therefore, cuts much deeper than that of the earlier one. Obviously the main impression one derives from the *Prufrock* poems is one of ubiquitous sterility; and the central symbol of this is the large city which is its proper environment. Cities are the carcasses of dead civilizations: they cannot grow; they merely swell. In this fetid, decaying atmosphere the poem of Gerontion opens. (Read.) As opposed to this, there is the longing for some principle of fertility, for something to make things grow and develop. This longing is an immemorial one, as it goes back to the dawn of agriculture, and it has created a host of rituals and gods. The religion which held together our civilization before it lost its grip on it and became spiritually rudderless was Christianity, and of all the symbolism which has gathered around the figure of Jesus not the least important is that concerned with him as a fertility god, an Adonis slain at the height of his powers whose body and blood, when eaten by his worshippers, unites them in a common bond. Thus, Gerontion goes on to speak of the decay of religion in the anonymous cosmopolitan society to which he belongs: (Read.) The same contrast is parodied in *Mélange Adultère de Tout*, the protean speaker of which announces that after being a professor in America, a journalist in England, a philosopher in Germany, and a "jemenfoutiste" in Paris:

> Je célébrai mon jour de fête
> Dans une oasis d'Afrique
> Vêtu d'une peau de girafe. [lines 16–18]

(Read the *Sunday Morning Service*.) This is a typical example of Eliot's technique: the fertility Christ baptized with the rain-giving water in the midst of the wilderness is set before us, but the accompanying summons of the Baptist to unconditional repentance has now passed into the collecting of pennies on a plate. The gaze wanders from the ushers extracting coins from children to the bumble-bees outside taking honey from the flowers. But the parallel between bee and usher is not quite perfect, for although the bee is an epicene in relation to the flower as the usher in relation to his god, still the bee does perform a fertilizing function. The thought of fertility leads us back to the image of Jesus standing in the water; but what rises in front of us instead are the buttocks of Sweeney.

The next step for Eliot was obviously to expand his symbolism into one long poem which should record his complete vision of the contemporary world, and this he did in *The Waste Land* (1922). The symbolism of the modern city has now clarified. A civilization is conceived as an organic growth rooted in a land which matures and finally becomes exhausted, and, in its last stage, separates itself from the land and enters a deracinated metropolitan phase, in which all sense of community has disappeared and an anarchic individualism takes its place. This is the thesis of Oswald Spengler's *Decline of the West*, though Eliot, with his contempt for Goethe and by implication for everything "Faustian,"[13] would probably be disinclined to admit that some knowledge of this book is necessary to a complete understanding of his poem. In any case, the sterility of the great city is the "waste land," and the scene is laid in London. We are shown sample attempts of city dwellers to engage in the only forms of communal activity left to them since the collapse of their belief in religion, love, and commerce. For the latter, a glance at the waste products of the Industrial Revolution is enough: for the former, there are the two upper-class lovers, bored nearly to madness, snarling at each other with their nerves jangling, to represent the courteous chivalry of the aristocracy; the account of the woman whose life was wrecked by a bungling attempt at abortion to represent domestic bliss; and the seduction of a typist by a carbuncular clerk to represent the ecstasy of romance. The remedy for this moral chaos and misery is the abandoning of a selfish individualism, the sterility of which produces the "waste land," for a communal consciousness, symbolized by the resurrection of Christ and by the coming of rain to the parched land. The past glories of our moribund culture, which contrast with the gloom of the present scene and emphasize its deadness, are suggested by interspersed quotations from famous poets, a scheme which, as Eliot handles it, is not at all as crude as it sounds.

There is no space here to make the full analysis of *The Waste Land* which would be necessary to clear up these sketchy notes on it: that would require a long paper in itself. The point is that here is a survey of society which can only be described as epic, packed into four hundred lines, of which about fifty are quotations, the economy being made possible by the allusiveness of the symbols and epigraphs and the aptness of the selected episodes. The result is no doubt a bookish, strained, and oversubtle poem, but a poet cannot always choose his own conventions: they are conditioned by the society in which he lives and limit his scope by the very fact that they create its form. A work of art is a synthesis; and a chaotic society no longer responsive to religious symbolism supplies the poet with incoherence and disorder as his primary data. Consequently, a successful poetic presentation of modern life not only has to make a synthesis: it has to reflect the difficulty of making one. The internal form, the natural organic growth of a great poem, is conditioned by an organically growing society: when the latter breaks down, the former can be attained directly only by parody, as it is in the jigsaw puzzle of literary echoes in *The Waste Land*. Other alternatives, such as subjective lyricism, attachment to the doctrines of some political organization, the attempt to find a communal symbolism in the subconscious, or any combination of these, are equally legitimate, but they are not more so, and they do not avoid the same central problem. *Ulysses*, published in the same year as *The Waste Land*, also parodies the idea of internal form by its application of the *Odyssey* pattern to a by no means heroic contemporary scene, but its method is the converse of that of Eliot's poem, which is a sort of microcosm of it. Eliot's technique is visionary, grouping episodes around a central symbol; Joyce's is dramatic, grouping symbols around an episode. Eliot makes his point by contracting to the limit; Joyce his by expanding to the limit: but both ridicule the disintegration of society by setting the perfected formal achievements of the past beside it, just as Pope showed how silly all the fuss made about cutting a lock of hair from a girl's head was by telling the story in mock-epic form.[14]

The symbolism employed in *The Waste Land*, in which an individualized society is associated with sterility and a group consciousness with fertility, points to a definite attitude toward society which Eliot began to develop in a series of critical writings. The point of view of these was declared to be "classicist in literature, royalist in politics, anglo-catholic in religion."[15] In full revolt against the Rousseauist or romantic heresy, the ancestor of modern humanism, which regards man as inherently good but restrained from being so by bad institutions, he regards man as essentially imperfect, depending for everything of education and discipline he has on a consolidated tradition. This attitude he calls classical. But the only way in which a tradition can remain consolidated is for it to be transmitted by a religion with a definite, solid dogma, an organized Church, and a stereotyped ritual, which by its conserving force gives direction to all historical advance. This religion must be Catholic, for the Protestant tendency is towards the discrete, anarchic individualism he is most concerned to attack: we have already seen how Eliot's poetry moves from the humanistic New England aristocracy which is the heir of Puritanism to the "waste land" of modern society as a whole. And just as a living culture is bound up with a religion, so it is bound up with a nation, and the political form which best expresses a national consciousness is a monarchy, for royalty provides a central catholic symbol as the more anonymous republic does not, and dictatorship, Eliot feels, represents the Napoleonic ideal, whose only criterion is "success" in the most vulgar sense of the word.

The present paper is concerned with Eliot's dogmas only as they have affected the form of his poetry. His analysis of the contemporary scene in *The Waste Land* had expanded the negative aspect of them to the limit. He had now to build up the positive side, to present a view of life in which the grounds for his satiric attack would be made explicit. Part of this would necessarily be concerned with portraying the advance of the individual through chaos to reintegration. He had made an impersonal survey of this chaos: his next step was to clear the ground for the individual's reaction to it by isolating its horror. This he did in *The Hollow Men*. (Read.) Then came what has frequently been called the purgatorio to this inferno: *Ash-Wednesday*, a sequence of meditations on the general theme of purification by suffering, which employs a religious symbolism derived chiefly from Dante and the Catholic Mass, the two most vital sources of Christian imagery.

Ash-Wednesday, however, was necessarily a transitional poem. It presents an individual's grasp of religious experience and, therefore, remains a lyric. To take full advantage of a Catholic religion, to escape completely, as an artist, from the disintegration of contemporary life, one should move on from the lyric to the communal art form of the drama, the only literary form which is, like music, an ensemble performance for an audience. A society with a flourishing music and drama, like England under Elizabeth, is likely to have a religious and national group-consciousness; and a society from which both arts have disappeared, like England under Victoria, is extremely unlikely to have one. *The Hollow Men* and *Ash-Wednesday*, therefore, present only one side of Eliot's problem of expressing the positive side of his "criticism of life." All great poets, Eliot points out in one of his essays, are restless until they arrive at the uncompromising objectivity of the dramatic attitude, however they express it;[16] and certainly Eliot himself did not, in either of the poems mentioned, attain to the impersonal balance of the poems up to and including *The Waste Land*, which had been purely dramatic in their approach. But the drama proper, the one genuinely catholic literary art form in which there can really be something for everybody, seemed to him the most satisfying medium of art, however unsuited to it he might be by temperament.

A developing fluency, a growing power over the larger rhythmic outlines of poetry, had been evident in his work ever since he had moved away from the tightly compressed quatrains of the Sweeney poems and the motionless echoing imagery of *The Waste Land*. Along with the alliance of his poetry with a religious tradition there went the problem of reshaping that tradition in new, vital, and popular forms. When Eliot, lecturing at Harvard, surveyed his cultivated listeners and announced that he himself would prefer an audience which could neither read nor write,[17] he was referring to a theme which he had already introduced into his poetry. Popular forms of literature and music in any age usually possess a strongly marked characteristic rhythm common to them all, and the twentieth century, of course, has found the word *jazz* to describe the one peculiar to it. *Sweeney Agonistes* is a remarkably successful experiment in jazz: to give any idea of its superb vitality it should be read as a whole, but the final chorus is all we have time for. (Read.)

The next step for Eliot was to combine the religious imagery of *Ash-Wednesday* and the popular idiom of *Sweeney Agonistes* into the form of a religious drama, and this he attempted in *The Rock*, a play intended to speed the project of building Anglo-Catholic churches in London as a means of reestablishing the Church among the common people and as at least a partial cure for unemployment. Finally, there appeared *Murder in the Cathedral*, a historical drama of the murder of Becket, whose martyrdom symbolizes the inexhaustible life of the Church as well as its contemporary neglect. This play is vastly superior to *The Rock*, and is undoubtedly one of the finest poetic dramas of our time: the amazing beauty of some of the choruses is unsurpassed in modern poetry. (Read.)

Fine as this is, it is probable that in *Murder in the Cathedral* the upward curve of Eliot's development begins to show a slope. The world is apparently developing a new form of society dependent on some sense of group-consciousness: what form this will take it is impossible to say, but many groups are putting forward their claims to represent it, and of these fascism, Communism, and Catholic Christianity are the largest. Now art forms change with the forms of society, and a group-consciousness in society will necessarily produce group art forms, of which two very important ones are music and drama, as already said. Hence, all these groups turn toward dramatic methods of expression; and the medium chosen is vulgar or subtle depending on the nature of the appeal. The circus, of which Eliot gives us an ironic picture in a poem called *Triumphal March*, seems to be the only one known to fascism, whether in its Caesarean or its Wagnerian form. Crude as it is, a modern Juvenal would find the circus more potent than ever, as it can evidently support a government accompanied by only a vague promise of bread. Soviet Communism elaborates on one of the less inspired logia of Lenin, to the effect that the central art form of the future proletarian state will be the cinema.[18] The more sophisticated Marxism of New York and of Auden in London has already a good deal of sound dramatic achievement to its credit. Eliot's drama, then, is by no means an isolated phenomenon. But there is another group art form infinitely more important than any that I have mentioned, and that is the ballet, which combines music and drama on the basis of the dance, the origin of both, and which is far more intellectually concentrated than the ordinary spoken drama, as every movement is controlled and related to the central rhythmic idea. This, whatever of spoken dialogue or chorus it may absorb, is the most highly organized art form the twentieth century is likely to produce. Auden, particularly in *The Dance of Death*, realizes perhaps more than Eliot the importance of pantomime, the integration of gesture with the drama; and even the cinema, so stultified by routine technical competence, immediately develops toward pantomime and ballet techniques as soon as an authentic genius, such as Walt Disney or Charlie Chaplin, is given a free hand. What steps, if any, Eliot will take in this direction, remains to be seen, but this is his direction. Possibly he may be hampered by his evident preference for the Latin side of Western culture as opposed to the Germanic tradition, which has produced most of our music. The musical impetus in the poetry of Goethe, Browning, and Hopkins Eliot is inclined to wince at; and perhaps it is best to read *Sweeney Agonistes* as a parody of this sort of technique.

Though Eliot himself has pointed out that the poet deals not with belief but with the emotional equivalent of belief,[19] most of the adverse criticism of him has been levelled directly at his religious and political opinions. I happen to embrace most of the tenets Eliot holds in peculiar abhorrence, but it is no part of my intention to explain in detail why I think them superior to his: still, it might be worth discussing two very obvious points, not because I wish to prove Eliot wrong about them, but because I wish to conclude with some estimate, however tentative, of his relation to contemporary culture as a whole.

In the first place, it might be objected that in forsaking Boston for Canterbury Eliot has merely exchanged one form of humanism for another and has not yet escaped from the overemphasis on social and moral criteria of religious experience, which is the real dilemma of humanism. This I mention because I feel that his close association of religion and morality has had an unfortunate effect on his work: there must be many others besides myself who find the preaching in *The Rock* irritating and such essays as *Thoughts After Lambeth* and *After Strange Gods* unreadable. It is rather ironic, too, that *Murder in the Cathedral*, which depicts the martyrdom of the Primate of England for withstanding the immoral purposes of his king, should be running in London at the very time when so radically different a relationship was being established between the Visitors of Magdalen and Merton.[20]

This leads me to the second point, or, if it does not, I am going to move on to it anyway. If the Christian Church is to be regarded primarily as a social institution, it takes its place in a political and economic conflict of reaction and revolution. Now whenever class lines have been sharply drawn in history, poets unable to accept the ideology of either side have found that the Church not only gave them a more acceptable doctrine, but also defined for them an impartial political attitude. That is why, to take a random example, we find a group of clerical and theological poets in England during the conflict of king and Parliament— Donne, Herbert, Vaughan, Milton, and the rest. In the nineteenth century the tension of capitalist society produced a somewhat similar situation, but this time the Christian Church as an institution was too disintegrated itself to satisfy many of the great artists of the time who could commit themselves to neither the bourgeois nor the proletarian outlook. But even at that one can hardly deny that the inspiration of Tolstoy and Dostoevsky was theological; and the same tonsure mark is on not only an orthodox Christian like César Franck, or an artist steeped in religious conceptions who later worked apart from them, like Van Gogh, but on those who attacked Christianity violently for essentially theological reasons, like Baudelaire and Nietzsche.

But now, it may be said, the Church affords an even more precarious foothold for the artist, not because it is weaker but because the economic conflict is stronger. There are two answers to this. In the first place, it could be argued that the very heat and fury of the economic struggle makes the Church an essential refuge for the artist who does not engage in it. Those artists of the past generation who remained aloof from religious as well as political groups spent their lives in complete spiritual isolation. That is a terrible price to pay, and many of the greatest geniuses of the nineteenth century paid for it with their sanity. In a world less a chaos than a womb of shaping forces it begins to look as though it were no longer worth paying, and though Eliot's refusal to do so after writing *The Hollow Men* has been criticized by many who can be very stark and terrible by proxy, he has definitely gained, as an artist, by declining to strike the expected pose. The sterile introspective abstraction of Picasso in his cubist period, of Joyce after *Ulysses*, of Stravinsky's contrapuntal exercises, has so far not been for Eliot. Whether or not that is because his own achievements have been made on a lower level is a matter of opinion. And certainly those who call him a reactionary can point to no D.H. Lawrence type of reaction: no *Plumed Serpent* with its schoolboyish Naziism, no Lady Chatterley mid-Victorian mamma fighting at bay and brandishing a contraceptive syringe.

The second answer is the stock—almost the automatic—revolutionary one. The economic struggle is rapidly absorbing all middle ground between reaction and revolution. As a social institution the Church is committed to reaction and will throw in its lot with fascism whenever the pressure is strong enough, which makes all Catholic poets today simply muddled fascists, unless they are so fortunate as to be muddled Catholics. But an assertion which depends for proof on future events is obviously impossible to discuss, and, in any case, nothing that Eliot may do will injure the quality of what he has already done. This is so high that it is rather a pity that he has to live in an age which can see no poetry because it keeps nervously peering behind it for lurking sociological hobgoblins. But then the poets are to blame for this as well, for they also belong to an age whose peculiar vanity it is to imagine that everything it does is charged with a portentous historical significance.

22

A Reconsideration of Chaucer

In 1938, according to John Ayre (147), Frye read a paper on Chaucer to the Graduate English Club at the University of Toronto, a paper originally written for his Oxford tutor, Edmund Blunden. "A Reconsideration of Chaucer," a revision and expansion of the earlier paper, incorporates about three-fifths of the essay Frye wrote for Blunden on Chaucer's early poems in October 1936, and it is about fifty percent longer than the earlier effort, a handwritten manuscript in the NFF, 1991, box 37, file 12. Frye wrote three essays on Chaucer for Blunden, and "A Reconsideration of Chaucer" might well incorporate portions of the other two papers, which have not been preserved. Frye's text for Chaucer was apparently the first edition (1933) of F.N. Robinson's The Works of Geoffrey Chaucer. *The references in square brackets following Frye's quotations (e.g., 1720–2: 478) are to the line and page numbers of Robinson's second edition (Boston: Houghton Mifflin, 1957). References to lines in* Troilus and Criseyde *are preceded by the number of the book (e.g., 5.1856–7: 479). The typescript is in the NFF, 1991, box 37, file 4.*

If I should be asked why I am reading a paper on Chaucer with so arrogant a title when so many among my audience know infinitely more about Chaucer than I do, I can only plead that I have a special interest in Blake. Blake's essay on *The Canterbury Tales*[1] outlines a method of criticizing Chaucer which I have ventured to apply to the minor poems and to *Troilus and Criseyde*, that is all. The original reconsideration of Chaucer is Blake's, not mine; and my approach to Chaucer includes a private conviction that Blake's essay is as revolutionary a document in the history of Chaucerian criticism as Tyrwhitt's edition itself.[2] Quotations from Chaucer will be given in modern English, for obvious reasons.[3]

It is always safe to begin with platitudes. In the history of European culture Renaissance succeeds to Gothic. Gothic culture is produced by a social system which also produces a landed aristocracy, a feudal economy, and a Catholic religion. Renaissance culture emerges in towns, among a strong mercantile class whose interests are generally protected by a despot—even big nations with many towns are strongly centralized in the Renaissance period. Renaissance religion may call itself Catholic or Protestant, but in either case is state religion. The feudal system was never so strongly entrenched in Italy as it was in northern Europe: Renaissance conditions prevailed there, more or less, from the Dark Ages on; and Italy, therefore, took the lead during the Renaissance proper. Chaucer, who owed so much to Italy, is on the threshold of the Italian Renaissance: he had not been dead many years when Masaccio was painting in the Brancacci Chapel. When anything like a Renaissance came to England, Chaucer had been dead so long that his prayer in *Troilus and Criseyde* had gone unanswered:

> So preye I god that noon miswrite thee,
> Ne the mismetre for defaute of tonge. [5.1795–6: 479]

And yet the fourteenth century in England was obviously as much on the eve of a Renaissance as it was in Italy. The middle class was rapidly growing in power and wealth, chiefly through the export of wool, and in the normal course of events we should expect that very soon after Chaucer's time it would, aided by a strong king, destroy the old landowner class. This revolution was achieved under the Tudors, but everything in Chaucer's time pointed directly towards it. The new spirit of nationalism which arose under Edward III was rapidly growing into a nationalistic religion. William of Occam proves in the schools that nations are realities and that Christendom is an abstraction; and the writings of Wycliffe and his followers urge the power of the secular state against that of the pope. *Piers Plowman* and *Richard the Redeless* are full of bitter reproaches against a weak king for not welding the nation into a single unit. However conservative Langland may be in his view of society, it is obvious that for him the king and a nation of industrious workers are the functional elements in it: the nobility and an ultramontane clergy are considered, more or less explicitly, as anarchic and disruptive forces.

This situation was, however, complicated by the Black Death, which raised the price of labour to such an extent that for the first time since the Norman Conquest the proletariat emerges as a second revolutionary class. In the face of this new threat to their interests, the landowning and mercantile classes combined and established the Lancastrian reaction. There was, perhaps, no more actual misery among the poorer classes in the fifteenth century than there was in the fourteenth under the Statute of Labourers,[4] though I am open to correction on this point. But there is something about a historical retrogression which crushes and stamps out culture, whatever the economic conditions are; for a change in a social system which may affect the working class very little may mean a great deal to the creative artist or scholar. In the fifteenth century the acknowledged poet laureate is not a Chaucer complaining about his empty purse, but a sleek and well-fed Lydgate. The one philosopher between Wycliffe and the Oxford reformers, Pecock, came much nearer the stake than ever Wycliffe did, in spite of his impeccable orthodoxy. We used to be told, of course, that the Middle Ages were full of fanatical obscurantism and a morbid liking for damnation and decomposition. That is no more true of the thirteenth and fourteenth centuries than of the age of Hitler and Salvador Dali; but, in that sense of the word *medieval*, the fifteenth century is the most medieval century in English culture. Its most original and typical art form is the *danse macabre*, and its only dispenser of impartial justice is death.

But the second half of the fourteenth century remains the prelude to the frustrated and postponed English Renaissance. Its vitality is amazing: the Peasants' Revolt and the rise of Lollardry are monuments of its genius quite as impressive as the poetry of Chaucer, Langland, the *Pearl* poet, and the Wakefield dramatist. In Duns Scotus scholastic philosophy had produced one of the finest critical intellects of any age; the startling and uncompromising paradoxes of William of Occam followed and led straight into the more explicitly revolutionary thought of Wycliffe. The intellectual development of England during this period was more exciting, more fearless—because less systematically restrained by censorship—and less sentimental than it was to be again for centuries—perhaps more centuries than have yet elapsed. The psychological effect of the Black Death as a catalyser for the revolutionary thought of the time must have been very great, but is a difficult factor to assess.

Similarly, literature seems to draw more vitality from all classes of society, from court to cottage, than it has ever done since. It is more truly

the expression of a national consciousness than even Elizabethan literature outside of Shakespeare, as it is much more firmly integrated with
the lower as well as with the upper and middle classes. The radical element in the thought of Langland, for instance, should not be underestimated, as it tends to be at present, because it has been wrongly
interpreted. Langland did not write a political poem; nor, in spite of his
insistence that there are good and bad in all classes, did he write a moral
poem. His work is theological, symbolic, and visionary, and only after
we have seen through the anagogic form of his argument as it develops
from the A to the C text[5] can we get any idea of the real power of his
mind. We have no space to discuss in detail all the points that Langland
makes in his poem, but we may refer to the well-known fact that in his
approach to Christianity he cuts straight through centuries of established hierarchy to the original proletarian cult recorded in the New
Testament. No other poet of English literature except Blake ever got this
far: even such great revolutionary geniuses as Milton and Shelley, to say
nothing of revolutionary poets of our own day, fall a long way short of
it. But Langland's is not an isolated achievement, even if we deny that a
committee sat on his poem, for the same thing is done, and done quite as
well in a different way, in *Secunda Pastorum*.

There is nothing of this in Chaucer, but even in Chaucer we are often
reminded that a unified religious impulse is almost emerging. We cannot call it Protestantism, for the simple reason that Protestantism arose
in the sixteenth century under very different social and intellectual conditions, but neither is it the Catholicism of the preceding century. Whatever we call it, it is a religious impulse much less dependent on class
selfishness than most religious impulses are and is capable of giving certain ultimate refinements in art which, say, the Elizabethan age does not
provide. Take the last words of Chaucer's Troilus:

> But trewely, Criseyde, swete may,
> Whom I have ay with al my myght yserved,
> That ye thus doon, I have it nat deserved. [5.1720–2: 478]

There is no sermon on original sin and the frailty of woman. Troilus
knows only that he has been hurt, and he sticks to that. According to
conventional Christian morality, Criseyde was a prostitute; according to
the morality of courtly love, she was something far worse. Troilus calls
her "maiden."

> O Cressid! O false Cressid! false, false, false!
> Let all untruths stand by thy stained name,
> And they'll seem glorious. [*Troilus and Cressida*, 5.2.178–80]

That is Shakespeare's Troilus. "O blood, blood, blood!" howls Othello [3.3.451]. Whether Shakespeare was capable of a touch like this of Chaucer or not, it is certain that no character he created ever was.

We shall come to this question of Chaucer's religious attitude again: all we are concerned with just now is the fact that the half-century between the Black Death and the death of Chaucer is a cultural unity as much as the baroque, rococo, or Victorian periods are. The inner conflicts are intense, but they are a sign of vitality, and from one very important point of view the resemblances are more profound and significant than the differences. It is an error of fact to call Langland a Lollard or a sympathizer with John Ball; but it is not an error of interpretation to see underlying connections among all three. Such a method of approach to any age in history is concerned above all to examine that age as far as humanly possible in terms of its own standards. We have had enough, for example, of the critic who ascribes to Chaucer a sneaking sympathy with the ideas of Voltaire because the critic himself is revolting against a Yahwistic mother. Even more responsible criticism is apt to assume an impossible antithesis between "medieval" and "modern" attitudes, in which case it is not difficult to prove that Chaucer was "essentially" either. Chaucer is not "essentially" anything but Chaucer, however, and Chaucer lived in the age of Wycliffe and Langland. At the same time it is undoubtedly true that he is a uniquely cosmopolitan figure. He drew both from the humanistic Italy of Petrarch and Boccaccio and from the still feudal and medieval France of Jean de Meung. The cultural unity of fourteenth-century England is expressed very well by Langland and Wycliffe; but if we want to see this period in its relation to European culture as a whole we have to turn to Chaucer.

A poem is a particular selection of universal experience: consequently, the real greatness of a poet is estimated in two ways: by the very general argument which presents the range and scope of his thought and his constructive ability and by the minute analysis of his technique. A critic who has the strength of mind to grapple with the former is generally not afraid to be pedantic about the latter. Chaucer begins his poetic career with translations: if we can construct out of these a working model of Chaucer's mind, we shall be better able to

understand his attitude as an independent poet. Let us take the very
early *ABC*, which is a translation of a French poem by one Deguilleville.[6]
I choose this largely because Professor Robinson says in his edition:
"The *ABC* being only a translation, reveals very little about Chaucer."[7]
We shall see.

In Deguilleville we at once notice that the rhyme is only part of a
much larger scheme of assonance. His stanza is longer than Chaucer's,
but he has only two rhymes against Chaucer's three, his scheme being
aaba abbb abba and Chaucer's *ababbcbc*. But the important difference is
that Deguilleville varies his rhymes as little as possible while Chaucer
contrasts his: some of Deguilleville's stanzas are actually constructed on
one rhyme alone, and when he does have two, rhyme *b* is as close to
rhyme *a*, both in sound and meaning, as he can get it. His rhymes for
stanza D are: misericorde, recorde, racordé, concorde, discorde, des-
cordé, accordé, concordé, corde, recordé, encordé, orde [37–48]. All this
ingenuity produces, of course, an extremely static effect—the rhymes
are wedged together so tightly that the poem hardly gives any sense of
movement or development.

Stanza G in Deguilleville opens with a quadruple pun. The poet
addresses the Virgin as "mother" (mère), says that she is never "marah"
or bitter (amere) in earth or sea (mer); and, of course, we are supposed
to remember that her name is Mary and that she is known as *stella maris*,
which reinforces the reference to the sea. That takes up three lines. Having run out of "mères," Deguilleville goes on to "père," and actually
succeeds in completing eight lines with that sound. The last line ends
with "frère," but then the bell rings, so to speak, and he has to start a
new stanza [73–84]. This is Chaucer:

> Glorious mayde and mooder, which that nevere
> Were bitter, neither in erthe nor in see,
> But ful of swetnesse and of merci evere,
> Help that my Fader be not wroth with me.
> Spek thou, for I ne dar not him ysee,
> So have I doon in erthe, allas the while!
> That certes, but if thou my socour bee,
> To stink eterne he wole my gost exile. [49–56: 525]

Deguilleville's stanza is based on the fact that "mère" rhymes with
"père"; Chaucer's, on the sharp antithesis between the mercy of the

divine mother and the wrath of the divine father. One of the most elemental of human emotions, which is not the less powerful for being called an Oedipus complex, vitalizes the dry bones of conventional piety, and the stanza takes on the organic tension of something alive. Notice how the thrust and counterthrust of "maid" and "mooder," "bitter" and "sweetness," "earth" and "sea," build up from the "mooder" of the first line to the climacteric "Fader" of the fourth. Notice how unobtrusive Chaucer's rhyme is, "never-ever," and yet how subtly it fits into the antithetical scheme. True, Deguilleville has most of the materials for these antitheses: "vierge mère," "en terre ne en mer," and "amere" against "douceur" [73, 75, 74, and 76]; but it is hard to achieve freedom under the dictatorship of one vowel, and any movement they might have given the stanza is completely lost in the roar of assonance.

In Chaucer's last line we have an association of three entirely negative ideas. To make hell a place of flames and torture adds a certain majestic splendor to horror, but a hell like a dung heap on which abandoned corpses are flung is merely degrading and shameful. There is some dignity to a human "soul" in hell, for the soul is immortal and intelligent, but a "ghost," the shadow of life, has no dignity and very little pathos. Again, to be "condemned" to hell suggests the Promethean rebel, but to be exiled there is merely to be contemptuously dismissed as undesirable. The picture of hopeless misery made from these three words is all the more poignant at the end of a stanza opening with the word "glorious." And of this last line there is not the slightest hint in Deguilleville.

If Chaucer can do this to a translation, it is hardly to be expected that when he emerges as an independent poet he should be less individual in his utterance. It is his business to carry on the poetic tradition as he finds it in his own way; but that tradition has been formed by poets he admires and respects: Machaut, Deschamps, and the authors of the *Roman de la Rose* in France, Dante, Petrarch, and Boccaccio in Italy. Here an entirely new problem arises.

Medieval culture before Chaucer had reached its highest development with the poetry of Dante and the philosophy of St. Thomas Aquinas. St. Thomas had constructed a system of thought in which everything focused on the proposition that reality lay in universals, in wholes rather than parts. The life of an individual is temporary and fluctuating, but at every moment he is in touch with realities which are eternal. The states of mind through which the individual passes are common to all men, therefore universal, therefore more real than the individual himself. The question, therefore, arises: what literary forms result from the belief that universals rather than individuals are real?

Two things immediately become obvious. In the first place, symbolism must be the basis of medieval art. In the second place, most of the mental energy of the time was absorbed in correlation. Medieval science was inclined to regard the world as complicated rather than complex, because a world in which universals were real would be one which could be explained in very simple formulae, such as the cardinal numbers. And we should expect this tendency to association of ideas, as shown in the endless attempts to interrelate all possible groups of three, four, seven, and twelve, to find counterparts in literature.

Thus, we find in Chaucer's poetry standard symbolic patterns like the game of chess and the elaborate anatomical description of the beloved lady which meet us in *The Book of the Duchess* [614–69, 939–60: 273, 276], and the astrological and mythological frameworks of such poems as the *Complaint of Mars*.[8] We find also a tendency to place a particular poem in a category, *The Legend of Good Women* being an obvious example; and on a smaller scale there is the convention of the catalogue. *The House of Fame* is full of catalogues, and its account of the wonders in the House of Rumour is of an exuberance surpassed only by the world's greatest master of the catalogue, Rabelais.[9]

Medieval poetry, then, like medieval philosophy and science, is based on a technique of correlating and associating ideas in a search for universals, and as this means the use of symbolism, there must be some transcendent symbol of perfect unity to hold all other symbols together. The required symbol would inevitably be love, for it is the function of love, in whatever aspect, to unite.

As regards form, the theme of love can be treated objectively or subjectively. The former gives us the epic or dramatic form of the love poem; the latter the lyric form. The objective treatment would require, we have seen, a symbolic framework, and would be more concerned with an archetypal love than with the frailties of individual lovers. It will, therefore, present a unity which holds up the mirror, not to nature, but to thought, or rather the imagination which produces thought. This gives us the form of the vision and the convention of the dream, as used by Chaucer in his four most important minor poems, *The Book of the Duchess*, *The House of Fame*, *The Parliament of Fowls*, and *The Legend of Good Women*. The lyric forms do not concern us: the most important is the complaint.

As regards subject matter, the love can obviously be either sacred or profane. In the latter case love poetry would be cast in the convention of courtly love. The present paper is forced, through exigencies of space, to omit all explanation of courtly love as it is set out in Mr. Lewis's brilliant work, *The Allegory of Love*. All we can say is that it was Chaucer's business as a court poet to produce poems in this convention.

But Chaucer came to the courtly love convention after many able French poets had exhausted its possibilities. Chaucer could add little organically new to the encyclopedic *Roman de la Rose*; yet he could not break away from it altogether. There was only one thing he could do—to transform courtly love poetry into visionary comedy, rich in humour and lightness. By comedy I do not mean parody or ridicule: there was far too much satire in the *Roman de la Rose* itself for Chaucer to be much interested in that approach. But many conventions do pass through a comic stage before they disappear; and when writers approach a convention in this indirect, sophisticated way it is a sign that the direct approach has become worn out. To Chaucer's minor poems perhaps *The Rape of the Lock* will offer an analogy. *The Rape of the Lock* is a comic adaptation of the classical epic, and while it is not a parody of Homer or Virgil, it does reflect Boileau's doctrine that a serious treatment of this form, whether in pagan or Christian terms, was no longer appropriate for poetry.[10]

And if Chaucer's poetry had ended with *The Parliament of Fowls*, there would be no more to say than this. But Chaucer also belongs to the period following St. Thomas and Dante; he comes after the assaults of Scotus, Occam, and Wycliffe on Thomism, and belongs to a world which had, outside the schools at least, begun to accept the doctrine of nominalism we hold today, that reality inheres in the individual and that the universal is an abstract idea or mental image. Chaucer's technique at its greatest, in *Troilus and Criseyde* and the later portions of *The Canterbury Tales*, is concerned primarily with individuals rather than symbols and is in spirit closer to the drama than the vision. We, therefore, have to expand our conception of Chaucer as a great master of comedy. Everybody knows that Shakespeare is one of a group of Elizabethan dramatists and that he is one of the three or four greatest poets of the world, but it is often difficult even for an experienced Shakespearean scholar to keep both ideas always in his head at the same time. We have to make similar intellectual effort in regard to Chaucer: he is a product of fourteenth-century England, but he is also one of the greatest masters of comedy who ever lived, his level being the level of Horace and Mozart. Like Mozart, he comes at a late stage of his particular culture, when the only possible attitude to the ideals of that culture was a quizzical and ironic attitude. And again like Mozart, he lived in a prerevolutionary time—the fact that the revolution did not come off for another century does not really alter Chaucer's position. He feels that some sort of upheaval is coming, but he presents his feeling in a summarized way, with exactly the same sort of indirect suggestion that he adopts toward the conventions of the past. Had such an upheaval come directly after Chaucer's time, a great revolutionary genius would doubtless have followed Chaucer as Beethoven followed Mozart, or, in our own day, as Picasso has followed Cézanne.

The difference of social conditions in Italy and France makes it difficult to see the transitional nature of the fourteenth century in Europe as a whole; and about the only place where a cultural development parallel to England's was taking place was in Siena. And of all the great men of the fourteenth century perhaps only two succeeded in making a unity out of Italian and French cultures, Chaucer and Simone Martini; and there are (to me) many parallels between these two artists. But the Sienese Renaissance also came to grief, though not so completely—witness the great Passion frescos of Simone's pupil Barna in the San Gimignano cathedral[11]—and the relation of Simone to Duccio or Giotto has not a little in common with the relation of Chaucer to Dante.

There are two Chaucers, then, that we have to deal with: the smaller Chaucer who transformed a great romantic convention into great comedy and the larger Chaucer who is, perhaps, the greatest creative artist of fourteenth-century Europe, the century of growing nations and vernacular literatures, a century as Franciscan as the thirteenth was Dominican. The former is the Chaucer of the minor poems; the latter the Chaucer of *Troilus and Criseyde*.

In *The Book of the Duchess*, a consolatory poem addressed to John of Gaunt on the death of his wife, we have an elegy which is a synthesis of complaint and vision forms, the symbolic setting being the enchanted garden which we enter at the opening of the *Roman de la Rose*. Here, first of all, is the typical or generic story, that of Ceyx and Alcyone, followed by a dream. Now while a vision may be tragic, the dream, the experience of someone in a recumbent posture, tends toward comedy—the comedy suggested by such a title as *Midsummer Night's Dream*. Chaucer heightens the humour by his introduction of Morpheus, the drowsy god who opens one eye when a messenger bawls in his ear [178–85: 269], and the dream itself opens in the peacefulness of a May morning, with the sun shining and the birds singing on the roof [291–325: 270]. Professors Lowes and Kittredge have both dwelt on a curious feature of this poem—its use of the irresponsible haziness and arbitrary associations of an actual dream.[12] But it seems to me that as the dreamer joins the hunt and enters the enchanted garden Chaucer is conveying a hint of a journey to an Elysium or a paradise. I would even venture the suggestion that the puppy, which comes running to meet the dreamer when he enters the garden, is the Cerberus of this paradise:

> Hyt com and crepte to me as lowe,
> Right as hyt hadde me yknowe,
> Helde doun hys hed and joyned hys eres,
> And leyde al smothe doun hys heres. [391–4: 271]

For, in spite of this puppy and in spite of Morpheus, the writing is only incidentally humourous: it really moves on a plane of easy serenity which is comedy at its finest and which, in spite of Arnold, is quite as high as the highest seriousness.[13] Again, Lowes has well spoken of the stroke of genius by which Chaucer represents the dreamer as dull, in order to draw out the black knight and thereby express at once the husband's grief and Chaucer's sympathy with it.[14] I think there is more to it than that. The dreamer gets everything all wrong because he does not understand what the knight is saying: my impression is that if the dreamer were really to get into his head the idea that someone was actually suffering, he would wake up, and the paradise around him, in which nothing suffers, would vanish. And the reason for laying the scene in Elysium is, of course, that it is the only way of expressing the inevitable consolation offered to bereaved people: "the dead are better off." For the poet to put his consolation in this form would be crude: for him to go to a place explicitly named paradise and see Blanche there would be equally crude. What this Elysian setting gives us is the suggestion that everything is all right in spite of the Man in Black's grief, which is exactly the correct touch. The genius of a great poet and the tact of a great gentleman united to make this poem.[15]

The extremely conventional lament, with its many stock patterns—the succession of oxymorons leading into the tirade against Fortune [617–709: 273–4], with the rather tedious conceit of the chess game, the

detailed description of the lady's soul and body, and the extremely varied lists of references—all lead us to suspect that the formalizing of personal grief characteristic of the great elegies of the language is a virtue
made of necessity. Death is so impartial and commonplace an event that
it is difficult to describe a particular death in particular terms.

To recapitulate: Chaucer modelled his earlier work on literary conventions which established love as the normal content and the vision
and complaint as standard forms of poetry. He came to these conventions, however, when they were worn out, and he broke through them
to the individualized technique of his two great masterpieces. He did
not take these conventions very seriously, and being a comic genius he
made comedies out of them, preparatory to outgrowing them. This process, which we have seen operating in *The Book of the Duchess*, was in all
essentials completed by *The House of Fame*, the Don Quixote of the medieval love vision.

Anyone who considers this an overstatement should simply read the
poem as a unity, not as puzzled editors read it, as an extravaganza arbitrarily tacked on to a dull summary of the *Aeneid*. First, with regard to
content. Chaucer, after hemming and hawing and clearing his throat for
a hundred and ten lines, in the best manner of medieval prolixity,
begins on a dream. He finds himself in a temple of glass, a perfect symbol of the imaginative, allegorical, visionary type of poetry he was
breaking away from. Inexorably engraved on the walls of this temple is
the well-worn story of Dido and Aeneas, the archetype of all lovers'
complaints. The poet plods along conscientiously, but finally announces
that he is bored, and that anyone who wants more of the story can read
it in Virgil. Then he says in effect: "I like this temple, but it is obviously
no place for me":

> "A, Lord!" thoughte I, "that madest us,
> Yet sawgh I never such noblesse
> Of ymages, ne swich richesse,
> As I saugh graven in this chirche;
> But not woot I whoo did hem wirche,
> Ne where I am, ne in what contree." [470–5: 286]

Feeling the need of fresh air, he goes out into the open and finds himself
alone in a desert. He does not say in so many words that the temple of
glass has been smashed to pieces, but it has; the Chaucer in that desert is

the potential author of *Troilus and Criseyde*. Then an eagle—Dante's own eagle—catches him in his claws and whirls him up through the air. He explains to the terrified poet that because he has tried to write love poems but has never regarded the love conventions very seriously, he is to be taken to the House of Fame where he will be properly instructed in the subject [529–699: 287–8]. But, as Lowes remarks, Chaucer hears, in that House of Rumour, rumours of everything but love;[16] he is utterly bewildered, and can make nothing of it beyond an immense confused noise. Just as he glimpses a man who seems to have some authority, and who looks as though he might explain everything, the poem ends. Or at least it stops, and editors say it is unfinished, but I am quite sure that there it ends, for it is exactly the right ending for this masterpiece of quizzical mockery. Surely the whole point about rumour is that it can always be tracked down to a source conveniently anonymous but alleged to be reputable, and it is never definite, though it is usually just going to be definite.

Similarly as regards form, the poem is the ultimate satire on the vision convention. Chaucer begins by solemnly enumerating the fifteen causes of dreams and making what we are to understand is a hair-splitting distinction between a "drem" and a "sweven" [1–65: 282], writes a double introduction to the first book as well as single ones to the other two, and impressively dates his dream twice. Now in a vision we have to make some sort of journey away from this world, and we can travel in one of three directions, down, up, or laterally. The vision of descent, the katabasis, is a common one: it meets us in classical journeys to the underworld, such as we find in the eleventh book of the *Odyssey* or the sixth book of the *Aeneid*, and in Biblical initiation symbols such as Daniel in the lion's den, his associates in the fiery furnace, and Jonah in the fish's belly. In book 1 Chaucer leaves Aeneas just at the entrance of his journey to the underworld, but refuses point blank to follow him.[17] The vision of ascent, which might be called, and which I am certainly going to call, the anabasis, the mounting up to a height from whence one may see all the kingdoms of the world and the glory of them, is equally common, and would, of course, be familiar to any reader of the *Paradiso*, including Chaucer. Book 2 is devoted to the poet's highly edifying but very reluctant journey through the spheres. And the visions of strange marvels in remote lands, which haunt us in so much medieval literature, and return to haunt us in the *Squire's Tale*, are the theme, more or less summarized, of the third book.

I wish I had time and space to analyse the technique of this superb *tour de force* in more detail. The dominating symbol is wind: even inside the breathless temple of glass Aeneas is blown out of Troy by Aeolus, wind ruffles the hair of Venus, and a tempest again drives Aeneas to the Cumaean Sibyl, where Chaucer abandons him [203–8, 229–30, 433–40: 284, 286]. Wind presumably sounds in Chaucer's ears along with aquiline oratory, and in book 3 Aeolus reappears as master of ceremonies, the House of Fame itself entering on a terrific sweep of wind [1583–1601: 297]. And with wind goes harangue: the preliminary harangues, the harangue of Dido in book 1, the endless harangues of the eagle, who incidentally points the connection by informing his charge that all words are air, and, finally, the rhetoric in the recital of the immense catalogue of things that go spinning and whirling around the poet's ears in the magnificent climax at the end.[18] The poem is, in one of its many aspects, a gorgeous satire on verbiage.

I am also inclined to think that if the poem were carefully examined from this point of view, it would turn out to be as profound as it is brilliant and exuberant. It has been called a parody of Dante,[19] but that hardly covers the ground: it is a parody of the whole world outlook which produced Dante. For the poet, confused as he may pretend to be, an old world is being blown out, a world of vague inchoate abstractions, and a new world of real people comes in on the tempest. That, at least in my opinion, is the reason for the apocalyptic symbolism of the armies summoned by the seven trumpets of Aeolus [1623–1817: 297–9]. And Aeolus is summoned by the goddess Fortune [1568–95: 297], for in medieval symbolism Fortune is frequently history, and the turning of her wheel the movement of historical events.

The medieval habit of classifying men into types and of giving symbolic value to outward objects combined to produce the popular art form of the bestiary. The serious treatment of the bestiary is bound up with the branch of allegory known as fable—an example of it in our literature is *The Hind and the Panther*. But obviously the form also makes an excellent vehicle for satire—usually vicious satire, as practically all our abusive and contemptuous epithets are derived from the animal world. There is a suggestion of the satiric bestiary in some of the caricatures of Rowlandson, and something more than a suggestion in the opening of *Volpone*.[20] *The Parliament of Fowls* has nothing of the *saeva indignatio*[21] of that splendid and terrible play, but in it the mocking smile of *The House of Fame* broadens to a good-humoured grin.

In the opening of the poem Chaucer ruefully admits, with all the irony of Burns's *Address to the Deil* [lines 109–14], that there must be many wonderful things concerning courtly love he knows nothing about, for the books say so. He reads of a dreamer who shoots up to the eighth sphere, where the ultimate certainties of heaven and hell are demonstrated to him. Chaucer, falling asleep, flies with that dreamer to the garden of romance, where he is to be similarly assured of the truth of bookish accounts of love. He conveniently forgets that he has tried this before.[22]

The poem eventually centres on a *demande d'amour*, or love debate, conducted by birds, with Mother Nature in the chair. Three tercel eagles love a formel eagle: only one can have her; which is it to be? Nearly all critics are convinced that Chaucer intended the different classes of birds to represent class distinctions in human society, and there seems no reason to doubt this.[23] There is a marked cleavage between conservative and radical opinion: the aristocracy believe, with the authors of the books that have overawed Chaucer, in a transcendental, superhuman state of love and in its absolute permanence: once in love, the "true" lover will never, never, love anyone else. The vulgar herd, being of the new school of nominalists, believe that is not an objective state, but a relation between individual men and women. On this assumption the duck points out that, as there are plenty of females, the two disappointed tercels can go and find other partners [594–5: 317]: similarly the goose— a deliciously flustered, spluttering Mistress Quickly of a goose— assumes that if love ceases on the woman's side it will tend to cease on the man's [566–7: 316]. The aristocrats run true to type. They receive this with shouts of laughter and annihilating snubs, and the gentle turtle is distressed [575–88: 317]. They, of course, have the last word, for the nicer points of *amour courtois* etiquette can be appreciated only by the leisured upper classes, and this particular *demande d'amour* is, quite properly, an affair of eagles. They must, then, be right, just as Chaucer's books must be right. So two of the tercels must remain loving and unloved. But as they all share equally in the state called love, it is unfair to give the preference to any, so all three should remain celibate. That seems to be the logical conclusion, but we have begun to suspect this logic, and we are hardly reassured when the ascetic solution is gravely propounded by that notorious emblem of all sexual unrighteousness, the cuckoo [603–9: 317]. A volley of abuse is immediately hurled at the cuckoo's head, but as his argument is unanswerable, the debate is at a standstill.

Through the clamour of quacks and clucks the voice of Nature makes itself heard. And the implications of Nature's speech [617–37, 659–65: 317, 318], which, because it is given to Nature, I take to represent Chaucer's own opinion, are that all arguments advanced are equally acute and equally irrelevant. Every speech, aquiline or anserine, is simply a priori moralizing: everyone has theories about what ought to be done, but no one seems to care about what is actually going to be done. The creator of Criseyde and the Wife of Bath delicately points out, through the words of the goddess who bore them, that the basis of this whole verbose structure of special pleading is the actual living female in front of them [621, 626–7: 317], whom they seem not to notice. What does she think about it?

All the birds are equally discomfited by this, but there is still time to save the face of the love convention when the lady makes her choice. But now comes the crowning touch of the whole uproarious farce: the lady calmly refuses to make any choice [652: 317]. The noise has all been made for nothing, and Chaucer has learned nothing from his dream about the subtleties of love etiquette except that they do not seem to work.

Then there is the little skit called *Anelida and Arcite*, which need not concern us long. The lady, Anelida, loves Arcite with all the fervent devotion required of her by courtly love: she gives him her whole soul. A modern writer would see that love of this sort is really a disguised masochism and that to adopt this attitude toward one's lover gives one a far subtler hold on him than any other approach could possibly do. A modern writer on this assumption would handle the situation exactly as Chaucer handles it. The man gets restive and deserts his affectionate lady for another one who makes him step lively. The long lament of the deserted Arcite follows [211–341: 306–7], tripping and bouncing along in almost every metre known to English poetry: she is obviously getting as much fun out of her desertion as she ever did out of her love affair.[24] She goes to the temple and is just about to begin another long complaint when the poem ends.

There are many Chaucerian critics who take nominalism, the belief that individuals are real, so much for granted that they are often not aware that another way of looking at things existed in Chaucer's time. And the *Prologue* to the *Legend of Good Women* is an excellent instance of how such critics can go wrong in reading Chaucer. The daisy turns out to be, not an orthodox Wordsworthian daisy recollected in tranquillity, but the emblem of a marguerite cult, and the passage celebrating it a mosaic of literary reminiscences. As a matter of fact this poem remains within the medieval love vision convention. It is a brilliant treatment of realistic symbolism (in the medieval sense of the word *realistic*) and constitutes a palinode in form as well as in content.

The daisy is introduced on the morning of the first of May, which means that it is a symbol, first of all, of the awakening of spring and the resurrection of life. The accretion of symbols around an object makes symbolic development a process of expansion, and the growth and unfolding of the flower is peculiarly appropriate to this. So the daisy is primarily the harbinger of an awakening world:

> And doun on knes anoon-ryght I me sette,
> And, as I koude, this fresshe flour I greete, . . .
> Forgeten hadde the erthe his pore estat
> Of wynter, that hym naked made and mat.[25]

But the daisy is much more. It is the harbinger also of the awakening day; it is an emblem of light, and with its white-rayed petals and its golden core it looks like a kind of microcosm of the sun. The daisy, says Chaucer, is the "day's eye": it opens to greet the sun in the morning and closes up at night, hating darkness [43–63: 483]. That is one aspect of the daisy. Then again, it is white, and white is the colour of purity and chastity, or red, which is the colour of passion. Thus, the daisy becomes a little goddess in her shrine of grass: Chaucer, in one of the supremely exquisite passages of English—surely of any—poetry, gets on his knees to her. He addresses her earlier as:

> of alle floures flour,
> Fulfilled of al vertu and honour. [53–4: 483]

Now symbolism is the relating of outward objects to inner experience, and even though Chaucer is ready to say of the daisy that:

> She is the clernesse and the verray lyght
> That in this derke world me wynt and ledeth. [84–5: 484]

still, as a symbol expands, there eventually comes a stage at which it has to be humanized. So the expansion of the symbolic daisy reaches its limit when the two qualities which the daisy possesses, light and virtue, appear in personal form, just as a vision of gods follows immediately the initiate's understanding of the symbolism of his rite. Chaucer takes advantage of a fact he has previously mentioned, that the daisy, being a flower of the sun, closes up at night, and with darkness the little emblem of light, "fulfilled of al vertu and honour," disappears, and the god of love enters in the form of a sun-god, with Alceste by his side [212–46: 487]. The one is associated with the passionate red and the other with the pure white of the daisy. In an initiation the epiphany is usually followed by a hymn of praise, and Chaucer's ballade appropriately follows their entry, enlarging the symbolism still further [249–69: 488]. He has already made the daisy the quintessential flower (which is what "of floures flour" means), less a flower than an incarnation of "flowerness." Now, when the virtue and honour of the daisy develop into the virtuous and honourable Alceste, she too is the quintessence of beauty, the ballade being a catalogue of the famous beauties she transcends. Chaucer takes pains to make it clear that Alceste is simply the soul of the daisy in anthropomorphic form:

> For of o perle fyn, oriental,
> Hire white coroune was ymaked al;
> For which the white coroune above the grene
> Made hire lyk a daysie for to sene. [221–4: 487]

The English word "daisy" (day's eye) refers only to the solar part of the symbolism: but the word "marguerite," which would be equally prominent in Chaucer's mind, is derived from the Greek word for *pearl*, which links it up with the "vertu and honour" part, as the pearl is, because of its colour, shape and delicacy, also an obvious symbol of pure womanhood.

With the entry of the gods the poem begins to take on the theological tone of the court of love. The first appearance of the God of Love almost recalls the triumphant Christ of the Apocalypse, and the long dialogue between the two divinities [341–534: 491–5] recalls those Italian primitives in which a precocious little manikin, with the piercing and accusing eyes of insulted godhead, is held in restraint by a gentle and kindly Madonna. We are, therefore, not surprised at the theological nature of the scheme projected: a martyrology of Cupid's saints.

Everything is demurely consistent with medieval philosophy and with its organizing principle that the individual is less real than his state of mind. If Chaucer the individual were the final reality, he could write a legend of good women whenever he wanted to. But *Troilus and Criseyde* and the translated *Romaunt of the Rose* were the products of a contrary state of mind, and that state has first to disappear and be replaced by its opposite. It can easily be seen how closely this doctrine is connected with the idea of purgatory, and the *Prologue*, as I hope I have made clear by this time, is a genuine initiation poem, initiation being always purgatorial. Love, the supremely integrating and unifying power in life, can be treated only in its pure state, and in that state it is, as Swedenborg was to say later, to the spiritual world what the sun is to the physical world: the source of its life.[26] In the daisy the light and the purity of love are symbolically connected, and the daisy is a flower of the spring, appearing when the world regains its youth and energy. By seeing the daisy, Chaucer is enabled to see the two divinities who embody its two symbolic attributes; then his own soul goes through a similar integration, and so, by that process of expansion, association, and synthesis which was perhaps the finest achievement of the medieval mind, we pass insensibly from the little meadow daisy to the ambition to write *The Legend of Good Women*. And when we get to the end we discover that the beginning was not as accidental or as haphazard as it looks. But medieval philosophy was much greater in conception than in application, and so is *The Legend of Good Women* greater in prologue than in illustration. We, therefore, stop where the interest of the poem largely stops.

Except for the fact that most epics are longer, *Troilus and Criseyde* is an epic poem. It is a complete artistic synthesis of life, containing all the religious, philosophical, social, and scientific ideas its author could pack into it. It is addressed, not only to "yonge fresshe folkes, he or she," but to the moralist Gower and the philosopher Strode [5.1835, 1856–7: 479]. In this poem Chaucer said essentially all that he had to say, and it is the unity of what he said, or the "argument" of the poem in the broad sense, that I wish to consider.

The unity of a poem is primarily connected with form, and in form *Troilus and Criseyde* is a tragedy, as is clearly stated by Chaucer in his envoy:

Go, litel bok, go, litel myn tragedye. [5.1786: 479]

We have a comparatively simple idea to start with, therefore, as tragedy in the Middle Ages was less a form than a formula, which is enunciated by the Monk in the *Canterbury Tales*:

> Tragedie is to seyn a certeyn storie
> As olde bookes maken us memorie,
> Of hym that stood in great prosperitee,
> And is yfallen out of heigh degree
> Into myserie, and endeth wrecchedly.[27]

However seriously Chaucer may have taken this, the fall of a hero from a high place to a low one is clearly the underlying pattern of *Troilus and Criseyde*:

> The double sorwe of Troilus to tellen,
> That was the kyng Priamus sone of Troye,
> In lovynge, how his aventures fellen
> Fro wo to wele, and after out of joie. [1.1–4: 389]

Now the first thing to notice about this medieval conception of tragedy is that it is not in any way a tragedy of character. It is true that in a good many cases medieval writers would give the fall of the hero a moral interpretation: he fell because he had done those things which he ought not to have done. But this is by no means invariably true, and even when it is, the sins are powerfully suggested by the environment of the high place. The fall of a given individual may not have been inevitable, but the fall of a certain number of individuals is inevitable; and, therefore, the fall, when it occurs, is automatic. The tragedy of Hamlet could not have happened to Othello, nor could the tragedy of Othello have happened to Hamlet, but the whole point about the medieval tragedy is that it could happen to anyone in a certain situation and always happens to someone. But, of course, tragedy is not the whole of life: there are rises as well as falls occurring continually, and these are also automatic. The obvious symbol for the entire operation of circumstance is, of course, the wheel, and the turning of the wheel of fortune appears in medieval art as well as in medieval history. Everyone is familiar with the drawings of it with men struggling up on the left, looking more and more secure and confident as they reach the top, gradually losing their balance on the right, and at the bottom either clinging desperately or falling out of the picture. One can see that wheel turning through the monotonous drone of the Monk's voice as hero after hero is brought down until he loses his grip and disappears. And in *Troilus and Criseyde* the rotary motion is even more explicitly indicated at the beginning:

> Fro wo to wele, and after out of joie. [1.4: 389]

Troilus gets a faint glimpse of the wheel when he is still far enough away from it to see it:

> For wel fynde I that Fortune is my fo;
> Ne all the men that riden konne or go
> May of hire cruel whiel the harm withstonde. [1.837–9: 398]

He is caught, however, in one swift movement: he falls in love with Criseyde at first sight, and then for two books the wheel inches slowly up and up, through all the despair and nervousness of Troilus, through all the doubts and hesitations of Criseyde, through all the subtle strategy of Pandarus, to the consummation of the first night the lovers spend together. Then the wheel begins relentlessly to lower:

> And whan a wight is from hire whiel ythrowe,
> Then laugheth she, and makyth hym the mowe. [4.6–7: 441]

Inch by inch, as Troilus waits, first days, then hours, for his Criseyde, until he is again forced to realize, this time in deadly earnest, the existence of the wheel:

> O ye loveris, that heigh upon the whiel
> Ben set of Fortune, in good aventure,
> God leve that ye fynde ay love of stiel,
> And longe mote youre lif in joie endure! [4.323–4: 444]

In Dante, lovers like Troilus and Criseyde, even when happy in this life, are whirled eternally in hell, but Troilus suffers before death the agony of being broken forever on a wheel:

> To bedde he goth, and walweth ther and torneth,
> In furie, as doth he Ixion in helle. [5.211–12: 461]

But before the wheel has caught Troilus it has caught Troy:

> And eft the Grekes founden nothing softe
> The folk of Troie; and thus Fortune on lofte,
> And under eft, gan hem to whielen bothe
> Aftir hir cours, ay whil that thei were wrothe. [1.137–40: 391]

Therefore, Troilus, as a Trojan warrior, is condemned to death before the story opens, as Diomede calmly informs Criseyde. It is a "double sorwe" in more than one sense that Chaucer has to tell: the tragedy of Troilus is not exhausted by the infidelity of Criseyde, a fact which is of the highest importance for our understanding of the poem. Behind the fortune of Troilus is the fortune of his city, his friends, and his relatives; so that the wheel, as we look at it, expands until we realize that it is not a wheel of fortune, in the sense of being chance or haphazard, but the spinning wheel of the Fates:

> And Troilus shal dwellen forth in pyne
> Til Lachesis his thred no lenger twyne. [5.6–7: 459]

Fatalism in philosophy is generally an inference from a mechanical or materialistic science, and of no age is that more true than of Chaucer's. To take one very concrete example: the medieval interpretation of love at first sight. A material substance leaves the eyes of Criseyde and enters those of Troilus: his love is no more romantic than getting shot with a bullet. But that is only one illustration of a universal principle. Everything in the world, organic or inorganic, is based on four aspects of existence, hot, cold, moist, and dry. The four possible combinations of these give us in the inorganic world the four elements; in the organic world, the four humours. Everyone is born with four humours, and their interrelation in any man determines what he is pleased to call his character. But the elements which compose everything in the world constitute only that part of the universe in which we live. Beyond us are the sun, moon, and stars, and these are made out of substances which are, by the process of special pleading in aesthetic metaphors dear to the medieval mind, "superior" to the elements, and therefore—for if you can bring in aesthetic metaphors you can bring in political ones—must necessarily "rule" them. We look at our flat, two-dimensional world, and in the process of historical events see the shape of a turning wheel.

We look up to the heavens, and see that there is no wheel, but spheres which continually mould all earthly events to the forms of their involutions. This way of looking at the world stems very largely, of course, from Boethius, who gave the Middle Ages the idea of the wheel of fortune, and Boethius's ideas and reflections concerning the ups and downs of fate have been closely woven into the poem. Every point of the tragedy of *Troilus and Criseyde* is, therefore, marked by the passage of the sun or moon through the zodiac, and at every point we are aware that the fall of Troy is not the result of the anger of gods, but of the movement of planets the unhappy pagans thought were also gods and hoped to propitiate by prayers and sacrifices. At the height of his ecstasy Troilus prays to Venus, Jupiter, Mars, Phoebus, Mercury, and Diana to help him in his love because, he thinks, they too have once loved, and will know how he feels [3.705–35: 428–9]. The Christian who reads Chaucer's poem knows that these alleged gods are only stars: they have never lived or loved and could not help Troilus even if they could hear him. An important symbol of the poem is, therefore, the stars hidden by clouds, with the inferred figure of the tempest which drives its victims to destruction. When Criseyde is first seen in her black cloak, there was never seen "under cloude blak so bright a sterre" [1.75: 391]. The tempest rises at the opening of book two:

> Owt of thise blake wawes for to saylle,
> O wynd, o wynd, the weder gynneth clere;
> For in this see the boot hath swych travaylle
> Of my connyng, that unneth I it steere. [2.1–4: 401]

The book rounds off with the tempest or "kankedort" in the breast of Troilus [2.752: 420]. The fatal conjunction of stars which occurs every six hundred years is concealed by rain.[28] In the final catastrophe Troilus is hurled toward Charybdis, in which the tempest and wheel symbols coincide [5.638–44: 466].

Now whether there is any possibility of escaping this wheel or not, there is no doubt that there is an intense desire to escape from it. Many methods have been tried, many others recommended, with deliverance guaranteed. The most obvious is death. As soon as Troilus is caught by the wheel he longs for death, as under the court of love code he was expected to do. After he feels the full horror of his situation, he longs for death in good earnest, in one of the most poignant utterances of the poem:

> O wery gooste, that errest to and fro,
> Why nyltow fleen out of the wofulleste
> Body that evere myghte on grounde go?
> O soule, lurkynge in this wo, unneste,
> Fle forth out of myn herte, and lat it breste. [4.302–6: 444]

The next step is to take matters into his own hands, kill himself and Criseyde, and cut himself loose from the wheel for good [4.1184–90: 453–4]. He draws his sword on his fainting mistress, but she revives, "and gan for fere crye" [4.225: 454], and Troilus is unable to go through with it. Suicide, then, is not a successful way out: the stars are too strong, and no man can die until the hour they have decreed. But the feeling of the immense relief of the escape through becoming dead or unconscious continues to haunt the poem. This is I think one reason for the numerous references to Ovid's *Metamorphoses*: the stories of lovers released from suffering. The fatal day on which Pandarus commences operations is announced by the swallow who is the changed Procne; the owl who is the changed Ascalaphus shrieks for the blood of Troilus; the lark who is the changed Scylla sings on the morning of Criseyde's tenth day of absence. Niobe is referred to in Troilus's first expression of longing for death; Myrrha when the lovers weep in each other's arms; Daphne and Herse in Troilus's prayer.[29]

The escape through knowledge is also hinted at and provides us with one of the most dramatic openings in literature. At the very beginning of the poem Calchas, Criseyde's father, divines the fortunes of the war, and deserts to the Greeks. I know of nothing more thrilling than Chaucer's handling of this: he opens quietly with his "bidding prayer" for true lovers and raises the curtain on the besieged Troy. In the expectant hush that follows Calchas suddenly scurries across the stage, leaving Troy to its fate, Troilus to his tragedy, and his own daughter in the lurch, at least for the time being. Knowing that he is free makes us realize at once how irretrievably the others are caught, and it assuredly heightens the irony of the feast of the Palladion which follows it [1.160 ff.: 391]. It has a more concrete reference still, for Calchas being Criseyde's father, his action suggests that "sliding courage" and a tendency to sacrifice loyalty to common sense run in the family, and so prepares the way for the escape of Criseyde herself, which we shall consider in a moment. And yet Calchas is a thoroughly contemptible character, the only one in the poem, which implies that one difficulty of escaping through knowledge is the one Faustus faced in a different way: gaining the world to lose one's soul.

A much more attractive method of escape by knowledge is that taken by the great poet or artist. Although the artist escapes the wheel by being an observer rather than a sufferer, he records the processes of the stars, not to save his own skin, like Calchas, but to help and console others. The story of Troilus immortalized by a great poet is an example, not in the vulgar sense of a nurse's bogey or a cautionary tale, but in the sense of an archetypal experience. The artist puts a pattern into the general chaos of life others may look to for guidance. The longer it lasts the more useful it will be. It is for this reason that Chaucer, who took such pains to revise and clarify his meaning in this poem, pleads with future ages to try to read him no matter how much the English language may change:

> And for ther is so gret diversite
> In Englissh and in writyng of our tonge,
> So prey I God that non myswrite the,
> Ne the mysmetre for defaute of tonge,
> And red wherso thow be, or elles songs,
> That thow be understonde, God I biseche! [5.1793–8: 479]

But the artist's pattern cannot last forever: sooner or later the larger rhythms of revolution whirl it away to oblivion, unless it is lucky enough to find, like the unknown and forgotten Lollius,[30] someone to recreate it:

> Ye knowe ek that in forme of speche is chaunge,
> Withinne a thousand yeer, and wordes tho
> That hadden pris, now wonder nyce and straunge
> Us thinketh hem, and yet thei spake hem so,
> And spedde as wel in love as men now do. [2.22–6: 401]

At the end of the poem Chaucer asserts that the promise of escape offered by the Christian religion to its followers does succeed where all others fail. Now, as the poem is written for a Christian society, for it is addressed to Gower and Strode rather than to an audience who did not like it much anyway, according to the *Legend of Good Women* prologue, and as it is primarily concerned with the problem of the relation of man to his destiny, it is obvious that the claim of Christianity to possess the only true solution of that problem cannot possibly be ignored or even subordinated. There is, thus, no way of regarding Chaucer's second envoy [5.1828–70: 479] as irrelevant to the poem, whether or not one agrees with him or believes in his sincerity. The tragedy of Troilus is the tragedy of the whole pagan world, as Chaucer is careful to point out:

> Lo here, of payens corsed olde rites,
> Lo here, what alle hire goddes may availle. [5.1849–50: 479]

Troilus believed in gods which had the power to deliver man from the working of fate, only to find that they do not exist. Since his time Christ has come, and he has that power. But how do we know that we are not deceiving ourselves just as Troilus did? The question is obviously so important for Chaucer's Christian audience, for the only people who could possibly understand his poem were Christians, that, had he ignored it, one might be justified in drawing the inference that he believed the stars to be stronger than the god of England as well as the gods of Troy.

If, however, the mere contrast between B.C. and A.D. had exhausted the issue, the question whether or not Chaucer's vindication of Christianity was a perfunctory gesture, made because it was the thing to do, would remain forever unsolved, as far as *Troilus and Criseyde* is concerned. But there is much more to it than that. The tragedy of Troilus is not solely a tragedy of paganism: the stars did not shift their courses or lose their influence at the Incarnation. Every six hundred years Jupiter and Saturn meet the crescent moon in Cancer and claim another victim.[31] Every six hundred years some Chaucer has to discover some dusty and forgotten Lollius and retell his story. And any contemporary hearer or reader of Chaucer would understand that the astrological dating of the *Troilus and Criseyde* consummation carried the subsidiary meaning that what happened long ago will happen in this year of grace 1385. Therefore, Christianity does not have things all its own way: it is faced with the challenge of astrological fatalism and has to defend itself. It has to prove all other attempts to escape from the wheel of destiny wrong; then it has to prove itself right. It first, however, has to concern itself with something more vital than a dead and gone paganism: for the use of a contemporary date implies that Christianity has a contemporary rival. This contemporary rival is, of course, the court of love.

That the court of love definitely set itself up as a rival to Christianity is quite clear. It had its own God, its own theology, its own moral code, its own symbolism; and its adherents, in worshipping it, carried out an extensive parody of the Christian ritual which for consistent and extended blasphemy has had no parallel since. Chaucer appropriates all he needs of this. He opens with a "bidding prayer" addressed to the Love God's devotees [1.15 ff.: 389]. When Troilus falls in love the process is described in terms of ecstatic religious conversion: Troilus goes on his knees before an angered deity to plead conviction of sin, to beg forgiveness, and to promise in future to lead a soberly adulterous and ungodly life. In fact, the omnipotence of the God of Love is manifest in his choice of victim:

> In hym ne deyned spare blood roial
> The fyr of love—the wherfro God me blesse—
> Ne him forbar in no degree for al
> His vertu or his excellent prowesse. [1.435–8: 394]

His worship, when Criseyde, after becoming converted to him, hears a nightingale singing a love song in her garden [2.18: 411], expands to a kind of pantheism. Pandarus piles the blasphemies up higher and higher: the saved of the God of Love are justified by their faith in him; Criseyde must forgive his strategy because Christ forgave his death, and so on till the climax is reached in the invocation to Venus at the opening of book three [1–49: 421], where love reaches its apotheosis as the sustainer and redeemer of the world: it has finally ousted divine love, the Holy Spirit, from its place. After that, we are hardly surprised to find that the opening of book 2 is taken from Dante's description of the entrance to purgatory from hell, nor to find that the progression of Troilus from conversion to consummation is one from purgatory to heaven:

> Thus sondry peynes bryngen folke to hevene, [3.1204: 434]

nor to find frequent references to his being in heaven scattered through this third book. A hymn of Dante's to the Blessed Virgin is appropriated by the God of Love,[32] and Boethius himself is called upon for homage.

Now the court of love promised, in the kind of love it recommended, deliverance from the wheel. And its kind of love attempted to combine the virtues, without the disadvantages, of the two ordinary forms of sexual union, marriage and the liaison. It forbade marriage, for it wanted to keep the ecstatic thrill of insecurity and it wanted to free the union of any taint of compulsion. On the other hand, it forbade the temporary liaison, for it wanted to keep the idea of sacramental fidelity and loyalty which the Church attaches to marriage. In other words, it tried, like art and religion, to create a pattern out of the chaos of life; and it found, in the rite of physical consummation, a continuous ecstasy of happiness. Like religion, it promised its followers ascent without descent: its true adherents, in the words of Pandarus, can no more come down on the other side of the wheel than the man can fall out of the moon [1.1023–6: 400]. It is also Pandarus who says that while a sinner may become a saint, it is very unlikely that a saint will later turn sinner [1.1002–8: 400].

It is one of the primary purposes of *Troilus and Criseyde* to expose the underlying fallacy of the court of love's theology. It does not escape from circumstances, for its crucial rite, physical union, is based on desire, and desire is a creature of time and mutability.[33] Very skilfully does Chaucer underscore the fact that the love of Troilus and Criseyde is essentially obedient to the law of kind, nature's objective impulse toward reproduction which, though it exploits human desire, overrides human will and makes hash of human idealistic reasoning. And Chaucer, like a diabolist painter, calmly introduces that as part of his reason for doing homage to the God of Love:

Forthy ensample taketh of this man,
Ye wise, proude, and worthi folkes alle,
To scornen Love, which that so soone kan
The fredom of youre hertes to hym thralle;
For evere it was, and evere it shal byfalle,
That Love is he that alle thing may bynde,
For may no man fordon the lawe of kynde. [1.232–8: 392]

And when Criseyde leaves Troilus, it is, in spite of all his religious phraseology, the absence of her body which is most vividly real to him:

Wher is myn owene lady, lief and deere?
Wher is hire white brest? wher is it, where?
Wher ben hire armes and hire eyen cleere,
That yesternyght this tyme with me were?
Now may I weepe allone many a teere,

> And graspe aboute I may, but in this place,
> Save a pilowe, I fynde naught t'enbrace. [5.218–24: 462]

Therefore, all attempts to make anything permanent or lasting out of a court of love attachment are quixotic. The operation of circumstances overrules it. Chaucer is not defending marriage, but if Troilus had married Criseyde he could have asserted the right to protect her, and would not have been forced to stand by helplessly when she was taken from him. Chaucer is not defending the liaison either, but had Troilus been the sort of man who could have profited by the example of Criseyde and the precept of Pandarus and taken another mistress, he might have suffered much less. Neither marriage nor the liaison are as ambitious as the court of love, but they go with the wheel: and, consequently, they make the best of a bad job, for escape from the wheel in that direction is impossible. The reason why Troilus suffers so at Criseyde's infidelity is that he keeps the idea of a permanent pattern in life always in front of him: he looks at the whole problem spatially, and, of course, when Criseyde's yielding to Diomede is compared with her professions of constancy to Troilus her action is abominable. But Criseyde does not see it in that way. She looks at it temporally: she yields to Troilus because she has yielded before and yields to Diomede because she has yielded to Troilus. When she swears fidelity to Troilus, she swears by symbols of constant inconstancy: the moon and a river [4.1545–54: 457]. She obeys the commands of a stronger force than the God of Love: and events work in her favour, not in that of Troilus. Troilus curses the day that follows his night of happiness with all the fervour of a Donne, [3.1450–70: 436–7], but the day comes for all that.

For Criseyde escapes. The fate of attractive women in a conquered city is not for her. She does not suffer too much to be consoled by another lover. We may not like Diomede as well as Troilus, but that is no reason to suppose that Criseyde did not. There is, thus, an additional significance in her swearing by the river Simois, for the river Simois, "that rennest ay downward to the se" [4.1549: 457], though unstable and sliding of courage, does escape from Troy. Now this fact of Criseyde's escape is an integral part of Chaucer's poem; and it is precisely this that makes the court of love moralists, and those later moralists like Henryson, who regarded the initial love of Troilus and Criseyde as essentially sacramental, like marriage, foam at the mouth.[34] Criseyde ought not to have escaped. She ought to have been horribly punished. But that is only a pious hope, not a fact, and however energetically the moralists may affirm that she was punished, do they really know whether she was or not? Logically the moralists have to concede this point and say that although Troilus was faithful and suffered for it, and although Criseyde was unfaithful and got away with it, nevertheless Criseyde ought to have remained faithful and suffered, because it would be the decent thing to do. But why? What god would justify her fidelity? The moralist may refuse to believe in the wheel of fortune, but his argument symbolizes it, for it circles like a boomerang.

The conventional moralist, who holds that all sexual attachments outside marriage, if he makes even that exception, are immoral, is no better off. Naturally, the centre of his obloquy is less Criseyde than Pandarus. But it is difficult to make out a case on purely moral grounds, without reference to religion, against Pandarus; for Chaucer is careful to show that if there is one thing Pandarus is not, it is a pander. The amount of work he puts into his stratagems is done with complete disinterest: he gains nothing by it and wants only to bring about the supreme happiness of Troilus and Criseyde as he understands happiness. And when things go all wrong, there is no doubt about the sincerity of his sympathy or of his contempt for the Criseyde who has broken his code. He is a servant of love, but if one puts that aside and considers only the moral implications of his attitude, they are seen to be quite simple and impeccable. Whatever brings happiness and does harm to no one cannot be wrong. It would do harm to Criseyde were her intrigue known, so Troilus is solemnly adjured to keep it secret. And if the moralist sulkily retreats from morality to convention and asserts that what has to be kept secret must have something wrong about it, what support, still on strictly moral grounds, can he offer except to say that somehow or other the voice of the people, which establishes conventions, is the voice of God? Public opinion goes on record exactly twice in *Troilus and Criseyde*. It roars at the desertion of Calchas [1.85–91: 390], and it roars for the traitor Antenor [4.183–6: 443]. As it is disastrously wrong both times, a love affair which kept itself secret from such a mob might well congratulate itself.

No, there is little use trying to wax righteously indignant over either Criseyde or Pandarus. Pandarus is as fine a man as this world, by itself, can offer: he is no Mephistopheles. Pandarus is the creation of a serene poet interpreting a sane and healthy morality: Mephistopheles, who comes from the lower world to point out the delights of this one, and who has much of his author's sympathy although he is an agent of evil, is the creation of a rebellious poet struggling with the warped and confused morality of the Renaissance. And if there is anything wrong with Criseyde's desertion, there is surely something much more wrong with the whole train of events that suggested it. It is significant that Criseyde and Pandarus both despise what we call superstition: Criseyde is contemptuous of her father's astrology [4.1401–14: 456]; Pandarus ridicules attempts to divine dreams [5.358–85, 1275–81: 463, 473]. They despise occult mysteries for the same reason that Edmund despises them:[35] they are children of nature, concerned with the world, not the heavens. It is futile to condemn them: it is the world we must condemn. This is the crucial difference between a religious tragedy like *Troilus and Criseyde* and a moral tragedy like *Romeo and Juliet*. In Shakespeare there is lip-service to the same astrological fatalism: the lovers are "star-crossed." But, nevertheless, our reaction is not purely fatalistic: we feel that in some way there has been a waste of two perfectly good lives. We feel like condemning the agents of the tragedy: if the Montagues and Capulets would stop their silly wrangles, young lovers would not be slaughtered. The prince who points this moral gets the last word. But in Chaucer the efficient causes of the catastrophe are less easy to locate. Again, the religious fatalism of *Troilus and Criseyde* is in sharp contrast to the atheistic fatalism of Hardy. In Hardy the machinery of fate is less intelligent and sensitive than the material it operates with: its most typical representatives, then, are projectiles of force and cunning rather than imagination, like Napoleon. The only escape from this unconscious power is through the increase of consciousness. Here the solution again is moral, though in a different way: the tragedy of Tess is also a waste, and had Angel been more intelligent, less subject to the automatic workings of instinct, the tragedy need not have happened.[36] But in Chaucer the chief characters are of the highest possible intelligence: not only their hopes and desires, but all their prudence and caution, their rationalizings and their idealisms, are adjusted with the most hair-splitting delicacy to the movements of the stars. As we have already said, the escape from the wheel through increase of knowledge does not work either.

Troilus and Criseyde, then, is not a moral tragedy but the tragedy of morality: it chooses the finest this world can produce only to show how useless and bankrupt it is. Good works are of no avail without something higher—faith. But is there any positive element in this whole dreary mess of Pandarus's miscalculations, Troilus's agony, Criseyde's infidelity, and the futility of all Trojan effort, which will lead us straight to the positive assurance which faith gives?

We can answer this by finding out what Chaucer is really interested in and, consequently, what he told the story for. He is not, like the moralists, like Henryson or even Boccaccio, primarily interested in Criseyde. He is usually considered to be sentimental about Criseyde, but what he says is:

> Ne me ne list this sely womman chyde
> Forther than the storye wol devyse, [5.1093–4: 471]

in which he implies that what really excuses Criseyde is not so much his tender heart as the formal requirements of his poem. It is Troilus who holds him, and it is the "double sorwe" of Troilus, of which Criseyde forms only part, that is his theme. Now the tragic love and death of Troilus is again, of course, more than the medieval fall of the illustrious man with a moral attached, for the last words of Troilus, chosen by Chaucer, I believe, with very great care, are as follows:

> But trewely, Criseyde, swete may,
> Whom I have ay with al my myght yserved.
> That ye thus doon, I have it nat deserved. [5.1720–2: 478]

The undeserved suffering of a tragic hero brings us to the concept of sacrifice. And sacrifice, a completely nonmoral act in its essence, is bound up with faith in religion as opposed to the routine practice of morality.

The symbolism by which Chaucer indicates that Troilus is a sacrificial victim is very subtle and very unobtrusive, but it is there. As usual, it slips in under cover of professed adoration for the God of Love. The bidding prayer at the opening states with bland reverence that the purpose of the sacrifice is to establish communion among devout believers in Eros. It is only in the double meaning of two lines that we begin to suspect anything, and we need not suspect that if we do not wish to:

> Thus biddeth God, for his benignite,
> So graunte hem soone owt of this world to pace,
> That ben despeired out of Loves grace. [1.40–1: 390]

Then the events begin to move, and the sun glides into the "white bull"

[2.55: 402]. Taurus, of course, but why white? A thousand lines intervene, and then comes Troilus's prayer to Jupiter, who loved Europa in
the form of a white bull, to aid him in his love.[37] Criseyde has to leave
Troilus, and then comes:

> Right as the wylde bole bygynneth sprynge,
> Now her, now ther, idarted to the herte,
> And of his deth roreth in compleynynge,
> Right so gan he aboute the chaumbre sterte. [4.239–42: 443]

The white bull is an emblem of a perfect sacrifice, and it is very difficult
to believe that these three interconnected passages are all accidents. But
the bull is not only a sacrificial animal; it is a symbol of fertility, and the
whole symbolism of sacrifice which through the death of one reinte-
grates and strengthens those who remain alive is connected with the
death and rebirth of the year. And the rhythm of the dying and reviving
year runs all through the tragedy of Troilus. Troilus is, as Chaucer takes
pains to point out, the appropriate victim of such a sacrifice, the king's
son. He first meets Criseyde in April, at the feast of Palladion which
bears a considerable resemblance to the festival in which we commemorate the year's rebirth, Easter [1.155–61: 391]. Chaucer's exquisite handling of the scene, too, recalls the immemorial nature myth of the
sleeping beauty: among all the handsomely dressed women the most
beautiful stands completely silent, dressed in the black of a widow's
cape [1.170: 391]. No wonder Troilus, as he gazes at her, unconsciously
refers to the ladies who "slepeth softe" while their lovers have insomnia
[1.195: 391]. In the next book we are in May, but it is still the awakening
spring when the wheel begins its movement. Chaucer adds a scene to
Boccaccio here: the hero who is to be sacrificed has to have his triumphant ride through the streets before it takes place; so Troilus, the conquering warrior, the flawless victim, rides directly under Criseyde's
window with the world temporarily at his feet [2.616 ff.: 408]. It is again
May, or at any rate spring, when the consummation takes place, and the
fertilizing rains pour all night.[38] When the catastrophe has occurred, the
emphasis is rather on the fertility god's descent to the underworld:

> But fro my soule shal Criseydes darte
> Out nevere mo; but down with Prosperpyne,
> Whan I am ded, I wol go wone in pyne. [4.472–4: 446]

Criseyde goes back to the black dress, and her departure is symbolized
by the sterility of winter:

> And as in wynter leves ben biraft,
> Ech after other, til the tree be bare,
> So that ther nys but bark and braunche ilaft,
> Lith Troilus, byraft of ech welfare,
> Ibounden in the blake bark of care. [4.225–9: 443]

The world wakes up again for the sacrifice as the final book opens in the
spring, with Diomede pleading with Criseyde "fresshe as braunche in
May" while Troilus gives orders for the imposing funeral pyre which is
at the same time his own altar:

> But of the fir and flaumbe funeral
> In which my body brennen shal to glede,
> And of the feste and pleyes palestral
> At my vigile, I prey the, tak good hede. [5.302–5: 462]

Adonis, the greatest of all dying gods, was slain by a boar, and, of
course, the boar is an emblem of the Diomede family: a good deal of
space is taken up with Troilus's dream of the fatal conquering boar and
Cassandra's interpretation of it [5.1233–1533: 472–6]. This is in Boccaccio, but it is Chaucer who ties it neatly into the general symbolism of the
poem when he makes Troilus pray to Venus, greatest of all divinities
according to his religion, for aid:

> For love of hym thow lovedest in the shawe,
> I meene Adoun, that with the boor was slawe. [3.720–1: 428]

There are even more Christian hints: in Criseyde's absence Troilus
spends three days in a condition of absolute despair, "and on the fourth
day he began to mend," and when he curses the gods responsible for his
fate [5.207–8: 461], he brings in two gods quite arbitrarily and by accident not mentioned elsewhere in the poem, Ceres and Bacchus, gods of
bread and wine [5.208: 461]. And there is one more curious fact. Most
dying gods are associated with some deep red flower that is thought to
spring from their blood, as Hyacinthus is associated with the "sanguine
flower inscrib'd with woe."[39] Troilus has no flower, but a recurrent sym-

bol of his hopeless love is a ruby ring. Pandarus says to Criseyde, apropos of nothing in particular:

> And, be ye wis as ye be fair to see,
> Wel in the ryng than is the ruby set. [2.584–5: 408]

Then we learn that Troilus possesses a ruby ring: it glows for an instant as he seals his first letter to Criseyde [2.1086–8: 413]. And it was a ruby, which Chaucer expressly says was "lik an herte" [3.1371: 436], which Criseyde gave Troilus as a pledge. And when Troilus is finally forced to realize something of his position, he says:

> O ryng, fro which the ruby is out falle,
> O cause of wo, that cause hast ben of lisse! [5.549–50: 465]

All four references to the ruby are Chaucer's additions, as, indeed, practically all of these fertility symbols are. For all this the inevitable appeal is, of course, to the "yonge fresshe folkes, he or she" at the end.

There is implicit in the tragedy of Troilus, then, the myth of the king's son sacrificed in the role of the dying god. The symbols we have noted are only a selection from a large network of images, a few phallic, most merely connected with the growth and death of vegetation, like the famous "hazelwood" one,[40] which form a pattern linking in at every point with movements, now precipitate, now hesitant, of the main characters, all slowly pushing the fatal wheel. But enough has been said to establish the main point. Now, the fatalism of Greek tragedy is a development of the sacrifice, and in it the suffering endurance of the hero is at once a statement and a solution of the problems that tragedy raises. So why should the sacrifice of Troilus point to the supersession of Greek by Christian religion? Or, to put it in another way, as Chaucer presumably knew nothing of Greek tragedy, why is Chaucer able to regard the Christian faith as anything beyond an expression of overwhelming fatalism?

The reason for this is to be found in another of those crucial stanzas at the close which we have not yet considered: Troilus's laugh as he is freed from the world. For our admiration of the endurance of Troilus and our sympathy with his suffering has to be qualified by the fact that he gets very little chance to pose. He belongs to the comic carnival as well as to the tragic sacrifice. To kill himself and Criseyde in a mad fit of

jealousy would give a rounded Sophoclean finish to the performance:
Troilus sets about this, but Criseyde cries, and Troilus makes a mess of
it. To go forth and wreak dire vengeance on Diomede would give it a
fine Euripidean swing: Troilus tries this too, but although he batters and
batters away at Diomede's helmet, he makes no impression on it [5.1762:
478]. Besides, Troilus is his own chorus; he weeps and wails and groans
over his real sufferings, and, on the principle that a hired mourner will
make more noise than a sorrowing relative, weeps and groans still more
over his conventional ones. Everything conspires to give the impression
that in spite of his very real agony, in spite even of that heartbreaking
wait, hour after hour, on the walls of Troy for the Criseyde who will
never return, the sentimental, honest Troilus, as nervous in love as he is
courageous in fighting, as shy a virgin as Criseyde is a sophisticated
widow, is a figure of fun.

For with Troilus a new figure emerges from the fabliaux into serious
English literature—the cuckold. It is true that the cuckold is married,
but Troilus belongs to an age in which the court of love was vanishing
and marriage was coming into its own as the normal form of sexual
love. Later writers tended to think of Troilus and Criseyde as really married. When the cuckold comes in the door, the court of love, like Horace,
jumps out the window. But the portents of his entry are more extensive
than that. The cuckold is subjected to the subtlest humiliation a man can
endure: he suffers, but his suffering is not dignified. In a comedy he is
always pathetic, however much the dramatist may guy him—even Sir
John Brute[41] is a pathetic figure—but in a tragedy he is always ridiculous, however much the dramatist may sympathize with him. In Greek
tragedy, the irony of fate is appreciated at second hand: the tragedy is a
very real centre, the irony a remote and inhuman circumference. But the
double sorrow of Troilus is a double-edged sorrow—there is another
way of looking at it, in which the irony is the central thing and the tragedy peripheral. We can see this double focus, because we can look at it
objectively; as soon as Troilus can look at himself objectively he laughs.
But an enlightenment gained by someone after death may be achieved
by someone else of a later age, who can take that objective view: we feel,
for instance, that Troilus, secure in the sphere of the moon,[42] is looking
at his story very much as Shakespeare looked at it. Dante says that when
he was on earth the universe appeared to be geocentric; but when he
was in heaven he knew that there was the real centre. Troilus is similarly
turned inside out. Now one step more leads us to the conclusion. Troilus

in his life saw only tragedy because he, a man, was being sacrificed in the role of a god. But the tragedy was not the whole story: the sacrifice was ineffectual, which, though it is an ironic fact, implies a still more horrible tragedy. It is only by means of an effectual sacrifice, that is, the sacrifice of a god in a form of a man, that the release of laughter comes.

One of the most solemn moments in the *St. Matthew Passion* occurs during the tenor recitativo which tells of Peter's denial and of his conviction by the crowing of the cock. And when the tenor comes to this, if he is any good, he does suddenly crow like a real rooster. A similar touch of supreme genius is in the conclusion of *Troilus and Criseyde*. Through the memorial of the sacrifice, the elevation of the host, and the hymn to the Christ triumphant in the Trinity, there sounds the laughter of Troilus, which, to a modern reader, carries a faint suggestion of the raucous cackle of Thersites.[43] Chaucer is the master of comedy, and could perhaps never have written the tragedy of Troilus had he not been able to balance everything on this laugh.

The ultimate solution is Catholic, of course, but it is a Catholicism arrived at by what is almost a Protestant route. The complete rejection not so much of the things of this world, for Chaucer is no ascetic, as of the entire machinery of the universe and the whole concept of a moral order, with the sacrifice of Christ and the faith in its effectiveness as the only things that make life intelligible: all this is at least as close to Calvin as to St. Thomas. It is another instance of the unity of culture that the fourteenth-century England, which had produced Wycliffe as its most representative thinker, should also produce *Troilus and Criseyde* as one of its most deeply considered and carefully thought-out works of art.

Notes

Introduction

1 See *Correspondence*, 2:603, 610, 688.

2 See *Correspondence*, 2:794, 803, 809, 825, 851, 855.

3 *Correspondence*, 2:689.

4 *Correspondence*, 1:300.

5 Ibid., 386.

6 *Correspondence*, 1:243.

7 David Cayley, *Northrop Frye in Conversation* (Concord, Ont.: Anansi, 1992), 61–2. On Malraux's remark, see *The Voices of Silence*, trans. Stuart Gilbert (Princeton: Princeton University Press, 1978), 619.

8 See "Wyndham Lewis: Anti-Spenglerian," *Canadian Forum*, 16 (June 1936): 21–2; rpt. in *Reading the World: Selected Writings, 1935–1976*, ed. Robert D. Denham (New York: Peter Lang, 1990), 277–82; "Oswald Spengler," in *Architects of Modern Thought*, 1st ser. (Toronto: Canadian Broadcasting Corp., 1955), 83–90; rpt. in *Reading the World*, 315–25; "New Directions from Old," in *Myth and Mythmaking*, ed. Henry A. Murray (New York: George Braziller, 1960), 117–18; rpt. in *Fables of Identity: Studies in Poetic Mythology* (New York: Harcourt, Brace and World, 1963), 53–4; and "*The Decline of the West* by Oswald Spengler," *Dædalus*, 103 (Winter 1974): 1–13; rpt. as "Spengler Revisited" in *Spiritus Mundi: Essays on Literature, Myth, and Society* (Bloomington: Indiana University Press, 1976), 179–98. This last essay NF describes as "an effort to lay a ghost to rest," but ten years later Spengler was still making occasional appearances in his essays.

9 "Spengler Revisited," 187.

10 Notebook 93.3.10, par. 26. Unpublished. NNF, 1993, box 3, file 10.

11 "Symbolism of the Unconscious" in *Northrop Frye on Culture and Literature*, ed. Robert D. Denham (Chicago: University of Chicago Press, 1978), 89; this essay appeared originally as "Sir James Frazer" in *Architects of Modern*

Thought, 3rd and 4th series (Toronto: Canadian Broadcasting Corp., 1959), 22–32.

12 *Correspondence*, 1:84.

13 NF had written a long paper on Blake for Pelham Edgar during his third year at Victoria; unfortunately the paper has not survived. See Ayre, 92–3, and *Correspondence*, 1:182.

14 (Princeton: Princeton University Press, 1947); see chap. 6, "Tradition and Experiment," esp. pp. 161–86.

15 "Towards Defining an Age of Sensibility," *ELH*, 23 (June 1956): 144–52; rpt. in *Fables of Identity: Studies in Poetic Mythology* (New York: Harcourt, Brace and World, 1963), 130–7; and "Varieties of Eighteenth-Century Sensibility," *Eighteenth-Century Studies*, 24 (Winter 1990–91): 157–72; rpt. in *The Eternal Act of Creation*, ed. Robert D. Denham (Bloomington: Indiana University Press, 1993), 94–108.

16 Although the prose style here seems to improve, NF's assertions about music are, as James Carscallen has pointed out to me, often either questionable or mistaken. James Carscallen to Robert D. Denham, 29 August 1996.

17 *The Decline of the West*, 1:126. The framework of Spengler's views on the spatial world of nature as over against the temporal world of organic life was derived from Kant, or rather Fichte's modification of Kant. See *Decline*, 1: 124–6, 170–5.

18 NF's transcript lists the following courses in philosophy: ethics (3d), philosophical texts (3e), history of philosophy (3f), types of aesthetic theory (3g), ethics (4e), and modern philosophy (4g). As his first course in honour philosophy is identified on his transcript only as "Phil." it is difficult to know which of the first- or second-year courses (ethics, logic, and history of philosophy) he took. The University of Toronto *Calendar* does not give reading lists for all of NF's courses, but the lists that are provided include texts by Plato, Aristotle, Hobbes, Locke, Spinoza, Leibnitz, Kant, Hume, Mill, and Spencer, T.H. Green, Mary Evelyn Clarke, Ralph Barton Perry, plus a number of other unspecified philosophers read from anthologies. The courses in ethics (3d) and history of philosophy (3f) also include readings from eight secondary sources, called "references."

19 *University of Toronto Quarterly*, 11 (January 1942), 167–79.

20 *Correspondence*, 1:52–3.

21 *Correspondence*, 1:397.

22 Ayre, 94.

23 See, e.g., Friedrich Schleiermacher, *On Religion: Speeches to Its Cultured Despisers*, trans. John Oman (New York: Harper, 1958), 282–3.

24 In a letter to Helen Kemp written on New Year's Day 1935 NF reported, "I arose in my wrath the last week of the Christmas term and smote theology hip and thigh—I had five essays and three term exams to get done in a week. So I wrote two Church History essays Monday, two New Testament essays

Tuesday, exams in Systematic Theology and Church History Wednesday, exam in New Testament and essay in Religious Pedagogy Thursday. Then I slept and slept" (*Correspondence*, 1:384).

25 Notebook 27, par. 445. Unpublished. NFF, 1991, box 25.

26 *Manitoba Arts Review*, 3 (Spring 1942): 35–47.

27 *Hudson Review*, 2 (Winter 1950): 582–95.

28 For the problems in dating "An Enquiry into the Art-Forms of Prose Fiction" see the headnote to the paper.

29 For an account of NF's relations to Eliot, largely antagonistic ones, see Imre Salusinszky, "Frye and Eliot," *Christianity and Literature*, 42 (Spring 1992): 299–311. NF's view of the central tradition of English poetry as being romantic, revolutionary, and Protestant is found everywhere in his work, and he states the principle explicitly in *Fables of Identity: Studies in Poetic Mythology* (New York: Harcourt, Brace and World, 1963), 1, 149. His book is *T.S. Eliot* (Edinburgh: Oliver and Boyd, 1963; rev. ed., 1968).

30 See *The Double Vision: Language and Meaning in Religion* (Toronto: University of Toronto Press, 1991), 40. About the insight from Spengler, NF wrote in a later notebook that Spengler's insight was "a vision of history as interpenetration, every historical phenomenon being a symbol of the totality of historical phenomena contemporary with it" (Notebook 1993.1. Unpublished. NFF, 1993, box 1).

31 *Science and the Modern World* (New York: New American Library, 1948), 93. NF would have read the 1925 ed. published by Macmillan; he later acquired the 1938 ed. published by Cambridge University Press. For NF's comment on this passage see *The Double Vision*, 40–1.

32 *The Double Vision*, 41. NF reflects on the meaning of interpenetration scores of times in his notebooks. See, for example, Notebook 19, pars. 130, 172, 182, 202 (NFF, 1991, box 24); Notebook 24, pars. 53, 57, 112, 165, 213 (NFF, 1991, box 25); Notebook 27, pars. 42, 164, 168, 230 (NFF, ibid.); and Notebook 1993.1, pars. 9, 31, 41, 172, 353, 359, 395, 415, 428, 501, 706, 709, 721 (NFF, 1993, box 1).

33 Copious notes for this book, to be called *The Critical Comedy*, among other proposed titles, are in NF's notebooks. He never completed the project.

1. The Basis of Primitivism

1 NF apparently takes his ideas about Johnson's antimusical biases from *Lives of the Poets*. The seen-but-not heard maxim, as it applies to children, perhaps derives from Johnson's remarks on children in the entry of 10 April 1776 of Boswell's *The Life of Samuel Johnson* (New York: Modern Library, n.d.), 628–9.

2 "Introduction: Of Taste," *A Philosophical Inquiry into the Origin of Our Ideas of the Sublime and Beautiful* (1757; rev. ed., 1759), in *Critical Theory since Plato*, ed. Hazard Adams, rev. ed. (Fort Worth: Harcourt Brace Jovanovich, 1992), 300.

3 Landscape artist.

4 Blake's *Book of Thel*, composed about the same time as his *Songs of Innocence* (1789), was written in what was to become Blake's typical seven-stress line, the fourteener; the story of Thel takes place against the backdrop of a dreamy, pastoral cycle of nature.

5 The ideas in this paragraph derive from Oswald Spengler, "The Soul of the City," *DW*, 2:87–110.

6 The reference is to Wordsworth's repeated statement—in his "Observations" prefixed to the 1800 edition of *Lyrical Ballads*—that his poetry relied on the language "really used by men."

7 In R.B. Sheridan's comic drama *The School for Scandal* (1777) Charles Surface represents good-naturedness and Joseph hypocrisy; similarly, in Henry Fielding's novel *Tom Jones* (1745), the hero is a generous soul, while Blifil is a cunning hypocrite.

8 NF is referring to various principles in Wordsworth's "Observations" prefixed to *Lyrical Ballads* (1800), including his pronouncement that "all good poetry is the spontaneous overflow of powerful feelings."

9 In the early 1760s James Macpherson had published "extremely literal" translations of the legendary Gaelic poet Ossian; Macpherson's "original" texts were later shown to be forgeries. Thomas Chatterton (1752–70) wrote and published forgeries of poems said to have been written by Thomas Rowley, a fifteenth-century monk. *Vortigern and Rowena* was a pseudo-Shakespearean play forged by W.H. Ireland (1775–1835).

10 Thomas Gray, who all his life had been interested in primitive verse, translated two Old Norse poems in 1761, *The Fatal Sisters* and *The Descent of Odin*; Thomas Percy's *Reliques of Ancient English Poetry*, a collection of ballads, sonnets, historical songs, and metrical romances, was published in 1765; Sir Walter Scott's interest in old ballads and tales was spurred by Percy's *Reliques* and medieval French romances.

11 *Blackwood's Magazine*, a Tory periodical founded by William Blackwood, began publication in 1817. Rather than the *Century*, NF must have intended to say the *Quarterly Review*, which, along with *Blackwood's*, the *Edinburgh Review*, and the *London Magazine*, was an influential periodical of the time.

12 Edgar has changed "no brains or ears" to "no brains but also without ears."

13 In October 1817, J.G. Lockhart, writing for *Blackwood's*, began a series of vicious attacks on Keats, Leigh Hunt, and William Hazlitt, labelling them members of the Cockney school of poetry; this meant simply that they were poets of no social rank.

14 See, for example, Byron's, *English Bards and Scotch Reviewers* (1809), Coleridge's *Biographia Literaria* (1817), and Poe's analysis of his own poem in "The Philosophy of Composition" (1845). Byron's critical opinions are to be found also in his *Letters and Journals*, rev. ed. (London: John Murray, 1922).

15 "Phrases and Philosophies for the Use of the Young," *The Complete Works of*

Oscar Wilde (New York: Harper and Row, 1989), 1205. NF has slightly altered the aphorism. What Wilde wrote was, "The first duty in life is to be as artificial as possible. What the second duty is no one has yet discovered."

16 Arturo Giovannitti's poem was published in *Arrows in the Gale* (Riverside, Conn.: Hillacre Bookhouse, 1914) and rpt. in *An Anthology of American Poetry*, ed. Alfred Kreymborg (New York: Tudor Publishing, 1930), 392–7.

17 "Walt Whitman," *The Works of Robert Louis Stevenson*, 10 vols. (New York: Davos Press, 1906), 10:87. Stevenson was introduced to the natives of Malua in 1889 as "Tusitala," meaning "The Master of Tales," and it was the name by which he was usually known in Samoa.

18 Omai from Tahiti (formerly known as Otaheite) was brought to England by the British navigator Thomas Furneaux in 1776; the first South Sea Islander to be seen in London, he received a warm welcome from people like Boswell. In 1870 Miller left Oregon for London, where he published *Pacific Poems*; he was warmly received by the Pre-Raphaelites, especially Dante Gabriel Rossetti; his *Songs of the Sierras*, which Rossetti helped him revise, made him famous.

19 A derisive name given by the Bloomsbury modernists to a literary establishment formed by J.C. Squire (1884–1958), editor of the *New Statesman* and of a number of successful anthologies, and his friends.

2. Romanticism

1 The date that the Paris mob, led by Camille Desmoulins, revolted and stormed the Bastille. NF himself was born on 14 July.

2 "Carthage must be destroyed," the repeated declaration to the Roman senate by Cato the Elder (234–149 B.C.), who was convinced that Rome's future could be secured only if Carthage was annihilated.

3 Much of what NF says about the culture-town, the soul of the city, and the metropolis derives from Spengler's *DW*; see esp. 1:32–5, 2:87–110.

4 The two volumes of Henry Thomas Buckle's *History of Civilization in England* were published in 1857 and 1861 (London: J.W. Parker and Son); Theodor Mommsen's *Romische Geschichte* (Berlin: Weidmann, 1855) was translated into English in 1862 as *The History of Rome*, 4 vols. (London: R. Bentley); both books were subsequently issued in numerous editions. NF had read Mommsen during his third year at Victoria College.

5 Brett's marginal query: "?opera."

6 Gustav Fechner (1801–87), German physicist and philosopher, best known as the founder of psychophysics; he maintained that the world of plants and other objects lower than the animal world have a soul as well as a body.

7 The ideas in this paragraph parallel those in the opening paragraph of NF's "The Romantic Myth," the first chapter of *A Study of English Romanticism* (New York: Random House, 1968), 3–49.

8 The idea I express by the word *blood* is usually rendered by *heart*, with an equal disregard of anatomical exactness, which I reject on account of its sentimental connotation. *Cerebellum* is perhaps less open to pedantic objection, but the essential meaning should be clear enough. [NF]. Compare the argument here with Spengler's in *DW*, 2:3–7.

9 Brett underlined "materialism" and wrote "mechanism" in the margin.

10 NF uses *skepsis* in Spengler's sense—the positivistic features of the "winter" phase of an epoch; it is an attitude of doubt that helps to extinguish the spiritual creative force of "culture," appearing at the dawn of megalopolitan "civilization." See, for example, *DW*, 1:45.

11 It is by no means fanciful to see how in history the soil clings to a religious growth, the Christian ascetics being an extreme but not surprising instance. The filth of a religious era is repellent and hideous to a late civilization, which always develops an extensive practice of bathing and bodily culture. The tradition of uncleanliness is associated with the artist, and nations which are commercially more advanced than others and consequently more saturated with the metropolitan spirit, such as the English, Dutch, and Americans, are noted for their personal fastidiousness. I mention this here because of the bearing it has on a fairly important question connected with the rise of romanticism—the collapse of literary obscenity. [NF].

12 *Elective Affinities* was a story Goethe began writing in 1808, expanding it finally into a novel. The title implies an analogy between chemical affinity and sexual passion. Max Weber (1864–1920) used "elective affinity" to describe the relationship between Protestantism and the ethos of capitalism: the former provides the soil in which the latter can flourish.

13 Brett underlined "implicate" and put a question mark in the margin.

14 We notice that the polite sceptics who helped destroy the eighteenth century and make the nineteenth possible were founders of modern history writing—Hume, Gibbon, and Voltaire. [NF]

15 The position argued by the medieval "realists" in their debate with the "nominalists." Scotus Erigena and William of Champeaux, among others, argued that universals, as opposed to particulars, were the essential and original reality.

16 In the case of Shakespeare the turn to musical form starts with *Hamlet*. *Julius Caesar* is a drama; *Coriolanus* a secular oratorio. Plot and underplot are antithetical and contrasting in the histories; in *King Lear* they are contrapuntal. *Romeo and Juliet* moves to a dramatic climax; *Macbeth* sweeps to a point of repose. The supreme example from this point of view is, however, *Coriolanus*, which is so concentrated in its form that the blocks of dramatic contrast we find earlier have practically disappeared with lyric "purple passages," the play being almost impossible to quote from. This play is Shakespeare's last in this style; the remaining three return to purely dramatic technique.

This is one reason for agreeing with Frank Harris in postulating a nervous breakdown in the dramatist around 1608. [NF]. For Harris's speculation see *The Man Shakespeare and His Tragic Life-Story* (New York: Horizon, 1969), 401.

17 The college freshman belongs here, I suppose, and the college is the epitome of the metropolis. [NF]

18 In a park adjoining the Petit Trianon near Versailles, Marie Antoinette engaged in a back-to-nature fantasy, establishing there eight small farms, complete with peasants, cows, and dung heaps.

19 Brett underlined "duofold" and put a question mark in the margin.

20 One of the many reasons for the tremendous influence of the Bible on English thought is that it insinuates a sense of the organic growth of the Hebrew culture into a book supposedly a transmitter of the most rigid and abstract truth. Similarly the Puritanic Revolt, which really starts romanticism in England, brings in the Old Testament. Law, prophecy, history, and poetry are organic; gospels, letters, and apocalypses belong to criticism. [NF]

21 *The Romantic School* (1833) in *The Portable Romantic Reader*, ed. Howard E. Hugo (New York: Viking Press, 1957), 67.

22 *Maximen und Reflexionen*, no. 1031, *Sämtliche Werke nach Epochen seines Schaffens*, Münchner Ausgabe, ed. Karl Richter (München: Carl Hanser, 1985–), 17:893; the well-known maxim also appears in a slightly different form in *Gespräche mit Eckermann*, 2 April 1929, Münchner Ausgabe, 19:300.

23 In other words, romanticism is to the life of a culture exactly what disease is to the individual: a manifestation of the supremacy of the time-force over its spatial cross-section of life. Which is of course why Goethe equated them. (Incidentally, it follows that romanticism could only deal with disease in terms of disease. This is a vindication of the penetrating suggestion, thrown out but not explained by Friedell, that the homeopathic or inoculative principle represents the romantic approach to medicine. The application of a narcotic to artistic production is the same thing.) [NF]. See Egon Friedell, *A Cultural History of the Modern Age*, 3 vols. (New York: Knopf, 1932), 3:52–3.

24 Schopenhauer wrote his chief work, *The World as Will and Idea* (1819), when he was thirty; he began teaching in 1820, but after failing at this, he retired to live a bitter, reclusive life for more than forty years.

25 After being imprisoned in 1830 for the revolutionary views expressed in his literary articles, Giuseppe Mazzini (1805–72) spent the next forty years, which included exile and arrest, in political agitation of one form or another.

26 In Berlin in the 1820s Schopenhauer (1788–1860) combatively staged his lectures at the same time as those of Hegel, who was eighteen years his senior, but he failed to attract many students. Camillo Benso di Cavour was five years younger than Mazzini, but his patient statesmanship made him a more dominating figure than the often exiled Mazzini in the events leading to the unification of Italy.

27 Hence, of course, the impulse to elaborate dress and bodily concealment disappears with the Directoire and again in the romantic rehabilitation of our own day. We have spoken before of the growth of a bodily culture—the distinction between it and the exercise of the fighters of the creative period is simply that the former, being the result of a merging of sexes, is centred on the narcissistic. (There is a weird anticipation of this in the pseudoclassical superstition that dead-white plasticity was the Greek ideal and consequently should be ours—the movement headed by Winckelmann.) [NF]. The Directoire style, which followed the downfall of the monarchy in France, abandoned the sumptuousness of the Louis XVI style in favour of simpler, less adorned designs. Johann Joachim Winckelmann's influential ideas about Greek art were developed in *Gedanken über die Nachahmung der griechischen Werke in der Malerei und Bildhauerkunst* (1755; English trans., *Reflections on the Paintings and Sculpture of the Greeks*, published by Fuseli in 1765) and *Geschichte der Kunst des Altertums* (1764).

28 Schopenhauer's attitude toward women seems to have grown out of his bitter relations with his mother; he was obsessed with the physical aspects of sex. The notes he left behind on love and marriage were burned by his literary executor, but his misogyny comes through clearly in his essay "On Women" in *Parerga* (1851).

29 Cf. the elegant little pastorale in "The Mikado":

> *Ko-ko*:   There is a beauty in extreme old age—
>   Do you fancy you are elderly enough?
>   Information I'm requesting
>   On a subject interesting;
>   Is a maiden all the better when she's tough? [NF]

The Complete Plays of Gilbert and Sullivan (New York: Modern Library, [1936]), act 2, lines 783–7.

30 Here NF is following Spengler, who sees Otto Weininger's *Geschlecht und Charakter* (1903) and August Strindberg's plays as two of the principal landmarks of nineteenth-century "ethical" positivism. See *DW*, 1:374.

31 NF's ellipsis.

32 It was a widespread belief in the positivistic period that the tomato, which was called a "love-apple," was poisonous. [NF]

33 In Voltaire's *Candide* (1759), a satire on Leibnitzian optimism, Pangloss repeatedly affirms that everything is best in the best of all worlds in spite of the countless examples of natural and moral evil he and Candide encounter.

34 In *The World as Will and Idea* (1819), Schopenhauer argues that just as ideas are a representation of human will, so the world is a representation of the cosmic will; both are "blind" insofar as they are unconscious driving forces.

35 In *The Critique of Pure Reason* (1781), Kant developed a fourfold division of

categories, each having three subcategories: quantity (unity, plurality, totality), quality (reality, negation, limitation), relation (inherence and subsis-
tence, causation and dependence, reciprocity between agent and patient),
and modality (possibility, existence, necessity).

36 Literally, leaning against or propping; in music, an embellishment consisting
of an unharmonized note falling or rising to an adjacent note.

37 This argument is developed in pt. 2 of Fichte's *Die Bestimmung des Menschen*
(1800); trans. by Roderick M. Chisholm as *The Vocation of Man* (Indianapolis:
Bobbs-Merrill, 1956).

38 Fichte's philosophy of history was developed in *Die Grundzüge des gegen-
wärtigen Zeitalters* (1804). Fichte actually gives five stages (reason as instinct,
reason as ruling authority, liberation from reason, reason as knowledge, and
reason as art). What NF calls the "normal nation" of barbarism apparently
corresponds to Fichte's first stage, the state of innocence; the "age of authority," to Fichte's second stage, the state of progressive sin; and the "age of
reasonable knowledge," to Fichte's fourth and/or fifth stages. NF derives his
account of Fichte, not from the *Grundzüge*, but from the three-stage summary
in Wilhelm Windelband, *A History of Philosophy*, trans. James H. Tufts, 2nd
ed. (New York: Macmillan, 1921), 605–6.

39 Again, NF's account here of Fichte derives from Windelband, 593–5.

40 On NF's analysis of Schelling here and in the following paragraphs, cf.
Windelband, 597–9, 607–10.

41 For Schelling's "dynamic atomistics," which he developed in opposition to
mechanistic physics, see his *Ideen zur einer Philosophie der Natur* (1797),
trans. by Errol E. Harris and Peter Heath as *Ideas for a Philosophy of Nature*
(Cambridge: Cambridge University Press, 1988).

42 Schelling advanced the idea of the "indifference" of nature and spirit in vol.
2 of *Zeitschrift für speculative Physik* (Jena and Leipzig: C.E. Gabler, 1800–1).
The work had not been translated into English in 1933, and it is highly
doubtful that NF consulted the original German. He perhaps encountered
the idea in one or both of the histories of philosophy with which he was
familiar: Windelband, 608, or Friedrich Ueberweg, *History of Philosophy from
Thales to the Present Time*, trans. G.S. Morris, 2 vols. (New York: Scribner,
Armstrong, 1875), 2:219–20.

43 In the margin at this point Brett wrote "cp Turgot," a reference to the French
statesman and economist Anne Robert Jacques Turgot (1727–81).

44 Cf. Chesterton: "The Victorians are somewhat excessively derided today,
because their notion of a novel was a story that ended well. The real vice of
the Victorians was that they regarded history as a story that ended well—
because it ended with the Victorians. They turned all human records into one
three-volume novel; and were quite sure that they themselves were the third
volume." —*Chaucer* [London: Faber and Faber, 1932], 38. [NF]

45 Shaftesbury makes the point in *Characteristics of Men, Manners, Opinions, Times* (1711); see especially pt. 3, sec. 2 of Treatise 5, "The Moralists."
46 "To shock the narrow-minded."
47 The point is made, though not so categorically, by W. Wallace in his *Life of Arthur Schopenhauer* (London: Walter Scott, 1890), 13–14.
48 See "On History," chap. 38 of *The World as Will and Idea*, trans. R.B. Haldane and J. Kemp, 3 vols. (London: Routledge and Kegan Paul, 1883), 3:220–30. "In all history," says Schopenhauer in the same book, though in another context, "the false outweighs the true" (1:317).
49 The words of Andrew Undershaft to Adolphus Cusins in act 3 of George Bernard Shaw's *Major Barbara* (1905).
50 This essay has not survived.
51 On Buckle and Mommsen, see n. 4. Buckle believed that general laws determined the course of human progress and that these laws could be shown, through the application of the scientific method, to operate in the histories of nations.
52 *DW*, 1:18–29.
53 Nordau, a Hungarian Zionist, was the author of *Entartung* (1893) (English trans., *Degeneration* [1895]), in which he argued that much of contemporary culture was pathologically degenerate; *Entartung* emerged as a racist term in the 1920s and a decade later became the chief slogan in the Nazis' campaign against the "degeneracy" of modern art.
54 *Traité de l'harmonie.*
55 In the piano sonata, op. 31, no. 3, the last movement, which an older composer would certainly have made a gigue, is a tarantelle, which appears and disappears with romanticism. The tarantelle is not a dance but the destruction of one, increasing its speed to the limit of endurance. Ravel did the same thing dynamically for the bolero, and finally annihilated the dance. [NF]
56 The famous *Dead March* of Handel shows how creative music deals with this. It is simply a succession of dominant and tonic chords in C major—a page of dead music. (The *Largo* is not a dead march, as an ardent church-goer might suspect; it is more like a slow waltz.) [NF]. The *Dead March* is from Handel's oratorio *Saul* (1739); *Handel's Largo*, as it is called in many arrangements, is the famous aria "Ombra mai fù" from the opera *Xerxes*.
57 After "Dickens" NF wrote "(see p.)," intending, apparently, to go back and fill in the page number where he refers to Dickens later in his paper.
58 The romantic undercurrent finds a peculiar expression in the well-known poem called *The Lost Chord*, which depicts an organist finding supreme solace and bliss in what must have been a highly complicated discord; otherwise the sufferer could have found it again easily enough. (Sullivan's setting, however, indicates that it was only a diminished seventh. Grieg as a child got a similar effect from a ninth and never got over it.) [NF]. *The Lost Chord*, a

poem by Adelaide A. Procter (1825–64), was set to music by Arthur Sullivan in 1876 and became the most popular ballad of the century. There may have been an actual incident behind the Mendelssohn anecdote, but the story is a generic one, having been told as often about Bach, Beethoven, Mozart, and Haydn as about Mendelssohn.

59 *Traité d'Instrumentation* (1844).

60 The final line of "Brander's Song," pt. 2, sc. 4.

61 It was not Frederick William IV but Prince Metternich who asked Berlioz whether he "composed music for five hundred players." The anecdote is recorded in *The Memoirs of Hector Berlioz*, trans. and ed. David Cairns (London: Gollancz, 1969), 481.

62 The title given to no. 30 of *Lieder ohne Worte*, one of thirty-six piano pieces that Mendelssohn began publishing in 1832.

63 Op. 45 (1834)—one of Chopin's many Preludes.

64 This celebrated religious tune was adapted by Gounod to the first prelude of Bach's *The Well-Tempered Clavier*; its original version, for violin and piano, was *Meditation* (1843).

65 In a letter to Abbé Girod. *Correspondance Inédite*, ed. Daniel Bernard (Paris: Calmann Levy, 1879), 238–9.

66 The opinions of André Ernest Modeste Grétry (1742–1813) on the sonata are to be found chiefly in his *Mémoires, ou essai sur la musique* (Paris, 1784).

67 Anton Diabelli (1781–1858) composed mainly for the piano, including a waltz on which fifty composers were invited to write a variation; Beethoven, uninvited, wrote thirty-three (op. 120).

68 Liszt's handling of the combination and interaction of representative themes can be heard in his *Dante Symphony* (1847–55) and *Faust Symphony* (1854–57); Wagner used leitmotifs in his operas to identify leading characters and important ideas.

69 The Second Ballade of Chopin, op. 38, is nothing less than a fight between a major and a minor theme in which the former, a gentle fragile weakling, is completely crushed and forced to express itself in a minor form. (Note the preference of the romanticist Burns for minor in the *Cotter's Saturday Night*.) [NF]. It is not clear what NF means by the parenthetical remark, except perhaps the contrast in st. 13 of Burns's poem between the "artless notes," by which the cotter and his family "tune their hearts," and the "Italian trills."

70 Many musicians and music lovers will not agree to any difference in character of the keys; but those who, like myself, have absolute pitch are in general more sympathetic to the idea. Plato, of course, propounds a corresponding theory for Greek music. [NF]. See Plato's *Sophist*, 253b.

71 James Carscallen has pointed out to me that many of NF's claims about music in this section are questionable—e.g., his assertions that the sonata developed from the suite, that the Beethoven scherzo is a parody of the min-

uet, that syncopation of a mazurka is an attack on rhythm, that the waltz is the most fundamental of dances, and that the march is necessarily a dance of death (James Carscallen to Robert D. Denham, 29 August 1996).

72 And of course the forms of the chief works of Milton and Bunyan reflect the struggle of a critical spirit in a creative age, and are half-way between the purely musical and the lyric-essay presentations on the one hand, and the dramatic and novelistic on the other. The first, which combines a tonal utterance with a personal world-picture, gives us the *Paradise Lost* type of philosophical epic; the second is evidently the allegory. [NF]

73 The sonnet is so purely pictorial that it has always been a favourite with painters, from Raphael and Michelangelo down to Rossetti. The Petrarchan sonnet is meant in the above; the Shakespearean is more musical, and a romantic does not handle it so well. [NF]

74 This idea appears, among other places in Blake, in his annotations to *The Works of Sir Joshua Reynolds*. See also NF's later commentary in *Fearful Symmetry* (Princeton: Princeton University Press, 1947), 91–106.

75 Experiments performed in 1732 when Rousseau was in Paris, as he records in bk. 4 of his *Confessions* (1765–70, pub. 1782).

76 St. 3 of pt. 1 of Coleridge's *The Rime of the Ancient Mariner* (1798). NF's emphases.

77 After "Browning" NF wrote "(see p.)," intending, apparently, to go back and insert the page numbers where he refers to Browning below.

78 The opening of Shelley's *Lines: "When the Lamp Is Shattered"* (1822).

79 In "The Critic as Artist," Gilbert remarks to Ernest, "Meredith is a prose Browning, and so is Browning. He used poetry as a medium for writing prose" (*The Literary Criticism of Oscar Wilde*, ed. Stanley Weintraub [Lincoln: University of Nebraska Press, 1968], 202).

80 NF's ellipsis.

81 After "scientist" NF wrote "(see p.)," intending to go back and insert the page number for his previous reference to the "hope of finding a rock-bottom formula" in pt. 1, sec. IV, above.

82 See Tennyson's *Idylls of the King* (1859, 1869), Swinburne's *Tristram of Lyonesse* (1882), Masefield's *Tristran and Isolt* (1927), and Robinson's *Lancelot* (1920) and *Tristram* (1927).

83 After "period" NF wrote "(see p.)," intending to go back and insert the page number for his treatment of the theme in pt. 1, sec. V.

84 By "part five" NF means his "Conclusion."

85 After "Stuarts" NF wrote "(see p.)," intending to go back and insert the page number for his statement about the enthusiasm of romanticism for the Middle Ages in pt. 1, sec. IV.

86 Madeleine de Scudéry (1608–1701) was a prolific writer of French heroic romances, the characters of which were notable persons of her own day.

87 *The Mystery of Edwin Drood*, which was being serialized when Dickens died in 1870.

88 NF has in mind a phrase from chap. 1 of George Meredith's *Diana of the Crossways*: "Rose pink and dirty drab will alike have passed away."

89 The primitivistic element in American literature is sustained a good deal by the Scandinavians, whose country forms the world's most typical province. The expression of peasant and proletariat alike in America is to a large extent in Scandinavian hands—Hamsun and Sandburg being respective examples. The importance of Ibsen as a dramatist lies in his having dealt with the repercussion of the world-city upon its environs. The present-day American primitivism is reflected in their choice of Scandinavian types to represent a rugged and strong masculinity and femininity in Lindbergh and Greta Garbo. [NF]

90 After "novel" NF wrote "(see p.)," intending to go back and insert the page number referring to the detective story in pt. 4, sec. II.

91 Giuseppe Mazzini (1805–72), known for his strong liberal, revolutionary, and republican views, was one of the leading figures in the unification of Italy; in his later years he was attracted to socialist doctrines, but he failed in his efforts to organize the working classes.

92 Marx, who thought Mazzini was long on rhetoric and short on practical aid for the Italians, especially the peasantry, did not expect the unification movement in Italy to advance his own aims; he also worried about Mazzini's popular support, and he feared that the independence of Italy would be at the expense of Austria, which Marx saw as a buffer against Russian expansion.

93 Mussolini was especially attracted to Nietzsche's *Also Sprach Zarathustra* and Sorel's *Réflexions sur la violence*; he wrote three articles on Nietzsche in 1908, and reviewed *Réflexions* when it was published in Italy in 1909.

3. Robert Browning: An Abstract Study

1 Edgar's revision: "reference to it. All the poetry of the last century or so is therefore to" for "reference to it, so that all the poetry of the last century to."

2 Edgar underlined "service of being."

3 In the margin beside this sentence Edgar wrote, "loose sentence structure."

4 Blake does not use the phrase "vegetable kingdom," though he often uses "vegetable," especially in *Milton* and *Jerusalem*, to refer to material things.

5 Edgar changed "cheap cynicism of Byron" to "cheaper cynicism that is to be found in Byron."

6 Edgar underlined "ash-," meaning perhaps that NF should not, as he had done, have hyphenated "ashcan."

7 Edgar marked through "only."

8 Edgar changed "stressing the liberal and wide-ranging education" to "stressing the need of liberalism and diversity in education."

9 Edgar underlined "tried" and "view."

10 Browning's line comes from *Pippa Passes* (1849), pt. 1, lines 227–8; Pope's from "Epistle 1" of *An Essay on Man* (1733), line 294.

11 Edgar marked through "petty."

12 "And yet God has not said a word!" (line 60).

13 *Épîtres à l'auteur du livre des trois imposteurs* (10 November 1770).

14 Edgar changed "back of" to "behind."

15 Edgar underlined "in their" and put an "X" in the margin.

16 In NF's typescript there is no paragraph break between this sentence and the previous one, but a paragraph mark (¶) has been inserted between them. Whether the mark is NF's or Edgar's is uncertain.

17 The dramatic monologues referred to in this paragraph are *A Grammarian's Funeral* (1855), *The Bishop Orders His Tomb at St. Praxed's Church* (1845), *Rabbi Ben Ezra* (1864), and *Johannes Agricola in Meditation* (1834).

18 In his *Enneads* Plotinus (ca. A.D. 205–70) maintains that the soul needs the deifying or enlightening virtues in order for it to have immediate knowledge of God, which is not possible through thought.

19 See Coleridge's *The Rime of the Ancient Mariner* (1798).

20 One of the readers of the manuscript of the *Student Essays* suggested that this is "perhaps a reference to the 'one needful thing' of Luke 10:42, which provides the title for bk. 1, chap. 1 of *Hard Times*, where Gradgrind makes his pronouncement about 'facts.'"

21 Above "it" Edgar wrote "itself" and put an "X" in the margin.

22 Compare with Browning's attitude the mysticism of Bunyan: "Then said Evangelist, pointing with his finger over a very wide field, Do you see yonder Wicket-gate? The man said, No. Then said the other, Do you see yonder shining light? He said, I think I do. Then said Evangelist, Keep that light in your eye, and go up directly thereto, so shalt thou see the gate." [NF]. The quotation comes from the opening episode of Bunyan's *The Pilgrim's Progress* (1678–84).

23 *An Epistle Containing the Strange Medical Experience of Karshish, the Arab Physician* (1855).

24 See *Death in the Desert* (1864). The quoted phrase comes from line 205.

25 Mrs. [Felicia Dorothea] Hemans, *The Poetical Works* (New York: Thomas Y. Crowell, [1890]). NF is referring to such words as "funerals," "dirge," "death," "grave," "mourner," and "departed" that appear in the titles of Mrs. Hemans's poems.

26 Edgar marked through "supreme."

27 Carlyle, in fact, drew several sympathetic portraits of his contemporaries; see, for example, his view of Coleridge in *Life of John Sterling* (1851), of

Wordsworth in *Reminiscences* (1867), and of Tennyson in a letter to Emerson (5 August 1844). On his high regard for Browning, see his letter to Browning, dated 21 June 1841, in *New Letters of Thomas Carlyle*, ed. Alexander Carlyle, 2 vols. (London: John Lane, 1904), 1:233–4.

28 Edgar wrote "and whom" above "that."
29 "Your friendship," Browning wrote to Carlyle, "will always seem, as it does now, enough to have lived for"—an attitude Browning maintained for forty years. The letter is quoted by Betty Miller in *Robert Browning: A Portrait* (New York: Scribner's, 1952), 59.
30 Edgar underlined "time" and "grasp" and put an "X" in the margin.
31 The quotation comes, not from *Sartor Resartus*, but from "The Hero as Poet," where Carlyle says, "Observe too how all passionate language does of itself become musical,—with a finer music than the mere accent; the speech of a man even in zealous anger becomes a chant, a song. All deep things are song. It seems somehow the very central essence of us, Song; as if all the rest were but wrappings and hulls!" (*On Heroes and Hero-Worship and the Heroic in History* [London: Oxford University Press, Geoffrey Cumberlege, 1935], 109).
32 In the margin beside this sentence Edgar wrote "meaning?"
33 Edgar corrected NF's spelling of "literate."
34 See, for example, Lamb's "A Chapter on Ears," *The Works of Charles and Mary Lamb*, ed. E.V. Lucas, 5 vols. (London: Methuen, 1903), 2:38–41.
35 Twain's views on music are found in *A Tramp Abroad* (1880), among other places; see especially chaps. 9, 10, and 16 for his tongue-in-cheek pronouncements; but see also "At the Shrine of St. Wagner" (1891), a more sober account that shows some appreciation of Wagner.
36 Here NF neglected to type "find," which Edgar inserted.
37 It will be remembered that the career of Schubert abruptly stopped when he came in contact with the work of Handel. [NF]. There seems to be no evidence for such a claim. Two weeks before he died Schubert, who had just been given a copy of Handel's works, reported to the Frölich family, "Ye gods! now I see what I still lack, what a lot I still have to learn" (*Schubert: Memoirs of His Friends*, ed. Otto Eric Deutsch [London: A. and C. Black, 1958], 255). Moreover, Schubert composed several of his major works during the final years of his short life.
38 Cf. Frye's remark in a letter to Helen Kemp during the summer of 1932: "Thank God for Bach and Mozart, anyway. They are a sort of common denominator in music,—the two you can't argue about. Beethoven, Chopin, Wagner—they give you an interpretation of music which you can accept or not as you like. But Bach and Mozart give you music, not an attitude toward it. If a man tells me that Beethoven or Brahms leaves him cold, I can still talk with him. But if he calls Bach dull and Mozart trivial I can't, not so much

because I think he is a fool as because his idea of music is so remote from mine that we have nothing in common" (*Correspondence*, 1:43).

39 Hallam Tennyson records this remark by his father in *Alfred Lord Tennyson: A Memoir by His Son*, 2 vols. (New York: Macmillan, 1897), 2:285.

40 In the margin beside this sentence Edgar put an "X."

41 For an unpublished essay on Byrd by NF, written in 1942, see Notebook 17. NFF, 1991, box 24.

42 Burns was notorious for flaunting his various sexual affairs.

43 *Master Hugues of Saxe-Gotha* (1855) is a dialogue between a church organist and the dead composer, Master Hugues, about the meaning of the fugues for which Hugues was well known. Browning himself said that Hugues was a dry-as-dust imitator of Bach.

44 See *Parleying with Charles Avison* (1887); Browning learned a great deal about music from Avison, an eighteenth-century organist and the composer of *Grand March*.

45 In the margin beside this sentence Edgar has put an "X."

46 *Our Theatres in the Nineties* (London: Constable, 1931), 1:28. [I am indebted to Marc Plamondon for this note. Ed.]

47 "The Critic as Artist," *The Literary Criticism of Oscar Wilde*, ed. Stanley Weintraub (Lincoln: University of Nebraska Press, 1968), 201–2.

48 The rhyme scheme of *Love Among the Ruins* (1855) is *aabbccddeeff*.

49 The rhyme schemes of the various poems in *Pacchiarotto, and How He Worked in Distemper: With Other Poems* (1876) are quite varied, but the most common patterns are rhymed couplets of varying lengths and quatrains of the form *abab*, *bcbc*, etc. Except for a variation in the first stanza of *The Glove* (1845), the poem is written in rhymed couplets.

50 A poem by Thomas Hood (1843), written in dactyllic dimeter, with nine different rhyming patterns, the most common being *abab* and *aabccb*.

51 When Eliot published *The Waste Land* in book form in 1922, he added an extensive series of notes that identified a large number of his sources and pointed to the relations between some of the poem's images and allusions.

52 Edgar underlined "would have," apparently questioning NF's use of the verb phrase.

53 "Meredith is prose Browning, and so is Browning. He used poetry as a medium for writing in prose" ("The Critic as Artist," 202).

54 Edgar underlined "back of" and wrote "behind" above it. In the next sentence he changed "due to" to "owing to."

55 Burns's *Jolly Beggars* is about a group of vagabonds who meet, drink, and indulge in unbridled revelry; Browning's *The Heretic's Tragedy* (1855) is about the burning at the stake of Jacques du Bourg-Molay by Philip IV of France; Molay (called "John" in the poem) seems to have been innocent of the charges of heresy, simony, and sodomy.

56 Edgar revised "can be traced back here" to "can be traced to this discordancy in his material."

57 Speakers in the three dramatic monologues whose titles come from their names: *Bishop Blougram's Apology* (1855), *Mr. Sludge, "The Medium"* (1864), and *Prince Hohenstiel-Schwangau, Saviour of Society* (1871).

58 *Pauline* (1833), Browning's first published work, was modelled on Shelley's confessional poems; it is an account of the conflict and ultimate defeat of a young boy who has renounced his mother's religion. John Stuart Mill annotated a review copy of the poem, and after Browning read Mill's comments about the morbid self-consciousness of the poem, he wrote no more confessional verse.

59 G.K. Chesterton, *Robert Browning* (London: Macmillan, 1926), 45.

60 In this connection it is interesting to examine the poem called *Wanting is— What?* which forms the prelude to *Jocoseria*, in which *Jochanan Hakkadosh* is found. Incidentally, bearing in mind what was said above concerning the pictorial nature of romanticism, it is not difficult to see why Browning was so inspired by Italy. [NF]. See line 6 of *Wanting is—What?* (1883): "—Framework which waits for a picture to frame."

61 Edgar enclosed the second syllable of "gotten" in parentheses.

62 *Samson Agonistes* (1671), lines 1640–5. The fortissimo notation is, of course, NF's.

63 The speech of Count Guido Franceschini in bk. 11 of *The Ring and the Book*.

64 The quotation about Schubert's modesty has not been located, but according to one Schubert scholar, "Schubert was not particularly known for his modesty or lack thereof. One could say that he quickly gained fame as a song composer and developed a natural self-confidence in this area." Moreover, "as a student of Salieri and others Schubert had fairly good training in composition" (Tilman Seebass to Robert D. Denham, 20 November 1996). What NF means by the opposition between "instrumental rhythm and song" is not clear.

65 Founded by Frederick James Furnivall and M.E. Mickey in 1881, the society tended to see Browning as a poet who, as Furnivall said in the society's inaugural meeting, "speaks the Spirit of his Time, and he speaks to his Time."

66 Two of Browning's most notoriously difficult poems, published, respectively, in 1840 and 1876.

67 G.K. Chesterton, *Robert Browning* (New York: Macmillan, 1914), 53.

68 Edgar cancelled "the" and made a mark in the margin beside the next sentence, where NF notes it is necessary to use the definite article with "novel" and "essay."

69 As Chesterton points out in his work on Chaucer, that poet has illustrated the plight of the critical subjectivist very wittily and delicately. Chaucer created others, but he has no story of his own, stammering only doggerel

and turgid prose. [NF]. G.K. Chesterton, *Chaucer* (Garden City, N.Y.: Doubleday, 1955), 178–9; NF would most likely have used the 1932 edition of the
book (London: Faber and Faber; New York: Farrar and Rinehart).

70 The opening paragraphs of Browning's "Essay on Shelley," written in 1851,
draw on the familiar nineteenth-century distinction, which Coleridge and
others had taken from the German romantics, between objective and subjective poets. The subjective poet is, among other things, "impelled to embody
the thing he perceives, not so much with reference to the many below as to
the One above him, the supreme Intelligence which apprehends all things
in their absolute truth." Browning's "Essay on Shelley" is included as
Appendix I of the Penguin edition of *The Poems*, 1:999–1013.

71 According to Elizabeth Barrett Browning, Browning said that he was more
indebted to Landor than to any other of his contemporaries. *Letters of
Elizabeth Barrett Browning*, ed. Frederic G. Kenyon, 2 vols. (New York:
Macmillan, 1897), 2:354.

72 The reference is to Tennyson's *Flower in the Crannied Wall* (1869).

73 NF is no doubt referring to the interrogative mode of *Song of Myself*, many
sections of which are answers to questions posed by Whitman. Cf. st. 46,
lines 1223–4, where Whitman writes, "You are also asking me questions and
I hear you, / I answer that I cannot answer, you must find out for yourself."

74 The exuberant and loquacious lawyer who serves as the defender of Guido
Franceschini in bk. 8 of *The Ring and the Book*.

4. The Concept of Sacrifice

1 My thanks to Kingsley Joblin for the information about the permission NF
had to submit late papers. Kingsley Joblin to Robert D. Denham, 17 November 1995.

2 W. Robertson Smith, *The Religion of the Semites: The Fundamental Institutions*
(New York: Meridian Books, 1956), 396, 439. NF probably used the 1927 ed.,
entitled *Lectures on the Religion of the Semites: The Fundamental Institutions*, 3rd
ed. (New York: Macmillan), though he could have read the 1st or the 2nd ed.
(1889, 1894).

3 NF is being ironic: Micawber, in Dickens's *David Copperfield*, is always given
to grandiloquence and would thus never say anything so ordinary as "eat
it."

4 In Leviticus 16:7–10 Aaron casts lots for two goats: one becomes a sacrificial
offering to the Lord; the other is driven away into the wilderness as a scapegoat for the evil spirit Azazel.

5 See Tylor's *Primitive Culture: Researches into the Development of Mythology,
Philosophy, Religion, Language, Art and Custom*, 2 vols. (New York: Holt, 1883),
2:375–6.

6 *The Religion of the Semites*, 137–9, 289–311.

7 Cup-marked rocks are found at many sites in Palestine, two of the most outstanding examples being at Gezer and Jerusalem. See R.A.S. Macalister, *A Century of Excavation in Palestine*, 2nd ed. (London: Religious Tract Society, 1930), 287–9.

8 The "great hypothesis" NF mentions is outlined in Alfred Loisy's *The Religion of Israel*, trans. Arthur Galton (London: T. Fisher Unwin, 1910), 44. Loisy, a French Biblical critic and ordained priest, was excommunicated in 1908 because his Biblical studies, based on the theories of higher criticism, were seen as heretical.

9 According to the documentary theory of the Pentateuch advanced by Julius Wellhausen and others in the nineteenth century, J represents the writings of the Jahwist source, the earliest strand of Old Testament narratives.

10 NF is referring to the creation story in Genesis 1, which is a part of the P or Priestly documents in the Pentateuch and was written centuries later than the J source.

11 "Crush the infamy," the famous challenge Voltaire hurled at the church; the phrase is found throughout his works, especially his letters; "infamy" refers, not so much to the church itself, but to the persecuting and privileged orthodoxy.

12 Which conjectures NF refers to are uncertain. For an account of early hypotheses on the relation between the alphabet and the lunar zodiac, see Hugh A. Moran and David H. Kelley, *The Alphabet and the Ancient Calendar Signs* (Palo Alto, Calif.: Daily Press, 1969).

13 Sir James Frazer, *The Scapegoat* (vol. 9 of *GB*), 412–23.

14 The household gods in Roman religion; the lar, a youth in a tunic carrying a cup and a drinking horn, seems originally to have been a god of the fields; the penates, dancing youths with drinking horns, were gods of the storeroom and kitchen. The images were placed in a niche together, the lar between the two penates.

5. The Fertility Cults

1 This is the position taken by Diotima, as reported by Socrates, in the *Symposium*, 201e–212c.

2 This and the preceding paragraph draw on Sir James Frazer, *The Dying God* (vol. 4 of *GB*), 14–46.

3 The source of the material in this paragraph is Sir James Frazer's *Adonis, Attis, Osiris*—the two volumes of *GB* devoted to dying and reviving gods; see especially pp. 1–12, 263–76.

4 John Milton, *Lycidas* (1637), line 106.

5 According to the documentary theory of the Pentateuch advanced by Julius

Wellhausen and others in the nineteenth century, P represents the writings
of the Priestly source, which was combined with the other earlier written
sources about 400 B.C.

6 In this story the children of Benjamin captured the virgins of Shiloh, who
were dancing at an annual festival, and took them as their wives. See Judges
21:16–24.

7 Against the Lord's injunction not to look back at the destroyed city of
Sodom, Lot's wife did so and was changed into a pillar of salt (Genesis
19:12–26). Similarly, when Orpheus descended to Hades to rescue Eurydice,
he looked back, against the injunction not to, and Eurydice disappeared.

8 The name Samson, for example, may be derived from the word for "sun."

9 The five Amorite kings who warred against Gibeon hid in a cave and were
brought forth and hanged by Joshua. See Joshua 10:3–26.

10 Iphigenia, the daughter of Agamemnon and Clytemnestra, was sacrificed by
her father so that he could sail to Troy to help recapture Helen, his brother's
wife, from Paris.

11 That is, any passionate censor. Cato the Elder (234–139 B.C.), the Roman
statesman, was strongly opposed to the contemporary fashion for all things
Greek; he was made censor in 184 B.C., and because of the vigour with which
he executed his office, he became known as "the Censor."

12 See Edvard Westermarck, *The History of Human Marriage*, 5th ed., 3 vols.
(New York: Allerton, 1922); and Edward Carpenter's two books, *Intermediate
Types among Primitive Folk: A Study in Social Evolution*, 2nd ed. (London:
George Allen and Unwin, 1919) and *Love's Coming of Age: A Series of Papers on
the Relations of the Sexes* (London: Swan Sonnenschein, 1909).

13 Solomon's revision of the administrative structure of the united kingdom
(1 Kings 4:7–19) led to a weakening of the old tribal ties and greater assimilation of the Canaanite population. The division of the united kingdom into
Judah and Israel occurred in 931 B.C.

14 The Book of Esther recounts the saga of the deliverance of the Jewish people
from their Persian enemies; the deliverance accounts for the annual Purim
feast on the fourteenth day of Adar.

15 Sir James Frazer, *The Scapegoat* (vol. 9 of *GB*), 417.

16 G.K. Chesterton, *The Everlasting Man* (Garden City, N.Y.: Doubleday, 1955),
178–9; NF would have used the 1925 ed. (New York: Dodd, Mead).

17 In Leviticus 16:7–10 Aaron cast lots for two goats: one became a sacrificial
offering to the Lord; the other was driven away into the wilderness as a
scapegoat for Azazel, an evil spirit or demon.

18 *Archetypal Patterns in Poetry: Psychological Studies of Imagination* (London:
Oxford University Press, 1934), 21.

19 NF is paraphrasing I.A. Richards, who said, "Besides the experiences which
result from the building up of connected attitudes, there are those produced

by the breaking down of some attitude which is a clog and bar to other activities. . . . The great masters of irony—Rabelais and the Flaubert of *Bouvard et Péuchet*—are the chief exponents of this kind of exorcism" (*Principles of Literary Criticism* [London: Kegan, Paul, French, 1925], 209–10).

20 No such title by James exists. Of James's several books on myth and ritual NF probably meant to list either *Primitive Ritual and Belief: An Anthropological Essay* (London: Methuen, 1917) or *Origins of Sacrifice: A Study in Comparative Religion* (London: John Murray, 1933).

6. The Jewish Background of the New Testament

1 "Whatever men do."

2 Auguste Comte believed that each science passed through theological, metaphysical, and positive stages. See his *Positive Philosophy*, trans. Harriet Martineau (New York: Calvin Blanchard, 1855), 26–7. Vol. 12 of *GB* is the bibliography and index. NF is referring, not to this vol., but to vol. 11, the second of two vols. entitled *Balder the Beautiful*; here Frazer, although not mentioning Comte by name, refers to the three stages of history as magic, religion, and science (305–6). See also the preface to vol. 10 (vol. 1 of *Balder the Beautiful*), where Frazer says that his own general concern is "the gradual evolution of human thought from savagery to civilization" (vi).

3 The line, slightly misquoted, comes from one of Voltaire's most successful verse satires, *Les Systèmes* (1772). Voltaire represents Spinoza as saying to God—the "grand Être": "Pardonnez-moi, dit-il en lui parlant tout bas, / Mais je pense, entre nous, que vous n'existez pas. / Je crois l'avoir prouvé par mes mathématiques" ["Pardon me, he said to him very softly, / But I think, between us, that you do not exist. / I believe that I have proved that by my mathematics"] (*Oeuvres complètes de Voltaire*, ed. Louis Moland, 52 vols. [Paris: Garnier Frères, 1877–85]: 10:170, lines 59–61).

4 G.K. Chesterton, *Chaucer* (London: Faber and Faber, 1932), 38.

5 In this paragraph NF repeats the familiar argument of Spengler's *DW*.

6 For a fuller treatment of the argument of this paragraph see NF's "The Augustinian Interpretation of History" in this volume (no. 10).

7 Philo of Alexandria (ca. 15 B.C.–A.D.50) was the most prominent representative of the form of Hellenistic Judaism that flourished in Alexandria for three hundred years, beginning about 200 B.C.; much of his work was devoted to allegorical interpretations of the Pentateuch.

8 Interesting overtone insofar as the word suggests Jacob, or the nation of Israel. The two names are not etymologically related.

9 That is, for almost three hundred years—from Saul's assuming the throne of Israel's united kingdom in ca. 1020 to the middle of the eighth century, when Jeroboam ruled in Israel after the kingdom was divided.

10 The inscription on the cliff of the Zagros mountains on the Baghdad-Hanadan road: "Thus saith Darius the King. That what I have done I have done altogether by the grace of Ahuramazda. Ahuramazda and the other gods that be, brought aid to me. For this reason did Ahuramazda and the other gods that be bring aid to me because I was not hostile nor a liar nor a wrongdoer, neither I nor my family, but according to Rectitude I have ruled." NF no doubt learned of the inscription from a footnote in Spengler's *DW*, 2:207.

11 King of Israel who killed the kings of Israel and Judah, executed Jezebel, and carried out other bloody deeds under a prophetic revolutionary mandate. See 2 Kings 9–10. Hosea 1:4–5 takes a different perspective on the revolt.

12 Malachi, which means "my messenger," seems to be a title rather than a name.

13 All are stories from the Apocrypha.

14 Both Judith and Jael defeat the enemies of Israel by literally taking matters into their own hands: the former, a devout widow, cuts off the head of Holofernes, one of Nebuchadnezzar's generals (Judith 13:7–8); the latter, the wife of Heber the Kenite, drives a tent-peg through the skull of Sisera, a Canaanite captain (Judges 4:17–22, 5:24–27).

15 Both Susanna and Tamar narrowly escape: the former, a devout and beautiful woman, is falsely accused of adultery but is saved by the clever cross-examination of Daniel; the latter, Er's widow, is condemned for playing the prostitute to trick Judah, but she escapes punishment because of her righteousness in upholding the principle of the levirate marriage (Genesis 38).

16 Regarding Joseph's resisting the temptation to lie with Potiphar's wife and his dream interpretations, see Genesis 39–41; Daniel resolves not to defile himself in Nebuchadnezzar's court (1:8); his interpretations of the king's dreams are recorded in chaps. 2 and 4.

17 Both festivals celebrate deliverance: the Passover commemorates the time when Yahweh, smiting the first-born of the Egyptians, passed over the habitations of the Hebrews (Exodus 12); Purim commemorates the deliverance of the Israelites when Haman's conspiracy against them is foiled by Esther and Mordecai (Esther 2–9).

18 Samson's name is similar to several Semitic words for sun.

19 NF means to refer, not to Genesis 4, but to Genesis 6:1–4, which speaks of the "sons of God," or the divine beings of the heavenly court, who descended into the human sphere to take the "daughters of men" as their wives. The fall of the angels is also recorded in the first of the three books of Enoch (the Ethiopic Book of Enoch).

20 Most conspicuously the flood episode in Genesis 6–8 derives in part from *Gilgamesh*.

21 "There is a tide in the affairs of men, / Which taken at the flood, leads on to fortune" (Shakespeare, *Julius Caesar*, 4.3.217).

22 The first period of the Cenozoic era, marked by the dominance of mammals on land.

23 The four "servant songs" in Second Isaiah (42:1–4, 49:1–6, 50:4–9, 52:13–53:12).

24 See 1 Enoch 37–71.

25 C.G. Montefiore, *The Old Testament and After* (London: Macmillan, 1923), 201–91. NF's characterization is not altogether accurate; although the thrust of Montefiore's argument is to illustrate the antecedents of the gospel in Judaism, he does say that the doctrine of losing one's life in order to save it was a new doctrine (256).

26 A Jewish religious group that emerged in Palestine at least as early as the second century B.C., the Essenes were ascetics who engaged in esoteric teachings and various ritual observances; as NF suggests, they resembled medieval monastic orders.

27 St. Dominic (1170–1221), a rigorous ascetic known for his piety and learning, founded the Dominicans, which began as a preaching order; St. Francis (ca. 1181–1226) founded the Franciscans and was primarily interested in ministering to the poor and the needy.

28 A Gnostic sect which originated near the Jordan River in the first or second century B.C.; the sect is perhaps connected with John the Baptist, who in any case is prominent in Mandean writings.

29 See especially Ecclesiastes 1.

30 Jonah 1:17–2:10; Daniel 6; the story of Shadrach, Meshach, and Abednego being cast into the fiery furnace by Nebuchadnezzar is in Daniel 3:8–30; Nebuchadnezzar's insanity, described in bestial terms, is recorded in Daniel 4:33.

31 Asmodeus, whose name means "destroyer," is described as an "evil demon" in Tobit 3:8; Abaddon and Apollyon are the Hebrew and Greek names for the "angel of the bottomless pit" in Revelation 9:11.

32 One of the Hellenic "mystery religions" in which personal rebirth was a chief theme. In the central story of Orpheus and Eurydice, the latter had to return to the underworld because the former failed to follow his instructions. See NF's essay "St. Paul and Orphism" in this volume (no. 9).

33 Mattathias (d. 166 B.C.), a priest of Modlin, who defied the efforts of Antiochus IV to Hellenize the Jews; Judas Maccabaeus, his son, who defeated the Syrian generals and in 165 B.C. recovered the temple for Jewish worship; and Jonathan, his brother, who consolidated the power of the Maccabees and the Jews. See 1 Maccabees 2–12.

34 As indicated in the headnote, this is almost certainly NF's paper "The Augustinian Interpretation of History," essay no. 10 in this volume.

35 This point is made by Spengler in *DW*, 2:222.
36 See n. 20 to essay no. 5, "The Fertility Cults."

7. The Age and Type of Christianity in the Epistle of James

1 The Ebionites were a Judaeo-Christian sect of the early Christian era that rigorously observed the Jewish law and believed Jesus was the Messiah, though not truly divine.
2 In this verse James alludes to the injunction against swearing in Matthew 5:34.
3 The Wisdom of Solomon was composed in Greek by an unknown Hellenistic Jew, probably in Alexandria during the late first century B.C.; Ecclesiasticus, or the Wisdom of Jesus the Son of Sirach, was written by a Jewish scribe, probably in Jerusalem, about 180 B.C. Philo Judaeus was a first-century Jewish Hellenistic philosopher who sought to synthesize Greek philosophy and Jewish scripture and who greatly influenced Clement and Origen. James Moffatt, throughout his commentary, points to James's familiarity with these sources.
4 Moffatt says that Origen was the first writer actually to quote from James and that it was "more than probable" that Hermas knew the Epistle. *The General Epistles: James, Peter, and Judas* (New York: Harper, 1928), 1. Origen was a third-century Biblical scholar and the leading theologian of Alexandria, where he became head of the catechetical school. *The Shepherd of Hermas* was a popular second-century work purportedly written by a freed Roman slave; it is divided into visions, mandates, and parables.
5 Joseph B. Mayor, *The Epistle of St. James: The Greek Text with Introduction, Notes, and Comments*, rev. 3rd ed. (London: Macmillan, 1913). NF's note is confused. The quotations from p. cxxi of Mayor are not from ante-Nicene writers quoting James but simply evidence that James was acquainted with Philo. Mayor does say that Origen "is apparently the first who cites the Epistle as Scripture and as written by St. James" (lxxxi), but he gives an extensive list of references to James by several dozen writers before the time of Origen (lxx–lxxxi).
6 Mayor claims that James was "written probably in the fifth decade of the Christian era by one who had been brought up with Jesus from his childhood and whose teaching is in many points identical with the actual words of our Lord as recorded in the Synoptic Gospels" (*The Epistle of St. James*, vii).
7 Two epistles were attributed to Clement of Rome (late first century); the first, written ca. A.D. 96, is generally accepted as his.
8 "Didache" is the short title for "The Teaching of the Lord through the Twelve Apostles," a brief manual of Christian moral teaching and church order written in the early second century.

9 For the publication information on Mayor and Moffat, see nn. 5 and 4 above. The other commentaries are: James Hardy Ropes, *The Apostolic Age in the Light of Modern Criticism* (New York: Charles Scribner's Sons, 1912); R.J. Knowling, *The Epistle of St. James, with an Introduction and Notes* (London: Methuen, 1904); and F.J.A. Hort, *The Epistle of St. James: The Greek Text* (London: Macmillan, 1909).

8. Doctrine of Salvation of John, Paul, and James

1 See Alan Hugh McNeile's *Introduction to the Study of the New Testament*, 2nd. ed., rev. by C.S.C. Williams (Oxford: Clarendon Press, 1953). NF was using the first edition of this book, entitled *Introduction to the New Testament* (1927).
2 *vide* Kautsky, *Beginnings of Christianity*. (A well-sustained Marxist attempt to prove that Christianity was basically a labour movement, making much of allegedly "socialistic" utterances in James tending to identify the poor with good and rich with evil.) [NF]. Unless NF is referring to the original German text, *Der Ursprung des Christentums* (1923), he means to cite the English trans., *Foundations of Christianity* (New York: International Publishers, 1925). NF does give the correct title in one of the notes to essay no. 13, "Relative Importance of the Causes of the Reformation."
3 Dow underlined "inherently a ritualist" and put a question mark beside it in the margin.
4 Dow placed parentheses around "the Pharisaic . . . ritual" and put a question mark beside it in the margin.
5 *vide* Kennedy, *St. Paul and the Mystery-Religions*. [NF]. Perhaps NF means "cf." rather than "vide," for H.A.A. Kennedy's *St. Paul and the Mystery-Religions* (London: Hodder and Stoughton, 1913) argues exactly the opposite of what NF claims.
6 Dow put parentheses around "Holy Spirit" and wrote "Word" above it.
7 Dow underlined "midway between" and put a question mark beside the phrase in the margin.
8 Dow put square brackets around "and the atonement of Jesus' death" and placed a question mark beside the phrase in the margin.
9 Dow underlined "John it is . . . salvation" and put a question mark beside the passage in the margin.

9. St. Paul and Orphism

1 The quotation from Gilbert's book (New York: Macmillan, 1928) comes from pp. 99–100.
2 See H.A.A. Kennedy, *St. Paul and the Mystery-Religions* (London: Hodder and Stoughton, 1913); Kennedy's actual position is that the influence of the Greek mystery religions on Paul was insignificant.

3 Alfred F. Loisy (1857–1940) was a French Catholic theologian whose books
  and articles on Biblical criticism were condemned by the Church and some of
  them placed on the Index; he was eventually excommunicated; from 1909 to
  1932 he was professor of Church history at the Collège de France; among his
  many books are *La naissance du christianisme* (1933; Eng. trans., 1948) and *Les
  origines du Nouveau Testament* (1936; Eng. trans., 1950). Salomon Reinach
  (1858–1932) was a French archaeologist whose *Orpheus: A History of Religions*
  (rev. ed., 1930) NF was familiar with. Richard Reitzenstein (1861–1931) was
  a German classical philologist and historian of religion; one of his better-
  known works, *Die hellenistischen Mysterienreligionen: nach ihre Grundgedanken
  und Wirkungen* (1910), was available only in the original German when NF
  was writing; H.A.A. Kennedy, to whom NF refers, is greatly indebted to
  Reitzenstein, even while disagreeing with many of his conclusions.
4 See especially chaps. 1–4 of *The Birth of Tragedy* (1870–71; 1st Eng. trans. 1909).
5 That is, designed to avert evil and ward off the anger of the gods.
6 Throughout "On Superstition," Plutarch's moralizing comments are set in
  opposition to the views of atheists and various superstitious people. See his
  Moralia (London: Dent, 1912), 371–88.
7 Plutarch's attitude toward war appears at many places in his *Lives*. See, to
  take one example, his account of Antony's foray into Ephesus, where Antony
  is described as "the Devourer and the Savage." *Plutarch's Lives*, the so-called
  "Dryden translation," corrected and rev. by A.H. Clough, 5 vols. (New York:
  A.L. Burt, n.d.), 5:74.
8 This paragraph derives from Sir James Frazer's *The Dying God* (vol. 4 of *GB*).
9 See Sir James Frazer's *Adonis, Attis, Osiris* (vol. 5 of *GB*), 1–12, 263–76.
10 See, for example, Isaiah 57:3–13.
11 The Hellenizing program of Antiochus Epiphanes IV, following his accession to the Syrian throne in 175 B.C., is recorded in 1 Maccabees 1:11–15 and 2
  Maccabees 5:11–26.
12 Sabazius was a Thraco-Phrygian god; the Vincentius frescoes at Rome associate him with certain Jewish eschatological ideas.
13 See par. 2 of Plutarch's life of Alexander, *Plutarch's Lives*, the so-called
  "Dryden translation," rev. by A.H. Clough, 5 vols. (New York: Hearst's
  International Library, 1914), 4:179–80.
14 NF's source here is Jane Ellen Harrison, *Ancient Art and Ritual* (New York:
  Holt, 1913), chaps. 3 and 4.
15 In the dramatic period the satyric drama was retained as the last play of the
  tetralogy. [NF]. On the etymology of *tragedy* and the relation of the Dionysian rite to satyric drama see NF's source, Jane Ellen Harrison, *Prolegomena to
  the Study of Greek Religion*, 3rd ed. (Cambridge: Cambridge University Press,
  1922), 420–1.
16 "Le Roi est mort! Vive le Roi!"—the words of the captain of Louis XIV's

bodyguard, exclaimed from the window of the state apartment after the king's death.

17 *Cyclops*, trans. William Arrowsmith, in *Euripides*, ed. David Grene and Richmond Lattimore, 4 vols. (Chicago: University of Chicago Press, 1959), 3:260, lines 643–8.

18 The vase depicting Orpheus and Apollo is reproduced in Harrison, *Prolegomena to the Study of Greek Religion*, 467, and in W.K.C. Guthrie, *Orpheus and Greek Religion* (London: Methuen, 1935), 38. The vase itself does not depict Apollo uttering the oracle: that comes rather from an account by Philostratus in his biography of Apollonius of Tyana (Harrison, ibid.).

19 This punning on σῶμα and σῆμα symbolizes, according to Macchioro, op. cit., the doctrine of the unity of opposites, made into a philosophical principle by Heraclitus, whom Macchioro claims as an Orphic. The opposites in this case are death and life. Life is the death of the soul; the death of the body, in the palingenesis or in actual death, the freeing of the soul into life. [NF]. The quotation is from the *Cratylus*, 400c (trans. H.N. Fowler), which was probably called to NF's attention by Guthrie, *Orpheus and Greek Religion*, 156–7, or perhaps by Harrison, *Prolegomena to the Study of Greek Religion*, 615. NF's reference to Macchioro is somewhat misleading. Although Macchioro does examine certain southern Italian *timboli* (burial mounds), which he sees as containing evidence of the Orphic views about the body as a prison, he says nothing about the punning on *soma* ("body)" and *sema* ("tomb" or "sign") that is implicit in the passage from the *Cratylus*. See Vittorio D. Macchioro, *From Orpheus to Paul: A History of Orphism* (New York: Holt, 1930), 109–21. Despite the "op. cit." NF has not previously cited Macchioro, whose work he lists in his bibliography at the end of the paper. For Macchioro's view on Heraclitus and Orphism, see pp. 169–76—a view, according to Guthrie, that is without merit (*Orpheus and Greek Religion*, 224–31).

20 See "The World of the Unborn," chap. 19 of *Erewhon* (1872; rev. by Butler in 1901).

21 *Odyssey*, bk. 11, line 598. "The cruel boulder bounding again to the level" (trans. Robert Fitzgerald).

22 NF doubtless read about this in vol. 1 of Sir James Frazer's translation of *Pausanias's Description of Greece*, 2nd ed., 6 vols. (London: Macmillan, 1913), bk. 10, chaps. 28–31. For Frazer's commentary on the passage, see vol. 5, 372–5. See also Harrison, *Prolegomena to the Study of Greek Religion*, 601–2.

23 See n. 10 in "The Jewish Background of the New Testament" (no. 6, above).

24 *Vide* Toynbee, A.J.: *A Study of History*, vol. 1. [NF]. See *A Study of History*, 3 vols., 2nd ed. (London: Oxford University Press, 1935), 1:63–7; only three volumes of Toynbee's eventual twelve-volume work had been published when NF was writing.

25 The point of NF's rhetorical question is apparently that just as Cyrus the

Great was largely responsible for the restoration of Israel after the Babylonian captivity, granting the Jews the return of Palestine and the rebuilding of Jerusalem and its temple, so Alaric II, the Visigoth king of Spain and southern Gaul (A.D. 485–507), was responsible for reversing the policy of his father, Euric, who had persecuted the Christians.

26 The ancient Greek city of southern Italy, which became a byword for the voluptuousness of its people. Kroton, with the aid of the Troezenians, recaptured Sybaris from the Achaeans in 510 B.C. On the Orphic tablets discovered at Sybaris, one of the ancient centres of Orphism, see Harrison, *Prolegomena to the Study of Greek Religion*, 583–8.

27 *Vide* Colin Still: *Shakespeare's Mystery Play*. [NF]. Still's book, which NF repeatedly referred to over the years in his discussions of *The Tempest*, was published in London by C. Palmer in 1921. The *danse macabre*, or dance of death, did not really develop in painting until after the Middle Ages, the Black Plague and the Hundred Years' War having helped to condition the response to such a theme.

28 After Socrates decides to admit Strepsiades into his school, there follows a long "initiation" scene that parodies a religious rite (lines 614 ff., B. Bickley Rogers translation). The point about the parody is made by Harrison, *Prolegomena to the Study of Greek Religion*, 511.

29 Jonson's play (1614) satirizes among other Puritan attitudes their attacks on the theatre.

30 An Orphic poem often quoted by Neoplatonic writers; its date and authorship are uncertain.

31 "Everything comes out to be of One and is resolved into One." The translation is by Guthrie, who quotes the Greek passage on pp. 74–5. The epigram is recorded by Diogenes Laertius in the "Prologue" to his *Lives of Eminent Philosophers*, 2 vols., rev. ed., trans. R.D. Hicks (London: Heinemann, 1950), 1:5. Hicks's translation: "All things proceed from unity and are resolved again into unity."

32 *Orpheus and Greek Religion*, p. 106. [NF]. Guthrie says, "The conception which seems to me to have the best right to be called an Orphic idea is that of a creator."

33 The vase is in the Kunsthistorisches Museum in Vienna. NF's source is doubtless Jane Ellen Harrison's *Prolegomena to the Study of Greek Religion*, which reproduces the amphora on p. 612.

34 For Heraclitus see Macchioro, op. cit., pp. 169 ff., and for Empedocles see Guthrie, op. cit., pp. 169 ff. [NF]

35 See H.A.A. Kennedy, "St. Paul's Relation to the Terminology of the Mystery-Religions," chap. 4 of *St. Paul and the Mystery-Religions* (London: Hodder and Stoughton, [1913]), and C.A. Anderson Scott, *Christianity according to St. Paul* (Cambridge: Cambridge University Press, 1927), 122–33.

36 Guthrie notes that Aristophanes is among those who "show by a turn of phrase or by a thought an acquaintance with Orphic literature" (74).

37 See Justin Martyr, *Dialogue with Trypho*, trans. Thomas B. Falls, in *Saint Justin Martyr*, vol. 16 of *The Fathers of the Church* (Washington, D.C.: Catholic University of America), 278. For Clement of Alexandria's views on false religions, see his *Exhortation to the Heathen*, in *The Ante-Nicene Fathers*, vol. 2 of *Fathers of the Second Century*, ed. Alexander Roberts and James Donaldson (Grand Rapids, Mich.: Eerdmans, 1956), 171–206.

10. The Augustinian Interpretation of History

1 See *City of God*, ed. David Knowles (New York: Penguin, 1972), bk. 18, sec. 2.

2 Although NF is being the devil's advocate here, Augustine does not actually ignore Greece and Egypt. He considers Rome and Assyria as earthly cities because they "present a kind of pattern of contrast, both historically and geographically." The other earthly cities are "appendages" of the Roman and Assyrian empires. See *City of God*, bk. 18, sec. 2.

3 Those who minimize the importance of Augustine's political and social views include three writers listed in NF's bibliography: Gierke, Carlyle, and Dunning. All three are cited by John Neville Figgis, *The Political Aspects of S. Augustine's "City of God"* (London: Longmans, Green, 1921), 2–3, which NF says in his bibliographic note was "the main commentary used." NF remarks that he consulted the three volumes "for the development of Augustine's thought during the medieval period." But NF could have learned very little about this development from any of the three. Gierke says almost nothing about Augustine, Carlyle is interested only in Augustine's views on law and justice, and Dunning, whom NF cites toward the end of his essay, calling him a superficial anticleric, devotes a mere three pages to pointing out how Augustine's conceptions of law and politics are formulated in the context of the spiritual life. NF may have consulted these three sources, or he may have simply relied on Figgis's brief account of them.

4 NF names none of the commentators on either side of the debate about Augustine as a philosophical historian; on this point he is doubtless following Figgis, 33–4.

5 Hegel's wording, at least in the English translation, is a bit different: "What experience and history teach is this,—that people and governments never have learned anything from history, or acted on principles deduced from it" ("Introduction," *Lectures on the Philosophy of History*, trans. J. Sibree [London: Henry G. Bohn, 1857], 6). NF, who had read a large portion of Shaw in his teenage years, may have first encountered the Hegelian maxim in the preface to *Heartbreak House*, where Shaw says, "Alas! Hegel was right when he said that we learn from history that men never learn anything from history" (*The*

Collected Works of Bernard Shaw, 30 vols. [New York: Wm. H. Wise, 1930],
15:38). A similar remark appears in Shaw's *The Revolutionist's Handbook*: "If
history repeats itself, and the unexpected always happens, how incapable
must Man be of learning from experience!" (*Collected Works*, 10:228).

6 In the margin beside this sentence Cousland wrote "obscure."

7 That is, from 336 B.C., when Alexander became king of Macedonia, until the
death of Hadrian in A.D. 138.

8 The Assyrian city of Nineveh fell to the Medes and Persians in 612 B.C.;
Sardis, the ancient city of Lydia, was captured in 499 B.C. by the Ionians in
the Persian Wars.

9 See Herodotus (484–420 B.C.), *History of the Persian Wars*, and Thucydides
(ca. 455–399 B.C.), *History of the Peloponnesian War*.

10 The point is made by Spengler in *DW*, 1:9–10, 18.

11 NF is apparently referring to the position taken by Glaucon in his first argument about justice in bk. 2 of the *Republic*, where he maintains that the nature
of a thing can be determined by its origin (357a–362c).

12 Civic degneration as revealed in the various corruptions of the ideal state:
timocracy, oligarchy, democracy, and tyranny.

13 Gilbert Murray, *The Greek View of Life*; C.N. Cochrane, *Thucydides and the
Science of History*. [NF]. No such title by Gilbert Murray exists. The book NF
apparently meant to cite was G. Lowes Dickinson, *The Greek View of Life*
(London: Methuen, 1896), a book which by 1932 had been issued in six subsequent editions. Dickinson, in any case, says that the Greeks, "supplied
with a general explanation of the world, . . . could put aside the question of
its origin and end, and devote themselves freely and fully to the art of living,
unhampered by scruples and doubts as to the nature of life" (Collier Books
edition, 1961, 51). NF's second citation is to Charles Norris Cochrane, *Thucydides and the Science of History* (London: Oxford University Press, 1929); the
point about history beginning with the Persian Wars is on p. 24.

14 Cf. Figgis, 42.

15 Cf. Figgis, 34: "No one who takes the Incarnation seriously can avoid some
kind of philosophy of history."

16 That is, on the borderland between primary causes (a universe based on a
divine plan or purpose) and secondary causes (material and instrumental
forces that can be studied scientifically).

17 Windelband, *History of Philosophy*. [NF]. Wilhelm Windelband maintains
that the world-movement of Christianity was based from the beginning on
the "experiences of personalities" or "the development of the relation of
person to person, and especially the relation of the finite spirit to the deity"
(*A History of Philosophy*, trans. James H. Tufts [New York: Macmillan,
1921], 256).

18 For some nine years before his conversion to Christianity Augustine was a

follower of Mani (ca. A.D. 217–76), who believed in the fundamental duality of mind and matter.

19 In the margin beside this paragraph Cousland wrote "a good paragraph."

20 Cf. Figgis, 36–7.

21 The most important of the voluminous writings of Giuseppe Mazzini (1805–72), Italian patriot, republican, and ardent liberal, are found in the partially autobiographical *The Life and Writings of Joseph Mazzini* (1864–70); the Whig thesis of Thomas Babington Macaulay (1800–59) is set down in his expansive *History of England* (vols. 1–2, 1848; vols. 3–4, 1855); the main principles of the humanistic religion of Auguste Comte (1798–1857) are developed in his *System of Positive Polity* (1852–54) and *Positivist Catechism* (1852).

22 "Kingdoms without justice are like criminal gangs." Figgis also calls the title of IV, iv, a "famous tag" (60).

23 This is the theme of the *Communist Manifesto*. [NF]. NF is referring to the first sentence of pt. 1 of Marx's *Communist Manifesto* (1848).

24 Cf. Figgis, 51–2.

25 *vide* Dunning, *Political Theories*, vol. 1. [NF]. William Archibald Dunning, *A History of Political Theories, Ancient and Medieval*, vol. 1 of the three-volume *A History of Political Theories* (London: Macmillan, 1902). On Dunning's reference to Augustine's view of slavery, see pp. 157–8.

26 This seems to be Augustine's general position on the question of political theory. Identifying, as he tacitly does, the (Stoic) Senecan theory of the organization of human society on force as a result of a fall from a Golden Age with the Christian doctrine of the Fall of Adam, he attaches comparatively little importance to justice, in practice, as the factor in holding the state together. At the same time, the only thing good in the *civitas terrena* is this same justice which, like the Church, is the only safeguard for the inhabitants of the city of God on earth (XIX, xxi, xxiv). [NF]

27 See A.J. Carlyle and R.W. Carlyle, *A History of Mediaeval Political Theory in the West*, vol. 1: *The Second Century to the Ninth*, 2nd ed. (London: W. Blackwood, 1927), 164–70. Carlyle, who argues that Augustine did not have any great influence on medieval political thought, is concerned mainly to illustrate that Augustine differs from St. Ambrose and other Church Fathers in seeing the essential quality of the state as authority rather than justice.

28 That is, an answer on the side of either the Church or the state. The Guelphs were a propapal, anti-imperial party in Italian cities in the thirteenth and fourteenth centuries; the Ghibellines were pro-imperialists, supporting the involvement of the Holy Roman Emperor in Italian politics.

29 Vico's *Scienza Nuova* (1725; trans. into English as *The New Science of Giambattista Vico*, 1949). This is the first reference in NF's writing to Vico, whose *New Science* was to become an important text for him in later years.

30 The dictum that every Jesuit would obey the pope and the general of the Jesuit order as unquestioningly "as a corpse."

31 Cousland underlined "Roman" and wrote "North African" in the margin.

32 I understand that the influence of Augustine on Descartes and Leibnitz has been traced by M. Gilson, but I have not been able to find anything containing this in any book bearing his name. [NF]. The book NF was unsuccessful in locating was Étienne Gilson's *Études sur la rôle de la pensée médiévale dans la formation du système cartésien* (Paris: Vrin, 1930).

33 Joachim of Floris's doctrine of the three ages—of the Father, the Son, and the Holy Spirit—is developed in his *Expositio in Apocalypsin* (1527). See Delno C. West and Sandra Zindars-Swartz, *Joachim of Fiore* (Bloomington: Indiana University Press, 1983), 10–29. NF was probably introduced to Joachim during his second year at Victoria College, when he read Spengler's *DW*.

34 On Machiavelli, More, and Vico, see Figgis, 48–50, 101.

35 This view of Hegel's philosophy of history was later promoted by Karl Popper in *The Open Society and Its Enemies*, 2 vols. (London: Routledge and Kegan Paul, 1945), 2:57–75. While there is support for the view of Hegel as a defender of the reactionary policies of Frederich Wilhelm III, other readers of Hegel, especially the left-wing Hegelians, have appealed to his work for its revolutionary and radical implications.

36 Hegel calls Fries the leader of "a superficial brigade of so-called philosophers" (*Elements of the Philosophy of Right*, ed. Allen W. Wood, trans. H.B. Nisbet [Cambridge: Cambridge University Press, 1991], 15).

37 Spengler's *Hour of Decision*, which NF read in the 1934 English translation, argues for the old German militarist position and attacks all forms of socialism, communism, and fascism.

38 The idea of opposing factors resolving in a synthesis, the great addition of Joachim to Augustine, appears not only in Hegel, but, with different context, in the Kantian and Comtian laws of three stages in thought. [NF]. Auguste Comte had proposed three stages in the development of each of the sciences—the theological, the metaphysical, and the positive. For Kant, the three stages were the dogmatic, the sceptical, and the critical. The tripartite scheme appeared also in Kant's critiques of knowledge, morality, and feeling, which he examined in turn in his *Critique of Pure Reason* (1781), *Critique of Practical Reason* (1788), and *Critique of Judgment* (1790).

39 Spengler conceived the thesis of his book before 1914 and worked it out by 1917; it was published a year later as *Untergang des Abendlandes: Gestalt und Wirklichkeit* and appeared in its English translation in 1926. NF read the revised 1928 edition. In this sentence NF's typescript reads "though written earlier, he culminates." Cousland noted the error by putting "he" in parentheses.

40 See Nietzsche, *Thus Spake Zarathustra* (1882–85), and Shaw, *Man and Superman* (1901, 1903; first performed in London in 1905).
41 Spengler outlines his basic thesis about the organic nature of culture in the
   introduction to vol. 1 of *DW*; see especially pp. 21–46.
42 That is, the deficiency of Spengler in treating St. Augustine as a Manichean.
   See *DW*, 2:227, 234.
43 For Spengler's outline of these correspondences see *DW*, 1:27, 112; they are
   summarized in more detail in the three tables at the end of vol. 1 of *DW*
   (following p. 428).
44 For Augustine's views on Varro and Seneca, see *The City of God*, bk. 6, chaps.
   2–6, 10–11, perhaps the source of NF's statement here.
45 "Mankind? It is an abstraction. There are, always have been, and always will
   be, men and only men" (Goethe to Luden, as quoted by Spengler, *DW*, 1:21).
46 NF seems to have constructed his bibliography at least partially from memory, which in some cases failed him. The books he lists, in addition to those
   of Hegel, Marx, and Spengler, are these: John Neville Figgis, *The Political
   Aspects of S. Augustine's "City of God"* (London: Longmans, Green, 1921);
   R.W. Carlyle and A.J. Carlyle, *A History of Mediaeval Political Theory in the
   West*, 6 vols. (London: R. Blackwood, 1903–36); Otto Friedrich von Gierke,
   Political Theories of the Middle Age (Cambridge: Cambridge University Press,
   1900); F.J.C. Hearnshaw, ed., *The Social and Political Ideas of Some Great
   Medieval Thinkers* (London: G.G. Harrap, 1923); William Archibald Dunning,
   A History of Political Theories, Ancient and Medieval, vol. 1 of the three-volume
   A History of Political Theories (London: Macmillan, 1902).

11. The Life and Thought of Ramon Lull

1 A work completed about 1272, this book was not translated into English
  when NF was writing (and has not yet been translated). *The Art of Contemplation*, trans. by E. Allison Peers (London: SPCK, 1925), is a different work
  altogether, being a section of Lull's prose romance *Blanquerna*.
2 This work had not been translated into English at the time NF was writing; it
  has since become the first volume of the *Selected Works of Ramon Lull*, 2 vols.
  (Princeton: Princeton University Press, 1985).
3 Wallace underlined "to" and wrote "than" in the margin.
4 Acre, the Palestinian seaport, was surrendered to the Saracens in 1291, thus
  marking the end of the crusades.
5 William Caxton's translation of a French version of Lull's *Book of the Ordre of
  Chyualrey* (ca. 1504) was reissued in 1926 by the Early English Text Society,
  and that edition was reprinted in 1991 by Sam Houston State University
  Press in Huntsville, Tex.; Sir Gilbert Hay's 1456 translation of the same book
  —*The Buke of the Ordre of Knychthede*—was also from a French text.

6 Long before Lull's time the Western and Eastern Churches disagreed over
the Latin Church's addition of the *filioque* clause to the Nicene Creed
("proceedeth from the Father *and the Son*").

7 Trans. E. Allison Peers (London: Jarrolds, 1926).

8 The most forceful of all papal claims, issued by Boniface VIII in 1302, that the
pope has authority over temporal powers.

9 E. Allison Peers translated a portion of this work, which was published as
The Tree of Love (London: SPCK, 1926).

10 In this paragraph NF is following Wilhelm Windelband, *A History of
Philosophy*, trans. James H. Tuft, 2nd ed. (New York: Macmillan, 1921), 323–5.
Windelband devotes a brief paragraph to Lull (321–2).

11 *BL*, 26. In Peers's 1945 edition, this passage was revised to read, "Propriety
and Community met, and joined together, that there might be love and
benevolence between Lover and Beloved."

12 Sebonde was a fifteenth-century Spanish theologian who, it is generally held,
owed a great debt to Lull; in the 1570s Montaigne translated and published
"La théologie naturelle de Raymond Sebon" and later wrote an "Apologie de
Raymond de Sebonde," which appeared in book 2 of his *Essais*. In the early
1580s Bruno lectured on Lull at the University of Paris and wrote a treatise
on his work.

13 "It is impossible for one metal to be changed into the form of another,"
says Lull. And again, "It is demonstrated that alchemy is not a science, but a
fabrication." NF quotes the Latin from Peers, 406n. 5.

14 Daniel 6:7–23; in *Pilgrim's Progress*, Christian, confronted by two lions, is
afraid to pass by until the porter of the house assures him that they are
chained.

15 Athanasius "the Great," the fourth-century bishop of Alexandria and vigorous opponent of Arianism, was exiled on five separate occasions by his
antagonists, among them Constantine and Julian.

12. Robert Cowton to Thomas Rondel

1 For Cowton, see Little, 222–3; for Rondel, 162. Of the eighteen manuscripts
in British collections containing Cowton's commentaries on Lombard's
Sentences, three are at Merton College. Nine Franciscans, five of whom were
laymen, arrived at Dover in 1224 and very soon established themselves in
and around Oxford.

2 The recipient of Cowton's letter was the Franciscan lector Thomas Rondel.
The role of a lector, according to Andrew G. Little, was "not unlike that of a
college tutor, except that he was always a man of proved ability and long
experience. To the friars he was far more than a theological lecturer; he was a
trusted friend, on whose advice and sympathy and help they might reckon

in all the conduct of life" (*The Grey Friars in Oxford*, 32). For brief biographical sketches of Cowton and Rondel, see the introduction to the present volume, pp. xxiv–xxv.

3 A port of Rome at the mouth of the Tiber.

4 Perugia is the province in central Italy in which Assisi, the birthplace of St. Francis and of the Franciscan order, is located; it is also the name of the capital of that province.

5 The much-visited pilgrimage church in Santiago de Compostela in north-western Spain.

6 The Franciscans were known as the Friars Minor.

7 Edward I (1239–1307), King of England, had assumed the throne in 1272. The French king was Philip IV ("The Fair"), who had succeeded his father in 1285.

8 Edward of Carnarvon, son of Edward I and Eleanor of Castile; he was made Prince of Wales in 1301 and became King of England in 1307. Edward II, as Cowton predicts, had an unfortunate reign, characterized by dissension among his barons and the loss of the English hold on Scotland. He was eventually deposed, and he abdicated in 1327. The henchmen of Queen Isabella and her lover, Roger de Mortimer, had him put to death shortly thereafter.

9 The feasts of the original four doctors of the Western Church—Ambrose, Augustine, Gregory the Great, and Jerome—had been imposed by Boniface VIII in 1298.

10 This is a variant of Chaucer: "And in a glass he haddé piggés bones." [NF]. The line comes from the portrait of the Pardoner in the "General Prologue" to *The Canterbury Tales*, line 702.

11 Edward I had accomplished the conquest of Wales in 1282 after a five-year campaign; in 1296 he began his long offensive against Scotland; following a number of campaigns against William Wallace, which eventually led to Wallace's defeat and execution, Edward died in 1307 as he was moving toward the border to engage Robert I (the Bruce), Wallace's successor as leader of the Scots. Duns Scotus, the celebrated scholastic philosopher, studied and taught at Oxford in the thirteenth century.

12 The Franciscans were known as the Grey Friars in England.

13 As Langland did in *Piers the Plowman*. [NF]. Langland's poem (ca. 1362) is in part a cry of social protest on behalf of the common person against abuses by the king and the courts; the poet particularly condemns the pride and the abuses of the clergy.

14 St. Paul's, which dates from Roman times. Construction on Old St. Paul's, the building that occupied the site in the thirteenth century, had begun in the late eleventh century; it was severely damaged by fire in 1561.

15 The medieval London Bridge, about sixty yards down the Thames from the present structure, was a stone bridge that had been completed in 1209; a row

of houses had sprung up on each side of the bridge, giving it the appearance of a continuous street.

16 Chaucer's pilgrims were also to set forth on their pilgrimage from the Tabard Inn to Canterbury Cathedral, the shrine of Thomas à Becket.

17 This is a reference to *The Second Shepherd's Play*, one of the mystery plays in the Wakefield cycle that was staged on movable pageant wagons. The manuscript for this play is dated mid-fifteenth century at the earliest; the earliest extant nativity play—from the York cycle—was not performed until 1376. The reference to *The Second Shepherd's Play* is, therefore, an anachronism—one of the few in Cowton's letter. (My thanks to Gail Gibson for the information about dating the nativity plays. Ed.)

18 Guienne was an old province in southwestern France, part of the older Aquitaine; it was disputed by England and France in the Middle Ages; between 1294 and 1296 Philip IV of France successfully overran the province, of which Edward I of England was duke; the territory finally passed to France in 1453. Calais, a fortified port on the Strait of Dover, played a prominent part in the early wars between England and France.

19 Edward I gave impetus to the development of law and built up the central administration of government; in response to the hostility of the merchants and other subjects, he issued in 1297 the confirmation of the charters granted by John and Henry III, including the Magna Carta. In 1302 Philip IV called together the nobility, clergy, and commons in a States General to explain his course of action against the papacy; twice more during his reign he summoned the States General.

20 The Franciscans were very strong in England and especially prominent around Oxford. Although the Dominicans (Black Friars) were widely dispersed across Europe by the late thirteenth century, St. Dominic's early missions had been in southern France, where he had preached especially against the reputed heresies of the Albigensians.

21 For Duns, see n. 11, above. William of Occam, an English scholastic philosopher and a Franciscan friar, studied at Oxford in the early fourteenth century.

22 Albertus Magnus (ca. 1193–1280) was a scholastic philosopher who joined the Dominicans in 1223. Bacon (ca. 1214–94) was a Franciscan scholar, scientist, and philosopher who studied at Oxford; his works were condemned for some unknown reason, perhaps because of his severe attacks on his contemporaries, and he was imprisoned for fifteen years; his scientific experiments led to his being seen as a magician in the popular imagination.

23 English Franciscan philosopher (d. 1245) and the first scholastic versed in the whole of Aristotle's work. Bacon had remarked that Alexander of Hales "was ignorant of natural philosophy and metaphysics."

24 A student of Albertus Magnus, Thomas Aquinas (1225–74) became the

greatest figure of medieval scholasticism; he joined the Dominican order in 1243 or 1244.

25 Construction of St. Peter's Cathedral in Beauvais, modelled on the cathedral at Amiens, began in 1227; the choir, begun in 1272, collapsed in 1284 but was rebuilt by doubling the number of pillars.

26 "Head of the world."

27 The *Sentences* of Peter Lombard (ca. 1100–ca. 1160) was one of the most important theological works of the Middle Ages; e.g., it enunciated the doctrine adopted by the Church at the Council of Trent that a sacrament was both a symbol and a means of grace; the book is arranged as a collection of opinions of theologians, often presenting unanimity on certain points of doctrine. On Cowton's later commentaries on the *Sentences* see the introduction, pp. xxiv–xxv, and n. 1, above.

28 Bonaventura (1221–74) was an Italian scholastic theologian who, as general of the Franciscans, was the principal curb on Roger Bacon's Aristotelianism, which he always mistrusted.

29 It was stamped out in the approved medieval way, when twenty-five of their numbers were burned as obstinate heretics in 1318. [NF]. The Zealots or Zelanti, also known as Spirituals, were a Franciscan faction that emerged in the 1240s intent on strict adherence to the convictions of St. Francis. Pope John XXII was determined to quash the group, and in 1318 twenty-five Zealots were handed over to the state for torture. Four of these were burned (not twenty-five, as NF says), but hundreds more were burned during the next several years. NF's source for his information about the Zealots was Vida D. Scudder's *The Franciscan Adventure: A Study of the First Hundred Years of the Order of St. Francis of Assisi* (London: J.M. Dent, 1931), chap. 10.

30 Philip IV conquered Flanders after Edward I of England withdrew in 1297; five years later the Flemish rebelled and defeated Philip at the Battle of Courtrai.

31 Philip IV was known as Philip the Fair.

32 The term was used as early as 1134. [NF]

33 Jews remained in France in spite of their being persecuted by Philip IV, who oppressed Templars and Italian bankers, as well as other wealthy groups.

34 It was actually Edward I who had ordered the Jews to leave England, resulting in a widespread exodus in 1290.

35 The historical Thomas Rondel was on the board or commission to investigate the Templars during the Philippian persecution, so I assume an antecedent interest. [NF]. The Knights Templar, members of the military religious order of the Poor Knights of Christ, were officially called the Knights of the Temple of Solomon after their house in Jerusalem. The order began during the period of the crusades and became one of the most powerful organizations in Europe: its goal was to protect Christianity, and the military exploits of the

Templars won them uncommon fame. Because of the Templars' great wealth they also became, in effect, the bankers of Europe, and it was this power that kindled the ire and greed of princes, such as Philip IV. Rondel did take part in the examination of the Templars in London in 1309, when he was a master of theology and perhaps a lector at the London Convent.

36 The Knights Hospitallers were members of the military religious Order of the Hospital of St. John in Jerusalem; the goal of the order was to aid pilgrims, but when military protection became necessary to fulfil this goal, the focus of the order changed. Like the Templars, the Hospitallers accumulated great wealth.

37 As indeed it did: Philip IV launched a persecution of the Templars from 1308 to 1314, confiscating their money, and Edward II suppressed the order in England.

38 Jacques De Molay had been elected grand master of the Templars in about 1295. Philip IV's final act against the Templars, which effectively ended the order, was to have De Molay burned to death in 1314.

39 The theologian Pelagius was believed to have been born in England about the middle of the fourth century. The heresies he was accused of had to do with his denial of original sin and with the questions of God's grace in justifying humanity and humanity's free will to choose between good and evil.

40 Bartholomew de Glanvilla (Bartholomaeus Anglicus), a Franciscan and author of the celebrated and popular medieval encyclopedia, *De proprietatibus rerum* (ca. 1220).

41 When Pelagius went to Rome in about A.D. 400, he wanted to improve the moral climate, and toward that end he claimed greater moral responsibility for individuals through a higher freedom of the will than the Church was willing to grant.

42 Dubois (ca. early 1250s–after 1313) was a propagandist for the interests of the French king; he began acting as permanent attorney for the king about 1300. The conflict between Pope Boniface and Philip IV, primarily an economic battle, was longstanding. It had begun with Philip's efforts to levy a permanent tax on the clergy and it eventuated in the seizure of Boniface in 1303 and, six years later, in the Avignon papacy.

43 Better known as Jean de Meung, father of French poetry, who continued the *Romaunt of the Rose* for some thirty or forty thousand lines. The derivation hazarded for his surname is pure guesswork. [NF]. Jean de Meung's dates are ca. 1250 to ca. 1305. NF's guesswork about the derivation of "de Meung" is correct. De Meung (or de Meun) continued the composition of the *Roman de la Rose* begun by Guillaume de Lorris, adding some 19,000 lines.

44 Giovanni Villani (1275–1348), author of a history of Florence (12 books), an early masterpiece of Italian prose.

45 The celebrations connected with the jubilee year 1300 drew thousands of pil-

grims to Italian cities; as many as thirty thousand pilgrims crossed the Tiber into Rome daily.

46 Cowton would have seen the most beautiful part of the church, the choir, which was begun in the thirteenth century. St. Peter's was not completed until four centuries later.

47 Dijon became the capital of the duchy of Burgundy in the eleventh century; it was brought to prominence, however, only after 1363 by Philippe le Hardi and the dukes who succeeded him.

48 St. Bénigne and the other church, Notre Dame, were both thirteenth-century churches. Notre Dame was actually built earlier (1229–40) than St. Bénigne (1271–88).

49 Anselm (ca. 1034–1109), the saintly and much beloved doctor of the church, was renowned for his patience in dealing with others.

50 Eckhart (ca. 1260–1327), the father of German mysticism, was widely known as a preacher; he taught at several places, including Paris, Strasbourg, and Cologne; his explanations of mysticism reveal that he was a better theologian than philosopher.

51 St. Francis was born and died in Assisi, and he founded his order there in 1208.

52 NF has let an anachronism slip in, or else this particular Charles of Savoy is a fictional character. The burghers of Geneva did call on the assistance of the dukes of Savoy in the thirteenth century, and the House of Savoy, in fact, aimed to establish a sovereign presence in Geneva. But Charles I, Charles II, and Charles III were fifteenth- and sixteenth-century dukes; and the various Charles Emmanuels came to power in Savoy in the seventeenth and eighteenth centuries. If NF meant to be historically accurate, as he almost everywhere else is, he should have referred to Amadeus V (1285–1323) of Savoy, who fought against the counts of Geneva. Or perhaps NF meant Peter of Savoy, the uncle of Amadeus V, who had entered into relations with the city of Geneva—though this would have been several decades before Cowton made his journey.

53 The Habsburg emperor during the time of Boniface VIII was King Albert I of Germany, who ruled from 1298 to 1308; he was the eldest son of Gertrude von Hohenberg and Rudolf I, founder of the Habsburg dynasty.

54 This is perhaps a little early for Eulenspiegel; there is a tradition that he died in 1350, and men of his type do not as a rule live to sixty-five or so. I use him here to symbolize the growing opposition of burgher and peasant. [NF]. Till Eulenspiegel, the north German peasant clown of the fourteenth century, was made famous by chapbooks describing his various tricks against the upper classes; he was not born until the end of the thirteenth or beginning of the fourteenth century.

55 The Viscontis were a powerful Ghibelline family in medieval Lombardy.

Matteo (1255–1322) became imperial vicar of Milan in 1294, and he extended
the Visconti domain through diplomacy; he was, however, eventually
excommunicated because of his opposition to the Church, whereupon he
abdicated. Piacenza held a high rank in the league of Lombard towns at the
time and was subject to fierce party struggles among the Scotti, Torriani, and
Visconti families. The "Scotto" to whom NF refers was Alberto Scotto, the
unscrupulous lord of Piacenza from 1290 until 1313.

56 The Ghibellines had been expelled from Florence before the time of Dante,
the Blacks and Whites then forming two factions within the Guelph party.

57 The allusion is to Proverbs 16:18.

58 The Cathari were members of an ascetic medieval religious group in southern Europe; their dualistic beliefs sprang from Gnosticism, Christianity, and
Manicheanism.

59 In the debate over concepts and individual things, the medieval realists held
that concepts had an existence independent of individuals: they existed *ante
rem*, or before the thing. The nominalists, on the contrary, held that concepts
existed only *post rem*; they were generalizations of individual things, and so
had no real existence at all.

60 The Albigensians were a Cathari sect in southern France; like other Cathari
in the Mediterranean world, they were ascetics and believed in the duality of
good and evil.

61 Duccio di Buoninsegna (ca. 1260–ca. 1319), whose painting represents the
culmination of the Byzantine tradition in Italian painting; his most famous
work is *La Maestà*, a double painting which hung over the high altar in the
Siena Cathedral until 1505 and is now housed in the Museo dell'Opera del
Duomo. About three years after NF wrote the present paper he saw *La
Maestà*—on a trip to Siena in March of 1937.

62 Cimabue's frescos, including *Madonna with Angels* and a painting of the saints,
among them St. Francis, are in the lower church of the Basilica of San Francesco. Cimabue was born about 1240, a fact that helps to date Cowton's journey. NF later saw the Cimabue frescos—on a trip to Assisi in March of 1937.

63 Perhaps a reference to a literal rendering of the parts of Cimabue's name:
cima (top) + *búe* (dunce).

64 i.e., in tempera. [NF]

65 The first recorded works of Giotto (ca. 1266–ca. 1337) are in the Basilica of
San Francesco.

66 The kingdom of the legendary Prester John was located variously in Asia
and Africa; one tradition placed him as the monarch of the kingdom of
Ethiopia.

67 Andrew III, with whom the royal Hungarian line descending from St.
Stephen died out (1301).

68 The first friar to reach the Mongol dynasty of central Asia was, so far as

records reveal, John of Monte Corvino, a Franciscan. The Eastern monarch would have been Kublai Khan (1216–94), who founded the Mongol dynasty in 1279 and who sought priests from Europe to instruct the Mongols.

69 Gunpowder, which had been used in the ninth century in China for fireworks, began to be used in firearms in Europe in the fourteenth century.

70 Ramon Lull (ca. 1236–1315) was a Mallorcan philosopher and missionary. See NF's essay on Lull in this volume (no. 11). Lull's educational treatises were *Doctrine for Boys* and *Book of the Order of Chivalry*, both written in 1274–75. His Utopian ideas are set forth in his long romance, *Blanquerna* (ca. 1283). In 1301 he sailed for Cyprus to preach against the heretics.

71 The reference is to Lull's *Ars Magna* (ca. 1275).

72 In its essential or universal nature; literally, "under the aspect of eternity."

73 This grotesque argument is attributed to William of Occam. [NF]. See Occam's *Reportatio*, 3, question 1, in *Opera Theologica*, vol. 6 (St. Bonaventure, N.Y.: Franciscan Institute, 1982), 9.34.

74 Since leaving St. Peter's Cowton has walked about one kilometre east along the Tiber to a position directly south of the Castel Sant'Angelo.

75 Dante was not exiled from Florence until 1302.

13. Relative Importance of the Causes of the Reformation

1 For a discussion of causation in history, see Spengler, *The Decline of the West*, vol. 1, pp. 117 ff. [NF]

2 A very bald statement of this is in Chesterton's *Victorian Spirit in English Literature*, p. 49. [NF]. The title of Chesterton's book is *The Victorian Age in Literature* (New York: Holt, 1913). But that book, while it does reveal Chesterton's Roman Catholic conservatism throughout, says nothing, on p. 49 or elsewhere, about the Reformation. Perhaps NF had in mind Chesterton's account of the Reformation in "Protestantism: A Problem Novel," in *The Thing: Why I Am a Catholic* (New York: Dodd, Mead, 1930), 96–102, or his remarks about the Reformation at other places in this book (e.g., pp. 23–5, 127–32).

3 This is the Marxist dialectic as developed by Kautsky: *Foundations of Christianity*, 11. [NF]. See especially bk. 2, "Society in the Roman Empire," of Kautsky's book (New York: International Publishers, 1925). In the margin beside this and the previous sentence Cousland wrote "not very clearly expressed."

4 NF apparently meant to say, "by no means less likely."

5 Froude is the standard exponent of this view: see chap. 6 of his *History of England*. [NF]. NF's reference is to chap. 6 of vol. 7 of Froude's *History* (New York: Scribner, 1871).

6 Smith, *Age of the Reformation*, p. 20. [NF]. Preserved Smith makes these points on pp. 20–9 of his book (New York: Holt, 1920).

7 Lindsay, *History of the Reformation*, p. 113. [NF]. It is not clear what NF means to cite in Thomas M. Lindsay's *A History of the Reformation*, 2 vols. (New York: Scribner's, 1907). Lindsay devotes chaps. 2 and 4 of vol. 1 to an analysis of the political and social conditions underlying the Reformation (chap. 4 ends on p. 113). But Lindsay says nothing explicitly about "a new religious idea."

8 Here Cousland has inserted the clause "which usually involves a restatement of theology."

9 This argument is applied to the Renaissance by Spengler, op. cit., vol. 1, p. 232, but his "Renaissance" is practically equivalent to the general cultural *Urgrund* spoken of above. [NF]

10 Lindsay, op. cit., p. 45. [NF]. For Lindsay's account of the relation of the Reformation to the Renaissance, see pp. 42–78 of vol. 1 of *A History of the Reformation*; for his account of capitalism, see pp. 84–9.

11 The Hanseatic League, a mercantile league of medieval German towns.

12 Here Cousland asked, "in a limited or wider sense?"

13 On the culture-town, see Spengler, *DW*, 1:32–5.

14 Smith, op. cit., p. 6. [NF]. The page reference here should be 5.

15 Friedell, *A Cultural History of the Modern Age*, pp. 152 and 230. [NF]. NF cites passages from vol. 1 of Egon Friedell's three-volume work, trans. Charles Francis Atkinson (New York: Knopf, 1930).

14. Gains and Losses of the Reformation

1 Cousland underlined "versus."

2 Cousland underlined "overthrow" and wrote "in part" beside it in the margin.

3 Cousland inserted "the" before "Protestant."

4 In the margin beside this sentence Cousland wrote "awkwardly expressed."

5 Johann Tetzel (ca. 1465–1519) was the Dominican monk whose ostentatious preaching an indulgence for the building of St. Peter's in Rome provoked Luther's Wittenberg theses.

6 The basis of the Roman Catholic practice of granting indulgences, merit having been accumulated by the good works of Christ and the saints.

7 St. Januarius was the Italian Christian martyr whose body is preserved in the cathedral at Naples; two phials supposedly containing his blood were said to liquefy on his feast day and at other times.

8 The efforts to reform the church by Cardinals Campeggio, Cajetan, Jiménez, and Wolsey largely failed, and it was not until Pope Paul III was elected in 1534 that substantial reform was possible; he convened the Council of Trent

in 1554, and this council, which also met in 1551–52 and 1562–63, was the primary impetus behind the Counter-Reformation, one of the chief arms of which was the Jesuit order.

9 Cousland underlined the repeated phrase "by no means."

10 That is, the mixed motives behind Henry VIII's desire for divorce, which led to the end of papal jurisdiction in England.

11 The principle stemming from Thomas Erastus (1524–83), who argued against Calvin's assertion that the state had the right to intervene in and control Church affairs, and against the Church's practice of excommunication.

12 The "you too" argument: a retort charging opponents with being or doing what they criticize in others.

13 Hugh O'Neill (ca. 1540–1616) was an Irish rebel who spread insurrection against Elizabeth I.

14 Philip II of Spain (1527–98) devoted much of his energy to the Spanish Inquisition, which he saw as a tool not simply to combat heresy but to extend control over his own dominions. The Valois were the members of the French royal house that ruled from 1328 to 1589.

15 Borgia (1476–1507), illegitimate son of Pope Alexander VI, was captain-general of the armies of the Church; he sought to seize all of central Italy through terror and treachery; Machiavelli saw him as a model prince. "Nephew" is a euphemism for illegitimate son.

16 See, for example, G.K. Chesterton's *Heretics* (1905) and *Orthodoxy* (1909); Hilaire Belloc's *The Servile State* (1912), *History of England* (1915), and *Europe and the Faith* (1920); and R.H. Tawney, *Religion and the Rise of Capitalism* (1926). Tawney, a Christian socialist, was not a Roman Catholic.

17 The analogy is to the period preceding the first ecumenical council of the Church at Nicaea in A.D. 325, which was called by Constantine to settle the doctrinal controversy between the Arians and the Orthodox about the person of Christ.

18 After Ferdinand II (king of Bohemia) issued the decree in 1627 that Bohemia should be purged of all non–Roman Catholics, the Jesuits began a systematic destruction of Bohemia's national literature. One Jesuit, Andrew Konias, boasted of having burned 60,000 Bohemian books himself.

19 The Index of Forbidden Books: the list of works that Catholics may not read, a list that originated in the Counter-Reformation.

20 In a section of his *Institutes* entitled "Faith assures us not of earthly prosperity," Calvin says, "Faith does not certainly promise itself with length of years or honour or riches in this life, since the Lord willed that none of these things be appointed for us. But it is content with this certainty: that, however many things fail us that have to do with the maintenance of this life, God will never fail" (*Institutes of the Christian Religion*, ed. John T. McNeill, 2 vols. [Philadelphia: Westminster Press, 1960], 3.2.27.574). This can hardly be taken

as evidence that for Calvin material prosperity was a sign of grace. In fact, there are numerous passages in the *Institutes* and elsewhere that negate the idea of a connection between election and material prosperity.

21 Following NF's final sentence Cousland wrote "Bibliography?"

15. A Study of the Impact of Cultural Movements upon the Church

1 John Bunyan, *The Pilgrim's Progress* (New York: Grossett and Dunlap, n.d.), 29–30.
2 See Oswald Spengler, *DW*, 1:3–50; 2:87–110.
3 Thomas Carlyle, "Signs of the Times," *A Carlyle Reader: Selections from the Writings of Thomas Carlyle*, ed. G.B. Tennyson (Cambridge: Cambridge University Press, 1984), 46–7.
4 Ibid., 54.
5 This paragraph is a summary of the position advanced by Kant in his *Critique of Pure Reason* (2nd ed., 1878).
6 *Select Poetry and Prose*, London, 1933, 187. [NF]. NF quotes from the Nonesuch Press edition, ed. Stephen Potter.
7 "To shock the narrow-minded."
8 Mario Praz, *The Romantic Agony*, trans. Angus Davidson (London: Oxford University Press, H. Milford, 1933).
9 The refrain appears at the end of six of the twelve stanzas in pt. 4 of Thomson's poem.
10 Herbert Spencer, *A System of Synthetic Philosophy*, vol. 1. *First Principles*, 3rd ed. (London: Williams and Norgate, 1870), 43, 44. The parenthetical phrase is NF's.
11 F.H. Bradley, *Appearance and Reality: A Metaphysical Essay*, 9th impression, corrected (Oxford: Clarendon Press, 1930), 392. NF's page reference is to the 2nd ed., rev. (London: Swan Sonnenschein, 1897).
12 Ibid., 306. NF's page reference is to the 2nd ed.
13 Thomas Hardy, *The Poetical Works of Thomas Hardy*, vol. 2. *The Dynasts: An Epic-Drama* (London: Macmillan, 1925), 6, 7. "S.D." (stage direction) is NF's interpolation.
14 A reference to the final two lines of John Keats's *Ode on a Grecian Urn* (1819).
15 John Ruskin, *The Crown of the Wild Olive: Three Lectures on Work, Traffic, and War* (New York: Merrill and Batzer, n.d.), 64–5.
16 Matthew Arnold, *Culture and Anarchy with Friendship's Garland and Some Literary Essays*, ed. R.H. Super (Ann Arbor: University of Michigan Press, 1965), 174–5.
17 "Ideals and Idealists" in *The Quintessence of Ibsenism. Collected Works of Bernard Shaw*, 30 vols. (New York: Wm. H. Wise, 1931), 19:28–35.
18 Joris-Karl Huysmans, *Là-bas* (1891).

19 Aubrey Beardsley's illustration for Malory's *Le Morte Darthur* appeared in F.J. Simmons's edition of the poem (London: Dent, 1893–94; 3rd ed., 1927).

20 *A Ballad of a Nun*, in *A Ballad of a Nun, and Other Poems*, ed. George Sylvester Viereck (Girard, Kansas: Haldeman-Julius, 1925), 12–17.

21 Madame Tussaud's Exhibition, a collection of wax figures in London.

22 *Literature and Dogma* (1873), chap. 1, sec. 2, par. 3.

23 W.P. Benson, *Walter Pater*, p. 58. [NF]. The quotation appears on p. 111 of the 1906 edition published in the English Man of Letters Series (London: Macmillan). Subsequent reprintings of the book (1907, 1911, 1926) have the same pagination. The author is Arthur C. Benson.

24 See especially chaps. 4–7 of Pater's *Gaston de Latour: An Unfinished Romance* (London: Macmillan, 1910).

25 Walter Pater, "Pico Della Mirandola," *The Renaissance: Studies in Art and Poetry* (London: Macmillan, 1910), 30–49. The phrase "Christian sentiment" appears in this essay: see, for example, pp. 30, 47.

26 For Pater's treatment of da Vinci's *La Gioconda* (*Mona Lisa*) see "Leonardo da Vinci," *The Renaissance: Studies in Art and Poetry*, 123–5.

27 From the *récit* of Bunthorne in act 1 of Gilbert and Sullivan's *Patience; or, Bunthorne's Bride* in *The Complete Plays of Gilbert and Sullivan* (New York: Modern Library, [1936]), 199.

28 *The Works of Oscar Wilde: De Profundis*, rev. ed. (New York: G.P. Putnam's Sons, 1909), 62, 72, 73, 78–9. NF's page references are to the 1905 edition.

29 *All Religions Are One* (1788), Blake's first illuminated work.

30 Thomas Carlyle, "The Everlasting Yea," *Sartor Resartus*, ed. Kerry McSweeney and Peter Sabor (Oxford: Oxford University Press, 1987), 149 (bk. 2, chap. 2).

31 The catchphrase for the utilitarian ethical theory advanced by Jeremy Bentham in *Principles of Morals and Legislation* (1789).

32 John Stuart Mill, *Essays on Ethics, Religion and Society*, ed. J.M. Robson (Toronto: University of Toronto Press, 1969), 95.

33 John Stuart Mill, *Essays on Politics and Society*, ed. J.M. Robson (Toronto: University of Toronto Press, 1977), 255, 256.

34 Sir James Frazer, *GB*, vol. 11 (vol. 2 of *Balder the Beautiful*), 305–6. On Comte's view of the three stages of history, see "The Jewish Background of the New Testament," n. 2, above.

35 *Rabbi Ben Ezra*, lines 145–50.

36 Thomas Hill Green, *Prolegomena to Ethics*, ed. A.C. Bradley (Oxford: Clarendon Press, 1906), 324–5.

37 Bernard Shaw, *Collected Works of Bernard Shaw: Plays*, 30 vols. (New York: Wm. H. Wise, 1930), 14:49.

38 William Morris, *The Collected Works of William Morris*, vol. 16 (New York: Russell and Russell, 1966), 230.

39 Ibid., 237.

40 Sir James Frazer, *GB*, vol. 11 (vol. 2 of *Balder the Beautiful*), 304–5.

41 *Mr. Sludge, "The Medium,"* lines 1112–22.

42 Thomas Hardy, *Tess of the d'Urbervilles*, ed. Scott Elledge, 3rd ed. (New York: Norton, 1991), 314 (chap. 59).

43 Samuel Butler, *The Works of Samuel Butler*, 20 vols. (London: Jonathan Cape, 1925), 2:35.

44 Ibid.

45 *Collected Works of Bernard Shaw*, 16:lxxx.

46 John Henry Newman, *The Idea of a University*, ed. I.T. Ker (Oxford: Clarendon Press, 1976), 121.

47 Ibid., 108.

48 Ibid., 259.

49 Ibid., 259–60.

50 Ibid., 262.

51 Ibid.

52 Ibid.

53 *Our Mutual Friend* (Oxford: Oxford University Press, 1952), 129 (chap. 11).

54 The secondary sources NF lists are as follows:

Mertz, John Theodore. *A History of European Thought in the Nineteenth Century*. 4 vols. Edinburgh: W. Blackwood, 1904–14. This book was issued and reprinted in various two- and four-volume editions.

Wingfield-Stratford, Esme Cecil. *Those Earnest Victorians*. New York: Morrow, 1930.

– *The Victorian Tragedy*. London: Routledge, 1930.

– *The Victorian Sunset*. London: Routledge, 1932.

Chesterton, G.K. *The Victorian Age in Literature*. New York: Holt, 1913.

Benson, Arthur C. *Walter Pater*. London: Macmillan, 1906.

Praz, Mario. *The Romantic Agony*. Trans. Angus Davidson. London: Oxford University Press, H. Milford, 1933.

Ward, Wilfrid Philip. *William George Ward and the Oxford Movement*. London: Macmillan, 1889.

De la Mare, Walter, ed. *The Eighteen-Eighties: Essays by Fellows of the Royal Society of Literature*. Cambridge: Cambridge University Press, 1930. The essay by Eliot in this collection is "The Place of Pater."

16. The Relation of Religion to the Arts

1 See, especially, chap. 16 of Leo Tolstoy's *What Is Art?* (1898).

2 On the back of the last page of this essay, which is a double-spaced typescript, NF typed the following single-spaced paragraph:

For the so-called separation of art from morals is as much a fallacy as its contemporary superstition, the conflict of religion and science. Sincerity is an example of a quality as valid as an artistic criterion as it is as a moral criterion. And it would be the most precarious kind of quibble to try to maintain that artistic sincerity is not fundamentally the same thing as moral sincerity. Again, when we say that Racine is economical and that Swinburne is extravagant, we are, although we are using a moral category, implying that Racine is a better artist than Swinburne, and it is difficult to see how art criticism could get along without such concepts. Here again it is impossible to urge that the words are metaphors when applied to art. Granting that it may be only accident that Racine was an exceptionally cool business head and that Swinburne was almost as incapable as an imbecile of looking after his own affairs, though that is a sizable cession, the question itself can have only one solution.

This paragraph is similar to the third paragraph in pt. 2 of "The Relation of Religion to the Art Forms of Music and Drama" (no. 17, below).

17. The Relation of Religion to the Art Forms of Music and Drama

1 The tripartite division of the "good" is found in various configurations throughout Plato, but is explicitly set forth in *Cratylus*, 439c–440e, *Phaedo*, 65c–d and 75d; see also the *Republic*, bk. 5, 476.
2 The argument for the dual aim of poetry is rooted in Horace's *Ars Poetica* (ca. 20 B.C.); in the British tradition it appears in such well-known critical texts as Sidney's *A Defence of Poetry* (1595) and Dryden's *Essay on Dramatic Poesy* (1688).
3 See, e.g., Sidney's account of the poet as *vates* (prophet) in *An Apology for Poetry* (1595).
4 The concept originated with Lessing's *Laokoön* (1766) and continued throughout the nineteenth century; during the last two decades of the century Oscar Wilde became a leading advocate of the idea that art is intrinsically valuable.
5 Diderot, d'Alembert, and other *philosophes* believed that rational behaviour was the only means for moral improvement.
6 *vide* Max Eastman: *Artists in Uniform*. [NF]. Eastman's book (New York: Knopf, 1934) is about the effects of Soviet bigotry and bureaucracy on arts and letters.
7 Montanism was an ascetic, enthusiastic Christian movement of the second century.
8 That is, the hope that some natural, direct passage into Shakespeare's mind can be discovered without considering the aesthetic qualities of his plays, which serve only as a barrier to his essence.
9 *vide* Wyndham Lewis: *Men without Art*. [NF]. Lewis announces in the introduction to *Men without Art* (London: Cassell, 1934) that "in the serious work

of art will be found . . . all the great intellectual departments of the human consciousness" (9). For his attacks on subjective expression, see especially the chapter on "The Terms 'Classical' and 'Romantic,'" 185–211.

10 The philosophy of Parmenides (ca. 515–450 B.C.) has come down to us through the fragments of his *On Nature*; for the views of Empedocles (ca. 493–433 B.C.) on attraction, see his *On Nature*.

11 The reference is to Walter Pater's essay on Leonardo da Vinci in *The Renaissance: Studies in Art and Poetry* (1873).

12 The dichotomy between poetry and science, feeling and reference, and connotation and denotation, which underlies NF's argument in this section, was a familiar opposition in the work of the New Critics, whose principles were beginning to be influential in the 1930s. NF appears to be drawing chiefly on the oppositions found in the work of I.A. Richards, including *The Meaning of Meaning*, with C.K. Ogden (1929), *Principles of Literary Criticism* (1924), *Practical Criticism* (1929), and *Science and Poetry* (1926).

13 *All Religions Are One* (1788).

14 NF is recalling, if a bit imperfectly, a passage from the introduction to Stuart Gilbert's *James Joyce's "Ulysses": A Study* (New York: Vintage Books, 1955), 42. NF had read the 1930 British ed. (London: Faber and Faber) or the first American ed. (New York: Knopf, 1931).

15 "Charges Toronto Chockful of Stupid Fundamentalism," *Toronto Daily Star*, 11 March 1936, 1, 7 (the quotation is from p. 7). The priest is Father E.J. McCorkell, principal of St. Michael's College and later director of the Pontifical Institute of Mediaeval Studies. [I am indebted to Jean O'Grady for locating this article. Ed.]

16 John Donne, *Goe and Catche a Falling Starre*, lines 1–9. NF is probably quoting from the Nonesuch Press edition (1929), edited by John Hayward from the 1633 edition of Donne's poetry (p. 4).

17 John Donne, *Holy Sonnets* (no. 4), lines 1–8 (Nonesuch Press ed., p. 282).

18 Jacobus Arminius (1560–1609) and his followers believed, as against the Calvinists, that Christ died not simply for the elect but for all people. For Friedrich Schleiermacher's views on election see *The Christian Faith*, ed. H.R. Mackintosh and J.S. Stewart (Edinburgh: T. and T. Clark, 1928), 536–60.

19 Joseph Haydn inscribed *In nomine Domine* at the beginning of all his scores and *Laus Deo* at the end.

20 *vide* William Empson: *Seven Types of Ambiguity*. [NF]. Empson's first book (London: Chatto and Windus, 1930) is a classic of the New Criticism; Empson deals systematically with the different forms of poetic ambiguity, a trope of compression that causes the reader to hold in suspension several complementary or contradictory meanings.

21 See Sir James Frazer, *GB*. NF's knowledge of Wilhelm Mannhardt's researches into myth and folklore probably derived from his reading of

Frazer, who frequently cites Mannhardt (1831–80). None of Mannhardt's books had been translated into English in 1935.

22 See Sir James Frazer, *GB*, vol. 7 (vol. 1 of *Spirits of the Corn and of the Wild*), 146, 171–7, and vol. 3, *Taboo and the Perils of the Soul*, 77–100.

23 (Letchworth, UK: Garden City Press, 1913).

24 *Theotokos* = the title of the Virgin Mary as the Mother of the incarnate Son of God.

25 Pisistratus was tyrant in Athens from 561 to 527 B.C.

26 Athenaeus, *Deipnosophistae*, 8.347e. It is assumed that Athenaeus took the line from a life of Aeschylus.

27 See especially the parados and the third episode of the *Bacchae*.

28 The source of NF's paragraphs on Dionysus is primarily Jane Ellen Harrison, *Prolegomena to the Study of Greek Religion*, 3rd ed. (Cambridge: Cambridge University Press, 1922), 363–453.

29 *vide* E.B. Tylor: *Primitive Culture*. [NF]. For Tylor's analysis of the sacrifice as gift, see *Primitive Culture: Researches into the Development of Mythology, Philosophy, Religion, Language, Art and Custom*, 3rd ed., 2 vols. (New York: Holt, 1883), 2:375–410.

30 The words of the captain of Louis XIV's bodyguard, exclaimed from the window of the state apartment after the king's death.

31 *vide* Maud Bodkin: *Archetypal Patterns in Poetry*. [NF]. See p. 17 of Bodkin's book (Oxford: Oxford University Press, 1934).

32 *vide* F.M. Cornford: *Origins of Attic Comedy*. [NF]. Cornford's chapter on "Classification of Types" in *The Origin of Attic Comedy* (Cambridge: Cambridge University Press, 1934) connects the beginnings of comedy with the fertility ritual. What follows in NF's paragraph derives from vol. 4 (*The Dying God*) and vol. 9 (*The Scapegoat*) of Sir James Frazer's *GB*.

33 A five-day festival during which the master and servant changed places. See Sir James Frazer, *GB*, vol. 4, *The Dying God*, 113.

34 Prince Hal, crowned Henry V at the end of *Henry IV, Part Two*, banishes Falstaff in act 5, sc. 5.

35 See Sir James Frazer, *GB*, vol. 9, *The Scapegoat*, 364–73, 397–407.

36 See Sir James Frazer, *GB*, vol. 9, *The Scapegoat*, 412–23.

37 *Comus*, Milton's pastoral drama, first printed anonymously in 1637.

38 *vide* William Lawrence: *Shakespeare's Problem Comedies*. [NF]. Lawrence's interpretation of *All's Well that Ends Well* draws on themes that are present in tales from the Italian, Indian, Turkish, Icelandic, and French traditions (New York: Macmillan, 1931), 32–77.

39 *vide* Colin Still: *Shakespeare's Mystery Play*. [NF]. NF seems to have first read Still's book (London: C. Palmer, 1921) after seeing T.S. Eliot's reference to it in his preface to Wilson Knight's *Wheel of Fire* (1930), and NF often noted the book in his subsequent commentaries on Shakespearean romance. Still

points to the parallels he sees between Shakespeare's plays and the ancient
mystery rites.

40 The source of this quotation, with its faulty French, remains unknown. The
passage NF may have had in mind is from sec. 39 of Baudelaire's *Mon coeur
mis à nu*: "La musique donne l'idée de l'espace. Tous les arts, plus ou moins;
puisqu'ils sont *nombre* et que le nombre est une traduction de l'espace"
["Music conveys the idea of space. All the arts do this, more or less; for
they employ *number* and number is an interpretation of space"] (Charles
Baudelaire, *Oeuvres complètes*, ed. Claude Pichois, rev. ed., 2 vols. [Paris:
Éditions Gallimard, 1961], 1:1296).

41 "The School of Giorgione," *The Renaissance: Studies in Art and Poetry* (New
York: Modern Library, n.d.), 111. Pater makes a similar point in his essay on
"Style" in *Appreciations* (1899): "If music be the ideal of all art whatever, precisely because in music it is impossible to distinguish the form from the substance or matter, the subject from the expression, then, literature, by finding
its specific excellence in the absolute correspondence of the term to its
import, will be but fulfilling the condition of all artistic quality in things
everywhere, of all good art."

42 *Iliad*, bk. 1, line 473; Robert Fitzgerald translates the word as "the One Who
Keeps the Plague Afar."

43 *vide* Nietzsche: *The Birth of Tragedy*. [NF]

44 *vide* Ruskin: *Crown of Wild Olive*. [NF]. NF is referring to John Ruskin's
lecture, "Traffic" in *The Crown of Wild Olive* (New York: Merrill and Batzer,
n.d.), 47–80; NF had read this book in English 1b during his first year at
Victoria College when he was enrolled in the pass course.

45 See Pierre de Nolhac, *Un poète rhépan ami de la Pléiade* (Paris: Librairie
Ancienne Honoré Champion, 1923), 18. [I am indebted to Jean O'Grady for
this note. Ed.]

46 For several years NF had been planning to do a B.D. thesis, either at
Emmanuel College or in England, on music. In April 1934, he wrote to
Helen Kemp, in connection with his thesis plans, that "there are two things
which are absolutely unique about the Christian religion and which guaran-
tee its truth—one is music, the other a philosophy of history, and, though I'll
do them both eventually, I don't care which I start on. They're intimately
connected, of course, and it may be better to get a solid musical background
first. We'll see how things turn out. The Catholic Church has four great
'doctors of the Church'—St. Ambrose, St. Gregory, St. Augustine, and St.
Jerome. The first two were musicians, the second two philosophers of history" (*Correspondence*, 1:199). By formal action of the Emmanuel College
executive council on 10 October 1934 NF's thesis proposal on "The Development of the Christian Tradition in Music" was approved (Minutes of the
Executive Council, United Church of Canada / Victoria University

Archives, 92.041v, box 1, file 1). Had NF written the thesis he would have been awarded the B.D. degree. But the thesis never materialized, NF having turned to literature instead, and he was awarded a "Diploma of the College" on 30 April 1936.

47 *vide* H.N. Frye: "Ballet Russe," *Acta Victoriana*, 60 (December 1935): 4–6; "Jooss Ballet," *Canadian Forum*, 16 (April 1936): 18–19. [NF]. NF cites two of his earliest published pieces. In "Ballet Russe," a review of two ballets by Tchaikovsky and one by Rimsky-Korsakov, NF analyses the function of rhythm, symbolism, and convention in ballet, concluding that the particular performance of the Ballet Russe under review was too allegorical and did not properly represent the emotional range of the form. "The Jooss Ballet" was ostensibly a review of four performances by the Jooss Ballet, but most of NF's remarks have to do with the ballet as a musical art. He speculates that in an age when the oratorio is dead and the opera moribund the ballet may emerge as a "genuinely new art-form."

48 "The Fertility Cults," paper no. 5 in the present collection.

49 See *DW*, 1:128–31, 227–32, 282–3, 320–3.

50 Reid McCallum, professor of philosophy at the University of Toronto.

18. The Diatribes of Wyndham Lewis

1 NF was granted permission by formal action of the executive council of Emmanuel College to take graduate courses in Honour English as elective subjects during his second year. See the Minutes of the Executive Council, Emmanuel College, 24 September 1934 and 9 October 1934. United Church of Canada / Victoria University Archives, 92.041v, box 1, file 1.

2 For a later essay by NF on Lewis see "Neo-Classical Agony," *Hudson Review*, 10 (Winter 1957–58): 592–8; rpt. in *Northrop Frye on Culture and Literature*, ed. Robert D. Denham (Chicago: University of Chicago Press, 1978), 178–87.

3 *The Diabolical Principle* and *The Dithyrambic Spectator* (London: Chatto and Windus, 1931), 32. These books, published together, are subsequently cited as *DPDS*.

4 Lewis's only volume of poetry was *One-Way Street* (London: Faber, 1933).

5 Portions of Joyce's *Work in Progress*, which was to become *Finnegans Wake* (1939), began appearing in the journal *transition* in 1927; fourteen instalments had been published at the time NF was writing.

6 The two numbers of *Blast* were issued in June 1914 and July 1915.

7 "Nietzsche as a Vulgarizer," *The Art of Being Ruled* (London: Chatto and Windus, 1926), 120–7. Subsequently cited as *ABR* within the text.

8 See the chapters on Hemingway and Faulkner in *ABR*, 17–64.

9 *Paleface: The Philosophy of the "Melting Pot"* (London: Chatto and Windus,

1929). On Gauguin, see pp. 211–12; on Lawrence, pp. 169–98. Subsequently cited as *PF*.

10 In *Antic Hay*, (1923) Aldous Huxley satirizes the cynicism of postwar Bohemia; for the London scenes of Lawrence's *Women in Love* (1920) see chaps. 5–7.

11 "To shock the narrow-minded."

12 The title of bk. 1 of *Time and Western Man* (London: Chatto and Windus, 1927); the "revolutionary simpleton" is described in chap. 6 of bk. 1. Subsequent citations, following *TWM*, are to the Beacon Press edition (Boston, 1957).

13 Mario Praz, *The Romantic Agony*, trans. Angus Davidson (London: Oxford University Press, 1933). On the so-called discipleship of Praz, see *Men without Art* (London: Cassell, 1934), 174–5. Subsequently cited as *MWA*.

14 The positions of Lewis summarized in this paragraph amount to an abstract of bk. 1 of *Time and Western Man*.

15 *TWM*, 136. NF used using the 1927 edition (London: Chatto and Windus). The page references given in the text and notes are to the Beacon Press edition (Boston, 1957). The practice of not capitalizing some proper nouns and their adjectival forms was a quirk of Lewis.

16 *TWM*, 121. "(*The Art of Being Ruled*)" is NF's interpolation.

17 "Mr. Wyndham Lewis: 'Personal-Appearance' Artist," *MWA*, 115–28.

18 *The Lion and the Fox: The Role of the Hero in the Plays of Shakespeare* (London: Methuen, 1951), 43, 47. Subsequently cited as *LF*.

19 The two books are Elliot Smith's *The Evolution of the Dragon* (West Orange, N.J.: Albert Saifer, 1918) and Jane Ellen Harrison's *Ancient Art and Ritual* (London: Williams and Norgate, 1913).

20 For the attack on Bergson, see pt. 3, chap. 6 of *TWM*; for the attack on Spengler, pt. 2 of the same book.

21 *Tarr*, 2nd ed., rewritten 1928 (London: Methuen, 1951), 1. Subsequently cited as *TR*.

22 See, for example, *MWA*, 127, and *PF*, 202.

23 For the split-man's litany, see *The Apes of God* (Baltimore: Penguin, 1956), 170–1; for the costume scene, see pt. 11, "Mr. Zagreus and the Split-Man," 343–62. NF was using the 1930 edition, published in London by the Arthur Press. Subsequently cited as *AG*.

24 *DPDS*, 4. In a letter to Helen Kemp, postmarked 4 December 1934, NF wrote: "I don't know whether it was you or your astral body that I told about Wyndham Lewis's "Apes of God," a book I'm busy with at the moment. It's a brilliant satire on literary charlatanism in London, imitates Rabelais particularly, with some Joyce—probably the best English novel since Ulysses, if that is in English. Sometimes it doesn't quite come off, but after reading it for half an hour I have to dash over to the library with a list of words a yard

long to look up in the dictionary, where they are not always to be found" (*Correspondence*, 1:374).

25 Edgell Rickword, "Wyndham Lewis," *Scrutinies*, by Various Writers, vol. 2, collected by Edgell Rickword (London: Wishart, 1931), 140–61. On the similarities between the styles of Lewis and Nashe, see p. 154.

26 *TWM*, 105. Lewis repeats the comparison in *ABR*, 402.

27 American Puritan writer (ca. 1578–1652); his *The Simple Cobler of Aggawam* (1647) is a satirical tirade against religious tolerance and other matters he considered irritants.

28 "John Galsworthy," *Scrutinies*, by Various Writers, collected by Edgell Rickword (London: Wishart, 1928), 60–2; rpt. in *Phoenix: The Posthumous Papers of D.H. Lawrence*, ed. Edward D. McDonald (New York: Viking, 1968), 540, 543–4.

29 In *The Man of Property*, the first volume of John Galsworthy's *The Forsyte Saga*, Bosinney is an architect with whom Soames Forsyte's wife, Irene, falls in love.

30 Aesop's "The Frog and the Ox" is a fable about a frog who bursts after continuing to puff himself up in order to become as large as the ox. The moral: "self-deceit may lead to self-destruction."

31 See, for example, "Romance and the Moralist Mind," chap. 3 of *TWM*, 15–19.

32 *The Destructive Element*, 3rd impression, reissued (London: Jonathan Cape, 1938), 216.

33 *TWM*, 94. The parenthetical phrase is NF's interpolation.

34 *TWM*, 6. The comment within parentheses is NF's interpolation. On Spengler's account of ahistorical cultures see *DW*, 1:8–12, 132–6.

35 "Wyndham Lewis," *Gog, Magog and Other Critical Essays* (London: J.M. Dent, 1933), 93.

36 *The Wild Body: A Soldier of Humour and Other Stories* (London: Chatto and Windus, 1927), 116–17.

37 See Blake's *A Descriptive Catalogue* (1809) and his annotations to *The Works of Sir Joshua Reynolds* (1798).

38 The phrase Lewis uses to refer to himself in *MWA*, 115.

39 Vilfredo Pareto, *The Mind and Society: A Treatise on General Sociology*, ed. Arthur Livingston, 4 vols. (New York: Harcourt, Brace, 1935), 1:92–9.

40 On Shakespeare as a "feminine genius" see *LF*, 149–58.

41 Lewis "seems aware that, by leaving out the moral element, he has simply constructed a satirist who is a sort of automaton. A satirist who attacks everyone (except the really significant), but who has no particular reason (except prejudice?) for attacking one set of people rather than another" (*The Destructive Element*, 208).

42 *MWA*, 126. The experimental quarterly *transition* was founded in Paris in

1927 by Eugène and Maria Jolas and edited for ten years by Eugène Jolas and Elliot Paul.

43 See especially chap. 6 of *MWA*, "The Bad-Lands in the Martyrs of the Marsh," 172–84. On Lewis's claim that Praz was influenced by *DPDS* see p. 175. On Praz, see also *MWA*, 69, 82, 89.

44 See the "Introduction" to *The Romantic Agony*.

45 J.S. Bach's Cantata no. 212, "Mer hahn en neue Oberkeet" (1742).

46 NF has in mind Eliot's remark in "Shakespeare and the Stoicism of Seneca": "Mr. Lewis has gone quite wrong if he thinks (I am not sure what he thinks) that Shakespeare, and Elizabethan England in general, was 'influenced' by the thought of Machiavelli" (*Selected Essays* [New York: Harcourt, Brace, 1950], 109).

47 That is, after Eliot announced his position, quoted in NF's next sentence, in the preface to *For Lancelot Andrewes* (Garden City, N.Y.: Doubleday, Doran, 1929), vii.

48 *Childermass*, pt. 1 (New York: Covici, Friede, 1928), 152–3.

49 *The Letters of Paul Gauguin to Georges Daniel de Monfreid*, trans. Ruth Pielkovo (New York: Dodd, Mead, 1922), 89. The letter is from October 1897. As NF wrote "Cambodians," rather than "*Cambodgiens*," he may have been quoting from another source.

50 *MWA*, 128; Lewis's ellipsis.

51 *Berkeley Square*, a 1933 film directed by Frank Lloyd and adapted from John L. Balderston's play of that title; the play, in turn, derives from Henry James's *A Sense of the Past*.

19. An Enquiry into the Art Forms of Prose Fiction

1 *Correspondence*, 2:693.

2 *Correspondence*, 2:809.

3 In a letter to Helen Kemp, NF said, "I ordered a typewriter, but it didn't come, so I think I'll let it go—Blunden never asks to see my papers" (*Correspondence*, 1:621). The only holograph manuscript that has survived NF's Oxford years is a paper on Chaucer's early poetry, which NF incorporated into "A Reconsideration of Chaucer" (no. 22).

4 Frye did, however, use different typewriters for the prose fiction paper and the one on Eliot.

5 It could not have been written before 1935 because NF refers to Briffault's *Europa* novels, the first of which was published during that year. Sandra Djwa reports that in his 1935 diary Roy Daniells notes that NF gave a lecture entitled "The English Anatomy" to the Graduate English Club on 16 December 1935. The present essay may have been adapted from that talk (Sandra Djwa to Ron Schoeffel, 23 July 1996).

6 Someone, perhaps NF's instructor, wrote "too conglomerate" in the margin beside this sentence, and below it, beside the next sentence, is a question mark. For two later paragraphs there is also a question mark in the margin.

7 T.S. Eliot, *The Sacred Wood* (London: Methuen, 1950), 140. [I am grateful to Marc Plamondon for locating this reference. Ed.]

8 Paul Valéry, "The Place of Baudelaire," *Leonardo, Poe, Mallarmé*, trans. James R. Lawler, vol. 8 in *The Collected Works of Paul Valéry* (Princeton: Princeton University Press, 1972), 201.

9 NF is punning on Buffon's aphorism, *Le style est l'homme même*.

10 "Whatever people do."

20. The Importance of Calvin for Philosophy

1 *Correspondence*, 1:427. In announcing his plans for his final year at Emmanuel College, Frye also wrote to Kemp on 28 June 1935 that he was "going to write a paper on Calvin and do some work on Arminius which should put me in good enough shape for Theology" (Ibid., 458).

2 Kingsley Joblin feels certain that this paper is the talk NF presented to the Emmanuel Theological Society (Kingsley Joblin to Robert D. Denham, 17 November 1995).

3 Thomas Erastus (d. 1583) and his followers advocated the doctrine of state supremacy in ecclesiastical matters.

4 The movement from culture-town to metropolis is an idea that NF took from Oswald Spengler's *DW*; see especially, vol. 2, chap. 4.

5 What Occam said was that the person of Christ can no more become or be the divine Word than it can become or be a donkey. In the Incarnation, he argued, one person is not formed by adding two natures—one human and one divine—to a single set of individuating principles. This would be as impossible as adding a donkey nature and a human nature to a single set of individuating principles. See William of Occam, *Reportatio III*, in *Opera Theologica*, vol. 6, ed. Francis E. Kelly and Girard I. Erzkorn (St. Bonaventure, N.Y.: Franciscan Institute, 1982), pt. 9, sec. 34.

6 See Article V of Aquinas's "Concerning Human Knowledge," in *Philosophical Writings*, ed. Allan Wolter (New York: Nelson, 1962), 122–30.

7 NF apparently has in mind Bacon's account of the "idols of the theatre" in the *Novum Organum* (1620); one such idol is the fallacious mode of thinking that introduces theological matters into science.

8 NF is referring to the neo-Thomism of such Catholic philosophers as Étienne Gilson, who founded the Pontifical Institute of Medieval Studies at the University of Toronto in 1929, and Jacques Maritain, who later taught at Toronto.

9 NF later referred to this idea as interpenetration, an idea he first encountered

in Whitehead's *Science and the Modern World* (New York: New American Library), 93.

21. T.S. Eliot and Other Observations

1 *Correspondence*, 2:699. Blunden was NF's tutor at Merton College.
2 Although Eliot's *Collected Poems, 1909–1935* had been issued in 1935 (New York: Harcourt, Brace), NF is referring to *Prufrock and Other Observations* (London: Egoist Press, 1917) and *Poems, 1909–1925* (London: Faber and Gwyer, 1925).
3 See Eliot's *Selected Essays, 1917–1932* (London: Faber and Faber, 1932), issued in a revised and enlarged edition by Faber and Faber in 1934.
4 The three books were Thomas McGreevy, *Thomas Stearns Eliot* (London: Chatto and Windus, 1931), Hugh Ross Williamson, *The Poetry of T.S. Eliot* (New York: Putnam, 1933), and F.O. Matthiessen, *The Achievement of T.S. Eliot* (London: Oxford University Press, 1935).
5 D.S. Mirsky, *Échanges*, 5 (December 1931).
6 J.R. Daniells, *University of Toronto Quarterly*, 2 (April 1933): 380–96. NF met J. Roy Daniells during the fall of 1934, when the latter had begun teaching at Victoria College. They became lifelong friends. For NF's account of his meeting Daniells see *Correspondence*, 1:353–4.
7 From stanza seven of *Mr. Eliot's Sunday Morning Service*: "Along the garden-wall the bees / With hairy bellies pass between / The staminate and the pistilate / Blest office of the epicene." NF means that as a critic he is performing a fertilizing function, but at the same time he is adopting Eliot's satiric pose and poking fun at his own effort.
8 A toast by John Collins Bossidy at the Midwinter Dinner of the Holy Cross Alumni in 1910: "And this is good old Boston, / The home of the bean and the cod, / Where the Lowells talk to the Cabots / And the Cabots talk only to God."
9 Slightly misquoted from Eliot's essay, "Francis Herbert Bradley" in *Selected Essays*, new ed. (New York: Harcourt, Brace, 1950), 404.
10 Ibid., 397.
11 As indicated in the headnote, this parenthetical instruction and those that follow are directives NF gives himself to read passages from the poems.
12 *Ara Vos Prec* (London: Ovid, 1920).
13 Spengler defines "Faustian" as the "soul whose prime-symbol is pure and limitless space, and whose 'body' is the Western culture that blossomed forth with the birth of the Romanesque style in the 10th century" (*DW*, 1:183).
14 *The Rape of the Lock* (1714).
15 "Preface," *For Lancelot Andrewes* (Garden City, N.Y.: Doubleday, Doran, 1929), vii.

16 This is the position taken by interlocutor "B" in Eliot's "A Dialogue on Dramatic Poetry," *Selected Essays* (1950), 38.

17 *The Use of Poetry and the Use of Criticism: Studies in the Relation of Criticism to Poetry in England* (London: Faber and Faber, 1933), 152.

18 "Of all art, the cinema is for us the most important." From a conversation with Lenin recorded by A.V. Lunacharsky in *Samoye Vazhnoye iz Vsekh Iskusstv* (Moscow, 1963), qtd. in *Not by Politics Alone . . . —The Other Lenin*, ed. Tamara Deutscher (London: George Allen and Unwin, 1973), 205.

19 In "Shakespeare and the Stoicism of Seneca," one of the many places Eliot addresses the issue of poetry and belief, he proposes that the "thinking" poet is the poet "who can express the emotional equivalent of thought" (*Selected Essays*, 115).

20 *Murder in the Cathedral* played at the West End Theatre from November 1935 to March 1937. The visitors of Magdalen and Merton Colleges were, respectively, Cyril Forster Garbett, the Bishop of Winchester, and Cosmo Gordon Lang, the Archbishop of Canterbury. (A visitor was a person to whom an appeal was made to settle a dispute that could not be resolved internally.) NF is perhaps referring to the conflict between Church and state that had been debated in the assembly of the Church of England during the summer of 1936. Archbishop Lang had presided at the assembly and Bishop Garbett had been an active participant; or NF may be referring to the fact that both Lang and Garbett had argued at the Convocation of Canterbury on 21 January 1937 that the Church of England should take a more liberal position on the matter of divorce than had been proposed by the Bishop of Ely, the debate having been occasioned by the proposed marriage of Edward VIII in December 1936 to Wallis Simpson, a divorcee. Although Lang had previously spoken out publicly against the king's intentions, he announced at the Convocation of Canterbury that he could not accept the Bishop of Ely's resolution that Edward VIII be barred from Holy Communion.

22. A Reconsideration of Chaucer

1 *A Descriptive Catalogue of Pictures, Poetical and Historical Inventions* (1809).

2 Thomas Tyrwhitt, *Canterbury Tales*, 5 vols. (London: T. Payne, 1775–78).

3 When presenting his paper, NF apparently read the passages from Chaucer in modern English; for the written text, however, he quotes from the Middle English.

4 An ordinance issued by King Edward III and his council in 1349 that required workers to accept jobs offered to them, the rate of payment being what was customary before the time of the Black Plague.

5 The various version of *Piers Plowman* are known as the A, B, and C texts, written by Langland over the course of about twenty years.

6 Guillaume Deguilleville, *The ABC*, from *Pélérinage de l'Ame*, pt. 1 of *Le Pélérinage de la Vie Humaine*, in *A One-Text Print of Chaucer's Minor Poems*, ed. Frederick J. Furnivall (London: Oxford University Press, 1880), 83–100; this is a parallel-text edition that prints the Deguilleville and Chaucer texts side by side. Subsequent references to Deguilleville's *ABC* are to the line numbers in this edition.

7 F.N. Robinson, *The Works of Geoffrey Chaucer*, 520.

8 See lines 29–154 of *The Complaint of Mars*, where the various positions and movements of Mars and Venus in relation to the sun (Phebus) are detailed (Robinson, 530–1).

9 For the description of the House of Rumour, see *The House of Fame*, 1920–2158: 300–2).

10 Nicholas Boileau-Despréaux, *The Art of Poetry* (1680–83), lines 373–428.

11 NF had seen Barna di Siena's fresco scenes from the New Testament in the Collegiata when he travelled to San Gimignano in April of 1937; Barna had worked on the frescos in the early 1380s, and they were completed by Giovanni d'Asciano. NF had also seen Martini's *Christ Blessing* in the Vatican picture gallery the previous month.

12 John Livingston Lowes, *Geoffrey Chaucer and the Development of His Genius* (Boston: Houghton Mifflin, 1934), 93–102; George Lyman Kittredge, "The Book of the Duchess," *Chaucer and His Poetry* (Cambridge: Harvard University Press, 1925), 37–72.

13 In *The Study of Poetry* (1880), Matthew Arnold claims that Chaucer "lacks the high seriousness of the great classics."

14 *Geoffrey Chaucer and the Development of His Genius*, 99–100.

15 NF's handwritten parentheses enclose the material from the beginning of this sentence through the end of the next paragraph. In the margin NF wrote "omit?"—no doubt a query to himself about the oral presentation.

16 *Geoffrey Chaucer and the Development of His Genius*, 112.

17 Chaucer actually takes the reader with Aeneas beyond the entrance to hell: "And also sawgh I how Sybile / And Eneas, besyde an yle, / To helle wente, for to see / His fader, Anchyses the free; / How he ther fond Palinurus / And Dido, and eke Deiphebus; / And every turment eke in helle / Saugh he" (439–46: 286). Chaucer goes on to recommend that readers consult Virgil, Claudius Claudianus, and Dante for the complete account.

18 Lines 311 ff. (Dido), 605 ff. (eagle), 766–8 (words are air), 2110–58 (catalogue) (Robinson, 285, 288, 289, 302).

19 In his explanatory notes to *The House of Fame*, F.N. Robinson says "several scholars have striven to show that [the poem] is a kind of parody of the Divine Comedy" (778).

20 The reference is to the speech of Mosca, which opens act 1, sc. 2 of Jonson's play, and the dialogue that follows.

21 "Raging indignation," a phrase from Jonathan Swift's epitaph.

22 1–112: 310–12. The poet is reading Macrobius' fourth-century commentary on Cicero's *The Dream of Scipio*.

23 The source of NF's claim is unclear. Two of NF's own sources, Robinson and Lowes, tend to dismiss the many allegorical interpretations of the birds that have been proposed. See Robinson, 309–10, 791–2, and Lowes, 124–6.

24 Anelida's complaint (220–350: 307–8), written in nine- and sixteen-line stanzas, as compared with the rhyme-royal pattern of the rest of the poem, is the most complicated stanzaic form in all of Chaucer.

25 *The Legend of Good Women* (115–16, 125–6: 485). NF quotes from the so-called "F Text" (sometimes referred to as the "B Text") of the poem.

26 Emanuel Swedenborg, *Divine Love and Divine Wisdom* (1763; English trans., 1788). NF may well have encountered the passage from Swedenborg in Blake's annotations to the book. In any case, he was later to cite Blake's annotation to the Swedenborg passage in *Fearful Symmetry* (Princeton: Princeton University Press, 1947), 140. The image of the sun of the spiritual world appears also in many places in Swedenborg's *The True Christian Religion* (1771).

27 "The Prologue of the Monk's Tale," lines 1973–7, Fragment 7 (Robinson, 189).

28 The conjunction of Saturn, Jupiter, and the crescent moon. See 3.624–9: 427.

29 Swallow, 2.64: 402; owl, 5.319: 463; lark, 5.1110: 471; Niobe, 1.759: 397; Myrrha, 4.1139: 453; Daphne and Herse, 3.726–29: 429.

30 The Latin author from whom Chaucer says he borrowed his story; the source of Chaucer's information about Lollius remains a mystery, in spite of numerous theories that have been advanced. Lollius is named twice in the poem: 1.394: 393, and 5.1653: 477.

31 This conjunction (see n. 28, above), which had occurred in A.D. 769, recurred in May 1385.

32 The reference, apparently, is to 3.1261 ff.: 434, lines which draw upon St. Bernard's praise to the Virgin Mary in the *Paradiso*, 33.

33 Between this sentence and the next NF wrote "Insert," apparently an instruction to himself to add some material.

34 Robert Henryson (1430–1506), one of the so-called Scottish Chaucerians, whose *Testament of Cresseid* (1593), a continuation of Chaucer's poem, depicts the notoriously unfaithful Cresseid as receiving her just retribution.

35 Edmund, the ambitious villain in Shakespeare's *King Lear*, is cynical about everything except his own advancement.

36 Angel Clare is the romantic idealist in Thomas Hardy's *Tess of the D'Urbervilles* (1891).

37 3.722–3: 428. Actually, some 2400 lines intervene.

38 John Ayre notes that when Frye read his essay to the Graduate English Club

it "impressed Margaret Roseborough as an intensely Freudian reading. She remembered his attention to the fertilizing rains associated with lovemaking and his own line that 'all night it rained'" (Ayre, 147).

39 John Milton, *Lycidas* (1638), line 106.

40 When Criseyde asks Pandarus to take Troilus her blue ring, Pandarus replies "A ryng? . . . ye, haselwodes shaken!" (3.890: 430). "Haselwode" also appears in 5.505: 465 and 5.1174: 472. Commentators are uncertain about the meaning; all three instances may be nothing more than commonplace expressions of scepticism.

41 The blundering rake in Sir John Vanbrugh's *The Provok'd Wife* (1696).

42 After his death Troilus's "lighte goost ful blisfully is went / Up to the holughnesse of the eighthe spere" (5.1808–9: 479). For Robinson's opinion that the eighth sphere was that of the moon, see p. 837.

43 The slanderous "slave" in Shakespeare's *Troilus and Cressida* (1601–2), who provides a satirical and cynical commentary on the action.

Emendations

86/3	was over and the *for* was over, and that the
89/10–11	Browning and Antony both have *for* Browning and Antony have both
89/35	as otherwise than a *for* as otherwise than as a
100/35	*The Waste Land for Waste Land*
118/26	waxing and waning make *for* waxing and waning makes
121/7	worked it into *for* worked into
125/30	stage in the development *for* stage in development
130/34	are the obverse *for* are obverse
132/10	undoubtedly reflect *for* undoubtedly reflects
132/16	are balanced *for* is balanced
135/9	on either a transcendent or an immanent *for* on either transcendent or immanent
142/10	only by the realization *for* only by realization
146/23–4	apologetics has *for* apologetics have
146/34–5	which together give us *for* which together gives us
147/26	in many respects *for* in many respect
147/29	who belong to *for* which belong to
148/5	to the older *for* to the other
156/5	If the Epistle were *for* If the Epistle was
157/30–1	religion, shows clearly *for* religion, show clearly
161/7	impress on the thought *for* impress of the thought
161/36	sin and a realization *for* sin and realization
176/37	vegetation, come *for* vegetation, comes
179/21	the most famous of which *for* most famous of which
181/36	Aristophanes' play *for* Aristophanes' play of
182/5	the Zagreus myth *for* the Zagreus
189/20	moral and historical senses *for* moral and historical sense
202/11	of God do *for* of God does
202/36	merely serves *for* merely serve
205/33	leading characteristics *for* leading characteristic
210/28–9	antithetical, and hinged *for* antithetical, hinged
212/32	This means that the ideal *for* Which means that the ideal
213/19	new lease on life *for* new lease of life
216/19	*Ages*; and Dunning *for Ages*; Dunning
230/15	possible questions *for* possible question
236/4	mishap befell him *for* mishap befall him
238/31	we crossed to France *for* we cross to France
239/14	Philip of France was preparing *for* Philip of France preparing
242/26	class are constant *for* class is constant
243/13	Jacques de Molay *for* Jacques du Bourg-Molay
246/38	against its overlord *for* against their overlord

247/21	Alps over an old *for* Alps over over an old
249/21–2	Provençal, which has had . . . its own *for* Provençal, who have had . . . their own
250/38	me, no painter *for* me, that no painter
251/20	pride of both *for* pride both of
253/37	knows is good *for* knows good
254/29	led eventually *for* lead eventually
260/15	are shaped *for* is shaped
265/14–15	scholarship, which were *for* scholarship, which was
269/33	what it thought . . . its Church *for* what they thought . . . their Church
275/27	pervading assumptions *for* pervading assumption
303/33	*Vita Sua* for *sua Vita*
306/22	its lapsing *for* it lapsing
310/7–8	strangle art *for* strangle it
311/30	art have never *for* art has never
318/16	Next to him *for* Next him
319/27	compel a certain conclusion *for* compel certain conclusion
322/33	data seem *for* data seems
323/5	all forms of activity *for* all form of activity
325/5	a "good" action *for* a "good" actions
329/29	those experiences *for* those experience
331/35	without it he *for* without he it
342/28	our own day makes *for* our own day make
348/5–6	life-forces are, of course *for* life-forces is, of course
356/31	misfire *for* miss fire
357/3	as well as the barking *for* and the barking
366/4	is he *for* is he is
375/6	implies puts it *for* implies put it
376/2	example, is Stein *for* example, is Gertrude
377/7	politics, and anglo-catholic *for* politics, anglo-catholic
389/33	term *fiction,* most *for* term, most
395/3	But classicism *for* But the classicism
395/15	manifest a pessimism *for* manifests a pessimism
396/7–8	require a style *for* requires a style
398/26–7	are also factors *for* is also a factor
400/11	renaissance of drama *for* renaissance of a drama
406/4–5	thinking and for any form *for* thinking, and of any form
406/38	and were in fact largely *for* and was in fact largely
408/12–13	completes its destruction *for* completes their destruction
411/11	those that can be *for* those than can be
421/10–11	sick melancholic nostalgia *for* sick melancholy nostalgia

Index

Another Way of Love (1855), 100;
Asolando (1889), 104; *Balaustion's
Adventures* (1871), 104; *Bishop Blou-
gram's Apology* (1855), 102; *The
Bishop Orders His Tomb at St.
Praxed's Church* (1845), 99, 103; *Cali-
ban upon Setebos* (1864), 98; *Cavalier
Tunes* (1842), 98; *Cleon* (1855), 99;
Confessions (1864), 103; *Death in the
Desert* (1864), 92n. 24; *An Epistle
Containing the Strange Medical Expe-
rience of Karshish, the Arab Physician*
(1855), 92; "Essay on Shelley"
(1852), 106; *The Flight of the Duchess*
(1845), 98–9; *The Glove* (1845), 99; *A
Grammarian's Funeral* (1855), 99,
289, 302; *Heretic's Tragedy* (1855),
101; *How They Brought the Good
News from Ghent to Aix* (1845), 98;
Ixion (1883), 98; *Jochanan Hakkadosh*
(1883), 102; *Johannes Agricola in
Meditation* (1836), 91; *The Last Ride
Together* (1855), 98; *Life in a Love*
(1855), 101; *Love Among the Ruins*
(1855), 99; *Master Hugues of
Saxe-Gotha* (1855), 97; *Mr. Sludge,
"The Medium"* (1864), 71–2, 92, 102,
292; *My Last Duchess* (1845), 99; *My
Star* (1855), 98; *Numpholeptos* (1876),
105; *Of Pacchiarotto, and How He
Worked in Distemper* (1876), 99;
Paracelsus (1835), 102; *Parleying with
Charles Avison* (1887), 97; *Pauline*
(1833), 102; *The Pied Piper of Hamelin*
(1842), 100; *Pippa Passes* (1841),
88–90, 102; *Porphyria's Lover* (1836),
90; *Prince Hohenstiel-Schwangau,
Saviour of Society* (1871), 102; *Rabbi
Ben Ezra* (1864), 91, 289; *The Ring
and the Book* (1868–9), 80, 97–8, 102,
103, 104, 106, 384, 386; *Saul* (1845),
292; *Sordello* (1840), 105; *A Soul's

Tragedy (1846), 102; *The Statue and
the Bust* (1855), 91, 102; *Through the
Metidja* (1863), 98; *Time's Revenges*
(1845), 93; *Waring* (1849), 98
Bruno, Giordano (1548–1600), 229,
230, 270
Buckle, Henry Thomas (1821–62), 16,
52
Buddha, 91
Buddhism, 173, 277
Bunyan, John (1628–88), xviii, 74, 93,
316, 329, 385; *Grace Abounding*
(1666), 393; *The Pilgrim's Progress*
(1678–84), 232, 273n. 1, 393
Burke, Edmund (1729–97), 4, 276
Burns, Robert (1759–96), 31, 97, 102;
Address to the Deil (1785), 445; *Jolly
Beggars* (1785), 97; *Tam o' Shanter*
(1792), 97
Burton, Robert (1577–1640), 389, 392,
394, 395; *Anatomy of Melancholy*
(1621), 384, 392, 394, 400
Butler, Samuel (1612–80), 361
Butler, Samuel (1835–1902), 361, 398;
Erewhon (1872), 178, 397, 399; *Ere-
whon Revisited* (1901), 397; *God the
Known and Unknown* (1900), 294–5,
Life and Habit (1877), 303; *Luck or
Cunning?* (1886), 303
Byrd, William (1543–1623), 62, 96
Byron, George Gordon Lord (1788–
1824), 7, 8, 31, 67, 79, 83, 87, 276

Caiaphas, 142
Cain and Abel, 116, 117, 207
Calverton, V.F. (1900–40): *The Making
of Man* (1931), 137, 154
Calvin, John (1509–64), xxiii, xxix, 15,
209, 269, 270, 281, 401–16, 467;
caricatures of, 402; his doctrine of
election, 409; doctrine of God's
sovereignty, 409–10, 413; features